D0164523

# STAFFING ORGANIZATIONS
## Eighth Edition

**Herbert G. Heneman III**
University of Wisconsin–Madison

**Timothy A. Judge**
University of Notre Dame

**John D. Kammeyer-Mueller**
University of Minnesota

Pangloss Industries
Mishawaka, IN

The McGraw-Hill Companies

Mc
Graw
Hill
Education

Dedication
*To Susan, Jill, and Mia*

STAFFING ORGANIZATIONS, EIGHTH EDITION

Published by Pangloss Industries, Inc., 2215 Waters Edge Court, Mishawaka, IN 46545, in collaboration with McGraw-Hill Education, 2 Penn Plaza, New York, NY 10121. Copyright © 2015 by Pangloss Industries, Inc. All rights reserved. Printed in the United States of America. Previous editions © 2012, 2009, and 2006. No part of this publication may be reproduced or distributed in any form or by any means, or stored in a database or retrieval system, without the prior written consent of the publisher, including, but not limited to, in any network or other electronic storage or transmission, or broadcast for distance learning.

Some ancillaries, including electronic and print components, may not be available to customers outside the United States.

This book is printed on acid-free paper.

This publication is designed to provide accurate and authoritative information in regard to the subject matter covered. It is sold with the understanding that the publisher is not engaged in rendering legal, accounting, or other professional services. If legal advice or other expert assistance is required, the services of a competent professional should be sought. (FROM A DECLARATION OF PRINCIPLES JOINTLY ADOPTED BY A COMMITTEE OF THE AMERICAN BAR ASSOCIATION AND A COMMITTEE OF PUBLISHERS.)

2 3 4 5 6 7 8 9 0 DOC/DOC 1 0 9 8 7 6 5 4

ISBN 978-0-07-786241-1
MHID 0-07-786241-4

Senior Vice President, Products & Markets:
    Kurt L. Strand
Vice President, General Manager, Products &
    Markets: *Michael Ryan*
Vice President, Content Production & Technology
    Services: *Kimberly Meriwether David*
Brand Manager: *Michael Ablassmeir*
Developmental Editor: *Jane Beck*
Marketing Manager: *Elizabeth Trepkowski*
Director, Content Production: *Terri Schiesl*
Senior Content Project Manager: *Melissa M. Leick*
Buyer: *Jennifer Pickel*
Cover Designer: *Studio Montage, St. Louis, MO*
Media Project Manager: *Shawn Coenen*

**Note to the Instructor:**

Pangloss and McGraw-Hill Education have combined their respective skills to bring *Staffing Organizations* to your classroom. This text is marketed and distributed by McGraw-Hill Education. For assistance in obtaining information or supplementary material, please contact your McGraw-Hill Education sales representative or the customer services division of McGraw-Hill Education at 800-338-3987.

Compositor: *Kinetic Publishing Services, LLC*
Typeface: *11/12.5 Times Roman*
Printer: *R. R. Donnelley*

*Address orders and customer service questions to:*
*McGraw-Hill Higher Education*
*1333 Burr Ridge Parkway*
*Burr Ridge, IL 60527*
*1-800-338-3987*

*Address editorial correspondence to:*
*Timothy A. Judge*
*Pangloss Industries*
*2215 Waters Edge Court*
*Mishawaka, IN 46545*
*tjudge@nd.edu*

**Library of Congress Cataloging-in-Publication Data**
Heneman, Herbert Gerhard, 1944-
    Staffing organizations / Herbert G. Heneman III, University of Wisconsin, Madison, Timothy A. Judge, University of Notre Dame, John Kammeyer-Mueller, University of Minnesota, Minneapolis.—Eighth Edition.
    pages cm
    ISBN 978-0-07-786241-1 (alk. paper)
    1. Employees—Recruiting.  2. Employee selection.  I. Judge, Tim.  II. Kammeyer-Mueller, John.
III. Title.
HF5549.5.R44H46 2014
658.3′11—dc23                                              2013038191

www.mhhe.com

# AUTHOR PROFILES

**Herbert G. Heneman III** is the Dickson-Bascom Professor Emeritus in the Management and Human Resources Department, School of Business, at the University of Wisconsin–Madison. He also serves as a senior researcher at the Wisconsin Center for Educational Research. Herb has been a visiting faculty member at the University of Washington and the University of Florida, and he was the University Distinguished Visiting Professor at The Ohio State University. His research is in the areas of staffing, performance management, compensation, and work motivation. He is currently investigating the design and effectiveness of teacher performance management and compensation systems. Herb was on the board of directors of the Society for Human Resource Management Foundation and served as its director of research. He is the senior author of three other textbooks on human resource management. Herb is a Fellow of the Society for Industrial and Organizational Psychology, the American Psychological Association, and the Academy of Management. He is also the recipient of career achievement awards from the Human Resources Division of the Academy of Management and from the Society for Human Resource Management.

**Timothy A. Judge** is the Franklin D. Schurz Professor, Department of Management, Mendoza College of Business, University of Notre Dame. Prior to receiving his PhD at the University of Illinois, Tim was a manager for Kohl's department stores. Tim has served on the faculties of Cornell University, the University of Iowa, and the University of Florida. Tim's teaching and research interests are in the areas of personality, leadership and influence behaviors, staffing, and job attitudes. He serves on the editorial review boards of the *Journal of Applied Psychology*; *Personnel Psychology*; *Academy of Management Journal*; *Academy of Management Discoveries*; *Human Resource Management Review*; and the *International Journal of Selection and Assessment*. Tim is a former program chair for the Society for Industrial and Organizational Psychology and a past chair of the Human Resources Division of the Academy of Management, and he recently served on the Academy of Management Board of Governors. Tim is a Fellow of the American Psychological Association, the Society for Industrial and Organizational Psychology, the American Psychological Society, and the Academy of Management.

**John D. Kammeyer-Mueller** is an associate professor in the Department of Work and Organizations in the Carlson School of Management at the University of Minnesota. John's primary research interests include the areas of organizational socialization and employee adjustment, personality and the stress process, employee retention, and career development. He has taught courses related to organizational staffing at the undergraduate, master's, and doctoral levels. His research work has appeared in *Academy of Management Journal*; the *Journal of Applied Psychology*; *Personnel Psychology*; the *Journal of Management*; and the *Journal of Organizational Behavior*, among other outlets. He serves on the editorial boards of the *Journal of Applied Psychology*; *Personnel Psychology*; and *Organizational Research Methods*. In addition to his scholarly work, John has performed consulting work in the areas of employee satisfaction, retention, and workplace safety and health for 3M Corporation, Allegiance Healthcare, Allina Healthcare, and the State of Minnesota. He has also worked with the Florida Nurses Association and the Florida Bar on research projects of interest to their professional membership.

# PREFACE

There has been a continual effort to incorporate strategic organizational concerns into every edition of the textbook. The eighth edition of *Staffing Organizations* develops these concepts significantly. Based on ideas from leading human resources thinkers, new discussions describe how to incorporate organizational strategy into every part of the staffing process. This material not only underlines the importance of strategic thinking for students, but provides specific guidance for specific actions that staffing decision makers can take to improve talent management.

This edition has been the benefactor of major restructuring and updating to ensure continuing alignment of the material with current in-the-field business practices. The changes range from small inclusions of new standards to major chapter revisions. The new structure will make it easier for students to see how each part of the staffing process proceeds from beginning to end, and it will also help them see how the topics fit together to create a cohesive staffing management system.

The landscape for human resources continues to be transformed by technology, and the latest edition reflects this influence. The use of human resources information systems for tasks like recruitment, selection, and forecasting is now thoroughly integrated into all sections. The role of social media, the Internet, and other information management tools is emphasized in several chapters, and new company examples keep the application of concepts fresh and current.

The changes for this edition reflect the integration of technology into core staffing functions. Many of the previous headings related to web-based topics have thus been eliminated to reflect the fact that these are no longer novel add-ons to staffing management but an integral part of the process.

Listed below are updates to each chapter.

## Chapter One: Staffing Models and Strategy

- New discussion on the indirect implications of effective staffing
- Updated Gore reference to reflect the company's current website
- New staffing system example—management trainees at Enterprise Rent-A-Car
- New example of a company keeping turnover to a minimum—SAS Institute
- Discussion of the effects of slow job recovery on staffing and company strategy

## Chapter Two: Legal Compliance

- New material on unpaid interns and trainees
- Updated information on EEOC determinations
- New exhibit with an updated consent decree case
- Revised and updated discussion on reasonable factors other than age (RFOA) and reasonableness standards
- New, replaced section on the definition of disability
- Updated definition of a qualified individual
- New information on reasonable accommodation
- New section on veterans with disabilities
- Updated potential state discrimination protections

## Chapter Three: Planning

- Emphasis on organizational strategy as a foundation for planning throughout the chapter
- New section that integrates internal and external influences
- New section addressing organizational culture in staffing
- New figure highlighting internal and external influences on staffing
- Restructuring and updating of methods for forecasting human resource requirements
- New material on scenario planning in forecasting
- New material on the aging workforce
- New figure showing a business case for effective diversity management

## Chapter Four: Job Analysis and Rewards

- New section on the purpose of various forms of job analyses and rewards
- New figure comparing job requirements, competency-based, and rewards job analysis techniques
- Updated discussion of the research on job analysis measurement
- Revised and updated discussion of job requirements, job analysis components, and the explanations of KSAOs
- Revised discussion of competency-based job analysis
- Updated discussion of best practices in collecting competency information
- New description and figures related to job rewards and job analysis

## Chapter Five: External Recruitment

- Emphasis on organizational strategy as a foundation for recruiting throughout the chapter
- New section on defining strategic recruiting goals
- Material reorganized to better match strategic recruiting processes
- New figure showing the process of implementing strategic recruiting
- New discussion on applicant reactions to job and organizational characteristics
- Revision of material on communication media to match current practices and the use of technology in reaching potential applicants
- Reorganization and revision of strategy implementation
- Updated discussion of use of human resources information systems in recruiting processes

## Chapter Six: Internal Recruitment

- Emphasis on organizational strategy as a foundation for recruiting throughout the chapter
- New section on defining strategic recruiting goals
- Material reorganized to better match strategic recruiting processes
- Updated discussion of team-based structures and their role in internal recruiting
- Updated and expanded discussion of the importance of applicant reactions to development and promotion policies
- Discussion of job postings revised to focus on web-based and intranet delivery
- New figure showing the format for intranet posting of job information

## Chapter Seven: Measurement

- Updated example of job information technology
- New discussion on issues associated with forced rankings
- Updated examples of objective versus subjective measures
- Revised coverage of key topics (e.g., goal of measurement; ratio scales, percentiles, standard scores, correlations, and reliability)
- New material on standard scores
- New discussion on sign of correlation coefficients
- New example for calculating the significance of the correlation coefficient
- New section on interrater agreement versus coefficient alpha
- New discussion on the drawbacks of content validation

### Chapter Eight: External Selection I

- Updated discussion on electronic testing
- New example of electronic résumé pitfalls
- New example for video résumé
- New discussion of the role of Twitter in résumé
- New section on the value of a college education
- New discussion of strategies to improve biodata questions
- New discussion on fraud in letters of recommendation
- New discussion on validity of credit scores

### Chapter Nine: External Selection II

- New discussion of test items on the Internet
- New paragraph on contextualizing Big Five measures
- New discussion on socially desirable responding and faking
- New discussion on the effects of warnings on faking personality tests
- New discussion on emotion regulation
- Revised discussion on the validity of integrity tests
- New discussion on the prevalence of unstructured interviews
- New section on structured video interviews
- Updated statistics on the use of drug testing by companies

### Chapter Ten: Internal Selection

- New example of promotion from within
- New discussion on the use of peer nominations to improve predictive validity
- New material on how mentors benefit from mentoring
- New discussion on job knowledge testing
- New example on performance appraisals for internal selection
- New discussion of strategies to improve performance appraisals
- New discussion on improving assessment center ratings

### Chapter Eleven: Decision Making

- Expanded introduction that integrates material from previous chapters
- New material on evidence-based management and decision making
- Updated discussion on the limitations of utility analysis
- Updated information on clinical decision making
- Revised discussion of hiring scoring in the selection process

### Chapter Twelve: Final Match

- Updated discussion of disclaimers in contracts and handbooks
- Updated information on the strategic approach to job offers and the employee value proposition
- New discussion of idiosyncratic deals tailored to individual employees
- New figure showing elements and examples of idiosyncratic deals
- New material on differential starting pay rates
- Updated discussion on employee orientation and socialization practices

### Chapter Thirteen: Staffing System Management

- Streamlined presentation of information
- Discussion of the strategic link between staffing and executive decision making
- New exhibit illustrating evidence-based principles for writing effective policies and procedures
- Updated discussion of human resource information systems and their role in staffing
- New examples of effective outsourcing
- New exhibit showing how metrics can be used for staffing process evaluation

### Chapter Fourteen: Retention Management

- Streamlined presentation of information
- Updated information on job openings and labor turnover
- Revised discussion of the costs and benefits of downsizing
- Revised and updated discussion of best practices in retention
- New figure illustrating the most and least effective retention initiatives

In preparing this edition, we have benefited greatly from the critiques and suggestions of numerous people whose assistance was invaluable. They helped us identify new topics, as well as clarify, rearrange, and delete material. We extend our many thanks to the following individuals:

- Amy Banta, Franklin University
- Fred Dorn, University of Mississippi
- Hank Findley, Troy University
- Diane Hagan, Ohio Business College
- Mark Lengnick-Hall, University of Texas–San Antonio

We wish to extend a special note of thanks to the McGraw-Hill Education publishing team—in particular, Michael Ablassmeir, Laura Spell, Melissa Leick, and

Jane Beck—for their hard work and continued support of the number-one staffing textbook in the market. Thanks also to the staff at Kinetic Publishing Services, LLC, for their dedicated work in this collaborative undertaking. We wish to thank Brent A. Scott of Michigan State University for his valuable input for this edition. We also appreciate the assistance of Lori Ehrman Tinkey and Virginia Brow in manuscript editing and preparation. Finally, we wish to thank you—the students and faculty who use the book. If there is anything we can do to improve your experience with *Staffing Organizations*, please contact us. We will be happy to hear from you.

# CONTENTS

## PART THREE

## Staffing Activities: Recruitment  203

### CHAPTER FIVE
### External Recruitment  205

### CHAPTER SIX
### Internal Recruitment  269

# STAFFING ORGANIZATIONS
Eighth Edition

# The Staffing Organizations Model

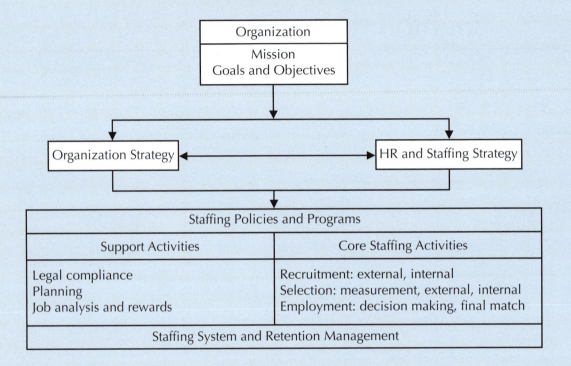

# PART ONE

## The Nature of Staffing

**CHAPTER ONE**
   Staffing Models and Strategy

# CHAPTER ONE

# Staffing Models and Strategy

**Learning Objectives and Introduction**
    Learning Objectives
    Introduction

**The Nature of Staffing**
    The Big Picture
    Definition of Staffing
    Implications of Definition
    Staffing System Examples

**Staffing Models**
    Staffing Quantity: Levels
    Staffing Quality: Person/Job Match
    Staffing Quality: Person/Organization Match
    Staffing System Components
    Staffing Organizations

**Staffing Strategy**
    Staffing Levels
    Staffing Quality

**Staffing Ethics**

**Plan for the Book**

**Summary**

**Discussion Questions**

**Ethical Issues**

**Applications**

**Endnotes**

## LEARNING OBJECTIVES AND INTRODUCTION

### Learning Objectives

- Define staffing and consider how, in the big picture, staffing decisions matter
- Review the five staffing models presented, and consider the advantages and disadvantages of each
- Consider the staffing system components and how they fit into the plan for the book
- Understand the staffing organizations model and how its various components fit into the plan for the book
- Appreciate the importance of staffing strategy, and review the 13 decisions that staffing strategy requires
- Realize the importance of ethics in staffing, and learn how ethical staffing practice is established

### Introduction

Staffing is a critical organizational function concerned with the acquisition, deployment, and retention of the organization's workforce. As we note in this chapter and throughout the book, staffing is arguably the most critical function underlying organizational effectiveness, because "the people make the place," because labor costs are often the highest organizational cost, and because poor hiring decisions are not easily undone.

This chapter begins with a look at the nature of staffing. This includes a view of the "big picture" of staffing, followed by a formal definition of staffing and the implications of that definition. Examples of staffing systems are given.

Five models are then presented to elaborate on and illustrate various facets of staffing. The first model shows how projected workforce head-count requirements and availabilities are compared to determine the appropriate staffing level for the organization. The next two models illustrate staffing quality, which refers to matching a person's qualifications with the requirements of the job or organization. The person/job match model is the foundation of all staffing activities; the person/organization match model shows how person/job matching could extend to how well the person will also fit with the organization. The core staffing components model identifies recruitment, selection, and employment as the three key staffing activities, and it shows that both the organization and the job applicant interact in these activities. The final model, staffing organizations, provides the entire framework for staffing and the structure of this book. It shows that organizations, human resources (HR), and staffing strategy interact to guide the conduct of staffing support activities (legal compliance, planning, and job analysis) and core staffing activities (recruitment, selection, and employment); employee retention and staffing system management are shown to cut across both types of activities.

Staffing strategy is then explored in detail by identifying and describing a set of 13 strategic staffing decisions that confront any organization. Several of the decisions pertain to staffing levels, and the remainder to staffing quality.

Staffing ethics—the moral principles and guidelines for acceptable practice—is discussed next. Several pointers that help guide ethical staffing conduct are indicated, as are some of the common pressures to ignore these pointers and compromise one's ethical standards. Suggestions for how to handle these pressures are also made.

Finally, the plan for the remainder of the book is presented. The overall structure of the book is shown, along with key features of each chapter.

## THE NATURE OF STAFFING

### The Big Picture

Organizations are combinations of physical, financial, and human capital. Human capital refers to the knowledge, skill, and ability of people and their motivation to use them successfully on the job. The term "workforce quality" refers to an organization's human capital. The organization's workforce is thus a stock of human capital that it acquires, deploys, and retains in pursuit of organizational outcomes such as profitability, market share, customer satisfaction, and environmental sustainability. Staffing is the organizational function used to build this workforce through such systems as staffing strategy, HR planning, recruitment, selection, employment, and retention.

At the national level, the collective workforces of US organizations total over 112 million (down from a peak of nearly 140 million in 2005), with employees spread across nearly 7.5 million work sites. The work sites vary considerably in size, with 18% of employees in work sites of fewer than 20 employees, 31% in work sites between 20 and 500 employees, and 51% in work sites over 500 employees.[1] Each of these work sites used some form of a staffing process to acquire its employees. Even during the Great Recession, which began in 2007 and ended in 2009, and its slow recovery, there were more than 4 million new hire transactions nationally each month, or over 50 million annually. This figure does not include internal transfers, promotions, or the hiring of temporary employees, so the total number of staffing transactions was much greater than the 50 million figure.[2] Even in difficult economic times, staffing is big business for both organizations and job seekers.

For most organizations, a workforce is an expensive proposition and cost of doing business. It is estimated that an average organization's employee cost (wages or salaries and benefits) is over 22% of its total revenue (and generally a higher percentage of total costs).[3] The percentage is much greater for organizations in labor-intensive industries—the service-providing as opposed to goods-producing industries—such as retail trade, information, financial services, professional and business services, education, health care, and leisure and hospitality. Since service-providing industries now dominate our economy, matters of employee cost and whether the organization is acquiring a high-quality workforce are of considerable concern.

A shift is gradually occurring from viewing employees as just a cost of doing business to valuing employees as human capital that creates competitive advantage for the organization. Organizations that deliver superior customer service, much of which is driven by highly knowledgcable employees with fine-tuned customer service skills, have a definite and hopefully long-term leg up on their competitors. The competitive advantage derived from such human capital has important financial implications.

In addition to direct bottom-line implications, an organization's focus on creating an effective selection system also has more indirect implications for competitive advantage by enhancing employees' well-being and retention. One recent study showed that employees who perceive their company uses effective selection practices such as formal selection tests and structured job interviews (practices that we will discuss in this book) are more committed to their organizations. In turn, those higher levels of commitment lead to more helping or citizenship behaviors on the part of employees, as well as stronger intentions to remain employed, both of which ultimately contribute to an organization's bottom line.[4]

Thus, organizations are increasingly recognizing the value creation that can occur through staffing. Quotes from several organization leaders attest to this, as shown in Exhibit 1.1.

## Definition of Staffing

The following definition of staffing is offered and will be used throughout this book:

> Staffing is the process of acquiring, deploying, and retaining a workforce of sufficient quantity and quality to create positive impacts on the organization's effectiveness.

This straightforward definition contains several implications which are identified and explained next.

## Implications of Definition

### Acquire, Deploy, Retain

An organization's staffing system must guide the acquisition, deployment, and retention of its workforce. Acquisition activities involve external staffing systems that govern the initial intake of applicants into the organization. These involve planning for the numbers and types of people needed, establishing job requirements in

---

**EXHIBIT 1.1**   **The Importance of Staffing to Organizational Leaders**

"Staffing is absolutely critical to the success of every company. To be competitive in today's economy, companies need the best people to create ideas and execute them for the organization. Without a competent and talented workforce, organizations will stagnate and eventually perish. The right employees are the most important resources of companies today."[a]

Gail Hyland-Savage, chief operating officer
Michaelson, Connor & Boul—real estate and marketing

"At most companies, people spend 2% of their time recruiting and 75% managing their recruiting mistakes."[b]

Richard Fairbank, CEO
Capital One

"I think about this in hiring, because our business all comes down to people. . . . In fact, when I'm interviewing a senior job candidate, my biggest worry is how good they are at hiring. I spend at least half the interview on that."[c]

Jeff Bezos, CEO
Amazon.com—Internet merchandising

"We missed a really nice nursing rebound . . . because we just didn't do a good job hiring in front of it. Nothing has cost the business as much as failing to intersect the right people at the right time."[d]

David Alexander, president
Soliant Health—health care

"Organization doesn't really accomplish anything. Plans don't accomplish anything, either. Theories of management don't much matter. Endeavors succeed or fail because of the people involved. Only by attracting the best people will you accomplish great deeds."[e]

Gen. Colin Powell (Ret.)
Former US secretary of state

[a]G. Hyland-Savage, "General Management Perspective on Staffing; The Staffing Commandments," in N. C. Burkholder, P. J. Edwards, Jr., and L. Sartain (eds.), *On Staffing* (Hoboken, NJ: Wiley, 2004), p. 280.
[b]J. Trammell, "CEOs Must Bring Own Recruiting: 10 Rules for Building a Top-Notch Function," *Forbes*, April 17, 2013 (www.forbes.com/sites/joeltrammell/2013/04/17/ceos-must-own-recruiting-10-rules-for-building-a-top-notch-function).
[c]G. Anders, "Taming the Out-of-Control In-Box," *Wall Street Journal*, Feb. 4, 2000, p. 81.
[d]J. McCoy, "Executives' Worst Mistakes in Staffing," *Staffing Industry Review*, Sept. 2010, pp. 1–2.
[e]C. Powell, "A Leadership Primer: Lesson 8," Department of the Army (www.frontiercapital.com/uploads/file/ColinPowellonLeadership%20PDF%20for%20Blog.pdf).

the form of the qualifications or KSAOs (knowledge, skill, ability, and other characteristics) needed to perform the job effectively, establishing the types of rewards the job will provide, conducting external recruitment campaigns, using selection tools to evaluate the KSAOs that applicants possess, deciding which applicants are the most qualified and will receive job offers, and putting together job offers that applicants will hopefully accept.

Deployment refers to the placement of new hires in the actual jobs they will hold, something that may not be entirely clear at the time of hire, such as the specific work unit or geographic location. Deployment also encompasses guiding the movement of current employees throughout the organization through internal staffing systems that handle promotions, transfers, and new project assignments. Internal staffing systems mimic external staffing systems in many respects, such as planning for promotion and transfer vacancies, establishing job requirements and job rewards, recruiting employees for promotion or transfer opportunities, evaluating employees' qualifications, and making job offers to employees for new positions.

Retention systems seek to manage the inevitable flow of employees out of the organization. Sometimes these outflows are involuntary on the part of the employee, such as through layoffs or the sale of a business unit to another organization. Other outflows are voluntary in that they are initiated by the employee, such as leaving the organization to take another job (a potentially avoidable turnover by the organization) or leaving to follow one's spouse or partner to a new geographic location (a potentially unavoidable turnover). Of course, no organization can or should seek to completely eliminate employee outflows, but it should try to minimize the types of turnover in which valued employees leave for "greener pastures" elsewhere—namely, voluntary-avoidable turnover. Such turnover can be very costly to the organization, as can turnover due to employee discharges and downsizing. Through various retention strategies and tactics, the organization can combat these types of turnover, seeking to retain those employees it thinks it cannot afford to lose.

## Staffing as a Process or System

Staffing is not an event, as in, "We hired two people today." Rather, staffing is a process that establishes and governs the flow of people into the organization, within the organization, and out of the organization. Organizations use multiple interconnected systems to manage the people flows. These include planning, recruitment, selection, decision making, job offer, and retention systems. Occurrences or actions in one system inevitably affect other systems. If planning activities show a forecasted increase in vacancies relative to historical standards, for example, the recruitment system will need to gear up for generating more applicants than previously, the selection system will have to handle the increased volume of applicants needing to be evaluated in terms of their KSAOs, decisions about job offers may have to be sped up, and the job offer packages may have to be sweetened to entice the necessary numbers of new hires. Further, steps will have to be taken to retain the new hires and thus avoid having to repeat the above experiences in the next staffing cycle.

## Quantity and Quality

Staffing the organization requires attention to both the numbers (quantity) and the types (quality) of people brought into, moved within, and retained by the organization. The quantity element refers to having enough people to conduct business, and the quality element refers to having people with the requisite KSAOs so that jobs are performed effectively. It is important to recognize that it is the combination of sufficient quantity and quality of labor that creates a maximally effective staffing system.

## Organization Effectiveness

Staffing systems exist and should be used to contribute to the attainment of organizational goals such as survival, profitability, and growth. A macro view of staffing like this is often lost or ignored because most of the day-to-day operations of staffing systems involve micro activities that are procedural, transactional, and routine in nature. While these micro activities are essential for staffing systems, they must be viewed within the broader macro context of the positive impacts staffing can have on organization effectiveness. There are many indications of this critical role of staffing.

Leadership talent is at a premium, with very large stakes associated with new leader acquisition. Sometimes leadership talent is bought and brought from the outside to hopefully execute a reversal of fortune for the organization or a business unit within it. For example, in 2012, Yahoo brought in Marissa Mayer, a former executive at Google, to turn around the aging tech giant. Organizations also acquire leaders to start new business units or ventures that will feed organizational growth. The flip side of leadership acquisition is leadership retention. A looming fear for organizations is the unexpected loss of a key leader, particularly to a competitor. The exiting leader carries a wealth of knowledge and skill out of the organization and leaves a hole that may be hard to fill, especially with someone of equal or higher leadership stature. The leader may also take other key employees along, thus increasing the exit impact.

Organizations recognize that talent hunts and loading up on talent are ways to expand organization value and provide protection from competitors. Such a strategy is particularly effective if the talent is unique and rare in the marketplace, valuable in the anticipated contributions to be made (such as product creations or design innovations), and difficult for competitors to imitate (such as through training current employees). Talent of this sort can serve as a source of competitive advantage for the organization, hopefully for an extended time period.[5]

Talent acquisition is essential for growth even when it does not have such competitive advantage characteristics. As hiring has steadily picked up since the Great

Recession ended, many companies are scrambling to staff positions in order to keep up with demand. For example, Amazon, Oracle, and Microsoft are each attempting to fill a whopping 2,000 positions that all pay at least $60,000 a year.[6] Shortages in the quantity or quality of labor can mean lost business opportunities, scaled-back expansion plans, inability to provide critical consumer goods and services, and even threats to the organization's survival.

Finally, for individual managers, having sufficient numbers and types of employees on board is necessary for the smooth, efficient operation of their work units. Employee shortages often require disruptive adjustments, such as job reassignments or overtime for current employees. Underqualified employees present special challenges to the manager, as they need to be trained and closely supervised. Failure of the underqualified to achieve acceptable performance may require termination, a difficult decision to make and implement.

In short, organizations experience and respond to staffing forces and recognize how critical these forces can be to organizational effectiveness. The forces manifest themselves in numerous ways: acquisition of new leaders to change the organization's direction and effectiveness, prevention of key leader losses, use of talent as a source of growth and competitive advantage, shortages of labor—both quantity and quality—that threaten growth and even survival, and the ability of individual managers to effectively run their work units.

## Staffing System Examples

### Staffing Jobs Without Titles

W. L. Gore & Associates is a Delaware-based organization that specializes in making products derived from fluoropolymers. Gore produces fibers (including dental floss and sewing threads), tubes (used, for example, in heart stents and oil exploration), tapes (including those used in space exploration), and membranes (used in Gore-Tex waterproof clothing).

In its more than half-century history, Gore has never lost money. Gore employs over 9,000 workers and appears on nearly every "best place to work" list. What makes Gore so special? Gore associates argue that it's the culture, and the culture starts with the hiring.

Gore has a strong culture, as seen in its structure: a team-based, flat lattice structure that fosters personal initiative. At Gore, no employee can ever command another employee—all commitments are voluntary, and any employee can say no to any request. Employees are called "associates" and managers are called "sponsors." How do people become leaders at Gore? "You get to be a leader if your team asks you to lead them."[7]

Gore extends this egalitarian, entrepreneurial approach to its staffing process. The focal point of Gore's recruitment process is the careers section of its website, which describes its core values and its unique culture. The website also provides position descriptions and employee perspectives on working at Gore, complete with pictures of the associates and videos. Three Gore associates—Janice, Katrin, and Mike—work on Gore's footwear products, striving to uphold the company's "keep you dry" guarantee. As Mike notes, "The reasons that I chose Gore from the start are the same reasons why I stay at Gore today, and continue to have fun every day: It's the people. Our team is a great team, and I think that is reflected or echoed across the entire enterprise." Hajo, Alicia, and Austin make up a team working on the clinical product Thoracic Endoprosthesis. As Hajo notes, "When you come to work each day, you don't have a boss to give you explicit instructions on what you need to accomplish."

Gore finds that its employee-focused recruitment efforts do not work for everyone, which is exactly what it intends. "Some of these candidates, or prospects in the fields we were recruiting for, told us 'this company probably isn't for me,'" says Steve Shuster, who helped develop the recruitment strategy. Shuster says that this self-selection is another benefit of its recruitment message. Potential recruits who prefer a more traditional culture quickly see that Gore isn't for them. Shuster says, "Rather than have them go through the interview process and invest their time and our time, we wanted to weed that out."

Of course, Gore is a culture that fits many. Says Gore associate Hannah, who works on the company's heart device team, "I feel like Gore is not just a job, that it's more of a lifestyle and a huge part of my life."[8]

## Pharmaceutical Industry Managers

Though Pfizer has been recognized by other pharmaceutical companies as a leader in selecting and developing its employees, it recently realized a need to dramatically overhaul its approach to staffing. Despite the previous success of its selection efforts, "Pfizer was not focused on managing the external environment," said Pfizer executive Chris Altizer. In the past, according to Altizer, Pfizer would project what kind of talent it would need in the next 10 years and then select employees whose skills matched the talent needs. Pfizer now believes the plan no longer works because there is increased global competition, especially from smaller start-up pharmaceutical firms that can rush products to market. That puts a premium on adaptability.

To address changing market conditions, Pfizer now looks at hiring employees who can jump from one position to another. This means that Pfizer focuses less on job descriptions (i.e., hiring for skills that fit a specific job) and more on general competencies that will translate from job to job. According to Altizer, Pfizer needs "a person who can switch from working on a heart disease product to one that helps people stop smoking"—in other words, rather than relying on past experience with one product (say, heart disease medications), Pfizer is looking for competencies that will allow the employee to quickly and proficiently move from one venture to the next.[9]

### Management Trainees

Enterprise Rent-A-Car is a private company founded in 1957 with locations in the United States, Canada, the UK, Ireland, and Germany. Enterprise boasts that its 5,500 offices in the United States are located within 15 miles of 90% of the population. Among its competitors, Enterprise frequently wins awards for customer satisfaction.

To staff its locations, Enterprise relies heavily on recruiting recent college graduates. In fact, Enterprise hires more college graduates—often between 8,000 and 9,000 a year—than any other company. New hires enter Enterprise's management training program, where they learn all aspects of running a branch, from taking reservations, picking up customers, developing relationships with car dealerships and body shops for future rentals, managing the fleet, handling customer issues, and even washing cars. Nearly all promotions at Enterprise occur from within and are strictly performance based, allowing management trainees to see a clear path from their current position to higher positions such as assistant manager, branch manager, and area manager. Typically, the first promotion occurs within 9 to 12 months of being hired, which speeds the climb up the corporate ladder.

To fill so many positions with college graduates, Enterprise relies on several strategies, including recruiting from an internship program of approximately 1,000 students a year, attending college recruitment fairs, using its website to highlight its performance-driven culture as well as employee testimonials, and devoting a large percentage of its television advertising to the NCAA basketball tournament that occurs each March and has a high college viewership. Although graduates' grades are important to Enterprise, communication skills are even more essential, says Dylan Schweitzer, northeast manager of talent acquisition.

Although the management trainee program at Enterprise has been described as a grueling process, with many trainees leaving prior to being promoted, its executives often describe it as an "MBA without the IOU" because trainees gain first-hand experience in sales, marketing, finance, and operations.[10]

## STAFFING MODELS

Several models depict various elements of staffing. Each of these is presented and described to more fully convey the nature and richness of staffing the organization.

## Staffing Quantity: Levels

The quantity or head-count portion of the staffing definition means organizations must be concerned about staffing levels and their adequacy. Exhibit 1.2 shows the basic model. The organization as a whole, as well as each of its units, forecasts workforce quantity requirements (the needed head count) and then compares these with forecasted workforce availabilities (the likely employee head count) to deter-

**EXHIBIT 1.2**   **Staffing Quantity**

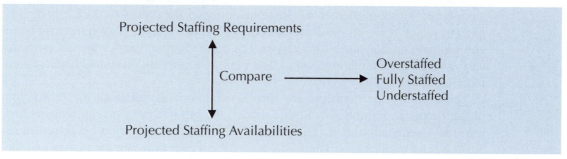

mine its likely staffing level position. If head-count requirements match availabilities, the organization will be fully staffed. If requirements exceed availabilities, the organization will be understaffed, and if availabilities exceed requirements, the organization will be overstaffed.

Making forecasts to determine appropriate staffing levels and then developing specific plans are the essence of planning. Being understaffed means the organization will have to gear up its staffing efforts, starting with accelerated recruitment and carrying on through the rest of the staffing system. It may also require developing retention programs that will slow the outflow of people, thus avoiding costly "turnstile" or "revolving door" staffing. Overstaffing projections signal the need to slow down or even halt recruitment, as well as to take steps to reduce head count, perhaps through early retirement plans or layoffs.

## Staffing Quality: Person/Job Match

The person/job match seeks to align characteristics of individuals with jobs in ways that will result in desired HR outcomes. Casual comments made about applicants often reflect awareness of the importance of the person/job match: "Clark just doesn't have the interpersonal skills that it takes to be a good customer service representative." "Mary has exactly the kind of budgeting experience this job calls for; if we hire her, there won't be any downtime while she learns our systems." "Gary says he was attracted to apply for this job because of its sales commission plan; he says he likes jobs where his pay depends on how well he performs." "Diane was impressed by the amount of challenge and autonomy she will have." "Jack turned down our offer; we gave him our best shot, but he just didn't feel he could handle the long hours and amount of travel the job calls for."

Comments like these raise four important points about the person/job match. First, jobs are characterized by their requirements (e.g., interpersonal skills, previous budgeting experience) and embedded rewards (e.g., commission sales plan, challenge and autonomy). Second, individuals are characterized by their level of qualification (e.g., few interpersonal skills, extensive budgeting experience) and motivation (e.g., need for pay to depend on performance, need for challenge and autonomy). Third, in each of the previous examples the issue was the likely degree of fit or match between the characteristics of the job and the person. Fourth, there are implied consequences for every match. For example, Clark may not perform very well in his interactions with customers; retention might quickly become an issue with Jack.

These points and concepts are shown more formally through the person/job match model in Exhibit 1.3. In this model, the job has certain requirements and rewards associated with it. The person has certain qualifications, referred to as KSAOs, and motivations. There is a need for a match between the person and the job. To the extent that the match is good, it will likely have a positive impact on HR outcomes, particularly with attraction of job applicants, job performance, retention, attendance, and satisfaction.

There is a need for a dual match to occur: job requirements to KSAOs, and job rewards to individual motivation. In and through staffing activities, there are attempts to ensure both of these. Such attempts collectively involve what will be referred to throughout this book as the matching process.

Several points pertaining to staffing need to be made about the person/job match model. First, the concepts shown in the model are not new.[11] They have been used

**EXHIBIT 1.3    Person/Job Match**

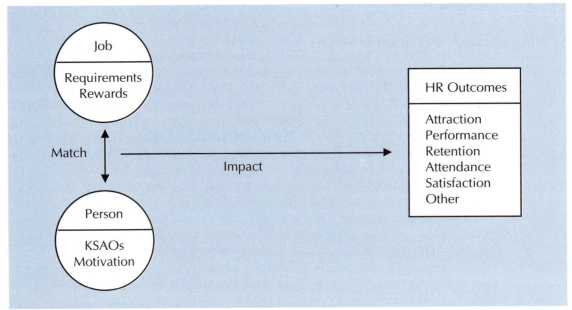

for decades as the dominant way of thinking about how individuals successfully adapt to their work environments. The view is that the positive interaction of individual and job characteristics creates the most successful match. Thus, a person with a given package of KSAOs is not equally suited to all jobs, because jobs vary in the KSAOs required. Likewise, an individual with a given set of needs or motivations will not be satisfied with all jobs, because jobs differ in the rewards they offer. Thus, in staffing, each individual must be assessed relative to the requirements and rewards of the job being filled.

Second, the model emphasizes a dual match of KSAOs to requirements and motivation to rewards. Both matches require attention in staffing. For example, a staffing system may be designed to focus on the KSAOs/requirements match by carefully identifying job requirements and then thoroughly assessing applicants relative to these requirements. While such a staffing system may accurately identify the probable high performers, problems could arise. By ignoring or downplaying the motivation/rewards portion of the match, the organization may have difficulty getting people to accept job offers (an attraction outcome) or having new hires remain with the organization for any length of time (a retention outcome). It does little good to identify the likely high performers if they cannot be induced to accept job offers or to remain with the organization.

Third, job requirements should be expressed in terms of both the tasks involved and the KSAOs needed to perform those tasks. Most of the time, it is difficult to establish meaningful KSAOs for a job without having first identified the job's tasks. KSAOs usually must be derived or inferred from knowledge of the tasks. An exception to this involves very basic or generic KSAOs that are reasonably deemed necessary for most jobs, such as literacy and oral communication skills.

Fourth, job requirements often extend beyond task and KSAO requirements. For example, the job may require punctuality, good attendance, safety toward fellow employees and customers, and travel. Matching an individual to these requirements must also be considered when staffing the organization. Travel requirements of the job, for example, may involve assessing applicants' availability for, and willingness to accept, travel assignments. Integrating this with the second point above, travel issues, which frequently arise in the consulting industry, play a role in both the attraction process (getting people to accept) and the retention process (getting people to stay). "Road warriors," as they are sometimes termed, may first think that frequent travel will be exciting, only to discover later that they find it taxing.

Finally, the matching process can yield only so much by way of impacts on the HR outcomes. The reason for this is that these outcomes are influenced by factors outside the realm of the person/job match. Retention, for example, depends not only on how close the match is between job rewards and individual motivation but also on the availability of suitable job opportunities in other organizations and labor markets. As hiring begins to improve and unemployment continues to drop, organizations are likely to face increased retention pressures as other opportunities present themselves to employees that were not previously present when economic conditions were poorer.

## Staffing Quality: Person/Organization Match

Often the organization seeks to determine how well the person matches not only the job but also the organization. Likewise, applicants often assess how well they think they will fit into the organization, in addition to how well they match the specific job's requirements and rewards. For both the organization and the applicant, then, there may be a concern with a person/organization match.[12]

Exhibit 1.4 shows this expanded view of the match. The focal point of staffing is the person/job match, and the job is the bull's eye of the matching target. Four

**EXHIBIT 1.4   Person/Organization Match**

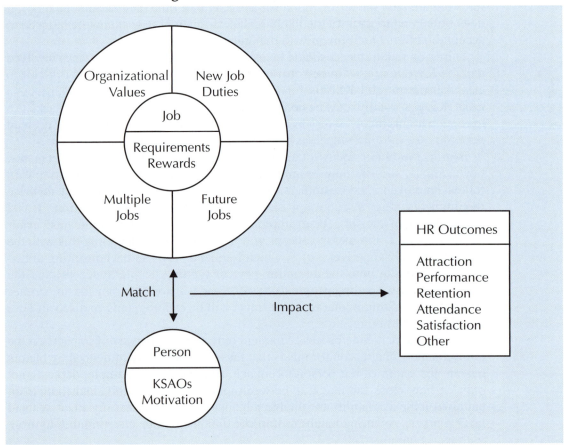

other matching concerns involving the broader organization also arise in staffing: organizational values, new job duties, multiple jobs, and future jobs.

Organizational values are norms of desirable attitudes and behaviors for the organization's employees. Examples include honesty and integrity, achievement and hard work, and concern for fellow employees and customers. Though such values may never appear in writing, such as in a job description, the likely match of the applicant to them is judged during staffing.

New job duties are tasks that may be added to the target job over time. Organizations desire new hires who will be able to successfully perform these new duties as they are added. In recognition of this, job descriptions often contain the catchall phrase "and other duties as assigned." These other duties are usually vague at the time of hire, and they may never materialize. Nonetheless, the organization would like to hire people it thinks could perform these new duties. Having such people will provide the organization the flexibility to complete new tasks without having to hire additional employees. As we will discuss later in this book, certain types of individuals are better than others at adapting to changing circumstances, and organizations with evolving job duties are well advised to select them.

Flexibility concerns also enter the staffing picture in terms of hiring people who can perform multiple jobs. Small businesses, for example, often desire new hires who can wear multiple hats, functioning as jacks-of-all-trades. Organizations experiencing rapid growth may require new employees who can handle several job assignments, splitting their time among them on an as-needed basis. Such expectations obviously require assessments of person/organization fit.

Future jobs represent forward thinking by the organization and the person as to which job assignments the person might assume beyond the initial job. Here the applicant and the organization are thinking of long-term matches over the course of transfers and promotions as the employee becomes increasingly seasoned for the long run. As technology and globalization cause jobs to change at a rapid pace, more organizations are engaging in "opportunistic hiring," where an individual is hired into a newly created job or a job that is an amalgamation of previously distributed tasks. In such cases, person/organization match is more important than person/job match.[13]

In each of the four concerns, the matching process is expanded to consider requirements and rewards beyond those of the target job as it currently exists. Though the dividing line between person/job and person/organization matching is fuzzy, both types of matches are frequently of concern in staffing. Ideally, the organization's staffing systems focus first and foremost on the person/job match. This will allow the nature of the employment relationship to be specified and agreed to in concrete terms. Once these terms have been established, person/organization match possibilities can be explored during the staffing process. In this book, for simplicity's sake, we will use the term "person/job match" broadly to encompass both types of matches, though most of the time we will be referring to the match with the actual job itself.

## Staffing System Components

As noted, staffing encompasses managing the flows of people into and within the organization, as well as retaining them. The core staffing process has several components that represent steps and activities that occur over the course of these flows. Exhibit 1.5 shows these components and the general sequence in which they occur.

As shown in the exhibit, staffing begins with a joint interaction between the applicant and the organization. The applicant seeks the organization and job opportunities within it, and the organization seeks applicants for job vacancies it has or anticipates having. Both the applicant and the organization are thus "players" in the staffing process from the very beginning, and they remain joint participants throughout the process.

At times, the organization may be the dominant player, such as in aggressive and targeted recruiting for certain types of applicants. At other times, the applicant may be the aggressor, such as when he or she desperately seeks employment with a particular organization and will go to almost any length to land a job with it. Most of the time, the staffing process involves a more balanced and natural interplay between the applicant and the organization.

The initial stage in staffing is recruitment, which involves identification and attraction activities by both the organization and the applicant. The organization

**EXHIBIT 1.5   Staffing System Components**

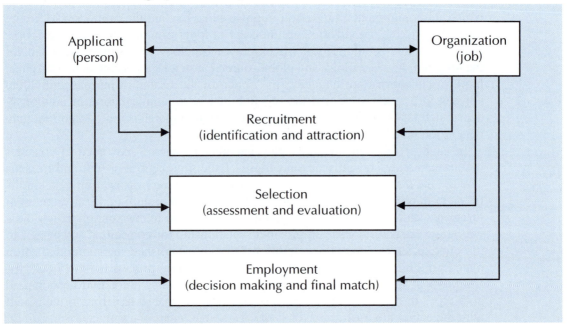

seeks to identify and attract individuals so that they become job applicants. Activities such as advertising, job fairs, use of recruiters, preparation and distribution of informational brochures, and "putting out the word" about vacancies among its own employees are undertaken. The applicant identifies organizations with job opportunities by reading advertisements, contacting an employment agency, mass mailing résumés to employers, and so forth. These activities are accompanied by attempts to make one's qualifications (KSAOs and motivation) attractive to organizations, such as by applying in person for a job or preparing a carefully constructed résumé that highlights significant skills and experiences.

Gradually, recruitment activities phase into the selection stage and its accompanying activities. Now, the emphasis is on assessment and evaluation. For the organization, this means the use of various selection techniques (interviews, application blanks, and so on) to assess applicant KSAOs and motivation. Data from these assessments are then evaluated against job requirements to determine the likely degree of person/job match. At the same time, the applicant is assessing and evaluating the job and organization on the basis of the information gathered from organizational representatives (e.g., recruiter, manager with the vacancy, and other employees), written information (e.g., brochures, employee handbook), informal sources (e.g., friends and relatives who are current employees), and visual inspection (e.g., a video presentation, a work site tour). This information, along with a self-assessment of KSAOs and motivation, is evaluated against the applicant's understanding of job requirements and rewards to determine whether a good person/job match is likely.

The last core component of staffing is employment, which involves decision making and final match activities by the organization and the applicant. The organization must decide which applicants to allow to continue in the process and which to reject. This may involve multiple decisions over successive selection steps or hurdles. Some applicants ultimately become finalists for the job. At that point, the organization must decide to whom it will make the job offer, what the content of the offer will be, and how it will be drawn up and presented to the applicant. Upon the applicant's acceptance of the offer, the final match is complete, and the employment relationship is formally established.

For the applicant, the employment stage involves self-selection, a term that refers to deciding whether to continue in the staffing process or drop out. This decision may occur anywhere along the selection process, up to and including the moment of the job offer. If the applicant continues as part of the process through the final match, the applicant has decided to be a finalist. His or her attention now turns to a possible job offer, possible input and negotiation on its content, and making a final decision about the offer. The applicant's final decision is based on overall judgment about the likely suitability of the person/job match.

Note that the above staffing components apply to both external and internal staffing. Though this may seem obvious in the case of external staffing, a brief elaboration may be necessary for internal staffing, where the applicant is a current employee and the organization is the current employer. As we discussed above, Enterprise Rent-A-Car staffs the overwhelming majority of its managerial positions internally. Job opportunities (vacancies) exist within the organization and are filled through the activities of the internal labor market. Those activities involve recruitment, selection, and employment, with the employer and the employee as joint participants. As another example, at the investment banking firm Goldman Sachs, candidates for promotion to partner are identified through a multistep process.[14] They are "recruited" by division heads identifying prospective candidates for promotion (as in many internal staffing decisions, it is assumed that all employees are interested in promotion). Candidates are then vetted on the basis of input from senior managers in the firm and are evaluated from a dossier that contains the candidate's photograph, credentials, and accomplishments. After this six-month process, candidates are recommended for partner to the CEO, who then makes the final decision and offers partnership to those lucky enough to be selected (partners average $7 million a year, plus perks). When candidates accept the offer of partnership, the final match has occurred, and a new employment relationship has been established.

## Staffing Organizations

The overall staffing organizations model, which forms the framework for this book, is shown in Exhibit 1.6. It depicts that the organization's mission, along with its goals and objectives, drives both organization strategy and HR and staffing strategy, which interact with each other when they are being formulated. Staffing policies and programs result from such interaction and serve as an overlay to both support activities and core staffing activities. Employee retention and staffing system management concerns cut across these support and core staffing activities. Finally, though not shown in the model, it should be remembered that staffing levels and staffing quality are the key focal points of staffing strategy, policy, and programs. A more thorough examination of the model follows next.

### Organization, HR, and Staffing Strategy

Organizations formulate strategy to express an overall purpose or mission and to establish broad goals and objectives that will help the organization fulfill its mission. For example, a newly formed software development company may have a mission to "help individuals and families manage all of their personal finances and records through electronic means." With this mission statement, the organization might develop goals and objectives pertaining to product development, sales growth, and competitive differentiation through superior product quality and customer service.

Underlying these objectives are certain assumptions about the size and types of workforces that will need to be acquired, trained, managed, rewarded, and retained. HR strategy represents the key decisions about how these workforce assumptions will be handled. Such HR strategy may not only flow from the organization strat-

**EXHIBIT 1.6**   **Staffing Organizations Model**

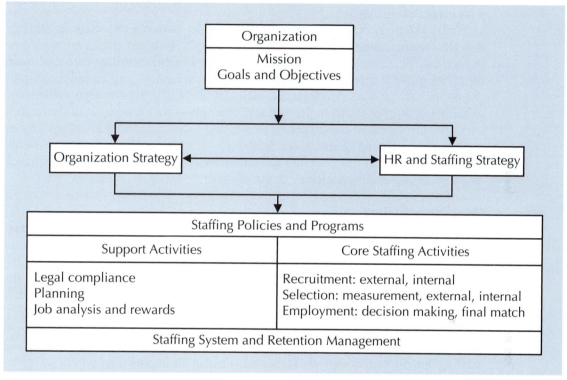

egy but also may actually contribute directly to the formulation of the organization's strategy.

Consider again the example of the software development company and its objective pertaining to new product development. Being able to develop new products assumes that sufficiently qualified product-development team members are available internally and externally, and that assurances from the HR department about availability may have been critical in helping the organization decide on its product development goals. From this general assumption, HR strategy may suggest (1) obtaining new, experienced employees from other software companies rather than going after newly minted college and graduate school graduates, (2) building a new facility for software development employees in a geographic area that is an attractive place to work, raise families, and pursue leisure activities, (3) developing relocation assistance packages and family-friendly benefits, (4) offering wages and salaries above the market average, plus using hiring bonuses to help lure new employees away from their current employers, (5) creating special training budgets for each employee to use at his or her own discretion for skills enhancement, and (6) putting in place a fast-track promotion system that allows employees to rise upward in either their professional specialty or the managerial ranks. In all these ways, HR strategy seeks to align acquisition and management of the workforce with organization strategy.

Staffing strategy is an outgrowth of the interplay between organization strategy and HR strategy, described above. It deals directly with key decisions regarding the acquisition, deployment, and retention of the organization's workforces. Such decisions guide the development of recruitment, selection, and employment programs. In the software development company example, the strategic decision to acquire new employees from the ranks of other organizations may lead the organization to develop very active, personalized, and secret recruiting activities for luring these experienced people away. It may also lead to the development of special selection techniques for assessing job experiences and accomplishments. In such ways, strategic staffing decisions shape the staffing process.

## Support Activities

Support activities serve as the foundation and necessary ingredients for the conduct of core staffing activities. Legal compliance represents knowledge of the myriad laws and regulations, especially equal employment opportunity and affirmative action (EEO/AA), and incorporation of their requirements into all phases of the core staffing activities. Planning serves as a tool for first becoming aware of key external influences on staffing, particularly economic conditions, labor markets, and labor unions. Such awareness shapes the formulation of staffing levels—both requirements and availabilities—the results of which drive planning for the core staffing activities. Job analysis represents the key mechanism by which the organization identifies and establishes the KSAO requirements for jobs, as well as the rewards that the jobs will provide, both first steps toward filling projected vacancies through core staffing activities.

Returning to our example of the software development company, if it meets various size thresholds for coverage (usually 15 or more employees), it must ensure that the staffing systems to be developed comply with all applicable federal, state, and local laws and regulations. Planning activities will revolve around first determining the major types of jobs that will be necessary for the product development venture, such as computer programmers, Internet specialists, and project managers. For each job, a forecast must be made about the number of employees needed and the likely availability of individuals both externally and internally for the job. Results of such forecasts serve as the key input for developing detailed staffing plans for the core staffing activities. Finally, job analysis will be needed to specify for each job exactly which KSAOs and rewards will be necessary for these sought-after new employees. Once all these support activities are in place, the core staffing activities can begin.

## Core Staffing Activities

Core staffing activities focus on recruitment, selection, and employment of the workforce. Since staffing levels have already been established as part of staffing planning, the emphasis shifts to staffing quality to ensure that successful person/ job and person/organization matches will be made. Accomplishment of this end result will require multiple plans, decisions, and activities, ranging from recruitment methods, communication with potential applicants with a special recruitment message, recruitment media, types of selection tools, deciding which applicants will receive job offers, and job offer packages. Staffing experts and the hiring manager will be involved in these core staffing activities. Moreover, it is likely that the activities will have to be developed and tailor-made for each type of job.

Consider the job of computer programmer in our software development company example. It will be necessary to develop specific plans for issues such as the following: Will we recruit only online, or will we use other methods such as newspaper ads or job fairs (recruitment methods)? What exactly will we tell applicants about the job and our organization (recruitment message), and how will we deliver the message, such as on our website or in a brochure (recruitment media)? What specific selection tools—such as interviews, assessments of experience, work samples, and background checks—will we use to assess and evaluate the applicants' KSAOs (selection techniques)? How will we combine and evaluate all the information we gather on applicants with these selection tools and then decide which applicants will receive job offers (decision making)? What exactly will we put in the job offer, and what will we be willing to negotiate (employment)?

## Staffing and Retention System Management

The various support and core staffing activities are quite complex, and they must be guided, coordinated, controlled, and evaluated. Such is the role of staffing system management. In our software development company example, what will be the role of the HR department, and what types of people will be needed to develop and manage the new staffing systems (administration of staffing systems)? How will we evaluate the results of these systems—will we collect and look at cost-per-hire and time-to-hire data (evaluation of staffing systems)? Data such as these are key effective indicators that both general and staffing managers are attuned to.

Finally, voluntary employee departure from the organization is usually costly and disruptive, and it can involve the loss of critical talent that is difficult to replace. Discharges can also be disruptive. Unless the organization is downsizing, replacements must be found in order to maintain desired staffing levels. The burden for such replacement staffing can be substantial, particularly if the turnover is unanticipated and unplanned. Other things being equal, greater employee retention means less staffing, and thus effective retention programs complement staffing programs.

In our software development company example, the primary focus will likely be on "staffing up" in order to keep producing existing products and developing new ones. Unless attention is also paid to employee retention, maintaining adequate staffing levels and quality may become problematic. Hence, the organization will need to monitor the amount and quality of employees who are leaving, along with the reasons they are leaving, in order to learn how much of the turnover is voluntary and avoidable; monitoring discharges will also be necessary. With these data, tailor-made retention strategies and programs to better meet employees' needs can be developed. If these are effective, strains on the staffing system will be lessened.

The remainder of the book is structured around and built on the staffing organizations model shown in Exhibit 1.6.

## STAFFING STRATEGY

As noted, staffing strategy requires making key decisions about the acquisition, deployment, and retention of the organization's workforce. Thirteen such decisions are identified and discussed below. Some decisions pertain primarily to staffing levels, and others pertain primarily to staffing quality. A summary of the decisions is shown in Exhibit 1.7. While each decision is shown as an either-or, each is more appropriately thought of as lying on a continuum anchored at the ends by these either-or extremes. When discussing the decisions, continued reference is made to the software development company example.

### Staffing Levels

#### Acquire or Develop Talent

A pure acquisition staffing strategy would have an organization concentrate on acquiring new employees who can "hit the ground running" and be at peak per-

---

**EXHIBIT 1.7    Strategic Staffing Decisions**

**Staffing Levels**
- Acquire or Develop Talent
- Hire Yourself or Outsource
- External or Internal Hiring
- Core or Flexible Workforce
- Hire or Retain
- National or Global
- Attract or Relocate
- Overstaff or Understaff
- Short- or Long-Term Focus

**Staffing Quality**
- Person/Job or Person/Organization Match
- Specific or General KSAOs
- Exceptional or Acceptable Workforce Quality
- Active or Passive Diversity

formance the moment they arrive. These employees would bring their talents with them to the job, with little or no need for training or development. A pure development strategy would lead to acquisition of just about anyone who is willing and able to learn the KSAOs required by the job. Staffing strategy must position the organization appropriately along this "buy or make your talent" continuum. For critical and newly created positions, such as might occur in the software development company example, the emphasis would likely be on acquiring talent because of the urgency of developing new products. There may be no time to train, and qualified internal candidates may not be available.

### Hire Yourself or Outsource

Increasingly, organizations are outsourcing their hiring activities, meaning they use outside organizations to recruit and select employees. Although there are variations of staffing outsourcing (we will have more to say about it in Chapter 3), in some cases, an organization wholly cedes decision-making authority to the vendor. Why might an organization do this? First, it may believe that the vendor can do a better job of identifying candidates than the organization itself can do. This is particularly true for small and mid-sized companies that lack a professional HR function. Second, in labor shortages, an organization may not be able to recruit enough employees on its own, so it may supplement its recruiting or selection efforts with those of a vendor that specializes in staffing. Finally, outsourcing may also have advantages for legal compliance, as many vendors maintain their own procedures for tracking compliance with equal-opportunity laws.

### External or Internal Hiring

When job vacancies occur or new jobs are created, should the organization seek to fill them from the external or internal labor market? While some mixture of external and internal hiring will be necessary in most situations, the relative blend could vary substantially. To the extent that the organization wants to cultivate a stable, committed workforce, it will probably need to emphasize internal hiring. This will allow employees to use the internal labor market as a springboard for launching long-term careers within the organization. External hiring might then be restricted to specific entry-level jobs, as well as newly created ones for which there are no acceptable internal applicants. External hiring might also be necessary when there is rapid organization growth, such that the number of new jobs created outstrips internal supply.

### Core or Flexible Workforce

The organization's core workforce is made up of individuals who are viewed (and view themselves) as regular full-time or part-time employees of the organization. They are central to the core goods and services delivered by the organization.

The flexible workforce is composed of more peripheral workers who are used on an as-needed, just-in-time basis. They are not viewed (nor do they view themselves) as regular employees, and legally, most of them are not even employees of the organization. Rather, they are employees of an alternative organization such as a staffing firm (temporary help agency) or independent contractor that provides these workers to the organization. The organization must decide whether to use both core and flexible workforces, what the mixture of core versus flexible workers will be, and in what jobs and units of the organization these mixtures will be deployed. Within the software development company, programmers might be considered part of the core workforce, but ancillary workers (e.g., clerical) may be part of the flexible workforce, particularly since the need for them will depend on the speed and success of new product development.

### Hire or Retain

There are trade-offs between hiring strategies and retention strategies for staffing. At one extreme, the organization can accept whatever level of turnover occurs and simply hire replacements to fill the vacancies. Alternatively, the organization can seek to minimize turnover so that the need for replacement staffing is held to a minimum. For example, SAS Institute, a company that frequently finds itself on *Fortune* magazine's "100 Best Companies to Work For" list, has an annual turnover rate of less than 3%, meaning that fewer than 3 out of 100 of its employees leave voluntarily within a 12-month period. The company's ability to retain its employees at such a high level is likely due in part to the generous perks it offers, including subsidized Montessori child care, unlimited sick time, a free health care center, and four cafeterias serviced by a local organic farm.[15] Since these strategies have costs and benefits associated with them, the organization could conduct an analysis to determine these and then strive for an optimal mix of hiring and retention. In this way the organization can control its inflow needs (replacement staffing) by controlling its outflow (retention).

### National or Global

As we noted earlier, one form of outsourcing is when organizations outsource staffing activities. Of course, many organizations outsource more than staffing activities—technical support, database management, customer service, and manufacturing are common examples. A growing number of computer-chip makers, such as IBM, Intel, and Motorola, contract with outside vendors to manufacture their chips; often these companies are overseas. Offshoring is related to, but distinct from, outsourcing. Whereas outsourcing is moving a business process (service or manufacturing) to another vendor (whether that vendor is inside or outside the organization's home country), offshoring is the organization setting up its own operations in another country (the organization is not contracting with an outside vendor; rather, it is establishing its own operations in another country). In the computer-chip example, outsourcing would be if the organization, say, IBM, contracted with an outside vendor to manufacture the chips. Offshoring would be if IBM set up its own plant in another country to manufacture the chips.

Increasingly, US organizations are engaged in both overseas outsourcing and offshoring, a trend spurred by three forces. First, most nations have lowered trading and immigration barriers, which has facilitated offshoring and overseas outsourcing. Second, particularly in the United States and western Europe, organizations find that by outsourcing or offshoring, they can manufacture goods or provide services more cheaply than they can in their own country. Third, some organizations cannot find sufficient talent in their home countries, so they have to look elsewhere. Many high-tech companies in the United States and western Europe are facing severe talent shortages. Siemens, the German engineering giant, has 2,500 positions for engineers open in Germany alone. These shortages have required many companies like Siemens to outsource overseas, to offshore, or to do both.[16]

### Attract or Relocate

Typical staffing strategy is based on the premise that the organization can induce sufficient numbers of qualified people to come to it for employment. Another version of this premise is that it is better (and cheaper) to bring the labor to the organization than to bring the organization to the labor. Some organizations, both established and new ones, challenge this premise and choose locations where there are ample labor supplies. The shift of lumber mills and automobile manufacturing plants to the southern United States reflects such a strategy. Likewise, the growth of high technology pockets such as Silicon Valley reflects the establishment or movement of organizations to geographic areas where there is ready access to highly skilled labor and where employees would like to live, usually locations with research universities nearby to provide the needed graduates for jobs. The software development company, for example, might find locating in such an area very desirable.

### Overstaff or Understaff

While most organizations seek to be reasonably fully staffed, some opt for being over- or understaffed. Overstaffing may occur when there are dips in demand for the organization's products or services that the organization chooses to ride out. Organizations may also overstaff in order to stockpile talent, recognizing that the staffing spigot cannot be easily turned on or off. Alternatively, understaffing may occur when the organization is confronted with chronic labor shortages, such as is the case for nurses in health care facilities. Also, prediction of an economic downturn may lead the organization to understaff in order to avoid future layoffs. Finally, the organization may decide to understaff and adjust staffing level demand spikes by increasing employee overtime or using flexible staffing arrangements such as temporary employees. Many have blamed the slow job recovery following the Great Recession on the reluctance of companies to put themselves in an overstaffing situation, instead asking current employees to work longer hours in order to handle increased demand in the company's products or services. The software development company might choose to overstaff in order to retain key employees and to be poised to meet the hopeful surges in demand as its new products are released.

## Short- or Long-Term Focus

Although any organization would want to have its staffing needs fully anticipated for both the short term and the long term, optimizing both goals is difficult, so trade-offs are often required. In this case, it often means addressing short-term labor shortages by identifying and developing talent for the long term. When forced to choose, organizations focus on their short-term needs. This is understandable because labor shortages can be debilitating. Even when the overall economy is sluggish, the pool of qualified applicants may be thin. One recruiting expert noted, "The weak labor market has really increased the noise level as more unqualified candidates apply for a decreasing number of job openings."[17] So, even in periods of economic duress, a labor shortage can happen in any industry. When business leaders in the trucking industry were asked to identify their top business concerns, 86% of executives listed the unavailability of drivers as one of their top three concerns.[18]

Balanced against this short-term "crisis management" focus are long-term concerns. Organizations with a long-term view of their staffing needs have put in place talent management programs. In some cases, this means thinking about the strategic talent, or future skill, needs for the entire organization. Bringing to mind John Maynard Keynes's comment, "In the long run we are all dead," the problem with a long-term focus is that long-term needs (demand) and availability (supply) are often unclear. Often, it seems as if calls for an upcoming labor shortage due to baby boomer retirements never end. As Peter Cappelli concludes, "They've been predicting a labor shortage since the mid-1990's and guess what, it's not happening." The Bureau of Labor Statistics (BLS) estimates that by 2018, the total labor force will shrink markedly, causing future labor shortages. However, BLS economist Ian Wyatt admits that whereas population and labor force growth can be forecasted fairly accurately, labor demand estimates are far less reliable. The future demand for workers "is a very tough question to answer," Wyatt said. "Perhaps because of this, while most organizations are aware of projected labor shortages, many fewer have any concrete plans to do anything about it."[19]

These long-term forecasting difficulties notwithstanding, growth will occur in some skill areas, while others will decrease in demand. Employers who make no efforts to project future supply and demand risk having their strategies derailed by lack of available labor. As a result of a lack of planning, some companies are facing unanticipated skilled labor shortages. For example, Linda Fillingham cannot find skilled laborers to work in her family's Bloomington, Illinois, steel plant.

Fillingham expresses puzzlement as to her labor shortage, given the alleged lack of job growth in manufacturing: "It's there if you want to do it," she says. Perhaps long-term planning would have avoided or ameliorated Fillingham's dilemma.[20]

## Staffing Quality

### Person/Job or Person/Organization Match

When acquiring and deploying people, should the organization opt for a person/job or person/organization match? This is a complex decision. In part, a person/job match will have to be assessed any time a person is hired to perform a finite set of tasks. In our software company example, programmers might be hired to do programming in a specific language such as Java, and most certainly the organization would want to assess whether applicants meet this specific job requirement. On the other hand, jobs may be poorly defined and fluid, making a person/job match infeasible and requiring a person/organization match instead. Such jobs are often found in technology and software development organizations.

### Specific or General KSAOs

Should the organization acquire people with specific KSAOs or more general ones? The former means focusing on job-specific competencies, often of the job knowledge and technical skill variety. The latter requires a focus on KSAOs that will be applicable across a variety of jobs, both current and future. Examples of such KSAOs include flexibility and adaptability, ability to learn, written and oral communication skills, and algebra/statistics skills. An organization expecting rapid changes in job content and new job creation, such as in the software company example, might position itself closer to the general competencies end of the continuum.

### Exceptional or Acceptable Workforce Quality

Strategically, the organization could seek to acquire a workforce that is preeminent KSAO-wise (exceptional quality) or that is more "ballpark" variety KSAO-wise (acceptable quality). Pursuit of the exceptional strategy would allow the organization to stock up on the "best and the brightest" with the hope that this exceptional talent pool would deliver truly superior performance. The acceptable strategy means pursuit of a less high-powered workforce and probably a less expensive one as well. If the software development company is trying to create clearly innovative and superior products, it will likely opt for the exceptional workforce quality end of the continuum.

### Active or Passive Diversity

The labor force is becoming increasingly diverse in terms of demographics, values, and languages. Does the organization want to actively pursue this diversity in the labor market so that its own workforce mirrors it, or does the organization want to more passively let diversity of its workforce happen? Advocates of an active diversity strategy argue that it is legally and morally appropriate and that a diverse workforce allows the organization to be more attuned to the diverse needs of the customers it serves. Those favoring a more passive strategy suggest that diversification of the workforce takes time because it requires substantial planning and assimilation activity. In the software company illustration, an active diversity strategy might be pursued as a way of acquiring workers who can help identify a diverse array of software products that might be received favorably by various segments of the marketplace.

## STAFFING ETHICS

Staffing the organization involves a multitude of individuals—hiring managers, staffing professionals, potential coworkers, legal advisors, and job applicants. During the staffing process, all of these individuals may be involved in recruitment, selection, and employment activities, as well as decision making. Are there, or should there be, boundaries on these individuals' actions and decisions? The answer is yes, for without boundaries, potentially negative outcomes and harmful effects may occur. For example, staffing is often a hurried process, driven by tight deadlines and calls for expediency (e.g., the hiring manager who says to the staffing professional, "Just get me someone now—I'll worry about how good they are later on"). Such calls may lead to negative consequences, including hiring someone without proper assessment and subsequently having him or her perform poorly, ignoring the many applicants who would have been successful performers, failing to advance the organization's workforce diversity initiatives and possible legal obligations, and making an exceedingly generous job offer that provides the highest salary in the work unit, causing dissatisfaction and possible turnover among other work unit members. Such actions and outcomes raise staffing ethics issues.

Ethics involves determining moral principles and guidelines for acceptable practice. Within the realm of the workplace, ethics emphasizes "knowing organizational codes and guidelines and behaving within these boundaries when faced with dilemmas in business or professional work."[21] More specifically, organizational ethics seeks to do the following:

- Raise ethical expectations
- Legitimize dialogue about ethical issues
- Encourage ethical decision making
- Prevent misconduct and provide a basis for enforcement

While organizations are increasingly developing general codes of conduct, it is unknown whether these codes contain specific staffing provisions. Even the general code will likely have some pertinence to staffing through provisions on such issues as legal compliance, confidentiality and disclosure of information, and use of organizational property and assets. Individuals involved in staffing should know and follow their organization's code of ethics. As pertains to staffing specifically, there are several points that can guide a person's ethical conduct. These points are shown in Exhibit 1.8 and elaborated on below.

The first point is that the person is serving as an agent of the organization and is duty bound to represent the organization first and foremost. That duty is to bring into being effective person/job and person/organization matches. The second point indicates that the agent must avoid placing his or her own interest, or that of a third party (such as an applicant or friend), above that of the organization. Point three suggests that even though the HR professional represents the organization, he or she should remember that the applicant is a participant in the staffing process. How the HR professional treats applicants may well lead to reactions by them that are favorable to the organization and further its interests, let alone those of applicants. Point four reminds the HR professional to know the organization's staffing policies and procedures and adhere to them. The fifth point indicates a need to be knowledgeable of the myriad laws and regulations governing staffing, to follow them, and to seek needed assistance in their interpretation and application. Point six guides the HR professional toward professional codes of conduct pertaining to staffing and HR. For example, the Society for Human Resource Management (SHRM) has a formal code of ethics. The Society for Industrial and Organizational Psychology (SIOP) follows the ethics code of the American Psychological Association (APA) and has issued a set of professional principles to guide appropriate use of employee selection procedures. The seventh point states that there is considerable useful research-based knowledge about the design and effectiveness of staffing systems and techniques that should guide

---

**EXHIBIT 1.8** **Suggestions for Ethical Staffing Practice**

1. Represent the organization's interests.
2. Beware of conflicts of interest.
3. Remember the job applicant.
4. Follow staffing policies and procedures.
5. Know and follow the law.
6. Consult professional codes of conduct.
7. Shape effective practice with research results.
8. Seek ethics advice.
9. Be aware of an organization's ethical climate/culture.

staffing practice. Much of that research is summarized in usable formats in this book. The eighth point suggests that when confronted with ethical issues, it is appropriate to seek ethical advice from others. Handling troubling ethical issues alone is unwise.

The final point is that one must be aware of an organization's climate and culture for ethical behavior. Organizations differ in their ethical climate/culture, and this has two implications for staffing.[22] First, an organization may have expectations for *how* staffing decisions are made. How an organization communicates with recruits (including those who are rejected) and whether selection decisions are made hierarchically or collaboratively are two examples of ethical staffing issues that may well vary from organization to organization. Second, an organization's ethics climate may well affect *which* staffing decisions are made. An organization that has high expectations for ethics may weight selection information differently (placing more weight on, say, background checks) than an organization with more typical expectations.

In both of these ways, one needs to realize that while some ethics considerations are universal, in other cases, what is considered ethical in one climate may be seen as a breach of ethics in another.

It should be recognized that many pressure points on HR professionals may cause them to compromise the ethical standards discussed above. Research suggests that the principal causes of this pressure are the felt need to follow a boss's directive, meet overly aggressive business objectives, help the organization survive, meet scheduling pressures, be a team player, save jobs, and advance the boss's career.[23]

The suggestions for ethical staffing practice in Exhibit 1.8 are a guide to one's own behavior. Being aware of and consciously attempting to follow these constitute a professional and ethical responsibility. But what about situations in which ethical lapses are suspected or observed in others?

One response to the situation is to do nothing—neither report nor attempt to change the misconduct. Research suggests a small proportion (about 20%) choose to ignore and not report misconduct.[24] Major reasons for this response include a belief that no action would be taken, a fear of retaliation from one's boss or senior management, not trusting promises of confidentiality, and a fear of not being seen as a team player. Against such reasons for inaction must be weighed the harm that has, or could, come to the employer, the employee, or the job applicant. Moreover, failure to report the misconduct may well increase the chances that it will be repeated, with continuing harmful consequences. Not reporting misconduct may also conflict with one's personal values and create remorse for not having done the right thing. Finally, a failure to report misconduct may bring penalties to oneself if that failure subsequently becomes known to one's boss or senior management. In short, "looking the other way" should not be viewed as a safe, wise, or ethical choice.

A different way to handle unethical staffing practices by others is to seek advice from one's boss, senior management, coworkers, legal counsel, ethics officer or ombudsperson, or an outside friend or family member. The guidelines in Exhibit 1.8 can serve as a helpful starting point to frame the discussion and make a decision about what to do.

At times, the appropriate response to others' misconduct is to step in directly to try to prevent or rectify the misconduct. This would be especially appropriate with employees whom one supervises or with coworkers. Before taking such an action, it would be wise to consider whether one has the authority and resources to do so, along with the likely support of those other employees or coworkers.

## PLAN FOR THE BOOK

The book is divided into six parts:

1. The Nature of Staffing
2. Support Activities
3. Staffing Activities: Recruitment
4. Staffing Activities: Selection
5. Staffing Activities: Employment
6. Staffing System and Retention Management

Each chapter in these six parts begins with a brief topical outline to help the reader quickly discern its general contents. The "meat" of the chapter comes next. A chapter summary then reviews and highlights points from the chapter. A set of discussion questions, ethical issues to discuss, applications (cases and exercises), and detailed endnotes complete the chapter.

The importance of laws and regulations is such that they are considered first in Chapter 2 (Legal Compliance). The laws and regulations, in particular, have become so pervasive that they require special treatment. Therefore, Chapter 2 reviews the basic laws affecting staffing, with an emphasis on the major federal laws and regulations pertaining to EEO/AA matters generally. Specific provisions relevant to staffing are covered in depth. Each subsequent chapter has a separate section labeled "Legal Issues," in which specific legal topics relevant to the chapter's content are discussed. This allows for a more focused discussion of legal issues while not diverting attention from the major thrust of the book.

The endnotes at the end of each chapter are quite extensive. They are drawn from academic, practitioner, and legal sources with the goal of providing a balanced selection from each of these sources. Emphasis is on the inclusion of recent references of high quality and easy accessibility. An overly lengthy list of references to each specific topic is avoided; instead, a sampling of only the best available is included.

The applications at the end of each chapter are of two varieties. First are cases that describe a particular situation and require analysis and response. The response may be written or oral (such as in class discussion or a group presentation). Second are exercises that entail small projects and require active practice of a particular task. Through these cases and exercises the reader becomes an active participant in the learning process and is able to apply the concepts provided in each chapter.

## SUMMARY

At the national level, staffing involves a huge number of hiring transactions each year, is a major cost of doing business (especially for service-providing industries), and can lead to substantial revenue and market value growth for the organization. Staffing is defined as "the process of acquiring, deploying, and retaining a workforce of sufficient quantity and quality to create positive impacts on the organization's effectiveness." The definition emphasizes that both staffing levels and labor quality contribute to an organization's effectiveness, and that a concerted set of labor acquisition, deployment, and retention actions guides the flow of people into, within, and out of the organization. Descriptions of three staffing systems help highlight the definition of staffing.

Several models illustrate various elements of staffing. The staffing level model shows how projected labor requirements and availabilities are compared to derive staffing levels that represent being overstaffed, fully staffed, or understaffed. The next two models illustrate staffing quality via the person/job and person/organization match. The former indicates there is a need to match (1) the person's KSAOs to job requirements and (2) the person's motivation to the job's rewards. In the person/organization match, the person's characteristics are matched to additional factors beyond the target job, namely, organizational values, new job duties for the target job, multiple jobs, and future jobs. Effectively managing the matching process results in positive impacts on HR outcomes such as attraction, performance, and retention. The core staffing components model shows that there are three basic activities in staffing: recruitment (identification and attraction of applicants), selection (assessment and evaluation of applicants), and employment (decision making and final match). The staffing organizations model shows that organization, HR, and staffing strategies are formulated and shape staffing policies and programs. In turn, these meld into a set of staffing support activities (legal compliance, planning, and job analysis), as well as the core activities (recruitment, selection, and employment). Retention and staffing system management activities cut across both support and core activities.

Staffing strategy is both an outgrowth of and a contributor to HR and organization strategy. Thirteen important strategic staffing decisions loom for any organization. Some pertain to staffing level choices, and others deal with staffing quality choices.

Staffing ethics involves determining moral principles and guidelines for practice. Numerous suggestions were made for ethical conduct in staffing, and many pressure points for sidestepping such conduct are in operation. There are appropriate ways to handle such pressures, which will be discussed.

The staffing organizations model serves as the structural framework for the book. The first part treats staffing models and strategy. The second part treats the support activities of legal compliance, planning, and job analysis. The next three parts treat the core staffing activities of recruitment, selection, and employment. The last section addresses staffing systems and employee retention management. As mentioned previously, each chapter has a section labeled "Legal Issues," as well as discussion questions, ethical issues questions, applications, and endnotes.

## DISCUSSION QUESTIONS

1. What are potential problems with having a staffing process in which vacancies are filled (1) on a lottery basis from among job applicants, or (2) on a first come–first hired basis among job applicants?

2. Why is it important for the organization to view all components of staffing (recruitment, selection, and employment) from the perspective of the job applicant?

3. Would it be desirable to hire people only according to the person/organization match, ignoring the person/job match?

4. What are examples of how staffing activities are influenced by training activities? Compensation activities?

5. Are some of the 13 strategic staffing decisions more important than others? If so, which ones? Why?

## ETHICAL ISSUES

1. Assume that you are either the staffing professional in the department or the hiring manager of a work unit. Explain why it is so important to represent the organization's interests (see Exhibit 1.8). What are some possible consequences of not doing so?

2. One of the strategic staffing choices is whether to pursue workforce diversity actively or passively. First suggest some ethical reasons for active pursuit of diversity, and then suggest some ethical reasons for a more passive approach. Assume that the type of diversity in question is increasing workforce representation of women and ethnic minorities.

## APPLICATIONS

### Staffing for Your Own Job

#### Instructions

Consider a job you previously held or your current job. Use the staffing components model to help you think through and describe the staffing process that led to your getting hired for the job. Trace and describe the process (1) from your own perspective as a job applicant and (2) from the organization's perspective. Listed below are some questions to jog your memory. Write your responses to these questions and be prepared to discuss them.

#### Applicant Perspective

Recruitment:

1. Why did you identify and seek out the job with this organization?
2. How did you try to make yourself attractive to the organization?

Selection:

1. How did you gather information about the job's requirements and rewards?
2. How did you judge your own KSAOs and needs relative to these requirements and rewards?

Employment:

1. Why did you decide to continue on in the staffing process, rather than drop out of it?
2. Why did you decide to accept the job offer? What were the pluses and minuses of the job?

#### Organization Perspective

Even if you are unsure of the answers to the following questions, try to answer them or guess at them.

Recruitment:

1. How did the organization identify you as a job applicant?
2. How did the organization make the job attractive to you?

Selection:

1. What techniques (application blank, interview, etc.) did the organization use to gather KSAO information about you?
2. How did the organization evaluate this information? What did it see as your strong and weak points, KSAO-wise?

Employment:

1. Why did the organization continue to pursue you as an applicant, rather than reject you from further consideration?
2. What was the job offer process like? Did you receive a verbal or written offer (or both)? Who made the offer? What was the content of the offer?

### Reactions to the Staffing Process

Now that you have described the staffing process, what are your reactions to it?

1. What were the strong points or positive features of the process?
2. What were the weak points or negative features of the process?
3. What changes would you like to see made in the process, and why?

## Staffing Strategy for a New Plant

Household Consumer Enterprises, Inc. (HCE) specializes in the design and production of household products such as brooms, brushes, rakes, kitchen utensils, and garden tools. It has its corporate headquarters in downtown Chicago, with manufacturing and warehouse/distribution facilities throughout the north-central region of the United States. The organization recently changed its mission from "providing households with safe and sturdy utensils" to "providing households with visually appealing utensils that are safe and sturdy." The new emphasis on "visually appealing" will necessitate new strategies for designing and producing products that have design flair and imagination built into them. One strategy under consideration is to target various demographic groups with different utensil designs. One group is 25- to 40-year-old professional and managerial people, who are believed to want such utensils for both their visual and conversation-piece appeal.

A tentative strategy is to build and staff a new plant that will have free rein in the design and production of utensils for this 25–40 age group. To start, the plant will focus on producing a set of closely related (design-wise) plastic products: dishwashing pans, outdoor wastebaskets, outdoor plant holders, and watering cans. These items can be produced without too large a capital and facilities investment, can be marketed as a group, and can be on stores' shelves and on HCE's store website in time for Christmas sales.

The facility's design and engineering team has decided that each of the four products will be produced on a separate assembly line, though the lines will share common technology and require roughly similar assembly jobs. Following the advice from the HR vice president, Jarimir Zwitski, the key jobs in the plant for staffing purposes will be plant manager, product designer (computer-assisted design), assemblers, and packers/warehouse workers. The initial staffing level for the plant will be 150 employees. Because of the riskiness of the venture and the low initial margins that are planned on the four products due to high start-up costs, the plant will run continuously six days per week (i.e., a 24/6 schedule), with the remaining day reserved for cleaning and maintenance. Pay levels will be at the low end of the market, except for product designers, who will be paid above market. Employees will have limited benefits, namely, health insurance with a 30% employee copay after one year of continuous employment and an earned time-off bank (for holidays, sickness, and vacation) of 160 hours per year. They will not receive a pension plan.

The head of the design team, Maria Dos Santos, and Mr. Zwitski wish to come to you, the corporate manager of staffing, to share their preliminary thinking and ask you some questions, knowing that staffing issues abound for this new venture. They ask you to discuss the following questions with them, which they have sent to you in advance so you can prepare for the meeting:

1. What geographic location might be best for the plant in terms of attracting sufficient quantity and quality of labor, especially for the key jobs?
2. Should the plant manager come from inside the current managerial ranks or be sought from the outside?
3. Should staffing be based on just the person/job match or also on the person/organization match?
4. Would it make sense to initially staff the plant with a flexible workforce by using temporary employees and then shift over to a core workforce if it looks like the plant will be successful?
5. In the early stages, should the plant be fully staffed, understaffed, or overstaffed?
6. Will employee retention likely be a problem, and if so, how will this affect the viability of the new plant?

Your task is to write out a tentative response to each question that will be the basis for your discussion at the meeting.

## ENDNOTES

1. "2010 County Business Patterns," *United States Census Bureau* (*www.census.gov/econ/susb/*), accessed 8/27/13.
2. M. deWolf and K. Klemmer, "Job Openings, Hires, and Separations Fall During the Recession," *Monthly Labor Review*, May 2010, pp. 36–44.
3. Saratoga Institute, *The Saratoga Review* (Santa Clara, CA: author, 2009), p. 10.

4. R. R. Kehoe and P. M. Wright, "The Impact of High-Performance Human Resource Practices on Employees' Attitudes and Behaviors," *Journal of Management*, 2013, 39, pp. 366–391.

5. J. B. Barney and P. M. Wright, "On Becoming a Strategic Partner: The Role of Human Resources in Gaining Competitive Advantage," *Human Resource Management*, 1998, 37(1), pp. 31–46; C. G. Brush, P. G. Greene, and M. M. Hart, "From Initial Idea to Unique Advantage: The Entrepreneurial Challenge of Constructing a Resource Base," *Academy of Management Executive*, 2001, 15(1), pp. 64–80.

6. J. Smith, "The Companies Hiring the Most Right Now," *Forbes*, Mar. 28, 2013 (*www.forbes.com/sites/jacquelynsmith/2013/03/28/the-companies-hiring-the-most-right-now-2/*), accessed 8/27/13.

7. C. Fleck, "Not Just a Job," *Staffing Management*, 2010, 6(1), (*www.shrm.org*); G. Hamel, "Inventing the Future of Management," Oct. 25, 2010, Ross School of Business, University of Michigan (*www.bus.umich.edu/NewsRoom/ArticleDisplay.asp?news_id=20780*).

8. "Mike's Story," W. L. Gore & Associates (*www.gore.com/en_xx/careers/associatestories/comfort/comfort_mike.html*); "Hajo's Story," W. L. Gore & Associates (*www.gore.com/en_xx/careers/associatestories/lives1/lives1_hajo.html*); "Our Culture," W. L. Gore & Associates, Inc., 2010 (*www.gore.com*).

9. J. Marquez, "A Talent Strategy Overhaul at Pfizer," *Workforce Management*, Feb. 12, 2007, pp. 1, 3.

10. A. Fisher, "Graduating This Spring? How to Stand Out From the Crowd," *Fortune*, Mar. 1, 2013 (*http://management.fortune.cnn.com/2013/03/01/college-grad-job-search-tips/*), accessed 8/28/13; S. Pathak, "Frat Boys Get an MBA Without the IOU at Enterprise," *Sales Job Watch*, Mar. 3, 2011 (*http://sales-jobs.fins.com/Articles/SB129866279544689937/Frat-Boys-Get-an-MBA-Without-the-IOU-at-Enterprise*), accessed 8/28/13.

11. D. F. Caldwell and C. A. O'Reilly III, "Measuring Person-Job Fit With a Profile-Comparison Process," *Journal of Applied Psychology*, 1990, 75, pp. 648–657; R. V. Dawis, "Person-Environment Fit and Job Satisfaction," in C. J. Cranny, P. C. Smith, and E. F. Stone (eds.), *Job Satisfaction* (New York: Lexington, 1992), pp. 69–88; R. V. Dawis, L. H. Lofquist, and D. J. Weiss, *A Theory of Work Adjustment (A Revision)* (Minneapolis: Industrial Relations Center, University of Minnesota, 1968).

12. T. A. Judge and R. D. Bretz, Jr., "Effects of Work Values on Job Choice Decisions," *Journal of Applied Psychology*, 1992, 77, pp. 1–11; C. A. O'Reilly III, J. Chatman, and D. F. Caldwell, "People and Organizational Culture: A Profile Comparison Approach to Assessing Person-Organization Fit," *Academy of Management Journal*, 1991, 34, pp. 487–516; A. L. Kristof, "Person-Organization Fit: An Integrative Review of Its Conceptualizations, Measurement, and Implications," *Personnel Psychology*, 1996, 49, pp. 1–50; A. K. Brown and J. Billsberry, *Fit: Key Issues and New Directions* (Malden, MA: John Wiley & Sons, 2013).

13. L. L. Levesque, "Opportunistic Hiring and Employee Fit," *Human Resource Management*, 2005, 44, pp. 301–317.

14. S. Craig, "Inside Goldman's Secret Rite: The Race to Become Partner," *Wall Street Journal*, Oct. 13, 2006, pp. A1, A11.

15. "100 Best Companies to Work For," *Fortune*, 2012 (*http://money.cnn.com/magazines/fortune/best-companies/2012/*), accessed 8/28/13.

16. M. Kessler, "More Chipmakers Outsource Manufacturing," *USA Today*, Nov. 16, 2006, p. B1; C. Dougherty, "Labor Shortage Becoming Acute in Technology," *New York Times*, Mar. 10, 2007, pp. 1, 4.

17. B. Leonard, "Economic Climate Provides Chance to Refine Recruiting Practices," *Staffing Management*, July 14, 2009 (*www.shrm.org*).

18. S. Wisnefski, "Truckers' Worries: Fuel, Driver Short-fall," *Wall Street Journal*, Oct. 25, 2006, p. B3A.

19. K. R. Lewis, "Recession Aside, Are We Headed for a Labor Shortage?" *The Fiscal Times*, Aug. 26, 2010 (*www.thefiscaltimes.com*); K. Gurchiek, "Few Organizations Planning for Talent Shortage as Boomers Retire," *SHRM News*, Nov. 17, 2010 (*www.shrm.org*).

20. C. Bowers, "Skilled Labor Shortage Frustrates Employers," *CBS Evening News*, Aug. 11, 2010 (*www.cbsnews.com/stories/2010/08/11/eveningnews/main6764731.shtml?tag=mncol;lst;1*).

21. *www.shrm.org/kc.*

22. A. Ardichvili and D. Jondle, "Ethical Business Cultures: A Literature Review and Implications for HRD," *Human Resource Development Review*, 2009, 8(2), pp. 223–244.

23. J. Joseph and E. Esen, *2003 Business Ethics Survey* (Alexandria, VA: Society for Human Resource Management, 2003), pp. 1–10.

24. Joseph and Esen, *2003 Business Ethics Survey*, pp. 10–11.

# The Staffing Organizations Model

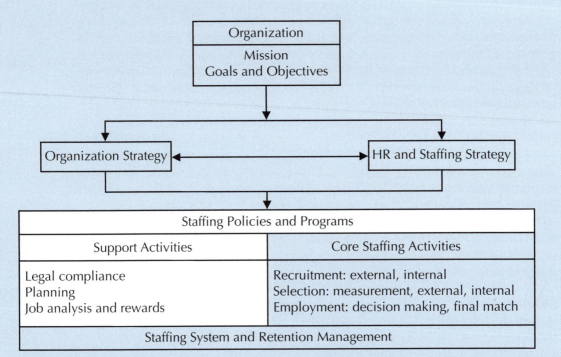

# PART TWO

## Support Activities

# CHAPTER TWO

## Legal Compliance

**Learning Objectives and Introduction**
Learning Objectives
Introduction

**The Employment Relationship**
Employer–Employee
Independent Contractors
Temporary Employees
Unpaid Interns and Trainees

**Laws and Regulations**
Need for Laws and Regulations
Sources of Laws and Regulations

**EEO/AA Laws: General Provisions and Enforcement**
General Provisions
Enforcement: EEOC
Enforcement: OFCCP

**EEO/AA Laws: Specific Staffing Provisions**
Civil Rights Acts (1964, 1991)
Age Discrimination in Employment Act (1967)
Americans With Disabilities Act (1990, 2008)
Genetic Information Nondiscrimination Act (2008)
Rehabilitation Act (1973)
Executive Order 11246 (1965)

**Other Staffing Laws**
Federal Laws
State and Local Laws
Civil Service Laws and Regulations

**Legal Issues in Remainder of Book**

**Summary**

**Discussion Questions**

**Ethical Issues**

**Applications**

**Endnotes**

# LEARNING OBJECTIVES AND INTRODUCTION

## Learning Objectives

- Contrast legal differences among employees, independent contractors, and temporary employees
- Appreciate why staffing laws are necessary, and their sources
- Review six major federal equal employment opportunity and affirmative action laws
- Distinguish between disparate treatment and adverse (disparate) impact approaches to enforcement
- Examine specific staffing provisions of the six major laws
- Look at other important staffing laws and regulations
- Gain an overview of legal issues covered in Chapters 3–14

## Introduction

When the organization selects people to do work for it, a legal employment relationship is established. The selected people may be employees, independent contractors, or temporary employees. Laws are needed to define how the employer may use each type of worker, as well as the rights of each type. In addition, laws have been developed to create fairness and nondiscrimination in staffing. The laws and accompanying regulations prohibit discrimination on the basis of many protected characteristics, such as race, sex, and disability. Actions based on these characteristics must be removed from staffing practices and decisions. Instead, employers must focus on job-related KSAOs (knowledge, skill, ability, and other characteristics) as the bases for those practices and decisions. Employers that ignore or sidestep these laws and regulations could potentially face stiff penalties.

This chapter begins by discussing the formation of the employment relationship from a legal perspective. It first defines what an employer is, along with the rights and obligations of being an employer. The employer may acquire people to work for it in the form of employees, independent contractors, and temporary employees. Legal meanings and implications for each of these terms are provided.

The employment relationship has become increasingly regulated, and reasons for the myriad laws and regulations affecting the employment relationship are suggested. Next, the major sources of the laws and regulations controlling the employment relationship are indicated.

Equal employment opportunity and affirmative action (EEO/AA) laws and regulations have become paramount in the eyes of many who are concerned with staffing organizations. The general provisions of six major EEO/AA laws are summarized, along with indications of how these laws are administered and enforced. While voluntary compliance is preferred by the enforcement agencies, if it fails, litigation may follow. Litigation is based on the key concepts of disparate treatment and disparate impact.

For these same six laws, their specific (and numerous) provisions regarding staffing are then presented in detail. Within this presentation the true scope, complexity, and impact of the laws regarding staffing become known.

Attention then turns to other staffing laws and regulations. These include myriad federal laws, state and local laws, and civil service laws and regulations. These laws, like federal EEO/AA laws, have major impacts on staffing activities.

Finally, the chapter concludes with a discussion of the "Legal Issues" section that appears at the end of each of the remaining chapters. In these sections, specific topics and applications of the law are presented. Their intent is to provide guidance and examples (not legal advice, per se) regarding staffing practices that are permissible, impermissible, and required.

## THE EMPLOYMENT RELATIONSHIP

From a legal perspective, the term "staffing" refers to formation of the employment relationship. That relationship involves several types of arrangements between the organization and those who provide work for it. These arrangements have special and reasonably separate legal meanings. This section explores those arrangements: employer–employee, independent contractor, temporary employee, and unpaid interns and trainees.[1]

### Employer–Employee

By far the most prevalent form of the employment relationship is that of employer–employee. This arrangement is the result of the organization's usual staffing activities—a culmination of the person/job matching process. As shown in Exhibit 2.1, the employer and the employee negotiate and agree on the terms and conditions that will define and govern their relationship. The formal agreement represents an employment contract, the terms and conditions of which represent the promises and expectations of the parties (job requirements and rewards, and KSAOs and motivation). Over time, the initial contract may be modified due to changes in requirements or rewards of the current job, or employee transfer or promotion. Either party may terminate the contract, thus ending the employment relationship.

Employment contracts come in a variety of styles. They may be written or oral (both types are legally enforceable), and their specificity varies from extensive to bare bones. In some instances where the contract is written, terms and conditions are described in great detail. Examples of such contracts are collective bargaining agreements and contracts for professional athletes, entertainers, and upper-level executives. At the other extreme, the contract may be little more than some simple

**EXHIBIT 2.1**  **Matching Process, Employment Contract, and Employment Relationship**

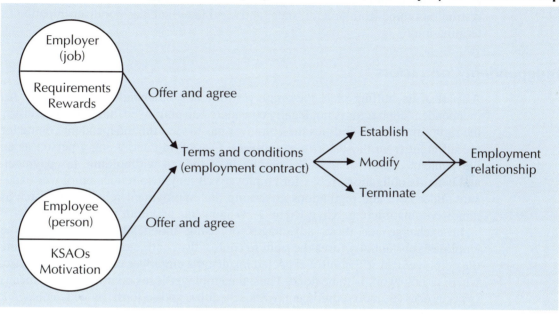

oral promises about the job, such as certain wages and hours, agreed to with a handshake.

From a legal perspective, an employer is an entity that employs others (employees or independent contractors) to do its work or work in its behalf. When these "others" are employees, the employer has the right to specify both the work output (results) expected and the work methods to be followed. In exchange for this right to control employees, the employer incurs certain legal responsibilities and liabilities. Specifically, the employer is (1) required to withhold employee payroll taxes (income, Social Security), (2) required to pay taxes (unemployment compensation, employer's share of Social Security and Medicare), (3) covered under the myriad laws and regulations governing the employment relationship, and (4) liable for the acts of its employees during employment.

When and how the employment relationship ends is very important to the employer and the employee. For the employer, it bears on the degree of staffing flexibility possible to quickly terminate employees without constraint. For the employee, the issue is the degree of continued employment and job security that will be expected. Under the common-law principle of employment-at-will, in the absence of any contract language to the contrary, the employment relationship is strictly an at-will one, meaning that either the employer or the employee may terminate the employment relationship at any time, for any reason, without prior notification. Restrictions on the employment-at-will right are usually established as part of the employment contract (such as termination for "just cause" only); other restrictions come from federal, state, and local laws (such as nondiscrimination in termination).[2]

## Independent Contractors

As part of its staffing plan, the employer may hire independent contractors.[3] An independent contractor is not legally considered an employee, however. Therefore, the rights and responsibilities the employer has toward the independent contractor are different from those for its employees. Classifying and using a person as an independent contractor frees the employer of the tax withholding, tax payment, and benefits obligations it has for employees. It may also reduce employer exposure under laws and regulations governing the employment relationship, such as nondiscrimination (e.g., Civil Rights Act) and wage and hour laws.

In exchange for these advantages of using independent contractors, the employer substantially loses the right to control the contractor. In particular, while the employer can still control expected results, the employer cannot dictate where, when, or how work is to be done. Thus, the employer loses control over the means (work processes, tools, equipment, work schedules, and so forth) by which the work is performed.

Beyond this crucial distinction, the line of demarcation between what constitutes an employee and what constitutes an independent contractor is often fuzzy. Numerous other factors come into play. For example, a person is more likely to be considered an independent contractor than an employee in the following situations:

- Working in a distinct occupation or business
- Working without supervision or oversight from the employer
- Paying one's own business and travel expenses
- Setting one's own work hours
- Possessing a high degree of skill
- Using one's own tools, materials, and office
- Working on a project with a definite completion date
- Working on relatively short projects
- Being paid by the project or commission rather than by the time spent

These examples are based on common-law interpretations and on a list of 11 criteria used by the Internal Revenue Service (IRS) to classify people as employees or independent contractors. Misclassifying people as independent contractors can result in substantial tax liabilities and fines for the employer. The IRS has stepped up its audit of employers to combat a trend of classifying people as independent contractors in order to gain staffing flexibility and save on labor costs.[4]

## Temporary Employees

Temporary employees do not have special legal stature. They are considered employees of the temporary help agency (staffing firm) that obtained them through its own staffing process. Temporary employees are given job assignments with other employers (clients) by the staffing firm. During these assignments, the temporary employee remains on the payroll of the staffing firm, and the client employer simply reimburses the staffing firm for its wage and other costs. The client employer has a severely limited right to control temporary employees that it utilizes because they are not its employees but employees of the staffing firm.

Use of temporary employees often raises issues of coemployment, in which the client employer and the staffing firm share the traditional role of employer.[5] Because both function as employers to an extent, their obligations and liabilities under various laws need to be sorted out. The Equal Employment Opportunity Commission (EEOC) provides guidance on coverage and responsibility requirements for staffing firms and their client organizations.[6] When both the firm and the client exercise control over the temporary employee and both have the requisite number of employees, they are considered employers and jointly liable under the Civil Rights Act, the Age Discrimination in Employment Act (ADEA), and the Equal Pay Act. The firm must make referrals and job assignments in a nondiscriminating manner, and the client may not set discriminatory job referral and job assignment criteria. The client must treat the temporary employees in a nondiscriminatory manner; if the firm knows this is not happening, it must take any corrective actions within its control. There are substantial penalties for noncompliance. There is special guidance for issues related to the Americans With Disabilities Act (ADA).

The demarcation between an employee and a temporary employee becomes increasingly blurred when an employer uses a set of temporary employees from a staffing firm on a long-term basis, resulting in so-called permatemps. Nationally, 29% of such employees work for the same client employer for a year or more, so they appear more like employees of the client than of the staffing firm. Which are they? Court cases suggest that these individuals are in fact employees of the client employer rather than of the staffing firm, particularly because of the strong degree of control the client employer typically exercises over those people. Hence, to help ensure that permatemps will not be legally considered the client's employees, the client must give up, or never exercise, direct control over these people and treat them as truly separate from regular employees. This may require, for example, not training or supervising them, not listing them in the phone directory, and not allowing them to use the organization's stationery. In practice, this is difficult to do.[7]

## Unpaid Interns and Trainees

The organization cannot simply say that a person is not an employee but rather an unpaid intern or trainee. In fact, a person must meet six requirements in order to be classified as an unpaid intern or trainee; otherwise the person is an employee. The requirements are that (1) the training must be similar to that given in school, (2) the training experience is to benefit the intern, (3) the trainee does not displace another person and works under close supervision of the employer's staff, (4) the employer does not gain an immediate advantage from the trainee's activities, and on occasion operations may be hampered, (5) the trainee is not entitled to a job at the end of training, and (6) the employer and the trainee must understand that the trainee is not entitled to any pay for time spent.[8]

## LAWS AND REGULATIONS

Establishing and maintaining the employment relationship involve exercising discretion by both the employer and the employee. Employment laws affecting that relationship spring from a need to define the scope of permissible discretion and place limits on it. The need for laws and regulations and the sources of them are explored below.

## Need for Laws and Regulations

### Balance of Power

Entering into and maintaining the employment relationship involve negotiating issues of power. The employer has something desirable to offer the employee (a job with certain requirements and rewards), and the employee has something to offer the employer (KSAOs and motivation). Usually, the employer has the upper hand in this power relationship since it controls the creation of jobs, the definition of jobs in terms of requirements and rewards, access to those jobs via staffing systems, movement of employees among jobs over time, and the retention or termination of employees. While employees participate in these processes and decisions, it is seldom as an equal or a partner of the employer. Employment laws and regulations exist, in part, to reduce or limit such employer power in the employment relationship.

### Protection of Employees

Laws and regulations seek to provide specific protections to employees that they are unlikely to get for themselves in an employment contract. These protections pertain to employment standards, individual workplace rights, and consistency of treatment. Employment standards represent the minimum acceptable terms and conditions of employment. Examples include minimum wage, nondiscrimination, overtime pay, and safety and health standards. Individual rights examples include organizing and collective bargaining, privacy protections, and constraints on unilateral termination. Finally, laws and regulations, in effect, guarantee consistency of treatment among employees. Hiring and promotion decisions, for example, cannot be made on the basis of protected employee characteristics (e.g., race, sex).

## Protection of Employers

Employers also gain protections from laws and regulations. First, they provide guidance to employers as to what are permissible practices and what are impermissible practices. The Civil Rights Act, for example, not only forbids certain types of discrimination on the basis of race, color, religion, sex, and national origin but also specifically mentions employment practices that are permitted. One of those practices is the use of professionally developed ability tests, a practice that has major implications for external and internal selection. Second, questions about the meaning of the law are clarified through many avenues—court decisions, policy statements from government agencies, informal guidance from enforcement officials, and networking with other employers. The result is increasing convergence on what is required to comply with the laws. This allows the employer to implement needed changes, which then become standard operating procedure in staffing systems. In this manner, for example, affirmative action programs (AAPs) have been developed and incorporated into the staffing mainstream for many employers.

# Sources of Laws and Regulations

Numerous sources of laws and regulations govern the employment relationship. Exhibit 2.2 provides examples of these as they pertain to staffing. Each of these is commented on next.

## Common Law

Common law, which has its origins in England, is court-made law, as opposed to law from other sources, such as the state. It consists of the case-by-case decisions of the court, which determine over time permissible and impermissible practices, as well as their remedies. There is a heavy reliance on common law in the precedence established in previous court decisions. Each state develops and administers its own common law. Employment-at-will and workplace tort cases, for example, are treated at the state level. As noted, employment-at-will involves the rights of the employer and the employee to terminate the employment relationship at will. A tort is a civil wrong that occurs when the employer violates a duty owed to its employees or customers that leads to harm or damages suffered by them. Staffing tort examples include negligent hiring of unsafe or dangerous employees, fraud and misrepresentation regarding employment terms and conditions, defamation of former employees, and invasion of privacy.

## Constitutional Law

Constitutional law is derived from the US Constitution and its amendments. It supersedes any other source of law or regulation. Its major application is in the area of the rights of public employees, particularly their due process rights.

**EXHIBIT 2.2   Sources of Laws and Regulations**

| Source | Examples |
| --- | --- |
| Common law | Employment-at-will<br>Workplace torts |
| Constitutional law | Fifth Amendment<br>Fourteenth Amendment |
| Statutory law | Civil Rights Act<br>Genetic Information Nondiscrimination Act<br>Age Discrimination in Employment Act<br>Americans With Disabilities Act<br>Rehabilitation Act<br>Immigration Reform and Control Act<br>Fair Credit Reporting Act<br>Employee Polygraph Protection Act<br>Uniformed Services Employment and Reemployment Rights Act<br>State and local laws<br>Civil service laws |
| Executive order<br>Agencies | 11246 (nondiscrimination under federal contracts)<br>Equal Employment Opportunity Commission (EEOC)<br>Department of Labor (DOL)<br>Office of Federal Contract Compliance Programs (OFCCP)<br>Department of Homeland Security<br>State fair employment practice (FEP) agencies |

## Statutory Law

Statutory law is derived from written statutes passed by legislative bodies. These bodies are federal (Congress), state (legislatures and assemblies), and local (municipal boards and councils). Legislative bodies may create, amend, and eliminate laws and regulations. They may also create agencies to administer and enforce the law.

## Agencies

Agencies exist at the federal, state, and local levels. Their basic charge is to interpret, administer, and enforce the law. At the federal level, the two major agencies of concern to staffing are the Department of Labor (DOL) and the EEOC. Housed within the DOL are several separate units for administration of employment law, notably the Office of Federal Contract Compliance Programs (OFCCP). The Department of Homeland Security handles issues regarding foreign workers and immigration in its agency, the US Citizenship and Immigration Services.

Agencies rely heavily on written documents in performing their functions. These documents are variously referred to as rules, regulations, guidelines, and policy statements. Rules, regulations, and guidelines are published in the *Federal Register*, as well as incorporated into the Code of Federal Regulations (CFR), and they have the weight of law. Policy statements are somewhat more benign in that they do not have the force of law. They do, however, represent the agency's official position on a point or question.

## EEO/AA LAWS: GENERAL PROVISIONS AND ENFORCEMENT

In this section, the major federal EEO/AA laws are summarized in terms of their general provisions. Mechanisms for enforcement of the laws are also discussed.[9] More details may be found online.

## General Provisions

The major federal EEO/AA laws are the following:

1. Title VII of the Civil Rights Acts (1964, 1991)
2. Age Discrimination in Employment Act (1967)
3. Americans With Disabilities Act (1990, 2008)
4. Genetic Information Nondiscrimination Act (2008)
5. Rehabilitation Act (1973)
6. Executive Order 11246 (1965)

Exhibit 2.3 contains a summary of the basic provisions of these laws pertaining to coverage, prohibited discrimination, and enforcement agency and to important rules, regulations, and guidelines. These laws are appropriately labeled "major" for several reasons. First, the laws are very broad in their coverage of employers. Second, they specifically prohibit discrimination on the basis of several individual characteristics (race, color, religion, sex, national origin, age, genetic information, disability, and handicap). Certain other factors that may be closely related to these protected characteristics may also be covered. The EEOC's opinion is that Title VII and the ADA may protect applicants and employees who are caregivers or who experience domestic or dating violence, sexual assault, or stalking. Third, separate agencies have been created for administration and enforcement of these laws. Finally, these agencies have issued numerous rules, regulations, and guidelines to assist in interpreting, implementing, and enforcing the law. The specifics of these regulations will be discussed in subsequent chapters.

Exhibit 2.3 shows that for some laws, the number of employees in the organization determines whether the organization is covered. To count employees, the EEOC has issued guidance indicating that the organization should include any

**EXHIBIT 2.3  Major Federal EEO/AA Laws: General Provisions**

| Law or Executive Order | Coverage | Prohibited Discrimination | Enforcement Agency | Important Rules, Regulations, and Guidelines |
|---|---|---|---|---|
| Civil Rights Act (1964, 1991) | Private employers with 15 or more employees<br>Federal, state, and local governments<br>Educational institutions<br>Employment agencies<br>Labor unions | Race, color, religion, national origin, sex | EEOC | Uniform Guidelines on Employee Selection Procedures<br>Sex Discrimination Guidelines<br>Religious Discrimination Guidelines<br>National Origin Discrimination Guidelines |
| Age Discrimination in Employment Act (1967) | Private employers with 20 or more employees<br>Federal, state, and local governments<br>Employment agencies<br>Labor unions | Age (40 and over) | EEOC | Interpretations of the Age Discrimination in Employment Act |
| Americans With Disabilities Act (1990, 2008) | Private employers with 15 or more employees<br>Federal, state, and local governments | Qualified individual with a disability | EEOC | ADA–Employment Regulations<br>Pre-Employment Disability-Related Questions and Medical Examinations |
| Genetic Information Nondiscrimination Act (2008) | Private employers with 15 or more employees<br>Federal, state, and local governments<br>Educational institutions<br>Employment agencies<br>Labor unions | Genetic information | EEOC | Final Regulations |
| Rehabilitation Act (1973) | Federal contractors with contracts in excess of $2,500 | Individual with a handicap | DOL (OFCCP) | Affirmative Action Regulations on Handicapped Workers |
| Executive Order 11246 (1965) | Federal contractors with contracts in excess of $10,000 | Race, color, religion, national origin, sex | DOL (OFCCP) | Sex Discrimination Guidelines<br>Affirmative Action Programs Regulations |

employee with whom the organization had an employment relationship in each of 20 or more calendar weeks during the current or preceding year. In essence, this means that full-time and part-time employees—and possibly temporary employees if there is true coemployment—should be included in the employee count.[10]

Individuals who oppose unlawful practices, participate in proceedings, or request accommodations are protected from retaliation under the laws shown in Exhibit 2.3. The term "retaliation" is broadly interpreted by the courts and the EEOC to include refusal to hire, denial of promotion, termination, other actions affecting employment (e.g., threats, unjustified negative evaluations), and actions that deter reasonable people from pursuing their rights (e.g., assault, unfounded civil or criminal charges). The EEOC has issued specific guidance on what constitutes evidence of retaliation, as well as special remedies for retaliatory actions by the employer.[11]

Three other general features of the EEO laws, as interpreted by the EEOC and the courts, should be noted.[12] First, state (but not local) government employers are immune from lawsuits by employees who allege violation of the ADA or the ADEA. State employees must thus pursue age and disability discrimination claims under applicable state laws. Second, organization officials and individual managers cannot be held personally liable for discrimination under the Civil Rights Act, the ADA, or the ADEA. They might be liable, however, under state law. Third, the ADA, the Civil Rights Act, and the ADEA extend to US citizens employed overseas by American employers. Also, a foreign company that is owned or controlled by an American employer and is doing business overseas generally must also comply with the Civil Rights Act, the ADA, and the ADEA.

An overview of the broad, sweeping nature of the specific employment practices affected by the federal EEO/AA laws is shown in Exhibit 2.4.

## Enforcement: EEOC

As shown in Exhibit 2.3, the EEOC is responsible for enforcing the Civil Rights Act, the ADEA, and the ADA. Though each law requires separate enforcement mechanisms, some generalizations about their collective enforcement are possible.[13]

### Disparate Treatment and Disparate Impact

Claims of discrimination in staffing ultimately require evidence and proof, particularly as these charges pertain to the staffing system itself and its specific characteristics as it has operated in practice. Toward this end, there are two avenues or paths to follow—disparate treatment and disparate impact.[14] Both paths may be followed for Title VII of the Civil Rights Act, ADA, and ADEA claims.

*Disparate Treatment.*   Claims of disparate treatment involve allegations of intentional discrimination in which the employer knowingly and deliberately discriminated against people on the basis of specific characteristics such as race or sex. Evidence for such claims may be of several sorts.

---

**EXHIBIT 2.4    Prohibited Employment Policies/Practices Under Federal Law**

Under the laws enforced by the EEOC, it is illegal to discriminate against someone (applicant or employee) because of that person's race, color, religion, sex (including pregnancy), national origin, age (40 or older), disability, or genetic information. It is also illegal to retaliate against a person because he or she complained about discrimination, filed a charge of discrimination, or participated in an employment discrimination investigation or lawsuit.

The law forbids discrimination in every aspect of employment.

The laws enforced by the EEOC prohibit an employer or other covered entity from using neutral employment policies and practices that have a disproportionately negative effect on applicants or employees of a particular race, color, religion, sex (including pregnancy), or national origin, or on an individual with a disability or class of individuals with disabilities, if the policies or practices at issue are not job related and necessary to the operation of the business. The laws enforced by the EEOC also prohibit an employer from using neutral employment policies and practices that have a disproportionately negative impact on applicants or employees age 40 or older, if the policies or practices at issue are not based on a reasonable factor other than age.

Covered practices:
- Job advertisements, recruitment, and job referrals
- Application and hiring
- Job assignments and promotion
- Employment references
- Pre-employment inquiries
- Discipline and discharge
- Pay and benefits
- Reasonable accommodation and disability, religion
- Training and apprenticeship programs
- Harassment
- Terms and conditions of employment, dress code
- Constructive discharge/forced to resign

SOURCE: Equal Employment Opportunity Commission, 2010.

First, the evidence may be direct. It might, for example, refer to an explicit written policy of the organization, such as one stating that "women are not to be hired for the following jobs."

The situation may not involve such blatant action but may consist of what is referred to as a mixed motive. Here, both a prohibited characteristic (e.g., sex) and a legitimate reason (e.g., job qualifications) are mixed together to contribute to a negative decision about a person, such as a failure to hire or promote. If an unlawful motive such as sex plays any part in the decision, it is illegal, despite the presence of a lawful motive as well.

Finally, the discrimination may be such that evidence of a failure to hire or promote because of a protected characteristic must be inferred from several situational factors. Here, the evidence involves four factors:

1. The person belongs to a protected class.
2. The person applied for, and was qualified for, a job the employer was trying to fill.
3. The person was rejected despite being qualified.
4. The position remained open and the employer continued to seek applicants as qualified as the person rejected.

Most disparate treatment cases involve and require the use of these four factors to initially prove a charge of discrimination.

***Disparate Impact.***   Disparate impact, also known as adverse impact, focuses on the effect of employment practices, rather than on the motive or intent underlying them. Accordingly, the emphasis here is on the need for direct evidence that, as a result of a protected characteristic, people are being adversely affected by a practice. Statistical evidence must be presented to support a claim of adverse impact.[15] Three types of statistical evidence may be used, and these are shown in Exhibit 2.5. Refer to "Legal Issues" in Chapters 3 and 7 for elaboration.

Shown first in the exhibit are applicant flow statistics, which look at differences in selection rates (proportion of applicants hired) among different groups for a particular job. If the differences are large enough, this suggests that the effect of the selection system is discriminatory. In the example, the selection rate for men is .50 (or 50%) and for women it is .11 (or 11%), suggesting the possibility of discrimination.

A second type of statistical evidence involves the use of stock statistics. Here, the percentage of women or minorities actually employed in a job category is compared with their availability in the relevant population. Relevant is defined in terms of such things as "qualified," "interested," or "geographic." In the example shown, there is a disparity in the percentage of minorities employed (10%) compared with their availability (30%), which suggests their underutilization.

The third type of evidence involves the use of concentration statistics. Here, the percentages of women or minorities in various job categories are compared to see if they are concentrated in certain workforce categories. In the example shown, women are concentrated in clerical jobs (97%), men are concentrated in production (85%) and managerial (95%) jobs, and men and women are roughly equally concentrated in sales jobs (45% and 55%, respectively).

## Initial Charge and Conciliation

Enforcement proceedings begin when an employee or job applicant files a charge (the EEOC itself may also file a charge). In states where there is an EEOC-approved fair enforcement practice (FEP) law, the charge is initially deferred to the state.

**EXHIBIT 2.5**    **Types of Disparate Impact Statistics**

**A. FLOW STATISTICS**

**Definition:**

Significant differences in selection rates between groups

**Example**

**Job Category: Customer Service Representative**

| No. of Applicants | | No. Hired | | Selection Rate (%) | |
|---|---|---|---|---|---|
| Men | Women | Men | Women | Men | Women |
| 50 | 45 | 25 | 5 | 50 | 11 |

**B. STOCK STATISTICS**

**Definition:**

Underutilization of women or minorities relative to their availability in the relevant population

**Example**

**Job Category: Management Trainee**

| Current Trainees (%) | | Availability (%) | |
|---|---|---|---|
| Nonminority | Minority | Nonminority | Minority |
| 90 | 10 | 70 | 30 |

**C. CONCENTRATION STATISTICS**

**Definition:**

Concentration of women or minorities in certain job categories

**Example**

| | **Job Category** | | | |
|---|---|---|---|---|
| | Clerical | Production | Sales | Managers |
| % Men | 3 | 85 | 45 | 95 |
| % Women | 97 | 15 | 55 | 5 |

The charge is investigated to determine whether there is reasonable cause to assume discrimination has occurred. If reasonable cause is not found, the charge is dropped. If reasonable cause is found, the EEOC attempts conciliation of the charge. Conciliation is a voluntary settlement process that seeks agreement by the employer to stop the practice(s) in question and abide by proposed remedies. This is the EEOC's preferred method of settlement. Whenever the EEOC decides not to pursue a claim further, it will issue a "right to sue" letter to the complaining party, allowing a private suit to be started against the employer.

Complementing conciliation is the use of mediation. With mediation, a neutral third party mediates the dispute between the employer and the EEOC and obtains an agreement between them that resolves the dispute. Participation in mediation is voluntary, and either party may opt out of it for any reason. Mediation proceedings are confidential. Any agreement reached between the parties is legally enforceable. More than 70% of complaints that go to mediation are resolved, and 96% of employers that use the EEOC mediation program say they would do so again.[16] In short, the EEOC prefers settlement to litigation.

### Litigation and Remedies

Should conciliation fail, suit is filed in federal court. The ensuing litigation process under Title VII is shown in Exhibit 2.6. As can be seen, the charge of the plaintiff (charging party) will follow either a disparate treatment or a disparate impact route.[17] In either event, the plaintiff has the initial burden of proof. Such a burden requires the plaintiff to establish a prima facie case that demonstrates reasonable cause to assume discrimination has occurred. Assuming this case is successfully presented, the defendant must rebut the charge and accompanying evidence.

In disparate treatment cases, the defendant must provide nondiscriminatory reasons during rebuttal for the practice(s) in question. In disparate impact cases, the employer must demonstrate that the practices in question are job related and consistent with business necessity.

**EXHIBIT 2.6**  **Basic Litigation Process Under Title VII: EEOC**

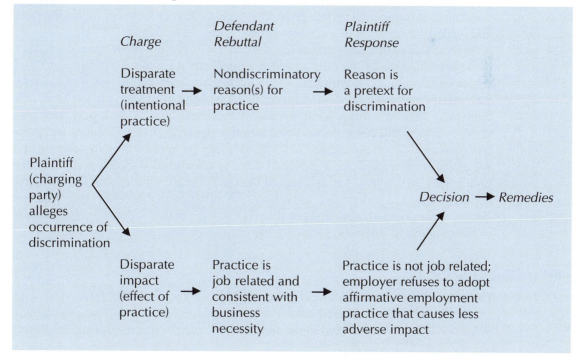

SOURCE: Equal Employment Opportunity Commission, May 26, 2004 (*www.eeoc.gov*).

Following rebuttal, the plaintiff may respond to the defense provided by the defendant. In disparate treatment cases, that response hinges on a demonstration that the defendant's reasons for a practice are a pretext, or smoke screen, for the practice. In disparate impact cases, the plaintiff's response will focus on showing that the defendant has not shown its practices to be job related and/or that the employer refuses to adopt a practice that causes less adverse impact.

Disparate impact litigation involving age discrimination charges is somewhat different. After the disparate impact claim (supported by disparate impact statistics) is made, the defendant rebuttal will involve an attempt to prove that the challenged practice is supported by a reasonable factor other than age, and the plaintiff response will attempt to prove that the factor cited is unreasonable and not the true reason for the practice.

Who bears the final, or ultimate, burden of proof? In disparate treatment cases, the plaintiff must ultimately prove that the defendant's practices are discriminatory. For disparate impact cases, on the other hand, the burden is on the defendant. That is, it is the defendant who must prove that its practices are not discriminatory.

The plaintiff and the defendant have an opportunity to end their dispute through a consent decree. This is a voluntary, court-approved agreement between the two parties. The consent decree may contain an agreement to not only halt certain practices but also implement certain remedies, such as various forms of monetary relief and AAPs. An example of a consent decree is shown in Exhibit 2.7.

In the absence of a consent decree, the court will fashion its own remedies from those permitted under the law, of which several are available. First, the court may enjoin certain practices, which means requiring the defendant to halt the practices. Second, the court may order the hiring or reinstatement of individuals. Third, the court may fashion various forms of monetary relief, such as back pay, front pay, attorney's fees, and compensatory and punitive damages. Compensatory and punitive damages, which are capped at $300,000, may be applied only in cases involving disparate treatment; front pay and back pay are excluded from the cap. Finally, under the Civil Rights Act and the ADA, the court may order "such affirmative action as may be appropriate," as well as "any other equitable relief" that the court deems appropriate. Through these provisions, the court has considerable latitude in the remedies it imposes, including the imposition of AAPs.

## Enforcement: OFCCP

Enforcement mechanisms used by the OFCCP are very different from those used by the EEOC. Most covered employers are required to develop and implement written AAPs for women and minorities. Specific AAP requirements for employers

**EXHIBIT 2.7   Example of a Consent Decree**

CLEVELAND—Presrite Corporation, a manufacturing company headquartered in Cleveland that makes gears and other industrial parts, will pay $700,000, offer jobs to no fewer than 40 women, and commit to other injunctive relief to settle a systemic class action lawsuit brought by the US Equal Employment Opportunity Commission (EEOC), the agency announced today.

The EEOC's lawsuit charged widespread discrimination against women who applied to work at one or more of Presrite's three plants in Cleveland and Ashtabula County. According to the EEOC, Presrite—a federal contractor—passed over female applicants in favor of less qualified males for entry-level positions at all three plants. The EEOC also cited evidence that women who were hired for such positions were harassed.

The EEOC charged the company with failing to keep applications and other employee data in violation of federal law. The EEOC alleged that Presrite failed to produce more than a thousand employment applications for persons the company hired and failed to maintain accurate or complete data about applicants. As a result, the EEOC said, it was unable to verify by name all of the female applicants who were unlawfully denied hire.

On April 24, Judge Patricia A. Gaughan signed a publicly filed consent decree resolving the case. Under the terms of the decree, Presrite will pay $700,000 in compensatory damages to establish a class fund for women who sought certain positions at Presrite and were denied hire. Over the course of the next three years, Presrite will also offer jobs to no fewer than 40 women identified by the EEOC during the claims process. The decree compels Presrite to give those females priority consideration and to offer them jobs before any current applicants.

The decree also requires Presrite to implement a number of measures designed to prevent future discrimination such as periodic reports to the EEOC disclosing the number of females and males who applied as compared to those who were hired; mandatory training; and compulsory retention of employment and applicant records, including creating and producing electronic data. The decree includes an injunction prohibiting Presrite from discriminating against women in the recruiting and hiring process, and compelling the company to make all good-faith, reasonably necessary efforts to find female candidates to fill vacancies in laborer and operative positions.

"We are pleased that we were able to reach an agreement with this defendant," said EEOC General Counsel David Lopez. "Moving forward, qualified female applicants will be judged by their talents and skill and not simply passed over because of their gender and women who were wrongfully denied positions will be compensated."

Source: Adapted from EEOC press release, April 30, 2013, (*www.eeoc.gov/eeoc/newsroom/release/4-30-13.cfm*), accessed 5/22/13.

under Executive Order 11246 are spelled out in Affirmative Action Programs Regulations, discussed in "Legal Issues" in Chapter 3.

To enforce these requirements, the OFCCP conducts off-site desk audits and reviews of employers' records and AAPs, and on-site visits and compliance reviews of employers' AAPs. It also investigates complaints charging noncompliance. Employers found to be in noncompliance are urged to change their practices through a conciliation process. Should conciliation be unsuccessful, employers are subject to various penalties that affect their status as a federal contractor. These include cancellation of contracts and debarment from bidding on future contracts.

## EEO/AA LAWS: SPECIFIC STAFFING PROVISIONS

Each of the major laws covered in the previous section contains specific provisions pertaining to staffing practices by organizations. This section summarizes those specific provisions, including agencies' and courts' interpretations of them. Phrases in quotation marks are from the laws themselves. Applications of these provisions to staffing policies, practices, and actions occur throughout the remainder of the book.

### Civil Rights Acts (1964, 1991)

The provisions of the Civil Rights Acts of 1964 and 1991 are combined for discussion purposes here. The 1991 law is basically a series of amendments to the 1964 law, though it does contain some provisions unique to it.

#### Unlawful Employment Practices

This section of the law contains a comprehensive statement regarding unlawful employment practices. Specifically, it is unlawful for an employer

1. "to fail or refuse to hire or to discharge any individual, or otherwise discriminate against any individual with respect to his compensation, terms, conditions, or privileges of employment, because of such individual's race, color, religion, sex, or national origin"; or
2. "to limit, segregate, or classify his employees or applicants for employment in any way which would deprive or tend to deprive any individual of employment opportunities or otherwise adversely affect his status as an employee because of such individual's race, color, religion, sex, or national origin."

These two statements are the foundation of civil rights law. They are very broad and inclusive, applying to virtually all staffing practices of an organization. There are also separate statements for employment agencies and labor unions.

### Establishment of Disparate Impact

As discussed previously, a claim of discrimination may be pursued via a disparate impact or disparate treatment approach. The law makes several points regarding the former approach.

First, staffing practices that may seem unfair, outrageous, or of dubious value to the employer but do not cause adverse impact are not illegal (assuming, of course, that no intention to discriminate underlies them). Thus, they are a matter of legal concern only if their usage causes disparate impact.

Second, staffing practices that the plaintiff initially alleges to have caused adverse impact are unlawful unless the employer can successfully rebut the charges. To do this, the employer must show that the practices are "job related for the position in question and consistent with business necessity." Practices that fail to meet this standard are unlawful.

Third, the plaintiff must show adverse impact for each specific staffing practice or component. For example, if an employer has a simple selection system in which applicants first take a written test and those who pass it are interviewed, the plaintiff must show adverse impact separately for the test and the interview, rather than for the two components combined.

### Disparate Treatment

Intentional discrimination with staffing practices is prohibited, and the employer may not use a claim of business necessity to justify intentional use of a discriminatory practice.

### Mixed Motives

An employer may not defend an action by claiming that while a prohibited factor, such as sex, entered into a staffing decision, other factors, such as job qualifications, did also. Such "mixed motive" defenses are not permitted. A plaintiff may pursue a mixed motive claim with either circumstantial or direct evidence of discrimination.

### Bona Fide Occupational Qualification

An employer may attempt to justify use of a protected characteristic, such as national origin, as being a bona fide occupational qualification (BFOQ). The law permits such claims, but only for sex, religion, and national origin—not race or color. The employer must be able to demonstrate that such discrimination is "a bona fide occupational qualification reasonably necessary to the normal operation of that particular business or enterprise." Thus, a maximum security prison with mostly male inmates might hire only male prison guards on the grounds that by doing so it ensures the safety, security, and privacy of inmates. However, it must be able to show that doing so is a business necessity.

## Testing

The law explicitly permits the use of tests in staffing. The employer may "give and act upon the results of any professionally developed ability test, provided that such test, its administration, or action upon the basis of results is not designed, intended, or used to discriminate because of race, color, religion, sex, or national origin."

Interpretation of this provision has been difficult. What exactly is a "professionally developed ability test"? How does an employer use a test to discriminate? Not discriminate? The need for answers to such questions gave rise to the Uniform Guidelines on Employee Selection Procedures (UGESP).

## Test Score Adjustments

Test scores are not to be altered or changed to make them more fair; test scores should speak for themselves. Specifically, it is an unlawful employment practice "to adjust the scores of, use different cutoff scores for, or otherwise alter the results of employment-related tests on the basis of race, color, religion, sex, or national origin." This provision bans so-called race norming, in which people's scores are compared only with those of members of their own racial group and separate cutoff or passing scores are set for each group.

## Seniority or Merit Systems

The law explicitly permits the use of seniority and merit systems as a basis for applying different terms and conditions to employees. However, the seniority or merit system must be "bona fide," and it may not be the result of an intention to discriminate.

This provision is particularly relevant to internal staffing systems. It in essence allows the employer to take into account seniority (experience) and merit (e.g., KSAOs, promotion potential assessments) when making internal staffing decisions.

## Employment Advertising

Discrimination in employment advertising is prohibited. Specifically, the employer may not indicate "any preference, limitation, specification, or discrimination based on race, color, religion, sex, or national origin." An exception to this is if sex, religion, or national origin is a BFOQ.

## Pregnancy

The Pregnancy Discrimination Act (PDA) is an amendment to Title VII. Under the PDA, an employer cannot refuse to hire a pregnant woman because of her pregnancy, because of a pregnancy-related condition, or because of the prejudices of coworkers, clients, or customers. There are also many provisions regarding pregnancy and maternity leave.

### Preferential Treatment and Quotas

The law does not require preferential treatment or quotas. Thus, the employer is not required to have a balanced workforce, meaning one whose demographic composition matches or mirrors the demographic makeup of the surrounding population from which the employer draws its employees.

Note that the law does not prohibit preferential treatment, AA, and quotas. It merely says they are not required. Thus, they may be used in certain instances, such as a voluntary AAP or a court-imposed remedy.

## Age Discrimination in Employment Act (1967)

### Prohibited Age Discrimination

The law explicitly and inclusively prohibits discrimination against those aged 40 and older. It is unlawful for an employer

1. "to fail or refuse to hire or to discharge any individual or otherwise discriminate against any individual with respect to his compensation, terms, conditions or privileges of employment, because of such individual's age"; and
2. "to limit, segregate, or classify his employees in any way which would deprive or tend to deprive any individual of employment opportunities or otherwise adversely affect his status as an employee, because of such individual's age."

These provisions are interpreted to mean that it is not unlawful to favor an older worker over a younger worker, even if both workers are aged 40 or older.

### Bona Fide Occupational Qualification

Like the Civil Rights Act, the ADEA contains a BFOQ provision. Thus, it is not unlawful for an employer to differentiate among applicants or employees on the basis of their age "where age is a bona fide occupational qualification reasonably necessary to the normal operation of the particular business."

### Reasonable Factors Other Than Age

The employer may use reasonable factors other than age (RFOA) in making employment decisions. Specific interpretation of this provision is given by the EEOC. In the case of disparate impact (but not disparate treatment) claims, the employer can seek to justify the adverse impact occurrence as being based on an RFOA (as opposed to business necessity). An employment practice is based on an RFOA if it is reasonably designed and administered to achieve a legitimate business purpose in light of circumstances. Reasonableness depends on the extent to which (1) a measured factor (e.g., job skill) is related to the employer's business purpose, (2) the factor has been accurately and fairly identified and applied, (3) managers and supervisors were given guidance or training about how to use the factor and avoid discrimination,

(4) limits were placed on supervisors' discretion to assess employees subjectively, (5) adverse impact against older workers was assessed, including the degree of harm to older workers, and (6) steps were taken to reduce the harm.

### Seniority Systems

The law permits the use of seniority systems (merit systems are not mentioned). Thus, the employer is permitted "to observe the terms of a bona fide seniority system that is not intended to evade the purposes" of the act.

### Employment Advertising

Employment advertising may not contain terms that limit or deter the employment of older individuals. It is permissible, however, to use terms or phrases that express a preference for older workers, such as "over age 60," "retirees," or "supplement your pension."

## Americans With Disabilities Act (1990, 2008)

The ADA's basic purpose is to prohibit discrimination against individuals with disabilities who are qualified for the job, and to require the employer to make reasonable accommodation for such individuals unless that would cause undue hardship for the employer.

### Prohibited Discrimination

The law contains a broad prohibition against disability discrimination. It specifically says that an employer may not "discriminate against an individual on the basis of disability in regard to job application procedures, the hiring, advancement, or discharge of employees, employee compensation, job training, and other terms, conditions, and privileges of employment." Also prohibited is discrimination based on an applicant's or employee's association with a person with a disability.

The law does not apply to all people with disabilities, only those with disabilities who are qualified for the job. To determine whether a person is covered under the ADA, it must be determined whether the person has a disability and is qualified for the job.

### Definition of a Disability

The EEOC provides considerable regulation and guidance on the complex issue of what is a disability. The definition is interpreted in favor of broad coverage of individuals. There are three prongs to the definition:

1. A physical or mental impairment that substantially limits one or more major life activities (an "actual disability")
2. A record of physical or mental impairment that substantially limited a major life activity (a "record of")

3. When an employer takes an action prohibited by the ADA because of an actual or perceived impairment that is not both transitory and minor ("regarded as")

Each of these three prongs is explained next.

***Actual Disability.*** An impairment is a physical or mental disorder, illness, or condition. A physical impairment is any physiological disorder or condition, cosmetic disfigurement, or anatomical loss affecting one or more body systems such as neurological, musculoskeletal, special sense organs, respiratory (including speech organs), cardiovascular, reproductive, digestive, genitourinary, immune, circulatory, hemic, lymphatic, skin, and endocrine. Also included (with special guidance) are cancer, diabetes, epilepsy, and intellectual disabilities. A mental or psychological disorder includes intellectual disability, organic brain syndrome, emotional or mental illness, and specific learning disabilities.

An impairment that is episodic or in remission is a disability if it substantially limits a major life activity when active (e.g., major depression, epilepsy). The use of mitigating measures (with the exception of eyeglasses and contact lenses) that eliminate or reduce the symptoms or impact of a disability must be ignored when determining whether there is an impairment that substantially limits a major life activity. The long list of mitigating measures includes medications, assistive devices, and various types of therapy. In terms of addiction as an impairment, current users of illegal drugs are not covered by the law; recovering drug users and both current and recovering alcoholics are covered.

Major life activities include caring for oneself, performing manual tasks, seeing, hearing, eating, sleeping, walking, standing, sitting, reaching, lifting, bending, speaking, breathing, learning, reading, concentrating, thinking, communicating, interacting with others, and working. Also included are major bodily functions (e.g., digestive, neurological), including the operation of an individual organ within a body system.

To determine whether an impairment substantially limits a major life activity, the person must be (or have been) substantially limited in performing a major life activity compared to most people in the general population. Temporary, nonchronic impairments of short duration with little or no residual effects usually are not considered disabilities (e.g., common cold, sprained joint, broken bone, and seasonal allergies). An impairment need not prevent or severely or significantly limit a major life activity to be considered substantially limiting.

Finally, in assessing whether a person has a disability, two guidelines should be followed. First, there should be an individualized assessment of the impairment. Second, the determination of a disability should not require extensive analysis.

***Record of a Disability.*** A person who does not currently have a substantially limiting impairment but had one in the past has a record of disability. Additionally, a person who was misclassified as having a substantially limiting impairment has a record of disability.

***Regarded as Disabled.*** A person is regarded as having a disability if the employer takes a prohibited action under the ADA (e.g., failure to hire or promote) based on an impairment the employer thinks the person has, unless the impairment is temporary (e.g., less than six months) and minor.

### Qualified Individual

A person is qualified for the job if he or she can meet the job's general requirements (e.g., skills, education, experience, licenses, and certification) and perform the job's essential functions (duties) with or without reasonable accommodation. Among qualified individuals, the employer can hire the most qualified person for the job.

### Essential Job Functions

The law provides little guidance as to what are essential job functions. It would seem that they are the major, nontrivial tasks required of an employee. The employer has great discretion in such a determination. Specifically, "consideration shall be given to the employer's judgment as to what functions of a job are essential, and if an employer has prepared a written description before advertising or interviewing applicants for the job, this description shall be considered evidence of the essential functions of the job." Subsequent regulations amplify what are essential job functions; these are explored in Chapter 4.

### Reasonable Accommodation and Undue Hardship

Unless it would pose an "undue hardship" on the employer, the employer must make "reasonable accommodation" for the "known physical or mental impairments of an otherwise qualified, disabled job applicant or employee." To qualify for reasonable accommodation, the person must be covered under the first (actual disability) or second (record of disability) prong of the disability definition. The law provides actual examples of reasonable accommodation. They include changes in facilities (e.g., installing wheelchair ramps), job restructuring, telework, changes in work schedules, employee reassignment to a vacant position, purchase of adaptive devices, provision of qualified readers and interpreters, and adjustments in testing and training material. For mental impairment and psychiatric disabilities, EEOC guidance indicates several types of reasonable accommodations: leaves of absence and other work schedule changes, physical changes in the workplace, modifications to company policy, adjustment of supervisory methods, medication monitoring, and reassignment to a vacant position. In general, only accommodations that would be difficult to make or that would require significant expense are considered to create an undue hardship.

A suggested four-step problem-solving approach for handling a reasonable accommodation request from an applicant or employee is as follows.[18] First, conduct a job analysis to determine the job's essential functions. Second, identify performance barriers that would hinder the person from doing the job. Third, work with the person to identify potential accommodations. Fourth, assess each accommodation and choose the most reasonable one that would not be an undue hardship.

## Selection of Employees

The law deals directly with discrimination in the selection of employees. Prohibited discrimination includes

1. "using qualification standards, employment tests or other selection criteria that screen out or tend to screen out an individual with a disability or a class of individuals with disabilities unless the standard, test, or other selection criteria, as used by the covered entity, is shown to be job related for the position in question and is consistent with business necessity"; and
2. "failing to select and administer tests concerning employment in the most effective manner to ensure that, when such a test is administered to a job applicant or employee who has a disability that impairs sensory, manual, or speaking skills, such results accurately reflect the skills, aptitude or whatever other factor of such applicant or employee that such test purports to measure, rather than reflecting the impaired sensory, manual, or speaking skills of such employee or applicant (except where such skills are the factors that the test purports to measure)."

These provisions seem to make two basic requirements of staffing systems. First, if selection procedures cause disparate impact against people with disabilities, the employer must show that the procedures are job related and consistent with business necessity. The requirement is similar to that for selection procedures under the Civil Rights Act. Second, the employer must ensure that employment tests are accurate indicators of the KSAOs they attempt to measure.

## Medical Exams for Job Applicants and Employees

Prior to making a job offer, the employer may not conduct medical exams of job applicants, inquire whether or how severely a person is disabled, or inquire whether the applicant has received treatment for a mental or emotional condition. Specific inquiries about a person's ability to perform essential job functions, however, are permitted.

After a job offer has been made, the employer may require the applicant to take a medical exam, including a psychiatric exam. The job offer may be contingent on the applicant successfully passing the exam. Care should be taken to ensure that all applicants are required to take and pass the same exam. Medical records should be confidential and maintained in a separate file.

For employees, medical exams must be job related and consistent with business necessity. Exam results are confidential.

## Direct Threat

The employer may refuse to hire an individual who poses a direct threat to himself or herself or to the health and safety of others.

## Affirmative Action

There are no affirmative action requirements for employers.

## Veterans

A veteran with a service-connected disability is covered by the ADA if the person meets the ADA definition of a disability and is qualified for the job. Vets with disabilities may also be covered under other laws and regulations that go beyond ADA requirements, such as asking an applicant to self-identify as a disabled veteran, and undertaking affirmative action on behalf of disabled veterans.

# Genetic Information Nondiscrimination Act (2008)

The Genetic Information Nondiscrimination Act (GINA) prohibits the use of genetic information in employment, as well as its acquisition; confidentiality of genetic information is required.

## Genetic Information

Genetic information includes an individual's genetic tests, genetic tests of family members, and the manifestation of a disease or disorder in family members (i.e., the family's medical history). Age and sex are not included as genetic information.

## Prohibited Practices

It is an unlawful employment practice for the employer to fail or refuse to hire; discharge; discriminate regarding terms and conditions of employment; and limit, segregate, or classify employees because of genetic information. There are no exceptions to this ban on usage.

It is also an unlawful employment practice to acquire (require, request, or purchase) genetic information about the employee or the employee's family members. There are several specific exceptions to this.

## Confidentiality of Information

Any genetic information is to be maintained in a separate file, but it is okay to use this same file for ADA purposes. There are strict limits on the disclosure of genetic information.

# Rehabilitation Act (1973)

The Rehabilitation Act applies to federal employees, contractors, and subcontractors, and most of them are also covered by the ADA. The Rehabilitation Act has many similarities to the ADA, including that the 2008 ADA amendments apply to the Rehabilitation Act. Hence, the Rehabilitation Act provisions are only briefly mentioned.

### Prohibited Discrimination

It is illegal to discriminate against a qualified individual with a disability. The definition of disability under the ADA applies here. Reasonable accommodation for a qualified individual with a disability must also be made.

### Affirmative Action

Employers are required to develop and implement written AAPs for employing and promoting qualified individuals with disabilities. The OFCCP monitors the plans and conducts employer compliance reviews.

## Executive Order 11246 (1965)

### Prohibited Discrimination

The federal contractor is prohibited from discriminating on the basis of race, color, religion, sex, and national origin. (A similar prohibition against age discrimination by federal contractors is contained in Executive Order 11141.)

### Affirmative Action

The order plainly requires affirmative action. It says specifically that "the contractor will take affirmative action to ensure that applicants are employed, and that employees are treated during employment, without regard to their race, color, religion, sex, or national origin. Such actions shall include, but not be limited to, the following: employment, upgrading, demotion, or transfer; recruitment or recruitment advertising; layoff or termination; rates of pay or other forms of compensation; and selection for training, including apprenticeship." (Executive Order 11141 does not require affirmative action.) Regulations for these affirmative action requirements are discussed in Chapter 3.

## OTHER STAFFING LAWS

In addition to the EEO/AA laws, a variety of other laws and regulations affect staffing. At the federal level are the Immigration Reform and Control Act (IRCA), the Employee Polygraph Protection Act, and the Fair Credit Reporting Act. At the state and local levels are a wide array of laws pertaining to EEO, as well as a host of other areas. Finally, there are civil service laws and regulations that pertain to staffing practices for federal, state, and local government employers.

## Federal Laws

### Immigration Reform and Control Act (1986)

The purpose of the IRCA and its amendments is to prohibit the employment of unauthorized aliens and to provide civil and criminal penalties for violations of this law. The law covers all employers regardless of size.

*Prohibited Practices.*   The law prohibits the initial or continuing employment of unauthorized aliens. Specifically,

1. "it is unlawful for a person or other entity to have, or to recruit or refer for a fee, for employment in the United States an alien knowing the alien is an unauthorized alien with respect to such employment"; and
2. "it is unlawful for a person or other entity, after hiring an alien for employment . . . to continue to employ the alien in the United States knowing the alien is (or has become) an unauthorized alien with respect to such employment." (This does not apply to the continuing employment of aliens hired before November 6, 1986.)

The law also prohibits employment discrimination on the basis of national origin or citizenship status. The purpose of this provision is to discourage employers from attempting to comply with the prohibition against hiring unauthorized aliens by simply refusing to hire applicants who are foreign-looking in appearance or have foreign-sounding accents.

*Employment Eligibility Verification System.*   The employer must verify that the individual is not an unauthorized alien and is legally eligible for employment by obtaining proof of identity and eligibility for work. The employer uses the I-9 form to gather documents from the new employee that establish proof of both identity and eligibility (authorization) for work. Documents that establish proof are shown on the back of the I-9 form. Documents should not be obtained until the person is actually hired, and they must be acquired within three business days of the date of employment. To verify eligibility information, federal contractors and subcontractors must use E-Verify, which conducts electronic verification checks against federal databases. Other employers may voluntarily participate in E-Verify. There are detailed record-keeping requirements. More information on verification is in the "Legal Issues" section of Chapter 12.

*Temporary Visas.*   The employer may apply for temporary visas for up to six years for foreign workers under two major visa categories (there are other, minor categories that are not covered here). The first category is H-1B visa. An H-1B nonimmigrant must have a bachelor's degree (or equivalent) or higher in a specific specialty. These workers are typically employed in occupations such as architect, engineer, computer programmer, accountant, doctor, or professor. The employer must pay the person the prevailing wage for employees working in a similar position for the employer and attest that the employee will not displace any other US employee. Congress sets an annual cap of 65,000 for the number of visas issued. H-1B nonimmigrants employed by universities and nonprofit (including government) organizations are exempt from the annual cap. There is also an exception (with a 20,000 annual cap) for workers with a master's degree or higher from a US university. H-1B visa holders may change jobs as soon as their employer files an approval petition, and they are not restricted to their current geographic area.

The H-2B visa category applies to nonagricultural temporary workers. It is for employers with peak load, seasonal, or intermittent needs to augment their regular workforce. Examples of such employers are construction, health care, resort/hospitality services, lumber, and manufacturing. There is an annual cap of 65,000 workers.

*Enforcement.*   The law is enforced by the US Citizenship and Immigration Services within the Department of Homeland Security. Noncompliance may result in fines of up to $10,000 for each unauthorized alien employed, as well as imprisonment for up to six months for a pattern or practice of violations. Federal contractors may be barred from federal contracts for one year.

## Employee Polygraph Protection Act (1988)

The purpose of the Employee Polygraph Protection Act is to prevent most private employers from using the polygraph or lie detector on job applicants or employees. The law does not apply to other types of "honesty tests," such as paper-and-pencil ones.

*Prohibited Practices.*   The law prohibits most private employers (public employers are exempted) from (1) requiring applicants or employees to take a polygraph test, (2) using the results of a polygraph test for employment decisions, and (3) discharging or disciplining individuals for refusing to take a polygraph test.

The polygraph may be used in three explicit instances. First, employers that manufacture, distribute, or dispense controlled substances, such as drugs, may use the polygraph. Second, private security firms that provide services to businesses affecting public safety or security, such as nuclear power plants or armored vehicles, may use the polygraph. Third, an employer that experiences economic loss due to theft, embezzlement, or sabotage may use the polygraph in an investigation of the loss.

*Enforcement.*   The law is enforced by the DOL. Noncompliance may result in fines of up to $10,000 per individual violation. Also, individuals may sue the employer, seeking employment, reinstatement, promotion, and back pay.

## Fair Credit Reporting Act (1970)

The Fair Credit Reporting Act, as amended, regulates the organization's acquisition and use of consumer reports on job applicants. A consumer report is virtually any information on an applicant that is compiled from a database by a consumer reporting agency and provided to the organization. The information may include not only credit characteristics but also employment history, income, driving record, arrests and convictions, and lifestyle; medical information may not be sought or provided without prior approval of the applicant. Specific requirements for gathering and using the information are provided in Chapter 8.

A second type of consumer report is investigative. It is prepared from personal interviews with other individuals, rather than a search through a database. There are separate compliance steps for this type of report.

*Enforcement.*    The law is enforced by the Consumer Financial Protection Bureau. Penalties for willful or negligent noncompliance go up to $1,000.

### Uniformed Services Employment and Reemployment Rights Act (1994)

The purpose of the Uniformed Services Employment and Reemployment Rights Act (USERRA) is to prohibit discrimination against members of the uniformed services and to extend reinstatement, benefit, and job security rights to returning service members.

*Coverage.*    Both private and public employers, regardless of size, are covered. All people who perform or have performed service in the uniformed services have USERRA rights, but only a person who was employed, is an applicant, or who is currently employed can invoke these rights.

*Requirements.*    Employers may not take negative job actions (e.g., firing, demoting, transferring, or refusing to hire) against members (and applicants for membership) in the uniformed services. The employer must reinstate (within two weeks of application for reinstatement) employees who have taken up to five total years of leave from their position in order to serve. These employees are entitled to be returned to the position they would have held if they had been continuously employed (this is called an "escalator" position). If the employee is not qualified for the escalator position, the employer must make a reasonable effort to help the employee qualify. Those employees are also entitled to promotions, raises, and other seniority-based benefits they would have received. There are many exceptions to both the five-year service limit and the reinstatement rights. Certain benefits must be made available to those who take leave for service, and benefits must be restored to those who return. An employee may not be fired, except for cause, for up to one year after returning from service.

*Enforcement.*    The law is enforced by the Veterans Employment and Training Service (VETS) within the DOL. There are also regulations for employer compliance.

## State and Local Laws

The emphasis in this book is on federal laws and regulations. It should be remembered, however, that an organization is subject to law at the state and local levels as well. This greatly increases the array of applicable laws to which the organization must attend.

### EEO/AA Laws

EEO/AA laws are often patterned after federal law. Their basic provisions, however, vary substantially from state to state. Compliance with federal EEO/AA law does not ensure compliance with state and local EEO/AA laws, and vice versa. Thus, it is the responsibility of the organization to be explicitly knowledgeable of the laws and regulations that apply to it.

Of special note is that state and local EEO/AA laws and regulations often provide protections beyond those contained in the federal laws and regulations. State laws, for example, may apply to employers with fewer than 15 employees, which is the cutoff for coverage under the Civil Rights Act. State laws may also prohibit certain kinds of discrimination not prohibited under federal law, for example, sexual orientation, gender identity or expression, breast feeding, and religious dress and grooming practices. For example, nearly half of all states, and many metropolitan areas where there is no state law, have prohibitions on employment discrimination on the basis of sexual orientation. The law for the District of Columbia prohibits 13 kinds of discrimination, including sexual orientation, physical appearance, matriculation, and political affiliation. Finally, state law may deviate from federal law with regard to enforcement mechanisms and penalties for noncompliance.

### Other State Laws

Earlier, reference was made to employment-at-will and workplace torts as matters of common law, which, in turn, are governed at the state law level. Statutory state laws applicable to staffing, in addition to EEO/AA laws, are also plentiful. Examples of areas covered in addition to EEO/AA include criminal record inquiries by the employer, polygraph and "honesty testing," drug testing, AIDS testing, and employee access to personnel records, unemployed applicants, and social media privacy.

## Civil Service Laws and Regulations

Federal, state, and local government employers are governed by special statutory laws and regulations collectively referred to as civil service. Civil service is guided by so-called merit principles that serve as the guide to staffing practices. Following these merit principles results in notable differences between public and private employers in their staffing practices.

## Merit Principles and Staffing Practices

The essence of merit principles relevant to staffing is fourfold:

1. To recruit, select, and promote employees on the basis of their KSAOs
2. To provide for fair treatment of applicants and employees without regard to political affiliation, race, color, national origin, sex, religion, age, or handicap
3. To protect the privacy and constitutional rights of applicants and employees as citizens
4. To protect employees against coercion for partisan political purposes[19]

Merit principles are codified in civil service laws and regulations.

## Comparisons With Private Sector

Merit principles and civil service laws and regulations combine to shape the nature of staffing practices in the public sector. This leads to some notable differences between the public and private sectors. Examples of public sector staffing practices are the following:

1. Open announcement of all vacancies, along with the content of the selection process that will be followed
2. Very large numbers of applicants due to applications being open to all persons
3. Legal mandate to test applicants only for KSAOs that are directly job related
4. Limits on discretion in the final hiring process, such as number of finalists, ordering of finalists, and affirmative action considerations
5. Rights of applicants to appeal the hiring decision, testing process, or actual test content and method[20]

These examples are unlikely to be encountered in the private sector. Moreover, they are only illustrative of the many differences in staffing practices and context between the private and public sectors.

# LEGAL ISSUES IN REMAINDER OF BOOK

The laws and regulations applicable to staffing practices by organizations are multiple in number and complexity. This chapter emphasized an understanding of the need for law, the sources of law, and general provisions of the law and presented in detail the specific provisions that pertain to staffing activities. Little has been said about practical implications and applications.

In the remaining chapters of the book, the focus shifts to the practical, with guidance and suggestions on how to align staffing practices with legal requirements. The "Legal Issues" sections in the remaining chapters discuss major issues from a compliance perspective. The issues so addressed, and the chapter in which they occur, are shown in Exhibit 2.8. Inspection of the exhibit should reinforce

**EXHIBIT 2.8**   **Legal Issues Covered in Other Chapters**

| Chapter Title and Number | Topic |
|---|---|
| Planning (3) | Affirmative action plans and diversity programs |
| | Legality of affirmative action plans and diversity programs |
| Job Analysis and Rewards (4) | Job relatedness and court cases |
| | Essential job functions |
| External Recruitment (5) | Definition of a job applicant |
| | Affirmative action programs |
| | Electronic recruitment |
| | Job advertisements |
| | Fraud and misrepresentation |
| Internal Recruitment (6) | Affirmative Action Programs Regulations |
| | Bona fide seniority systems |
| | The glass ceiling |
| Measurement (7) | Determining adverse impact |
| | Standardization |
| External Selection I (8) | Disclaimers |
| | Reference checks |
| | Background checks |
| | Preemployment inquiries |
| | Bona fide occupational qualifications |
| External Selection II (9) | Uniform Guidelines on Employee Selection Procedures (UGESP) |
| | Selection under the ADA |
| | Drug testing |
| Internal Selection (10) | UGESP |
| | The glass ceiling |
| Decision Making (11) | UGESP |
| | Diversity and hiring decisions |
| Final Match (12) | Employment eligibility verification |
| | Negligent hiring |
| | Employment-at-will |
| Staffing System Management (13) | Record keeping and privacy |
| | EEO report |
| | Legal audits |
| | Training for managers and employees |
| | Dispute resolution |
| Retention Management (14) | Separation laws and regulations |
| | Performance appraisal |

the importance accorded laws and regulations as an external influence on staffing activities.

It should be emphasized that there is a selective presentation of the issues in Exhibit 2.8. Only certain issues have been chosen for inclusion, and only a summary of their compliance implications is presented. It should also be emphasized that the discussion of these issues does not constitute professional legal advice.

## SUMMARY

Staffing involves the formation of the employment relationship. That relationship involves the employer acquiring individuals to perform work for it as employees, independent contractors, temporary employees, and unpaid interns and trainees. The specific legal meanings and obligations associated with these various arrangements were provided.

Myriad laws and regulations have come forth from several sources to place constraints on the contractual relationship between employer and employee. These constraints seek to ensure a balance of power in the relationship, as well as provide protections to both the employee and the employer.

Statutory federal laws pertaining to EEO/AA prohibit discrimination on the basis of race, color, religion, sex, national origin, age, genetic information, and disability. This prohibition applies to staffing practices intentionally used to discriminate (disparate treatment), as well as to staffing practices that have a discriminatory effect (disparate or adverse impact). The EEO/AA laws also contain specific provisions pertaining to staffing, which specify both prohibited and permissible practices. In both instances, the emphasis is on use of staffing practices that are job related and focus on the person/job match.

Other laws and regulations also affect staffing practices. At the federal level, there is a prohibition on the employment of unauthorized aliens and on the use of the polygraph (lie detector), constraints on the use of credit reports on job applicants, and specification of the employment rights of those in the uniformed services. State and local EEO/AA laws supplement those found at the federal level. Civil service laws and regulations apply to government employees. Many other staffing practices are also addressed by state and local laws. Finally, civil service laws and regulations govern staffing practices in the public sector. Their provisions create marked differences in certain staffing practices between public and private employers.

Legal issues will continue to be addressed throughout the remainder of this book. The emphasis will be on explanation and application of the laws' provisions to staffing practices. The issues will be discussed at the end of each chapter, beginning with the next one.

# DISCUSSION QUESTIONS

1. Do you agree that the employer usually has the upper hand when it comes to establishing the employment relationship? When might the employee have maximum power over the employer?
2. What are the limitations of disparate impact statistics as indicators of potential staffing discrimination?
3. Why is each of the four situational factors necessary for establishing a claim of disparate treatment?
4. What factors would lead an organization to enter into a consent agreement rather than continue pursuing a suit in court?
5. What are the differences between staffing in the private sector and staffing in the public sector? Why would private employers probably resist adopting many of the characteristics of public staffing systems?

# ETHICAL ISSUES

1. Assume that you're the staffing manager in an organization that informally, but strongly, discourages you and other managers from hiring people with disabilities. The organization's rationale is that people with disabilities are unlikely to be high performers or long-term employees and are costly to train, insure, and integrate into the work unit. What is your ethical assessment of the organization's stance? Do you have any ethical obligations to try to change the stance, and if so, how might you go about that?
2. Assume the organization you work for strictly adheres to the law in its relationships with employees and job applicants. The organization calls it "staffing by the book." But beyond that it seems anything goes in terms of tolerated staffing practices. What is your assessment of this approach?

# APPLICATIONS

## Age Discrimination in a Promotion?

The Best Protection Insurance Company (BPIC) handles a massive volume of claims each year in the corporate claims function, as well as in its four regional claims centers. Corporate claims is headed by the senior vice president of corporate claims (SVPCC); reporting to the SVPCC are two managers of corporate claims (MCC-Life and MCC-Residential) and a highly skilled corporate claims specialist (CCS). Each regional office is headed by a regional center manager (RCM); the

RCM is responsible for both supervisors and claims specialists within the regional office. The RCMs report to the vice president of regional claims (VPRC). Here is the structure of the organization:

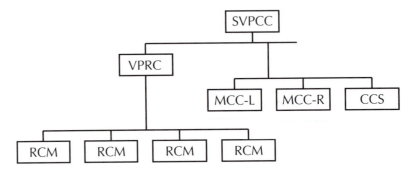

BPIC decided to reorganize its claims function by eliminating the four regional offices (and the RCM position) and establishing numerous small field offices throughout the country. The other part of the reorganization involved creating five new CCS positions. The CCS job itself was to be redesigned and upgraded in terms of knowledge and skill requirements. These new CCS positions would be staffed through internal promotions from within the claims function.

The SVPCC asked Gus Tavus, a 52-year-old RCM, to apply for one of the new CCS positions since his job was being eliminated. The other RCMs, all of whom were over 40 years of age, were also asked to apply. Neither Gus nor the other RCMs were promoted to the CCS positions. Other candidates, some of whom were also over age 40, were also bypassed. The promotions went to five claims specialists and supervisors from within the former regional offices, all of whom were under age 40. Two of these newly promoted employees had worked for, and reported to, Gus as RCM.

Upon learning of his failure to be promoted, Gus sought to find out why. What he learned led him to believe that he had been discriminated against because of his age. He then retained legal counsel, attorney Bruce Davis. Bruce met informally with the SVPCC to try to determine what had happened in the promotion process and why his client had not been promoted. He was told that there were numerous candidates who were better qualified than Gus and that Gus lacked adequate technical and communication skills for the new job of CCS. The SVPCC refused to reconsider Gus for the job and said that all decisions were etched in stone. Gus and Bruce then filed suit in federal district court, claiming a violation of the Age Discrimination in Employment Act. They also subpoenaed numerous BPIC documents, including the personnel files of all applicants for the CCS positions.

After reviewing the documents and discussing things with Gus, Bruce learned more about the promotion process actually used by BPIC. The SVPCC and the two MCCs conducted the entire process; they received no input from the VPRC or the HR department. There was no formal, written job description for the new CCS position, nor was there a formal internal job posting as required by company policy. The SVPCC and the MCCs developed a list of employees they thought might be interested in the job, including Gus, and then met to consider the list of candidates. At that meeting, the personnel files and previous performance appraisals of the candidates were not consulted. After deciding on the five candidates who would be offered the promotion (all five accepted), the SVPCC and MCCs scanned the personnel files and appraisals of these five (only) to check for any disconfirming information. None was found. Bruce's inspection of the files revealed no written comments suggesting age bias in past performance appraisals for any of the candidates, including Gus. Also, there was no indication that Gus lacked technical and communication skills. All of Gus's previous appraisal ratings were above average, and there was no evidence of decline in the favorability of the ratings. Finally, an interview with the VPRC (Gus's boss) revealed that he had not been consulted at all during the promotion process, that he was "shocked beyond belief" that Gus had not been promoted, and that there was "no question" but that Gus was qualified in all respects for the CCS job.

1. Prepare a written report that presents a convincing disparate treatment claim that Gus had been intentionally discriminated against on the basis of his age. Do not address the claim as one of disparate impact.
2. Present a convincing rebuttal, from the viewpoint of BPIC, to this disparate treatment claim.

## Disparate Impact: What Do the Statistics Mean?

Claims of discrimination can be pursued under an allegation of disparate impact. According to this approach, the effect or impact of staffing practices can be discriminatory and thus in violation of the Civil Rights Act. Such an impact could occur even though there may be no underlying intention to discriminate against members of a protected group or class (e.g., women or minorities). Pursuit of a disparate impact claim requires the use of various statistics to show that, in effect, women or minorities are being treated differently than men or nonminorities under the law.

Exhibit 2.5 shows three types of disparate impact statistics: flow statistics, stock statistics, and concentration statistics. Also shown is a statistical example of disparate impact for each type. For each of these three types of statistics, prepare a report in which you discuss the following:

1. How can an organization collect and report these statistics in the form shown in Exhibit 2.5?
2. What standards or guidelines would you recommend for deciding whether statistical differences between men and women, or nonminorities and

minorities, reflect discrimination occurring throughout an organization's staffing system?

3. What types of staffing activities (recruitment, selection, and employment) might be causing the statistical differences? For example, in Exhibit 2.5 the selection rate is 50% for men and 11% for women. How would the organization collect the data necessary to compute these selection rates, how would you decide whether the difference in selection rates (50% vs. 11%) is big enough to indicate possible discrimination, and what sorts of practices might be causing the difference in selection rates?

## ENDNOTES

1. M. W. Bennett, D. J. Polden, and H. J. Rubin, *Employment Relationships: Law and Practice* (Frederick, MD: Aspen, 2004), pp. 1-1 to 3-50; D. J. Walsh, *Employment Law for Human Resource Practice*, 4th ed. (Mason, OH: South-Western, 2013), pp. 31–60.
2. Walsh, *Employment Law for Human Resource Practice*, pp. 625–628.
3. S. Bates, "A Tough Target: Employee or Independent Contractor?" *HR Magazine*, July 2001, pp. 69–74; Bennett, Polden, and Rubin, *Employment Relationships: Law and Practice,* pp. 1-4 to 1-7; K. D. Meade, J. W. Pegano, I. M. Saxe, and J. A. Moskowitz, "Revisit Independent Contractor Classifications," *Legal Report*, Society for Human Resource Management, Oct./Nov. 2007, pp. 7–8.
4. A. R. Midence, "A Risky New Trend: Replacing Employees With Independent Contractors," *Workforce Management Online*, Nov. 2009, accessed 5/18/2010; J. Smith, "Labor Crackdown Heats Up," *Wall Street Journal*, Mar. 4, 2013, p. B6.
5. Walsh, *Employment Law for Human Resource Practice*, pp. 40–41.
6. Equal Employment Opportunity Commission, *EEOC Policy Guidance on Temporary Workers* (Washington, DC: author, 1997); Equal Employment Opportunity Commission, *Enforcement Guidance: Application of the ADA to Contingent Workers Placed by Temporary Agencies and Other Staffing Firms* (Washington, DC: author, 2000); N. Greenwald, "Use of Temporary Workers Also Invites Exposure to Lawsuits," *Workforce Management Online*, Mar. 2010 (*www.workforce.com*), accessed 3/25/2010.
7. R. J. Bohner, Jr., and E. R. Salasko, "Beware the Legal Risks of Hiring Temps," *Workforce*, Oct. 2003, pp. 50–57; Walsh, *Employment Law for Human Resource Practice,* pp. 40–46; L. E. O'Donnell, "Is Our Unpaid Intern Legit?" *HR Magazine*, Apr. 2013, pp. 77–79.
8. US Department of Labor, "Fact Sheet # 71: Internship Programs Under the Fair Labor Standards Act," Apr. 2010 (*www.dol.gov/whd/regs/compliance/whdfs71.htm*).
9. L. Guerin and A. DelPo, *The Essential Guide to Federal Employment Laws*, 4th ed. (Berkeley, CA: Nolo, 2013); D. D. Bennett-Alexander and L. P. Hartman, *Employment Law for Business*, 6th ed. (New York: McGraw-Hill Irwin, 2009).
10. Equal Employment Opportunity Commission, *EEOC Enforcement Guidance on How to Count Employees When Determining Coverage Under Title VII, the ADA, and the ADEA* (Washington, DC: author, 1997).
11. Equal Employment Opportunity Commission, *EEOC Guidance on Investigating, Analyzing Retaliation Claims* (*www.eeoc.gov*).

12. W. Bliss, "The Wheel of Misfortune," *HR Magazine*, May 2000, pp. 207–218; W. A. Carmell, "Application of U.S. Antidiscrimination Laws to Multinational Employers," *Legal Report*, Society for Human Resource Management, May/June 2001; S. Lash, "Supreme Court Disables State Employees," *HR News*, Apr. 2001, p. 6.

13. Bennett, Polden, and Rubin, *Employment Relationships: Law and Practice*, pp. 4-75 to 4-82.

14. Walsh, *Employment Law for Human Resource Practice*, pp. 66–87.

15. R. K. Robinson, G. M. Franklin, and R. F. Wayland, *Employment Regulation in the Workplace* (Armonk, NY: M. E. Sharpe, 2010), pp. 84–103.

16. K. Tyler, "Mediating a Better Outcome," *HR Magazine*, Nov. 2007, pp. 63–66.

17. Bennett, Polden, and Rubin, *Employment Relationships: Law and Practice*, pp. 4-75 to 4-82; Walsh, *Employment Law for Human Resource Practice*, pp. 66–87.

18. J. R. Mook, "Accommodation Paradigm Shifts," *HR Magazine*, Jan. 2007, pp. 115–120.

19. J. P. Wiesen, N. Abrams, and S. A. McAttee, *Employment Testing: A Public Sector Viewpoint* (Alexandria, VA: International Personnel Management Association Assessment Council, 1990), pp. 2–3.

20. Wiesen, Abrams, and McAttee, *Employment Testing: A Public Sector Viewpoint*, pp. 3–7.

# CHAPTER THREE

## Planning

**Learning Objectives and Introduction**
Learning Objectives
Introduction

**Internal and External Influences**
Organizational Strategy
Organizational Culture
Labor Markets
Technology

**Human Resource Planning**
Process and Example
Initial Decisions
Forecasting HR Requirements
Forecasting HR Availabilities
Reconciliation and Gaps

**Staffing Planning**
Staffing Planning Process
Core Workforce
Flexible Workforce
Outsourcing

**Diversity Planning**
Demography of the American Workforce
Business Case for Diversity
Planning for Diversity

**Legal Issues**
Affirmative Action Plans
Legality of AAPs and Diversity Programs
AAPs for Veterans and Individuals With Disabilities
EEO and Temporary Workers

**Summary**

**Discussion Questions**

**Ethical Issues**

**Applications**

**Endnotes**

# LEARNING OBJECTIVES AND INTRODUCTION

## Learning Objectives

- Recognize internal and external influences that will shape the planning process
- Understand how strategic plans integrate with staffing plans
- Become familiar with statistical and judgmental techniques for forecasting HR requirements and availabilities
- Know the similarities and differences between replacement and succession planning
- Understand the advantages and disadvantages of a core workforce, a flexible workforce, and outsourcing strategies for different groups of employees
- Learn how to incorporate diversity into the planning process
- Recognize the fundamental components of an affirmative action plan

## Introduction

Human resource (HR) planning is the process of forecasting the organization's future employment needs and then developing action plans and programs for fulfilling these needs in ways that align with the staffing strategy. HR plans form the basis of all other activities conducted during staffing. An organization that thoroughly considers its staffing needs and how these needs fit with the external environment will find it much easier to recruit the right number and type of candidates, develop methods for selecting the right candidates, and evaluate whether its programs are successful.

Essentially, HR planning involves learning about the employment environment, determining how many employees an organization will need in the future, and assessing the availability of employees in both the internal and external markets. The HR planning process involves several specific components that we cover in this chapter, including making initial planning decisions, forecasting HR requirements and availabilities, determining employee shortages and surpluses, and developing action plans.

The chapter begins with an overview of internal and external influences on the HR planning process, like organizational strategy and culture, labor markets, and technology. Next, we provide an overview of the process of HR planning, including a review of methods for forecasting HR requirements and availability. The staffing planning process includes distinguishing between the core and flexible workforces, as well as understanding the environment for outsourcing. Diversity programs have become an increasingly important part of the staffing planning process, so they are also discussed. The major legal issue for HR staffing planning is that of affirmative action plans (AAPs). A different legal issue, that of equal employment opportunity (EEO) coverage for temporary employees and their agencies, is also discussed.

## INTERNAL AND EXTERNAL INFLUENCES

Planning does not occur in a vacuum. All aspects of the planning process must consider both internal and external influences. The two most important internal influences on the planning process are the organization's strategy and the organization's culture. There are three major sources of external influence on HR and staffing planning, namely, product market conditions, labor markets, and technology. Exhibit 3.1 provides specific examples of these influences, which are discussed next.

## Organizational Strategy

The first, and most important, influence on the planning process is the organization's overall strategy. Staffing managers must be intimately familiar with all aspects of the organization's future plans and goals so they can respond by hiring

---

**EXHIBIT 3.1    Examples of Internal and External Influences on Staffing**

### ORGANIZATIONAL STRATEGY
- Current financial and human resources in the organization
- Demand for products and/or services
- Competitors and partners
- Financial and marketing goals

### ORGANIZATIONAL CULTURE
- The expressed vision of executives
- The degree of hierarchy and bureaucracy
- Style of communication

### LABOR MARKETS
- Labor demand: employment patterns, KSAOs sought
- Labor supply: labor force, demographic trends, KSAOs available
- Labor shortages and surpluses
- Employment arrangements

### TECHNOLOGY
- Elimination of jobs
- Creation of jobs
- Changes in skill requirements

the right number of people with the right KSAOs (knowledge, skill, ability, and other characteristics) in a timely manner. Some of the techniques we will review for staffing planning are based on a view of the organization's historical staffing levels. This is a good place to start, because previous practice is an important guide to setting a baseline for future needs. However, all planning must be conducted with an eye to the future as well.

The Society for Human Resource Management proposes that strategic planning involves a thorough knowledge of the organization's current situation as well as a sense of the strategic vision of the organization.[1] Breaking down the organization's strengths, weaknesses, opportunities, and threats (SWOT) is a common method for understanding strategy. The internal assessment phase of the SWOT analysis focuses on physical and financial resources, as well as structure and culture. The external assessment phase looks to learn about economic, demographic, and technological trends that will influence the organization in the future.

Effective staffing planning must begin with a dialogue between HR representatives and organizational leaders.[2] HR managers should be aware of core aspects of the organization's operations, including financial and marketing considerations. Additionally, it is important to see how the organization sees itself changing in the future so that staffing strategies to meet these needs can be developed. Participating in activities like annual planning meetings and reviewing financial statements are essential. Strategic HR experts emphasize that this dialogue must be a two-way communication. In many cases, the current workforce and its capabilities will influence overall organizational plans. HR managers who are aware of internal human capital resources will be much more effective in an advisory capability when discussing future plans with the other executives.

## Organizational Culture

Organizational culture is a very complex topic, in part because culture is so difficult to define. In essence, culture is the set of intangibles that influences attitudes and behavior in organizations. Some of the factors that can influence an organization's culture include the expressed vision of executives, the degree of hierarchy and bureaucracy, the history of interactions among departments, and the style of communication throughout the organization. For example, an organization in which structure and predictability are emphasized will call for a very different set of staffing practices relative to an organization in which flexibility and innovation are core values. The relationship between the organization and labor unions or other employee organizations (such as professional organizations like the American Medical Association or the state Bar Association) is also an extremely important part of culture. To understand culture, HR managers should spend time talking with senior executives, administer and evaluate employee survey data, and conduct focus groups.

Just because culture is intangible does not mean it is not important. Michael Davis, the chief human resources officer at General Mills, encourages HR managers to build "an integrated set of programs and policies that reinforce and bring value to life." He further notes that when the company's espoused values are inconsistent with the practices that employees encounter on a day-to-day basis, problems with motivation, communication, and retention will follow.[3] Matching culture to planning occurs in numerous ways. Deciding the types of attitudes and values that employees should have in order to achieve a person/organization fit is entirely dependent on culture. An organization with a participative culture should ensure that planning involves representatives from many different perspectives. Decisions related to how succession planning should be managed are also influenced by the degree to which the organization's members value opportunities for growth and development relative to stability and predictability. These are just a few of the ways in which culture can impact the planning process.

In conjunction with the staffing planning process, the organization's staffing philosophy should be reviewed. The results of this review help shape the direction and character of the specific staffing systems implemented. The review should focus on internal versus external staffing and diversity philosophy.

External and internal staffing is a critical matter because it directly shapes the nature of the staffing system, as well as sends signals to applicants and employees alike about the organization as an employer. Exhibit 3.2 highlights the advantages and disadvantages of external and internal staffing. Clearly there are trade-offs to consider in deciding the optimal internal-external staffing mix. The point regarding time to reach full productivity warrants special comment. Any new hire, either internal or external, will require time to learn the new job and reach a full productivity level. In some ways, external hires may be able to reach job productivity faster. This is because external hires are usually selected because they have experience in a job similar to the one they will be taking, whereas internal hires are promoted into jobs they have not previously held. On the other hand, internal new hires have an advantage in terms of person/organization fit because they are already familiar with the culture, policies, procedures, and relationships among organizational members. Internal hires may have also received special training and development to prepare them for the new job.

In terms of diversity, the organization must be sure to consider or develop a sense of importance attached to being a diversity-conscious employer and the commitment it is willing to make in incorporating diversity elements into all phases of the staffing system. As we describe later in the chapter, an organization's overall philosophy toward diversity will be shaped by the cultural value the organization attaches to diversity as well as the business-related consequences of diversity-related practices. Many choices throughout the staffing process will follow from the organization's attitudes toward diversity, ranging from deciding where to recruit to what types of qualifications are most important for new hires.

**EXHIBIT 3.2** **Staffing Philosophy: Internal Versus External Staffing**

|  | Advantages | Disadvantages |
|---|---|---|
| **Internal** | • Positive employee reactions to promotion from within<br><br>• Quick method to identify job applicants<br><br>• Less expensive<br><br>• Less time required to reach full productivity | • No new KSAOs into the organization<br><br>• May perpetuate current underrepresentation of minorities and women<br><br>• Small labor market to recruit from<br><br>• Inexperienced employees may require more training time |
| **External** | • Brings in employees with new KSAOs<br><br>• Larger number of minorities and women to draw from<br><br>• Large labor market to draw from<br><br>• Experienced employees may require less training time | • Negative reaction by internal applicants<br><br>• Time-consuming to identify applicants<br><br>• Expensive to search external labor market<br><br>• More time required to reach full productivity |

## Labor Markets

In and through labor markets, organizations express specific labor preferences and requirements (labor demand), and persons express their own job preferences and requirements (labor supply). Ultimately, person/job matches occur from the interaction of demand and supply forces. Both labor demand and supply contain quantity and quality components, as described below. Labor shortages, labor surpluses, and a variety of possible employment arrangements are also discussed.

## Labor Demand: Employment Patterns

Labor demand is a derived demand, meaning it is a result of consumer demands for the organization's products and services. Knowing the organization's strategy and projections for future KSAO needs will guide the search for labor demand information. In particular, the labor market for the occupations the organization needs to staff will be greatly affected by the product market. For example, in the field of software design, the increased use of tablet computers since 2010 increased demand for programmers who gained skills in designing applications for related operating systems.

To learn about labor demand, national employment statistics are collected and analyzed. They provide data about employment patterns and projections for industries, occupations, and organization size. Most organizations will need to examine not just aggregated statistics, like the overall unemployment rate, but also occupational and regional employment data. As an example, the Bureau of Labor Statistics in 2013 estimated that the unemployment rate for structural iron and steel workers was 21.9% and the rate for telemarketers was 23.1%. At the other extreme, the unemployment rate for physician assistants was 1.2% and the rate for petroleum engineers was 0.6%.[4]

Projections to year 2018 indicate that most job growth will occur in the services sector, led by the education and health services industries, followed by business and professional services. Manufacturing and federal government employment will remain steady, and declines will occur in mining and agriculture.[5]

## Labor Demand: KSAOs Sought

KSAO requirements or preferences of employers are not widely measured, except for education requirements. Data collected by the Bureau of Labor Statistics suggest a continued increase in demand for individuals with college degrees or higher. The number of jobs requiring a bachelor's degree is expected to increase 17%, the number requiring a master's degree is expected to increase 19%, and the number requiring a doctoral degree is expected to increase 22%. In contrast, the number of jobs requiring only short-term on-the-job training is expected to increase by only 9%.[6] The increasing demand for education most likely reflects advances in technology that have made many jobs more complex and technically demanding.[7]

A very thorough and systematic source of information about KSAOs needed for jobs is the Occupational Outlook Handbook. It does not indicate KSAO deficiencies; rather, it provides detailed information about the nature of work and the training and KSAOs required for the entire spectrum of occupations in the United States. Surveys of HR professionals and employees consistently reveal that critical thinking skills, creativity, diversity, ethics, and lifelong learning are seen as especially relevant skills for today's employees.[8]

## Labor Supply: The Labor Force and Its Trends

Quantity of labor supplied is measured and reported periodically by the Bureau of Labor Statistics in the US Department of Labor. An example of basic results for July 2002–2012 is given in Exhibit 3.3. It shows that the labor force, including both full- and part-time employees, reached about 155 million individuals (employed and unemployed) and that unemployment ranged from 4.6% to 9.6%. The data for 2009–2010 clearly show the effects of a major economic slowdown. The subsequent gradual economic recovery is reflected by the decreased unemployment rate in 2012.

Data reveal several labor force trends that have particular relevance for staffing organizations. Labor force growth is slowing, going from an annual growth rate of around 2% in the early 1990s to a projected rate of 1% by the year 2018. There are increasingly fewer new entrants to the labor force. This trend, coupled with the severe KSAO deficiencies that many of the new entrants will have, creates major adaptation problems for organizations.

Demographically, the labor force has become more diverse, and this trend will continue. Data starting in the 1980s and projected through 2018 show a slow trend toward nearly equal labor force participation for men and women, a slight decrease in the proportion of whites in the workforce, and large proportional growth in the representation of Hispanics and Asians. There will also be a dramatic shift toward fewer younger workers and more workers over the age of 55.

Other, more subtle labor force trends are also under way. There has been a slight upward movement overall in the average number of hours that people work and a strong rise in the proportion of employees who work very long hours in certain

## EXHIBIT 3.3  Labor Force Statistics

|  | 2002 | 2004 | 2006 | 2008 | 2010 | 2012 |
|---|---|---|---|---|---|---|
| Civilian noninstitutional population (in millions) | 218 | 223 | 229 | 234 | 238 | 243 |
| Civilian labor force (in millions) | 145 | 147 | 152 | 155 | 154 | 155 |
| Employed (in millions) | 136 | 140 | 145 | 147 | 139 | 142 |
| Unemployed (in millions) | 8.4 | 8.1 | 7.0 | 8.9 | 14.8 | 12.5 |
| Labor force participation rate (%) | 67 | 66 | 66 | 63 | 65 | 64 |
| Unemployment rate (%) | 5.8 | 5.5 | 4.6 | 5.8 | 9.6 | 8.1 |

SOURCE: US Department of Labor, "The Employment Situation," July 2002, July 2004, July 2006, July 2008, July 2010, July 2012.

occupations, such as managers and professionals. Relatedly, there is an increase in holding multiple jobs, with 6.2% of employed people holding more than one job. The number of immigrants in the population is growing; nearly 1 in 10 people is foreign born, the highest rate in more than 50 years. New federal and state policies are increasingly pushing welfare recipients into the labor force, and they are mostly employed in low-wage jobs with low educational requirements. People historically out of the labor force mainstream—such as those with disabilities and the growing number of retirees—may assume a greater presence in the labor force.[9]

## Labor Supply: KSAOs Available

A survey of 431 HR professionals found that 40% of employers indicated that high school graduates lack basic skills in reading comprehension, writing, and math required for entry-level jobs, and that 70% of employers said high school graduates are deficient in work habits such as professionalism, critical thinking, personal accountability, and time management.[10] Most respondents believed college graduates were somewhat better prepared for work, but 44% of applicants with college degrees were still rated as having poor writing skills. There are also shortages of employees with the high skill levels required in contemporary manufacturing environments.[11] Economists and sociologists are quick to note that these skills shortages are being reported despite consistent gains in standardized test scores and educational attainment in the labor force since the 1960s.[12] Thus, it appears the problem is that demand for advanced skills is increasing, as we noted earlier, not that the supply of skilled workers is decreasing. This idea is reinforced by another survey of 726 HR professionals which found 98% of respondents reported that the competition for talented workers has increased in recent years.[13] Data such as these reinforce the serious KSAO deficiencies reported by employers in at least some portions of the labor force.

## Labor Shortages and Surpluses

When labor demand exceeds labor supply for a given pay rate, the labor market is said to be "tight" and the organization experiences labor shortages. Shortages tend to be job or occupation specific. Low unemployment rates, surges in labor demand in certain occupations, and skill deficiencies fuel labor quantity and labor quality shortages for many organizations. The shortages cause numerous responses:

- Increased pay and benefit packages
- Hiring bonuses and stock options
- Alternative work arrangements to attract and retain older workers
- Use of temporary employees
- Recruitment of immigrants
- Lower hiring standards

- Partnerships with high schools, technical schools, and colleges
- Increased mandatory overtime work
- Increased hours of operation

These types of responses are lessened or reversed when the labor market is "loose," meaning there are labor surpluses relative to labor demand.

## Employment Arrangements

Though labor market forces bring organizations and job seekers together, the specific nature of the employment arrangement can assume many forms. One form is whether the person will be employed full time or part time. Data show that about 83% of people work full time and 17% work part time.[14] Although many people prefer part-time work, approximately 23% of part-time workers are seeking full-time employment.

A second arrangement involves the issue of flexible scheduling and shift work. The proportion of the workforce covered by flexible shifts has steadily grown from 12.4% in 1985 to 27.5% in 2004. Many of these workers are covered by formal flextime programs. Work hours are often put into shifts, and about 15% of full-time employed adults work evening, night, or rotating shifts.[15]

Two other types of arrangements, often considered in combination, are (1) various alternative arrangements to the traditional employer–employee relationship, and (2) the use of contingent employees. Alternative arrangements include the organization filling its staffing needs through the use of independent contractors, on-call workers and day laborers, temporary help agency employees, and employees provided by a contract firm that provides a specific service (e.g., accounting). Contingent employees do not have an explicit or implicit contract for long-term employment; they expect their employment to be temporary rather than long term.

National data on the use of alternative employment arrangements and contingent employees were gathered by the US Bureau of Labor Statistics in 2005. It found that 89.3% of surveyed individuals worked in a traditional employer–employee arrangement, and the vast majority of these individuals (97.1%) considered themselves noncontingent. The most prevalent alternative was to work as an independent contractor (7.5%), followed by on-call employees and day laborers (1.7%), temporary help agency employees (.9%), and employees provided by a contract firm (.6%). The percentage of contingent employees in these alternative arrangements ranged from 3.4% (independent contractors) to 60.7% (temporary help employees). Unfortunately, there has not been a data collection effort on the use of alternative employment arrangements since 2005, but most indicators suggest that alternative employment arrangements have increased over time.

Exhibit 3.4 shows several other workforce trends identified in a survey of 1,247 HR professionals. The cost of health care has long been an issue identified in this survey, which is conducted every two years. The aging workforce has also

---
**EXHIBIT 3.4    Major Workforce Trends**

- Continuing high cost of health care in the United States
- Increased global competition for jobs, markets, and talent
- Growing complexity of legal compliance for employers
- Large numbers of baby boomers leaving the workforce at around the same time
- Economic growth of emerging markets
- Greater need for cross-cultural understanding in business settings

SOURCE: J. Schramm, *Workplace Forecast, 2011* (Alexandria, VA: Society for Human Resource Management, 2011).

been an issue of note. More recent surveys focus on global issues such as international competition for talent as well as the economic growth of emerging markets.

## Technology

Changes in technology can influence the staffing planning process significantly. In some cases, technology can serve as a substitute for labor by either eliminating or dramatically reducing the need for certain types of workers. The economy as a whole has shown decreased demand for positions like clerical workers, telephone operators, and manufacturing operators as technology has replaced labor as an input to production. Ironically, changes in software that have made computers easier for nonspecialists to use have eliminated many jobs in computer programming.

At the same time, technology can serve to create new jobs as new business opportunities emerge. In place of the jobs that are eliminated, demand for technical occupations like robotics engineers, systems and database analysts, and software engineers has increased. The expansion of e-commerce and other Internet-based services has increased demand for those who design and manage websites. Increasing productivity as a result of technological change can also spur increased firm performance, which in turn will create more jobs. Often these new jobs will require a completely different set of KSAOs than previous jobs, meaning that increased staffing resources will have to be devoted to either retraining or replacing the current workforce. Research conducted in both the United States and Germany shows that computerization has led to an increase in the demand for highly educated specialists, leading to an overall increased market demand for skills in science and mathematics, which has led to dramatic increases in wages for individuals with these skills.[16] Employers that adopt new technology for any aspect of their operations will also have to consider how to tap into labor markets that have these skills.

## HUMAN RESOURCE PLANNING

After a solid understanding of the internal and external environments has been acquired, a more detailed set of plans to address organizational needs in light of these environmental influences can be considered. Human resource planning (HRP) is a process and set of activities undertaken to forecast an organization's labor demand (requirements) and internal labor supply (availabilities), to compare these projections to determine employment gaps, and to develop action plans for addressing these gaps. Action plans include planning to arrive at desired staffing levels and staffing quality.

A general model depicting the process of HRP is presented first, followed by an operational example of HRP. Detailed discussions of the major components of HRP are then given.[17]

### Process and Example

The basic elements of virtually any organization's HRP are shown in Exhibit 3.5. As can be seen, the HRP process involves four sequential steps:

1. Determine future HR requirements
2. Determine future HR availabilities
3. Reconcile requirements and availabilities—that is, determine gaps (shortages and surpluses) between the two
4. Develop action plans to close the projected gaps

An example of HRP, including results from forecasting requirements and availabilities, is shown in Exhibit 3.6. The exhibit shows a partial HRP conducted by an organization for a specific unit (sales and customer service). It involves only two job categories (sales [A] and customer service [B]) and two hierarchical levels

---

**EXHIBIT 3.5   The Basic Elements of Human Resource Planning**

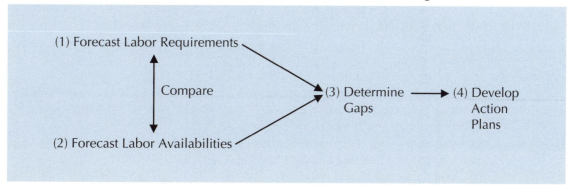

**EXHIBIT 3.6    Operational Format and Example of Human Resource Planning**

Organizational Unit: Sales and Customer Service

| Job Category and Level | Current Workforce | Forecast for Workforce— One Year | | Reconciliation and Gaps | Action Planning |
|---|---|---|---|---|---|
| | | Requirements | Availabilities | | |
| A1 (Sales) | 100 | 110 | 71 | −39 (shortage) | Recruitment Selection |
| A2 (Sales manager) | 20 | 15 | 22 | +7 (surplus) | Employment Retention |
| B1 (Customer service representative) | 200 | 250 | 140 | −110 (shortage) | Compensation Training and |
| B2 (Customer service manager) | 15 | 25 | 22 | −3 (shortage) | development |
| | 335 | 400 | 255 | −145 (shortage) | |

for each category (entry level [1] and managerial level [2]). All of the HRP steps are confined to this particular organizational unit and its job categories/levels, as shown.

The current workforce size (number of employees) is given for each job category/level. Requirements and availabilities are predicted for one year, and the results are shown in the relevant columns. After the reconciliation process, final gap figures are agreed on and entered into the gap column.

These gap data serve as the basic input to action planning. Because the gaps show both shortages and a surplus, and because the gaps vary in severity relative to the current workforce, a specific action plan will probably have to be developed and implemented for each job category/level. The resulting four staffing (and other) plans should bring staffing into an orderly balance of requirements and availabilities over the course of the planning period.

The above process and example identify and illustrate the rudiments of HRP. Within them are several distinct components that require elaboration. We turn now to these components, emphasizing that each one represents a factor that must be considered in HRP and that specific choices must be made regarding the operational details for each component.

## Initial Decisions

Before HRP per se can be undertaken, several critical decisions must be made. These decisions will shape the nature of the resultant HRP process, and they will influence the output of the process, namely, the gap estimates. The quality and potential effectiveness of the action plans developed from the gap estimates are thus at stake when these initial decisions are confronted and made.

### Strategic Planning

We have already discussed the need to integrate organizational strategy into the HRP process. In addition, the development of a strategy for HR should also be the first element of HRP. Several key decisions should be made before more concrete plans are considered.[18] First, a vision based on the overall organizational strategy should be developed. This often means deciding what values and core competencies all members of the organization should possess, and considering principles that will support these. Second, potential strategies for achieving planning process goals should be discussed. It is best at this point to think of whole systems of goals (e.g., integrate all KSAO information for the workforce and future planning needs) rather than specific concrete goals (e.g., conduct recruiting at a local college campus). Too much focus on implementation details early in the strategic planning process can lead to a patchwork approach that involves elements that do not fit together well. Third, contingency plans should be developed and considered. For example, what happens if certain key employees leave the organization? What happens if there is a change in the economy that reduces the supply of needed KSAOs in the labor market? Use of simulation software that shows potential future outcomes for a variety of actions and responses is one way to evaluate the likelihood of potential worst-case scenarios and plan for how to respond should they arise. Fourth, methods for obtaining feedback relative to goals and objectives should be in place. This is a crucial stage, as it involves specifying the types of data that will be used to determine whether the planning process is successful or whether changes need to be made.

HRP can be performed on a plan-basis, project-basis, or population-basis. When HRP takes place as an integral part of an organization's strategic planning process, it is referred to as plan-based HRP. This is a wise approach because it helps integrate the organization's strategic planning process with HR implications. However, not all important business developments are captured in formal business plans, particularly if they occur rapidly or unexpectedly. Organizational responses to these changes that occur in the form of special projects, rather than in changes to the total business plan, are referred to as project-based HRP. In addition, many organizations do HRP outside the formal planning cycle for critical groups of employees on a regular basis. This often occurs for jobs in which there are perennial shortages of employees. Planning focused on a specific employee group is referred to as population-based HRP.

### Planning Time Frame

Since planning involves looking into the future, the logical question for an organization to ask is, How far into the future should our planning extend? Typically, plans are divided into long term (three years and more), intermediate (one to three years), or short term (one year or less). Organizations vary in their planning time frame, often depending on which of the three types of HRP is being undertaken.

For plan-based HRP, the time frame will be the same as that of the business plan. In most organizations, this is between three and five years for so-called strategic planning and something less than three years for operational planning. Planning horizons for project-based HRP vary depending on the nature of the projects involved. Solving a temporary shortage of, say, salespeople for the introduction of a new product might involve planning for only a few months, whereas planning for the start-up of a new facility could involve a lead time of two or more years. Population-based HRP will have varying time frames, depending on the time necessary for labor supply (internal as well as external) to become available. As an example, for top-level executives in an organization, the planning time frame will be lengthy.

### Job Categories and Levels

The unit of HRP and analysis is composed of job categories and hierarchical levels among jobs. These job category/level combinations, and the types and paths of employee movement among them, form the structure of an internal labor market.

Management must choose which job categories and hierarchical levels to use for HRP. In Exhibit 3.6, for example, the choice involves two jobs (sales and customer service) and two levels (entry and managerial) for a particular organizational unit.

Job categories are created and used on the basis of the unit of analysis for which projected shortages and surpluses are being investigated. Hierarchical levels should be chosen so they are consistent with or identical to the formal organizational hierarchy. The reason for this is that these formal levels define employee promotions (up levels), transfers (across levels), and demotions (down levels). Having gap information by level facilitates planning of internal movement programs within the internal labor market. For example, it is difficult to have a systematic promotion-from-within program without knowing probable numbers of vacancies and gaps at various organizational levels.

## Head Count (Current Workforce)

The basic unit of analysis for workforce planning is not the number of employees needed. Rather, to account for the amount of scheduled time worked by each employee, staffing needs are stated in terms of full-time equivalents (FTEs). To determine FTEs, simply define what constitutes full-time work in terms of hours per week (or other time unit) and count each employee in terms of scheduled hours worked relative to a full workweek. If full time is defined as 40 hours per week, a person who normally works 20 hours per week is counted as a .50 FTE, a person normally working 30 hours per week is a .75 FTE, and so on. It is also often advisable to take current authorized vacancies into account when assessing head count.

## Roles and Responsibilities

Both line managers and staff specialists (usually from the HR department) become involved in HRP, so the roles and responsibilities of each must be determined as part of HRP. Most organizations take the position that line managers are ultimately responsible for the completion and quality of HRP, but the usual practice is to have HR staff assist with the process. As noted previously, in an ideal situation there will be a constant flow of information among those involved in HRP, with line managers indicating how needs are expected to change, and HR staff describing the KSAO resources within and outside the organization that can be used to meet these needs in the future.

The process begins with line staff evaluating their current capabilities and future needs based on strategic plans for the organization. The HR staff then takes the lead in proposing which types of HRP will be undertaken and when, and in making suggestions with regard to comprehensiveness, planning time frame, and job categories and levels. Final decisions on these matters are usually the prerogative of line management. Once an approach has been decided on, task forces of both line managers and HR staff are assembled to design an appropriate forecasting and action planning process and to do any other preliminary work.

Once these processes are in place, the HR staff typically assumes responsibility for collecting, manipulating, and presenting the necessary data to line management and for laying out alternative action plans (including staffing plans). Action planning usually becomes a joint venture between line managers and HR staff, particularly as they gain experience with, and trust for, one another.

## Forecasting HR Requirements

Forecasting HR requirements is a direct derivative of business and organizational planning. As such, it becomes a reflection of projections about a variety of factors, such as sales, production, technological change, productivity improvement, and the regulatory environment. Many specific techniques may be used to forecast HR requirements; these are either statistical or judgmental in nature, and they are usually tailor-made by the organization. In forecasting future needs, it is essential to consider not just the status of the workforce but also the expected changes in needs due to strategic considerations. Forward-thinking HR experts note that data can inform HRP when it comes to prior needs and trends, but effective planning also entails considering how changes in the internal and external environments will alter forecasts.[19]

### Statistical Techniques

A wide array of statistical techniques are available for use in HR forecasting. Prominent among these are regression analysis, ratio analysis, trend analysis, time series analysis, and stochastic analysis. Brief descriptions of three of these techniques are given in Exhibit 3.7.

The use of integrated workforce planning software, which can be combined with data from other organizational databases, has made it easier to use these statistical techniques than it was in the past. As we noted earlier, HR practitioners are also increasingly expected to support their proposals and plans with hard data. The three techniques shown in Exhibit 3.7 have different strengths and weaknesses, as we will see. We present these approaches in order from those requiring the least data collection to those requiring the most.

Trend analysis is the simplest approach, because it uses data only on previous staffing levels over time to predict future needs. Trend analysis is useful when organizations have data mostly on historical staffing levels with less detailed information on specific predictors. The decomposition of data into specific time periods of demand is often used in health care and retail settings, where staffing levels vary greatly over the course of a year or even at different times of the day.

The trend analysis approach implicitly assumes that the pattern of staffing needs in the past will be predictive of the future but does not take any external factors, like the overall state of the economy or product market demand, into account.

Ratio analysis is a more sophisticated approach that uses data from prior sales figures or other operational data to predict expected head count. In the example in Exhibit 3.7, estimates of sales growth are used to predict how many employees will

---

**EXHIBIT 3.7    Examples of Statistical Techniques to Forecast HR Requirements**

**(A)  Trend Analysis**

1. Gather data on staffing levels over time and arrange in a spreadsheet with one column for employment levels and another column for time.
2. Predict trend in employee demand by fitting a line to trends in historical staffing levels over time (this can be done by using regression or graphical methods in most spreadsheet programs).
3. Calculate period demand index by dividing each period's demand by the average annual demand.

   Example: January demand index = Avg. January FTE/Avg. annual FTE

4. Multiply the previous year's FTEs by the trend figure, then multiply this figure by the period's demand index.

   Example: A retail store finds that the average number of employees over the past five years has been 142, 146, 150, 155, and 160. This represents a consistent 3% increase per year; to predict the next year's average demand, multiply 160 by 1.03 to show a 3% expected increase. Over this same time period, it averaged 150 FTEs per month, with an average of 200 FTEs in December. This means the December demand index is 200/150 = 1.33, so its estimate for next year's December FTE demand will be (160 × 1.03) × 1.3 = 219 FTEs.

**(B)  Ratio Analysis**

1. Examine historical ratios involving workforce size.

   Example:   $\dfrac{\$ \text{ sales}}{1.0 \text{ FTE}} = ?$     $\dfrac{\text{No. of new customers}}{1.0 \text{ FTE}} = ?$

2. Assume ratio will be true in future.
3. Use ratio to predict future HR requirements.

   Example:   (a) $\dfrac{\$40{,}000 \text{ sales}}{1.0 \text{ FTE}}$ is past ratio
   (b) Sales forecast is $4,000,000
   (c) HR requirements = 100 FTEs

**(C)  Regression Analysis**

1. Statistically identify historical predictors of workforce size.

   Example:   FTEs = $a + b_1$ sales + $b_2$ new customers

2. Only use equations with predictors found to be statistically significant.
3. Predict future HR requirements, using equation.

   Example:   (a) FTEs = 7 + .0004 sales + .02 new customers
   (b) Projected sales = $1,000,000
       Projected new customers = 300
   (c) HR requirements = 7 + 400 + 6 = 413

be needed. This technique is useful for incorporating data from other functional areas to predict the future. However, this model cannot directly account for any changes in technology or skill sets that might change these ratios.

The regression analysis technique can be used with historical predictors and can make more statistically precise estimates of future expectations by taking several factors into account simultaneously. In the example, sales data and new customer data from organizational records are used to predict staffing needs in the past. Then the estimates from these predictions are combined with projections for the future to generate future FTE requirements. This procedure is more thorough than the ratio analysis approach, which incorporates only a single predictor of workforce size. However, collecting enough data to make good estimates can be time-consuming and requires judgment calls.

## Judgmental Techniques

Judgmental techniques represent human decision-making models that are used for forecasting HR requirements. Unlike statistical techniques, judgmental techniques use a decision maker who collects and weighs the information subjectively and then turns it into forecasts of HR requirements. The decision maker's forecasts may or may not agree very closely with those derived from statistical techniques. This is not necessarily a weakness of either approach. Ideally, the precision of statistical techniques should be coupled with on-the-ground knowledge represented by judgmental techniques to provide estimates that have both rigor and relevance.

Implementation of judgmental forecasting can proceed from either a top-down or bottom-up approach. In the former, top managers of the organization, organizational units, or functions rely on their knowledge of business and organizational plans to predict what future head counts should be. At times, these projections may, in fact, be dictates rather than estimates, necessitated by strict adherence to the business plan. Such dictates are common in organizations undergoing significant change, such as restructuring, mergers, and cost-cutting actions.

In the bottom-up approach, lower-level managers make initial estimates for their unit (e.g., department, office, or plant) on the basis of what they have been told or presume are the business and organizational plans. These estimates are then consolidated and aggregated upward through successively higher levels of management. Then, top management establishes the HR requirements in terms of numbers.

## Scenario Planning

Scenario planning is a technique that has been explored in a variety of fields to predict future outcomes in an uncertain environment.[20] The previous methods we have described are all designed to give a specific estimate for the number of people who will be needed in the organization in the future. Scenario planning provides a range of estimates based on various possible changes in the external and internal environments. For example, ratio analysis uses forecasts of future product demand to predict how many FTEs will be required; in our example in Exhibit 3.7, 100 FTEs will be required based on sales forecasts. Scenario planning provides a range of possible FTE requirements based on a variety of potential product demand levels; thus, three distinct estimates of FTE requirements will be developed for worst-case, expected, and best-case demand levels.

The advantage of scenario planning is that it allows HRP to incorporate uncertainty and prepare for the unexpected. Because it explicitly acknowledges ways that the future might be different from the past, it also incorporates judgmental techniques. Considering all the complex factors that go into various scenarios is often challenging, so simulation software is often part of the process. These programs allow managers to change various features of a situation to see how an outcome (in this case, projected FTEs) will change. Evidence suggests that the process of doing scenario planning can change the ways decision makers think by promoting more holistic views of a problem that incorporate a wide range of factors.[21]

## Forecasting HR Availabilities

In Exhibit 3.6, head-count data are given for the current workforce and their availability as forecast in each job category/level. These forecasted figures take into account movement into and out of each job category/level and exit from the organizational unit or the organization. Described below are three approaches for forecasting availabilities: manager judgment, Markov Analysis, and replacement and succession planning.

### Manager Judgment

Individual managers may use their judgment to make availability forecasts for their work units. This is especially appropriate in smaller organizations or in ones that lack centralized workforce internal mobility data and statistical forecasting capabilities. Continuing the example from Exhibit 3.6, assume the manager is asked to make an availability forecast for the entry sales job category A1. The template to follow for making the forecast and the results of the forecast are shown in Exhibit 3.8. To the current staffing level in A1 (100) is added likely inflows to A1 (10), and then likely outflows from A1 (37) are subtracted to yield the forecasted staffing availability (73). Determining the inflow and outflow numbers requires judgmental estimates as to the numbers of promotions, transfers, demotions, and exits. As shown at the bottom of Exhibit 3.8, promotions involve an upward change of job level within or between job categories, transfers are lateral moves at the same job level across job categories, and demotions are downward changes of job level within or between job categories. Separate forecasts may be done for the other job category/levels (A2, B1, and B2).

To provide reliable estimates, the manager must be very knowledgeable about both organizational business plans and individual employee plans or preferences for

## EXHIBIT 3.8    Manager Forecast of Future HR Availabilities

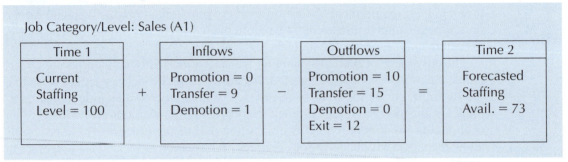

Job Category/Level: Sales (A1)

| Time 1 | | Inflows | | Outflows | | Time 2 |
|---|---|---|---|---|---|---|
| Current Staffing Level = 100 | + | Promotion = 0 Transfer = 9 Demotion = 1 | − | Promotion = 10 Transfer = 15 Demotion = 0 Exit = 12 | = | Forecasted Staffing Avail. = 73 |

NOTE: Promotion is A1 to A2, A1 to B2, B1 to B2, or B1 to A2; transfer is A1 to B1, A2 to B2, B1 to A1, or B2 to A2; demotion is A2 to A1, A2 to B1, B2 to B1, or B2 to A1.

staying in their current job versus moving to another job. Knowledge of business plans will be helpful in judging the likely internal mobility opportunities for employees. Business expansion, for example, will likely mean expanding internal mobility opportunities. Knowledge of employee plans or preferences will help pinpoint which employees are likely to change jobs or leave the work unit or organization.

The estimated staffing availability (n = 73) in Exhibit 3.8 coincides closely with the availability estimate (n = 71) derived from forecasting based on Markov Analysis results, discussed below. This is intentional. Markov Analysis uses historical mobility data and probabilities to forecast future availabilities, while managers' judgment uses current knowledge of business and employees' plans to forecast employee movements person by person. Results from these two approaches to availability forecasts will not necessarily coincide, but they can be quite close if the manager is knowledgeable about past mobility patterns, employee mobility intentions, and mobility opportunities.

A major problem with using manager judgment to forecast availabilities is that the manager may lack the necessary business plan and employee intention information to provide solid estimates, as opposed to casual guesstimates. In addition, if there are large numbers of employees and job category/levels in the work unit, the sheer complexity of the forecasting task may overwhelm the manager. Markov Analysis presents a way out of this dilemma, since it substitutes historical data about internal mobility and exit rates for the manager's judgment as a basis for making availability forecasts, and it simultaneously considers all types of possible employee movement in the forecasts.

### Markov Analysis

Markov Analysis is used to predict availabilities on the basis of historical patterns of job stability and movement among employees. Consider again the four job category/levels (A1, A2, B1, and B2) in the sales and customer service unit in

Exhibit 3.6. Note that between any two time periods, the following possibilities exist for each employee in the internal labor market:

1. Job stability (remain in A1, A2, B1, or B2)
2. Promotion (move to a higher level: A1 to A2, A1 to B2, B1 to B2, or B1 to A2)
3. Transfer (move at the same level: A1 to B1, B1 to A1, A2 to B2, or B2 to A2)
4. Demotion (move to a lower level: A2 to A1, A2 to B1, B2 to B1, or B2 to A1)
5. Exit (move to another organizational unit or leave the organization)

These possibilities may be thought of in terms of flows and rates of flow or movement rates. Past flows and rates may be measured and then used to forecast the future availability of current employees, based on assumptions about the extent to which past rates will continue unchanged in the future. For example, if it is known that the historical promotion rate from A1 to A2 is .10 (10% of A1 employees are promoted to A2), we might predict that A1 will experience a 10% loss of employees due to promotion to A2 over the relevant time period. To conduct Markov Analysis we must know all of the job stability, promotion, transfer, demotion, and exit rates for an internal labor market before we can forecast future availabilities.

The elements of Markov Analysis are shown in Exhibit 3.9 for the organizational unit originally presented in Exhibit 3.6. Refer first to part A of Exhibit 3.9, where movement rates between two time periods (T and T+1) are calculated for four job category/level combinations. This is accomplished as follows. For each job category/level, take the number of employees at time period T, and use this number as the denominator for calculating job stability and movement rates. Next, for each of these employees, determine which job category/level they were employed in at T+1. Then, sum up the number of employees in each job category/level at T+1, and use these as the numerators for calculating stability and movement rates. Finally, divide each numerator separately by the denominator. The result is the stability and movement rates expressed as proportions, also known as transition probabilities. The rates for any row (job category/level) must add up to 1.0.

For example, consider job category/level A1. Assume that at time T in the past, A1 had 400 people. Further assume that at T+1, 240 of these employees were still in A1, 40 had been promoted to A2, 80 had been transferred to B1, 0 had been promoted to B2, and 40 had exited the organizational unit or the organization. The resulting transition probabilities, shown in the row for A1, are .60, .10, .20, .00, and .10. Note that these rates sum to 1.00.

By referring to these figures, and the remainder of the transition probabilities in the matrix, an organization can begin to understand the workings of the unit's internal labor market. For example, it becomes clear that 60%–80% of employees experienced job stability and that exit rates varied considerably, ranging from 10% to 35%. Promotions occurred only within job categories (A1 to A2, B1 to B2), not between

---

**EXHIBIT 3.9   Use of Markov Analysis to Forecast Availabilities**

| A. **Transition Probability Matrix** Job Category and Level | | A1 | A2 | **T + 1** B1 | B2 | Exit |
|---|---|---|---|---|---|---|
| | A1 | .60 | .10 | .20 | .00 | .10 |
| | A2 | .05 | .60 | .00 | .00 | .35 |
| **T** | B1 | .05 | .00 | .60 | .05 | .30 |
| | B2 | .00 | .00 | .00 | .80 | .20 |

| B. **Forecast of Availabilities** | Current Workforce | | | | |
|---|---|---|---|---|---|
| A1 | 100 | 60 | 10 | 20 | 0 |
| A2 | 20 | 1 | 12 | 0 | 0 |
| B1 | 200 | 10 | 0 | 120 | 10 |
| B2 | 15 | 0 | 0 | 0 | 12 |
| | | 71 | 22 | 140 | 22 |

job categories (A1 to B2, B1 to A2). Transfers were confined to the lower of the two levels (A1 to B1, B1 to A1). Only occasionally did demotions occur, and only within a job category (A2 to A1). Presumably, these stability and movement rates reflect specific staffing policies and procedures that were in place between T and T+1.

With these historical transitional probabilities, it becomes possible to forecast the future availability of the current workforce over the same time interval, T and T+1, assuming that the historical rates will be repeated over the time interval and that staffing policies and procedures will not change. Refer now to part B of Exhibit 3.9. To forecast availabilities, simply take the current workforce column and multiply it by the transition probability matrix shown in part A. The resulting availability figures (note these are the same as those shown in Exhibit 3.6) appear at the bottom of the columns: A1 = 71, A2 = 22, B1 = 140, and B2 = 22. The remainder of the current workforce (80) is forecast to exit and will not be available at T+1.

***Limitations of Markov Analysis.***   Markov Analysis is an extremely useful way to capture the underlying workings of an internal labor market and then use the results to forecast future HR availabilities. It is, however, subject to some limitations that must be kept in mind.[22]

The first and most fundamental limitation is that of sample size, or the number of current workforce employees in each job category/level. As a rule, it is desirable to have 20 or more employees in each job category/level. Since this number serves as the denominator in the calculation of transition probabilities, with small sample sizes there can be substantial differences in the values of transition probabilities, even though the numerators used in their calculation are not that different (e.g., 2/10 = .20 and 4/10 = .40). Thus, transition probabilities based on small samples yield unstable estimates of future availabilities.

A second limitation of Markov Analysis is that it does not detect multiple moves by employees between T and T+1; it only classifies employees and counts their movement according to their beginning (T) and ending (T+1) job category/level, ignoring any intermittent moves. To minimize the number of undetected multiple moves, therefore, it is necessary to keep the time interval relatively short, preferably no more than two years.

A third limitation pertains to the job category/level combinations created to serve as the unit of analysis. These must be meaningful to the organization for the HRP purposes of both forecasting and action planning. Thus, extremely broad categories (e.g., managers or researchers) and categories without any level designations should be avoided. Note that this recommendation may conflict somewhat with organizations with a non-bureaucratic or team-based structure.

Finally, the transition probabilities reflect only gross, average employee movement and not the underlying causes of the movement. Stated differently, all employees in a job category/level are assumed to have an equal probability of movement. This is unrealistic because organizations take many factors into account (e.g., seniority, performance appraisal results, and KSAOs) when making movement decisions about employees. Because of these factors, the probabilities of movement may vary among specific employees.

## Individual Internal Forecasts

Both the managerial judgment and Markov Analysis approaches are designed to estimate future internal HR availabilities for large numbers of employees. Replacement and succession planning focus on identifying individual employees who will be considered for promotion, along with a thorough assessment of their current capabilities and deficiencies, coupled with training and development plans to erase any deficiencies. Through replacement and succession planning, the organization constructs internal talent pipelines that ensure steady and known flows of qualified employees to higher levels of responsibility and impact. Replacement planning precedes succession planning, and the organization may choose to stop at just replacement planning rather than proceeding into the more complex succession planning process.[23]

Replacement and succession planning can occur at any and all levels of the organization. They are most widely used at the management level, starting with the chief executive officer and extending downward to the other officers or top managers. They can also be used throughout the entire management team, including the identification and preparation of individuals for promotion into entry-level management. They may also be used for linchpin positions—ones that are critical to organization effectiveness (such as senior scientists in the research and development function of a technology-driven organization) but not necessarily housed within the management structure.

***Replacement Planning.***   Replacement planning focuses on identifying individual employees who will be considered for promotion and thoroughly assessing their current capabilities and deficiencies. Training and development plans to improve the fit between capabilities and requirements are also developed. The focus is thus on both the quantity and the quality of availability. The results of replacement planning are shown on a replacement chart, an example of which is shown in Exhibit 3.10. The chart is based on the previous sales–customer service unit in Exhibit 3.6. The focus is on replacement planning for the sales manager (A2) from the ranks of sales associates (A1) as part of the organization's "grow your own," promotion-from-within HR strategy. The top part of the chart indicates the organizational unit and jobs covered by replacement planning, as well as the minimum criteria for promotion eligibility. The next part shows the actual replacement chart information for the incumbent department manager (Woo) and the two eligible sales associates (Williams and Stemke) in the menswear department at the Cloverdale store. The key data are length of service, overall performance rating, and promotability rating. When the incumbent sales manager (Woo) is promoted to group sales manager, both sales associates will be in the promotion pool. Williams will likely get the position because of her "ready now" promotability rating. Given his relatively short length of service and readiness for promotion in less than one year, Stemke is probably considered a "star" or a "fast tracker" whom the organization will want to promote rapidly. Similar replacement charts could be developed for all departments in the store and for all hierarchical levels up to and including store manager. Replacement chart data could then be aggregated across stores to provide a corporate composite of talent availability.

The process of replacement planning has been greatly accelerated by human resources information systems (HRISs). Many HRISs make it possible to keep data on KSAOs for each employee based on job history, training, and outside education. Software also allows organizations to create lists of employees who are ready to move into specific positions, and to assess potential risks that managers or leaders will leave the organization. The ability to keep track of employees across the organization by standardized inventories of skill sets means that staffing managers will be able to compare a variety of individuals for new job assignments quickly and consistently. A large database of candidates also makes it possible to seek out passive internal job candidates who are not actively looking for job changes but might be willing to take new positions if offered. Many organizations that use integrated database systems to track candidates across a variety of locations report they are able to consider a larger pool of candidates than they would with a paper-based system. Some HRISs automatically alert HR when key positions become open, and thus the process of finding a replacement can get under way quickly. The development of comprehensive replacement planning software is typically quite expensive, with costs reaching hundreds of thousands of dollars. The software is probably most useful for large organizations that are able to capitalize on the costs of a large system. However, smaller organizations may

**EXHIBIT 3.10  Replacement Chart Example**

Organizational Unit: Merchandising—Soft Goods
Replacement for: Department Sales Manager (A2)
Pipelines for Replacement: Department Sales (A1)—preferred; External Hire—last resort
Minimum Eligibility Requirements: Two years' full-time sales experience; overall performance rating of "exceeds expectations"; promotability rating of "ready now" or "ready in < 1 yr."

Department: Menswear
Store: Cloverdale

| **Incumbent Manager** | **Years in Job** | **Overall Performance Rating** | | |
|---|---|---|---|---|
| Seng Woo | 7 | X  Exceeds expectations | Meets expectations | Below expectations |
| **Promote to** | | **Promotability Rating** | | |
| Group Sales Manager | | X  Ready now | Ready in < 1 yr. | Ready in 1–2 yrs. | Not promotable |

| **Replacement** | **Years in Job** | **Overall Performance Rating** | | |
|---|---|---|---|---|
| Shantara Williams | 8 | X  Exceeds expectations | Meets expectations | Below expectations |
| **Promote to** | | **Promotability Rating** | | |
| Sales Manager | | X  Ready now | Ready in < 1 yr. | Ready in 1–2 yrs. | Not promotable |

| **Replacement** | **Years in Job** | **Overall Performance Rating** | | |
|---|---|---|---|---|
| Lars Stemke | 2 | X  Exceeds expectations | Meets expectations | Below expectations |
| **Promote to** | | **Promotability Rating** | | |
| Sales Manager | | Ready now | X  Ready in < 1 yr. | Ready in 1–2 yrs. | Not promotable |

find it possible to create their own databases of skills as a means of facilitating the internal replacement process.[24]

***Succession Planning.***    Succession plans build on replacement plans and directly tie into leadership development. The intent is to ensure that candidates for promotion will have the specific KSAOs and general competencies required for success in the new job. The key to succession planning is assessing each promotable employee for KSAO or competency gaps, and where there are gaps, creating employee training and development plans that will close the gap. A survey conducted by the Society for Human Resource Management showed that over half of HR professionals indicated that their organization had implemented some form of succession planning.[25]

Continuing the example from replacement planning, Exhibit 3.11 shows a succession plan for the two promotable sales associates. The organization has developed a set of general leadership competencies for all managers, and for each management position (such as department sales manager), it indicates which of those competencies are required for promotion, in addition to the minimum eligibility requirements. It is the focus on these competencies, and the development plans to instill them in candidates for promotion who lack them, that differentiates replacement and succession planning.

It can be seen that Williams, who is "ready now," has no leadership competency gaps, with the possible exception of an in-house training course on budget preparation and monitoring, which she is currently completing. Stemke, while having "star" potential, must undertake development work. When he successfully completes that work, he will be promoted to sales manager as soon as possible. Alternatively, he might be placed in the organization's acceleration pool. This pool contains high-potential individuals like Stemke from within the organization who are being groomed for management positions generally, and for rapid acceleration upward, rather than progressing through the normal promotion paths.

It should be noted that replacement and succession planning require managers' time and expertise to conduct, both of which the organization must be willing to provide to those managers. Moreover, there must be effective performance appraisal and training and development systems in place to support replacement and succession planning. For example, overall performance and promotability ratings, plus assessment of competency gaps and spelling out development plans, could occur annually as part of the performance appraisal process conducted by management. In addition to identifying the skills needed immediately, succession plans should also identify skills needed in the future. Finally, promotability and development assessments require managers to make tough and honest decisions. A study of successful succession management in several Fortune 500 organizations concluded, "Succession management is possible only in an organizational culture that encourages candor and risk taking at the executive level. It depends on a willingness to differentiate individual performance and a corporate culture in which the truth is valued more than politeness."[26]

**EXHIBIT 3.11   Succession Plan Example**

Organizational Unit: Merchandising—Soft Goods
Department: Menswear
Position to Be Filled: Department Sales Manager (A2)
Leadership Competencies Required
  • Plan work unit activities
  • Budget preparation and monitoring
  • Performance management of sales associates

| Eligible Replacement | Promotability Rating | Competency Gaps | Development Plans |
|---|---|---|---|
| S. Williams | Ready now | Budget prep | Now completing in-house training course |
| L. Stemke | Ready in < 1 year | Plan work | Shadowing sales manager |
| | | Budget prep | Starting in-house training course |
| | | Perf. mgt. | Serving as sales manager 10 hours per week |
| | | | Taking course on performance management at university extension |

## Reconciliation and Gaps

The reconciliation and gap determination process is best examined by means of an example. Exhibit 3.12 presents intact the example in Exhibit 3.6. Attention is now directed to the reconciliation and gaps column. It represents the results of bringing together requirements and availability forecasts with the results of external and internal environmental scanning. Gap figures must be decided on and entered into the column, and the likely reasons for the gaps need to be identified.

Let's first consider job category/level A1. A relatively large shortage is projected due to a mild expansion in requirements coupled with a substantial drop in availabilities. This drop is not due to an excessive exit rate but to losses through promotions and job transfers (refer back to the availability forecast in Exhibit 3.9).

For A2, decreased requirements coupled with increased availabilities lead to a projected surplus. Clearly, changes in current staffing policies and procedures will have to be made to stem the availability tide, such as a slowdown in the promotion

**EXHIBIT 3.12    Operational Format and Example of Human Resource Planning**

### Organizational Unit: Sales and Customer Service

| Job Category and Level | Current Workforce | Forecast for Workforce— One Year | | Reconciliation and Gaps | Action Planning |
|---|---|---|---|---|---|
| | | Requirements | Availabilities | | |
| A1 (Sales) | 100 | 110 | 71 | −39 (shortage) | Recruitment Selection |
| A2 (Sales manager) | 20 | 15 | 22 | +7 (surplus) | Employment Retention |
| B1 (Customer service representative) | 200 | 250 | 140 | −110 (shortage) | Compensation Training and development |
| B2 (Customer service manager) | 15 | 25 | 22 | −3 (shortage) | |
| | 335 | 400 | 255 | −145 (shortage) | |

rate into A2 from A1, or to accelerate the exit rate, such as through an early retirement program.

Turning to B1, note that a huge shortage is forecast. This is due to a major surge in requirements and a substantial reduction in availabilities. To meet the shortage, the organization could increase the transfer of employees from A1. While this would worsen the already-projected shortage in A1, it might be cost effective and would beef up the external staffing for A1 to cover the exacerbated shortage. Alternately, a massive external staffing program could be developed and undertaken for B1 alone. Or, a combination of internal transfers and external staffing for both A1 and B1 could be attempted. To the extent that external staffing becomes a candidate for consideration, this will naturally spill over into other HR activities, such as establishing starting-pay levels for A1 and B1. Finally, a very different strategy would be to develop and implement a major retention program for employees in customer service.

For B2 there is a small projected shortage. This gap is so small, however, that for all practical purposes it can be ignored. The HRP process is too imprecise to warrant concern over such small gap figures.

In short, the reconciliation and gap phase of HRP involves coming to grips with projected gaps and the likely reasons for them. Quite naturally, thoughts about future implications begin to creep into the process. Even in the simple example shown, it can be seen that considerable action will have to be contemplated and undertaken to respond to the forecasting results for the organizational unit. That will involve mixtures of external and internal staffing, with compensation as another likely HR ingredient. Through action planning, these possibilities become real.

## STAFFING PLANNING

After the HRP process is complete, it is time to move toward the development of specific plans for staffing. This is a vital phase of the planning process, in which staffing objectives are developed and alternative staffing activities are generated. The objectives are the targets the organization establishes to determine how many employees will be needed and in which job categories. The activities are the specific methods, including recruiting and selection strategies, that will be used to meet these objectives. We devote special attention in this section to one of the most critical decisions made during staffing planning: Should the organization use a core workforce or a flexible workforce, or should parts of the workforce be outsourced?

### Staffing Planning Process

#### Staffing Objectives

Staffing objectives are derived from identified gaps between requirements and availabilities. Thus, these objectives respond to both shortages and surpluses. They may require the establishment of quantitative and qualitative targets.

Quantitative targets should be expressed in head count or FTE form for each job category/level and will be very close in magnitude to the identified gaps. Indeed, to the extent that the organization believes in the gaps as forecast, the objectives will be identical to the gap figures. A forecast shortage of 39 employees in A1, for example, should be transformed into a staffing objective of 39 accessions (or something close to it) to be achieved by the end of the forecasting time interval. Exhibit 3.13 illustrates these points. For each cell, enter a positive number for head-count additions and a negative number for head-count subtractions.

Qualitative staffing objectives refer to the qualities of people in KSAO-type terms. For external staffing objectives, these may be stated in terms of averages, such as average education level for new hires and average scores on ability tests. Internal staffing objectives of a qualitative nature may also be established. These may reflect desired KSAOs in terms of seniority, performance appraisal record over a period of years, types of on- and off-the-job training, and so forth.

The results of replacement and succession planning, or something similar to that, will be very useful to have as well.

## Generating Alternative Staffing Activities

With quantitative and, possibly, qualitative objectives established, it is necessary to begin identifying possible ways of achieving them. At the beginning stages of generating alternatives, it is not wise to close the door prematurely on any of them. Exhibit 3.14 provides a full range of options for dealing with employee shortages and surpluses. As with previous planning processes, the focus is not on specific programs at this stage but rather on broad classes of potential activities.

As shown in the exhibit, both short- and long-term options for shortages, involving a combination of staffing and workload management, are possible. Short-term options include utilizing current employees better (through more overtime, productivity

---

**EXHIBIT 3.13**   **Setting Numerical Staffing Objectives**

| Job Category and Level | Gap | Objectives | | | | | Total |
|---|---|---|---|---|---|---|---|
| | | New Hires | Promotions | Transfers | Demotions | Exits | |
| A1 | −39 | 52 | −6 | −3 | 0 | −4 | +39 |
| A2 | +7 | 0 | +2 | −8 | 0 | −1 | −7 |
| B1 | −110 | +140 | −5 | −3 | −2 | −20 | +110 |
| B2 | −3 | +2 | +4 | −1 | 0 | −2 | +3 |

NOTE: The objective is to close each gap exactly.

**EXHIBIT 3.14** **Staffing Alternatives to Deal With Employee Shortages and Surpluses**

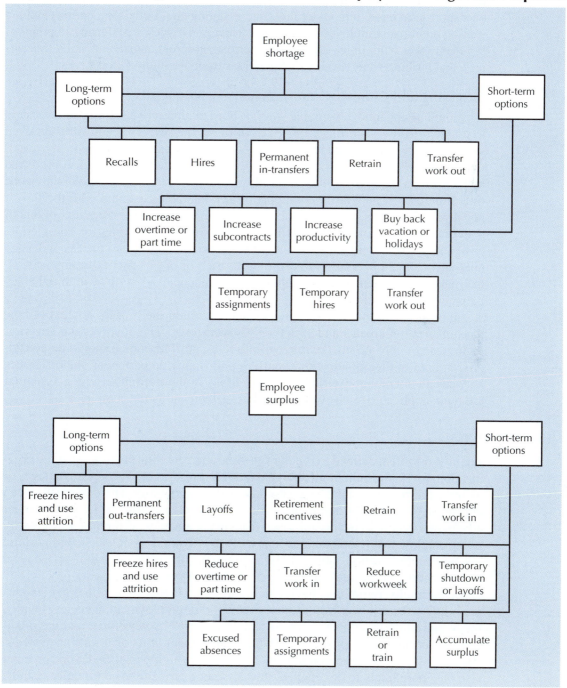

increases, and buybacks of vacation and holidays), outsourcing work to other organizations (subcontracts, transferring work out), and acquiring additional employees on a short-term basis (temporary hires and assignments). Long-term options include staffing additional employees (recalling former employees, transferring in employees from other work units, adding new permanent hires), enhancing skills (retraining), and pushing work to other organizations (transferring work out).

### Assessing and Choosing Alternatives

As should be apparent, a veritable smorgasbord of alternative staffing activities are available to address staffing gaps. Each of these alternatives needs to be assessed systematically to help decision makers choose from among them.

The goal of assessment is to identify one or more preferred activities. A preferred activity offers the highest likelihood of attaining the staffing objective within the time limit established, at the least cost or at a tolerable cost, and with the fewest negative side effects. A wide variety of metrics are available to assess potential activities. First, a common set of assessment criteria (e.g., time for completion, cost, and probability of success) should be identified and agreed on. Second, each alternative should be assessed according to each of these criteria. In this way, all alternatives will receive equal treatment, and tendencies to jump at an initial alternative will be minimized.

All of these alternatives must be considered within the broader context of how the organization creates and structures its workforce. This involves the key strategic issue of core versus flexible workforce usage. The choice should be considered in light of the organization's staffing philosophy, in particular, the difference between an internal or external emphasis. Many of the staffing activity alternatives are more applicable to one type of workforce than another.

## Core Workforce

A core workforce, defined as regular full-time and part-time employees of the organization, forms the bulk of most organizations' workforces. The key advantages of a core workforce are stability, continuity, and predictability. The organization can depend on its core workforce and build strategic plans based on it. Several other advantages accrue to the organization from using a core workforce. The regularity of the employment relationship fosters a sense of commitment and shared purpose toward the organization's mission. In addition, the organization maintains the legal right to control employees working in its behalf, in terms of both work process and expected results, rather than having to divide or share that right with organizations providing a flexible workforce, such as temporary employment agencies. Finally, the organization can directly control how it acquires its workforce and the qualifications of those it employs through the management of its own staffing systems. By doing so, the organization may build not only a highly qualified workforce but also one more likely to be retained, thus lessening pressure to continually restaff.

Several disadvantages of a core workforce exist. The implied permanence of the employment relationship "locks in" the organization's workforce, with a potential loss of staffing flexibility to rapidly increase, reduce, or redeploy its workforce in response to changing market conditions and project life cycles. Reducing the core workforce, in particular, can be very costly in terms of severance pay packages, low morale, and damage to the organization's reputation as a good employer. Additionally, the labor costs of the core workforce may be greater than that of the flexible workforce due to (1) higher wages, salaries, and benefits for the core workforce, and (2) the fixed nature of these labor costs, relative to the more variable costs associated with a flexible workforce. By using a core workforce, the organization incurs numerous legal obligations—particularly taxation and employment law compliance—that could be fully or partially avoided through the use of flexible workforce providers, which would be the actual employer. Finally, use of a core workforce may deprive the organization of new technical and administrative knowledge that could be infused into it by use of flexible workers such as programmers and consultants.

Consideration of these numerous advantages and disadvantages needs to occur separately for various jobs and organizational units covered by the HR plan. In this way, usage of a core workforce proceeds along selective, strategic lines. Referring back to the original example in Exhibit 3.6, staffing planners should do a unique core workforce analysis for the sales and customer service unit, and within that unit, for both sales and customer service jobs at the entry and managerial levels. The analysis may result in a decision to use only full-time core workers for the managerial jobs, both full-time and part-time core workers for sales jobs, and a combination of full-time core customer service representatives augmented by both full-time and part-time temporary customer service representatives during peak sales periods. Once the job and work unit locations of the core workers have been determined, specific staffing planning for effective acquisition must occur. This involves planning of recruitment, selection, and employment activities; these topics will be covered in subsequent chapters.

## Flexible Workforce

The two major components of the flexible workforce are temporary employees provided by a staffing firm and independent contractors. Planning for usage of the flexible workforce must occur in tandem with core workforce planning; hence, it should begin with a review of the advantages and disadvantages of a flexible workforce.[27] The key advantage is staffing flexibility. The flexible workforce may be used for adjusting staffing levels quickly in response to changing technological or consumer demand conditions and to ebbs and flows of orders for products and services. Other flexibility advantages are the ability to quickly staff new areas or projects and the ability to fill in for core workers absent due to illness, vacations, and holidays. Relative to the core workforce, the flexible workforce may also present labor cost advantages in the form of lower pay and benefits, more variable labor costs, and reduced training costs. It should be noted, however, that the temporary workforce provider shoulders many of these costs and simply passes them on to the organization through the fees it charges for its services. Another advantage for the organization is possibly being relieved of many tax and employment law obligations, since flexible workers are often not considered employees of the organization. For temporary employees, however, the organization may be considered a co-employer subject to some legal obligations, especially pertaining to EEO. An emerging advantage is that the flexible workforce, especially in the professional and technical ranks, may be an important source of new knowledge about organizational best practices and new skills not present in the core workforce, especially "hot skills" in high market demand. In a related vein, organizations use temporary or interim top executives to fill in until a permanent hire is found and on board, to spur change, and to launch special projects requiring their expertise.[28] Finally, usage of a flexible workforce relieves the organization of the need to design and manage its own staffing systems, since this is done by the flexible workforce provider. An added advantage here is that the organization might use flexible workers on a tryout basis, much like a probationary period, and then hire into its core workforce those who turn out to be a solid person/job match. Many temporary workers are "temp-to-perm," meaning that the organization will hire them permanently if they perform successfully in the temporary role. Such an arrangement is usually negotiated up front with the staffing services company.

These numerous advantages must be weighed against several potential disadvantages. Most important is the legal loss of control over flexible workers because they are not employees of the organization. Thus, although the organization has great flexibility in initial job assignments for flexible workers, it is very limited in the amount of supervision and performance management it can conduct for them. Exacerbating the situation, frictions between core and flexible workers may also arise. Core workers, for example, may feel that flexible workers lack knowledge and experience, are just "putting in time," receive the easy job assignments, and do not act like committed team players. Also, flexible workers may lack familiarity with equipment, policies, procedures, and important customers; such deficiencies may be compounded by a lack of training in specific job requirements. Finally, it should be remembered that the quality of the flexible workforce depends heavily on the quality of the staffing and training systems used by the provider of the flexible workers. The organization may end up with flexible but poorly qualified workers.

If the review of advantages and disadvantages of flexible workers confirms the strategic choice to use them in staffing, plans must be developed for the organization units and jobs in which they will be used, and for how they will be acquired. Acquisition plans normally involve the use of staffing firms and independent contractors, both of which perform the traditional staffing activities for the organization. Hence, in contrast to the substantial and sustained staffing planning that must occur for the core workforce, planning for the flexible workforce is primarily a matter of becoming knowledgeable about potential sources and lining them up in advance of when they will be needed.

### Staffing Firms

Recall that staffing firms (also called temporary help agencies) are the legal employers of the workers being supplied, though matters of co-employment may arise. Hence, the staffing firm conducts recruitment, selection, training, compensation, performance appraisal, and retention activities for the flexible workers. The firm is also responsible for on-site supervision and management, as well as all payrolling and the payment of legally required insurance premiums. For such services, the firm charges the organization a general fee for its labor costs (wages and benefits) plus a markup percentage of labor costs (usually 40%–50%) to cover these services' costs plus provide a profit. There may be additional charges for specially provided services, such as extra testing or background checks, or skill training. Temp-to-perm workers may be hired away from the firm (with its permission and for a special fee) by the organization to become regular employees in the core workforce. For larger clients the firm may provide an on-site manager to help the organization plan its specific staffing needs, supervise and appraise the performance of the temporary workers, handle discipline and complaints, and facilitate firm–organization relations. With such additional staffing services, the firm functions increasingly like a staffing partner rather than just a staffing supplier.

Use of a staffing firm requires advanced planning, rather than a panicky phone call to a firm at the moment of staffing need. In addition to becoming aware of firms that might be accessed, it is wise to become familiar with their characteristics and services. Shown in Exhibit 3.15 are the various factors and issues to become knowledgeable about for any firm.

When the organization chooses a firm, both parties should enter into a formal written agreement. The agreement should cover such matters as specific services to be provided, costs, steps to ensure that the flexible workers are employees of the firm (such as having an on-site manager for them), and the process for terminating the firm–organization relationship. It is best to have legal counsel prepare and review the agreement.

The organization may decide to establish its own in-house staffing firm. When this is done, the employees of the firm may even be employees of the organization. Managers thus have readily available flexible workers to whom they can turn, without having to go through all the planning steps mentioned above.

### Independent Contractors

An independent contractor (IC) provides specific task and project assistance to the organization, such as maintenance, bookkeeping, advertising, programming, and consulting. The IC can be a single individual (self-employed, freelancer) or an

---

**EXHIBIT 3.15**    **Factors to Consider When Choosing a Staffing Firm**

| Factor | Issues |
|---|---|
| Agency and Its Reputation | How long in business; location; references from clients available. |
| Types of Workers Provided | What occupation and KSAO levels; how many available. |
| Planning and Lead Time | Does agency help client plan staffing levels and needs; how quickly can workers be provided. |
| Services Provided | |
|     Recruitment | What methods are used; how targeted and truthful is recruitment process. |
|     Selection | What selection techniques are used to assess KSAOs. |
|     Training | What types of training, if any, are provided before workers are placed with client. |
|     Wages and Benefits | How are wages determined; what benefits are provided. |
|     Orientation | How does the agency prepare workers for assignment with client; does agency have an employee handbook for its workers. |
|     Supervision | How does agency supervise its workers on site of client; does agency provide on-site manager. |
|     Temp-to-Perm | Does agency allow client to hire its temporary workers as permanent employees. |
|     Client Satisfaction | How does agency attempt to gauge client satisfaction with services, workers, costs. |
| Worker Effectiveness | |
|     Punctuality and Attendance | Does the agency monitor these; what is its record with previous clients. |
|     Job Performance | Is it evaluated; how are the results used. |
|     Retention | How long do workers remain on an assignment voluntarily; how are workers discharged by the agency. |
| Cost | |
|     Markup | What is the percentage over base wage charged to client (often it is 50% to cover benefits, overhead, profit margin). |
|     For Special Services | What services cost extra beyond the markup (e.g., temp-to-perm); what are those costs. |

employer with its own employees. Neither the IC nor its employees are intended to be employees of the organization utilizing the IC's services, and care should be taken to ensure that the IC is not treated as an employee (see Chapter 2).[29]

As with staffing firms, the organization must take the initiative to identify and check out ICs for possible use in advance of when they are actually needed. It is desirable to solicit and examine references from past or current clients of the IC. In addition, as much as possible the organization should seek to determine how the IC staffs, trains, and compensates its employees. This could occur during a preliminary meeting with the IC. In these ways, the organization will have cultivated and screened ICs prior to when they are actually needed.

## Outsourcing

Outsourcing of work functions can be defined as the transfer of a business process to an external organization. This is a more drastic step than simply using ICs or temporary employees. The primary difference is that when processes are outsourced, the organization expects to receive a completely finished product from the external source. This means the organization does not direct or control the way in which work is performed; rather, it only receives the end result of the work. Within the HR department, it has become the norm for organizations to completely outsource payroll tasks, meaning that data from the organization are sent to a third-party vendor that assesses taxes and withholdings and takes care of either directly depositing or sending out paychecks for employees.[30]

Organizations outsource for a variety of reasons. An obvious reason for outsourcing of manufacturing and routine information-processing tasks is the availability of less expensive labor in the global market. Often, specialized vendors can achieve economies of scale for routine tasks that are performed across a variety of organizations. Organizations also outsource functions that have highly cyclical demand so that they do not have to make major capital outlays and go through the cost of hiring and training permanent workers to perform tasks that may not be needed in the future. Sometimes organizations outsource functions that require specific expertise that cannot be economically generated in-house. Smaller organizations that require legal services, for example, often choose to hire an external law firm rather than establish their own pool of legal specialists. As we have noted, many organizations also outsource routine business functions, such as having third-party vendors take care of payroll or benefits administration tasks.

One variant of outsourcing is termed "offshoring," which means that products or services are provided by an external source outside of the country where the organization's core operations take place.[31] The outsourcing of manufacturing to lower-wage countries has a long history, and this practice is likely to continue unabated. For example, in the computer industry it is common for large companies to have many subcomponent electronic parts manufactured by third-party vendors overseas, with final assembly of products performed domestically. Many companies have outsourced routine computer programming and telephone help services to third-party providers in India because of the availability of a highly skilled labor force that typically draws only a fraction of the wages paid in North America. Offshoring is no longer limited to blue- and pink-collar jobs. There has been a dramatic increase in offshoring white-collar technical and professional work in the twenty-first century, fueled by improvements in global education, an increasingly positive climate for business in China and India, and increased demand for products and services in multinational organizations.

The decision to outsource is likely to be controversial.[32] Outsourcing is usually done for activities that have low added value for the organization. Normal transactional or procedural work that is easily replicated is likely to be outsourced. High-value-added operations that are core to the organization's business strategy almost certainly should not be outsourced. Although most managers are aware that it is unwise to outsource work that is fundamental to a business's core operations, there are still many cases where organizations discover, too late, that they outsourced work that should have been done internally. Additionally, offshoring has been the focus of media and political scrutiny. Extremely low wages and dangerous working conditions provided by external partners in foreign countries have created a backlash against certain companies that have offshored manufacturing jobs. Negative press about poor working conditions in overseas "sweatshops" has been especially prominent in the clothing industry. When outsourcing, an organization needs to make certain that it is not losing too much control over its major work processes. Just because a business process has been outsourced does not mean that the organization has lost the responsibility (and this sometimes includes legal liability) for the actions of external partners.

## DIVERSITY PLANNING

Diversity programs arise out of a recognition that the labor force is becoming more demographically and culturally diverse. Diversity planning in staffing requires developing a strategy to recruit and select a diverse group of employees. Another major focus of diversity programs is the assimilation and adaptation of a diverse workforce.

To foster workforce diversity and to help strengthen the diversity–organizational effectiveness link, organizations have designed and implemented a wide variety of diversity initiatives and programs. Many of these initiatives involve staffing, as a diverse workforce must be actively identified, acquired, deployed, and retained. Most organizations supplement the staffing component of their diversity initiatives with many other programs, including diversity training for managers and employees to heighten awareness and acceptance of diversity, mentoring relationships, work/life balance actions such as flexible work schedules, team building, and special career and credential-building job assignments.

### Demography of the American Workforce

In part, organizations need to take diversity into account because the workforce has become more diverse. There has been a massive shift in the makeup of the American workforce over the past 30 years.[33] Once excluded from large portions of the workforce, women now make up half of the labor force, along with making up a majority of university graduates. There has also been a dramatic increase in the ethnic and racial diversity of the workforce. Immigration into the United States has brought large numbers of Latinos and Asians, and the progress of civil rights legislation has removed previous barriers to employment faced by African Americans. Legislation and technology have combined to make accommodations that allow the entry of individuals with disabilities into the workforce more feasible. The age diversity of the workforce has increased over time, as greater numbers of individuals continue working into their sixties and seventies. There has also been an increased presence of openly lesbian, gay, bisexual, and transgender (LGBT) employees in the workforce, which has been accompanied by numerous state and local statutes making sexual orientation and/or gender identity a protected class.[34]

These shifts in the makeup of the workforce have permanently altered the requirements for successful HR management. Surveys conducted by the Society for Human Resource Management suggest that managers are especially concerned about the loss of skills due to the retirement of baby boomers, increases in medical expenses that arise as the workforce ages, and employee elder-care responsibilities.[35] A host of other issues have been identified as arising from demographic changes, including providing work-life benefits for dual-career couples and developing multilingual training materials for workers who primarily speak a language other than English.

## Business Case for Diversity

There is a strong impetus for effectively managing a diverse workforce. In fact, many argue that above and beyond the ethical need to treat all employees fairly and with respect, there is a financial imperative to manage diversity effectively.[36] As we noted in the introductory chapter, there are two ways organizations can address issues related to diversity. In passive diversity planning, the organization reviews all policies and practices to ensure there is no discrimination on the basis of race, religion, national origin, gender, disability status, age, or other protected classes covered locally. In active diversity planning, the organization goes a step further by encouraging underrepresented groups to apply for positions, actively recruiting from a variety of sources that are likely to be seen by underrepresented groups, and providing additional training and mentoring to encourage the advancement of underrepresented groups.

There are certain advantages to an active diversity management strategy. Exhibit 3.16 illustrates ways in which an effective diversity management strategy can enhance organizational effectiveness in several domains. It should be noted that these are not speculative staffing outcomes—all are supported by prior research findings. In some areas, like legal compliance, the goal is to minimize negative consequences. However, the foundation of diversity management should be based on the potential advantages of effective diversity management. It is more productive for an organization to emphasize diversity management as an opportunity for gain, rather than as a way of protecting against a threat. Emphasizing

**EXHIBIT 3.16    Making the Business Case for Diversity**

| Area of Concern | Effective Diversity Management |
|---|---|
| Legal and policy compliance | • Avoids lawsuits<br>• Minimizes operational disturbances<br>• Prevents negative press due to government investigations |
| Staffing levels | • Broadens base of candidates from which to select<br>• Increases diversity of employee KSAOs<br>• Improves potential to respond to environmental change<br>• Improves retention of employees |
| Employee attitudes and behavior | • Enhances engagement<br>• Creates perceptions of justice<br>• Fosters cooperation and collaboration among employees |
| Product/service market | • Increases insight into diverse customer groups' preferences<br>• Heightens sensitivity in interacting with the public<br>• Improves relationships with communities and regulatory agencies |

the positive impact that all workers will see when diversity is managed effectively will also enhance managerial motivation to implement diversity-oriented policies.[37]

At the same time, there are costs associated with these active diversity efforts that must be considered, as additional recruiting, selection, and training programs do not come for free. Empirical evidence suggests that despite the conceptual advantages of having more diverse points of view in work groups, demographically diverse teams are not more effective than more homogenous teams. Active diversity efforts that are specifically directed to some groups of employees and not others may unintentionally send a message to members of the demographic majority that they are less welcome in the organization. Therefore, an organization needs to carefully consider how to engage in active diversity planning and select the right mix of passive and active strategies to maximize organizational effectiveness.

## Planning for Diversity

Whether an organization adopts an active or passive diversity strategy, there are several ways that workforce diversity should be taken into account in the staffing planning process. First and foremost, top management must state that diversity goals are important and will be measured.[38] Clear communications regarding diversity strategies should be made, and updated frequently, to remind employees of the importance of nondiscrimination for the organization's mission.

Many recruiting activities can help enhance the diversity of the workforce. One such activity is to advertise positions in media sources that target a variety of demographic groups.[39] Organizations that wish to increase the diversity of their workforce may also consider recruiting at colleges, universities, and other institutions that have large numbers of underrepresented minorities. These efforts can have a major impact on employee attitudes. Studies show that women and minorities prefer to work at companies that show a commitment to diversity in their recruiting efforts. Internally, organizational promotion efforts should target qualified members of underrepresented groups, possibly supplemented with mentoring programs to overcome gaps in skills.[40]

There are also techniques that can incorporate diversity into the selection process. Requirements that might lead to lower representation of traditionally underrepresented groups should be considered carefully, and eliminated when they are not absolutely necessary for job performance. Additionally, efforts to incorporate objective standards for judging candidate qualifications and policies that encourage nondiscrimination have been shown to diminish the extent of discrimination in the hiring process.[41]

Unfortunately, evidence suggests that many organizations do not take demographic shifts in the workplace into account when developing staffing plans. Programs to help dual-career couples manage work and child-care arrangements are implemented in a rather scattered fashion, with some organizations doing little to recognize the needs of such families. Other organizations have failed to adequately address the needs of employees with disabilities, even though disability rights advocates note that most accommodations are relatively inexpensive and do not affect core job tasks. Often, the needs of older workers are also overlooked. A survey of over 700 organizations found that 77% of companies had not analyzed projected retirement rates of their workforce or had done so to only a limited extent.[42] Similarly, data show that about a third of employers report that they do not have enough programs for the recruitment and training of older workers.[43]

Research shows that diversity-oriented practices, including targeted recruitment, inclusion of women and African Americans on the top management team, work/family accommodations, the creation of AAPs, and diversity councils, can increase the racial and gender diversity of the organization's entire managerial workforce.[44] The effects of such practices on the composition of the nonmanagerial workforce are not well known, nor have the effects of these practices on organizational performance been documented. Similar programs with a strong behavioral component designed to improve the representation of individuals with disabilities and older workers should also be considered. It is interesting to note that while concrete programs like those mentioned above have been highlighted as improving workforce diversity, attitude-based diversity training interventions have not shown as much effectiveness.

### The Aging Workforce

A recent staffing challenge facing organizations (and individuals seeking employment) is that of the aging workforce. It is estimated that the number of individuals who are 75 years old or older and still employed has increased by a whopping 76.7% over the past 20 years. Although many older individuals continued to work after the Great Recession out of financial necessity (many saw their retirement portfolios shrink to substandard levels), their continued push for employment, even as the economy has rebounded, is also due to other factors. Not only are people living longer, but many jobs are not as physically demanding as they were in previous generations, allowing individuals to work well past the traditional retirement age.

Although the supply of older workers has sharply increased, demand has not, leading to higher unemployment. In 2007, 3.1% of US workers aged 65 or older were unemployed; in 2012, that number grew to 6.2%. From the perspective of the older worker, the statistics can be discouraging. From the perspective of the organization, the abundant supply means that it can have the "pick of the litter." Older workers bring with them a multitude of experience and tacit, difficult to articulate knowledge from their previous professions. However, older workers are also frequently accompanied by myths and stereotypes that may influence employers' perceptions of their competence and potential for success. Such myths include perceptions that older workers are poorer performers, unmotivated, unhealthy, and resistant to change and skill acquisition. A recent meta-analysis of these stereotypes found that most are exaggerations. A general unwillingness to train on the part of older workers was the sole exception, as this stereotype was supported by the available data. Thus, the increasing number of older individuals seeking employment presents both opportunities and challenges for selection systems.[45]

## LEGAL ISSUES

The major legal issues in HR and staffing planning are AAPs and diversity programs. AAPs originate from many sources—voluntary employer efforts, court-imposed remedies for discriminatory practices, conciliation or consent agreement, and requirements as a federal contractor. Regardless of the source, all AAPs seek to rectify the effects of past employment discrimination by increasing the representation of certain groups (minorities, women, and individuals with disabilities) in the organization's workforce. This is achieved through establishing and actively pursuing hiring and promotion goals for these groups. As described above, diversity programs are undertaken for competitive reasons, rather than as a legal response to discrimination. However, diversity programs may share components with AAPs.

This section describes the general content of AAPs, discusses the affirmative action requirements for federal contractors under AAP regulations, and provides some general indications as to the legality of AAPs and diversity programs.

## Affirmative Action Plans

AAPs are organization-specific plans that, as noted above, have a legal origin and basis. They precede diversity programs, which organizations typically undertake for strategic business reasons rather than legal ones. Often, however, the structure and content of AAPs and diversity programs are very similar. While AAPs are organization specific, they all share a common architecture composed of three major components—availability analysis of women and minorities, placement (hiring and promotion) goals derived from comparing availability with incumbency (percentages of women and minority employees), and action-oriented programs for meeting the placement goals. These components, and accompanying details, are spelled out in the federal regulations put forth and enforced by the Office of Federal Contract Compliance Programs (OFCCP). The Federal Contractor Compliance Manual may also be consulted.

### Affirmative Action Programs Regulations

All but very small federal contractors must develop and implement AAPs according to the OFCCP's affirmative action regulations. Below are a summary of those regulations and a sample of an AAP for small employers from the OFCCP website. The contractor must develop a separate AAP for each of its establishments with more than 50 employees. With advance approval from the OFCCP, the contractor may sidestep separate establishment plans by developing a functional plan that covers employees in discrete functional or business units, even though in different locations. All employees must be included in either AAP. The description that follows is for an establishment plan. It uses race, ethnicity, and job category designations on the EEO-1 form (see Chapter 13). OFCCP race, ethnicity, and job category designations are somewhat different. Usage of either EEOC or OFCCP designations is acceptable.

***Organization Display.*** An organization display depicts the staffing pattern within an establishment. It provides a profile of the workforce at the establishment, and it assists in identifying units in which women or minorities are underrepresented. Key elements are a showing of organizational structure of lines of progression (promotion) among jobs or organization units, the total number of job incumbents, the total number of male and female incumbents, and the total number of male and female incumbents in each of the following groups: Hispanic and Latino, white, black or African American, Native Hawaiian or other Pacific Islander, Asian, American Indian or Alaskan Native, and two or more races.

*Job Group Analysis.* Jobs with similar content, wage rates, and opportunities (e.g., promotion, training) must be combined into job groups, and each group must include a list of job titles. Small establishments (fewer than 150 employees) may use the categories on the EEO-1 form: executives/senior level officials and managers, first/mid-level officials and managers, professionals, technicians, sales workers, administrative support workers, craft workers, operatives, laborers and helpers, and service workers. The percentage of minorities and the percentage of women (determined in the previous step) employed in each job group must be indicated.

*Availability Determination.* The availability of women and minorities must be determined separately for each job group. At a minimum, the following two factors should be considered when determining availability:

1. The percentage of minorities or women with requisite skills in the reasonable recruitment area
2. The percentage of minorities or women among those promotable, transferable, and trainable within the organization

Current census data, job service data, or other data should be consulted to determine availability. When there are multiple job titles in a job group, with different availability rates, a composite availability figure for the group must be calculated. This requires summing weighted availability estimates for the job titles.

Exhibit 3.17 shows an example of availability determination for a single job group based on the EEO-1 form. Listed on the left are the two availability factors that must be considered. Shown next are the raw statistic availability estimates for females and minorities (summed across the four minority groups) for both of the availability factors (refer to the "Source of Statistics" column to see the sources of data for these estimates). Next, the value weights represent an estimate of the percentages of the total females and minorities available according to each availability factor (50% for each group). The weighted statistics represent the raw statistics multiplied by the value weight (e.g., 41.8% × .50 = 20.9%). A summing of the weighted statistics yields the total availability estimate percentages (47.6% for female, 18.1% for minority).

*Comparison of Incumbency With Availability.* For each job group, the percentages of women and minority incumbents must be compared with their availability. When the percentage employed is less than would reasonably be expected by the availability percentage, a placement goal must be established.

Exhibit 3.18 compares incumbency with availability for eight job groups, including job group 1. The comparisons are shown separately for females and minorities. Where incumbency is less than availability, it may be decided to establish a placement goal. In job group 1, it was concluded that the differences between availability

**EXHIBIT 3.17  Determining Availability of Minorities and Women**

| Job Group: 1 | Raw Statistics | | Value Weight | Weighted Statistics | | Source of Statistics | Reason for Weighting |
| --- | --- | --- | --- | --- | --- | --- | --- |
| | Female | Minority | | Female | Minority | | |
| 1. Percentage of minorities or women with requisite skills in the reasonable recruitment area | 41.8% | 9.4% | 50.0% | 20.9% | 4.7% | 2000 Census Data<br><br>The reasonable recruitment area for this job group is the St. Louis, MO–IL metropolitan statistical area (MSA). | 50% of placement into this job group is made from external hires. |
| 2. Percentage of minorities or women among those promotable, transferable, and trainable within the contractor's organization | 53.3% | 26.7% | 50.0% | 26.7% | 13.4% | The group of promotable employees in job group 2 | 50% of placement into this job group is made from internal promotions. |
| Totals: | | | 100% | **47.6%** | **18.1%** | <Final Factor | |

SOURCE: Sample Affirmative Action Program for Small Employers, 2004, *www.dol.gov/ofccp.*

**EXHIBIT 3.18**   **Determining Affirmative Action Goals: Comparing Incumbency With Availability and Annual Placement Goals**

| Job Group | Female Incumbency | Female Availability | Establish Goal? Yes/No | If Yes, Goal for Females | Minority Incumbency | Minority Availability | Establish Goal? Yes/No | If Yes, Goal for Minorities |
|---|---|---|---|---|---|---|---|---|
| 1 | 0.0% | 47.6% | Yes | 47.6% | 11.1% | 18.1% | Yes | 18.1% |
| 2 | 45.5% | 43.8% | No | | 18.2% | 8.2% | No | |
| 4 | 20.0% | 34.5% | Yes | 34.5% | 0.0% | 12.4% | Yes | 12.4% |
| 5 | 83.3% | 87.7% | No | | 43.3% | 27.6% | No | |
| 6 | 9.3% | 5.5% | No | | 34.9% | 23.2% | No | |
| 7 | 10.0% | 6.3% | No | | 30.0% | 37.5% | No | |
| 8 | 6.3% | 19.1% | Yes | 19.1% | 37.5% | 26.3% | No | |

NOTE: The 80% rule of thumb is followed in declaring underutilization and establishing goals when the actual employment of minorities or females is less than 80% of their availability. If the female/minority incumbency percentage (%) is less than the female/minority availability percentage (%) and the ratio of incumbency to availability is less than 80%, a placement goal should be included in the appropriate "If Yes" column.

SOURCE: Sample Affirmative Action Program for Small Employers, 2004, www.dol.gov/ofccp.

and incumbency percentages for both females and minorities were sufficient to warrant placement goals (47.6% for females and 18.1% for minorities). Note that an incumbency percentage less than an availability percentage does not automatically trigger a placement goal (e.g., females in job group 5).

How does the organization decide whether to set a placement goal for females or minorities in a job group? The OFCCP permits some latitude. One possibility is to set a placement goal whenever incumbency is less than availability, on the theory that any differences between availability and incumbency represent underutilization of females and minorities. A second possibility is based on the theory that some differences in percentages are due to chance, so some amount of tolerance of differences is permissible. The suggested rule is 80% tolerance. This means that if the ratio of incumbency percentage to availability percentage is greater than 80%, no placement goal is needed. If the ratio is less than 80%, a placement goal must be set. The 80% rule was followed in Exhibit 3.18. Though the incumbency percentage for females was less than the availability percentage in both job groups 1 and 5, the difference was less than 80% in only job group 1, triggering a placement goal just for that group.

**Placement Goals.** If an annual placement goal is set, it should at least equal the availability percentage for women or minorities in a job group. Placement goals may not be rigid or inflexible quotas; quotas are expressly forbidden. Placement goals do not require hiring a person who lacks the qualifications to perform the job successfully, or hiring a less qualified person in preference to a more qualified one.

**Designation of Responsibility.** An official of the organization must be designated as responsible for the implementation of the AAP.

**Identification of Problem Areas.** The organization must evaluate the following:

1. Problems of minority or female utilization or distribution in each job group
2. Personnel activity (applicant flow, hires, terminations, and promotions) and other personnel actions for possible selection disparities
3. Compensation systems for possible gender-, race-, or ethnicity-based disparities
4. Selection, recruitment, referral, and other procedures to see whether they result in disparities in employment or advancement of minorities or women

**Action-Oriented Programs.** The organization must develop and execute action-oriented programs to correct any identified problem areas and attain placement goals. Specific examples of these programs are shown in Exhibit 3.19.

**Internal Audit and Reporting.** An auditing system must be developed that periodically measures the effectiveness of the total AAP.

---

**EXHIBIT 3.19** **Examples of Action-Oriented Programs for an AAP**

1. Conducting annual analyses of job descriptions to ensure they accurately reflect job functions;
2. Reviewing job descriptions by department and job title using performance criteria;
3. Making job descriptions available to recruiting sources and to all members of management involved in the recruiting, screening, selection, and promotion processes;
4. Evaluating the total selection process to ensure freedom from bias through:
   a. Reviewing job applications and other preemployment forms to ensure information requested is job related;
   b. Evaluating selection methods that may have a disparate impact to ensure that they are job related and consistent with business necessity; and
   c. Training in EEO for management and supervisory staff.
5. Using techniques to improve recruitment and increase the flow of minority and female applicants:
   a. Include the phrase "Equal Opportunity/Affirmative Action Employer" in all printed employment advertisements;
   b. Place help-wanted advertisements, when appropriate, in local minority news media and women's interest media;
   c. Disseminate information on job opportunities to organizations representing minorities, women, and employment development agencies when job opportunities occur;
   d. Encourage all employees to refer qualified applicants;
   e. Actively recruit at secondary schools, junior colleges, and colleges and universities with predominantly minority or female enrollment; and
   f. Request employment agencies to refer qualified minorities and women.
6. Hiring a statistical consultant to perform a self-audit of compensation practices; and
7. Ensuring that all employees are given equal opportunity for promotion:
   a. Post promotional opportunities;
   b. Offer counseling to assist employees in identifying promotional opportunities, and offer training and educational programs to increase promotions and opportunities for job rotation or transfer; and
   c. Evaluate job requirements for promotion.

SOURCE: Adapted from Sample Affirmative Action Program for Small Employers, 2010, *www.dol.gov/ofccp*.

## Legality of AAPs and Diversity Programs

AAPs have been controversial since their inception, and there have been many challenges to their legality. Questions of legality involve complex issues of constitutionality, statutory interpretations, differences in the structure of the AAPs being challenged in the courts, claims that affirmative action goals represent hiring quotas, and, very importantly, differences in the amount of weight placed on race or gender in the ultimate selection decisions made about job applicants.

Despite these problems, it is possible to provide several conclusions and recommendations regarding affirmative action. AAPs in general are legal in the eyes of the Supreme Court. However, to be acceptable, an AAP should be based on the following guidelines:[46]

1. The plan should have as its purpose the remedying of specific and identifiable effects of past discrimination.
2. The plan should address the current underutilization of women and/or minorities in the organization.
3. Regarding nonminority and male employees, the plan should not unsettle their legitimate expectations, should not result in their discharge and replacement with minority or women employees, and should not create an absolute bar to their promotion.
4. The plan should be temporary and should be eliminated once affirmative action goals have been achieved.[47]
5. All candidates for positions should be qualified for those positions.
6. The plan should include organizational enforcement mechanisms as well as a grievance procedure.

Court rulings on the constitutionality of federal and state government AAPs suggest that even more strict guidelines than these may be necessary. Insofar as these programs are concerned, racial preferences are subject to strict constitutional scrutiny. They may be used only when there is specific evidence of identified discrimination, when the remedy has been narrowly tailored to only the identified discrimination, when only those who have suffered discrimination may benefit from the remedy, and when other individuals will not carry an undue burden, such as job displacement, from the remedy. Lesser scrutiny standards may apply for gender preferences.[48] Some states have even banned the use of AAPs by government employers, contractors, and educational institutions.[49]

Turning to diversity programs, the EEOC states the following about how they differ from AAPs, as well as their permissibility:

> Diversity and affirmative action are related concepts, but the terms have different origins and legal connotations. Workforce diversity is a business

management concept under which employers voluntarily promote an inclusive workplace. Employers that value diversity create a culture of respect for individual differences in order to "draw talent and ideas from all segments of the population" and thereby potentially gain a "competitive advantage in the increasingly global economy." Many employers have concluded that a diverse workforce makes a company stronger, more profitable, and a better place to work, and they implement diversity initiatives for competitive reasons rather than in response to discrimination, although such initiatives may also help to avoid discrimination.

Title VII permits diversity efforts designed to open up opportunities to everyone. For example, if an employer notices that African Americans are not applying for jobs in the numbers that would be expected given their availability in the labor force, the employer could adopt strategies to expand the applicant pool of qualified African Americans such as recruiting at schools with high African American enrollment. Similarly, an employer that is changing its hiring practices can take steps to ensure that the practice it selects minimizes the disparate impact on any racial group. For example, an employer that previously required new hires to have a college degree could change this requirement to allow applicants to have a college degree or two years of relevant experience in the field. A need for diversity efforts may be prompted by a change in the population's racial demographics, which could reveal an underrepresentation of certain racial groups in the work force in comparison to the current labor pool.[50]

## AAPs for Veterans and Individuals With Disabilities

There are specific AAP regulations for federal contractors under the Vietnam Era Veterans' Readjustment Assistance Act and the Rehabilitation Act. The regulations were recently updated to strengthen them and improve the hiring of veterans and individuals with disabilities (IWDs).

For veterans, updates to the regulations include:

1. Requiring contractors to annually adopt a benchmark based on either the national percentage of veterans in the workforce (currently 8%) or the best available data
2. Collecting annual data on the number of veterans who apply and are hired in order to increase accountability for staffing practices and decisions
3. Making contractor job listings in formats that can be easily used by state employment service agencies
4. Creating flexibility in "linage agreements" with organizations that provide recruiting or training services to veterans
5. Repealing regulations in Part 60-250 of the Code of Federal Regulations

For IWDs, the new regulations include:

1. Establishing a 7% utilization goal at the job group level
2. Inviting applicants to self-identify as IWDs at both the pre-offer and post-offer phases of the staffing process; inviting employees to self-identify on a regular basis
3. Collecting annual data on the number of IWDs who apply and are hired in order to increase accountability for staffing practices and decisions
4. Revising the definition of "disability" to be consistent with the new amendments to the Americans With Disabilities Act (ADA)

## EEO and Temporary Workers

The EEOC has provided guidance on coverage and responsibility requirements for temporary employment agencies (and other types of staffing firms) and their client organizations.[51] When both the agency and the client exercise control over the temporary employee and both have the requisite number of employees, they are considered employers and jointly liable under the Civil Rights Act, the Age Discrimination in Employment Act (ADEA), the ADA, and the Equal Pay Act. It should be noted that these laws also apply to individuals placed with organizations through welfare-to-work programs. The agency is obligated to make referrals and job assignments in a nondiscriminatory manner, and the client may not set discriminatory job referral and job assignment criteria. The client must treat the temporary employees in a nondiscriminatory manner; if the agency knows this is not happening, the agency must take any corrective actions within its control. The agency, the client, or both parties could face substantial penalties for noncompliance (e.g., back pay, front pay, and compensatory damages). There is special guidance for ADA-related issues.

## SUMMARY

Internal and external forces shape the conduct and outcomes of HRP. The key forces and trends that emerge are organizational strategy, organizational culture, labor markets, and technology.

HRP is a process and set of activities undertaken to forecast future HR requirements and availabilities, resulting in the identification of likely employment gaps (shortages and surpluses). Action plans are then developed for addressing the gaps. Before HRP begins, initial decisions must be made about its comprehensiveness, planning time frame, job categories and levels to be included, how to "count heads," and the roles and responsibilities of line and staff (including HR) managers.

A variety of statistical and judgmental techniques may be used in forecasting. Those used in forecasting requirements are typically used in conjunction with business and organization planning. For forecasting availabilities, techniques must be used that take into account the movements of people into, within, and out of the organization, on a job-by-job basis. Here, manager judgment, Markov Analysis, and replacement and succession planning are suggested as particularly useful techniques.

Staffing planning is a form of action planning. It is shown to generally require setting staffing objectives, generating alternative staffing activities, and assessing and choosing from among those alternatives. A fundamental alternative involves the use of core or flexible workforces, as identified in staffing strategy. Plans must be developed for acquiring both types of workforces, and the advantages and disadvantages of each type should be reviewed to reaffirm strategic choices about the use of each. After this step, planning can begin. For the core workforce, this involves matters of staffing philosophy that will guide the planning of recruitment, selection, and employment activities. For the flexible workforce, the organization should establish early contact with the providers of the flexible workers (i.e., staffing firms and independent contractors). Organizational leaders should also consider the advantages and disadvantages of outsourcing some jobs at this point.

Changes in the demographic makeup of the workforce suggest that organizations need to take employee diversity into account in the planning process. Activities to address a diverse workforce include recruiting, selection, training, development, and retention.

AAPs are an extension and application of general HR and staffing planning. AAPs have several components. The Affirmative Action Programs Regulations, which apply to federal contractors, specify requirements for these components. The legality of AAPs has been clearly established, but the courts have fashioned limits to their content and scope. To clarify how EEO laws apply to temporary employees and agencies, the EEOC has issued specific guidance.

## DISCUSSION QUESTIONS

1. What are ways that the organization can ensure that KSAO deficiencies do not occur in its workforce?
2. What types of experiences, especially staffing-related ones, will an organization be likely to have if it does not engage in HR and staffing planning?
3. Why are decisions about job categories and levels so critical to the conduct and results of HRP?
4. What are the advantages and disadvantages of doing succession planning for all levels of management instead of just top management?
5. What is meant by reconciliation, and how can it be useful as an input to staffing planning?

6. What criteria would you suggest using for assessing the staffing alternatives shown in Exhibit 3.14?
7. What problems might an organization encounter in creating an AAP that it might not encounter in regular staffing planning?

## ETHICAL ISSUES

1. Does an organization have an ethical responsibility to share with all of its employees the results of its forecasting of HR requirements and availabilities? Does it have an ethical responsibility not to do this?
2. Identify examples of ethical dilemmas an organization might confront when developing an AAP.

## APPLICATIONS

### Markov Analysis and Forecasting

The Doortodoor Sports Equipment Company sells sports clothing and equipment for amateur, light sport (running, tennis, walking, swimming, badminton, and golf) enthusiasts. It is the only company in the nation that does this door-to-door, seeking to bypass the retail sporting goods store and sell directly to the customer. Its salespeople have sales kits that include both sample products and a full-line catalog they can use to show the products and discuss them with customers. The sales function is composed of full-time and part-time salespeople (level 1), assistant sales managers (level 2), and regional sales managers (level 3).

The company has decided to study the internal movement patterns of people in the sales function, as well as forecast their likely availabilities in future time periods. The results will be used to help identify staffing gaps (surpluses and shortages) and to develop staffing strategy and plans for future growth.

To do this, the HR department first collected data for 2013 and 2014 to construct a transition probability matrix, as well as the number of employees for 2015 in each job category. It then wanted to use the matrix to forecast availabilities for 2016. The following data were gathered:

| Job Category | Level | Transition Probabilities (2013–14) | | | | | Current (2015) No. Employees |
|---|---|---|---|---|---|---|---|
| | | SF | SP | ASM | RSM | Exit | |
| Sales, Full-time (SF) | 1 | .50 | .10 | .05 | .00 | .35 | 500 |
| Sales, Part-time (SP) | 1 | .05 | .60 | .10 | .00 | .25 | 150 |
| Ass't. Sales Mgr. (ASM) | 2 | .05 | .00 | .80 | .10 | .05 | 50 |
| Region. Sales Mgr. (RSM) | 3 | .00 | .00 | .00 | .70 | .30 | 30 |

Use these data to answer the following questions:

1. Describe the internal labor market of the company in terms of job stability (staying in same job), promotion paths and rates, transfer paths and rates, demotion paths and rates, and turnover (exit) rates.
2. Forecast the numbers available in each job category in 2016.
3. Indicate potential limitations to your forecasts.

## Deciding Whether to Use Flexible Staffing

The Kaiser Manufacturing Company (KMC) has been in existence for over 50 years. Its main products are specialty implements for use in both the crop and the dairy herd sides of the agricultural business. Products include special attachments for tractors, combines, and discers and add-on devices for milking and feeding equipment that enhance the performance and safety of the equipment.

KMC has a small corporate office and four manufacturing plants (two in the Midwest and two in the South). It has a core workforce of 725 production workers, 30 clerical workers, 32 engineers and professional workers, and 41 managers. All employees are full time, and KMC has never used either part-time or temporary workers. Those in charge of staffing feel very strongly that the strategy of using only a core workforce has paid big dividends over the years in attracting and retaining a committed and highly productive workforce.

Sales have been virtually flat at $175 million annually since 2008. At the same time, KMC has begun to experience more erratic placement of orders for its products, making sales less predictable. This appears to be a reflection of more turbulent weather patterns, large swings in interest rates, new entrants into the specialty markets, and general uncertainty about the future direction and growth of the agricultural industry. Increased unpredictability in sales has been accompanied by steadily rising labor costs. This is due to KMC's increasingly older workforce, as well as shortages of all types of workers (particularly production workers) in the immediate labor markets surrounding the plants.

Assume you are the HR manager responsible for staffing and training at KMC. You have just been contacted by a representative of the Flexible Staffing Services (FSS) Company, Mr. Tom Jacoby. Mr. Jacoby has proposed meeting with you and the president of KMC, Mr. Herman Kaiser, to talk about FSS and how it might be of service to KMC. You and Mr. Kaiser agree to meet with Mr. Jacoby. At that meeting, Mr. Jacoby makes a formal presentation to you in which he describes the services, operation, and fees of FSS and highlights the advantages of using a more flexible workforce. During that meeting, you learn the following from Mr. Jacoby.

FSS is a recent entrant into what is called the staffing industry. Its general purpose is to furnish qualified employees to companies (customers) on an as-needed basis, thus helping the customer implement a flexible staffing strategy. It furnishes employees in four major groups: production, clerical, technical, and professional/managerial. Both full-time and part-time employees are available in each of these groups. Employees may be furnished to the customer on a strictly temporary basis ("temps") or on a "temp-to-perm" basis, in which the employees convert from being temporary employees of FSS to being permanent employees of the customer after a 90-day probationary period.

For both the temp and the temp-to-perm arrangements, FSS offers the following services. In each of the four employee groups it will recruit, select, and hire people to work for FSS, which will in turn lease them to the customer. FSS performs all recruitment, selection, and employment activities. It uses a standard selection system for all applicants, composed of an application blank, reference checks, drug testing, and a medical exam (given after making a job offer). It also offers customized selection plans in which the customer chooses from among a set of special skill tests, a personality test, an honesty test, and background investigations. Based on the standard and/or custom assessments, FSS refers to the customer what it views as the top candidates. FSS tries to furnish two people for every vacancy, and the customer chooses from between the two.

New hires at FSS receive a base wage that is similar to the market wage, as well as close to the wage of the customer's employees with whom they will be directly working. In addition, new hires receive a paid vacation (one week for every six months of employment, up to four weeks), health insurance (with a 25% employee co-pay), and optional participation in a 401(k) plan. FSS performs and pays for all payroll functions and deductions. It also pays the premiums for workers' compensation and unemployment compensation.

FSS charges the customer as follows. There is a standard fee per employee furnished of $1.55 \times$ base wage $\times$ hours worked per week. The 1.55 is labeled "markup"; it covers all of FSS's costs (staffing, insurance, benefits, and administration) plus a profit margin. On top of the standard fee is an additional fee for customized selection services. This fee ranges from $.50$ to $.90 \times$ base wage $\times$ hours worked per week. Finally, there is a special one-time fee for temp-to-perm employees (a finder's fee of one month's pay), payable after the employee successfully completes the 90-day probationary period and becomes an employee of the customer.

Mr. Jacoby concludes his presentation by stressing three advantages of flexible staffing as provided by FSS. First, use of FSS employees on an as-needed basis will give KMC greater flexibility in its staffing to match fluctuating product demand, as well as movement from completely fixed labor costs to more variable labor costs. Second, FSS provides considerable administrative convenience, relieving KMC of most of the burden of recruitment, selection, and payrolling. Finally, KMC will experience considerable freedom from litigation (workers' comp, EEO, torts) since FSS and not KMC will be the employer.

After Mr. Jacoby's presentation, Mr. Kaiser tells you he is favorably impressed, but that the organization clearly needs to do some more thinking before it embarks on the path of flexible staffing and the use of FSS as its provider. He asks you to prepare a brief preliminary report including the following:

1. A summary of the possible advantages and disadvantages of flexible staffing
2. A summary of the advantages and disadvantages of using FSS as a service provider
3. A summary of the type of additional information you recommend gathering and using as part of the decision-making process

## ENDNOTES

1. W. Bliss, "Engaging in Strategic Planning," *SHRM Templates and Toolkits*, Mar. 21, 2013 (*www.shrm.org*).
2. D. Ulrich, J. Younger, W. Brockbank, and M. Ulrich, *HR From the Outside In* (New York: McGraw-Hill, 2012); M. Fiester, "Practicing Strategic Human Resources," *SHRM Templates and Toolkits*, Mar. 21, 2013 (*www.shrm.org*); D. Ulrich, J. Allen, W. Brockbank, J. Younger, and M. Nyman, *HR Transformation: Building Human Resources From the Outside In* (New York: McGraw-Hill, 2009); D. Ulrich, J. Younger, W. Brockbank, and M. Ulrich, *HR Transformation* (New York: McGraw-Hill, 2009); P. M. Wright, J. W. Boudreau, D. A. Pace, E. Sartain, P. McKinnon, and R. L. Antoine, *The Chief HR Officer: Defining the New Role of Human Resource Leaders* (San Francisco: Jossey-Bass, 2011).
3. M. L. Davis, "The CHRO as Cultural Champion," in P. M. Wright, J. W. Boudreau, D. A. Pace, E. Sartain, P. McKinnon, and R. L. Antoine (eds.), *The Chief HR Officer: Defining the New Role of Human Resource Leaders* (San Francisco: Jossey-Bass, 2011), pp. 93–97.
4. S. Hargreaves, "Jobs With the Lowest (and Highest) Unemployment," *CNN Money*, Jan. 7, 2013 (*money.cnn.com*).
5. T. A. Lacey and B. Wright, "Occupational Employment Projections to 2018," *Monthly Labor Review*, May 2009, pp. 86–125.
6. Lacey and Wright, "Occupational Employment Projections to 2018."
7. A. Spitz-Oener, "Technical Change, Job Tasks, and Rising Educational Demands: Looking Outside the Wage Structure," *Journal of Labor Economics*, 2006, 24, pp. 235–270.
8. Society for Human Resource Management, *Critical Skills Needs and Resources for the Changing Workforce* (Alexandria, VA: author, 2008).
9. M. Toossi, "Labor Force Projections to 2018: Older Workers Staying More Active," *Monthly Labor Review*, Nov. 2009, pp. 30–51; P. L. Rones, R. E. Ilg, and J. M. Garner, "Trends in Hours of Work Since the Mid-1970s," *Monthly Labor Review*, Apr. 1997, pp. 3–14; J. Schramm, *SHRM Workplace Forecast* (Alexandria, VA: Society for Human Resource Management, 2008); P. J. Kiger, "With Baby Boomers Graying, Employers Are Urged to Act Now to Avoid Skills Shortages," *Workforce Management*, 2005, 84(13), pp. 52–54; J. F. Stinson, Jr., "New Data on Multiple Job Holding Available From the CPS," *Monthly Labor Review*, Mar. 1997, pp. 3–8; Manpower Inc., *Employment Outlook Survey: United States* (Milwaukee, WI: author, 2007).
10. T. Minton-Eversole and K. Gurchiek, "New Workers Not Ready for Prime Time," *HR Magazine*, Dec. 2006, pp. 28–34.
11. M. Rich, "Factory Jobs Return, but Employers Find Skills Shortage," *New York Times Online*, July 1, 2010.

12. M. J. Handel, "Skills Mismatch in the Labor Market," *Annual Review of Sociology*, 2003, 29, pp. 135–165.

13. BMP Forum and Success Factors, *Performance and Talent Management Trend Survey 2007* (San Mateo, CA: author, 2007).

14. Bureau of Labor Statistics, "Employed and Unemployed Full- and Part-Time Workers by Age, Race, Sex and Hispanic or Latino Ethnicity," Dec. 2007 (*www.bls.gov*).

15. US Department of Labor, "Workers on Flexible and Shift Schedules in May 2004," *News*, July 1, 2005.

16. T. Dunne, L. Foster, J. Haltiwanger, and K. R. Troske, "Wage and Productivity Dispersion in United States Manufacturing: The Role of Computer Investment," *Journal of Labor Economics*, 2004, 22, pp. 397–429; Spitz-Oener, "Technical Change, Job Tasks, and Rising Educational Demands: Looking Outside the Wage Structure."

17. C. R. Greer, *Strategic Human Resource Management*, 2nd ed. (Upper Saddle River, NJ: Prentice Hall, 2001); International Personnel Management Association, *Workforce Planning Guide for Public Sector Human Resource Professionals* (Alexandria, VA: author, 2002); D. W. Jarrell, *Human Resource Planning* (Englewood Cliffs, NJ: Prentice Hall, 1993); J. W. Walker, *Human Resource Strategy* (New York: McGraw-Hill, 1992).

18. L. Rubis, "Strategic Planning Not So Hard if Done Right," *HR News*, June 26, 2011, (*www.shrm.org*).

19. F. Hansen, "Strategic Workforce Planning in an Uncertain World," *Workforce Management Online*, Sept. 7, 2011 (*www.workforce.com*).

20. S. Overman, "Staffing Management: A Better Forecast," *Staffing Management Magazine*, Apr. 1, 2008 (*www.shrm.org*); T. J. Chermack, *Scenario Planning in Organizations: How to Create, Use, and Assess Scenarios* (San Francisco: Berrett-Koehler, 2011).

21. M. B. Glick, T. J. Chermack, H. Luckel, and B. Q. Gauck, "Effects of Scenario Planning on Participant Mental Models," *European Journal of Training and Development*, 2012, 36, pp. 488–507.

22. H. G. Heneman III and M. H. Sandver, "Markov Analysis in Human Resource Administration: Applications and Limitations," *Academy of Management Review*, 1977, 2, pp. 535–542.

23. J. A. Conger and R. M. Fuller, "Developing Your Leadership Pipeline," *Harvard Business Review*, Dec. 2003, pp. 76–84; International Public Management Association–Human Resources, *Succession Planning* (Alexandria, VA: author, 2003); S. J. Wells, "Who's Next?" *HR Magazine*, Nov. 2003, pp. 45–50.

24. E. Frauenheim, "Software Products Aim to Streamline Succession Planning," *Workforce Management*, Jan. 2006 (*www.workforce.com*).

25. S. Fegley, *2006 Succession Planning* (Alexandria, VA: Society for Human Resource Management, 2006).

26. Conger and Fuller, "Developing Your Leadership Pipeline," p. 84.

27. S. F. Matusik and C.W.L. Hill, "The Utilization of Contingent Work, Knowledge Creation, and Competitive Advantage," *Academy of Management Review*, 1998, 23, pp. 680–697; Society for Human Resource Management, *Alternative Staffing Survey* (Alexandria, VA: author, 2000); C. V. von Hippel, S. L. Mangum, D. B. Greenberger, R. L. Heneman, and J. D. Skoglind, "Temporary Employment: Can Organizations and Employees Both Win?" *Academy of Management Executive*, 1997, 11, pp. 93–104.

28. G. Weber, "Temps at the Top," *Workforce*, Aug. 2004, pp. 27–31; M. Frase-Blunt, "Short Term Executives," *HR Magazine*, June 2004, pp. 110–114.

29. J. Brown, "Contingent Workers: Employing Nontraditional Workers Requires Strategy," *IPMA-HR News*, June 2004, pp. 9–11; A. Davis-Blake and P. P. Hui, "Contracting for Knowledge-Based Competition," in S. E. Jackson, M. A. Hitt, and A. S. DeNisi (eds.), *Managing Knowledge for Sustained Competitive Advantage* (San Francisco: Jossey-Bass, 2003), pp. 178–206.

30. D. Arthur, *Recruiting, Interviewing, Selecting, and Orienting New Employees*, 4th ed. (New York: Arthur Associates Management Consultants Limited, 2006); E. Esen, *Human Resource Outsourcing Survey Report* (Alexandria, VA: Society for Human Resource Management, 2004); J. Schramm, *Workplace Forecast, 2005–2006* (Alexandria, VA: Society for Human Resource Management, 2006).

31. P. Babcock, "America's Newest Export: White-Collar Jobs," *HR Magazine*, Apr. 2004, pp. 50–57; B. Tai and N. R. Lockwood, *Outsourcing and Offshoring HR Series Part I* (Alexandria, VA: Society for Human Resource Management, 2006); R. J. Moncarz, M. G. Wolf, and B. Wright, "Service-Providing Occupations, Offshoring, and the Labor Market," *Monthly Labor Review*, Dec. 2008, pp. 71–86.

32. M. Belcourt, "Outsourcing—The Benefits and the Risks," *Human Resource Management Review*, 2006, 16, pp. 269–279; B. M. Testa, "Tales of Backshoring," *Workforce Management*, Dec. 2007 (*www.workforce.com*); A. Fox, "The Ins and Outs of Customer Contact Centers," *HR Magazine Online*, May 2010.

33. L. Lieber, "Changing Demographics Will Require Changing the Way We Do Business," *Employment Relations Today*, Fall 2009, pp. 91–96; A. Fox, "At Work in 2020," *HR Magazine Online*, Jan. 1, 2010.

34. M. P. Bell, M. F. Özbilgin, T. A. Beauregard, and O. Sürgevil, "Voice, Silence, and Diversity in 21st Century Organizations: Strategies for Inclusion of Gay, Lesbian, Bisexual, and Transgender Employees," *Human Resource Management*, 2011, 50, pp. 131–146.

35. J. Schramm, *SHRM Workplace Forecast* (Alexandria, VA: Society for Human Resource Management, 2006).

36. E. Esen, *2005 Workforce Diversity Practices* (Alexandria, VA: Society for Human Resource Management, 2005).

37. R. R. Hastings, "Diversity Efforts Should Include White Employees," *SHRM HR Topics and Strategy*, July 7, 2012 (*www.shrm.org*); Society for Human Resource Management, *Global Diversity and Inclusion: Perceptions, Practices, and Attitudes* (Alexandria, VA: author, 2009).

38. Society for Human Resource Management, *2007 State of Workplace Diversity Management* (Alexandria, VA: author, 2007).

39. D. R. Avery, "Reactions to Diversity in Recruitment Advertising: Are the Differences Black and White?" *Journal of Applied Psychology*, 2003, 88, pp. 672 679; D. R. Avery and P. F. McKay, "Target Practice: An Organizational Impression Management Approach to Attracting Minority and Female Job Applicants," *Personnel Psychology*, 2006, 59, pp. 157–187.

40. S. B. Welch, "Diversity as Business Strategy: Company Faced Racial Tensions Head On," *Workforce Management Online*, Apr. 2009; Lieber, "Changing Demographics Will Require Changing the Way We Do Business."

41. J. M. Sacco, C. R. Scheu, A. M. Ryan, and N. Schmitt, "An Investigation of Race and Sex Similarity Effects in Interviews: A Multilevel Approach to Relational Demography," *Journal of Applied Psychology*, 2003, 88, pp. 852–865; J. C. Ziegert and P. J. Hanges, "Employment Discrimination: The Role of Implicit Attitudes, Motivation, and a Climate for Racial Bias," *Journal of Applied Psychology*, 2005, 90, pp. 553–562.

42. P. J. Kiger, "Few Employers Addressing Impact of Aging Workforce," *Workforce Management*, Jan. 2010, pp. 6–7.

43. A. Nancherla, "Getting to the Foundation of Talent Management," *T + D*, Feb. 2010, p. 20.

44. M.E.A. Jayne and R. L. Dipboye, "Leveraging Diversity to Improve Business Performance: Research Findings and Recommendations for Organizations," *Human Resource Management*, 2004, 43, pp. 409–424; A. Kalev, F. Dobins, and E. Kelley, "Best Practices or Best Guesses? Assessing the Efficacy of Corporate Affirmative Action and Diversity Policies," *American Sociological Review*, 2006, 71, pp. 589–617; N. R. Lockwood and J. Victor, *Recruiting for Workplace Diversity: A Business Strategy* (Alexandria, VA: Society for Human Resource Management, 2007).

45. C. Dugas, "Tips for Gray-Haired Job Searchers; It Can Be Tough, but Programs Are Out There to Help," *USA Today,* Apr. 24, 2013, p. 6B; C. Dugas, "More Older Americans Remaining Part of the Workforce," *USA Today,* Jan. 14, 2013, p. 2B; T.W.H. Ng and D. C. Feldman, "Evaluating Six Common Stereotypes about Older Workers with Meta-Analytical Data," *Personnel Psychology*, 2012, 65, pp. 821–858.

46. D. Bennett-Alexander and L. B. Pincus, *Employment Law for Business*, 6th ed. (Burr Ridge, IL: Irwin McGraw-Hill, 2009), p. 245; C. R. Gullett, "Reverse Discrimination and Remedial Affirmative Action in Employment," *Public Personnel Management*, 2000, 29(1), pp. 107–118; T. Johnson, "Affirmative Action as a Title VII Remedy: Recent U.S. Supreme Court Decisions, Racial Quotas and Preferences," *Labor Law Journal*, 1987, 38, pp. 574–581; T. Johnson, "The Legal Use of Racial Quotas and Gender Preferences by Public and Private Employers," *Labor Law Journal*, 1989, 40, pp. 419–425; D. J. Walsh, *Employment Law for Human Resource Practice*, 2nd ed. (Mason, OH: Thomson Higher Education, 2007).

47. For an example of eliminating an AAP once affirmative action goals have been achieved, see A. R. McIlvaine, "Court: Boston Must Hire White Firefighters," *Human Resource Executive*, Feb. 2004, p. 13.

48. R. T. Seymour and B. B. Brown, *Equal Employment Law Update* (Washington, DC: Bureau of National Affairs, 1997), pp. 23-553 to 23-558; R. U. Robinson, G. M. Franklin, and R. F. Wayland, *Employment Regulation in the Workplace* (Armonk, NY: M. E. Sharpe, 2010), pp. 182–219.

49. M. P. Crockett and J. B. Thelen, "Michigan's Proposal 2: Affirmative Action Law Shifts at the State Level," *Legal Report*, Society for Human Resource Management, July/Aug. 2007, pp. 5–8.

50. EEOC Compliance Manual, 2006 (*www.eeoc.gov/policy/docs/race-color.html*).

51. Equal Employment Opportunity Commission, *EEOC Policy Guidance on Temporary Workers* (Washington, DC: author, 1997); Equal Employment Opportunity Commission, *Enforcement Guidance: Application of the ADA to Contingent Workers Placed by Temporary Agencies and Other Staffing Firms* (Washington, DC: author, 2000).

# CHAPTER FOUR

## Job Analysis and Rewards

## LEARNING OBJECTIVES AND INTRODUCTION

### Learning Objectives

- Understand the rationale behind job analysis
- Know the difference between a job description and a job specification
- Learn about methods for collecting job requirements
- Understand why competency-based job analysis has grown in prominence
- Learn about methods for collecting competencies
- Recognize the types of rewards associated with jobs
- Become familiar with the legal issues surrounding job analysis

### Introduction

Once the planning process is complete, the next step in developing an effective, strategic staffing system is to develop a thorough understanding of the jobs to be filled. The process of studying and describing the specific requirements for a job is called job analysis. Anyone who has ever looked for a job is familiar with a traditional job description, which lists the major tasks, duties, and responsibilities of a job. Such descriptions are just part of the wealth of information collected during the job analysis process. As we will see later in the book, job analysis information can be used for identifying recruiting pools, designing selection tools, and assessing and improving employee performance.

At first blush, describing a job may seem to be a straightforward task. However, there are some important considerations that will determine which techniques should be employed for collecting this information. In many cases, a traditional task-based job analysis is sufficient to cover both the operational and the legal requirements of an organization's staffing strategy. In other cases, it will make more sense to focus on a general set of KSAOs (knowledge, skill, ability, and other characteristics) that span a wide variety of jobs in the organization. The choice of techniques will depend on both the nature of the jobs involved and the organization's plans for the future.

The chapter begins by explaining the rationale behind job analysis and reviewing the challenges that arise when developing a description of jobs in a changing environment. Then, methods for performing job analysis are discussed. The first approach, job requirements job analysis, is guided by the job requirements matrix, which includes tasks, KSAOs, and job context. Next, competency-based job analysis is described. This approach to job analysis starts from the organization's mission and goals and then develops a list of the general KSAOs that will help the organization meet these needs. Attention then turns to job rewards, including both intrinsic and extrinsic rewards that jobs may provide to employees. Finally, legal issues pertaining to job analysis are addressed.

# THE NEED FOR JOB ANALYSIS

Jobs are the building blocks of an organization, in terms of both job content and the hierarchical relationships that emerge among them. They are explicitly designed and aligned in ways that enhance the production of the organization's goods and services. Job analysis thus must be considered within the broader framework of the design of jobs and the organization as a whole, for it is through their design that jobs acquire their requirements and rewards. The information from job analysis will be used in every single phase of the staffing process. In this sense, job analysis is a support activity to the various functional staffing activities. Indeed, without thorough and accurate information about job requirements and/or competencies, the organization is greatly hampered in its attempts to acquire a workforce that will be effective in terms of human resource (HR) outcomes such as performance, satisfaction, and retention. Thus, job analysis is the foundation upon which successful staffing systems are constructed.

## Types of Job Analysis

Job analysis may be defined as the process of studying jobs in order to gather, analyze, synthesize, and report information about job requirements and rewards. Note in this definition that job analysis is an overall process as opposed to a specific method or technique. A job requirements job analysis seeks to identify and describe the specific tasks, KSAOs, and job context for a particular job. This type of job analysis aims to be objective and has a very well-developed body of techniques to support its implementation. A second type of job analysis, competency-based, attempts to identify and describe job requirements in the form of general KSAOs required across a range of jobs; task and work context requirements are of little concern. Competency-based approaches focus on how jobs relate to organizational strategy. A third approach to job analysis focuses on the rewards employees receive from their work. Unlike the job requirements and competency-based approaches, the rewards-based approach is used to assess what types of positive outcomes employees receive from performing a job. From a staffing perspective, knowing the rewards of a job can be very useful in attracting individuals to apply for, and ultimately accept, jobs in the organization.

To help show the differences and similarities among task job requirements, competency-based, and job rewards methods of job analysis, Exhibit 4.1 describes the method, process, and staffing implications of each of the three types. As can be seen, every phase of the staffing process is rooted in job analysis, from initial planning to retention. Each technique contributes different information and uses different sources. Job requirements analysis is mostly rooted in documenting what employees currently do, competency analysis focuses on how executives see work roles contributing to strategy, and rewards analysis determines what employees get from their jobs. These techniques are not mutually exclusive, of course, and organizations can benefit from using all three methods of analysis simultaneously.

**EXHIBIT 4.1   Comparison of Types of Job Analysis**

| | Job Analysis Technique | | |
| --- | --- | --- | --- |
| | **Job Requirements** | **Competency** | **Job Rewards** |
| **Method** | Collect information on activities performed on the job and use this information to assess needed KSAOs for each job | Collect information on company strategy and use this information to determine KSAOs and behavioral capabilities needed across the organization | Collect information from employees on preferences and outcomes of jobs and combine with preferences identified in the labor market as a whole |
| **Process** | Review occupational requirements; collect data on tasks, duties, and responsibilities from incumbents and supervisors; develop job requirements matrix | Discuss strategy with executives to determine overall goals, then meet with division or department leaders to review how each job fits with the overall goals | Develop a list of potential rewards for a job and survey job incumbents and leaders |
| **Staffing Implications** | Documents task requirements for legal purposes and determines specific KSAOs for selection | Links organizational strategy with planning process and determines broad KSAOs for selection | Provides guidance for how to develop recruiting materials and retention strategies |

## The Changing Nature of Jobs

The traditional way of designing a job is to identify and define its elements and tasks precisely and then incorporate them into a job description. The core task includes virtually all tasks associated with the job, and from it a fairly inclusive list of KSAOs will flow. Thus defined, there are clear lines of demarcation between jobs in terms of both tasks and KSAOs, and there is little overlap between jobs. Each job also has its own set of extrinsic and intrinsic rewards. Such job design is marked by formal organization charts, clear and precise job descriptions and specifications, and well-defined relationships between jobs in terms of mobility (promotion and transfer) paths. Also, traditional jobs are very static, with little or no change occurring in tasks or KSAOs.

One challenge to this traditional perspective is that jobs are constantly evolving.[1] Generally, these changes are not so radical that a job ceases to exist, and they are often due to technological or workload changes. An excellent example of such an evolving job is that of secretary. Traditional or core tasks associated with the job include typing, filing, taking dictation, and answering phones. However, in nearly all organizations the job has evolved to include new tasks such as managing multiple projects, creating spreadsheets, purchasing supplies and office technology, and gathering information on the Internet. These task changes led to new KSAO requirements such as planning and coordination skills and knowledge of spreadsheet software. Accompanying these changes is a switch in job title to that of "administrative assistant." Note that jobs may also evolve due to changing organizational and technology requirements, as well as employee-initiated changes through a process of job crafting.

Another challenge to the traditional view is the need for flexibility. Flexible jobs have frequently changing task and KSAO requirements. Sometimes these changes are initiated by the job incumbent who constantly adds and drops (or passes off) new assignments or projects in order to work toward moving targets of opportunity. Other times the task changes may be dictated by changes in production schedules, client demands, or technology. Many small-business owners, general managers of start-up strategic business units, and top management members perform such flexible jobs.

Team-based work enhances the need for flexibility and further complicates the process of job analysis. A work team is an interdependent collection of employees who share responsibility for achieving a specific goal. Examples of such goals include developing a product, delivering a service, winning a game, conducting a process, developing a plan, or making a joint decision. No matter its form or function, every team is composed of two or more employees and has an identifiable collection of tasks to perform. Usually, these tasks are grouped into specific clusters, and each cluster constitutes a position or job. A project management team, for example, may have separate jobs and job titles for budget specialists, technical specialists, coordinators, and field staff. While teams differ in many respects, two differences are very important in terms of their job analysis and staffing implications. Many team members perform multiple jobs (rather than a single job). In such cases, staffing must emphasize recruitment and selection for both job-specific KSAOs and job-spanning KSAOs. Many job-spanning KSAOs involve flexibility, adaptability, and the ability to quickly learn skills that will facilitate performing, and switching between, multiple jobs.[2] Therefore, job analysis for team-based work has to account for this highly varied and constantly evolving set of task demands.

Finally, the more open and flexible nature of work described above has suggested a need to identify factors that make people go beyond what is simply written in a job description. Job analysis has typically focused on skills and abilities to a greater degree than motivational factors. As more and more organizations emphasize employee engagement—or the degree to which an employee identifies with and has enthusiasm for his or her work—our analysis of jobs needs to take motivational factors into account. A large-scale study of 7,939 business units showed that organizations whose employees reported above-average levels of engagement performed significantly better (63% of such organizations had above-average levels of performance) than those whose employees were below average on engagement (37% of such organizations had above-average levels of performance).[3] One way to incorporate engagement is to consider it a general competency in competency-based job analysis coupled with job rewards analysis. As one reviewer of the engagement literature suggests, "Identify those candidates who are best-suited to the job and your organization's culture."[4]

## JOB REQUIREMENTS JOB ANALYSIS

### Overview

As noted earlier, job requirements job analysis identifies the tasks, KSAOs, and context for a job. Due to the ambiguous and fluid nature of some jobs, organizations may focus on defining them in terms of competencies rather than specific tasks and KSAOs. Recent developments in job analysis encourage raters to explicitly describe potential changes in future job requirements in an effort to adapt to these jobs.[5]

Concepts underlying job requirements can be arranged in a hierarchy from observable tasks up to job families. Job requirements job analysis starts with tasks, which are identifiable work activities that are logical and necessary steps in the performance of the job. Task dimensions are groups of similar types of tasks. A job is a grouping of positions that have similar tasks. Jobs that are similar to one another can be grouped into job categories. Finally, a job family is a grouping of jobs according to function. For example, within the community and social service job family there are categories of jobs like health workers, counselors, and social workers. Under this category are specific jobs like mental health counselor and rehabilitation counselor. Tasks like collecting information, developing treatment plans, and counseling clients make up the job of mental health counselor. A position is a grouping of task dimensions that constitutes the total work assignment of a single employee; there are as many positions as there are employees.

A framework depicting job requirements job analysis is shown in Exhibit 4.2. As can be seen, the job analysis begins by identifying the specific tasks and job context for a particular job.[6] After these have been identified, the KSAOs necessary for performing these tasks within the work context are inferred. For example, after identifying the task of "developing and writing monthly sales and marketing plans" for a sales manager's job, the job analysis would proceed by inferring which KSAOs would be necessary to perform this task. The task might require knowledge of intended customers, arithmetic skills, creative ability, and willingness and availability to travel frequently to various organizational units. No particular job context factors, such as physical demands, may be relevant to performance of this

**EXHIBIT 4.2   Job Requirements Approach to Job Analysis**

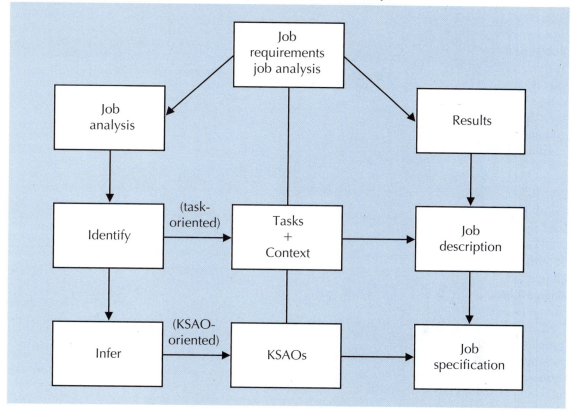

task or to its required KSAOs. The task and job context information is recorded in a job description, whereas the KSAO requirements are placed into a job specification. In practice, these are often contained within a single document.

## Job Requirements Matrix

The job requirements matrix shows the key components of job requirements job analysis, each of which must be explicitly considered for inclusion in any job requirements job analysis. Completion of the cell entries in the matrix represents the information that must be gathered, analyzed, synthesized, and expressed in usable written form.

A completed job requirements matrix, a portion of which is shown in Exhibit 4.3 for the job of administrative assistant, serves as the basic informational source or document for any job in terms of its requirements. The resultant information serves as a basic input and guide to all subsequent staffing activities.

**EXHIBIT 4.3    Portion of Job Requirements Matrix for Job of Administrative Assistant**

| Tasks | | | KSAOs | |
|---|---|---|---|---|
| Specific Tasks | Task Dimensions | Importance (% time spent) | Nature | Importance to Tasks (1–5 rating) |
| 1. Arrange schedules with office assistant/volunteers to ensure that office will be staffed during prescribed hours | A. Supervision | 30% | 1. Knowledge of office operations and policies | 4.9 |
| | | | 2. Ability to match people to tasks according to their skills and hours of availability | 4.6 |
| 2. Assign office tasks to office assistant/volunteers to ensure coordination of activities | A. Supervision | | 3. Skill in interaction with diverse people | 2.9 |
| | | | 4. Skill in determining types and priorities of tasks | 4.0 |
| 3. Compose and edit letters, memos, and reports based on supervisory direction | B. Document preparation | 20% | 1. Knowledge of typing formats | 3.1 |
| | | | 2. Knowledge of grammar and style rules | 5.0 |
| 4. Prepare graphs and other visual material to supplement reports | B. Document preparation | | 3. Knowledge of graphics display software | 2.0 |
| | | | 4. Ability to proofread and correct work | 5.0 |
| 5. Proofread typed copy and correct grammar, punctuation, and typographical errors in order to produce high-quality materials | B. Document preparation | | 5. Skill in use of MS Word (most current version) | 4.3 |
| | | | 6. Skill in creating visually appealing and understandable graphs | 3.4 |

**Job Context:** Indoors, cubicle, business clothes, mostly sitting and standing, no environmental or job hazards.

Referring to Exhibit 4.3, five specific tasks identified via job analysis are listed. Note that only a portion of the total tasks for the job is shown. In turn, these have been categorized into two general task dimensions—supervision and word processing. Their importance to the overall job is indicated with the percentage of time spent on each—30% and 20%, respectively. For each task dimension and its specific tasks, several KSAOs have been inferred to be necessary for performance. The nature of these KSAOs is presented, along with a 1–5 rating of how important each KSAO is for performance of the task dimension. At the bottom of the matrix are indications of job context factors pertaining to work setting (indoors), privacy of work area (cubicle), attire (business clothes), body positioning (mostly sitting and standing), and physical work conditions (no environmental or job hazards).

## Task Statements

Job analysis begins with the development of task statements. Task statements are objectively written descriptions of the major tasks an employee performs in a job. They serve as the building blocks for the remainder of the job requirements job analysis. The statements are made in simple declarative sentences.

Ideally, each task statement will show several things:

1. What the employee does, using a specific action verb at the start of the task statement
2. To whom or what the employee does what he or she does, stating the object of the verb
3. What is produced, indicating the expected output of the verb
4. What equipment, materials, tools, or procedures are used

In addition to the preceding four requirements, there are several other suggestions for effectively writing task statements. First, use specific action verbs that have only one meaning. Examples of verbs that do not conform to this suggestion include "supports," "assists," and "handles."

Second, focus on recording tasks, as opposed to specific elements that compose a task. This requires the use of considerable judgment because the distinction between a task and an element is relative and often fuzzy. Note that most jobs can be adequately described within a range of 15–25 task statements. A task statement list exceeding this range is a warning that it may be too narrow in terms of activities defined.

Third, do not include minor or trivial activities in task statements; focus only on major tasks and activities. An exception to this recommendation occurs when a so-called minor task is judged to have great importance to the job (see the following discussion).

Fourth, ensure that the list of task statements is reliable.[7] A good way to do this is to have two or more people (analysts) independently evaluate the task statement list in terms of both inclusiveness and clarity. Close agreement between people signifies high reliability. If there is disagreement, the nature of the disagreement can be discussed and the task statements can be appropriately modified. It should be acknowledged that differences in task statements are not necessarily an indication of error. Different incumbents may perform their jobs in different ways.[8] The final job analysis document should reflect these varying perspectives clearly. Failure to acknowledge this variety can lead to an overly narrow set of desired KSAOs, and may even lead to legal problems if the job analysis documents used to make decisions do not reflect the various ways jobs are actually performed.

### Task Dimensions

Task statement lists may be maintained in list form and subsequently incorporated into the job description. Often, however, it is useful to group sets of task statements into task dimensions and then attach a name to each such dimension. Other terms for task dimensions are "duties," "accountability areas," "responsibilities," and "performance dimensions."

A useful way to facilitate the grouping process is to create a task dimension matrix. Each column in the matrix represents a potential task dimension, and a label is tentatively attached to it. Each row in the matrix represents a particular task statement. Cell entries in the matrix represent the assignment of task statements to task dimensions (the grouping of tasks). The goal is to have each task statement assigned to only one task dimension.

Several things should be kept in mind about task dimensions. First, their creation is optional and should occur only if they will be useful. Second, there are many different grouping procedures, ranging from straightforward judgmental ones to highly sophisticated statistical ones.[9] For most purposes, a simple judgmental process is sufficient, such as having the people who created the task statements also create the groupings as part of the same exercise. As a rule, there should be four to eight dimensions, depending on the number of task statements, regardless of the specific grouping procedure used. Third, it is important that the grouping procedure yield a reliable set of task dimensions acceptable to managers, job incumbents, and other organizational members.

### Importance of Tasks/Dimensions

Rarely are all tasks/dimensions of a job thought to be of equal weight or importance. It is generally felt that these differences must be captured, expressed, and incorporated into job information, especially the job description. Normally, assessments of importance are made just for task dimensions, though it is certainly possible to make them for individual tasks as well.

Before actual weighting can occur, two decisions must be made: (1) the specific attribute to be assessed in terms of importance must be decided (e.g., time spent on the task/dimension or importance), and (2) whether the attribute will be measured in categorical terms (e.g., essential or nonessential) or continuous terms (e.g., per-

**EXHIBIT 4.4   Examples of Ways to Assess Task/Dimension Importance**

**A.   Relative Time Spent**

For each task/dimension, rate the amount of time you spend on it, relative to all other tasks/dimensions of your job.

| 1 | 2 | 3 | 4 | 5 |
|---|---|---|---|---|
| Very small amount | | Average amount | | Very large amount |

**B.   Percentage (%) of Time Spent**

For each task/dimension, indicate the percentage (%) of time you spend on it (percentages must total to 100%).

Dimension  _____          % Time spent  _____

**C.   Importance to Overall Performance**

For each task/dimension, rate its importance to your overall job performance.

| 1 | 2 | 3 | 4 | 5 |
|---|---|---|---|---|
| Minor importance | | Average importance | | Major importance |

**D.   Need for New Employee Training**

Do new employees receive a standard, planned course of training for performance of this task, other than a customary job orientation?

_____ Yes

_____ No

centage of time spent, 1–5 rating of importance). Exhibit 4.4 shows examples of the results of these two decisions in terms of commonly used importance attributes and their measurement. Task importance judgments are likely to vary across raters even more than task statements, so it is necessary to collect judgments from several sources.[10]

## KSAOs

KSAOs are inferred or derived from knowledge of the tasks and task dimensions themselves. The inference process requires that the analysts think explicitly in specific cause-and-effect terms. For each task or dimension, the analyst must in essence ask, "Exactly which KSAOs do I think will be necessary for (will cause) performance on this task or dimension?" Then the analyst should ask, "Why do I think this?" in order to think through the soundness of the inferential logic. Discussions among analysts about these questions are encouraged.

Our discussion of KSAOs will be grounded in information provided by the US Department of Labor's Occupational Information Network, or O*NET. The development and refinement of the O*NET database is ongoing, and many new observations from both job incumbents and trained analysts are being added regularly.[11] O*NET contains extensive research-based taxonomies in several categories: occupational tasks, knowledges, skills, abilities, education and experience/training, work context, organizational context, occupational interests and values, and work styles.[12] Additionally, O*NET contains ratings of the specific factors within each category for many occupations, and ratings for additional occupations are continually being added. There are statistical techniques that link O*NET KSAO ratings for a job to specific selection tools, like standardized literacy tests.[13] Use of O*NET information is a helpful starting point in preparing KSAO statements, but they will probably have to be supplemented with more job-specific statements crafted by the job analyst. Analysts should be particularly wary of using global terms such as "knowledge of accounting principles" and should instead indicate which accounting principles are being utilized and why each is necessary for task performance.

***Knowledge.*** Knowledge is a body of information (conceptual, factual, procedural) that can be applied directly to the performance of tasks. It tends to be quite focused or specific in terms of job, organization, or occupation. O*NET provides definitions of 33 knowledges that might generally be necessary, in varying levels, in occupations. Exhibit 4.5 lists these knowledges. Knowledge is often divided into declarative and procedural categories. Declarative knowledge is factual in nature, whereas procedural knowledge concerns processes. A surgeon, for example, has declarative knowledge of the symptoms of heart disease and can state them, and also has procedural knowledge of the steps one would take to perform open-heart surgery. Both declarative and procedural knowledge should be reflected in job analysis documents.[14]

***Skill.*** Skill refers to an observable competence for working with or applying knowledge to perform a particular task or a closely related set of tasks. A skill is not an enduring characteristic of the person; it depends on experience and practice. Skill requirements are directly inferred from observation or knowledge of tasks performed. Returning to our example, skill refers to the actual demonstrated capacity of the surgeon to perform an operation in an efficient and competent manner.

Considerable research has been devoted to identifying particular job-related skills and organizing them into taxonomies. Job analysts should begin the skills inference process by referring to the results of this research.

**EXHIBIT 4.5   Knowledges Contained in O\*NET**

- Business and management
    - Administration and management
    - Clerical
    - Economics and accounting
    - Sales and marketing
    - Customer and personal service
    - Personnel and human resources
- Manufacturing and production
    - Production and processing
    - Food production
- Engineering and technology
    - Computers and electronics
    - Engineering and technology
    - Design
    - Building and construction
    - Mechanical
- Mathematics and science
    - Mathematics
    - Physics
    - Chemistry
    - Biology
    - Psychology
    - Sociology and anthropology
    - Geography
- Health services
    - Medicine and dentistry
    - Therapy and counseling
- Education and training
    - Education and training
- Arts and humanities
    - English language
    - Foreign language
    - Fine arts
    - History and archaeology
    - Philosophy and theology
- Law and public safety
    - Public safety and security
    - Law, government, and jurisprudence
- Communications
    - Telecommunications
    - Communications and media
- Transportation
    - Transportation

SOURCE: Adapted from National Center for O\*NET Development, "The O\*NET Content Model" (*www.onetcenter.org/content.html#cm6*), accessed 8/29/13.

O\*NET identifies and defines 42 skills applicable across the occupational spectrum. Exhibit 4.6 lists these skills. The first 10 are basic skills involving acquiring and conveying information; the remaining 32 are cross-functional skills used to facilitate task performance.

*Ability.*   An ability is an underlying, enduring trait of the person that is useful for learning about and performing a range of tasks. It differs from a skill in that it is less likely to change over time and that it is applicable across a wide set of tasks encountered in many different jobs. One can think of ability as the underlying personal characteristics that determine how quickly one can acquire and to what degree one can master the knowledge and skills required for a job.[15] Four general categories of abilities are commonly recognized: cognitive, psychomotor, physical, and sensory. O\*NET contains a complete taxonomy of these four categories, shown in Exhibit 4.7.

**EXHIBIT 4.6** **Skills Contained in O*NET**

### Basic Skills

- Content skills
  - Reading comprehension
  - Active listening
  - Writing
  - Speaking
  - Mathematics
  - Science

- Process skills
  - Critical thinking
  - Active learning
  - Learning strategies
  - Monitoring

### Cross-Functional Skills

- Social skills
  - Social perceptiveness
  - Coordination
  - Persuasion
  - Negotiation
  - Instructing
  - Service orientation
- Complex problem-solving skills
  - Problem identification
  - Information gathering
  - Information organization
  - Synthesis/reorganization
  - Idea generation
  - Idea evaluation
  - Implementation planning
  - Solution appraisal
- Resource management skills
  - Time management
  - Management of financial resources
  - Management of material resources
  - Management of personnel resources

- Technical skills
  - Operations analysis
  - Technology design
  - Equipment selection
  - Installation
  - Programming
  - Equipment maintenance
  - Troubleshooting
  - Repairing
  - Operation monitoring
  - Operation and control
  - Quality control analysis
- Systems skills
  - Judgment and decision making
  - Systems analysis
  - Systems evaluation

SOURCE: Adapted from National Center for O*NET Development, "The O*NET Content Model" (*www.onetcenter.org/content.html#cm6*), accessed 8/29/13.

*Other Characteristics.* "Other characteristics" is a catchall category for factors that do not fit neatly into the knowledge, skills, and abilities categories. Despite the catchall nature of these requirements, they are very important for having the right personality to perform job tasks well, values and interests that are consistent with social and organizational priorities, and the specific training and experience requirements to take a job. Numerous examples of these factors are shown in

**EXHIBIT 4.7   Abilities Contained in O*NET**

**Cognitive Abilities**
- Verbal abilities
  - Oral comprehension
  - Written comprehension
  - Oral expression
  - Written expression
- Idea generation and reasoning abilities
  - Fluency of ideas
  - Originality
  - Problem sensitivity
  - Deductive reasoning
  - Inductive reasoning
  - Information ordering
  - Category flexibility
- Quantitative abilities
  - Mathematical reasoning
  - Number facility
- Memory
  - Memorization
- Perceptual abilities
  - Speed of closure
  - Flexibility of closure
  - Perceptual speed
- Spatial abilities
  - Spatial organization
  - Visualization
- Attentiveness
  - Selective attention
  - Time sharing

**Psychomotor Abilities**
- Fine manipulative abilities
  - Arm-hand steadiness
  - Manual dexterity
  - Finger dexterity
- Control movement abilities
  - Control precision
  - Multilimb coordination
  - Response orientation
  - Rate control

- Reaction time and speed
  - Reaction time
  - Wrist-finger dexterity
  - Speed of limb movement

**Physical Abilities**
- Physical strength
  - Static strength
  - Explosive strength
  - Dynamic strength
  - Trunk strength
- Endurance
  - Stamina
- Flexibility, balance, and coordination
  - Extent flexibility
  - Dynamic flexibility
  - Gross body coordination
  - Gross body equilibrium

**Sensory Abilities**
- Visual abilities
  - Near vision
  - Far vision
  - Visual color discrimination
  - Night vision
  - Peripheral vision
  - Depth perception
  - Glare sensitivity
- Auditory and speech abilities
  - Hearing sensitivity
  - Auditory attention
  - Sound localization
  - Speech recognition
  - Speech clarity

Source: Adapted from National Center for O*NET Development, "The O*NET Content Model" (*www.onetcenter.org/content.html#cm6*), accessed 8/29/13.

Exhibit 4.8. Care should be taken to ensure that these factors truly are job requirements, as opposed to whimsical and ill-defined preferences of the organization.

### KSAO Importance

As suggested in the job requirements matrix, the KSAOs of a job may differ in their weight or contribution to task performance. Hence, their relative importance must be explicitly considered, defined, and indicated. Failure to do so means that all KSAOs will be assumed to be of equal importance by default.

As with task importance, deriving KSAO importance requires two decisions. First, what will be the specific attribute(s) on which importance is judged? Second, will the measurement of each attribute be categorical (e.g., required-preferred) or continuous (e.g., 1–5 rating scale)? Examples of formats for indicating KSAO importance are shown in Exhibit 4.9. O*NET uses a 1–5 rating scale format and also provides actual importance ratings for many jobs.

Ratings of KSAO importance generally can be divided into time and importance.[16] Time-oriented measures include things like time spent, frequency, and duration scales. Importance includes things like criticality, difficulty, and overall importance. In most organizations, time spent and importance are completely distinct, and so both should be measured to get a full picture of the job's requirements. It should be noted that there are systematic differences in ratings of time spent and importance across observers. For example, new employees may spend more time developing relationships, whereas established employees spend time maintaining relationships. Thus, multiple perspectives will need to be integrated.

### Job Context

As shown in the job requirements matrix, tasks and KSAOs occur within a broader job context. A job requirements job analysis should include consideration of the job context and the factors that are important in defining it. Such consideration

---

**EXHIBIT 4.8**   **Examples of Other Job Requirements**

**Personality**
- Conscientiousness
- Extraversion
- Agreeableness
- Confidence/assertiveness

**Training and Experience**
- Licensing
- Certificates
- Registrations
- Clean criminal background

**Values and Interests**
- Moral and ethical principles
- Independence
- Creativity

---

**EXHIBIT 4.9   Examples of Ways to Assess KSAO Importance**

**A.   Importance to (acceptable) (superior) task performance**
   1 = minimal importance
   2 = some importance
   3 = average importance
   4 = considerable importance
   5 = extensive importance

**B.   Should the KSAO be assessed during recruitment/selection?**
   ☐ Yes
   ☐ No

**C.   Is the KSAO required, preferred, or not required for recruitment/selection?**
   ☐ Required
   ☐ Preferred
   ☐ Not required (obtain on job and/or in training)

is necessary because these factors may have an influence on tasks and KSAOs; further, information about the factors may be used in the recruitment and selection of job applicants. For example, the information may be given to job applicants to provide them a realistic job preview during recruitment, and consideration of job context factors may be helpful in assessing likely person/organization fit during selection.

O*NET contains a wide array of job and work context factors useful for characterizing occupations. The job context information contained in O*NET involves interpersonal, physical, and structural characteristics, as shown in Exhibit 4.10. These characteristics can be useful for determining additional KSAO requirements and may be especially important for determining whether a job can or cannot be modified to accommodate an individual who is disabled.

## Job Descriptions and Job Specifications

As previously noted, it is common practice to express the results of job requirements job analysis in written job descriptions and job specifications. Referring back to the job requirements matrix, note that its sections pertaining to tasks and job context are similar to a job description, and the section dealing with KSAOs is similar to a job specification.

There are no standard formats or other requirements for either job descriptions or job specifications. In terms of content, however, a job description should include the following: job family, job title, job summary, task statements and dimensions,

---

**EXHIBIT 4.10 Job Context Contained in O*NET**

**Interpersonal Relationships**
- Communication
- Role relationships
- Responsibility for others
- Conflictual contact

**Physical Work Conditions**
- Work setting
- Environmental conditions
- Job hazards
- Body positioning
- Work attire

**Structural Job Characteristics**
- Criticality of position
- Routine vs. challenging work
- Competition
- Pace and scheduling

---

importance indicators, job context indicators, and the date that the job analysis was conducted. A job specification should include job family, job title, job summary, KSAOs (separate section for each), importance indicators, and date conducted. An example of a combined job description/specification is shown in Exhibit 4.11.

## Collecting Job Requirements Information

Job analysis involves consideration of not only the types of information (tasks, KSAOs, and job context) to be collected but also the methods, sources, and processes to be used for such collection. These issues are discussed next, and as will be seen, there are many alternatives to choose from for developing an overall job analysis system for any particular situation. Potential inaccuracies and other limitations of the alternatives will also be pointed out.[17]

### Methods

Job analysis methods represent procedures or techniques for collecting job information. Many specific techniques and systems have been developed and named (e.g., Functional Job Analysis, Position Analysis Questionnaire [PAQ]). Rather than discuss each technique separately, we will concentrate on the major generic methods that underlie all specific techniques and applications. Many excellent descriptions and discussions of the specific techniques are available.[18]

*Prior Information.* For any job, there is usually some prior information available that could and should be consulted. Indeed, this information should routinely be searched for and used as a starting point for a job analysis.

Existing information is a natural starting point for conducting a job requirements job analysis. Organizations that have performed job analysis in the past will

**EXHIBIT 4.11   Example of Combined Job Description/Specification**

### FUNCTIONAL UNIT: CHILDREN'S REHABILITATION
### JOB TITLE: REHABILITATION SPECIALIST
### DATE: 12/5/14

**JOB SUMMARY**

Works with children with disabilities and their families to identify developmental strengths and weaknesses, develop rehabilitation plans, deliver and coordinate rehabilitation activities, and evaluate effectiveness of those plans and activities.

**PERFORMANCE DIMENSIONS AND TASKS**                          **Time Spent (%)**

**1. Assessment**                                                    **10%**

Administer formal and informal motor screening and evaluation instruments to conduct assessments. Perform assessments to identify areas of strengths and need.

**2. Planning**                                                      **25%**

Collaborate with parents and other providers to directly develop the individualized family service plan. Use direct and consultative models of service in developing plans.

**3. Delivery**                                                      **50%**

Carry out individual and small-group motor development activities with children and families. Provide service coordination to designated families. Work with family care and child care providers to provide total services. Collaborate with other staff members and professionals from community agencies to obtain resources and specialized assistance.

**4. Evaluation**                                                    **15%**

Observe, interpret, and report on client to monitor individual progress. Assist in collecting and reporting intervention data in order to prepare formal program evaluation reports. Write evaluation reports to assist in developing new treatment strategies and programs.

**JOB SPECIFICATIONS**

**1. License:**    License to practice physical therapy in the state

**2. Education:**   B.S. in physical or occupational therapy required; M.S. preferred

**3. Experience:**  Prefer (not required) one year experience working with children with disabilities and their families

**4. Skills:**     Listening to and interacting with others (children, family members, coworkers)
Developing treatment plans
Organizing and writing reports using Microsoft Word

**JOB CONTEXT:** Indoors, office, business clothes, no environmental or job hazards.

have information on the tasks, duties, and responsibilities of the job as well as the corresponding KSAOs. While such information can be helpful, the changing nature of work suggests that all older information should be considered carefully and evaluated relative to the current set of requirements. In fact, organizations that rely excessively on old information can get into legal trouble if there is a discrepancy between the job on record and the job as it is actually performed.

O*NET, which we discussed in detail earlier, is another starting point for job analysis information. Obvious advantages of O*NET are its flexibility (it can be applied to many different types of jobs) and its ease of use.[19] Because the data were collected by professionals across a wide variety of locations, it is also considered to be of high quality. The chief disadvantage of O*NET is that it describes occupations and not jobs. Occupational information indicates what individuals performing a certain job title do across a wide variety of organizational contexts, whereas job information reflects the unique characteristics of how work is done in a specific company. In other words, while O*NET has a very well-developed description of what marketing managers do, it cannot say anything about the specific nature of a marketing manager job at Apple.

The ready availability of prior job information needs to be balanced with its limitations. Existing information within the organization may be out of date, and information from O*NET does not take the organization's unique context into account. While prior information should be the starting point for job analysis, it should not be the stopping point.

***Observation.***   Simply observing job incumbents performing the job is an excellent way to learn about tasks, KSAOs, and context. It provides a thoroughness and richness of information unmatched by any other method. It is also the most direct form of gathering information because it does not rely on intermediary information sources, as would be the case with other methods (e.g., interviewing job incumbents and supervisors).

The following potential limitations to observation should be kept in mind. First, observation is most appropriate for jobs with physical (as opposed to mental) components and ones with relatively short job cycles (i.e., amount of time required to complete job tasks before repeating them). Second, the method may involve substantial time and cost. Third, the ability of the observer to do a thorough and accurate analysis is open to question; it may be necessary to train observers prior to the job analysis. Fourth, the method will require coordination with, and approval from, many people (e.g., supervisors and incumbents). Finally, the incumbents being observed may distort their behavior during observation in self-serving ways, such as making tasks appear more difficult or time-consuming than they really are.

***Interviews.***   Interviewing job incumbents and others, such as their managers, has many potential advantages. It respects the interviewee's vast source of information. The interview format allows the interviewer to explain the purpose of the job analysis and how the results will be used, thus enhancing likely acceptance of the process by the interviewees. It can be structured in format to ensure standardization of collected information.

As with any job analysis method, the interview is not without potential limitations. It is time-consuming and costly, and this may cause the organization to skimp on it in ways that jeopardize the reliability and content validity of the information gathered. The interview, not providing anonymity, may lead to suspicion and distrust on the part of interviewees. The quality of the information obtained, as well as interviewee acceptance, depends on the skill of the interviewer. The interviewers should thus be carefully selected and trained. Finally, the success of the interview also depends on the skills and abilities of the interviewee, such as the person's verbal communication skills and the ability to recall tasks performed.

*Task Questionnaire.*   A typical task questionnaire contains a lengthy list of task statements that cut across many different job titles and is administered to incumbents (all or samples of them) in these job titles. For each task statement, the respondent is asked to indicate (1) whether the task applies to the respondent's job (respondents should always be given a DNA [does not apply] option) and (2) task importance (e.g., a 1–5 scale rating difficulty or time spent).

A questionnaire-based job analysis tool known as the PAQ is perhaps the single most popular specific job analysis method. The PAQ consists of 300 items and is completed by job incumbents. The items are sorted into six major divisions: (1) information input (e.g., use of written materials), (2) mental processes (e.g., use of reasoning and problem solving), (3) work output (e.g., use of keyboard devices), (4) interpersonal activities (e.g., serving/catering), (5) work situation and job context (e.g., working in low temperatures), and (6) miscellaneous aspects (e.g., irregular hours). After the employees evaluate how well each of the 300 items applies to their jobs, the completed questionnaires are scored by computer and a report is generated that provides scores for the divisions (and more finely grained subdivisions).[20]

The advantages of task questionnaires are numerous. They are standardized in content and format, thus yielding a standardized method of information gathering. They can obtain considerable information from large numbers of people, as well as being economical to administer and score, and the availability of scores creates the opportunity for subsequent statistical analysis. Additionally, task questionnaires are (and should be) completed anonymously, thus enhancing respondent participation, honesty, and acceptance.

The development of task questionnaires like the PAQ has also facilitated the development of linkages between task dimensions and required KSAOs. Some of these developments have involved a technique called synthetic validation, which helps determine the most appropriate types of selection tools for a job.[21] As the databases linking task dimensions to KSAOs have increased in size and scope over time, it has become increasingly possible to know which selection predictors are most appropriate for a given job without having to resort to a local validation study, as will be discussed in Chapter 7.

A task questionnaire is potentially limited in certain ways. The most important limitation pertains to task statement content. Care must be taken to ensure that the questionnaire contains task statements of sufficient content relevance, representativeness, and specificity. This suggests that if a tailor-made questionnaire is to be used, considerable time and resources must be devoted to its development to ensure accurate inclusion of task statements. If a preexisting questionnaire (e.g., the PAQ) is considered, prior to its use the task statement content should be assessed relative to the task content of the jobs to be analyzed.

A second limitation of task questionnaires pertains to potential respondent reactions. Respondents may react negatively if they feel the questionnaire does not contain task statements covering important aspects of their jobs. Respondents may also find completion of the questionnaire to be tedious and boring; this may cause them to commit rating errors. Interpretation and understanding of the task statements may also be problematic for respondents who have reading and comprehension skill deficiencies.

A third limitation is that questionnaires such as the PAQ assume that the incumbent is reasonably intelligent, experienced in the job, and sufficiently educated to evaluate the items. To the extent incumbents are less intelligent, lack experience, or have little education, the familiar dictum "garbage in, garbage out" may apply.

***Committee or Task Force.*** Job analysis is often guided by an ad hoc committee or task force. Members of this group typically include job experts—both managers and employees—as well as an HR representative. They may conduct a number of activities, including (1) reviewing existing information and gathering sample job descriptions, (2) interviewing job incumbents and managers, (3) overseeing the administration of job analysis surveys and analyzing the results, (4) writing task statements, grouping them into task dimensions, and rating the importance of the task dimensions, and (5) identifying KSAOs and rating their importance. A committee or task force brings considerable job analysis expertise to the process, facilitates reliability of judgment through conversation and consensus building, and enhances acceptance of the final results.

***Criteria for Choice of Methods.*** Some explicit choices regarding methods of job analysis need to be made. One set of choices involves deciding whether to use a particular method of information collection. An organization must decide whether to use an off-the-shelf method or its own particular method that is suited to its own needs and circumstances. A second set of choices involves how to blend together a set of methods that will be used in varying ways and degrees in the actual job analysis. Some criteria for guidance in such decisions are shown in Exhibit 4.12. In practice, job analysis is usually conducted through a combination of these methods so that the weaknesses of any one method are offset by the strengths of another.

**EXHIBIT 4.12** **Criteria for Guiding Choice of Job Analysis Methods**

| Method | Sources | Advantages and Disadvantages |
|---|---|---|
| Prior information | Current job descriptions<br>Training manuals<br>Performance appraisals<br>O*NET | Readily available<br>Inexpensive<br>External sources may not match jobs in your organization<br>Focus is on how jobs have been done previously, not how they will be done in the future |
| Observation | Trained job analysts or HR professionals watch incumbents perform the job | Thorough, rich information<br>Does not rely on intermediary information sources<br>Not appropriate for jobs that are largely mental in character<br>Incumbents may behave differently if they know they're being observed |
| Interviews | HR professionals discuss job requirements with job incumbents and managers | Takes the incumbent's knowledge of the position into account<br>Time-consuming and costly<br>Quality depends on the knowledge and ability of the interviewee and skill of the interviewer |
| Task questionnaire | Job incumbents, managers, and HR professionals fill in a standardized form with questions regarding job | Standardized method across a variety of jobs<br>Can combine information from large numbers of incumbents quickly<br>Developing questionnaires can be expensive and time-consuming<br>Requires that incumbents be capable of completing the forms accurately |
| Committee or task force | Managers, representatives from HR, and incumbents meet to discuss job descriptions | Brings expertise of a variety of individuals into the process<br>Increases reliability of the process<br>Enhances acceptance of the final product<br>Significant investment of staff time |

### Sources to Be Used

Choosing sources of information involves considering who will be used to provide the information sought. While this matter is not entirely independent of job analysis methods (e.g., use of a task questionnaire normally requires use of job incumbents as the source), it is treated this way in the sections that follow.

*Job Analyst.*    A job analyst is someone who, by virtue of job title and training, is available and suited to conduct job analyses and to guide the job analysis process. The job analyst is also "out of the loop," being neither manager nor incumbent of the jobs analyzed. Thus, the job analyst brings a combination of expertise and neutrality to the work.

Despite such advantages and appeals, reliance on a job analyst as the job information source is not without potential limitations. First, the analyst may be perceived as an outsider by incumbents and supervisors, a perception that may result in questioning the analyst's job knowledge and expertise, as well as trustworthiness. Second, the job analyst may, in fact, lack detailed knowledge of the jobs to be analyzed, especially in an organization with many different job titles. Lack of knowledge may cause the analyst to bring inaccurate job stereotypes to the analysis process. Finally, having specially designated job analysts (either employees or outside consultants) tends to be expensive.

*Job Incumbents.*    Job incumbents seem like a natural source of information to be used in job analysis, and indeed they are relied on in most job analysis systems. The major advantage of working with incumbents is their familiarity with tasks, KSAOs, and job context. In addition, job incumbents may become more accepting of the job analysis process and its results through their participation in it.

Some skepticism should be maintained about job incumbents as a source of workplace data, as is true for any source. They may lack the knowledge or insights necessary to provide inclusive information, especially if they are probationary or part-time employees. Some employees may also have difficulty describing the tasks involved in their job or being able to infer and articulate the underlying KSAOs necessary for the job. There are also concerns about job incumbents not responding to job analysis surveys; most studies show that fewer than half of job incumbents voluntarily respond to job analysis surveys. Response rates are lower among lower-level employees and those with less education.[22] Another potential limitation of job incumbents as an information source pertains to their motivation to be a willing and accurate source. Feelings of distrust and suspicion may greatly hamper employees' willingness to function capably as sources. For example, incumbents may intentionally fail to report certain tasks as part of their job so that those tasks are not incorporated into the formal job description. Incumbents may also deliberately inflate the importance ratings of tasks in order to make the job appear more difficult than it actually is.

*Supervisors.*   Supervisors are excellent sources for use in job analysis. They not only supervise employees performing the job to be analyzed but also have played a major role in defining it and in adding or deleting job tasks (as in evolving and flexible jobs). Moreover, because supervisors ultimately have to accept the resulting descriptions and specifications for jobs they supervise, including them as a source is a good way to ensure such acceptance.

*Subject Matter Experts.*   Often, job analysts, job incumbents, and supervisors are called subject matter experts (SMEs). Other individuals may also be used as SMEs. These people bring particular expertise to the job analysis process, an expertise not thought to be available through standard sources. Though the exact qualifications for being designated an SME are far from clear, examples of sources so designated include previous jobholders (e.g., recently promoted employees), private consultants, customer/clients, and citizens-at-large for some public sector jobs (e.g., superintendent of schools for a school district). Whatever the sources of SMEs, a common requirement is that they have recent, firsthand knowledge of the job being analyzed.[23]

## Job Analysis Process

Collecting job information through job analysis requires development and use of an overall process. Unfortunately, there is no set or best process to be followed; the process has to be tailor-made to suit the specifics of the situation in which it occurs. Many key issues must be dealt with in the construction and operation of the process.[24] Each of these is briefly commented on next.

*Purpose.*   The purpose(s) of job analysis should be clearly identified and agreed on. Since job analysis is a process designed to yield job information, the organization should ask exactly what job information is desired and why. Here, it is useful to refer back to the job requirements matrix to review the types of information that can be sought and obtained in a job requirements job analysis. Management must decide exactly what types of information are desired (task statements, task dimensions, and so forth) and in what format. Once the desired output and the results of job analysis have been determined, the organization can then plan a process that will yield the desired results.

*Scope.*   The issue of scope involves which job(s) to include in the job analysis. Decisions about actual scope should be based on (1) the importance of the job to the functioning of the organization, (2) the number of job applicants and incumbents, (3) whether the job is entry level and thus subject to constant staffing activity, (4) the frequency with which job requirements (both tasks and KSAOs) change, and (5) the amount of time that has lapsed since the previous job analysis.

***Internal Staff or Consultant.*** The organization may use its own staff to conduct the job analysis or it may procure external consultants. This is a difficult decision because it involves not only the obvious consideration of cost but also many other considerations. Exhibit 4.13 highlights some of these concerns and the trade-offs involved.

***Organization and Coordination.*** Any job analysis project, whether conducted by internal staff or external consultants, requires careful organization and coordination. Two key steps help ensure that this is achieved. First, an organizational

**EXHIBIT 4.13    Factors to Consider in Choosing Between Internal Staff and Consultants for Job Analysis**

| Internal Staff | Consultant |
|---|---|
| Cost of technical or procedural failure is low | Cost of technical or procedural failure is high |
| Project scope is limited | Project scope is comprehensive and/or large |
| Need for job data ongoing | Need for job data is a one-time, isolated event |
| There is a desire to develop internal staff skills in job analysis | There is a need for assured availability of each type and level of job analysis skill |
| Strong management controls are in place to control project costs | Predictability of project cost can depend on adhering to work plan |
| Knowledge of organization's norms, "culture," and jargon are critical | Technical innovativeness and quality are critical |
| Technical credibility of internal staff is high | Leverage of external "expert" status is needed to execute project |
| Process and products of the project are unlikely to be challenged | Process and products of the project are likely to be legally, technically, or politically scrutinized |
| Rational or narrative job analysis methods are desired | Commercial or proprietary job analysis methods are desired |
| Data collected are qualitative | Data collection methods are structured, standardized, and/or quantitative |

Source: D. M. Van De Vort and B. V. Stalder, "Organizing for Job Analysis," in S. Gael (ed.), *The Job Analysis Handbook for Business, Industry and Government.* Copyright © 1988 by John Wiley & Sons, Inc. Reprinted by permission of John Wiley & Sons, Inc.

member should be appointed as project manager for the total process (if consultants are used, they should report to this project manager). The project manager should be assigned overall responsibility for the total project, including its organization and control. Second, the roles and relationships for the various people involved in the project—HR staff, project staff, line managers, and job incumbents—must be clearly established.

***Communication.***   Clear and open communication with all concerned will facilitate the job analysis process. Some employees will liken job analysis to an invasive, exploratory surgical procedure, which, in turn, naturally raises questions in their minds about its purpose, process, and results. These questions and concerns need to be anticipated and addressed forthrightly.

***Work Flow and Time Frame.***   Job analysis involves a mixture of people and paper in a process in which they can become entangled very quickly. The project manager should develop and adhere to a work flowchart that shows the steps to be followed in the conduct of the job analysis. This should be accompanied by a time frame showing critical completion dates for project phases, as well as a final deadline.

***Analysis, Synthesis, and Documentation.***   Once collected, job information must be analyzed and synthesized through the use of various procedural and statistical means. These should be planned in advance and incorporated into the work-flow and time-frame requirements. Likewise, provisions need to be made for preparation of written documents, especially job descriptions and job specifications, and their incorporation into relevant policy and procedure manuals.

***Maintenance of the System.***   Job analysis does not end with completion of the project. Rather, mechanisms must be developed and put into place to maintain the job analysis and information system over time. This is critical because the system will be exposed to numerous influences requiring response and adaptation. Examples include (1) changes in job tasks and KSAOs—additions, deletions, and modifications, (2) job redesign, restructuring, and realignment, and (3) creation of new jobs. In short, job analysis must be thought of and administered as an ongoing organizational process.

***Example of Job Analysis Process.***   Because of the many factors involved, there is no best or required job analysis process. Rather, the process must be designed to fit each particular situation. Exhibit 4.14 shows an example of the job analysis process with a narrow scope, namely, for a single job—that of administrative assistant (secretary). This was a specially conducted job analysis that used multiple methods (prior information, observation, and interviews) and multiple sources (job analyst,

**EXHIBIT 4.14    Example of Job Requirements Job Analysis**

1. Meet with manager of the job, discuss project → 2. Gather existing job information from O*NET, current job description, observation of incumbents → 3. Prepare tentative set of task statements →

4. Review task statements with incumbents and managers; add, delete, rewrite statements → 5. Finalize task statements, get approval from incumbents and managers → 6. Formulate task dimensions, assign tasks to dimensions, determine % of time spent (importance) for each dimension →

7. Infer necessary KSAOs, develop tentative list → 8. Review KSAOs with incumbents and managers; add, delete, and rewrite KSAOs → 9. Finalize KSAOs, get approval from incumbents and manager →

10. Develop job requirements matrix and/or job description in usable format → 11. Provide matrix or job description to parties (e.g., incumbents, managers, HR department) → 12. Use matrix or job description in staffing activities, such as communicating with recruits and recruiters, developing the selection plan →

job incumbents, and supervisors). A previous job holder (SME) conducted the job analysis, and it took about 20 hours over a 30-day period to conduct and prepare a written job description as the output of the process.

## COMPETENCY-BASED JOB ANALYSIS

Job requirements job analysis is a technique that was originally developed in the first half of the twentieth century to catalog the requirements for well-defined job roles with very specific and observable characteristics that would be the same across many organizations. As the pace of change increased, new technology rendered many of these jobs obsolete, and organizations adopted more flexible roles; thus, the relevance of job requirements job analysis came into question.[25] As a result, the competency-based type of job analysis came into being. Usage of competencies and competency models in staffing reflects a desire to (1) connote job requirements in ways that extend beyond the specific job itself, (2) design and implement staffing programs focused around competencies (rather than just specific jobs) as a way of increasing staffing flexibility in job assignments, and (3) make it easier to adapt jobs to a changing organizational context.

## Overview

The chief difference between job requirements and competency-based job analyses is the direction of information flow. The job requirements analysis begins by looking at very specific tasks and then aggregates these from the bottom up to form jobs and job categories that are found throughout an organization. Due to its linkage with overall organizational capacities, competency-based job analysis has become closely aligned with the strategic perspective on HR management. Because of this explicit link to organizational strategy, and the use of terminology that is consistent with strategic plans, most job analysts in the field find that executives are much more supportive of competency-based analysis relative to job requirements analysis.[26]

Over time, many techniques have been developed that facilitate competency-based job analysis, and it has progressively become a much more rigorous approach than it once was. From this development, a standard set of best practices for conducting and using a competency analysis perspective has emerged.[27] The competency analysis begins by considering the organization's goals and strategies and then determines how each job corresponds to these strategic goals. Competency models should explicitly consider the organizational context. This is a key point, because the top-down approach of competency modeling makes it much easier to address how jobs fit together and complement one another to produce goods and services compared to the task focus of job requirements job analysis. Finally, because competency models are tied to the organization's strategy, it is important to emphasize how requirements can potentially change over time. The competencies assessed in the process should be sufficiently general to address both present and future organizational needs.

## Nature of Competencies

A competency is an underlying characteristic of an individual that contributes to job or role performance and to organizational success.[28] Competencies specific to a particular job are the familiar KSAO requirements established through job requirements job analysis. Competency requirements may extend beyond job-specific ones to those of multiple jobs, general job categories, or the entire organization. These competencies are much more general or generic KSAOs, such as technical expertise or adaptability. A competency model is a combination of the several competencies deemed necessary for a particular job or role.

Despite the strong similarities between competencies and KSAOs, there are two notable differences. First, competencies may be job spanning, meaning that they contribute to success in multiple jobs. Members of a work team, for example, may each hold specific jobs within the team but may be subject to job-spanning competency requirements, such as adaptability and teamwork orientation. Such requirements ensure that team members will interact successfully with one another and will even perform portions of others' jobs if necessary. As another example, competency requirements may span jobs within the same category, such as sales jobs or managerial jobs. All sales jobs may have product knowledge as a competency requirement, and all managerial jobs may require planning and results orientation. Such requirements allow for greater flexibility in job placements and job assignments within the category.

Second, competencies can contribute not only to job performance but also to organizational success. These are very general competencies applicable to, and required for, all jobs. They serve to align requirements for all jobs with the mission and goals of the organization. A restaurant, for example, may have "customer focus" as a competency requirement for all jobs as a way of indicating that servicing the needs of its customers is a key component of all jobs.

### Competency Example

An illustration of the competency approach to job requirements is shown in Exhibit 4.15. The Green Care Corporation produces several lawn maintenance products. The organization is in a highly competitive industry. To survive and grow, it has product innovation and product reliability as its core mission; its goals are to achieve 10% annual growth in revenues and 2% growth in market share. To help fulfill its mission and goals, the organization has established four general (strategic) workforce competencies—creativity/innovation, technical expertise, customer focus, and results orientation. These requirements are part of every job in the organization. At the business unit (gas lawn mowers) level, the orga-

**EXHIBIT 4.15    Examples of Competencies**

Company: Green Care Corporation
Products:  Gas and electric lawn mowers, gas and electric weed whackers, manual lawn
           edgers, electric hedge trimmers

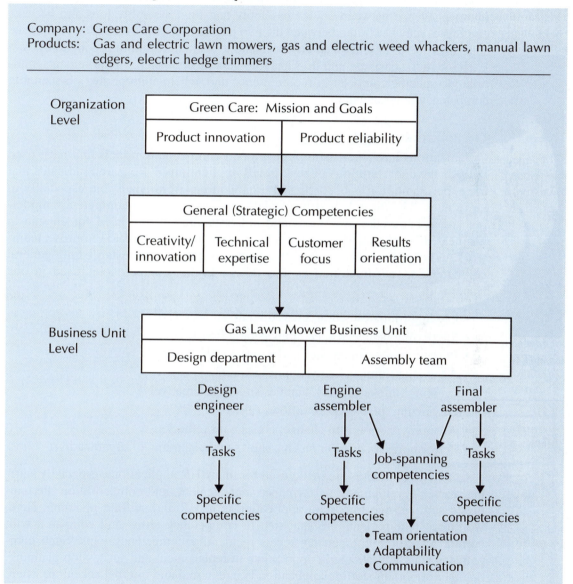

nization has also established job-specific and job-spanning requirements. Some
jobs, such as design engineer, are traditional or slowly evolving jobs and, as such,
have only job-specific KSAO or competency requirements. Because the products
are assembled via team processes, jobs within the assembly team (such as engine
assembler or final assembler) have both job-specific and job-spanning competency

requirements. The job-spanning competencies—team orientation, adaptability, and communication—are general and behavioral. They are necessary because of task interdependence between engine assembly and final assembly jobs and because employees may be shifted between the two jobs in order to cover sudden employee shortages due to unscheduled absences and to maintain smooth production flows. Each job in the business unit thus has four general competency requirements, multiple job-specific competency requirements, and, where appropriate, job-spanning competency requirements.

### Organization Usage

Organizations have increasingly developed competency models and have used them as the underpinnings of several HR applications.[29] Research indicates that the experimentation is occurring in organizations of all sizes, but especially in large ones. The three key strategic HR reasons for doing competency modeling are to (1) create awareness and understanding of the need for change in business, (2) enhance the skill levels in the workforce, and (3) improve teamwork and coordination. Most of the emphasis has been on establishing general competencies, as illustrated by the "Great Eight" competencies used in one framework:[30]

- Leading (initiates action, gives direction)
- Supporting (shows respect, puts people first)
- Presenting (communicates and networks effectively)
- Analyzing (thinks clearly, applies expertise)
- Creating (thinks broadly, handles situations creatively)
- Organizing (plans ahead, follows rules)
- Adapting (responds to change, copes with setbacks)
- Performing (focuses on results, shows understanding of organization)

Competency models are being used for many HR applications, especially staffing, career development, performance management, and compensation. Pertaining to staffing, one important application is in HR and staffing planning. Here, workforce requirements are specified in competency terms and compared with current workforce competency levels to identify competency gaps. Such comparisons may be particularly appropriate in replacement and succession planning. Another important staffing application is in external and internal selection, where applicants are assessed not only for job-specific competencies but also for general competencies. For external hiring, competency-based interviews with applicants are conducted to gauge general competencies as a key factor in selection decisions and then in job placement decisions for those hired. For promotion decisions, competency-based interviews are used in conjunction with supervisory assessments of promotability.[31]

## Collecting Competency Information

Techniques and processes for collecting competency information are continually being developed.[32] General competencies at the organization (strategic) level are likely to be established by top management, with guidance from strategic HR managers. At a minimum, effective establishment of general competency requirements would seem to demand the following. First, it is crucial that the organization establish its mission and goals prior to determining competency requirements; this will help ensure that general competencies are derived from knowledge of mission and goals, much as job-specific competencies are derived from previously identified job tasks. Second, the general competencies should be truly important at all job levels so that their usage as job requirements will focus and align all jobs with the organization's mission and goals. This principle also holds in the case where general competency requirements are at the strategic business unit or subunit level instead of the organization level. Third, all general competencies should have specific behavioral definitions, not just labels. These definitions provide substance, meaning, and guidance to all concerned.

For job-spanning competencies, these definitions will necessarily be more task specific. To ensure effective identification and definition, several tasks should be undertaken. First, it is crucial to know the major tasks for which the competencies are to be established, meaning that some form of job analysis should occur first. For now, the organization will have to craft that process since we lack prototypes or best-practice examples as guidance. Second, SMEs familiar with all the jobs or roles to which the competencies will apply should be part of the process. Third, careful definition of the competencies will be necessary. Acquiring definitions from other organizations, consultants, or O*NET will be useful here. Training programs can improve the quality of competency information. Specifically, managers who attended a program that included an explanation of the competency modeling approach, specific guidance in translating the required behaviors of a role into competencies, and feedback on the quality of practice exercises produced competency data that were more accurate, more detailed, and more consistent across raters relative to competency data produced by managers who had not received training.[33]

When competency modeling first appeared, staffing experts expressed concern about the lack of agreement across multiple raters when evaluating the same job's competencies. One rater might claim that a job entailed a high level of interpersonal skill, while another might emphasize the analytical demands of the job. Increasingly, it has been recognized that this inconsistency might be an accurate reflection of the many ways people can do the same job.[34] In particular, in complex jobs with high levels of personal autonomy and discretion, different job incumbents engage in completely different behaviors requiring completely different skills. Competency data may be more likely to show differences across raters than job requirements analysis because competency analysis is more likely to focus on complex jobs with high autonomy. Indeed, evidence suggests that decisions based on well-designed and implemented competency-based job analyses can be as rigorous and accurate as those based on job requirements approaches.[35]

# JOB REWARDS

In the person/job match model, jobs are composed of requirements and rewards. The focus so far in this chapter has been on job requirements vis-à-vis the discussion of job analysis. Attention now turns to job rewards. Providing and using rewards is a key staffing strategy for motivating several HR outcomes—applicant attraction, employee performance, and employee retention in particular. Successfully matching rewards provided with rewards desired will be critical in attaining the HR outcomes. Doing so first requires specifying the types of rewards potentially available and desired.

## Types of Rewards

Organizations and jobs provide a wide variety of rewards. It is common to classify each reward as either extrinsic or intrinsic in nature. Extrinsic rewards are tangible factors external to the job itself that are explicitly designed and granted to employees by representatives of the organization (e.g., pay, benefits, work schedule, advancement, job security). Intrinsic rewards are the intangibles that are more internal to the job itself and experienced by the employee as an outgrowth of actually doing the job and being a member of the organization (e.g., variety in work duties, autonomy, feedback, coworker and supervisor relations).[36]

## Employee Value Proposition

The totality of rewards, both extrinsic and intrinsic, associated with the job constitutes the employee value proposition (EVP).[37] The EVP is akin to the "package" or "bundle" of rewards provided to employees and to which employees respond by joining, performing, and remaining with the organization. It is the "deal" or "bargain" struck between the organization and the employee, first as a promise to the prospective employee, later as a reality to the actual new employee, and later still as a new deal as the EVP changes due to reward improvements and/or internal job changes. The EVP thus functions as a glue that binds the employee and the organization, with the employee providing certain behaviors (attraction, performance, retention, and so forth) in exchange for the EVP.

The challenge to the organization is to create EVPs for various employee groups that, on average, are both attractive and affordable (how to create an individual EVP in the form of a formal job offer to a prospective employee is considered in Chapter 12). No reward, extrinsic or intrinsic, is costless, so the organization must figure out what it can afford as it creates its EVPs. Regardless of cost, however, the rewards must also be attractive to those for whom they are intended, so attraction and cost must be considered jointly when developing EVPs. The dual affordable-attractive requirements for EVPs may create some potential problems: wrong magnitude, wrong mix, or not distinctive.[38]

Wrong magnitude refers to a package of rewards that is either too small or too great monetarily. To the prospective or current employee, too small a package may be viewed as simply inadequate, noncompetitive, or an insult, none of which are desirable perceptions to be creating. Such perceptions may arise very early in the applicant's job search, before the organization is even aware of the applicant, due to word-of-mouth information from others (e.g., former applicants or employees) or information obtained about the organization, such as through its print or electronic recruitment information. Alternatively, too small a package may not become an issue until fairly late in the job search process, as additional bits of reward package information become known to the applicant. Regardless of when the too-small perceptions emerge, they can be deal killers that lead the person to self-select out of consideration for the job, turn down the job, or quit. While too-small packages may be unattractive, they often have the virtue of being affordable for the organization.

Too large a package creates affordability problems for the organization. Those problems may not surface immediately, but long term they can threaten the organization's financial viability and possibly even its survival. Affordability problems may be particularly acute in service-providing organizations, where employee compensation costs are a substantial percentage of total operating costs.

Wrong mix refers to a situation in which the composition of the rewards package is out of sync with the preferences of prospective or current employees. A package that provides excellent retirement benefits and long-term performance incentives to a relatively young and mobile workforce, for example, is most likely a wrong mix. Its attraction and retention power in all likelihood is minimal. It might also be relatively expensive to provide.

Not distinctive refers to individual rewards packages that are viewed as ho-hum in nature. They have no uniqueness or special appeal that would either win or retain employees. They do not signal anything distinctive about the organization or give the job seeker or employee any special reason to think the "deal" is one that simply cannot be passed up.

In short, creating successful EVPs is a challenge, and the results can have important implications for workforce attraction, retention, and cost. To create successful EVPs, the organization should seek to systematically collect information about rewards that are important or unimportant to employees and the extent to which these rewards are currently provided.

## Collecting Job Rewards Information

Unlike job analysis as a mechanism for collecting job requirements information, mechanisms for collecting job rewards information are more fragmentary. Nonetheless, several things can be done to assess employee preferences and the rewards employees associate with their work. Armed with knowledge about employee preferences and perceived rewards, the organization can begin to build EVPs that are of the right magnitude, mix, and distinctiveness. Learning about job rewards involves looking both within and outside the organization. It is important to note that a meaningful job rewards analysis must be specific to each job category—overall preferences and rewards in the organization as a whole will tend to be too vague and will not be useful for assessing person/job fit.

### Within the Organization

To learn about employee reward perceptions within the organization, interviews with employees, or surveys, might be used.

*Interviews With Employees.* The interview approach requires decisions about who will guide the process, interview content, sampling confidentiality, data recording and analysis, and reporting of the results. The following are a few suggestions to guide each of those decisions. First, a person with special expertise in the employee interview process should guide the total process. This could be a person within the HR department, a person outside HR with the expertise (such as in marketing research), or an outside consultant. The person guiding the process may be the only interviewer; if not, he or she should carefully select and train those who will do the interviews, including supervising a dry run of the interview.

Second, the interviews should be structured and guided. The major content areas and specific questions should be decided in advance, tested on a small sample of employees as to their clarity and wording, and then placed in a formal interview protocol to be used by the interviewer. Potential questions are shown in Exhibit 4.16. Note that the major content areas covered in the interview are rewards offered, reward magnitude, reward mix, and reward distinctiveness.

Third, employees from throughout the organization should be part of the sample. In small organizations, it might be possible to include all employees; in larger organizations, random samples of employees will be necessary. When sampling, it is important to include employees from all job categories, organizational units, and organizational levels.

Fourth, it is strongly recommended that the interviews be treated as confidential and that the responses of individuals be seen only by those recording and analyzing the data. At the same time, it would be useful to gather (with their permission) interviewees' demographic information (e.g., age, gender) and organizational information (e.g., job title, organizational unit) since this will permit breakouts of responses during data analysis. Such breakouts will be very useful in decisions about whether to create separate EVPs for separate employee groups or organizational units.

*Surveys of Employees.* A survey of employees should proceed along the same lines, following many of the same recommendations, as for an employee interview process. The biggest difference will be the mechanism for gathering the data—

---

**EXHIBIT 4.16**  **Examples of Job Rewards Interview Questions**

**Rewards Offered**
- What are the most rewarding elements of your job? Consider both the work itself and the pay and benefits associated with your job.
- Looking ahead, are there any changes you can think of that would make your job more rewarding?

**Reward Magnitude**
- Overall, do you think the level of complexity and challenge in your job is too much, too little, or about right, compared to other jobs in the organization?
- Describe the amount of potential for growth and development in your job.
- Do you feel like the pay and benefits provided for your job are adequate for the work you do? If not, what would you change?

**Reward Mix**
- If you could change the mix of rewards provided in your job, what would you add?
- Of the rewards associated with your job, which two are the most important to you?
- What types of rewards associated with your job are irrelevant to you?

**Reward Distinctiveness**
- Which rewards that you receive in your job are you most likely to tell others about?
- Which of our rewards really stand out to you? To job applicants?
- What rewards could we start offering that would be unique?

namely, a written set of questions with response scales rather than a verbally administered set of questions with open-ended responses. To construct the survey, a listing of the rewards to be included on the survey must be developed. These could be chosen from a listing of the job's current extrinsic rewards, plus some questions about intrinsic rewards for the job. An example of a partial employee reward preferences survey is shown in Exhibit 4.17. Note that questions involve both extrinsic and intrinsic rewards and ask about the importance of various rewards as well as the extent to which each job provides these rewards.

As with interviews, it is recommended that a person with special expertise guide the project, that the survey content be specially constructed (rather than canned), that sampling include employees throughout the organization, that employees be assured of confidentiality, that thorough analysis of results be undertaken, and that reports of findings be prepared for organizational representatives.

***Which to Use?***   Should the organization opt to use interviews, surveys, or both? The advantages of an interview are numerous: it is of a personal nature; employees

**EXHIBIT 4.17**   Example of Job Rewards Survey

To what extent are the following job rewards important to you?

| | Not at All Important | Unimportant | Somewhat Important | Important | Very Important |
|---|---|---|---|---|---|
| **Extrinsic Rewards** | | | | | |
| Base pay | 1 | 2 | 3 | 4 | 5 |
| Incentive pay | 1 | 2 | 3 | 4 | 5 |
| Health insurance | 1 | 2 | 3 | 4 | 5 |
| **Intrinsic Rewards** | | | | | |
| Using my skills | 1 | 2 | 3 | 4 | 5 |
| Doing significant tasks | 1 | 2 | 3 | 4 | 5 |
| Relationships with coworkers | 1 | 2 | 3 | 4 | 5 |

To what extent does your job provide the following rewards to you?

| | Very Low Extent | Low Extent | Moderate Extent | High Extent | Very High Extent |
|---|---|---|---|---|---|
| **Extrinsic Rewards** | | | | | |
| Base pay | 1 | 2 | 3 | 4 | 5 |
| Incentive pay | 1 | 2 | 3 | 4 | 5 |
| Health insurance | 1 | 2 | 3 | 4 | 5 |
| **Intrinsic Rewards** | | | | | |
| Using my skills | 1 | 2 | 3 | 4 | 5 |
| Doing significant tasks | 1 | 2 | 3 | 4 | 5 |
| Relationships with coworkers | 1 | 2 | 3 | 4 | 5 |

are allowed to respond in their own words; it is possible to create questions that probe perceptions regarding reward magnitude, mix, and distinctiveness; and a very rich set of data is obtained that provides insights beyond mere rating-scale responses. On the downside, interviews are costly to schedule and conduct, data analysis is messy and time-consuming, and statistical summaries and analysis of the data are difficult. Surveys are easier to administer (especially online), and they permit statistical summaries and analyses that are very helpful in interpreting responses. The biggest downsides to surveys are the lack of richness of data and the difficulty in constructing questions that tap into employees' preferences about reward magnitude, mix, and distinctiveness.

Assuming adequate resources and expertise, a combined interview and survey approach would be best. This would allow the organization to capitalize on the unique strengths of each approach, as well as offset some of the weaknesses of each. In such cases, interviews usually are done first and then the information gathered from the open-ended responses is used as a springboard to develop specific survey questions.

A final cautionary note is that both interviews and surveys of current employees miss out on two other groups from whom reward preference information would be useful. The first group is departing or departed employees, who may have left due to dissatisfaction with the EVP. Chapter 14 discusses the exit interview as a procedure for learning about this group. The second group is potential job applicants. Presumably the organization could conduct interviews and surveys with this group, but that could be administratively challenging (especially with Internet applicants). Additionally, applicants might feel they are "tipping their hand" to the organization in terms of what they desire or would accept in a job offer. The more common way to learn about applicant reward preferences is from surveys of employees outside the organization, who might represent the types of applicants the organization will encounter.

## Outside the Organization

*Other Employees.*   Data on the reward preferences of employees outside the organization are available from surveys of employees in other organizations. To the extent these employees are similar to the organization's own applicants and employees, the data will likely provide a useful barometer of preferences. An example is the Job Satisfaction survey conducted by the Society for Human Resource Management (SHRM). It administered an online survey to a national random sample of 600 employees. The employees rated the importance of 25 extrinsic and intrinsic rewards to their overall satisfaction on a 1–5 (very unimportant to very important) scale. The percentage of employees rating each reward as "very important" is shown in Exhibit 4.18.

Possibly reflecting employee anxiety surrounding the poor economic conditions in 2010, job security was ranked as the top aspect of satisfaction. Next came the extrinsic reward of "benefits," which was closely followed by intrinsic rewards of "opportunities to use skills and abilities" and "the work itself." Note that relationships with supervisors, recognition, and communication were all rated highly.

**EXHIBIT 4.18**  "Very Important" Aspects of Employee Job Satisfaction (Employees)

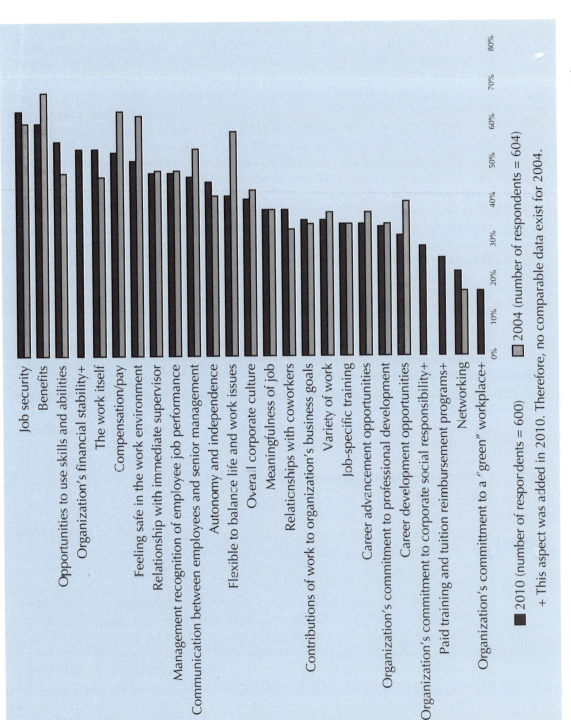

SOURCE: Society for Human Resource Management, *2010 Employee Job Satisfaction* (Alexandria, VA: author), p. 7; E. Essen, *Job Satisfaction Series* (Alexandria, VA: Society for Human Resource Management, 2004), p. 156. Used with permission.

Not shown in Exhibit 4.18 are two other important findings. First, a sample of HR professionals was asked to predict the importance that employees attached to the rewards, and the HR professionals' predictions did not correspond all that closely to the actual employee ratings. A second finding was that there were some differences in reward importance as a function of employee age, tenure, gender, and industry; these differences, however, were relatively small.

Additional information regarding the rewards associated with jobs can be found in O*NET. Every job in O*NET has accompanying salary information. There is also a set of work values associated with each job, evaluating the extent to which a job provides intrinsic rewards like achievement, independence, recognition, relationships, support, and working conditions. As with other O*NET information, these data are collected at the occupational level rather than the job level, so they will need to be supplemented with information from the organization as well.

***Organizational Practices.*** A less direct way to assess the importance of rewards to employees is to examine the actual rewards that other organizations provide their employees. The assumption here is that these organizations are attuned to their employees' preferences and try to provide rewards that are consistent with them. Since pay and benefits loom large in most employees' reward preferences, it is particularly important to become knowledgeable of other organizations' pay and benefit practices to assist in the development of the EVP.

The best single source of pay and benefit information comes from the National Compensation Survey, conducted by the Bureau of Labor Statistics within the Department of Labor. The pay part of the survey reports average pay for employees, broken out by occupation, private-public sector, organization size, and geographic area. The benefits part of the survey presents detailed data about the percentage of employees who have access to a benefit or the average benefit provision. Data about the following benefits are provided: retirement, health care coverage (medical, dental, and vision) and required employee contributions, short- and long-term disability, paid holidays, paid vacation, child care, flexible workplace, wellness programs, and several others. The data are broken out by occupation, industry, and geographic area.

Another important source of information about benefits is the SHRM Annual Benefits Survey. It provides very detailed information about specific benefits provided in each of the following areas: family friendliness, housing and relocation, health care and wellness, personal services, financial, business travel, leave, and other benefits. The data are broken out by organization size.

## LEGAL ISSUES

Job analysis plays a crucial role in establishing the foundations for staffing activities, and that role continues from a legal perspective. Job analysis becomes intimately involved in court cases involving the job relatedness of staffing activities.

It also occupies a prominent position in the Uniform Guidelines on Employee Selection Procedures (UGESP). Additionally, the Americans With Disabilities Act (ADA) requires that the organization determine the essential functions of each job, and job analysis can play a pivotal role in that process. The job requirements matrix and its development are very relevant to these issues.

## Job Relatedness and Court Cases

In equal employment opportunity and affirmative action (EEO/AA) court cases, the organization is confronted with the need to justify its challenged staffing practices as being job related. Common sense suggests that this requires the organization to conduct some type of job analysis to identify job requirements. If the case involves an organization's defense of its selection procedures, the UGESP require conducting a job analysis. In addition, specific features or characteristics of the job analysis make a difference in the organization's defense. Specifically, an examination of court cases indicates that for purposes of legal defensibility the organization should conform to the following recommendations:

1. "Job analysis must be performed and must be for the job for which the selection instrument is to be utilized.
2. Analysis of the job should be in writing.
3. Job analysts should describe in detail the procedure used.
4. Job data should be collected from a variety of current sources by knowledgeable job analysts.
5. Sample size should be large and representative of the jobs for which the selection instrument is used.
6. Tasks, duties, and activities should be included in the analysis.
7. The most important tasks should be represented in the selection device.
8. Competency levels of job performance for entry-level jobs should be specified.
9. Knowledge, skills, and abilities should be specified, particularly if a content validation model is followed."[39]

These recommendations are consistent with our view of job analysis as the basic foundation for staffing activities. Moreover, even though these recommendations were made many years ago, there is little reason to doubt or modify any of them on the basis of more recent court cases.

## Essential Job Functions

Recall that under the ADA, the organization must not discriminate against a qualified individual with a disability who can perform the "essential functions" of the job, with or without reasonable accommodation. This requirement raises three questions: What are essential functions? What is the evidence of essential functions? What is the role of job analysis?

## Essential Functions

The ADA employment regulations provide the following statements about essential functions:

1. "The term essential functions refers to the fundamental job duties of the employment position the individual with a disability holds or desires. The term essential function does not include the marginal functions of the position; and
2. A job function may be considered essential for any of several reasons, including but not limited to the following:
   1. The function may be essential because the reason the position exists is to perform the function;
   2. The function may be essential because of the limited number of employees available among whom the performance of that job function can be distributed; and/or
   3. The function may be highly specialized so that the incumbent in the position is hired for his or her expertise or ability to perform the particular function."

## Evidence of Essential Functions

The employment regulations go on to indicate what constitutes evidence that any particular function is in fact an essential one. That evidence includes, but is not limited to, the following:

1. The employer's judgment as to which functions are essential
2. Written job descriptions, prepared before advertising the job or interviewing applicants for the job
3. The amount of time spent on the job performing the function
4. The consequences of not requiring the incumbent to perform the function
5. The terms of a collective bargaining agreement
6. The work experience of past incumbents in the job
7. The current work experience of incumbents in similar jobs

## Role of Job Analysis

What role(s) might job analysis play in identifying essential functions and establishing evidence of their being essential? The employment regulations are silent on this question. However, the Equal Employment Opportunity Commission (EEOC) has provided substantial and detailed assistance to organizations to deal with this and many other issues under the ADA.[40] The specific statements regarding job analysis and essential functions of the job are shown in Exhibit 4.19.

Examination of the statements in Exhibit 4.19 suggests the following. First, while job analysis is not required by law as a means of establishing the essential functions of a job, it is strongly recommended. Second, the job analysis should focus on tasks associated with the job. Where KSAOs are studied or specified,

---

**EXHIBIT 4.19**   **Job Analysis and Essential Functions of the Job**

The ADA does not require that an employer conduct a job analysis or any particular form of job analysis to identify the essential functions of a job. The information provided by a job analysis may or may not be helpful in properly identifying essential job functions, depending on how it is conducted.

The term "job analysis" generally is used to describe a formal process in which information about a specific job or occupation is collected and analyzed. Formal job analysis may be conducted by a number of different methods. These methods obtain different kinds of information that is used for different purposes. Some of these methods will not provide information sufficient to determine if an individual with a disability is qualified to perform "essential" job functions.

**For example:** One kind of formal job analysis looks at specific job tasks and classifies jobs according to how these tasks deal with data, people, and objects. This type of job analysis is used to set wage rates for various jobs; however, it may not be adequate to identify the essential functions of a *particular* job, as required by the ADA. Another kind of job analysis looks at the kinds of knowledge, skills, and abilities that are necessary to perform a job. This type of job analysis is used to develop selection criteria for various jobs. The information from this type of analysis sometimes helps to measure the importance of certain skills, knowledge and abilities, but it does not take into account the fact that people with disabilities often can perform essential functions using other skills and abilities.

Some job analysis methods ask current employees and their supervisors to rate the importance of general characteristics necessary to perform a job, such as "strength," "endurance," or "intelligence," without linking these characteristics to *specific* job functions or specific tasks that are part of a function. Such general information may not identify, for example, whether upper body or lower body strength is required, or whether muscular endurance or cardiovascular endurance is needed to perform a particular job function. Such information, by itself, would not be sufficient to determine whether an individual who has particular limitations can perform an essential function with or without an accommodation.

As already stated, the ADA does not require a formal job analysis or any particular method of analysis to identify the essential functions of a job. A small employer may wish to conduct an informal analysis by observing and consulting with people who perform the job, or have previously performed it, and their supervisors. If possible, it is advisable to observe and consult with several workers under a range of conditions, to get a better idea of all job functions and the different ways they may be performed. Production records and workloads also may be relevant factors to consider.

*(continued)*

**EXHIBIT 4.19   Continued**

To identify essential job functions under the ADA, a job analysis should focus on the purpose of the job and the importance of actual job functions in achieving this purpose. Evaluating importance may include consideration of the frequency with which a function is performed, the amount of time spent on the function, and the consequences if the function is not performed. The analysis may include information on the work environment (such as unusual heat, cold, humidity, dust, toxic substances, or stress factors). The job analysis may contain information on the manner in which a job currently is performed, but should not conclude that ability to perform the job in that manner is an essential function, unless there is no other way to perform the function without causing undue hardship. A job analysis will be most helpful for purposes of the ADA if it focuses on the results or outcome of a function, not solely on the way it customarily is performed.

**For example:**
- An essential function of a computer programmer job might be described as "ability to develop programs that accomplish necessary objectives," rather than "ability to manually write programs." Although a person currently performing the job may write these programs by hand, that is not the essential function, because programs can be developed directly on the computer.
- If a job requires mastery of information contained in technical manuals, this essential function would be "ability to learn technical material," rather than "ability to read technical manuals." People with visual and other reading impairments could perform this function using other means, such as audiotapes.
- A job that requires objects to be moved from one place to another should state this essential function. The analysis may note that the person in the job "lifts 50-pound cartons to a height of 3 or 4 feet and loads them into truck-trailers 5 hours daily," but should not identify the "ability to manually lift and load 50-pound cartons" as an essential function unless this is the only method by which the function can be performed without causing an undue hardship.

A job analysis that is focused on outcomes or results also will be helpful in establishing appropriate qualification standards, developing job descriptions, conducting interviews, and selecting people in accordance with ADA requirements. It will be particularly helpful in identifying accommodations that will enable an individual with specific functional abilities and limitations to perform the job.

SOURCE: Equal Employment Opportunity Commission, *Technical Assistance Manual for the Employment Provisions (Title I) of the Americans With Disabilities Act* (Washington, DC: author, 1992), pp. II-18 to II-20.

they should be derived from an explicit consideration of their probable links to the essential tasks. Third, with regard to tasks, the focus should be on the tasks themselves and the outcome or results of the tasks, rather than the methods by which they are performed. Finally, the job analysis should be useful in identifying potential reasonable accommodations.[41]

## SUMMARY

Organizations design and use various types of jobs—as jobs change and evolve, new design approaches are sometimes needed. All design approaches result in job content in the form of job requirements and rewards. Job analysis is described as the process used to gather, analyze, synthesize, and report information about job content. The job requirements approach to job analysis focuses on job-specific tasks, KSAOs, and job context. Competency-based job analysis seeks to identify more general KSAOs that apply across jobs and roles. The job rewards approach focuses on understanding the outcomes of work for employees.

The job requirements approach is guided by the job requirements matrix. The matrix calls for information about tasks and task dimensions, as well as their importance. In a parallel fashion, it requires information about KSAOs required for the tasks, plus indications about the importance of those KSAOs. The final component of the matrix deals with numerous elements of the job context.

When gathering the information called for by the job requirements matrix, the organization is confronted with a multitude of choices. Those choices are shown to revolve around various job analysis methods, sources, and processes. The organization must choose from among these; all have advantages and disadvantages associated with them. The choices should be guided by a concern for the accuracy and acceptability of the information being gathered.

Competency-based job analysis seeks to identify general competencies (KSAOs) necessary for all jobs because the competencies support the organization's mission and goals. Within work units, other general competencies (job-spanning KSAOs) may also be established that cut across multiple jobs. Potential techniques and processes for collecting competency information were suggested.

Jobs offer a variety of rewards, both extrinsic and intrinsic. The totality of these rewards constitutes the EVP. To help form EVPs, it is necessary to collect information about employee reward preferences and rewards given to employees at other organizations. Numerous techniques for doing this are available.

From a legal perspective, job analysis is very important in creating staffing systems and practices that comply with EEO/AA laws and regulations. The employer must ensure (or be able to show) that its practices are job related. This requires not only conducting a job requirements job analysis but also using a process that itself has defensible characteristics. Under the ADA, the organization must identify the essential functions of the job. Though this does not require a job analysis, the organization should strongly consider it as one of the tools to be used. Over time, we will learn more about how job analysis is treated under the ADA.

## DISCUSSION QUESTIONS

1. What is the purpose of each type of job analysis, and how can the three types described in this chapter be combined to produce an overall understanding of work in an organization?
2. How should task statements be written, and what sorts of problems might you encounter in asking a job incumbent to write these statements?
3. Would it be better to first identify task dimensions and then create specific task statements for each dimension, or should task statements be identified first and then used to create task dimensions?
4. What would you consider when trying to decide what criteria (e.g., percentage of time spent) to use for gathering indications about task importance?
5. What are the advantages and disadvantages of using multiple methods of job analysis for a particular job? Multiple sources?
6. What are the advantages and disadvantages of identifying and using general competencies to guide staffing activities?
7. Referring back to Exhibit 4.18, why do you think HR professionals were not able to accurately predict the importance of many rewards to employees? What are the implications for creating the EVP?

## ETHICAL ISSUES

1. It has been suggested that ethical conduct be formally incorporated as a general competency requirement for any job within the organization. Discuss the pros and cons of this suggestion.
2. Assume you are assisting in the conduct of job analysis as an HR department representative. You have encountered several managers who want to delete certain tasks and KSAOs from the formal job description that have to do with employee safety, even though they clearly are job requirements. How should you handle this situation?

## APPLICATIONS

### Conducting a Job Requirements or Job Rewards Job Analysis

Job analysis is defined as "the process of studying jobs in order to gather, synthesize, and report information about job content." Based on the person/job match model, job content consists of job requirements (tasks and KSAOs) and job rewards (extrinsic and intrinsic). The goal of a job requirements job analysis is to produce the job requirements matrix.

Choose a job you want to study and conduct either a job requirements or job rewards job analysis. Write a report of your project that includes the following sections:

1. The job—What job (job title) did you choose to study and why?
2. The methods used—What methods did you use (prior information, observation, interviews, task questionnaires, committee, combinations of these), and exactly how did you use them?
3. The sources used—What sources did you use (job analyst, job incumbent, supervisor, SMEs, or combinations of these), and exactly how did you use them?
4. The process used—How did you go about gathering, synthesizing, and reporting the information? Refer back to Exhibit 4.14 for an example.
5. The matrix—Present the actual job requirements matrix.

## Maintaining Job Descriptions

The InAndOut, Inc., company provides warehousing and fulfillment services (order receiving and filling) to small publishers of books with small print runs (number of copies of a book printed). After the books are printed and bound at a printing facility, they are shipped to InAndOut for handling. The books are initially received by handlers who unload them from the trucks, place them on pallets, and move them via forklifts and conveyors to their assigned storage space in the warehouse. The handlers also retrieve books and take them to the shipping area when orders are received. The shippers package the books, place them in cartons, and load them onto delivery trucks (to take to air or ground transportation providers). Book orders are taken by customer service representatives via printed, phone, or electronic (e-mail, fax) forms. New accounts are generated by marketing representatives, who also service existing accounts. Order clerks handle all the internal paperwork. All these employees report to either the supervisor of operations or the supervisor of customer service, who in turn reports to the general manager.

The owner and president of InAndOut, Inc., Alta Fossom, is independently wealthy and delegates all day-to-day management matters to the general manager, Marvin Olson. Alta requires, however, that Marvin clear any new ideas or initiatives with her before taking action. The company is growing and changing rapidly, along with adding many new, and often larger, accounts. Publishers are demanding more services and faster order fulfillment. Information technology is constantly being upgraded, and new machinery (forklifts, computer-assisted conveyor system) is being utilized. The workforce is growing in size to meet the business growth. There are now 37 employees, and Marvin expects to hire another 15–20 new employees within the next year.

Job descriptions for the company were originally written by a consultant about eight years ago. They have never been revised and are hopelessly outdated. The job of marketing representative does not even have a job description, because the job was created only five years ago. As general manager, Marvin is responsible for all HR management matters, but he has little time to devote to them. To get a better grip on HR responsibilities, Marvin has hired you as a part-time HR intern. He has a gut feeling that the job descriptions need to be updated or, in some cases, created and has assigned this project to you. Since Marvin has to clear new projects with Alta, he wants you to prepare a brief proposal that he can take to her for approval and that suggests the following:

1. Reasons why it is important to update or write new job descriptions
2. An outline of a process for doing this that will yield a set of thorough, current job descriptions
3. A process to be used in the future for periodically reviewing and updating job descriptions

Marvin wants to meet with you and discuss each of these points. He wants the proposal to contain specific suggestions and ideas. What exactly would you suggest to Marvin?

# ENDNOTES

1. J. I. Sanchez and E. L. Levine, "The Rise and Fall of Job Analysis and the Future of Work Analysis," *Annual Review of Psychology*, 2012, 63, pp. 397–425.
2. M. T. Brannick, E. L. Levine, and F. P. Morgeson, *Job and Work Analysis* (Thousand Oaks, CA: Sage, 2007).
3. J. K. Harter, F. L. Schmidt, and T. L. Hayes, "Business-Unit-Level Relationship Between Employee Satisfaction, Employee Engagement, and Business Outcomes: A Meta-Analysis," *Journal of Applied Psychology*, 2002, 87, pp. 268–279.
4. P. Bobko, P. L. Roth, and M. A. Buster, "A Systematic Approach for Assessing the Currency of Job Analytic Information," *Public Personnel Management*, 2008, 37, pp. 261–277.
5. R. J. Vance, *Employee Engagement and Commitment* (Alexandria, VA: Society for Human Resource Management, 2006), pp. 1, 13; Harter, Schmidt, and Hayes, "Business-Unit-Level Relationship Between Employee Satisfaction, Employee Engagement, and Business Outcomes: A Meta-Analysis."
6. For excellent overviews and reviews, see Brannick, Levine, and Morgeson, *Job and Work Analysis*; R. D. Gatewood, H. S. Feild, and M. Barrick, *Human Resource Selection*, 7th ed. (Orlando, FL: Harcourt, 2010), pp. 267–363; P. R. Sackett and R. M. Laczo, "Job and Work Analysis," in W. Borman, D. Ilgen, and R. Klimoski (eds.), *Handbook of Psychology: Industrial and Organizational Psychology*, Vol. 12 (New York: Wiley, 2003), pp. 21–37.
7. E. T. Cornelius III, "Practical Findings From Job Analysis Research," in S. Gael (ed.), *The Job Analysis Handbook for Business, Industry and Government,* Vol. 1 (New York: Wiley, 1988), pp. 48–70.

8. Sanchez and Levine, "The Rise and Fall of Job Analysis and the Future of Work Analysis."

9. C. J. Cranny and M. E. Doherty, "Importance Ratings in Job Analysis: Note on the Misinterpretation of Factor Analysis," *Journal of Applied Psychology*, 1988, 73, pp. 320–322.

10. Sanchez and Levine, "The Rise and Fall of Job Analysis and the Future of Work Analysis."

11. F. P. Morgeson and E. C. Dierdorff, "Work Analysis: From Technique to Theory," in S. Zedeck (ed.), *APA Handbook of Industrial and Organizational Psychology*, Vol. 2 (Washington, DC: American Psychological Association, 2011), pp. 3–41; Sanchez and Levine, "The Rise and Fall of Job Analysis and the Future of Work Analysis."

12. N. G. Peterson, M. D. Mumford, W. C. Borman, P. R. Jeanneret, E. A. Fleishman, K. Y. Levin, M. A. Campion, M. S. Mayfield, F. S. Morgeson, K. Pearlman, M. K. Gowing, A. R. Lancaster, M. B. Silver, and D. M. Dye, "Understanding Work Using the Occupational Information Network: Implications for Research and Practice," *Personnel Psychology*, 2001, 54, pp. 451–492.

13. C. C. LaPolice, G. W. Carter, and J. W. Johnson, "Linking O*NET Descriptors to Occupational Literacy Requirements Using Job Component Validation," *Personnel Psychology*, 2008, 61, pp. 405–441.

14. Morgeson and Dierdorff, "Work Analysis: From Technique to Theory."

15. Morgeson and Dierdorff, "Work Analysis: From Technique to Theory."

16. Sanchez and Levine, "The Rise and Fall of Job Analysis and the Future of Work Analysis."

17. F. P. Morgeson, K. Delaney-Klinger, M. S. Mayfield, P. Ferrara, and M. A. Campion, "Self-Presentations Processes in Job Analysis: A Field Experiment Investigating Inflation in Abilities, Tasks, and Competencies," *Journal of Applied Psychology*, 2004, 89, pp. 674–686.

18. For detailed treatments, see Brannick, Levine, and Morgeson, *Job Work Analysis*; Gael (ed.), *The Job Analysis Handbook for Business, Industry and Government*, pp. 315–468; Gatewood, Feild, and Barrick, *Human Resource Selection*, pp. 267–363; M. Mader-Clark, *The Job Description Handbook* (Berkeley, CA: Nolo, 2006).

19. R. Reiter-Palmon, M. Brown, D. L. Sandall, C. B. Buboltz, and T. Nimps, "Development of an O*NET Web-Based Job Analysis and Its Implementation in the U.S. Navy," *Human Resource Management Review*, 2006, 16, pp. 294–309.

20. Brannick, Levine, and Morgeson, *Job and Work Analysis*.

21. T. A. Stetz, J. M. Beaubien, M. J. Keeney, and B. D. Lyons, "Nonrandom Response and Variance in Job Analysis Surveys: A Cause for Concern?" *Public Personnel Management*, 2008, 37, pp. 223–241.

22. P.D.G. Steel and J. D. Kammeyer-Mueller, "Using a Meta-Analytic Perspective to Enhance Job Component Validation," *Personnel Psychology*, 2009, 62, pp. 533–552; P.D.G. Steel, A. I. Huffcutt, and J. D. Kammeyer-Mueller, "From the Work One Knows the Worker: A Systematic Review of the Challenges, Solutions, and Steps to Creating Synthetic Validity," *International Journal of Selection and Assessment*, 2006, 14, pp. 16–36.

23. R. G. Jones, J. I. Sanchez, G. Parameswaran, J. Phelps, C. Shop-taught, M. Williams, and S. White, "Selection or Training? A Two-fold Test of the Validity of Job-Analytic Ratings of Trainability," *Journal of Business and Psychology*, 2001, 15, pp. 363–389; D. M. Truxillo, M. E. Paronto, M. Collins, and J. L. Sulzer, "Effects of Subject Matter Expert Viewpoint on Job Analysis Results," *Public Personnel Management*, 2004, 33(1), pp. 33–46.

24. See Brannick, Levine, and Morgeson, *Job and Work Analysis*; Gael (ed.), *The Job Analysis Handbook for Business, Industry and Government*, pp. 315–390; Gatewood, Feild, and Barrick, *Human Resource Selection*, pp. 267–363.

25. G. W. Stevens, "A Critical Review of the Science and Practice of Competency Modeling," *Human Resource Development Review*, 2013, 12, pp. 86–107.

26. M. A. Campion, A. A. Fink, B. J. Ruggeberg, L. Carr, G. M. Phillips, and R. B. Odman, "Doing Competencies Well: Best Practices in Competency Modeling," *Personnel Psychology*, 2011, 64, pp. 225–262.

27. Campion, Fink, Ruggeberg, Carr, Phillips, and Odman, "Doing Competencies Well: Best Practices in Competency Modeling."

28. J. S. Schippman, "Competencies, Job Analysis, and the Next Generation of Modeling," in J. C. Scott and D. H. Reynolds (eds.), *Handbook of Workplace Assessment* (San Francisco: Jossey-Bass, 2010), pp. 197–231; J. S. Schippman, R. A. Ash, M. Battista, L. Carr, L. D. Eyde, B. Hesketh, J. Kehoe, K. Pearlman, E. P. Prien, and J. I. Sanchez, "The Practice of Competency Modeling," *Personnel Psychology*, 2000, 53, pp. 703–740.

29. Schippman, "Competencies, Job Analysis, and the Next Generation of Modeling."

30. D. Bartram, "The Great Eight Competencies: A Criterion-Centric Approach to Validation," *Journal of Applied Psychology*, 2007, 90, pp. 1185–1203.

31. Schippman et al., "The Practice of Competency Modeling."

32. Schippman et al., "The Practice of Competency Modeling."

33. F. Lievens and J. I. Sanchez, "Can Training Improve the Quality of Inferences Made by Raters in Competency Modeling? A Quasi-Experiment," *Journal of Applied Psychology*, 2007, 92, pp. 812–819.

34. F. Lievens, J. I. Sanchez, D. Bartram, and A. Brown, "Lack of Consensus Among Competency Ratings of the Same Occupation: Noise or Substance?" *Journal of Applied Psychology*, 2010, 95, pp. 562–571; Sanchez and Levine, "The Rise and Fall of Job Analysis and the Future of Work Analysis."

35. V. M. Catano, W. Darr, and C. A. Campbell, "Performance Appraisal of Behavior-Based Competencies: A Reliable and Valid Procedure," *Personnel Psychology*, 2007, 60, pp. 201–230.

36. R. V. Dawis, "Person-Environment Fit and Job Satisfaction," in C. J. Cranny, P. C. Smith, and E. F. Stone (eds.), *Job Satisfaction* (New York: Lexington, 1992), pp. 69–88; G. Ledford, P. Mulvey, and P. LeBlanc, *The Rewards of Work* (Scottsdale, AZ: WorldatWork/Sibson, 2000).

37. E. E. Ledford and M. I. Lucy, *The Rewards of Work* (Los Angeles: Sibson Consulting, 2003).

38. Ledford and Lucy, *The Rewards of Work*, p. 12.

39. D. E. Thompson and T. A. Thompson, "Court Standards for Job Analysis in Test Validation," *Personnel Psychology*, 1982, 35, pp. 865–874.

40. Equal Employment Opportunity Commission, *Technical Assistance Manual on the Employment Provisions (Title 1) of the Americans With Disabilities Act* (Washington, DC: author, 1992), pp. II-19 to II-21.

41. K. E. Mitchell, G. M. Alliger, and R. Morgfopoulos, "Toward an ADA-Appropriate Job Analysis," *Human Resource Management Review*, 1997, 7, pp. 5–26; F. Lievens, J. I. Sanchez, and W. De Corte, "Easing the Inferential Leap in Competency Modelling: The Effects of Task-Related Information and Subject Matter Expertise," *Personnel Psychology*, 2001, 57, pp. 847–879; Lievens and Sanchez, "Can Training Improve the Quality of Inferences Made by Raters in Competency Modeling: A Quasi-Experiment," pp. 812–819.

# The Staffing Organizations Model

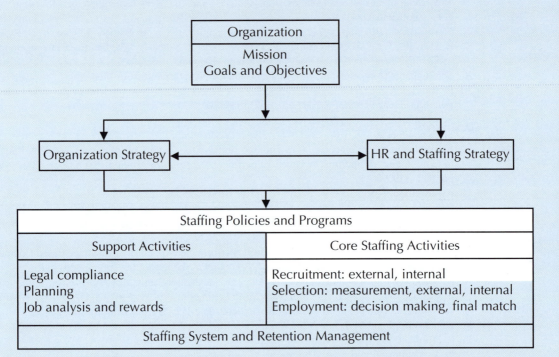

# PART THREE

## Staffing Activities: Recruitment

**CHAPTER FIVE**
External Recruitment

**CHAPTER SIX**
Internal Recruitment

# CHAPTER FIVE

## External Recruitment

# LEARNING OBJECTIVES AND INTRODUCTION

## Learning Objectives

- Engage in strategic recruitment planning activities
- Understand the difference between open and targeted recruitment
- Create a persuasive communication message
- Learn about a variety of recruitment media
- Recognize how applicant reactions influence the effectiveness of a recruiting plan
- Utilize a variety of recruitment sources
- Evaluate recruiting based on established metrics

## Introduction

An effective recruiting process is the cornerstone of an effective staffing system. If the recruiting system works, high-quality applicants will be attracted to the organization, the best candidates will be available for selection and eventual hiring, and the organization will have a much easier time reaching its strategic staffing goals. Conversely, if recruiting fails to attract enough qualified applicants, none of the other components of the staffing system can function properly—after all, you can't hire people who don't apply.

In external recruiting, the organization is trying to sell itself to potential applicants, so many marketing principles are applied to improve recruiting yields. You'll learn how recruiters choose from three types of messages—realistic, employment brand, or targeted—to attract the right types of candidates. Over the course of this chapter, you'll also learn about the advantages and disadvantages of recruiting methods such as corporate websites, employee referrals, college job fairs, and many others.

The recruitment process begins with a strategic planning phase, during which strategic recruiting goals are defined, a decision is made about whether an open or targeted technique will be employed, and organizational and administrative plans are developed. Following the formation of a strategy, the message to be communicated to job applicants is established, along with the media that will be used to convey the message. Special consideration must be given to applicant reactions to recruiters and the recruitment process in undertaking each of these phases of the external recruitment process. Finally, the organization will implement its chosen strategy, based on careful consideration of all the factors that have been mentioned previously. Close attention must also be given to legal issues. This includes consideration of the definition of job applicant, disclaimers, targeted recruitment, electronic recruitment, job advertisements, and fraud and misrepresentation.

## STRATEGIC RECRUITMENT PLANNING

Recruiting is a process that attracts potential future employees who have KSAOs (knowledge, skill, ability, and other characteristics) that will help the organization achieve its strategic goals. If strategic goals are going to be fulfilled, each step must flow from the foundation established during the recruitment planning process. Exhibit 5.1 provides an overview of how this process should operate.

Consistent with this model, three issues must be resolved before attracting applicants to the organization. First, the organization needs to define its strategic goals for the recruiting process. The needs that were identified in the planning process will guide the process of identifying exactly what types of employees need to be recruited, how quickly these needs will be fulfilled, and the time frame for the recruiting process. Next, the organization needs to decide how broadly it will

**EXHIBIT 5.1** **Planning, Communicating, and Implementing Strategic Recruiting**

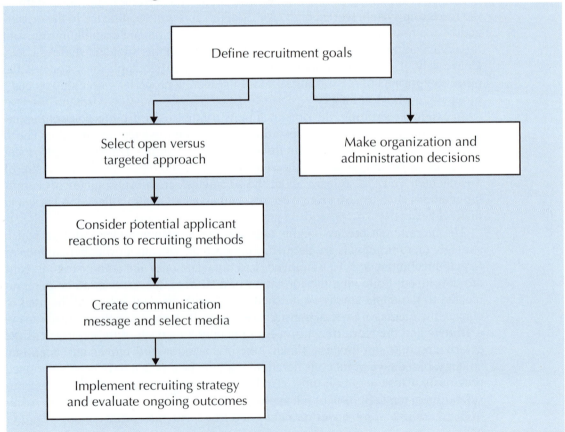

recruit. Finally, organizational and administrative issues need to be considered, including who will do the recruiting and budgeting.

## Defining Strategic External Recruiting Goals

Any recruiting drive must begin from a careful consideration of the organization's strategic goals.[1] Defining specific desired outcomes for the process can ensure that the organization can concentrate its efforts on applicants who will contribute most to overall organizational success. The definition of strategic goals includes developing goals for attraction, goals for speed, and a time frame.

### Goals for Attraction

Knowing how to recruit effectively and strategically begins by knowing the organization's current needs and future needs. For example, a global computer hardware manufacturer considering international expansion will need to consider what national cultures and languages its employees will need to understand. A pharmaceutical company in a dynamic market will need to think of the expertise of current employees as well as recruits' ability to learn and develop as the business environment evolves. The key issues an organization needs to resolve in defining its goals for attraction involve consideration of the fit issues we have discussed throughout the book.

In terms of person/job fit, the organization will need to determine what types of applicants are most likely to have the required KSAOs identified through the process of job analysis. At this stage in the process, goals should proceed from general statements to specifics. Determine whether you need a highly educated workforce or one with lots of practical experience, and then get more specific about what types of degrees employees should have or specific jobs employees should have previously held. After the KSAOs have been well defined, think about which of the recruiting sources we discuss later in the chapter are most likely to attract interested individuals with the right competencies.

In terms of person/organization fit, the techniques for recruiting should closely match the organization's culture and values. Companies that pride themselves on environmental sustainability and a team-oriented environment want to send a much different message to new recruits relative to companies that promote an aggressive growth and revenue-driven culture. Everything from the areas of the country where recruiting will take place to the types of media that are employed will send a message to potential applicants regarding what the organization's culture is like, so choices about recruiting should always take these considerations into account.

### Goals for Speed

While goals for attraction answer the question of job seekers the organization needs to attract, goals for speed answer the question of how fast the organization needs to attract applicants. When an organization needs to fill a position quickly with an employee who will contribute right away, recruiting will have to focus on methods that contact highly qualified and experienced individuals who are probably doing similar work already. Attracting these candidates does not involve the same strategy that would be employed if an organization wants to attract applicants with raw talent and ability who can be molded to fit the needs of the organization with training and experience.

Goals for speed can also influence the ways an organization recruits in more immediate ways as well. When an organization needs to fill a position quickly, techniques that identify a large pool of interested individuals who want to start right away should be implemented. On the other hand, the organization's long-term hiring strategy should include establishing personal relationships with a broad pool of talented individuals, regardless of their immediate availability, through ongoing networking. Some technology companies start the process of recruiting by providing scholarships and mentoring opportunities for college students, with the hope of identifying and attracting individuals who will be interested in a job when they graduate.

### Time Frame

The last issue that needs to be resolved in defining strategic goals is the time frame during which recruitment will take place. This can be particularly important in a legal sense because the applicant pool definition depends on the length of time applicants will have to apply. Defining a time frame means determining how long the position will be advertised prior to consideration of applications, and at what point a final offer for selection tests and interviews will be sent to applicants. During the time-frame goal development phase, general principles for determining how long a job will remain open are considered in light of strategic goals for the recruiting process. Finally, specific decisions about timing are left for the organization and administration phase.

When an organization is seeking applicants for a very specific, in-demand position, the time frame should be similarly specific, with applications accepted only until a firm deadline is reached, after which no other applications will be accepted or considered. When an organization is seeking a larger number of applicants for an entry-level managerial or professional job category, recruiters might attend job fairs and encourage applications from attendees. If an organization has the goal of filling a large number of positions that traditionally have relatively high turnover, such as most sales or customer service jobs, then recruiting may not have a termination point at all. Instead, recruiting will be considered ongoing, as with a policy of "always taking applications."

## Open Versus Targeted Recruitment

One of the most difficult aspects of recruitment is knowing where to look for applicants. In theory, the pool of potential job applicants is the eligible labor force (i.e., employed, unemployed, discouraged workers, new labor force entrants, and labor force reentrants). In practice, the organization must narrow down this vast pool into segments or strata of workers believed to be the most desirable applicants. To do so, organizations can use open or targeted recruitment methods.

## Open Recruitment

With an open recruitment approach, organizations cast a wide net to identify potential applicants for specific job openings. Very little effort is made in segmenting the market into applicants with the most desirable KSAOs. This approach is very passive in that anyone can apply for an opening, and all who apply for a position are considered, regardless of their qualifications. An advantage of the open recruitment method is that applicants often see it as being "fair" in that everyone has the opportunity to apply. Open recruitment helps ensure that a diverse set of applicants—including minorities, teens, former retirees, veterans, people with disabilities, and other potentially overlooked employee groups—are given a fair shot at being considered. Another advantage of open recruitment is that it is useful—perhaps even essential—when large numbers of applicants must be hired. The disadvantage to this approach is that a large number of applications must be considered, so it is possible that qualified applicants may be overlooked in the process. Unfortunately, with the growth of web-based recruiting, many employers have found that open recruiting yields too many applicants, making it very time-consuming to review all the résumés and other application materials.[2]

## Targeted Recruitment

A targeted recruitment approach is one whereby the organization identifies segments in the labor market where qualified candidates are likely to be. Often, this is done to find applicants with specific characteristics pertinent to person/job or person/organization match. Some experts propose that a targeted strategy may be more effective because it allows the organization to prepare a specific message that appeals to the audience, rather than relying on a general message that is mildly appealing to some candidates but strongly appealing to none.[3]

Following is a list of some of the potential target recruitment groups (of course, these categories are not mutually exclusive):

- *Key KSAO shortages*—the objective here is to identify applicants with specific new areas of knowledge or "hot" skills
- *Workforce diversity gaps*—often, one must go beyond open recruitment to reach diverse groups and make special efforts
- *Passive job seekers or noncandidates*—sometimes excellent candidates can be found in "trailing spouses" or other dual-career couples
- *Former military personnel*—especially those with key competencies such as leadership
- *Employment-discouraged*—long-term unemployed, homemakers, welfare recipients, teenagers, and people with disabilities

- *Reward-seekers*—those who are attracted to the organization's employee value proposition, which might offer benefits such as flexible work schedules and fully paid health care
- *Former employees*—those with good track records while they were employees
- *Reluctant applicants*—some individuals may have interest in an organization but are conflicted; research shows that flexible work arrangements may help attract such individuals[4]

### Making the Choice

The choice between open and targeted recruitment is important, as it dictates recruiting methods and sources. This is not to suggest open and targeted recruitment necessarily achieve different goals. Targeted recruitment can achieve the same ends of inclusion as open recruitment, though by a different mechanism. Whereas open recruitment achieves inclusiveness by encouraging everyone to apply, targeted recruitment may actually seek out particular groups that would not respond in an open recruitment environment. In theory, open and targeted recruitment can be used in combination. For example, an organization may encourage all applications by posting jobs on its website and advertising broadly, while still making special efforts to reach certain populations. Of course, by seeking out one group, another may be inadvertently overlooked from consideration. So, before targeted recruitment is undertaken, the organization needs to carefully consider which groups to target, as well as the job skills necessary to perform the job(s) in question. Similarly, before open recruitment is selected, the organization needs to decide whether it is prepared to handle and fairly consider the large number of applications that may flow in.

Recruiting experts say it is not necessary to use just one strategy.[5] Organizations might choose a very open strategy for jobs that are not core to their performance, such as clerical and administrative functions, but then use a much more targeted approach for employees who need highly specific KSAOs. Accenture Consulting, for example, suggests that retailers identify the most critical segments of the workforce, analyze the performance of the most successful employees, and then target the recruiting to attract employees sharing relevant characteristics with star performers in these high-leverage positions. For less critical positions, a less resource-intensive process might be advisable. Exhibit 5.2 reviews the advantages of open and targeted recruitment and suggests when each approach is appropriate.

## Organization and Administration

Once the organization has a good idea of which types of candidates to recruit, decisions must be made regarding how the process will proceed. Recruiting can be coordinated in-house or by an external recruitment agency. An organization can also do its own recruiting or cooperate with other organizations in a recruitment

---

**EXHIBIT 5.2**   **Choosing Between Open and Targeted Recruiting**

|  | Technique | Advantages | Best When |
|---|---|---|---|
| **Open** | Advertising positions with a message appealing to a wide variety of job seekers in a variety of media outlets that will reach the largest possible audience | Ensures that a diverse set of applicants are contacted and considered<br><br>Lower resource and personnel cost per applicant located | Large numbers of applicants are required<br><br>Pre-entry qualifications are not as important |
| **Targeted** | Focusing advertising and recruiting efforts by tailoring message content to attract segments of the labor market with specific KSAOs or demographic characteristics | Narrows the pool of potential applicants, allowing the organization to concentrate efforts on the most qualified<br><br>Facilitates a more personal approach to each applicant | The organization needs specific skill sets that are in short supply<br><br>Hiring for high-leverage positions |

alliance. Given the flexibility of this process, authority to recruit may be centralized or decentralized in the organization.

### In-House Versus External Recruitment Agency

Most recruiting in large organizations is done in-house. Smaller organizations may rely on external recruitment agencies rather than an in-house function, as smaller organizations may not have the staff, expertise, or budget to run their own recruitment functions. Organizations with low turnover rates may also prefer to use external recruitment agencies because they recruit so infrequently it doesn't make sense to have their own recruitment function.

Outsourcing the recruiting function has grown significantly over time.[6] Specialized recruiting firms are constantly in touch with a wide variety of applicants and therefore have detailed knowledge of many potential candidates. Recruiting firms also often have databases of available applicants they have collected over time, which can mean very rapid access to many interested individuals. However, an in-house recruiting agency has definite advantages. In particular, in-house recruiters know much more about their organization's culture and can convey that information to recruits more credibly because it is delivered by people who actually work for the company. Additionally, employees may perceive that a company that does its own recruiting is more interested in applicants and has a more people-oriented culture than an organization that leaves this process to an outside firm. Each organization needs to decide, based on its recruiting strategy, budget, and needs, whether an in-house or external agency is better.

## Centralized Versus Decentralized Recruitment

An organization can centralize or decentralize the recruitment of external job applicants. In centralized recruitment, one group coordinates the recruitment activities, usually human resources (HR) professionals in the corporate offices. In a decentralized recruitment system, individual business units or managers coordinate the recruitment activities. Although the ultimate hiring decisions reside in the business unit, most organizations centralize the administrative activities associated with recruiting and screening applicants.

One advantage to centralized recruitment is that efforts are not duplicated. For example, when recruiting at a school, only one advertisement is placed, rather than separate ads for multiple organizational business units. Another advantage is that a centralized approach ensures that policy is being interpreted consistently across business units. For example, GM centralized its recruiting system in order to convey a consistent message to applicants.[7] Along these same lines, a centralized function helps ensure compliance with relevant laws and regulations. Another factor that facilitates centralized recruiting is the growth in staffing software (see Chapter 13).

Some organizations prefer decentralized recruitment functions. Case studies suggest that research and development departments, for example, often develop specialized recruiting practices to attract talent. These strategies are more focused on university recruiting and emphasize projects that are likely to interest highly educated and intrinsically motivated researchers.[8] One advantage of decentralized recruitment is that when there are fewer people to recruit, placement can take place more quickly than when a centralized approach is used. Also, the recruitment search may be more responsive to the business unit's specific needs because the local managers involved with recruitment may be closer to the day-to-day operations of the business unit than are their corporate counterparts.

## Timing

Two factors that drive the decision of when to look for job applicants are lead time concerns and time sequence concerns. As staffing managers have been increasingly called on to show concrete results for their work, the importance of documenting the time to fill requisitions has grown. These deadlines are very important for procedural justice and even legal defensibility, as both current employees and potential applicants will expect the organization to abide by the specified date requirements. Once a goal for the time frame is established, the organization should not pursue a certain applicant before the deadline or consider applicants who apply after the deadline.

***Lead Time Concerns.*** Although managers would like to fill each position immediately on approval of the requisition, this is not possible since recruiters handle a large number of vacancies at any one time. It is possible, however, to minimize the delay in filling vacancies by planning for openings well in advance of their actual occurrence. Effective planning requires that top management prioritize job openings so that they can be filled in the order that best meets the needs of the business. It also requires that recruiters be fully prepared to conduct the searches. Therefore, recruiters must be aware of the deadlines for placing ads in the appropriate periodicals, and they should be knowledgeable about the availability of labor in the marketplace. With the growth of Internet recruiting, much hiring is now continuous.[9] For example, many large organizations keep a list of job openings on their websites that are continually updated through their HR information systems.

*Time Sequence Concerns.*  In a successful recruitment program, the steps involved in the process are clearly defined and sequenced in a logical order. A staffing flowchart should be used to organize all components of the recruitment process. The sequence of recruitment activities will affect the amount of time needed to fill job vacancies.

A very useful set of indicators for time sequence concerns is known as time-lapse statistics. These statistics provide data on the average length of time between various phases in the recruitment process. Organizations should routinely collect these data in order to assist managers in planning when vacancies are to be filled.

## Recruitment Budget and Return on Investment

The recruitment process is a very expensive component of organizational staffing. Costs include staff time developing a recruitment message, a website, advertising, personal contacts and follow-up with potential candidates, and logistics for on-site candidate visits. Because recruiting is such an expensive proposition, it is vital for HR to track both the costs and the returns of its recruiting practices.[10] The use of applicant tracking systems makes it easier for leaders to estimate metrics from a variety of recruiting practices.

The high costs of recruitment also point to the importance of establishing a well-developed recruitment budget. An example of a recruitment budget is shown in Exhibit 5.3. Two issues need to be addressed in establishing a recruitment budget. First, a top-down or bottom-up procedure can be used to gather the information needed to formulate the budget. With a top-down approach, top management sets the budget for recruitment activities on the bases of the business plan for the organization and projected revenues. With a bottom-up approach, the budget for recruitment activities is set on the basis of the specific needs of each business unit. The former approach works well when the emphasis is on controlling costs. The latter approach works better when commitment to the budget by business unit heads is the goal.

A second issue is deciding whether to charge recruitment costs to business unit users. That is, should recruitment expenses be charged to HR or to the business unit using HR services? Most organizations charge the HR department. One reason for this may be to encourage each business unit to use the recruitment services of

**EXHIBIT 5.3   Example of a Recruitment Budget for 500 New Hires**

**Administrative Expenses**

| | |
|---|---|
| Staff | 32,000 |
| Supplies | 45,000 |
| Equipment | 10,000 |
| | $87,000 |

**Recruiter Expenses**

| | |
|---|---|
| Salaries | 240,000 |
| Benefits | 96,000 |
| Expenses | 150,000 |
| | $486,000 |

**Candidate Expenses**

| | |
|---|---|
| Travel | 320,000 |
| Lodging | 295,000 |
| Fees | 50,000 |
| Relocation | 150,000 |
| | $815,000 |

**Total Recruitment Expenses**

87,000 + 486,000 + 815,000 = $1,388,000

**Total Cost per Hire**

$1,388,000 / 500 new hires = $2,776

the HR group. However, in organizations where HR is charged, business unit users may not be as concerned about minimizing recruitment costs.

Once a budget is in place and the recruiting techniques are implemented, the organization should take the additional step of assessing the effectiveness of various techniques. Applicant tracking systems make it possible to assess how many individuals are attracted and hired through each source. An applicant tracking system helps identify which recruiting sources lead applicants to the organization. For example, it is possible to determine how many candidates learned about the job opening from media advertisements, the organization's website, campus visits and job fairs, employee referrals, or other sources. It is also possible to track how many candidates are hired from each source. From this information on the number of applicants and hires, coupled with budget figures, it is possible to calculate the cost per applicant (total media cost divided by number of applicants) and the cost per hire (total media cost divided by number of hires). Cost-effective methods for attracting candidates can then become the focal part of the organization's recruiting strategy, and those that have lower returns on investment can be eliminated.

## Development of a Recruitment Guide

A recruitment guide is a formal document that details the process to be followed to attract applicants to a job. It should be based on the organization's staffing flow-charts, if available. Included in the guide are details such as the time, money, and staff required to fill the job as well as the steps to be taken to do so. An example of a recruitment guide is shown in Exhibit 5.4.

Although a recruitment guide takes time to produce—time that may be difficult to find in the face of an urgent requisition to be filled—it is an essential document.

---

**EXHIBIT 5.4**   **Recruitment Guide for Director of Claims**

**Position:**   Director, Claims Processing

**Reports to:**   Senior Director, Claims Processing

**Qualifications:**   4-year degree in business
8 years' experience in health care, including 5 in claims, 3 of which should be in management

**Relevant labor market:**   Regional Midwest

**Timeline:** week of 1/17: Conduct interviews with qualified applicants
2/1/11: Targeted hire date

**Activities to undertake to source well-qualified candidates:**

Regional newspaper advertising

Post job opening on company website

Request employee referrals

Contact regional health and life insurance associations

Call HR departments of regional health and life insurance companies to see if any are outplacing any middle managers

Contact, if necessary, executive recruiter to further source candidates

**Staff members involved:**

HR Recruiting Manager
Senior Director, Claims Processing
VP, Human Resources
Potential peers and direct reports

**Budget:**
$3,000–$5,000

It clarifies expectations for both the recruiter and the requesting department as to what will be accomplished, what the costs will be, and who will be held accountable for the results. It also clarifies the steps that need to be taken in order to ensure that they are all followed in a consistent fashion and in accordance with organization policy as well as relevant laws and regulations. In short, a recruitment guide safeguards the interests of the employer, the applicant, and the recruiter.

### Process Flow and Record Keeping

Before deciding where and how to look for applicants, it is essential that the organization prepare for the high volume of data that accompanies the filling of vacancies. This high volume of data results from the use of multiple sources to identify candidates (e.g., advertisements, walk-ins, employment agencies), the need to circulate the applicant's credentials to multiple parties (e.g., hiring managers, HR), and the need to communicate with candidates regarding the status of their applications. If process flow and record-keeping issues are not addressed before the recruitment search, the organization may become overwhelmed with correspondence that is not dealt with in a timely and professional manner; in turn, the organization may lose well-qualified applicants.

To manage the process flow and record-keeping requirements, an information system must be created for recruitment efforts. An effective system allows the candidate, the hiring manager, and HR representatives to know the candidate's status at any time. The information system tracks the applicant's file as it flows through the organization's recruitment process. The information system can also periodically issue reports on how timely and accurately the applicant information is being processed.

The process of managing data and records has been transformed by online applications.[11] Indeed, one might characterize it as a double-edged sword. On the one hand, data entry and record maintenance are facilitated in that applications are immediately transferred into a searchable standardized database. Online applications often permit candidate screening by checking qualifications and administering online skills tests. This can greatly reduce the time spent weeding out résumés sent in by unqualified candidates. On the other hand, online applications generate much more data, including applications from individuals who are poorly motivated to join the organization or are obviously unqualified for the position. To facilitate combing through all this information, many web-based recruiting systems have integrated screening tools to eliminate unqualified applicants early in the process.

As the applicant progresses through the hiring process, additional record keeping is required, such as who has reviewed the file, how long each individual has had the file to be reviewed, what decision has been reached (e.g., reject, invite for a visit, conduct a second interview), and what step needs to be taken next (e.g., arrange for a flight and accommodations, schedule an interview). Throughout the process, communications with the applicant must also be tracked so the applicant knows whether his or her credentials will receive further review and whether he or she needs to take any additional steps to secure employment.

Even when an applicant is rejected for a position, there are record-keeping responsibilities. The applicant's file should be stored in the event that another search arises that requires someone with the applicant's qualifications. Such storage should be for a maximum of one year (see "Legal Issues" at the end of the chapter).

## APPLICANT REACTIONS

After the organization has a clear idea of its strategic plan, the possible reactions of applicants should be considered. Organizations should try to collect as much information about potential applicant reactions at all phases of the process, including initial intentions to apply, interest in taking a job if offered, and final choice. Different factors can be important at different stages. For example, the influence of the recruiter on the applicant is more likely to occur in the initial stage rather than the latter stages of the recruitment process. In the latter stages, actual job characteristics carry more weight in the applicant's decision.

Understanding how applicants will react to various features of the recruiting process will help determine which type of communication message content and media should be employed, as well as help facilitate implementation of effective strategies. Thus, we review applicant reactions to job and organization characteristics, recruiters, the recruitment process, and diversity issues in turn before turning to communicating a message and receiving applications.

### Reactions to Job and Organizational Characteristics

In a marketing sense, the job and the organization are the products the organization is trying to "sell" to potential applicants, so any recruiting strategy will have to take these characteristics into account.

At the job level, research suggests that applicants are most interested in working for organizations that offer sufficient wages, opportunities for growth and development, and interesting work characteristics.[12] In particular, opportunities for challenge and development are most strongly associated with applicant attraction. Of course, not all jobs have these desired features, so managers will need to decide exactly how much information about the job should be shared. This issue will be discussed in detail shortly. In some industries, the payment strategy may also help attract candidates who match the job demands. For example, to attract entrepreneurial financial advisors, some financial services firms entice potential applicants with a well-publicized opportunity to run their shops independently and keep 100% of their advisory fees.[13] Attracting such individuals supports an organizational strategy that focuses on innovation, personal initiative, and achievement.

At the organization level, applicants are most drawn to prestigious organizations that have a reputation for treating their employees well.[14] The social environment of the organization also matters, with most applicants being attracted to companies where they believe they will work with good coworkers in a positive social environment. Although some research suggests that most potential applicants prefer a supportive organizational culture to a competitive culture, a large proportion of workers clearly prefer an organization that emphasizes individual work and ambition.[15] Most experts advise that organizations should accurately portray their culture in recruiting so they attract employees who will fit well within the organization.

## Reactions to Recruiters

Considerable research has been conducted and carefully reviewed on the reactions of job applicants to the behavior and characteristics of recruiters.[16] The data collected have been somewhat limited by the fact that they focus primarily on reactions to college recruiters rather than noncollege recruiters. Despite this limitation, several key themes emerge in the literature.

First, though the recruiter does indeed influence job applicant reactions, he or she does not have as much influence on them as do actual job characteristics. This indicates that the recruiter cannot be viewed as a substitute for a well-defined and well-communicated recruitment message showing the actual characteristics of the job.

Second, the influence of the recruiter is more likely to be felt in the attitude rather than in the behavior of the job applicant. That is, an applicant who has been exposed to a talented recruiter is more likely to walk away with a favorable impression of the recruiter than to accept a job on the basis of the interaction with a recruiter. This attitudinal effect is important, however, as it may lead to good publicity for the organization. In turn, good publicity may lead to a larger applicant pool to draw from in the future.

Third, two behaviors of the recruiter seem to have the largest influence on applicant reactions. The first is the level of warmth that the recruiter shows toward the job applicant. Warmth can be expressed by being enthusiastic, personable, empathetic, and helpful in dealings with the candidate. The second behavior is communicating knowledge about the job. This can be conveyed by being well versed with the job requirements matrix and the job rewards matrix. Additionally, recruiters who show interest in the applicant are viewed more positively.

Organizations can use this information to their advantage by selecting and training recruiters well. Recruiters should be knowledgeable regarding forms and reports, organization and job characteristics, recruitment targets, policies and procedures, and the legal environment around recruiting.[17] Recruiters also need to receive training in marketing and interpersonal aspects of recruiting. Recruiters can be trained on how to do market research, how to find job candidates in the market, and how to identify what candidates want. In developing their marketing skills, recruiters can be shown how to link up with other departments, such as marketing and public relations. Recruiters may be able to collaborate with marketing efforts to achieve a brand image that not only sells products to customers but sells the organization to prospective hires as well. Interpersonal skills training should include practice scripts, strategies to put recruits at ease, and role-playing exercises.

Finally, in their efforts to recruit more creatively, recruiters need training on ethical issues in recruitment. Is it ethical for a recruiter to recruit at a competitor's place of business? In parking lots? At weddings or funerals? Some recruiters will even lie to applicants in an effort to lure them. To ensure that recruiters behave ethically, standards should be developed and recruiters should be trained on these standards.[18]

## Reactions to the Recruitment Process

Only some administrative components of the recruitment process have been shown to have an impact on applicant reactions.[19] Research suggests that above all else, applicants want a system that is fair. First, job applicants are more likely to have favorable reactions to the recruitment process when the screening devices used to narrow the applicant pool are seen as job related. That is, the process used should be closely related to the content of the job as spelled out in the job requirements matrix. Applicants also see recruiting processes as more fair if they have an opportunity to perform or demonstrate their ability to do the job.

Second, delays in the recruitment process have a negative effect on applicants' reactions. In particular, when long delays occur between the applicant's expression of interest and the organization's response, the applicant forms negative reactions about the organization but not about himself or herself. For example, an applicant who experiences a long delay between an on-site visit and a job offer is more likely to believe that something is wrong with the organization rather than with his or her personal qualifications. This is especially true of the better-qualified candidate, who is likely to act on these feelings by accepting another job offer.

Finally, though little research is available, the increasing use of the Internet in recruitment, and that it is often the applicant's first exposure to an organization, suggest that applicants' reactions to an organization's website will increasingly drive their reactions to the recruitment process.

Indeed, studies reveal that applicants are able to locate more relevant jobs on the Internet than in traditional sources such as print media. Moreover, applicants generally like using the Internet for evaluating companies and submitting applications, if some provisos are kept in mind. As with general recruiting, perhaps the most important factor is the degree and speed of follow-up; delays greatly harm the image of the recruiting organization, so organizations need to make sure that online applications are followed up. Also, research shows that job seekers are more satisfied with organization websites when specific job information is provided and security precautions are taken to preserve the confidentiality of the information submitted. One key assurance is that the organization will not share résumés with vendors that will spam applicants with various solicitations.[20]

## Reactions to Diversity Issues

In addition to tailoring messages to reach employees with specific KSAO profiles, some organizations also target specific underrepresented groups, such as women and racioethnic minorities. Most research suggests that the race or gender of a recruiter has relatively little influence on applicant attraction, and there is not strong support for the idea that individuals react more positively when recruited by someone of their own demographic group. However, the content of the recruiting message and choice of recruiting sources can have an influence.

Research suggests that applicants react more positively to ads that reflect their own demographic group, which should be taken into account when developing a media campaign.[21] Such efforts are among the most effective, and the least controversial, elements of affirmative action programs (AAPs). One of the most common methods for increasing the diversity of applicant pools is to advertise in publications targeted at women and minorities. Surveys of job seekers show that women and minorities are especially interested in working for employers that endorse diversity through policy statements and in recruiting materials. Advertisements depicting groups of diverse employees are seen as more attractive to women and racioethnic minorities, which is probably why most organizations depict workforce diversity prominently in their recruiting materials. Effective depiction of diversity should take job functions into account as well; diversity advertisements that fail to show women and minorities in positions of organizational leadership send a negative message about the diversity climate at an organization.[22]

Some organizations are also aiming to increase the age diversity of the workforce by targeting older workers. Many traditional recruiting methods, like campus recruiting and job fairs, draw in a primarily younger workforce. However, as noted in Chapter 3, there has been an increase in the proportion of the workforce over 50 years of age that is likely to persist. These older workers are often highly qualified and experienced, and thus attractive candidates for recruiting, but a different targeted approach is required to bring them in. Mature workers are attracted by flexible schedules, health and pension benefits, and part-time opportunities, so the presence of such programs should be noted in recruiting advertisements.

## COMMUNICATION

Once the strategic planning phase is completed, it is time to consider how the position will be marketed to potential applicants. Reaching out to the job market first requires developing a message and then selecting a medium to communicate that message. Both phases are considered in turn.

# Communication Message

### Types of Messages

Recruiting experts have studied the ways in which the content of the recruiting message can influence potential applicants' thinking about the position. The communication message to applicants can focus on conveying realistic, employment brand, or targeted information. Each method involves different content and tone, and these differences can affect the eventual applicant pool.

***Realistic Recruitment Message.*** A realistic recruitment message portrays the organization and the job as they really are, rather than describing what the organization thinks job applicants want to hear. Organizations continue to describe themselves to applicants in overly positive terms, overstating desired values such as risk taking and understating undesirable values such as rules orientation. Some would argue that this is not the best message to send applicants on moral or practical grounds. While hyping the benefits of joining up may work for the army, where recruits are obligated to remain for three to five years, this is not the best approach for the organization.

A very well-researched recruitment message is known as a realistic job preview (RJP).[23] According to this practice, job applicants are given a "vaccination" by being told verbally, in writing, or on videotape what the actual job is like.[24] An example of the numerous attributes in an RJP for the job of elementary school teacher is shown in Exhibit 5.5. Note that the attributes are quite specific and that they are both positive and negative. Information like this "tells it like it is" to job applicants.

After receiving the vaccination, job applicants decide whether they want to work for the organization. The hope with the RJP is that job applicants will

**EXHIBIT 5.5** **Example of Job Attributes in an RJP for Elementary School Teachers**

**Positive Job Attributes**
Dental insurance is provided
Innovative teaching strategies are encouraged
University nearby for taking classes
Large support staff for teachers

**Negative Job Attributes**
Salary growth has averaged only 2% in past three years
Classes are large
The school day is long
Interactions with community have not been favorable

self-select into or out of the organization. By selecting into the organization, the applicant may be more committed to working there than he or she might otherwise have been. When an applicant self-selects out, the organization does not face the costs associated with recruiting, selecting, training, and compensating an employee, only to then have him or her leave because the job did not meet his or her expectations.

A great deal of research has been conducted on the effectiveness of RJPs, which appear to lead to somewhat higher job satisfaction and lower turnover. This appears to be true because providing applicants with realistic expectations about future job characteristics helps them better cope with job demands once they are hired. RJPs also appear to foster the belief in employees that their employer is honest and concerned with employee well-being, which leads to higher levels of organizational commitment.

RJPs may lead applicants to withdraw from the recruitment process, although a recent review suggests that RJPs have little effect on such attrition. This may be good news for employers interested in using RJPs: Providing applicants with realistic information provides employers with more satisfied and committed employees while still maintaining applicant interest in the position. Where the situation may become problematic is when one considers the type of applicant scared away by the realistic message. It appears plausible that the applicants most likely to be dissuaded by the realistic message are high-quality applicants, because they have more options. In fact, research suggests that the negative effects of RJPs on applicant attraction are particularly strong for high-quality applicants (those whose general qualifications are especially strong) and those with direct experience or familiarity with the job.

Although RJPs appear to have both weakly positive consequences (slightly higher job satisfaction and lower turnover among new hires) and negative consequences (slightly reduced ability to hire high-quality applicants), these outcomes have been found to be affected by a number of factors. A review of 40 studies on the effectiveness of RJPs offers more insight into the effect of RJPs:

- RJPs presented very early in the recruitment process are less effective in reducing posthire turnover than those presented just before or just after hiring.
- Posthire RJPs lead to higher levels of job performance than do RJPs presented before hiring.
- Verbal RJPs tend to reduce turnover more than written or videotaped RJPs.
- RJPs are less likely to lead to turnover when the organization "restricts" turnover for a period of time after the RJP (with contracts, above-market salaries, etc.).

In general, these findings suggest that RJPs should be given verbally (rather than in writing or by showing a video) and that it is probably best to reserve their use for later in the recruiting process (RJPs should not be part of the initial exposure of the organization to applicants).[25]

***Employment Brand Message.***   Organizations wishing to portray an appealing message to potential applicants may develop an employment brand to attract applicants. An employment brand is a good-company tag that places the image of being a great place to work or "employer of choice" in the minds of job candidates. An organization's employment brand is closely tied to its product market image. And like general product awareness, the more "customers" (in this case, potential applicants) are aware of an organization's employment brand, the more interested they are in pursuing a job.[26] Organizations that are well known by potential applicants may not need to engage in as much advertising for their jobs. Big-name organizations that market well-known products, such as Microsoft, Apple, Sony, and Disney, often have many more applicants than they need for most openings. Organizations with lower profiles may have to actively advertise their employment brand to bring in more applicants. One of the best ways for smaller organizations to emphasize their unique brand is to emphasize their most attractive attributes. Experts in corporate branding also encourage employers to compare their own organizational employment offerings with the competition to see how they are unique, and then highlight these unique advantages in organizational recruiting messages. For example, under a branding strategy, the US Marine Corps emphasized the Marines as an elite group of warriors rather than focusing on the financial advantages of enlistment, which had been done in the past.

Beyond reputation, another employment brand may be value or culture based. For example, GE has long promoted its high performance expectations in order to attract achievement-oriented applicants seeking commensurate rewards. Organization websites are often used to convey information regarding an organization's culture and emphasize the employment brand. Most organizational websites provide information regarding the organization's history, culture, diversity, benefits, and specific job information under a "careers" heading. It is informative to look through a series of these organizational websites to see how organizations cater to applicants. For example, Merck's corporate website shows an organization that conveys a message of professional development and social responsibility, whereas Goldman Sachs emphasizes performance and success, and Coca-Cola emphasizes global opportunities and fun.

There are several possible benefits of branding. Of course, establishing an attractive employment brand may help attract desired applicants to the organization. Moreover, having an established brand may help retain employees who were attracted to the brand to begin with. Research suggests that identifiable employment brands may breed organizational commitment on the part of newly hired employees.[27] Employment brands associated with empowerment and high compensation have been shown to be especially attractive to applicants.[28]

Research shows that having an employment brand can attract applicants to an organization, even beyond job and organizational attributes. Evidence also suggests that employers are most able to get their brand image out when they engage in early recruitment activities such as advertising or generating publicity about the organization.[29]

***Targeted Message.*** One way to improve upon matching people with jobs is to target the recruitment message to a particular audience. Different audiences may be looking for different rewards from an employer. This would appear to be especially true of special applicant populations, such as teenagers, older workers, welfare recipients, people with disabilities, homeless individuals, veterans, and displaced homemakers, all of whom may have special needs. Older workers, for example, may be looking for employers that can meet their financial needs (e.g., supplement Social Security), security needs (e.g., retraining), and social needs (e.g., place to interact with people). College students appear to be attracted to organizations that provide rewards and promotions on the basis of individual rather than group performance. Also, most college students prefer to receive pay in the form of a salary rather than in the form of incentives.[30] Unlike the branded recruiting message, where the focus is on the organization and what it offers, the targeted message focuses on the potential applicant and his or her individual preferences and how the organization can match those preferences.

## Choice of Messages

The different types of messages—realistic, branded, and targeted—are not likely to be equally effective under the same conditions. Which message to convey depends on the labor market, vacancy characteristics, and applicant characteristics.

The three types of messages are summarized in Exhibit 5.6. If the labor market is tight and applicants are difficult to come by, realism may not be an effective message, because to the extent that applicants self-select out of the applicant pool, fewer are left for an employer to choose from. Hence, if the employment objective is simply to fill job slots in the short run and worry about turnover later, a realistic message will have counterproductive effects. Obviously, then, when applicants are abundant and turnover is an immediate problem, a realistic message is appropriate.

In a tight labor market, branded and targeted messages are likely to be more effective in attracting job applicants. Attraction is strengthened, as there are inducements in applying for a job. In addition, individual needs are more likely to be perceived as met by a prospective employer. Hence, the applicant is more motivated to apply to organizations with an attractive or targeted message than those without. During loose economic times when applicants are plentiful, the branded or targeted approaches may be more costly than necessary to attract an adequate supply of labor. Also, they may set up false expectations concerning what life will be like on the job, and thus lead to turnover.

Job applicants will know more about the characteristics of highly visible jobs versus those of less visible jobs. For example, service sector jobs, such as that of

## EXHIBIT 5.6  Comparing Types of Messages

|  | Information Conveyed | Applicant Reactions | Potential Drawback | Best For |
|---|---|---|---|---|
| **Realistic** | Both positive and negative aspects of a job and organization are described | Some applicants self-select out; those who remain will have a better understanding of the job and will be less likely to leave | The best potential applicants may be more likely to leave | Loose labor markets or when turnover is costly |
| **Branded** | An appealing description is developed based on marketing principles, emphasizing unique features of the organization | Positive view of the organization, increased intention to apply for jobs, and better prehire information about benefits of the job | Overly positive message may result in employee dissatisfaction after hire | Tight labor markets or higher-value jobs |
| **Targeted** | Advertising themes are designed to attract a specific set of employees | Better fit between application message and specific applicant groups | May dissuade applicants who aren't interested in the work attributes featured in the message from applying | Specific KSAOs, or seeking a specific type of applicant |

cashier, are highly visible to people, and thus it may be redundant to give a realistic message. Other jobs, such as an outside sales position, are far less visible to people. These jobs may seem glamorous (e.g., sales commissions) to prospective applicants who fail to see the less glamorous aspects of the job (e.g., a lot of travel and paperwork).

The value of the job to the organization also has a bearing on the selection of an appropriate recruitment message. Inducements for jobs of higher value or worth to the organization are easier to justify in a budgetary sense than inducements for jobs of lower worth. The job may be of such importance to the organization that it is willing to pay a premium through inducements to attract well-qualified candidates.

In regard to the effectiveness of certain messages, some applicants are less likely than others to be influenced in their attitudes and behaviors by the recruitment message. For example, one study showed that a realistic message is less effective for those with considerable previous job experience.[31] Highly experienced candidates are more likely to be persuaded by high-quality, detailed advertisements than are less experienced candidates.[32] A targeted message does not work very well if the source is seen as not credible.[33] Other tactics have varying degrees of effectiveness as well. Inducements, for example, may not be particularly effective with applicants who do not have a family or who have considerable wealth.

## Communication Media

Not only is the message itself an important part of the recruitment process, so, too, is the selection of media to communicate the message. The most common communication media include advertisements, organizational websites, videoconferencing, and direct contact. Although these are all potential ways to get the message out, the most common method of learning about a job is through word of mouth, which is a difficult communication medium for an organization to manage.

Effective communication media are high in richness and credibility. Rich media channels allow for timely personal feedback and a variety of methods for conveying messages (e.g., visual images, text, figures and charts), and they are customized to each respondent's specific needs. Credible media channels transmit information that is honest, accurate, and thorough. Research has shown that respondents will have more positive images of organizations that transmit information that is rich and credible.[34] If the information is seen as coming directly from the employees, rather than from the organization's recruiting offices, the message will likely be seen as more honest and unbiased. Experts on advertising advise recruiters to remember that they need to constantly promote their brand to potential employees, because sheer repetition and consistency of a promotional message increase its effectiveness.

Our review of communication media below proceeds from the media that tend to have the least credibility and richness to the media that have the most credibility and richness. Research has shown that greater employer involvement with prospective applicants is likely to improve the image of the organization. In turn, a better image of the organization is likely to result in prospective applicants pursuing employment with the organization.[35] The media with the least richness and credibility usually have an advantage in that they can reach a large number of people at low cost, so they should not be overlooked. Given the various advantages and disadvantages of the methods we review below, organizations usually select a variety of media that support one another. For example, some organizations use the broad reach of advertising to get the word out to many potential candidates, and then direct these candidates to the organization's website for a richer presentation.

## Advertisements

Given space limitations for some online and printed media, and the potentially limited attention spans of readers, ads are often short and to the point. Unfortunately, because of the short duration of most advertisements, they typically cannot provide rich information. Because advertisements are obvious attempts at persuasion, they tend to have relatively low credibility. They can have a very broad reach, though, so they should be seriously considered if the organization wishes to reach a broad market.

Ads appear in a variety of places other than business publications and can be found in local, regional, and national news media; on television and radio; and in bargain shoppers, door hangers, direct mail, and welcome wagon packets. Advertisements can thus be used to reach a broad market segment. There are many different types of ads:

1. *Classified advertisements.* These ads appear in the "help wanted" section of the newspaper or online at sites like Craigslist. Newspaper ads, whether in print or online, are often limited in length and style, but some online sites allow for much more information. These ads are used most often for quick résumé solicitation for low-level jobs at a low cost. Although there has been a major shift toward the use of electronic recruiting, and all newspapers have online resources as well, surveys suggest that print ads remain a significant presence in the recruiting of hourly workers.[36] An example of a classified ad is shown in Exhibit 5.7. The length of this ad is more typical of online sources that do not limit words or characters.

2. *Banner ads.* Banner ads are online advertisements placed on websites that an organization believes will be visited by potential applicants, including social media sites, occupation-specific websites, or news media sites. They are limited in size, but viewers can easily click over to the organization's official site for a more extensive description of the job. Depending on the website where the banner ad is placed, these can be either relatively cheap or quite expensive.

3. *Display ads.* Display ads are larger and more involved than classified ads, and they are usually developed in conjunction with a professional advertising agency. These ads allow for freedom of design and placement in a publication. Thus, they are very expensive and begin to resemble recruitment brochures. These ads are typically used when an employer is searching for a large number of applicants to fill multiple openings. They are often found in professional publications as part of a targeted marketing strategy.

**EXHIBIT 5.7   Classified Ad for Human Resource Generalist**

### HUMAN RESOURCE GENERALIST

ABC Health, a leader in the health care industry, currently has a position available for an experienced **Human Resource Generalist.**

This position will serve on the human resources team, which serves as a business partner with our operational departments. Our team prides itself on developing and maintaining progressive and impactful human resources policies and programs.

Qualified candidates for this position will possess a bachelor's degree in business with an emphasis on human resource management, or a degree in a related field, such as industrial psychology. In addition, a minimum of three years of experience as a human resource generalist is required. This experience should include exposure to at least four of the following functional areas: compensation, employment, benefits, training, employee relations, and performance management.

In return for your contributions, we offer a competitive salary as well as comprehensive, flexible employee benefits. If you meet the qualifications and our opportunity is attractive to you, please forward your résumé and salary expectations to:

Human Resource Department
ABC Health
P.O. Box 123
Pensacola, FL 12345
An Equal Opportunity/Affirmative Action Employer

4. *Radio and television ads.* Organizations that advertise on the radio or on television purchase a 30- or 60-second time slot to advertise openings in specific job categories. Choice of stations and broadcast times will target specific audiences. For example, a classical music radio station will likely draw in different applicants than would a contemporary pop music radio station; an all-sports network will draw in different applicants than would a cooking program. Radio and television stations often have detailed demographic information available to potential advertisers. The advantage of radio and television advertisements is their reach. Individuals who are already searching for jobs generally read help-wanted ads, whereas those who are not currently looking for jobs are more likely to hear radio and television ads. Being able to expand the potential job pool to include those who are not actively looking for work can be a real advantage in a tight labor market.

Although most recruiters are familiar with the advantages of the techniques described above, there are other media outlets that have been explored less frequently that might offer a recruiter a competitive advantage for attracting candidates. For example, BNSF Railway finds that advertising for jobs in movie theaters is an effective way to reach a diverse group of candidates who might not otherwise consider working in the rail industry. A large technology firm in Belgium experimented with a decidedly old-fashioned method of recruiting by sending handwritten postcards to potential applicants rather than using e-mail. This "strange" strategy paid off, with applicants recruited through the postcard method being more likely to reply, more qualified on average, and, among those who did apply, more likely to be invited for a job interview. In another unusual example of innovative media recruiting, the US Army has used a very popular online video game called *America's Army* to draw in thousands of recruits.[37]

Advertisements can be very costly and need to be monitored closely for yield. Using marketing data on audience demographics, employers can diversify their applicant pool by placing ads in media outlets that reach a variety of applicant populations. By carefully monitoring the results of each ad, the organization can make a more informed decision as to which ads should be run in the future. To track ads, each should be coded. Then, as résumés come into the organization in response to the ad, they can be organized according to the codes, and the yield for that ad can be calculated. This information will help the organization weed out less effective ads and focus on the more productive ones.

## Recruitment Brochures

A recruitment brochure is often sent or given directly to job applicants, or it is included as part of the organization's website. Information in the brochure may be very detailed, and hence, the brochure may be lengthy. A brochure not only covers information about the job but also communicates information about the organization and its location. It may include pictures in addition to written narrative in order to illustrate various aspects of the job, such as the city in which the organization is located and actual employees. These various means of demonstrating the features of the organization enhance the richness of this recruiting technique. The advantage of a brochure is that the organization controls who receives a copy. Also, it can be lengthier than an advertisement. A disadvantage is that it can be quite costly to develop, and because it is obviously a sales pitch made by the organization, it might be seen as less credible.

A successful brochure possesses (1) a unique theme or point of view relative to other organizations in the same industry and (2) a visual distinctiveness in terms of design and photographs. A good format for the brochure is to begin with a general description of the organization, including its history and culture (values, goals, "brand"). A description of the hiring process should come next, followed by a characterization of pay/benefits and performance reviews. Finally, the brochure should conclude with contact information.

## Organizational Websites

It may not be an overstatement to conclude that organizational websites have become the single most important medium through which organizations communicate with potential applicants. Nearly every large organization has a "career opportunities" page on its website, and many small organizations have company and point-of-contact information for job seekers. Websites are a powerful means of not only communicating information about jobs but also reaching applicants who otherwise would not bother (or know how or where) to apply. Thus, care must be taken to ensure that the organizational website is appealing to potential job candidates. The web is unique in that it may function as both a recruitment source and a recruitment medium. When a web page only serves to communicate information about the job or organization to potential applicants, it serves as a recruitment medium. However, when a web page attracts actual applicants, particularly when applicants are allowed to apply online, it also functions as a recruitment source.

Research has shown that organizations can successfully convey cultural messages on their websites by describing organizational policies, showing pictures, and including testimonials. Effective websites also permit users to customize the information they receive by asking questions about their preferences and providing relevant information.[38]

How can web designers put these findings into practice? The three core attributes driving the appeal of an organizational website are engagement, functionality, and content. First, the website must be vivid and attractive to applicants. Second, while engagement is important, at the same time the website must be functional, meaning that it is quick to load, easily navigated, and interactive. A website that is overly complcx may be vivid, but it will only generate frustration if it is hard to decipher or slow to load. Third, an organizational website must convey the information prospective applicants want to see, including current position openings, job requirements, and steps for applying. Many organizations also integrate video testimonials from current employees as a way to lure potential applicants. In industries where competition for talent is fierce, a textual job description may simply not be compelling enough to compete with a well-produced video featuring enthusiastic current employees.[39]

Of course, there is more to designing an organizational website than the three attributes discussed above. Exhibit 5.8 provides a thorough list of factors to keep in mind when designing a website for organizational recruitment.

## Videoconferencing

Videoconferencing is another way to communicate with applicants.[40] Rather than meet in person with applicants, organizational representatives meet with applicants

**EXHIBIT 5.8   Factors for Designing Organizational Websites**

1. *Keep it simple*—surveys reveal that potential job candidates are overwhelmed by complex, difficult-to-navigate websites; never sacrifice clarity for a flashy display—remember, a good applicant is there for the content, not for the bells and whistles.
2. *Make access easy; the web page and links should be easy to download*—studies reveal that individuals will not wait more than eight seconds for a page to download, so the four-color page that looks great will backfire if it takes the user too much time to download it (also make sure that the link to the recruiting site on the home page is prominently displayed).
3. *Provide an online application form*—increasingly, potential candidates expect to be able to submit an application online; online forms are not only desired by candidates, organizations can load responses directly into searchable databases.
4. *Provide information about company culture*—allow applicants to self-select out if their values clearly do not match those of your organization.
5. *Include selected links to relevant websites*—the words "selected" and "relevant" are key here; links to include might be a cost-of-living calculator and a career advice area.
6. *Make sure necessary information is conveyed to avoid confusion*—clearly specify job title, location, etc., so applicants know the job for which they are applying and, if there are several jobs, they don't apply for the wrong job.
7. *Keep the information current*—make sure position information is updated regularly (e.g., weekly).
8. *Evaluate and track the results*—periodically evaluate the performance of the website on the basis of various criteria (number of hits, number of applications, application/hits ratio, quality of hires, cost of maintenance, user satisfaction, time to hire, etc.) or set up a software program to track the response data.

face-to-face on a monitor, in separate locations. Nearly all laptop and tablet computers have the technology needed for videoconferencing, so most applicants can participate quite easily. Moreover, this technology makes it possible for the organization to screen applicants at multiple or remote locations without actually having to travel to those locations. Company representatives who will participate in these videoconferences should be carefully selected and trained so they can answer questions thoroughly and communicate in a compelling manner. Videoconferencing has most of the advantages of face-to-face communication. It has high richness because the recruiter can answer questions, and it is highly credible because most people trust personal communication with an identifiable person more than they trust a prepackaged message from an organization.

## Direct Contact

The most expensive, but potentially the most powerful, method for communicating with potential applicants is through direct contact. The two most common media for direct contact are telephone messages and e-mail. These techniques are much more personal than the other methods of recruiting because the applicants are specifically approached by the organization. Personal contacts are likely to be seen as more credible by respondents. In addition, messages delivered through direct contact often allow respondents to ask personally relevant questions, which obviously should enhance the richness of the information.

However, in the age of spamming, it is important to remember that most individuals will regard mass e-mailings or automated telephone messages with even less enthusiasm than that for junk mail. Most e-mail programs filter spam, and the more mass messages you send, the more likely it is that mail servers will identify your address as a problem. Therefore, e-mail contact should be used only for very specific individuals. Direct contact should be communicated in a way that makes it clear that the receiver is one of a small number of people who will receive the message. The messages should be highly personal, reflecting an understanding of the candidate's unique qualifications. Providing a response e-mail address or telephone number that allows respondents to ask questions about the job opening will also help increase the yield for the direct contact method. However, personalization and customized responding to questions obviously will increase the cost per individual contacted, so the trade-offs in terms of cost must be considered.

## Word of Mouth

One of the most powerful methods for communicating about a potential job opportunity is one that organizations cannot directly control: word of mouth.[41] This refers to the informal information regarding an organization's reputation, employment practices, and policies that can exert a powerful impact on job seekers' impressions of an employer. Because word of mouth usually comes from individuals who do not have a vested interest in "selling" the job, the messages are likely to be seen as more credible. The fact that job seekers can ask and have questions answered also makes word of mouth a very rich source of information. Some word of mouth is no longer conveyed face-to-face, as blogs and social networking sites can also be used to communicate information about employers.

How can organizations influence word of mouth? One technique is to carefully cultivate relationships with current employees, recognizing that the way they are treated will come to influence the ways that other potential applicants believe they will be treated. This means making certain that jobs are as intrinsically and extrinsically satisfying for the current workforce as possible. Organizations should also make conscious efforts to shape the perception of their employment brand by using online testimonials from current employees. These testimonials act as a sort of virtual equivalent of word of mouth. Although job seekers will likely be somewhat skeptical of any information on a corporate website, a testimonial from someone who works at the organization is still likely to be more persuasive than a conventional sales pitch.

## STRATEGY IMPLEMENTATION

Once the recruitment planning phase is complete and the organization has spread the word about the job opening through various communication media, the next phase is implementing the recruiting strategy. This process involves gathering applications from a variety of sources and evaluating the quantity of applicants, the quality of applicants, the cost of using each source, and the impact on HR outcomes.

## Individual Recruiting Sources

The first category of recruiting sources we consider are those that focus on the individuals the organization is attempting to contact. These sources target active job seekers who are submitting applications to a number of potential employers. This means that it is incumbent on the job seeker to actively participate in the process early on. Applicants generally apply only to organizations they believe are hiring, so effective use of communication media is necessary to elicit enough applications.

### Applicant Initiated

Applicant-initiated recruiting is among the most traditional and well-accepted techniques for finding a job. Most employers accept applications from job applicants who physically walk into the organization to apply for a job, who call the organization, or who contact the organization through the corporate website.

The usual point of contact for walk-ins or phone inquiries is the receptionist in smaller organizations and the employment office in larger organizations. When applications are accepted, a contact person responsible for processing such applicants needs to be assigned. If the applications will be completed on paper or through an electronic on-site application system like a job kiosk, space must be created for walk-ins to complete applications and preemployment tests. Additionally, hours must be established when applicants can apply for jobs, and procedures must be in place to ensure that data from these individuals are entered into the applicant flow process. If walk-ins or résumé senders are treated like intruders, they may communicate a very negative image about the organization to the community.

As we noted previously, a company's website can blend the process of spreading information about a job opening with the process of submitting an application. Although surveys reveal that most employers believe their websites do a better job of attracting applicants than do job boards, many of these websites do not live up to their potential.[42] Many have been likened to little more than post office boxes where applicants can send their résumés. It is important to remember that communication with an applicant shouldn't end with his or her online application. Apple's website, for example, allows applicants to track the status of their application for 90 days after they apply. Procter and Gamble does the same thing, using a process eased by software that automatically scores its online applications and provides feedback to the applicants.[43]

All of the principles we described earlier in website design should be kept in mind when it comes to the application pages. In particular, the application portal should be simple, easy to use, informative, and up-to-date. To assess job seeker preferences, consultants from Brass Ring watched applicants go through the process of visiting organization websites, with the applicants describing their thought processes aloud. The consultants' research indicates that recruits are often frustrated by complex application systems, especially those that require them to enter the same data multiple times. To keep potential applicants from feeling disconnected from the online recruiting process, it is advisable to keep in touch with them at every stage of the process. To speed things up, some organizations inform applicants immediately if there is a mismatch between the information they provided and the job requirements; thus they can know immediately that they are not under consideration. Quickly eliminating unacceptable candidates also allows recruiters to respond more quickly to applicants who do have sufficient KSAOs. A review of online job solicitation found that the best website advertising offered special features to potential applicants, including opportunities to check where they are in the hiring process, examples of a typical "day in the life" at an organization, and useful feedback to applicants regarding their potential fit with the organization and job early in the process.

Many organizations have taken these suggestions to heart and are working to improve the functionality of their online application process. For example, Red Lobster's recruiting site was revised as part of a comprehensive effort to better leverage the organization's brand-based recruiting strategy. To facilitate exploring work options, candidates are directed through several job options on the basis of their level of experience and are provided detailed descriptions and requirements for each position before they apply. Comparing multiple jobs parallels the format many job seekers might be familiar with from e-commerce sites; essentially, applicants can "shop" for jobs. Encouraging potential applicants to carefully consider a variety of work options should lead to a better eventual person/job match. Research also shows that candidates prefer organizational websites that allow them to customize the information they receive. Candidates considering many jobs might self-select out of jobs that are not really of interest to them, which might help reduce the applicant pool to a set of more interested, qualified candidates and also reduce turnover down the line.

### Employment Websites

Employment websites have evolved from their original function as job boards and database repositories of jobs and résumés to become fully featured recruiting and screening centers.[44] For employers that pay a fee, many employment websites provide services like targeted advertising, video advertising, preemployment screening examinations, and applicant tracking. For job seekers, there are resources to facilitate exploring different career paths, information about the communities where jobs are offered, and access to message boards where current and former employees can sound off on the culture and practices of different organizations.

Millions of job seekers submit their résumés to employment websites every year, and there are thousands of job sites to which they can apply. Although it is difficult to obtain precise data on the use of employment websites, some estimates suggest that they are second only to referrals as a source of new hires. On the other hand, research suggests that solicitations for employment from electronic bulletin boards are seen as especially low in credibility and informativeness relative to organization websites or face-to-face meetings at campus placement offices. Therefore, these methods should not be used without having some supporting practices that involve more interpersonal contact.[45]

One difficulty in the use of the Internet in recruiting is that many sites specifically designed for recruitment become defunct. Conversely, new employment websites come online almost daily. Thus, one cannot assume that the sites an organization used in the past will be the best options in the future, or that they will even exist. Any attempt to summarize the current state of the Internet job posting board scene needs to be taken with a grain of salt, since the landscape for Internet recruiting is shifting very rapidly. Another difficulty with Internet recruiting is the growing problem of identity theft, where fake jobs are posted online in order to obtain vital information on a person or to extract a fake fee.

*General Employment Websites.*  Most readers of this book are likely familiar with the biggest employment websites, so it is easy to forget that they have only had a major impact on the job search process over the past 10 or 20 years. Since that time, a few early movers and larger entrants have grabbed the lion's share of the market. Three of the biggest employment websites are Monster, CareerBuilder, and Indeed, which collectively are estimated to be responsible for a large portion of external Internet hires. Glassdoor is another very popular employment website that has done an especially good job of integrating various social media into its approach.

General employment websites are not limited to simple advertising, as noted earlier. Services are rapidly evolving for these sites, and many now offer the ability to create and approve job requisitions online, manage recruiting tasks, track the progress of open positions and candidates, and report on recruiting metrics like time to hire, cost per hire, and equal employment opportunity (EEO). Several of the larger employment websites have developed extensive cross-listing relationships with local newspapers, effectively merging the advantages of local media in terms of credibility and name recognition with the powerful technological advances and large user base of employment websites.[46]

***Niche Employment Websites.*** Although there are advantages to open recruitment, as described earlier, it is also possible to conduct a more targeted web-based recruitment effort through niche employment websites.[47] These sites focus on specific occupations (there are employment websites for jobs ranging from nurses to geologists to metal workers), specific industries (sports, chemicals, transportation, human services), and specific locations (cities, states, or regions often have their own sites). Increasingly, employment websites are targeting blue-collar jobs as well. Recruiters looking for examples of niche job sites for a specific occupation can simply do an Internet search of "employment websites" coupled with the occupation of interest. Although any one niche job board is unlikely to have a huge number of posters, collectively these more specific websites have been estimated to account for two-thirds of Internet hiring. Experienced recruiters claim that the audience for niche employment websites is often more highly qualified and interested in specific jobs than are applicants from more general job sites.

Niche job sites have also been developed that cater to specific demographic groups, including women, African Americans, and Hispanics. Organizations that want to improve the diversity of their work sites or that are under an AAP should consider posting in a variety of such specialized employment websites as part of their search strategy. Survey data suggest that applicants believe that companies that advertise on these targeted websites are more positively disposed toward workforce diversity, further serving to enhance the usefulness of diversity-oriented advertising.[48]

***Searching Employment Website Databases.*** As opposed to actively posting jobs online, another (but not mutually exclusive) means of recruiting on the web is to search for applicants without ever having posted a position. Under this process, applicants submit their résumés online, which are then forwarded to employers when they meet the employer's criteria. Such systems allow searching the databases according to various search criteria, such as job skills, years of work experience, education, major, grade-point average, and so forth. It costs applicants anywhere from nothing to hundreds of dollars to post their résumé or other information on the databases. For organizations, there is always a cost. The exact nature of the cost depends on both the database(s) to which the organization subscribes and the services requested.

## Social Recruiting Sources

A second major type of recruiting source is social networks. These recruiting sources rely on the relationships that potential employees have with either those who currently work for the organization or others who might endorse the organization. Although it's generally the case that these interpersonal recruiting sources will yield fewer applicants than broader media-based recruiting sources used in the individual approaches, there are some distinct advantages to social networks that we review below.

### Employee Referrals

Employees currently working for an employer are a valuable source for finding job applicants.[49] Employees can refer people they know to their employer for consideration. Most estimates suggest that referrals are one of the most commonly used recruiting methods. The vast majority of organizations accept referrals, though only about half have formal programs. In some organizations, a cash bonus is given to employees who refer job candidates who prove to be successful on the job for a given period of time. Most bonuses range from a few hundred dollars to thousands of dollars. To ensure adequate returns on bonuses for employee referrals, it is essential to have a good performance appraisal system in place to measure the performance of the referred new hire. There also needs to be a good applicant tracking system to ensure that new hire performance is maintained over time before a bonus is offered.

Referral programs have many potential advantages, including low cost per hire, high-quality hires, decreased hiring time, and an opportunity to strengthen bonds with current employees. Research also shows that individuals hired through referrals are less likely to leave.

Employee referral programs may fail to work for any number of reasons. Current employees may lack the motivation or ability to make referrals. Additionally, employees sometimes don't realize the importance of recruitment to the organization. As a result, the organization may need to encourage employee participation by providing special rewards and public recognition along with bonuses for successful referrals. And finally, employees may not be able to match people with jobs, because they do not know about vacancies or the requirements needed to fill them. Hence, employees must regularly be notified of job vacancies and their requirements.

Former employees can be an ideal source of future applicants, either by recruiting them to come back to the organization or by asking them to provide referrals. As return employees, they will know the organization, its jobs, and its culture and will also be well known to those inside the organization. This not only cuts down on orientation costs but also means they can get into the flow of work more quickly. As referral sources, they can convey their personal observations to other job seekers, and thus those who decide to apply will be better informed. Using former employees as a recruiting source naturally means that the organization must remain on good terms with departing employees and keep channels of communication open after employees leave. Many organizations that undergo cyclical layoffs or downsizing in lean times might also seek to rehire those who were laid off previously when the organization returns to an expansionary strategy.[50]

## Social Networking Sites

Another way of finding applicants is through social networking sites, where friends or acquaintances are used to connect those looking for applicants to those looking for jobs. Many recruiters have turned to social networking websites such as Twitter, LinkedIn, and Facebook as sources for finding qualified job candidates.[51] The use of social networking has become so prevalent that recruiting software integrates these sites into the applicant tracking process. Recruiters can automatically post openings to these social networking sites and receive reports on which channels are resulting in the most leads and the best candidates.[52] The use of social networking sites has a number of advantages. Because many of the connections between users are based on professional background or shared work experiences, networking sites often provide access to groups of potential employees with specific skill sets. Some social networking websites geared toward professionals encourage users to indicate the industry and area in which they work. Recruiters can set up their own profile pages with these websites, encouraging potential applicants to apply by making personal contacts. By accessing the social networks of those already employed in the organization, it is possible to locate passive candidates who are already employed and not necessarily looking for a new job. In fields where the unemployment rate is very low, such as engineering, health care, and information technology (IT), these passive candidates may be the primary source of potential applicants.

However, some recruiters find that these networking sites are not very efficient, because of the large number of passive candidates who are not interested in alternative employment offers. Organizations can face troubling legal and ethical quandaries when using social networking sites, because candidates' personal information, such as marital status, health status, or demographics, is often publicly available on personal pages. To avoid these problems, recruiters are strongly advised not to ask potential applicants to provide access to personal information when conducting networking-based recruiting. Only publicly available information should be viewed. Companies should establish strong guidelines for the use of social media, because managers may be using personal information without the company's knowledge or consent.[53]

## Professional Associations and Meetings

Organizations can take advantage of the relationships their employees have with professional associations. Through networking with others who do similar work, employees can develop contacts with potential new recruits. This contact can be established informally by reaching individuals via e-mail or through message boards. Professional associations sometimes have a formal placement function that is available throughout the year. For example, the websites of professional associations often advertise both positions available and interested applicants. Others may have a computerized job and application bank.

Many technical and professional organizations meet around the country at least once a year. Many of these groups run a placement service for their members, and some may charge a fee to recruit at these meetings. This source represents a way to attract applicants with specialized skills or professional credentials. Also, some meetings are an opportunity to attract underrepresented groups.

## Organizational Recruiting Sources

External organizations form a third major category of potential recruiting sources. These connections tend to be more formal than social networks, and so they tend not to provide some of the relational advantages of individual contact. However, external organizations are more likely to provide access to a large number of potential applicants. Organizational recruiting sources can also help narrow down the applicant pool by providing formal screening services.

### Colleges and Placement Offices

Colleges are a source of people with specialized skills for professional positions. Most colleges have a placement office or officer who is in charge of ensuring that a match is made between the employer's interests and the graduating student's interests. Research has shown that campus recruiting efforts are seen as more informative and credible than organization websites or electronic bulletin boards.[54] In fact, recruiting experts found that members of the tech-savvy millennial generation are reluctant to use social networking and other Internet job search tools, and that they prefer campus career placement offices to find jobs.[55]

In most cases, the placement office is the point of contact with colleges. It should be noted, however, that not all students use the services of the placement office. Students sometimes avoid placement offices because they believe they will be competing against the very best students and will be unlikely to receive a job offer. Additional points of contact for students at colleges include professors, department heads, professional fraternities, honor societies, recognition societies, and national professional societies. Organizations sometimes overlook small colleges as a recruitment source because the small number of students does not make it seem worth the effort to visit. In order to present a larger number of students to choose from, some small colleges have banded together in consortia. For example, the Oregon Liberal Arts Placement Consortium provides a centralized recruitment source for nine small public and private colleges and universities. It is essential that appropriate colleges and universities be selected for a visit.

A difficult choice for the employer is deciding which colleges and universities to target for recruiting efforts. Some organizations focus their efforts on schools with the best return on investment and invest in those programs more heavily. Other organizations, especially large ones with relatively high turnover, find they need to cast a much broader net. In the end, the decision of breadth versus depth comes down to the number of individuals who need to be hired, the recruiting budget, and a strategic decision about whether to invest deeply in a few programs or more broadly in more programs. Some factors to consider when deciding which colleges and universities to target include the following:[56]

1. Past experiences with students at the school—including the quality of recent hires (measured in terms of performance and turnover), offer acceptance rates, skills, experience, and training in the areas where job openings exist—should be factored in.
2. Rankings of school quality. *U.S. News and World Report*, *The Gorman Report*, and *Peterson's Guide* are comprehensive rankings of colleges and universities and various degree programs. *BusinessWeek*, the *Wall Street Journal*, and the *Financial Times* rank business schools. Applicants recruited from highly ranked programs almost always come at a premium, so organizations need to make sure they are getting a good return on their investment.
3. The costs of recruiting at a particular school must be assessed. Colleges and universities that are nearby often mean substantially fewer resources expended on travel (both for recruiters traveling to the school and for bringing applicants in for interviews).

There are several ways an organization can establish a high-quality relationship with a school. A critical task is to establish a good relationship with the placement director. Although most placement directors are eager to make the organization's recruitment process productive and pleasant, there are many aspects where they exert additional influence over the success of the organization's recruitment of high-quality graduates (e.g., informal discussions with students about good employers, alerting recruiters to impressive candidates). Another way to establish a high-quality relationship with a school is to maintain a presence. This presence can take various forms, and organizations are increasingly becoming more creative and aggressive in establishing relationships with universities and their students. Some investment banks, consulting firms, and other companies shell out $500,000 and more per school to fund career seminars, gifts for students, and fancy dinners. Ernst & Young built a study room at Columbia University, and GE sponsored an e-commerce lab at the University of Connecticut.[57] Other companies are using nonconventional approaches. UPS has hired massage therapists to give students massages at job fairs. Ford has allowed students to test-drive Fords and Jaguars. Dow has even held crayfish boils.

Some organizations develop a talent pipeline that includes individuals in educational institutions who may not take a job immediately but may be attracted into the organization in the future. Managing an organization's talent pipeline means establishing effective relationships even before positions open up. Some organizations try to develop early relationships with incoming college freshmen in hopes that they will consider the organization as a potential employer when they graduate. Organizations that engage in large-scale collaborative research and development efforts with universities cultivate relationships with faculty, with the hope of eventually luring them into private sector work. Many organizations establish folders or databases of high-potential individuals who are still receiving an education or who work for other companies and then regularly send materials to these individuals about potential career prospects within the organization. Intel has run a competition called "Cornell Cup" in which student teams from a number of universities compete to design the best engineering projects. Those who perform well are not only given cash prizes but also invited to take on summer jobs or internships.[58]

## Employment Agencies

One traditional source of nonexempt employees and lower-level exempt employees is employment agencies. These agencies contact, screen, and present applicants to employers for a fee. The fee is contingent on successful placement of a candidate with an employer and is usually a percentage of the candidate's starting pay. In a temp-to-hire arrangement, the employee has a trial period in which his or her contract will be contingent on performance, and then after a period of time the employee will be taken on as permanent employee of the organization. This gives both the applicant and the employer a chance to observe each other and assess the quality of the fit. Many jurisdictions have specific duration requirements for these arrangements, such as laws stating that employees may be classified as "temporary" for only 90 days.

Care must be exercised in selecting an employment agency. It is a good idea to check references, as allegations abound regarding the shoddy practices of some agencies. A poor agency may, for example, flood the organization with résumés of both qualified and unqualified applicants. A good agency will screen out unqualified applicants and not attempt to dazzle the organization with a large volume of résumés. Poor agencies may misrepresent the organization to the candidate and the candidate to the organization. Misrepresentation may take place when the agency is only concerned about a quick placement (and fee) and pays no regard to the costs of poor future relationships with clients. A good agency will be in business for the long run and not misrepresent information and invite turnover. A good agency will not pressure managers, make special deals, or avoid the HR staff. Finally, it is important to have a signed contract in place in which mutual rights and responsibilities are laid out.

Although employment agencies have traditionally focused on individuals with comparatively low skill levels, many agencies have expanded to include individuals with specialized or technical skills. There are even employment agencies that specialize in areas like health care or engineering, which require very high levels of expertise. Some of these agencies provide recruiting and screening services for potential employers, and then employees receive an offer of a permanent position like recruits from any other source. However, even for these technical fields, temp-to-hire arrangements are not unheard of.

## Executive Search Firms

For higher-level professional positions or jobs with salaries of $100,000 and higher, executive search firms, or "headhunters," may be used. Like employment agencies, these firms contact and screen potential applicants and present résumés to employers. The difference between employment agencies and search firms lies in two primary areas: (1) search firms typically deal with higher-level positions than those of employment agencies, and (2) search firms are more likely to operate on the basis of a retainer than on a contingency. Search firms that operate on a retainer are paid regardless of whether a successful placement is made. The advantage of operating this way, from the hiring organization's standpoint, is that it aligns the interests of the search firm with those of the organization. Thus, search firms operating on retainer do not feel compelled to put forward candidates just so their contingency fee can be paid. Moreover, a search firm on retainer may be less likely to give up if the job is not filled in a few weeks. Of late, business has been slow for executive search firms, partly due to the moderate economic growth and the bustling online recruiting business. Thus, organizations have been able to negotiate smaller fees (retainers or contingencies).[59]

Increasingly, executive search firms are getting into the appraisal business, where an organization pays the search firm to provide an assessment of the organization's top executives. On one level this makes sense, since executive search firms are in the assessment business. The problem is that since the executive assessment pays much less than the retainer or contingency fees for hiring an executive, the search firms have an incentive to pronounce top executives substandard so as to justify bringing in an outsider. This is exactly what happened with a top executive search firm whose executive recruiters negatively evaluated an executive, only to recommend hiring an outsider, for which the recruiters were compensated handsomely. Given these inherent conflicts of interest, organizations should avoid using the same search firm to hire new executives and to appraise its existing executive team.[60]

## Social Service Agencies

All states have an employment or job service. These services are funded by employer-paid payroll taxes and are provided by the state to help secure employment for those seeking it, particularly those currently unemployed. Typically, these services refer low- to middle-level employees to employers. For jobs to be filled properly, the hiring organization must maintain a close relationship with the employment service. Job qualifications need to be clearly communicated to ensure that proper screening takes place by the agency. Positions that have been filled must be promptly reported to the agency so that résumés are not sent for closed positions. The federal Job Corps program is another option. Job Corps is designed to help individuals between 16 and 24 years of age obtain employment. The program targets individuals with lower levels of education and prepares them for entry-level jobs through a combination of work ethic training and general job skills. For employers, Job Corps can provide specialized training, prescreening of applicants, and tax benefits. Some agencies in local communities may also provide outplacement assistance for the unemployed who cannot afford it. Applicants who use these services may also be listed with a state employment service. Community agencies may also offer counseling and training.

The US Department of Labor has provided funding for states to develop one-stop career centers that will provide workers with various programs, benefits, and opportunities related to finding jobs. The centers' emphasis is on providing customer-friendly services that reach large segments of the population and are fully integrated with state employment services. These centers now offer a variety of skills certification programs, such as the National Work Readiness Credential and the National Career Readiness Certificate, which are highly sought after by employers.[61] For example, when Honda decided to build its Odyssey plant in Alabama, part of the deal was that the state would establish a close partnership with Honda to recruit and train employees.[62] Nissan has established similar relationships with the states of Mississippi and Tennessee. The state of Illinois provides customized applicant screening and referral to employers so efficiently that some employers, such as Jewel-Osco, use the service as an extension of their HR department.[63]

## Job Fairs

Industry associations, schools, groups of employers, the military, and other interested organizations often hold career or job fairs to attract applicants. Typically, the sponsors of a job fair will meet in a central location with a large facility in order to provide information, collect résumés, and screen applicants. Often, there is a fee for employers to participate. Job fairs may provide both short- and long-term gains. In the short run, the organization may identify qualified applicants. In the long run, it may be able to enhance its visibility in the community, which, in turn, may improve its image and ability to attract applicants for jobs.

For a job fair to yield a large number of applicants, it must be advertised well in advance. Moreover, advertisements may need to be placed in specialized publications likely to attract minorities and women. To attract quality candidates from all those in attendance, the organization must be able to differentiate itself from all the other organizations competing for applicants at the job fair. Items such as mugs and key chains with the company logo can be distributed to remind the applicants of employment opportunities at a particular organization. An even better promotion may be to provide attendees at the fair with assistance in developing their résumés and cover letters.

One strength of job fairs is also a weakness—although a job fair enables the organization to reach many people, the typical job fair has around 1,600 applicants vying for the attention of about 65 employers. Given the ratio of 25 applicants for every employer, the typical contact with an applicant is probably shallow. In response, some employers instead (or also) devote their resources to information sessions geared toward a smaller group of specially qualified candidates. During these sessions, the organization presents information about itself, including its culture, work environment, and career opportunities. Small gifts and brochures are also typically given out. One recent research study showed that applicants who were favorably impressed by an organization's information session were significantly more likely to pursue employment with the organization. Other studies show that job fairs that allow for interpersonal interactions between job seekers and organization representatives are seen as especially informative by job seekers. Thus, both applicants and employers find information sessions a valuable alternative, or complement, to job fairs.[64]

Increasingly, job fairs are being held online, with preestablished time limits. One online recruiting site held a job fair that included 240 participating companies. In these virtual job fairs, recruiters link up with candidates through chat rooms.

### Co-ops and Internships

A large number of educational institutions, including many high schools and nearly all technical colleges and universities, require some or all of their students to get work experience as part of their degree programs. Co-ops and internships are two potential ways that employers can recruit applicants. Under a co-op arrangement, the student works with an employer on an alternating quarter basis. In one quarter the student works full time, and in the next quarter the student attends school full time. Under an internship arrangement, the student has a continuous period of employment with an employer for a specified period of time. These approaches allow an organization to not only obtain services from a part-time employee for a short period of time but also assess the person for a full-time position after graduation. One manager experienced in working with interns commented, "Working with them is one of the best talent-search opportunities available to managers."[65] In turn, interns have better employment opportunities as a result of their experiences.

Internships and co-op assignments can take a variety of forms. One type of assignment is to have the student perform a part of the business that occurs periodically. For example, some amusement parks that operate only in the summer in northern climates may have a large number of employees who need to be hired and trained in the spring. A student with a background in HR could perform these hiring and training duties. Increasingly, colleges and universities are giving students college credit for—in some cases, even instituting a requirement for—working as part of their professional degree.[66] A student in social work, for example, might be required to work in a welfare office for a summer. Occasionally, some internships and co-op assignments do not provide these meaningful experiences that build on the qualifications of the student. Research shows that school-to-work programs often do not provide high utility to organizations in terms of benefit-cost ratios. Thus, organizations need to evaluate co-ops and internships not only in terms of quality for the student but in terms of the cost-benefit economic perspective as well.[67]

Meaningful experiences benefit both the organization and the student. The organization gains from the influence of new ideas the student has been exposed to in his or her curriculum, and the student gains from the experience of having to apply concepts while facing the realities of organizational constraints. For both parties to gain, a learning contract must be developed and signed by the student, the student's advisor, and the corporate sponsor. The learning contract becomes, in essence, a job description to guide the student's activities. Also, it establishes the criteria by which the student's performance is assessed for purposes of grading by the academic advisor and for purposes of successful completion of the project for the organization. In the absence of a learning contract, internships can result in unrealistic expectations by the corporate sponsor, which, in turn, can result in disappointment when these unspoken expectations are not met.[68]

To secure the services of students, organizations can contact the placement offices of high schools, colleges, universities, and vocational technology schools. Also, teachers, professors, and student chapters of professional associations can be contacted to obtain student assistance. Placement officials can provide the hiring organization with the policies that need to be followed for placements, while teachers and professors can give guidance on the types of skills students could bring to the organization and the organizational experiences the students would benefit from the most.

## Recruiting Metrics

Each recruiting source has strengths and weaknesses. Determining the best method for an organization entails assessing the costs and benefits of each method and then selecting the optimal combination of sources to meet the organization's strategic needs. Exhibit 5.9 provides an overview of the metrics that might be expected for the categories of recruiting activities, along with issues considered relevant to each source. Conclusions for the number and types of applicants drawn by each method are informed by a number of studies comparing recruiting sources.[69] Although broad generalizations can be made regarding quantity, quality, cost, and impact on HR outcomes for different recruiting methods, each organization's unique labor market situation will need to be considered since the meta-analytic evidence shows considerable variety in the effects of recruiting variables on applicant attraction.

### Sufficient Quantity

The more broadly transmitted the organization's search methods, the more likely it is that a large number of individuals will be attracted to apply. Other methods of recruiting naturally tend to be more focused and will draw a comparatively small number of applicants. While broad recruiting methods such as advertising and Internet postings are able to reach thousands of individuals, it might be to an

**EXHIBIT 5.9**    Potential Recruiting Metrics for Different Sources

| Recruiting Source | Quantity | Quality | Costs | Impact on HR |
|---|---|---|---|---|
| Applicant initiated | Contingent on how widely the company's brand is known | Highly variable KSAO levels if no skill requirements are posted | Application processing and clerical staff time | Higher training costs, lower performance, higher turnover |
| Employment websites | Often opens to very large pool, although niche sites have a more narrow pool | Can provide specific keywords to limit applications to those with specific KSAOs | Subscription fees or user fees from database services | Good tracking data, potentially lower satisfaction, and higher turnover |
| Employee referrals | Generates a small number of applicants | Better fit because current employees will inform applicants about the culture | Signing bonuses are sometimes provided to increase quantity | Higher performance, higher satisfaction, lower turnover, lower diversity |
| Social networking sites | Potentially a large number of individuals, depending on employee use of networks | Depends on whether networks are made up of others with similar skills and knowledge | Time spent searching through networks and soliciting applications | Potentially similar results to referrals, although results are unknown |
| Professional associations and meetings | Comparatively few candidates will be identified for each job opening | Those attending professional meetings will be highly engaged and qualified | Cost of attending meetings and direct interviewing with staff can be very high | Superior performance, although those seeking jobs at meetings may be "job hoppers" |
| Colleges and placement offices | About 50 individuals can be contacted at each university per day | High levels of job-relevant human capital, usually screened on the basis of cognitive ability, little work experience | Time costs of establishing relationships, traveling to college locations | Initial training and development for inexperienced workers; can increase average KSAO levels |

(continued)

**EXHIBIT 5.9**   Continued

| Recruiting Source | Quantity | Quality | Costs | Impact on HR |
|---|---|---|---|---|
| Employment agencies | Many applicants for lower-level jobs, fewer applicants available for managerial or executive positions | Applicants will be prescreened; organizations are often able to try out candidates as temps prior to hiring | Fees charged by employment agencies | Reduced costs of screening candidates, improved person/job match |
| Executive search firms | Only a small number of individuals will be contacted | Search firms will carefully screen applicants, usually experienced candidates | Fees for executive searches can be more than half of the applicant's annual salary | Reduced staff time required because the search firm finds applicants; very high costs for firms |
| Social service agencies | There are usually a limited number of individuals available, although this varies by skill level | Applicants may have had difficulty finding jobs through other routes because of lack of skills | Often there are direct financial incentives for hiring from these agencies | Potentially greater training costs, higher levels of diversity |
| Job fairs | About 40 applicants can be contacted per recruiter per day | Often draws in individuals with some knowledge of the company or industry | Advertising and hosting costs are considerable, although this is an efficient way to screen many candidates | Higher levels of diversity if targeted to diverse audiences; effects on performance, satisfaction unknown |
| Co-ops and internships | Only a small number of interns can be used in most organizations | High levels of formal educational preparation, but few interns will have work experience | Cost of paid interns can be very high; unpaid interns are a huge cost savings although they often require staff time | Those who are hired will be prescreened, and should have higher performance and lower turnover |

organization's advantage not to attract too many applicants, because of the costs associated with processing all the applications.

### Sufficient Quality

Recruiting methods that link employers to a database of employees with exceptional skills will enable an employer to save money on screening and selection processes. But if the search is too narrow, the organization will likely be engaged in a long-term process of looking.

### Cost

The costs of any method of recruiting are the direct expenses involved in contacting job seekers and processing their applications. Some sources, such as radio advertisements, search firms, and sophisticated website portals that customize information and provide employees with feedback, are quite expensive to develop. These methods may be worth the cost if the organization needs to attract a large number of individuals, if KSAOs for a job are in short supply, or if the job is crucial to the organization's success. On the other hand, organizations that need fewer employees or that require easily found KSAOs discover that lower-cost methods like applicant-initiated recruiting or referrals are sufficient to meet their needs. Some fee-based services, like employment agencies, are able to process applications inexpensively because the pool of applicants is prescreened for relevant KSAOs.

### Impact on HR Outcomes

A considerable amount of research has been conducted on the effectiveness of various recruitment sources and can be used as a starting point for which sources are likely to be effective. Research has defined effectiveness as the impact of recruitment sources on increased employee satisfaction, job performance, diversity, and retention. Evidence suggests that, overall, referrals and job trials are likely to attract employees who have a better understanding of the organization and its culture, and therefore they tend to result in employees who are more satisfied, more productive, and less likely to leave. Conversely, sources like employment agencies can produce employees who are less satisfied and productive. Any general conclusions regarding the effectiveness of recruitment sources should be tempered by the fact that the location of an organization, the compensation and benefits packages provided, the type of workers, and the typical applicant experience and education levels will moderate the efficacy of these practices.

## TRANSITION TO SELECTION

Once a job seeker has been identified and attracted to the organization, the organization needs to prepare the person for the selection process. In preparation, applicants need to be made aware of the next steps in the hiring process and what will be required of them. If the recruiting organization overlooks this transition step, it may lose qualified applicants who mistakenly think that delays between steps in the hiring process indicate that the organization is no longer interested in them or who are fearful that they "didn't have what it takes" to successfully compete in the next steps.

The city of Columbus, Ohio, has done an excellent job preparing job seekers from external recruitment sources to apply for the position of firefighter. To become a firefighter, an applicant must pass a series of physical ability exams in which he or she completes an obstacle course, carries heavy equipment up stairs, and performs a number of other timed physical exercises. Many applicants have never encountered these types of tests before and are afraid that they don't have the physical ability to successfully complete them.

To prepare job seekers and applicants for these tests, videos were developed that give instructions for taking the tests and show a firefighter taking the tests. The videos are shown to those who have applied for the position, and they are also shown on public access television for those who are thinking about applying for the job. The city of Columbus also provides upper-body strength training, as this is a stumbling point for some job applicants in the selection process.

This example indicates that to successfully prepare people for the transition to selection, organizations should consider reviewing the selection method instructions with the applicants, showing them actual samples of the selection method, and providing them with practice or training if necessary. These steps should be followed not just for physical ability tests but for all selection methods in the hiring process that are likely to be unfamiliar to applicants or uncomfortable for them.

## LEGAL ISSUES

External recruitment practices are subject to considerable legal scrutiny and influence. During recruitment there is ample room for the organization to exclude certain applicant groups (e.g., minorities, women, and people with disabilities) as well as to deceive in its dealings with applicants. Various laws and regulations seek to limit these exclusionary and deceptive practices.

Legal issues regarding several of the practices are discussed in this section. These include definition of job applicants, AAPs, electronic recruitment, job advertisements, and fraud and misrepresentation.

### Definition of a Job Applicant

Both the Equal Employment Opportunity Commission (EEOC) and the Office of Federal Contract Compliance Programs (OFCCP) require the organization to keep applicant records. Exactly what is a job applicant and what records should be kept? It is necessary to provide guidance on the answer to this question in terms of both traditional hard-copy applicants and electronic applicants.

### Hard-Copy Applicants

The original (1979) definition of an applicant by the EEOC is in the Uniform Guidelines on Employee Selection Procedures (UGESP). It reads as follows: "The precise definition of the term 'applicant' depends on the user's recruitment and selection procedures. The concept of an applicant is that of a person who has indicated an interest in being considered for hiring, promotion, or other employment opportunities. This interest may be expressed by completing an application form, or might be expressed orally, depending on the employer's practice."

This definition was created prior to the existence of the electronic job application. It remains in force for hard-copy applications. Because it is so open-ended, it could create a substantial record-keeping burden for the organization since any contact with the organization by a person might count as an application for enforcement purposes. Hence, it is advisable for the organization to formulate and strictly adhere to written application policies and procedures that are communicated to organizational representatives and to all persons acting as though they are job applicants. Several suggestions for doing this follow.

First, require a written application from all who seek to be considered, and communicate this policy to all potential applicants. Inform people who apply by other means that they must submit a written application in order to be considered. If this policy is not defined, virtually anyone who contacts the organization or expresses interest by any means could be considered an applicant. Second, require that the applicant indicate the precise position applied for, and establish written minimum qualifications for each position. This way, the organization can legitimately refuse to consider as applicants those who do not meet these requirements. Third, establish a definite period for which the position will remain open, communicate this clearly to applicants, and do not consider those who apply after the deadline. Also, do not keep applications on hold or on file for future consideration. Fourth, return unsolicited applications through the mail. Finally, keep track of applicants who drop out of the process due to lack of interest or acceptance of another job. Such suggestions will help the organization limit the number of "true" applicants and reduce record keeping while also fostering legal compliance.[70]

### Internet Applicants

The OFCCP regulations (the Internet Applicant rule) provide a definition of an Internet applicant for federal contractors, as well as establish record-keeping requirements.[71] The EEOC has not yet provided a definition of an Internet applicant, though it is in the process of developing one.

According to the OFCCP, an individual must meet all four of the following criteria to be considered an Internet applicant:

- The individual submits an expression of interest in employment through the Internet or related electronic data technologies.
- The employer considers the individual for employment in a particular position.

- The individual's expression of interest indicates that the individual possesses the basic qualifications for the position.
- At no point in the employer's selection process prior to receiving an offer of employment from the employer does the individual remove himself or herself from further consideration or otherwise indicate that he or she is no longer interested in the position.

"Internet or related electronic data technologies" includes electronic mail/e-mail, résumé databases, job banks, electronic scanning technology, applicant tracking system/applicant service providers, applicant screeners, and résumé submission by fax. Mobile and hand-held devices such as cell and smart phones are also likely included. "Basic qualifications for the position" are those established in advance and advertised to potential applicants. They must be non-comparative across applicants, objective (e.g., BS in biology), and relevant to performance in the specific position.

The employer must keep records of the following:

- All expressions of interest submitted through the Internet and contacts made with the job applicant
- Internal résumé databases—including date of entry, the position for which each search was made, the date of the search, and the search criteria used
- External résumé databases—position for which each search was made, the date of the search, search criteria used, and the records for each person who met the basic qualifications for the position

The OFCCP regulations also require the employer to make every reasonable effort to gather race/gender/ethnicity data from both traditional and Internet applicants. The preferred method for doing so is voluntary self-disclosure, such as through tear-off sheets on an application form, postcards, or short forms to request the information or as part of an initial telephone screen. Observation may also be used. A series of questions and answers to the regulations provide additional information and clarification. Notable issues covered in this section include searching large databases, searching niche and diversity databases, and using employment agencies and recruitment firms, campus recruitment, job fairs, and applicants' noninterest in and self-removal from consideration for the position. The employer must keep records relating to adverse impact calculations for Internet applicants and for all test takers.

## Affirmative Action Programs

As discussed in Chapter 2, AAP regulations from the OFCCP require that the organization identify problem areas impeding EEO and undertake action-oriented programs to correct these problem areas and achieve the placement (hiring and promotion) goals. The regulations say little else specifically about recruitment activities. Based on former (now expired) regulations, however, the OFCCP offered considerable guidance to the organization for its recruitment actions:

- Update job descriptions and ensure their accuracy
- Widely circulate approved job descriptions to hiring managers and recruitment sources
- Carefully select and train all personnel included in staffing
- Reach out to organizations prepared to refer women and minority applicants, such as the Urban League, state employment (job) services, National Organization for Women, sectarian women's groups, and so forth
- Conduct formal briefings, preferably on organization premises, for representatives from recruiting sources
- Encourage women and minority employees to refer job applicants
- Include women and minorities on the HR department staff
- Actively participate in job fairs
- Actively recruit at secondary schools and community colleges with predominantly minority and female enrollment
- Use special employment programs, such as internships, work/study, and summer jobs
- Include minorities and women in the planning and production of recruitment brochures
- Expand help-wanted advertising to include female and minority news media

Taken in total, the OFCCP suggestions indicate that organizations with AAPs should undertake targeted recruitment programs using recruitment staff trained in affirmative action recruiting.

## Electronic Recruitment

Technology has flooded the recruitment process for both the organization and job applicants. Numerous legal issues may arise.

### Access

The use of electronic recruitment technologies may potentially create artificial barriers to employment opportunities.[72] It assumes that potential applicants have access to computers and the skills necessary to apply online. These may be poor assumptions, especially for some racial minorities and the economically disadvantaged. To guard against legal challenge and to ensure accessibility, the organization might do several things. One action is to supplement online recruitment with other widely used sources of recruitment, such as newspaper advertisements or other sources that organizational experience indicates are frequently used by women and minorities. Alternately, online recruitment and application could be restricted to certain jobs that have strong computer-related KSAO requirements. Applicants in all likelihood will have easy access to computers and online recruitment, as well as the skills necessary to successfully navigate and complete the application.

Another access issue is the use of recruitment software that conducts résumé searches within an applicant database using keyword search criteria. Staffing specialists or hiring managers often specify the search criteria to use, and they could select non-job-related criteria that cause adverse impact against women, minorities, or people with disabilities. Examples of such criteria include preferences for graduation from elite colleges or universities, age, and physical requirements. To guard against such a possibility, the organization should set only job-related KSAO requirements, restrict the search criteria to those KSAOs, and train recruiters in the appropriate specification and use of search criteria.

### People With Disabilities

The OFCCP provides specific regulations for people with disabilities.[73] If the employer routinely offers applicants various methods (including online) of applying for a job and all are treated equally, that may be sufficient for compliance purposes. If only an online application system is used, however, it must be made accessible to all. Examples here include making the organization's website compatible with screen readers and using assistive technology and adaptive software.

The regulations also indicate that the employer is obligated to provide reasonable accommodation to the applicant, if requested. Examples include the following:

- Making job vacancy application information available in Braille and responding to job inquiries via telecommunications devices for the deaf (TDDs) or use of the telephone relay system
- Providing readers, interpreters, or similar assistance during the application process
- Extending the time limit for completing an online examination
- Making testing locations fully accessible to those with mobility impairments

### Social Media and Networks

Recruiters might be tempted to troll for and access private information placed on social networks. The scope of social media and networks is broad. It includes social and professional networking websites (e.g., Facebook, LinkedIn, and Twitter), personal Internet accounts, photos, video clips and résumés, blogs, podcasts, text messages, e-mails, and website profiles. In total, social media and networks provide potential access to an incredible array of information about job applicants—information that is obtained outside of a traditional, carefully constructed recruitment/application process. Problems may arise.[74]

Social networks may contain applicant pools of limited diversity, creating adverse impact possibilities. Another problem is the quality and legality of information obtained. Legally protected characteristics are readily available, ranging from demographics to marital status, citizenship, and sexual orientation. On top of that, applicant information may not be accurate or job related and may even be maliciously planted. Finally, use of the information may run afoul of state/local statutes prohibiting the consideration of lawful off-duty conduct by the applicant (e.g., smoking, drinking, medical use of marijuana, political activity).

How might the organization proceed down this new, evolving legal path? The first suggestion is to learn about the many social media privacy laws states have or will soon have. Generally, these laws

- Identify the specific types of social media and networks covered
- Prohibit asking applicants or employees to disclose information (such as username or password) that would allow access to personal media information
- Prohibit taking an adverse action against an applicant (e.g., failure to hire) or employee (e.g., failure to promote; discharge) for not providing protected information

Second, decide whether the organization should use legally acquired social media information in recruitment and screening. For example, consider the type and quality of information likely to be gathered about applicants: Is it KSAO-focused, and can it be gathered in a thorough and systematic way for all applicants? Also, if social media information is gathered, will the organization be able to show that it was gathered legally by recruiters and hiring managers?

Third, if it is decided to gather and use social media information, develop policies and practices to safeguard the process. Address such topics as (1) which social media will be accessed and how, (2) when social media will be accessed in the recruitment process, (3) who will be allowed to access the information, (4) how the information will be evaluated and used, and (5) what guidelines and training will be given to those allowed to access the information.

Consensus on best practices for these topics has not yet emerged. A set of suggestions as food for thought, however, is as follows:

1. Avoid early screening of applicants via social media
2. Inform job applicants that the organization may gather and use social media information about them
3. Gather and evaluate only job-related, KSAO-focused information
4. Prohibit hiring managers from accessing and evaluating social media information
5. Have only trained staffing professionals gather and evaluate social media information
6. Gather and evaluate social media information only late in the recruitment process so that EEO-related information about applicants is already known
7. Conduct a social media review only for finalists for the job as part of a formal background check

These suggestions show there is much to be considered as the organization develops appropriate and legally defensible practices.

Finally, the organization should examine its own social media practices for recruiting applicants. It should ensure that its recruitment messages do not discourage applications based on EEO protected characteristics and, conversely, that the messages portray a welcoming of applicant diversity. In addition, the organization should make sure that its recruitment information is accurate and does not make any false promises about job offer content or future business and employment opportunities (see "Fraud and Misrepresentation" below).[75]

## Job Advertisements

Job advertising that indicates preferences or limitations for applicants based on legally protected characteristics is generally prohibited (see Chapter 2). Questions continually arise as to exceptions or less blatant forms of advertising, as the following examples indicate.[76]

Title VII permits indicating preferences based on sex, religion, or national origin (but not race or color) if they are bona fide occupational qualifications (BFOQs). The organization should be sure about the legality and validity of any BFOQ claims before conducting such advertising. Use of gender-specific job titles such as waitress or repairman, however, generally should be avoided.

Using the phrase "women and minorities are encouraged to apply" in a job advertisement is okay because it is an inclusive effort to generate the largest pool of qualified applicants. An indication that the organization is "seeking" a particular type of applicant (e.g., stay-at-home moms), however, is not permitted, because it connotes a preference for a particular group rather than an encouragement to apply.

Regarding age preferences, advertisements cannot limit or deter potential older applicants from seeking a position. It is permissible, however, to show a preference for older workers, using phrases such as "over age 60," "retirees," or "supplement your pension."

These examples show that the line between permissible and prohibited ad content is quite murky. The organization thus should monitor the construction and content of all its job advertisements.

## Fraud and Misrepresentation

Puffery, promises, half-truths, and even outright lies are all encountered in recruitment under the guise of selling the applicant on the job and the organization. Too much of this type of selling can be legally dangerous. When it occurs, under workplace tort law, applicants may file suit claiming fraud or misrepresentation.[77] Claims may cite false statements of existing facts (e.g., the nature and profitability of the employer's business) or false promises of future events (e.g., promises about terms and conditions of employment, pay, promotion opportunities, and geographic location). It does not matter if the false statements were made intentionally (fraud) or negligently (misrepresentation). Both types of statements are a reasonable basis for a claim by an applicant or newly hired employee.

To be successful in such a suit, the plaintiff must demonstrate that

1. A misrepresentation of a material fact occurred
2. The employer knew, or should have known, about the misrepresentation
3. The plaintiff relied on the information to make a decision or take action
4. The plaintiff was injured because of reliance placed on the statements made by the employer

Though these four requirements may appear to be a stiff set of hurdles for the plaintiff, they are by no means insurmountable, as many successful plaintiffs can attest. Avoidance of fraud and misrepresentation claims in recruitment requires straightforward action by the organization and its recruiters. First, provide applicants with the job description and specific, truthful information about the job rewards. Second, be truthful about the nature of the business and its profitability. Third, avoid specific promises about future events regarding terms and conditions of employment or business plans and profitability. Finally, make sure that all recruiters follow these suggestions when they recruit job applicants.

## SUMMARY

The objective of the external recruitment process is to identify and attract qualified applicants to the organization. To meet this objective, the organization must conduct strategic recruitment planning. The single most important issue at this stage is developing a strong link between organizational strategy and the goals of the recruiting process. The organization will also choose whether to implement an open strategy or a targeted strategy. At this stage, attention must also be given to both organizational issues (e.g., centralized versus decentralized recruitment function) and administrative issues (e.g., size of the budget).

The next stage is to develop a message for the job applicants and to select a medium to convey that message. The message may be realistic, branded, or targeted. There is no one best message; it depends on the characteristics of the labor market, the job, and the applicants. The message can be communicated through several different media, each of which has strengths and weaknesses.

Applicants are influenced by characteristics of recruiters and the recruitment process. Through proper attention to these characteristics, the organization can help provide applicants with a favorable recruitment experience.

Choices the organization makes about which sources to use follow from the previous stages. The strategy implementation process involves comparing individual, social, and organizational sources and evaluating their effectiveness through a variety of recruiting metrics. After a sufficient number of individuals have applied, the organization begins the process of transition to selection. Recruitment practices and decisions come under intense legal scrutiny because of their potential for discrimination at the beginning of the staffing process. The legal definition of a job applicant creates record-keeping requirements for the organization that, in turn, have major implications for the design of the entire recruitment process. Affirmative Action Programs Regulations likewise affect the entire recruitment process, prodding the organization to set targeted placement goals for women and minorities and to be aggressive in recruitment outreach actions. Job advertisements may not contain applicant preferences regarding protected characteristics such as age and gender. Finally, recruitment communication with applicants must be careful to avoid false statements or promises, lest problems of fraud and misrepresentation arise.

## DISCUSSION QUESTIONS

1. List and briefly describe each of the administrative issues that needs to be addressed in the planning stage of external recruiting.
2. List 10 sources of applicants that organizations turn to when recruiting. For each source, identify needs specific to the source, as well as pros and cons of using the source for recruitment.
3. In designing the communication message to be used in external recruiting, what kinds of information should be included?
4. What are the advantages of conveying a realistic recruitment message as opposed to portraying the job in a way that the organization thinks that job applicants want to hear?
5. What strategies are organizations using to ensure that they attract women and underrepresented racioethnic groups?

## ETHICAL ISSUES

1. Many organizations have adopted a targeted recruitment strategy. For example, some organizations target workers 50 years of age and older in their recruitment efforts, which includes advertising specifically in media outlets frequented by older individuals. Other organizations target recruitment messages at women, minorities, or those with the desired skills. Do you think targeted recruitment systems are fair? Why or why not?
2. Most organizations have job boards on their web page where applicants can apply for jobs online. What ethical obligations, if any, do organizations have to individuals who apply for jobs online?

## APPLICATIONS

### Improving a College Recruitment Program

The White Feather Corporation (WFC) is a rapidly growing consumer products organization that specializes in the production and sales of specialty household items such as lawn furniture cleaners, spa (hot tub) accessories, mosquito and tick repellents, and stain-resistant garage floor paints. The organization has 400 exempt employees and 3,000 nonexempt employees, almost all of whom are full time. In addition to its corporate office in Clucksville, Arkansas, the organization has five plants and two distribution centers at various rural locations throughout the state.

Two years ago WFC created a corporate HR department to provide centralized direction and control for its key HR functions—planning, compensation, training, and staffing. In turn, the staffing function is headed by the senior manager of staffing, who receives direct reports from three managers: the manager of nonexempt employment, the manager of exempt employment, and the manager of EEO/AA. Marianne Collins, the manager of exempt employment, has been with WFC for 10 years and has grown with the organization through a series of sales and sales management positions. She was chosen for her current position as a result of WFC's commitment to promotion from within, as well as her broad familiarity with the organization's products and customers. When Marianne was appointed, her key area of accountability was defined as college recruitment, with 50% of her time to be devoted to it.

In her first year, Marianne developed and implemented WFC's first-ever formal college recruitment program. Working with the HR planning person, WFC set a goal of 40 college graduate new hires by the end of the year. They were to be placed in the production, distribution, and marketing functions; specific job titles and descriptions were to be developed during the year. Armed with this forecast, Marianne began the process of recruitment planning and strategy development. The result was the following recruitment process.

Recruitment was to be conducted at 12 public and private schools throughout the state. Marianne contacted the placement office at each school and set up a one-day recruitment visit. All visits were scheduled during the first week in May. The placement office at each school set up 30-minute interviews (16 at each school) and made sure that applicants completed and had on file a standard application form. To visit the schools and conduct the interviews, Marianne selected three young, up-and-coming managers (one each from production, distribution, and marketing) to be the recruiters. Each manager was assigned to four of the schools. Since none of the managers had any recruiting experience, Marianne conducted a recruitment briefing for them. During that briefing she reviewed the overall recruitment (hiring) goal, provided a brief rundown on each of the schools, and explained the specific tasks the recruiters were to perform. Those tasks were to pick up the application materials of the interviewees at the placement office prior to the interviews, review the materials, conduct the interviews in a timely manner (the managers were told they could ask any questions they wanted to that pertained to qualifications for the job), and at the end of the day complete an evaluation form on each applicant. The form asked for a 1–7 rating of overall qualifications for the job, written comments about strengths and weaknesses, and a recommendation of whether to invite the person for a second interview in Clucksville. These forms were to be returned to Marianne, who would review them and decide which applicants to invite for a second interview.

After the campus interviews were conducted, problems began to surface. Placement officials at some of the schools contacted Marianne and lodged several complaints. Among those complaints were that (1) one of the managers failed to pick up the application materials of the interviewees, (2) none of the managers were able to provide much information about the nature of the jobs they were recruiting for, especially jobs outside their own functional area, (3) the interviewers got off schedule early on, so some applicants were kept waiting and others had shortened interviews as the managers tried to make up time, (4) none of the managers had any written information describing the organization and its locations, (5) one of the managers asked female applicants very personal questions about marriage plans, use of drugs and alcohol, and willingness to travel with male coworkers, (6) one of the managers talked incessantly during the interviews, leaving the interviewees little opportunity to present themselves and their qualifications, and (7) none of the managers were able to tell interviewees when they might be contacted regarding a second interview. In addition to these complaints, Marianne had difficulty getting the managers to complete and turn in their evaluation forms (they claimed they were too busy, especially after being away from the job for a week). From the reports she did receive, Marianne extended invitations to 55 of the applicants for a second interview. Of these, 30 accepted the invitation. Ultimately, 25 people were given job offers, and 15 accepted.

To put it mildly, the first-ever college recruitment program was a disaster for WFC and Marianne. In addition to her embarrassment, Marianne was asked to meet with her boss and the president of WFC to explain what went wrong and to receive "guidance" from them as to their expectations for next year's recruitment program. Marianne subsequently learned that she would receive no merit pay increase for the year and that the three managers all received above-average merit increases.

To turn things around for the second year of college recruitment, Marianne realized that she needed to engage in a thorough process of recruitment planning and strategy development. As she began this undertaking, her analysis of past events led her to conclude that one of her key mistakes was to naïvely assume that the three managers would actually know how to be good recruiters and were motivated to do the job effectively. Marianne first decided to use 12 managers as recruiters, assigning one to each of the 12 campuses. She also decided that more than a recruitment briefing was needed. She determined that an intensive, one-day training program must be developed and given to the managers prior to the beginning of the recruitment "season."

You work in HR at another organization in Clucksville and are a professional acquaintance of Marianne's. Knowing that you have experience in both college recruiting and training, Marianne calls you for some advice. She asks you if you would be willing to meet and discuss the following questions:

1. What topics should be covered in the training program?
2. What materials and training aids will be needed for the program?
3. What skills should the trainees actually practice during the training?
4. Who should conduct the training?
5. What other changes might have to be made to ensure that the training has a strong impact on the managers and that during the recruitment process they are motivated to use what they learned in training?

## Internet Recruiting

Selma Williams is a recruiter for Mervin/McCall-Hall (MMH), a large publisher of educational textbooks (K–12 and college). Fresh out of college, Selma has received her first big assignment at MMH, and it is a tough one—develop an Internet recruitment strategy for the entire organization. Previously, MMH had relied on the traditional recruitment methods—college recruiting, word of mouth, newspaper advertisements, and search firms. As more and more of MMH's textbook business is connected to the web, however, it became clear to Selma's boss, Jon Beerfly, that MMH needs to consider upgrading its recruitment process. Accordingly, after Selma had acclimated herself to MMH and had worked on a few smaller recruitment projects (including doing a fair amount of recruiting at college campuses in the past three months), Jon described her new assignment to her, concluding, "Selma, I really don't know much about this. I'm going to leave it to you to come up with a set of recommendations about what we ought to be doing. We just had a new intern come into the office for a stint in HR, and I'm going to assign this person to you to help on this project." Assume that you are the intern.

At your first meeting, you and Selma discuss many different issues and agree that regardless of whatever else is done, MMH must have a recruitment area on the corporate website. After further discussion, Selma gives you several assignments toward this objective:

1. Look at three to five corporate websites that have a recruitment area and note their major features, strengths, and weaknesses.

2. Interview three to five students who have used the recruitment area on a corporate website and ask them what they most liked and disliked about the recruitment areas.

3. Prepare a brief report that (1) summarizes your findings from assignments #1 and #2 and (2) recommends the design features that you and Selma will develop for inclusion in the MMH website.

## ENDNOTES

1. G. Dessler, *A Framework for Human Resource Management*, 7th ed. (Upper Saddle River, NJ: Pearson, 2013); E. Page, "Linking Business Strategy to Recruiting Strategy," *Journal of Corporate Recruiting Leadership*, May 2010, pp. 3–6; J. Sullivan, "The 20 Principles of Strategic Recruiting," ERE, July 7, 2008 (*www.ere.net/2008/07/07/the-20-principles-of-strategic-recruiting/*).

2. D. H. Freedman, "The Monster Dilemma," *Inc.*, May 2007, pp. 77–78; J. Barthold, "Waiting in the Wings," *HR Magazine*, Apr. 2004, pp. 89–95; A. M. Chaker, "Luring Moms Back to Work," *New York Times*, Dec. 30, 2003, pp. D1–D2; B. McConnell, "Hiring Teens? Go Where They Are Hanging Out," *HR-News*, June 2002, p. 16; J. Mullich, "They Don't Retire Them, They Hire Them," *Workforce Management*, Dec. 2003, pp. 49–57; R. Rodriguez, "Tapping the Hispanic Labor Pool," *HR Magazine*, Apr. 2004, pp. 73–79; C. Wilson, "Rehiring Annuitants," *IPMA-HR News*, Aug. 2003, pp. 1–6.

3. L. Ryan, "10 Ways to Fix Broken Corporate Recruiting Systems," *BusinessWeek*, June 13, 2011, p. 3.

4. B. L. Rau and M. M. Hyland, "Role Conflict and Flexible Work Arrangements: The Effects on Applicant Attraction," *Personnel Psychology*, 2002, 55, pp. 111–136.

5. F. Hansen, "Recruiting the Closer: Dealing With a Deal Maker," *Workforce Management Online*, Oct. 2007 (*www.workforce.com*).

6. R. J. Grossman, "How to Recruit a Recruitment Outsourcer," *HR Magazine*, July 1, 2012 (*www.shrm.org*); R. J. Grossman, "Alternatives to Recruitment Process Outsourcing," *HR Magazine*, July 1, 2012 (*www.shrm.org*).

7. M. N. Martinez, "Recruiting Here and There," *HR Magazine*, Sept. 2002, pp. 95–100.

8. P. O. Ángel and L. S. Sánchez, "R&D Managers' Adaptation of Firms' HRM Practices," *R&D Management*, 2009, 39, pp. 271–290.

9. "Cutting Corners to the Best Candidates," *Weddle's*, Oct. 5, 2004 (*www.weddles.com*).

10. J. Whitman, "The Four A's of Recruiting Help Enhance Search for Right Talent," *Workforce Management Online*, Nov. 2009 (*www.workforce.com*).

11. D. Dahl, "Recruiting: Tapping the Talent Pool . . . Without Drowning in Résumés," *Inc.*, Apr. 2009, pp. 121–122.

12. D. S. Chapman, K. L. Uggerslev, S. A. Carroll, K. A. Piasentin, and D. A. Jones, "Applicant Attraction to Organizations and Job Choice: A Meta-Analytic Review of the Correlates of Recruiting Outcomes," *Journal of Applied Psychology*, 2005, 90, pp. 928–944; K. L. Uggerslev, N. E. Fassina, and D. Kraichy, "Recruiting Through the Stages: A Meta-Analytic Test of Predictors of Applicant Attraction at Different Stages of the Recruiting Process," *Personnel Psychology*, 2012, 65, pp. 597–660.

13. Anonymous, "Recruiting Today: In a Tight Marketplace, the Lures Come Out," *Financial Planning*, Aug. 2013, pp. 14–16.

14. Uggerslev, Fassina, and Kraichy, "Recruiting Through the Stages: A Meta-Analytic Test of Predictors of Applicant Attraction at Different Stages of the Recruiting Process."

15. D. Catanzaro, H. Moore, and T. R. Marshall, "The Impact of Organizational Culture on Attraction and Recruitment of Job Applicants," *Journal of Business and Psychology*, 2010, 25, pp. 649–662; J. E. Slaughter and G. J. Greguras, "Initial Attraction to Organizations: The Influence of Trait Inferences," *International Journal of Selection and Assessment*, 2009, 17, pp. 1–18.

16. S. L. Rynes, "Recruitment, Job Choice, and Post-Hire Decisions," in M. D. Dunnette and L. M. Hough (eds.), *Handbook of Industrial and Organizational Psychology*, Vol. 2 (Palo Alto, CA: Consulting Psychologists Press, 1991), pp. 399–444; J. L. Scott, "Total Quality College Relations and Recruitment Programs: Students Benchmark Best Practices," *EMA Journal*, Winter 1995, pp. 2–5; J. P. Wanous, *Organizational Entry*, 2nd ed. (Reading, MA: Addison-Wesley, 1992).

17. S. L. Rynes and J. W. Boudreau, "College Recruiting Practices in Large Organizations: Practice, Evaluation, and Research Implications," *Personnel Psychology*, 1986, 39(3), pp. 286–310; S. A. Carless and A. Imber, "The Influence of Perceived Interviewer and Job and Organizational Characteristics on Applicant Attraction and Job Choice Intentions: The Role of Applicant Anxiety," *International Journal of Selection and Assessment*, 2007, 15, pp. 359–371.

18. C. Patton, "Recruiter Attack," *Human Resource Executive*, Nov. 2000, pp. 106–109; E. Zimmerman, "Fight Dirty Hiring Tactics," *Workforce*, May 2001, pp. 30–34.

19. Chapman, Uggerslev, Carroll, Piasentin, and Jones, "Applicant Attraction to Organizations and Job Choice: A Meta-Analytic Review of the Correlates of Recruiting Outcomes"; W. R. Boswell, M. V. Roehling, M. A. LePine, and L. M. Moynihan, "Individual Job-Choice Decisions and the Impact of Job Attributes and Recruitment Practices: A Longitudinal Field Study," *Human Resource Management*, 2003, 42, pp. 23–37; A. M. Ryan, J. M. Sacco, L. A. McFarland, and S. D. Kriska, "Applicant Self-Selection: Correlates of Withdrawal From a Multiple Hurdle Process," *Journal of Applied Psychology*, 2000, 85, pp. 163–179; Rynes, "Recruitment, Job Choice, and Post-Hire Decisions"; S. L. Rynes, "Who's Selecting Whom? Effects of Selection Practices in Applicant Attitudes and Behaviors," in N. Schmitt, W. Borman, and Associates (eds.), *Personnel Selection in Organizations* (San Francisco: Jossey-Bass, 1993), pp. 240–276; S. L. Rynes, R. D. Bretz, Jr., and B. Gerhart, "The Importance of Recruitment and Job Choice: A Different Way of Looking," *Personnel Psychology*, 1991, 44, pp. 487–521; M. S. Taylor and T. J. Bergmann, "Organizational Recruitment Activities and Applicant Reactions to Different Stages of the Recruiting Process," *Personnel Psychology*, 1988, 40, pp. 261–285.

20. B. R. Dineen, S. R. Ash, and R. A. Noe, "A Web of Applicant Attraction: Person-Organization Fit in the Context of Web-Based Recruitment," *Journal of Applied Psychology*, 2002, 87, pp. 723–734; D. C. Feldman and B. S. Klaas, "Internet Job Hunting: A Field Study of Applicant Experiences With On-Line Recruiting," *Human Resource Management*, 2002, 41, pp. 175–192; K. Maher, "The Jungle," *Wall Street Journal*, July 18, 2002, p. B10; D. L. Van Rooy, A. Alonso, and Z. Fairchild, "In With the New, Out With the Old: Has the Technological Revolution Eliminated the Traditional Job Search Process?" *International Journal of Selection and Assessment*, 2003, 11, pp. 170–174.

21. D. R. Avery, "Reactions to Diversity in Recruitment Advertising: Are the Differences Black and White?" *Journal of Applied Psychology*, 2003, 88, pp. 672–679; D. R. Avery and P. F. McKay, "Target Practice: An Organizational Impression Management Approach to Attracting Minority and Female Job Applicants," *Personnel Psychology*, 2006, 59, pp. 157–187.

22. P. F. McKay and D. R. Avery, "What Has Race Got to Do With It? Unraveling the Role of Racioethnicity in Job Seekers' Reactions to Site Visits," *Personnel Psychology*, 2006, 59, pp. 395–429; Avery, "Reactions to Diversity in Recruitment Advertising: Are the Differences

Black and White?"; Avery and McKay, "Target Practice: An Organizational Impression Management Approach to Attracting Minority and Female Job Applicants."

23. S. L. Premack and J. P. Wanous, "A Meta-Analysis of Realistic Job Preview Experiments," *Journal of Applied Psychology*, 1985, 70, pp. 706–719; J. M. Phillips, "Effects of Realistic Job Previews on Multiple Organizational Outcomes: A Meta-Analysis," *Academy of Management Journal*, 1998, 41, pp. 673–690.

24. J. P. Wanous, *Recruitment, Selection, Orientation, and Socialization of Newcomers*, 2nd ed. (Reading, MA: Addison-Wesley, 1992).

25. R. D. Bretz, Jr., and T. A. Judge, "Realistic Job Previews: A Test of the Adverse Self-Selection Hypothesis," *Journal of Applied Psychology*, 1998, 83, pp. 330–337; D. M. Cable, L. Aiman-Smith, P. W. Mulvey, and J. R. Edwards, "The Sources and Accuracy of Job Applicants' Beliefs About Organizational Culture," *Academy of Management Journal*, 2000, 43, pp. 1076–1085; Y. Ganzach, A. Pazy, Y. Ohayun, and E. Brainin, "Social Exchange and Organizational Commitment: Decision-Making Training for Job Choice as an Alternative to the Realistic Job Preview," *Personnel Psychology*, 2002, 55, pp. 613–637; P. W. Hom, R. W. Griffeth, L. E. Palich, and J. S. Bracker, "An Exploratory Investigation Into Theoretical Mechanisms Underlying Realistic Job Previews," *Personnel Psychology*, 1998, 51, pp. 421–451; B. M. Meglino, E. C. Ravlin, and A. S. DeNisi, "A Meta-Analytic Examination of Realistic Job Preview Effectiveness: A Test of Three Counter-Intuitive Propositions," *Human Resource Management Review*, 2000, 10, pp. 407–434.

26. C. J. Collins, "The Interactive Effects of Recruitment Practices and Product Awareness on Job Seekers' Employer Knowledge and Application Behaviors," *Journal of Applied Psychology*, 2007, 92, pp. 180–190; C. J. Collins and C. K. Stevens, "The Relationship Between Early Recruitment-Related Activities and the Application Decisions of New Labor-Market Entrants: A Brand Equity Approach to Recruitment," *Journal of Applied Psychology*, 2002, 87, pp. 1121–1133; P. J. Kiger, "Talent Acquisition Special Report: Burnishing the Brand," *Workforce Management*, Oct. 22, 2007, pp. 39–45.

27. Corporate Leadership Council, *The Employment Brand: Building Competitive Advantage in the Labor Market* (Washington, DC: author, 1999); E. Silverman, "Making Your Mark," *Human Resource Executive*, Oct. 16, 2004, pp. 32–36; M. Spitzmüller, R. Hunington, W. Wyatt, and A. Crozier, "Building a Company to Attract Talent," *Workspan*, July 2002, pp. 27–30.

28. R. K. Agrawal and P. Swaroop, "Effect of Employer Brand Image on Application Intentions of B-School Undergraduates," *VISION*, 2009, 13(3), pp. 41–49.

29. Collins and Stevens, "The Relationship Between Early Recruitment-Related Activities and the Application Decisions of New Labor-Market Entrants: A Brand Equity Approach to Recruitment"; F. Lievens and S. Highhouse, "The Relation of Instrumental and Symbolic Attributes to a Company's Attractiveness as an Employer," *Personnel Psychology*, 2003, 56, pp. 75–102.

30. R. D. Bretz, Jr., and T. A. Judge, "The Role of Human Resource Systems in Job Applicant Decision Processes," *Journal of Management*, 1994, 20, pp. 531–551; D. M. Cable and T. A. Judge, "Pay Preferences and Job Search Decisions: A Person-Organization Fit Perspective," *Personnel Psychology*, 1994, 47, pp. 648–657; T. J. Thorsteinson, M. A. Billings, and M. C. Joyce, "Matching Recruitment Messages to Applicant Preferences," Poster presented at 16th annual conference of the Society for Industrial and Organizational Psychology, San Diego, 2001.

31. R. J. Vandenberg and V. Scarpello, "The Matching Model: An Examination of the Processes Underlying Realistic Job Previews," *Journal of Applied Psychology*, 1990, 75(1), pp. 60–67.

32. H. J. Walker, H. S. Feild, W. F. Giles, and J. B. Bernerth, "The Interactive Effects of Job Advertisement Characteristics and Applicant Experience on Reactions to Recruitment Messages," *Journal of Occupational and Organizational Psychology*, 2008, 81, pp. 619–638.

33. D. R. Ilgen, C. D. Fisher, and M. S. Taylor, "Consequences of Individual Feedback on Behavior in Organizations," *Journal of Applied Psychology*, 1979, 64, pp. 349–371.

34. Cable and Yu, "Managing Job Seekers' Organizational Image Beliefs: The Role of Media Richness and Media Capability."

35. R. D. Gatewood, M. A. Gowen, and G. Lautenschlager, "Corporate Image, Recruitment Image, and Initial Job Choice Decisions," *Academy of Management Journal*, 1993, 36(2), pp. 414–427.

36. G. Ruiz, "Print Ads See Resurgence as Hiring Source," *Workforce Management*, Mar. 26, 2007, pp. 16–17.

37. J. Pont, "Online, In-house," *Workforce Management*, May 2005, pp. 49–51; S. Cromheeke, G. Van Hoye, and F. Lievens, "Changing Things Up in Recruitment: Effects of a 'Strange' Recruitment Medium on Applicant Pool Quantity and Quality," *Journal of Occupational and Organizational Psychology*, 2013, 86, pp. 410–416.

38. G. Ruiz, "Studies Examine the Online Job Hunting Experience," *Workforce Management Online*, July 2006 (*www.workforce.com*); D. G. Allen, R. V. Mahto, and R. F. Otondo, "Web-Based Recruitment: Effects of Information, Organizational Brand, and Attitudes Toward a Web Site on Applicant Attraction," *Journal of Applied Psychology*, 2007, 92, pp. 1696–1708; P. W. Braddy, A. W. Meade, J. J. Michael, and J. W. Fleenor, "Internet Recruiting: Effects of Website Content on Viewers' Perception of Organizational Culture," *International Journal of Selection and Assessment*, 2009, 17, pp. 19–34; B. R. Dineen and R. A. Noe, "Effects of Customization on Application Decisions and Applicant Pool Characteristics in a Web-Based Recruitment Context," *Journal of Applied Psychology*, 2009, 94, pp. 224–234.

39. M. Wisniewski, "In Battle for IT Talent, Banks Deploy High-Tech Recruiting Tactics," *American Banker*, Aug. 1, 2013, p. 8.

40. E. Baker and J. Demps, "Videoconferencing as a Tool for Recruiting and Interviewing," *Journal of Business and Economics Research*, 2009, 7(10), pp. 9–14.

41. G. van Hoye and F. Lievens, "Social Influences on Organizational Attractiveness: Investigating If and When Word of Mouth Matters," *Journal of Applied Social Psychology*, 2007, 37, pp. 2024–2047; G. van Hoye, "Nursing Recruitment: Relationship Between Perceived Employer Image and Nursing Employees' Recommendations," *Journal of Advanced Nursing*, 2008, 63, pp. 366–375; H. J. Walker, H. S. Feild, W. F. Giles, A. A. Armenakis, and J. B. Bernerth, "Displaying Employee Testimonials on Recruitment Websites: Effects of Communication Media, Employee Race, and Job Seeker Race on Organizational Attraction and Information Credibility," *Journal of Applied Psychology*, 2009, 94, pp. 1354–1364.

42. R. T. Cober, D. J. Brown, P. E. Levy, and J. H. Shalhoop, *HR Professionals' Attitudes Toward and Use of the Internet for Employee Recruitment*, Executive Report, University of Akron and Society for Human Resource Management Foundation, 2003.

43. R. T. Cober, D. J. Brown, and P. E. Levy, "Form, Content, and Function: An Evaluative Methodology for Corporate Employment Web Sites," *Human Resource Management*, 2004, 43, pp. 201–218; R. T. Cober, D. J. Brown, P. E. Levy, A. B. Cobler, and K. M. Keeping, "Organizational Web Sites: Web Site Content and Style as Determinants of Organizational Attraction," *International Journal of Selection and Assessment*, 2003, 11, pp. 158–169.

44. Freedman, "The Monster Dilemma," pp. 77–78; R. Zeidner, "Companies Tell Their Stories in Recruitment Videos," *HR Magazine*, Dec. 2007, p. 28; J. Borzo, "Taking On the Recruiting Monster," *Fortune Small Business*, May 2007, p. 89; E. Frauenheim, "Logging Off Job Boards," *Workforce Management*, June 2009, pp. 25–29.

45. D. M. Cable and K.Y.T. Yu, "Managing Job Seekers' Organizational Image Beliefs: The Role of Media Richness and Media Credibility," *Journal of Applied Psychology*, 2006, 91, pp. 828–840.

46. G. Ruiz, "Newspapers, Job Boards Step Up Partnerships," *Workforce Management*, Dec. 11, 2006, pp. 17–18.

47. P. Babcock, "Narrowing the Pool: Employers Ponder Worth of Niche Job Sites, and Many Take the Plunge," *SHRM Online HR Technology Focus Area*, May 2007 (*www.shrm.org*).

48. Avery and McKay, "Target Practice: An Organizational Impression Management Approach to Attracting Minority and Female Job Applicants."

49. I. Weller, B. C. Holtom, W. Matiaske, and T. Mellewigt, "Level and Time Effects of Recruitment Sources on Voluntary Employee Turnover," *Journal of Applied Psychology*, 2009, 94, pp. 1146–1162; S. Overman, "Use the Best to Find the Rest," *Staffing Management Magazine*, June 2008 (*www.shrm.org*).

50. P. Weaver, "Tap Ex-Employees' Recruitment Potential," *HR Magazine*, July 2006, pp. 89–91.

51. T. Cote and T. Armstrong, "Why Tweeting Has Become an Ad Agency's Main Job-Posting Strategy," *Workforce Management Online*, May 2009 (*www.workforce.com*); F. Hansen, "Using Social Networking to Fill the Talent Acquisition Pipeline," *Workforce Management Online*, Dec. 2006 (*www.workforce.com*); E. Frauenheim, "Company Profile: Recruiters Get LinkedIn in Search of Job Candidates," *Workforce Management Online*, Nov. 2006 (*www.workforce.com*).

52. S. F. Gale, "In E-Recruiting, There's a New Recruit in Town," *Workforce Management*, Aug. 2013, p. 8.

53. B. Busch, "Professional Employer Organizations, Social Media, and the Workplace," *Business People*, Aug. 2013, p. 72.

54. Cable and Yu, "Managing Job Seekers' Organizational Image Beliefs: The Role of Media Richness and Media Credibility."

55. S. Overman, "Do Your Hiring Homework," *Staffing Management Magazine*, Jan. 1, 2009 (*www.shrm.org/publications/staffingmanagementmagazine*).

56. J. Flato, "Key Success Factors for Managing Your Campus Recruiting Program: The Good Times and Bad," in N. C. Burkholder, P. J. Edwards, Sr., and L. Sartain (eds.), *On Staffing* (Hoboken, NJ: Wiley, 2004), pp. 219–229; J. Floren, "Constructing a Campus Recruiting Network," *EMT*, Spring 2004, pp. 29–31; C. Joinson, "Red Hot College Recruiting," *Employment Management Today*, Oct. 4, 2002 (*www.shrm.org/emt*); J. Mullich, "College Recruitment Goes for Niches," *Workforce Management*, Feb. 2004 (*www.workforce.com*).

57. A. Sanders, "We Luv Booz," *Forbes*, Jan. 24, 2000, p. 64; M. Schneider, "GE Capital's E-Biz Farm Team," *BusinessWeek*, Nov. 27, 2000, pp. 110–111.

58. B. Perkins, "Jousting for Jobs," *Computerworld*, Aug. 12, 2013, p. 40.

59. D. L. McLain, "Headhunters Edge Toward Consulting," *Wall Street Journal*, May 5, 2002, pp. B4–B18; S. J. Wells, "Slow Times for Executive Recruiting," *HR Magazine*, Apr. 2003, pp. 61–68.

60. L. Gomes, "Executive Recruiters Face Built-In Conflict Evaluating Insiders," *Wall Street Journal*, Oct. 14, 2002, p. B1.

61. D. Cadrain, "Admit One," *Staffing Management Magazine*, July 2009 (*www.shrm.org*).

62. R. J. Grossman, "Made From Scratch," *HR Magazine*, Apr. 2002, pp. 44–52.

63. L. Q. Doherty and E. N. Sims, "Quick, Easy Recruitment Help—From a State?" *Workforce*, May 1998, pp. 35–42.

64. D. Aberman, "Smaller, Specialized Recruiting Events Pay Off in Big Ways," *EMA Today*, Winter 1996, pp. 8–10; T. A. Judge and D. M. Cable, "Role of Organizational Information Sessions in Applicant Job Search Decisions," Working paper, Department of Management and Organizations, University of Iowa; Cable and Yu, "Managing Job Seekers' Organizational Image Beliefs: The Role of Media Richness and Media Credibility."

65. S. Armour, "Employers Court High School Teens," *Arizona Republic*, Dec. 28, 1999, p. E5; C. Hymowitz, "Make a Careful Search to Fill Internships: They May Land a Star," *Wall Street Journal*, May 23, 2000, p. B1; "In a Tight Job Market, College Interns Wooed," *IPMA News*, Nov. 2000, p. 22.

66. P. J. Franks, "Well-Integrated Learning Programs," in Burkholder, Edwards, Sr., and Sartain (eds.), *On Staffing*, pp. 230–238.

67. L. J. Bassi and J. Ludwig, "School-to-Work Programs in the United States: A Multi-Firm Case Study of Training, Benefits, and Costs," *Industrial and Labor Relations Review*, 2000, 53, pp. 219–239.

68. G. Beenen and D. M. Rousseau, "Getting the Most From Internships: Promoting Intern Learning and Job Acceptance," *Human Resource Management*, 2010, 49, pp. 3–22.

69. Chapman, Uggerslev, Carroll, Piasentin, and Jones, "Applicant Attraction to Organizations and Job Choice: A Meta-Analytic Review of the Correlates of Recruiting Outcomes"; M. A. Zottoli and J. P. Wanous, "Recruitment Source Research: Current Status and Future Directions," *Human Resource Management Review*, 2000, 10, pp. 353–382.

70. R. H. Glover and R. A. Schwinger, "Defining an Applicant: Maintaining Records in the Electronic Age," *Legal Report*, Society for Human Resource Management, Summer 1996, pp. 6–8; G. P. Panaro, *Employment Law Manual*, 2nd ed. (Boston: Warren Gorham Lamont, 1993), pp. I-51 to I-57.

71. OFCCP, "Frequently Asked Questions About the Internet Applicant Rule," periodically updated (*www.dol.gov/ofccp/regs/compliance/faqs/empefaqs.htm*), accessed 3/18/2010; V. J. Hoffman and G. M. Davis, "OFCCP's Internet Applicant Definition Requires Overhaul of Recruitment and Hiring Policies," *Legal Report*, Society for Human Resource Management, Jan./Feb. 2006; D. Reynolds, "OFCCP Guidance on Defining a Job Applicant in the Internet Age: The Final Word?" *The Industrial/Organizational Psychologist*, 2006, 43(3), pp. 107–113.

72. J. Arnold, "Online Job Sites: Convenient but Not Accessible to All," Society for Human Resource Management, July 31, 2007 (*www.shrm.org*).

73. OFCCP, "Frequently Asked Questions About Disability Issues Related to Online Application Systems," periodically updated (*www.dol.gov/ofccp/regs/compliance/faqs/empefaqs.htm*), accessed 3/18/10.

74. J. Deschenaux, "Attorney: Using Social Networking Sites for Hiring May Lead to Discrimination Claims" (*www.shrm.org*), accessed 3/23/2010; K. A. Gray, "Searching for Candidate Information," (*www.hreonline.com/HRE/*), accessed 1/29/2010; F. Hansen, "Discriminatory Twist in Networking Sites Puts Recruiters in Peril" (*www.workforce.com*), accessed 2/23/2010.

75. L. S. Rosen, *The Safe Hiring Manual*, 2nd ed. (Tempe, AZ: BRP Publications, 2013), pp. 413–436; J. A. Segal, "Dancing on the Edge of a Volcano," *HR Magazine*, 2011, April, pp. 83–86; J. A. Segal, "Widening Web of Social Media," *HR Magazine*, 2012, June, pp. 117–120.

76. EEOC, "Title VII and ADEA: Job Advertisements" (3/8/2008) and "ADEA: Job Advertisements Seeking Older Workers" (7/11/2007), informal discussion letters (*www.eeoc.gov/eeoc/foia/letters/index.cfm*), accessed 7/28/2010.

77. R. M. Green and R. J. Reibstein, *Employer's Guide to Workplace Torts* (Washington, DC: Bureau of National Affairs, 1992), pp. 40–61, 200, 254–255; D. J. Walsh, *Employment Law for Human Resource Practice*, 4th ed. (Mason, OH: South-Western, 2013), pp. 122–126.

# CHAPTER SIX

## Internal Recruitment

## LEARNING OBJECTIVES AND INTRODUCTION

### Learning Objectives

- Be able to engage in effective internal recruitment planning activities
- Apply concepts of closed, open, and hybrid recruitment to the internal recruiting process
- Recognize which recruitment sources are available for internal candidates
- Evaluate internal recruiting based on established metrics
- Be able to evaluate communication messages for internal selection
- Recognize how applicant reactions influence the effectiveness of a recruiting plan
- Understand how affirmative action plans are implemented for internal recruiting

### Introduction

Internal recruitment is the process of identifying and attracting current employees for open jobs. Internal recruits have numerous advantages: they already know the organization's culture, they have already developed relationships with coworkers, and they may require less training than external hires. The nearly ubiquitous presence of internal labor markets underscores the importance of effective internal recruiting. One survey of 725 human resource (HR) professionals found that as a result of recruiting, selection, training, and development costs, organizations are increasingly looking internally to staff positions.[1] A majority of those surveyed reported that managing their internal talent pool was either a high (45.6%) or a very high (27.7%) strategic priority in their organization. The development of internal talent was seen as one of the top talent management tasks (63% of respondents), even more so than the acquisition of talent (49.4% of respondents).

Unfortunately, despite the imperative placed on improving talent management, this survey also showed that only 25.7% of organizations have a formal talent management strategy, and only 13.8% of small businesses have a formal talent management system. This relatively limited implementation of effective formal talent management systems means there is much room for improvement. At the same time, a poorly managed internal talent management system can lead to accusations of favoritism, bias, or discrimination. Great care must be taken to ensure that any internal recruiting system is seen as fair.

The first step in the internal recruiting process is recruitment planning. The second step is developing a strategy for where, how, and when to look. Knowing where to look requires an understanding of open, closed, and hybrid internal recruitment systems. Knowing how to look requires an understanding of job postings, intranets and intraplacement, a talent management system, nominations, in-house temporary pools, replacement and succession plans, and career development centers. Knowing when to look requires an understanding of lead time and time sequence concerns.

The third step consists of the communication message and medium for notification of the job vacancy. The fourth step in the process is developing a job posting system and providing applicants with an understanding of the selection process and how to best prepare for it. The fifth step in the process is the consideration of legal issues. Specific issues to be addressed include Affirmative Action Programs Regulations, bona fide seniority systems, and the glass ceiling.

# STRATEGIC RECRUITMENT PLANNING

Like the external recruitment process, the internal recruitment process involves matching employee KSAOs (knowledge, skill, ability, and other characteristics) to organizational needs. Unlike external recruiting, the management of an internal recruiting process is directed toward channeling and enhancing existing capabilities rather than bringing in new capabilities from the external market. Internal recruiting must be integrated with employee training and development programs. Before identifying and attracting internal applicants to vacant jobs, attention must be directed to organizational and administrative issues that facilitate the effective matching of those applicants with available positions.

## Defining Strategic Internal Recruiting Goals

The goals for an internal recruiting system will flow from the organization's overall strategic goals. An internal perspective on recruiting entails defining goals for attraction, goals for speed, and a time frame, much like external recruiting, but the operative issues for each of these topics will change.

## Mobility Paths and Policies

The internal recruiting system will be crucially dependent on the mobility paths and policies that have been established in the organization. Just as the external labor market can be divided into segments or strata of workers believed to be desirable job applicants, so, too, can the internal labor market of an organization be divided into segments. This division is often done informally inside organizations. For example, managers might talk about the talented pool of managerial trainees this year and refer to some of them as "high-potential employees." As another example, people in the organization talk about their "techies," an internal collection of employees with the technical skills needed to run the business.

At a more formal level, organizations must create a structured set of jobs for their employees and paths of mobility for them to follow as they advance in their careers.

### Mobility Paths

A mobility path consists of possible employee movements within the internal labor market structure. Mobility paths are determined by many factors, including KSAO requirements, workforce characteristics, organizational culture, and labor market characteristics. Mobility paths are of two types: hierarchical and alternative. Both types determine who is eligible for a new job in the organization.

***Hierarchical Mobility Paths.***    Examples of hierarchical mobility paths are shown in Exhibit 6.1. As can be seen, the emphasis is primarily on upward mobility in the organization. Due to their upward nature, hierarchical mobility paths are often labeled promotion ladders. This label implies that each job is a step toward the top of the organization. Employees often see upward promotions as prizes because of the promotions' desirable characteristics. Employees receive these prizes as they compete against one another for job vacancies. For example, a promotion might lead to a higher rate of pay, and a transfer may result in a move to a better work location. There has been a great deal of research on these types of "tournaments" for higher pay and promotions, with evidence clearly suggesting that individuals increase their effort when faced with the prospect of a large payoff.[2] However, this same research suggests that competition can lead to counterproductive behavior, like sabotaging other employees or turnover among those who do not receive promotions.

An exception to the primarily upward mobility in the promotion ladders in Exhibit 6.1 shows the lateral moves that sometimes occur for the staff member who has both generalist and specialist experience as well as corporate and division

**EXHIBIT 6.1    Hierarchical Mobility Paths**

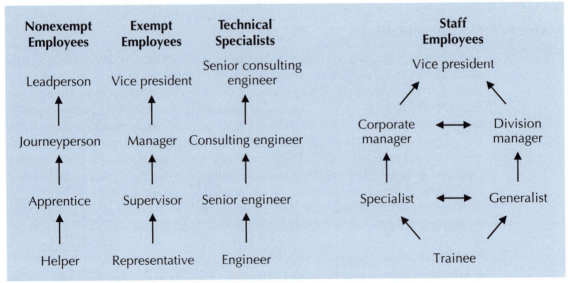

experience. This staff member is considered more well rounded and better able to work within the total organization. Experience as a specialist gives the person familiarity with technical issues that arise. Experience as a generalist gives the employee a breadth of knowledge about many matters in the staffing function. Corporate experience provides a policy and planning perspective, whereas division experience provides greater insight on day-to-day operational matters.

Hierarchical mobility paths make it very easy, from an administrative vantage point, to identify where to look for applicants in the organization. For promotion, one looks at the next level down in the organizational hierarchy, and for transfer, one looks over. Although such a system is straightforward to administer, it is not very flexible and may inhibit matching the best person to the job. For example, the best person for the job may be two levels down and in another division from the vacant job. It is very difficult to locate such a person under a hierarchical mobility path.

*Alternative Mobility Paths.* Examples of alternative mobility paths are shown in Exhibit 6.2. The emphasis here is on movement in the organization in any direction—up, down, and side to side. Employee movement is emphasized to ensure that each employee is continuously learning and that he or she can make the greatest contribution to the organization. This is in direct contrast to the hierarchical promotion ladder, where the goal is for each person to achieve a position with ever-higher status. Many organizations have shifted to alternative mobility paths for two reasons: (1) there is a need to be flexible given global and technological changes, and (2) slower organizational growth has made it necessary to find alternative ways to utilize employees' talents. Parallel tracks allow for employees to specialize in technical work or management work and advance within either. Historically, technical specialists had to shift away from technical work to managerial work if they wanted to receive higher-status job titles and pay. In other words, a technical specialist was a dead-end job. Under a parallel track system, however, job titles and salaries of technical specialists are elevated to be commensurate with their managerial counterparts.

With a lateral track system, there may be no upward mobility at all. The individual's greatest contribution to the organization may be to stay at a certain level for an extended period of time while serving in a variety of capacities, as shown in Exhibit 6.2.

A lattice mobility path has upward, lateral, and even downward movement. For example, a recruiter may be promoted to a recruitment supervisor position, but to continue to contribute to the organization, the person may need to take a lateral step to become knowledgeable about all the technical details in compensation. After mastering these details, the person may then become a supervisor again, this time in the compensation area rather than in recruitment. From a previous organization, the person may have experience in training and be ready to move to training manager without training experience internal to the organization. Finally,

**EXHIBIT 6.2** **Alternative Mobility Paths**

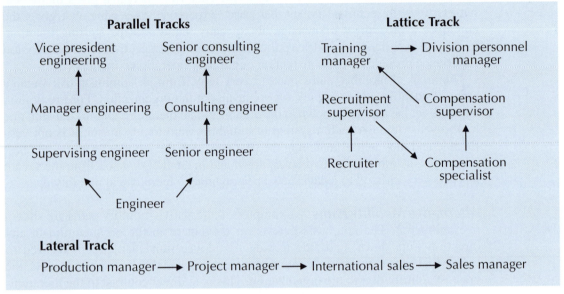

the person may make a lateral move to manage all the HR functions in a division (recruitment, compensation, and training) as a division personnel manager.

Some organizations, hoping to maximize information flow, increase flexibility, and minimize boundaries among employees, have adopted a team-based structure.[3] These organizations may do away with formal job titles and ranks altogether, with workers being reassigned to different roles in various project teams as needed. Such a structure is generally found mainly in research and development environments. The role of internal recruiting in such organizations changes completely, as talent management is focused on pairing employee KSAOs with unique project demands that are constantly in flux. This means there is a dramatic increase in the need for assessment of employee KSAOs and collaboration with team leaders to reconfigure groups quickly and efficiently. Such team-focused arrangements can be highly motivational for highly skilled individuals who are self-directed and engaged in their profession.

The downside to alternative mobility paths is that they are very difficult to administer. Neat categories of where to look do not exist to the same degree as with hierarchical mobility paths. On the positive side, however, talented inside candidates who may not have been identified within a hierarchical system are identified because of the flexibility of the system.

When upward mobility is limited in an organization, as in those using alternative mobility paths, special steps need to be taken to ensure that work remains meaningful to employees. If steps are not taken, the organization with limited promotional opportunities risks turnover of good employees. Examples of steps to make work more meaningful include the following:

1. *Alternative reward systems.* Rather than basing pay increases on promotions, pay increases can be based on an individual's knowledge and skill acquisition and contribution to the organization as a team member. Research has shown that these programs are successful at encouraging employees to develop job-relevant skills.[4]

2. *Team building.* Greater challenge and autonomy in the workplace can be created by having employees work in teams where they are responsible for all aspects of work involved in providing a service or product, including self-management.

3. *Counseling.* Workshops, self-directed workbooks, and individual advising can be used to ensure that employees have a well-reasoned plan for movement in the organization.

4. *Alternative employment.* Arrangements can be made for employee leaves of absence, sabbaticals, and consulting assignments to ensure that workers remain challenged and acquire new knowledge and skills.

## Mobility Policies

Mobility paths show the relationships among jobs, but they do not show the rules by which people move between jobs. These rules are specified in written policies, which must be developed and should specify eligibility criteria.

***Development.***   A well-defined mobility path policy statement is needed for both hierarchical and alternative mobility paths and has the following characteristics:

1. The intent of the policy is clearly communicated.
2. The policy is consistent with the philosophy and values of top management.
3. The scope of the policy, such as coverage by geographic region, employee groups, and so forth, is clearly articulated.
4. Employees' responsibilities and opportunities for development are clearly defined.
5. Supervisors' responsibilities for employee development are clearly stated.
6. Procedures are clearly described, such as how employees will be notified of openings, deadlines, and data to be supplied; how requirements and qualifications will be communicated; how the selection process will work; and how job offers will be made.
7. Rules regarding compensation and advancement are included.
8. Rules regarding benefits and benefit changes as they relate to advancement are included.

Employees are likely to see a well-articulated and well-executed mobility path policy as fair. A poorly developed or nonexistent policy is likely to lead to employee claims of favoritism and discrimination.

*Eligibility Criteria.*   An important component of an effective mobility policy is a listing of the criteria by which the organization will decide who is eligible to be considered for a vacancy in a mobility path. In essence, these criteria restrict eligibility for recruitment to certain individuals. Usually these criteria are based on the amount of seniority, level of experience, KSAOs, or job duties required. For example, to be considered for an international assignment, the applicant may be required to have been with the organization a certain length of time, have experience in a functional area where there is a vacancy, be proficient in a foreign language, and be interested in performing new duties. These criteria need to be made very clear in the policy; otherwise, unqualified people will apply and be disappointed when they are not considered. In addition, the organization may be flooded with the paperwork and processing of applicants who are not eligible.

## Closed, Open, and Hybrid Recruitment

The decision of how to communicate a job announcement to employees is a key component of an internal recruiting system. The choices among closed, open, and hybrid systems can affect employee motivation and perceptions of fairness, so each possibility should be carefully considered.

### Closed Internal Recruitment System

Under a closed internal recruitment system, employees are not made aware of job vacancies. The only people made aware of promotion or transfer opportunities are those who oversee placement in the HR department, line managers with vacancies, and contacted employees. Exhibit 6.3 shows how a vacancy is typically filled under a closed system.

A closed system is very efficient. There are only a few steps to follow, and the time and cost involved are minimal. However, a closed system is only as good as the files showing candidates' KSAOs. If the files are inaccurate or out of date, qualified candidates may be overlooked. Thus, maintaining accurate human resource information systems (HRISs) that track KSAOs regularly is vital.

### Open Internal Recruitment System

Under an open internal recruitment system, employees are made aware of job vacancies. Usually this is accomplished by a job posting and bidding system. Exhibit 6.4 shows the typical steps followed in filling a vacancy under an open internal recruitment system.

An open system gives employees a chance to measure their qualifications against those required for advancement. It helps minimize the possibility that supervisors

**EXHIBIT 6.3**   **Closed Internal Recruitment System**

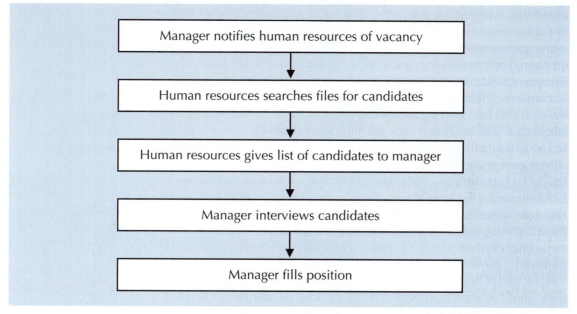

will select favorite employees for promotion or transfer, and it often uncovers hidden talent.

An open system may, however, create unwanted competition among employees for limited advancement opportunities. It is a very lengthy and time-consuming process to screen all candidates and provide them with feedback. Employee morale may decrease among those who do not advance.

## Hybrid System of Internal Recruitment

Under a hybrid system, both open and closed steps are followed at the same time. Job vacancies are posted, and the HR department conducts a search outside the job posting system. Both systems are used in order to cast as wide a net as possible. The large applicant pool is then narrowed down by KSAOs, seniority eligibility, demographics, and availability of applicants.

Merico Hotels uses a hybrid system that includes both training and developing promising employees for specific higher-level positions alongside job posting methods.[5] The organization's performance management system encourages employees to specify their potential internal career tracks and indicate which developmental opportunities will help them progress. Those identified as high-potential employees receive special training within a formal succession planning system. When jobs come open, they are posted via an internal job vacancy software program developed

**EXHIBIT 6.4   Open Internal Recruitment System**

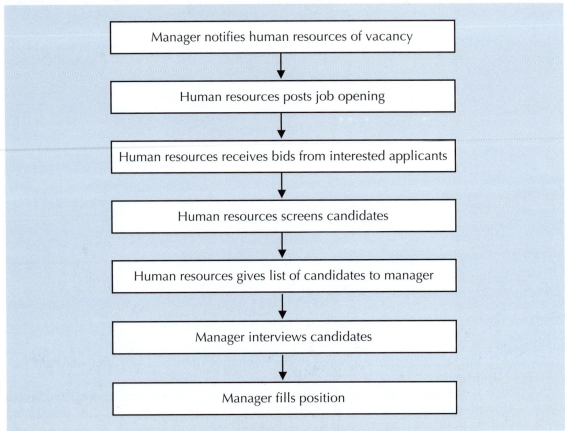

Manager notifies human resources of vacancy

Human resources posts job opening

Human resources receives bids from interested applicants

Human resources screens candidates

Human resources gives list of candidates to manager

Manager interviews candidates

Manager fills position

specifically by Merico. Employees who are especially qualified for these openings are alerted by the organization and encouraged to apply.

A hybrid system has four advantages: qualified candidates are identified in advance, a thorough search is conducted, people have equal opportunity to apply for postings, and hidden talent is uncovered. The major disadvantage of a hybrid system is that it entails a time-consuming and costly process.

### Criteria for Choice of System

In an ideal world with unlimited resources, one would choose a hybrid system of internal recruitment. However, due to resource constraints, most organizations must choose between open and closed systems. Several criteria need to be thoroughly considered before selecting an internal recruitment system. Exhibit 6.5 reviews these criteria.

---

**EXHIBIT 6.5**    **Choosing Among Open, Closed, and Hybrid Internal Recruiting**

| Technique | Advantages | Best When |
|---|---|---|
| Open | Identifies more candidates, including those who might be overlooked in a closed system | Issues exist about perceived fairness |
| | | Hidden talent might be overlooked |
| | Makes rules and regulations explicit and open to all employees | |
| | Sometimes required by labor agreements | |
| Closed | Less expensive in terms of search costs | Managers need the new candidate to start immediately |
| | Offers a quicker response | Jobs require a very narrow and specialized set of KSAOs |
| | Less cumbersome when only a select few meet the minimum requirements | |
| Hybrid | Finds a large number of candidates | There are adequate resources to run such a hybrid system |
| | Everyone has an opportunity to apply | |
| | | Jobs are especially key to organizational success |

Although the choice of system is important, use of staffing software (see Chapter 13) allows bridges between these systems to be built to take advantage of the best features of each.

## Organization and Administration

Mobility paths and mobility policies must be established as part of the planning process, and so, too, must administrative matters. Administrative matters include coordination, the budget, and the recruitment guide.

### Coordination

Internal and external recruitment efforts need to be coordinated and synchronized via the organization's staffing philosophy. If this is not done, disastrous results can occur. For example, if independent searches are conducted internally and externally, two people may be hired for one vacancy. If only an external recruitment search is conducted, the morale of current employees may suffer if they feel that they have been passed over for a promotion. If only an internal recruitment search is conducted, the person hired may not be as qualified as someone from the external market. Because of these possibilities, internal *and* external professionals must work together with the line manager to coordinate efforts before the search for candidates begins.

To coordinate activities, policies need to be created that specify the number and types of candidates sought both internally and externally. External recruiters should stay in frequent contact with internal placement professionals.

### Budget

An organization's budgeting process for internal recruitment should closely mirror that for external recruitment. The cost per hire may, however, differ between internal and external recruitment. The fact that internal recruitment targets candidates already working for the organization does not mean that the cost per hire is necessarily less than the cost per hire for external recruitment. Sometimes internal recruitment can be more costly than external recruitment because the methods involved in internal recruitment can be quite expensive. For example, when internal candidates are considered for the job but not hired, they need to be counseled on what to do to further develop their careers to become competitive for the position the next time it is vacant. When an external candidate is rejected, a simple and less costly rejection letter usually suffices.

### Recruitment Guide

As with external recruitment, internal recruitment activities involve the development of a recruitment guide, a formal document that details the process to be followed to attract applicants to a vacant job. Included in the plan are details such as the time, money, and staff activities required to fill the job, as well as the steps to be taken to fill the vacancy created by the internal candidate leaving to take the new job. An example of an internal recruitment guide is shown in Exhibit 6.6.

## Timing

A final strategic consideration an organization must make is determining when to look for internal candidates. As with external recruitment, consideration involves calculation of lead time and time sequence concerns.

### Lead Time Concerns

A major difference between internal and external recruitment is that internal recruitment not only fills vacancies but also creates them. Each time a vacancy is filled with an internal candidate, a new vacancy is created in the spot vacated by the internal candidate.

Because of this difference, it is incumbent on the organization to do HR planning along with internal recruitment. This planning involves elements of succession planning (see Chapter 3) and is essential for effective internal recruitment.

**EXHIBIT 6.6** **Internal Recruitment Guide**

### Position Reassignments Into New Claims Processing Center

**Goal:** Transfer all qualified medical claims processors and examiners from one company subsidiary to the newly developed claims processing center. Terminate those who are not well qualified for the new positions and whose existing positions are being eliminated.

**Assumptions:** That all employees have been notified that their existing positions in company subsidiary ABC are being eliminated and they will be eligible to apply for positions in the new claims processing center.

**Hiring responsibility:** Manager of Claims Processing and Manager of Claims Examining.

**Other resources:** Entire human resource department staff.

**Time frames:**
Positions posted internally on April 2, 2015
Employees may apply until April 16, 2015
Interviews will be scheduled/coordinated during week of April 19, 2015
Interviews will occur during the week of April 26, 2015
Selections made and communicated by last week in May
Total number of available positions: 60

**Positions available and corresponding qualification summaries:**

**6 claims supervisors**—4-year degree with 3 years of claims experience, including 1 year of supervisory experience.

**14 claims data entry operators**—6 months of data entry experience. Knowledge of medical terminology helpful.

**8 hospital claims examiners**—12 months of claims data entry/processing experience. Knowledge of medical terminology necessary.

**8 physician claims examiners**—12 months of claims data entry/processing experience. Knowledge of medical terminology necessary.

**8 dental claims examiners**—12 months of claims data entry/processing experience and 6 months of dental claims examining experience. Knowledge of dental terminology necessary.

**8 mental health claims examiners**—12 months of claims data entry/processing experience and 6 months of mental health claims experience. Knowledge of medical and mental health terminology necessary.

**8 substance abuse claims examiners**—12 months of claims data entry/processing experience and 6 months of substance abuse experience. Knowledge of medical terminology necessary.

*(continued)*

**EXHIBIT 6.6    Continued**

**Transfer request guidelines:** Internal candidates must submit internal transfer requests and an accompanying cover page listing all positions for which they are applying, in order of preference.

Internal candidates may apply for no more than five positions.

Transfer requests must be complete and be signed by the employee and the employee's supervisor.

**Candidate qualification review process:** Transfer requests from internal candidates will be reviewed on a daily basis. Those not qualified for any positions for which they apply will be notified by phone that day, due to the large volume of requests.

All transfer requests and accompanying cover pages will be filed by the position to which they refer. If internal candidates apply for more than one position, their transfer packet will be copied so that one copy is in each position folder.

Once all candidate qualifications have been received and reviewed, each candidate's transfer packet will be copied and transmitted to the managers for review and interview selection. Due to the large number of candidates, managers will be required to interview only those candidates with the best qualifications for the available positions. Managers will notify human resources with the candidates with whom they would like interviews scheduled. Whenever possible, the manager will interview the candidate during one meeting for all of the positions applied and qualified for.

**Selection guidelines:** Whenever possible, the best-qualified candidates will be selected for the available positions.

The corporation has committed to attempting to place all employees whose positions are being eliminated.

Managers reserve the right to not select employees currently on disciplinary probationary periods.

Employees should be slotted in a position with a salary grade comparable to their current salary grade. Employees' salaries shall not be reduced due to the involuntary nature of the job reassignment.

**Notification of nonselection:** Candidates not selected for a particular position will be notified by electronic message.

**Selection notifications:** Candidates selected for a position will be notified in person by the human resource staff and will be given a confirmation letter specifying starting date, position, reporting relationship, and salary.

Internal and external lead time considerations also differ because in an internal market, the employer can actively participate in identifying and developing knowledge and skills of the pool of eligible internal employees. Strategic talent management means that the organization identifies crucial skills that will be needed for future positions and begins cultivating these skills in the workforce well in advance.[6] By proactively developing needed skills in advance, the organization will be able to significantly reduce the lead time to fill positions with very specific KSAO requirements.

### Time Sequence Concerns

As previously noted, it is essential that internal and external recruitment activities be properly coordinated. This is especially true with the timing and sequencing of events that must be carefully laid out for both recruitment and placement personnel. Many organizations start with internal recruitment followed by external recruitment to fill a vacancy. Issues to be addressed include how long the internal search will take place, whether external recruitment can be done concurrently with internal recruitment, and who will be selected if an internal candidate and an external candidate with relatively equal KSAOs are identified.

## APPLICANT REACTIONS

A glaring omission in the research literature is the lack of attention paid to studying the reactions of applicants to the internal recruitment process. This lapse stands in stark contrast to the quantity of research conducted on reactions to the external recruitment process.

Perceived fairness of an internal recruiting process is extremely important. A potential applicant who feels that a company's external recruiting policy is unfair will be less likely to pursue a job opportunity, but that generally will mark the end of the interaction. An employee who feels that his or her company's internal recruiting policy is unfair will remain an employee, and the negative perceptions may spill over to reduce motivation, engagement, and performance and might even lead to turnover. Issues of fairness can be broken down into the categories of distributive and procedural justice. Distributive justice refers to how fair the employee perceives the actual decision to be (e.g., promote or not promote). Procedural justice refers to how fair the employee perceives the process (e.g., policies and procedures) that leads to the promotion or transfer decision to be. Reviews of the evidence suggest that procedures may be nearly as great a source of dissatisfaction to employees as decisions.[7] In some organizations, dissatisfaction arises because there is no formal policy regarding promotion and transfer opportunities. In other organizations, there may be a formal policy, but it is not closely followed.

In yet other organizations, it may be who you know rather than what you know that serves as the criterion for advancement. Finally, in some organizations there is outright or subtle discrimination against women and minorities. All these examples are violations of procedural justice and are likely to be perceived as unfair. To prevent these negative reactions, the organization should ensure that policies and procedures are clearly stated, based on objective criteria, widely communicated, and consistently followed.

## COMMUNICATION

Once the planning and strategy development phases have been conducted, it is time to conduct the search. As with external recruitment, informing potential applicants about the existence of an opening and the characteristics of the position will have a strong influence on the types of individuals who will apply. However, the content of the message and the media through which it will be transmitted are quite different.

### Communication Message

Like the external recruitment message, the internal recruitment message to be communicated can be realistic, branded, or targeted. A realistic message portrays the job as it really is, including positive and negative aspects. A targeted message points out how the job matches the needs of the applicant. A branded message emphasizes the value, culture, and identity of the unit to attract applicants who fit the brand label. For internal recruitment, information will be presented regarding the culture of the work unit or division and how it may differ from other areas of the organization. The internal applicant will have more information about the organization and its practices than would most external applicants, but any additional information about the job itself might not be accurate and might arrive via rumors or other unreliable internal communication methods. Therefore, any recruiting message should take the internal image of the job into account.

Realistic messages can be communicated using a technique such as a realistic job preview (RJP). This technique needs to be carefully applied for internal recruitment because applicants may already have a picture of the job since they are already a member of the organization. It should not be automatically assumed that all internal candidates have accurate information about the job and organization. In fact, word-of-mouth information, such as rumors, within the organization can lead internal recruits to have inaccurate perceptions about a job that need to be corrected. RJPs are particularly appropriate for internal applicants when they move to an unknown job, a newly created job, or a new geographic area, including an international assignment. Alternatively, it is often possible to give internal recruits informational interviews with future coworkers, site visits, or even hands-on experience in the new work environment, which is less feasible with external recruits.

Branded messages can emphasize how a specific area of the organization offers unique opportunities to internal applicants. This information can be communicated in a way that takes advantage of what employees already know about the job and organization. For example, a company expanding into a new regional market can describe how taking on a position in this new region will be a unique opportunity for personal and professional growth, with detailed information regarding specific products, initiatives, and even mention of key individuals involved in the process whose reputations might be known in the organization.

Targeted messages along with inducements are likely to attract experienced internal employees. Because internal applicants will be personally known by coworkers and supervisors, messages can be specifically targeted around each person's identified needs and desires. Targeted messages about the desirability of a position and the actual rewards should come directly from the job rewards matrix. The hiring manager needs to clearly communicate factual information in the job rewards matrix, rather than offers of potential rewards that the manager may not be able to provide.

## Communication Media

The actual methods or media used to communicate job openings internally include a formal job posting, direct contact with potential supervisors and peers, and word of mouth. In most cases, all three media should be considered as potential parts of the process, although only the first two are encouraged.

A job posting should clearly define the duties and requirements of the job as well as the eligibility requirements. To ensure consistency and fair treatment, job postings are usually coordinated by the HR department. Other documents used to communicate a vacancy may include a description of the work unit and its location as well as a description of the job. A brochure or video can also be created to show and describe what the job and its location are like. Such a message would be important to applicants asked to relocate to a new geographic area or to accept an international assignment.

Potential supervisors and peers can be used to describe to the internal applicant how the position he or she is considering fits into the larger organizational picture. Supervisors are knowledgeable about how the position fits with the strategic direction of the organization. Hence, they can communicate information regarding the expansion or contraction of the business unit within which the job resides. Moreover, supervisors can convey the mobility paths and requirements for future movement by applicants within the business unit, should they be hired. Peers can supplement these supervisory observations by giving candidates a realistic look at what actually happens by way of career development.

Word of mouth, which is difficult for the organization to control when it comes to external applicant searches, can be much more problematic for internal searches. This can be a highly selective, inaccurate, and haphazard method of communicating information. It is selective because, by accident or design, not all employees hear about vacant jobs. Talented personnel, including underrepresented groups, may thus be overlooked. It is inaccurate because it relies on second- or thirdhand information; important details, such as actual job requirements and rewards, are omitted or distorted as they are passed from person to person. Informal methods are also haphazard in that there is no regular communication channel specifying set times for communicating job information. As a result of these problems, the organization should be aware of word of mouth and attempt to minimize its influence on the applicant identification and attraction process.

## STRATEGY IMPLEMENTATION

After a strategic focus of the search has been established and communication messages and media have been evaluated, an organization must develop a strategy to access viable internal job applicants.

## Recruitment Sources

Choice of recruitment sources in an internal search is closely related to whether a closed, open, or hybrid system is employed. Some of the techniques described below are clearly more appropriate for a closed search, while others are more suited to an open search. One unique feature of the internal recruitment effort is that various sources overlap with one another and will likely be used simultaneously.

### Job Postings

A job posting system is very similar to the use of organizational websites in external recruitment. A posting spells out the duties and requirements of available jobs and provides a portal through which internal applicants can submit their materials. Organizations do not have to build these internal systems from the ground up; many HRIS developers integrate internal job posting systems into their programs. This means that when a job that has been designated as part of the internal market comes open, full posting information based on job analysis records can easily be put onto the company intranet in one integrated process. Smaller organizations with less robust internal labor markets may post jobs through e-mails rather than establishing a dedicated internal recruiting site. E-mail contact to selected individuals can also be used as part of a closed recruiting system as well.

An example of the type of information found in an internal job posting is shown in Exhibit 6.7. Such information includes job title, category, compensation, and work schedule. A brief overview of desired qualifications and a job description can

---

**EXHIBIT 6.7   Example of Job Posting Information**

| | |
|---|---|
| **Job code and title** | (75593) Administrative Specialist II |
| **Position title** | Assistant to Director of Marketing |
| **Position category** | Administrative and clerical |
| **Compensation category** | Nonexempt C [$15.00 to $20.00 per hour to start, depending on qualifications] |
| **Work hours** | 8:30 am–5:00 pm |
| **Work days** | MTWThF |
| **Required/preferred qualifications** | Prior experience as Administrative Specialist I or II |
| | Excellent professional communication skills |
| | Proficiency with word processing, spreadsheet, asset management, database, electronic mail, and Internet browser software |
| | Knowledge of management principles and functions |
| **Job description** | Assist the Director of Marketing with clerical and administrative tasks, including preparing correspondence, organizing a calendar of appointments, communicating with individuals within and external to the organization |
| **Work unit description** | The Director of Marketing works in the corporate offices in downtown Chicago. Employees work closely with one another in the marketing department and support one another through their efforts. There is a formal dress code for all employees in this division and professionalism is emphasized. |
| **Application instructions** | Click to enter submission portal: ENTER |
| | Click to submit appraisal information from records: ENTER |
| | Click to request recommendations: ENTER |

be pulled directly into the system from job analysis files. Work unit descriptions can also be developed and standardized to make the process of uploading a new position more efficient. Finally, application instructions link the user to three different portals. The submission portal leads to a series of pages where applicants can submit their qualifications and statement of interest. The appraisal information portal allows applicants to link their individual application to previous performance appraisal information in the HRIS. Finally, the recommendation portal allows the applicant to request recommendations from other individuals within the organization; these requests generate e-mail messages to the relevant parties with information on how to submit a recommendation to the system. This example shows a very basic, utilitarian format for the posting, but many organizations supplement their postings with images or personal messages from individuals working in similar roles.

At Home Depot, job openings are listed on computer kiosks in break rooms. Employees can view these job postings during breaks or before or after shifts. An employee who is interested in one of the jobs can take a computerized test for the opening at the kiosk. If the employee makes the cut, his or her application is forwarded. If the employee fails, the supervisor is notified and the employee may be offered training so he or she can compete successfully for the position in the future.[8]

Despite their advantages, internal job posting systems have some drawbacks. Examples of such difficulties include situations where employees believe that someone was selected before the job was posted (a "bagged" job), cumbersome systems where managers and HR personnel are overwhelmed with résumés of unqualified candidates, and criticisms that the HR department is not doing an effective job of screening candidates for positions.

Another important issue with posting systems is feedback. Not only do employees need to know whether they have received the job, but those who did not receive the job need to be made aware of *why* they did not. Providing this feedback serves two purposes. First, it makes job posting part of the career development system of the organization. Second, it invites candidates to bid on future postings. If employees are not given feedback, they may be less likely to bid for another job because they feel that their attempts are futile.

### Talent Management System

A talent management system is a comprehensive method for monitoring and tracking the utilization of employee skills and abilities throughout the organization.[9] The process of talent management is closely aligned with replacement and succession planning—talent management systems track the KSAOs of the workforce, and then replacement and succession planning translates this information into concrete action plans for specific job roles. Although talent management involves performance management and training processes in addition to managing the internal recruiting process, tracking employees' KSAOs and their use in the organization is the key component of talent management systems.

Although a number of different models for implementing talent management systems exist, there are a few key processes common to most. The first stage of the process is identifying the KSAOs required for all jobs in the organization. This information can be obtained from job descriptions and job specifications. The complete set of KSAOs required across the organization will then be compiled into a master list. The current workforce will need to be assessed for its competence in this set of KSAOs, usually as an adjunct to routine performance evaluations. When positions come open, managers make a query to the talent management system to determine which employees are eligible. A process should be in place to make regular comprehensive examinations of the changing nature of KSAO requirements throughout the organization. Information from these analyses can then be used as a springboard for developing comprehensive plans for training and development experiences.

There has been such a strong integration of database software for talent management systems that when staffing managers refer to talent management systems, they are often talking about the specific HRIS that is used to facilitate tracking KSAOs in the workforce. While these database applications offer great promise for coordinating information, many managers find operating talent management systems challenging. Most of the problems in implementing the systems in practice do not come from a lack of technology but from an excess of technology that cannot be understood by line managers. A few principles should be borne in mind when developing or evaluating a user-friendly talent management system:

- Keep the format for entering data as simple as possible.
- Have an easy method for updating basic information with each performance evaluation cycle.
- Make it easy to perform database queries.
- Provide varied formats for obtaining reports.
- Ensure that information is confidential.
- Make it possible to perform statistical analyses using relational databases.
- Integrate data with other HR files.

## Nominations

Nominations for internal candidates to apply for open positions can be solicited from potential supervisors and peers. These individuals are an excellent source of names of internal candidates, as they are familiar with what is required to be successful in the position. They can help establish the criteria for eligibility and then, through their contacts in the organization, search for eligible candidates. Self-nominations are also very useful in that they ensure that qualified candidates are not inadvertently overlooked using other applicant searching methods. Self-nomination is an especially important consideration in the internal recruitment of minorities and women.

## In-House Temporary Pools

In-house temporary pools are important to the temporary staffing of organizations, and they are also an excellent source of permanent internal employment. Unlike employees hired through external staffing agencies, those employed through in-house temporary pools are legally treated as employees. Therefore, the full legal liability for these employees falls exclusively on the employer. Using in-house temporary employees has a number of advantages.[10] Internal temporary employees require less orientation to the organization than external hires. Staffing agencies typically charge an employer an hourly fee for each temporary employee. But with an internal system, because the employer does not have to pay an hourly fee to an external agency, the cost savings can be applied to higher levels of compensation and benefits. It is also easier for an organization to ensure the quality and person/ organization fit for employees from an in-house pool relative to a pool of external hires. Temporary employment can also serve as an "audition" for full-time employment, allowing the temporary employees to try out a number of positions until the employee and the organization agree on a good person/job match. Carroll County, Maryland, set up an in-house temporary pool to deal with absences, vacations, and vacancies. Rather than relying on costly temporary agencies, Carroll County has five entry-level employees who fill in wherever needed. The city of Little Rock, Arkansas, has a similar program.[11] In health care, it is common to have "float" staff who are assigned to different units regularly, depending on the organization's needs. Substitute teachers are staffed in a similar manner. Such employees must be adaptable to different situations, and the organization must ensure that the employees have sufficient work. In addition, extra training may be needed for these employees since they are expected to have a broad range of skills in their repertoire.

## Replacement and Succession Plans

A critical source of internal recruitment is provided by the results of replacement and succession planning. Most succession plans include replacement charts (see Chapter 3), which indicate positions and who is scheduled to fill those slots when they become vacant. Replacement charts usually also indicate when the individual will be ready for the assignment. Succession plans are organized by position and list the skills needed for the prospective position (i.e., "for the employee to be promoted into this position from her current position, she needs to develop the following skills"). Dow Chemical's succession plan, for example, includes a list of "now ready" candidates; for jobs with similar competencies, it clusters roles and lists candidates for these roles as well. Dow has formal succession plans for 50–60 jobs that are identified as critical corporate roles and also has plans for another 200–300 jobs that are identified as needing continuity.

It is critical that succession planning be future oriented, lest the organization plan be based on historical competencies that fail to meet new challenges. Software exists to assist organizations with succession planning. Saba Succession is a succession planning package used by many Fortune 500 companies that interfaces with an organization's HRIS to provide replacement charts and competency libraries that allow an organization to identify developmental activities and assignments for individuals in the replacement charts.

CEO succession has always been an important issue for organizations, but never more so than today. The need for employee development has heightened as an increasing proportion of the workforce is approaching retirement. There is a very strong concern among career development specialists that the mass retirement of baby boomers will lead to a loss of organizational memory and knowledge built up with experience. Having strong succession planning techniques that will enable the more recently hired workforce to acquire knowledge from its experienced coworkers before moving into managerial positions is one way to minimize the impact of mass retirements. For example, Bristol-Myers Squibb developed a talent management program that provides employees with feedback on how to learn from great managers and leaders, and widely announces internal promotions with descriptions of the demonstrated leadership skills that led to the promotion being granted.[12] Many large, successful corporations lack clear succession plans. The problem may be even more severe in Asia, where many large conglomerates and family-owned businesses are run by aging chief executives without a clear succession plan in place.[13]

The key to avoiding potential fiascoes is to have a succession plan for CEOs. However, according to a poll of 518 organizations conducted by the National Association of Corporate Directors, only 42% of responding organizations have a formal succession plan in place. A succession plan should begin with a thorough job analysis and a listing of the characteristics and behaviors of a successful CEO.[14] The organization should not leave it to the CEO to identify a successor. CEOs are typically not trained or experienced in staffing, and they may have selfish motives in appointing a successor. Alternatively, they may avoid appointing a successor altogether, thus keeping themselves in the job. Therefore, the board must be deeply involved in the selection process. Boards also need to realize that the succession process should begin well before the CEO departs; in fact, it should be a continuous process.

## Career Development Centers

To facilitate internal transfers, many organizations have an internal office of career development that helps employees explore career options available within the organization.[15] Career development centers provide employees with opportunities to take interest inventories, assess their personal career goals, and interview with representatives across the organization. The goal of career development centers is twofold. First, employees learn about themselves and have a chance to think about what they really want to achieve in their careers. Second, employers have a chance to explain the career options within the organization and develop methods to structure internal career paths that match the interests of their employees. Surveys conducted in numerous organizations consistently demonstrate that employees are more satisfied when their employers provide them with ample communication and opportunities for internal advancement—an interactive career development center can do both.[16]

The interest inventories provided in career development centers often take the form of multiple-choice questionnaires that ask employees to indicate their preferred work activities. For example, respondents might be asked whether they prefer tasks that involve analytical processes like analyzing financial data or more social tasks like motivating a group of workers. After completing these surveys, employees compare their work preferences with the profiles of activities in a variety of jobs. Career development counselors can help talk employees through their thoughts and concerns about job options. Ideally, these career development inventories, coupled with careful analysis of KSAOs, will be paired with job analysis information to improve the person/job match. If employees lack the required KSAOs, career development counselors can suggest developmental work experiences or training opportunities.

Any assessment of career development centers needs to take the organization's bottom line into account.[17] Having full-time career development staff is a significant cost for any organization, and it is unlikely that small or medium-sized organizations will find it cost effective to develop a comprehensive career development center. For smaller organizations, it is more advisable to develop smaller-scale informal initiatives based on personal interactions. Smaller organizations can make use of some career development tools by bringing in external career coaches or consultants to work with individuals who are especially interested in career development within the organization. To reduce costs, employees could take their career development profiles and receive initial feedback through web-based surveys. These electronic survey options save money by reducing staff needs, and employees will not need to go to the career development offices to receive initial counseling.

Although career development centers are complicated to develop and expensive to maintain, they do offer organizations an opportunity to help employees learn about a large spectrum of careers. By providing employees with a clear sense of how they can direct their own careers, it is hoped that job satisfaction will increase and thus lead to increased retention. Because of the cost of career development services, it is especially important to keep track of the return on investment for these services.

## Recruiting Metrics

Like external recruiting sources, each internal recruiting source has strengths and weaknesses. Exhibit 6.8 provides an overview of the metrics that might be expected for the categories of recruiting activities, along with issues considered relevant to each source. There is far less research on the costs and benefits of internal recruiting techniques, so our comments here are necessarily somewhat speculative; it is likely that each organization will need to consider its unique needs even more thoroughly than it would when selecting external recruiting methods.

### Sufficient Quantity

Because the organization's pool of employees will necessarily be smaller than the general labor market, most internal recruiting methods will have far lower quantity

**EXHIBIT 6.8**   **Potential Recruiting Metrics for Different Sources**

| Recruiting Method | Quantity | Quality | Costs | Impact on HR |
|---|---|---|---|---|
| Job posting | Often will be the company's entire workforce | Because all employees will be able to apply, quality is variable | Staff time to develop the recruiting message | May reduce turnover, reduced time to full performance |
| Talent management system | Identifies knowledge, skills, and abilities across all employees | High; preselection of applicants based on identified skill sets | Maintenance of databases can be very time and resource intensive | Higher performance, reduced downtime, reduced training costs |
| Nominations | Limited to those who receive positive appraisals by supervisors or coworkers | If supervisors make accurate assessments, will be very good person/job match | Many companies keep routine records of employee performance | Can actively identify those who will be good performers and target identified training needs |
| In-house temporary pools | Based on organization's need for temporary staff coverage | Higher quality if in-house temps receive better benefits than what external staffing firms provide | Start-up costs can be significant; reduces payments to external agencies | More accountability relative to external agencies; increased internal flexibility |
| Replacement and succession plans | A small number of select workers seen as having high potential | Able to assess skill sets very carefully and consider configurations | HRIS start-up costs, data entry, and checking | Reduces gaps in leadership, protects against shocks due to turnover, reduced turnover |
| Career development centers | The set of employees who are interested in career development | Assesses employee KSAOs and preferences | Start-up costs, cost of staff, system maintenance | Significant reduction in turnover, increased match between KSAOs and work requirements |

yields. Techniques that permit job postings and intranets will likely produce far more candidates for promotion and advancement than will succession plans.

### Sufficient Quality

The degree to which the organization utilizes its own internal information on candidate qualifications and job performance to narrow the pool will determine how qualified the applicants will be. In assessing applicant characteristics, organizations that have internal recruiting systems have a huge advantage over organizations that use external recruiting systems, so the ability of each source to draw in qualified internal candidates should capitalize on the additional capacity to carefully observe candidates. Regular performance appraisals of all employees, coupled with talent management systems to track KSAOs, are a vital part of an effective internal recruiting system.

### Cost

Internal recruitment methods have a completely different set of costs than external recruitment methods. In some ways, internal recruitment can be far less expensive than external recruitment because the organization's own internal communication systems can usually be utilized. It costs very little to send an e-mail to all qualified staff informing them of job opportunities or to post job advertisements on either a physical or an electronic bulletin board. However, more sophisticated systems, such as a corporate intranet or comprehensive talent management systems, take more personnel resources to set up and maintain. Career development centers are very costly propositions, and only organizations with considerable internal placement needs will find them cost effective.

### Impact on HR Outcomes

Very little research has been done on the effectiveness of various internal recruitment sources. Thus, it is imperative that organizational leaders consider how their internal recruiting systems are affecting turnover rates, job performance, and diversity. Despite the lack of research, it should be easier to monitor these outcomes directly, because it is easier to directly measure the applicant pool contacted through internal methods. From anecdotal observations, some preliminary conclusions can be drawn regarding the advantages of internal placement. There is some evidence that internal career opportunities can reduce turnover intentions. Internal recruitment methods may reduce the time it takes for employees to reach full performance once placed, because they will already be familiar with the organization and may know more about the job in question than would an external hire. Any costs of internal recruitment should be compared against the costs of external recruiting, and the replacement of the employee who takes an internal position should also be taken into account.

## TRANSITION TO SELECTION

As with external recruitment, once a job seeker has been identified and attracted to a new job, the organization needs to prepare the person for the selection process. It should not be assumed that just because job seekers come from inside the organization they automatically know and understand the selection procedures. With the rapid advances being made in selection methods, the applicant might encounter methods that are different from those used to hire the applicant to a previous job. Even if the same selection methods are used, the applicant may need to be refreshed on the process since much time may have elapsed between the current and previous selection decisions.

An organization that has done an excellent job of preparing internal job seekers to become applicants is the Public Works Agency for the county of Sacramento, California.[18] The county uses a panel of interviewers together, rather than a series of individual interviews, to make selection decisions. For many lower-level employees in the maintenance department, this approach was a first-time experience. Consequently, they were apprehensive about this process because they had no previous experience with the internal selection process. In response to this situation, the HR group initially conducted training classes to describe the process to applicants. However, as this was a very time-consuming process for the staff, they replaced the classroom training with videos. One major component of the video was the preparation required prior to the panel interview. Instructions here included appropriate dress and materials to review. Another major component of the video depicted what happens to the applicant during the panel interview. This component included instructions on types of questions that would be asked, the process to be followed, and dos and don'ts in answering the panel interview questions. A final component of the video was testimonials from previous exam takers who became managers. They explain from an organizational perspective what the organization is looking for, as well as provide study tips and strategies.

## LEGAL ISSUES

The mobility of people within the organization, particularly upward, has long been a matter of equal employment opportunity/affirmative action (EEO/AA) concern. The workings of the internal labor market rely heavily on internal recruitment activities. Like external recruitment activities, internal recruitment activities can operate in exclusionary ways, resulting in unequal promotion opportunities, rates, and results for certain groups of employees, particularly women and minorities. The Affirmative Action Programs Regulations specifically address internal recruitment as part of the federal contractor's affirmative action plan (AAP). Seniority systems are likewise subject to legal scrutiny, particularly regarding what constitutes a bona fide system under the law. More recently, promotion systems have been studied as they relate to the glass ceiling effect and the kinds of barriers that have been found to stifle the rise of minorities and women upward in organizations.

## Affirmative Action Programs Regulations

Regulations on Affirmative Action Programs from the Office of Federal Contract Compliance Programs (OFCCP) require promotion placement goals where there are discrepancies between percentages of minorities and women employed and available internally in job groups. Accompanying these goals must be an identification of problem areas and action-oriented programs to correct these areas. As in the case of external recruitment, the regulations are virtually silent on indications of specific steps the organization might take to correct promotion system problems. Previous (now expired) regulations provided many useful ideas, including the following:

- Post or otherwise announce promotion opportunities.
- Make an inventory of current minority and female employees' academic, skill, and experience levels.
- Initiate necessary remedial job training and work-study programs.
- Develop and implement formal employee evaluation programs.
- Make certain that "worker specifications" have been validated on job performance–related criteria (neither minority nor female employees should be required to possess higher qualifications than those of the lowest-qualified incumbent).
- When apparently qualified minority or female employees are passed over for upgrading, require supervisory personnel to submit written justification.
- Establish formal career counseling programs to include attitude development, education aid, job rotation, buddy systems, and similar programs.
- Review seniority practices and seniority clauses in union contracts to ensure such practices or clauses are nondiscriminatory and do not have a discriminatory effect.

As can be seen, the previous regulations contained a broad range of suggestions for reviewing and improving promotion systems. In terms of recruitment itself, the previous regulations appeared to favor developing KSAO-based information about employees as well as an open promotion system characterized by job posting and cautious use of seniority as a basis for governing upward mobility.

## Bona Fide Seniority Systems

Title VII (see Chapter 2) explicitly permits the use of bona fide seniority systems as long as they are not the result of an intention to discriminate. This position presents the organization with a serious dilemma. Past discrimination in external staffing may have resulted in a predominantly white male workforce. A change to a nondiscriminatory external staffing system may increase the presence of women and minorities within an organization, but they will still have less seniority than the white males. If eligibility for promotion is based on seniority and/or if seniority is an actual factor considered in promotion decisions, those with less seniority will have a lower incidence of promotion. Thus, the seniority system will have an adverse impact on women and minorities, even though there is no current intention to discriminate. Is such a seniority system bona fide?

Two points are relevant here. First, the law does not define "seniority system." Generally, however, any established system that uses length of employment as a basis for making decisions (such as promotion decisions) is interpreted as a seniority system. Promotions based on ad hoc judgments about which candidates are "more experienced," however, would not likely be considered a bona fide seniority system.[19] Seniority systems can and do occur outside the context of a collective bargaining agreement.

Second, current interpretation is that, in the absence of a discriminatory intent, virtually any seniority system is likely to be bona fide, even if it causes adverse impact.[20] This interpretation incentivizes the organization not to change its current seniority-based practices or systems. Other pressures, such as the Affirmative Action Program Regulations or a voluntary AAP, create an incentive to change in order to eliminate the occurrence of adverse impact in promotion. The organization thus must carefully consider exactly what its posture will be toward seniority practices and systems within the context of its overall AAP.

Under the Americans With Disabilities Act (ADA) there is potential conflict between needing to provide reasonable accommodation to an employee (such as job reassignment) and provisions of the organization's seniority system (such as bidding for jobs based on seniority). According to the Supreme Court, it will ordinarily be unreasonable (undue hardship) for a reassignment request to prevail over the seniority system unless the employee can show some special circumstances that warrant an exception.

## The Glass Ceiling

The "glass ceiling" is a term used to characterize strong but invisible barriers to promotion in the organization, particularly to the highest levels, for women and minorities. Evidence demonstrating the existence of a glass ceiling is substantial. The overall labor force is 74% white and 54% male. At the very top in large corporations, senior-level managers are overwhelmingly white males. As one goes down the hierarchy and across industries, a more mixed pattern of data emerges. Equal Employment Opportunity Commission (EEOC) data show that nationwide the percentage of women who are officials and managers has increased to over 36.4%. In some industries, particularly health care, retail, legal services, and banking, the percentage of women managers is substantially higher. Women account for over 51% of employees in management, professional, and related occupations. In other industries, such as manufacturing, trucking, and architectural/engineering services, the percentage of women managers is much lower (13%–18%).[21] Unfortunately, similar kinds of data for minorities are not available, though few doubt a general underrepresentation of minorities in managerial roles as well. Thus, the closer to the top of the hierarchy, the thicker the glass in the ceiling. At lower levels, the glass becomes much thinner. Across industries, there are substantial variations in this pattern.

Where glass ceilings exist, there are two important questions to ask: What are the reasons for a lack of upward mobility and representation for minorities and women at higher levels of the organization? What changes need to be made, especially staffing-related ones, to help shatter the glass ceiling?

### Barriers to Mobility

An obvious conclusion from such data is that there are barriers to mobility, many of them originating within the organization. The Federal Glass Ceiling Commission conducted a four-year study of glass ceilings and barriers to mobility. It identified many barriers: lack of outreach recruitment practices, lack of mentoring training in revenue-generating areas, and lack of access to critical developmental assignments; initial selection for jobs in staff areas outside the upward pipeline to top jobs; biased performance ratings; little access to informal networks; and harassment by colleagues.[22] Added to this list should be another important barrier, namely, child rearing and domestic responsibilities that create difficult work/life balance choices.

An instructive illustration of these barriers, particularly the internal ones, comes from a 21-company study of men and women in sales careers.[23] The study found that 41% of women and 45% of men were eager to move into management, but the women were much less optimistic of their chances of being promoted. Whereas the sales forces studied were 26% female, only 14% of sales managers were female. The study portrayed "a survivalist culture where career paths are more like obscure jungle trails and where most women say they experience sexual harassment." The study also found "recruiters' use of potentially discriminatory screening tests, managers' negative stereotypes about women, women's lack of access to career-boosting mentors and networks, and difficulty entertaining customers in traditional ways such as fishing and golf outings." Saleswomen were also highly dependent on their mostly male managers for job and territory assignments, which were often based on stereotypes about willingness to travel, relocate, and work long hours.

### Overcoming Barriers

It is generally recognized that multiple actions, many of them beyond just staffing-system changes, will be needed to overcome barriers to mobility. Exhibit 6.9 shows a listing of such actions, many of which are consistent with recommendations of the Glass Ceiling Commission.[24]

**EXHIBIT 6.9**   **Ways to Improve Advancement for Women and Minorities**

**Examine the Organizational Culture**
- Review HR policies and practices to determine if they are fair and inclusive.
- Examine the organization's informal culture: look at subtle behaviors, traditions, and norms that may work against women.
- Discover men's and women's perceptions about the organization's culture, their career expectations, and what drives their intentions to stay or leave.
- Identify the organization's best practices that support women's advancement.

**Drive Change Through Management Commitment**
- Support top-management commitment to talent management, including women in senior positions.
- Ensure that diversity (including women in senior positions) is a key business measurement for success that is communicated to all employees by top management.
- Require line management accountability for advancement of women by incorporating it in performance goals.
- Train line managers to raise awareness and understand barriers to women's advancement.

**Foster Inclusion**
- Establish and lead a change-management diversity program for managers and employees.
- Affirm diversity inclusion in all employment brand communications.
- Develop a list of women for succession planning.
- Develop and implement retention programs for women.

**Educate and Support Women in Career Development**
- Emphasize the importance of women acquiring line management experience.
- Encourage mentoring via informal and formal programs.
- Acknowledge successful senior-level women as role models.
- Support the development and utilization of women's networks inside and outside the organization.
- Create and implement leadership development programs for women, including international assignments, if applicable.

**Measure for Change**
- Monitor the impact of recruiting strategies designed to attract women to senior levels of the organization.
- Track women's advancement in the organization (hiring, job rotation, transfers, international assignments, promotions).
- Determine who gets access to leadership and management training and development opportunities.
- Evaluate differences between salary of men and women at parallel levels within the organization.
- Measure women's turnover against men's.
- Explore reasons why women leave the organization.

SOURCE: Adapted from N. Lockwood, *The Glass Ceiling* (Alexandria, VA: Society for Human Resource Management, 2004), pp. 8–9. Used with permission.

In terms of specific staffing practices that may help eliminate the glass ceiling, we offer the following suggestions. Barriers to upward mobility can be addressed and removed, at least in part, through internal recruitment activities. Internal recruitment planning needs to involve the design and operation of internal labor markets that facilitate the identification and flows of people to jobs throughout the organization. This may very well conflict with seniority-based practices or seniority systems, both of which are likely to be well entrenched. Organizations simply have to make hard and clear choices about the role(s) that seniority will play in promotion systems.

In terms of recruitment strategy, where to look for employees looms as a major factor in potential change. The organization must increase its scanning capabilities and horizons to identify candidates to promote throughout the organization. In particular, this requires looking across functions for candidates, rather than merely promoting within an area (from sales to sales manager to district manager, for example). Candidates should thus be recruited through both hierarchical and alternative career paths.

Recruitment sources have to be more open and accessible to far-ranging sets of candidates. Informal, word-of-mouth, and "good old boy" sources do not suffice. Job posting and other recruitment strategies that encourage openness of vacancy notification and candidate application are necessary.

Recruitment changes must be accompanied by many other changes.[25] Top male managers need to fully understand that women executives differ from them in what they perceive to be the major barriers to advancement. Research suggests that women executives are more likely to see an exclusionary climate (male stereotyping and preconceptions of women, exclusion from informal networks, and inhospitable corporate culture) as a critical barrier, whereas top male managers are more likely to point to experience deficiencies (lack of significant general management and line experience, not being in the pipeline long enough) as the culprit. Hence, top management must take steps to not only create better experience-generating opportunities for women, but also develop and foster a more inclusive climate for women, such as through mentoring and providing access to informal networks. To encourage such changes and improve advancement results for women and minorities, managers must be held formally accountable for their occurrence.

An example of a far-reaching diversity initiative to expand the internal diversity pipeline is the "Championing Change for Women: An Integrated Strategy" program at Safeway, a retail grocery giant. A focal point is the Retail Leadership Development (RLD) program, a formal full-time career development program for entry-level grocery store employees to prepare them for moving up into the management ranks (90% of store managers and above come through the program). The program has a particular focus on women and people of color. Employees apply for the program by taking a retail knowledge and skill exam. Those who complete the program are immediately assigned to a store as an assistant manager—the stepping stone to further advancement. To support the advancement program, all managers attend a managing diversity workshop, receive additional on-the-job education, and have access to a toolkit to help them incorporate diversity discussions into their staff meetings. Managers are evaluated in part on their success in meeting diversity goals, and bonus money is riding on that success. Every manager is also expected to serve as a mentor, helping mentees acquire the KSAOs necessary for continued advancement. Other elements of the program include strong support and participation from the CFO, women's leadership network groups (for black, Asian, Hispanic, and LGBT [lesbian, gay, bisexual, and transgender] employees), modification of a requirement to relocate in order to gain experience, and work/life balance initiatives for employees with and without children. Since the program was initiated, the number of women who qualified for and completed the RLD program has risen 37%, and the number of women store managers has increased by 42% (31% for white women and 92% for women of color).[26]

In summary, solutions to the glass ceiling problem require myriad points of attack. First, women and minorities must have visibility and support at top levels—from the board of directors, the CEO, and senior management. That support must include actions to eliminate prejudice and stereotypes. Second, women and minorities must be provided the job opportunities and assignments that will allow them to develop the depth and breadth of KSAOs needed for ascension to, and success in, top management positions. These developmental experiences include assignments in multiple functions, management of diverse businesses, line management experience with direct profit-loss and bottom-line accountability, diverse geographic assignments, and international experience. Naturally, the relative importance of these experiences will vary according to the type and size of the organization. Third, the organization must provide continual support for women and minorities to help ensure positive person/job matches. Included here are mentoring, training, and flexible work-hour systems. Fourth, the organization must gear up its internal recruitment to aggressively and openly track and recruit women and minority candidates for advancement. Finally, the organization must develop and use valid methods of assessing the qualifications of women and minority candidates (see Chapters 8 and 9).[27]

## SUMMARY

The steps involved in the internal recruitment process—planning, strategy development, and communication—closely parallel those in the external recruitment process. With internal recruitment, the search is conducted inside rather than outside the organization. Where both internal and external searches are conducted, they need to be coordinated with each other.

The planning stage requires that the applicant population be identified. As before, the process begins by understanding strategic recruiting goals. Next, an understanding of mobility paths in the organization and mobility path policies is a vital part of deciding how to implement internal recruiting. To get access to the internal applicant population, attention must be devoted in advance of the search to number and types of contacts, the budget, development of a recruitment guide, and timing. Understanding applicant reactions to internal recruiting policies is also crucial to develop effective systems.

When searching for candidates, the message to be communicated can be realistic, targeted, or branded. Which approach is best to use depends on the applicants, job, and organization. The message is usually communicated with a job posting. It should, however, be supplemented with other media, including other potential peers' and supervisors' input. Informal communication methods with information that cannot be verified or that is incomplete are to be discouraged.

There are a variety of internal methods for taking applications in the strategy implementation phase. These range from posting information about jobs on the company intranet to career development centers with interest inventories and counseling staff. Just as with external recruitment, multiple criteria must be considered in choosing internal sources.

The organization needs to provide the applicant with assistance for the transition to selection. This assistance requires that the applicant be made fully aware of the selection process and how to best prepare for it. Taking this step, along with providing well-developed job postings and clearly articulated mobility paths and policies in the organization, should help applicants see the internal recruitment system as fair.

Internal recruitment activities have long been the object of close legal scrutiny. Past and current regulations make several suggestions regarding desirable promotion system features. The relevant laws permit bona fide seniority systems, as long as they are not intentionally used to discriminate. Seniority systems may have the effect of impeding promotions for women and minorities because these groups have not had the opportunity to accumulate an equivalent amount of seniority as compared to that of white males. The glass ceiling refers to invisible barriers to upward advancement, especially to the top levels, for minorities and women. Studies of promotion systems indicate that internal recruitment practices contribute to this barrier. As part of an overall strategy to shatter the glass ceiling, changes are now being experimented with for opening up internal recruitment. These include actions to eliminate stereotypes and prejudices, training and developmental experiences, mentoring, aggressive recruitment, and use of valid selection techniques.

## DISCUSSION QUESTIONS

1. Traditional career paths emphasize strict upward mobility within an organization. How does mobility differ in organizations with innovative career paths? List three innovative career paths discussed in this chapter and describe how mobility occurs in each.

2. A sound promotion policy is important. List the characteristics necessary for an effective promotion policy.
3. Compare and contrast a closed internal recruitment system with an open internal recruitment system.
4. What information should be included in the targeted internal communication message?
5. Exhibit 6.9 contains many suggestions for improving the advancement of women and minorities. Choose the three suggestions you think are most important and explain why.

## ETHICAL ISSUES

1. MDN, Inc., is considering two employees for the job of senior manager. An internal candidate, Julie, has been with MDN for 12 years and has received very good performance evaluations. The other candidate, Raoul, works for a competitor and has valuable experience in the product market into which MDN wishes to expand. Do you think MDN has an obligation to promote Julie? Why or why not?
2. Do organizations have an ethical obligation to have a succession plan in place? If no, why not? If so, what is the ethical obligation, and to whom is it owed?

## APPLICATIONS

### Recruitment in a Changing Internal Labor Market

Mitchell Shipping Lines is a distributor of goods on the Great Lakes. It also manufactures shipping containers used to store the goods while in transit. The subsidiary that manufactures these containers is Mitchell-Cole Manufacturing, and the president and CEO is Zoe Brausch.

Brausch is in the middle of converting the manufacturing system from an assembly line to autonomous work teams. Each team will be responsible for producing a separate type of container and will have different tools, machinery, and manufacturing routines for its particular type of container. Members of each team will have the job title "assembler," and each team will be headed by a permanent leader. Brausch would like all leaders to come from the ranks of current employees, in terms of both the initial set of leaders and the leaders in the future as vacancies arise. In addition, she wants to discourage employee movement across teams in order to build team identity and cohesion. The current internal labor market, however, presents a formidable potential obstacle to her internal staffing goals.

In the long history of the container manufacturing facility, employees have always been treated like union employees even though the facility is nonunion. Such treatment was desired many years ago as a strategy to remain nonunion. It was management's belief that if employees were treated like union employees, there should be no need for employees to vote for a union. A cornerstone of the strategy is use of what everyone in the facility calls the "blue book." The blue book looks like a typical labor contract, and it spells out all terms and conditions of employment. Many of those terms apply to internal staffing and are very typical of traditional mobility systems found in unionized work settings. Specifically, internal transfers and promotions are governed by a facility-wide job posting system. A vacancy is posted throughout the facility and remains open for 30 days; an exception to this is identified entry-level jobs that are filled only externally. Any employee with two or more years of seniority is eligible to bid for any posted vacancy; employees with less seniority may also bid, but they are considered only when no two-year-plus employees apply or are chosen. Internal applicants are assessed by the hiring manager and a representative from the HR department. They review applicants' seniority, relevant experience, past performance appraisals, and other special KSAOs. The blue book requires that the most senior employee who meets the desired qualifications receive the transfer or promotion. Thus, seniority is weighted heavily in the decision.

Brausch is worried about this current internal labor market, especially for recruiting and choosing team leaders. These leaders will likely be required to have many KSAOs that are more important than seniority, and KSAOs likely to not even be positively related to seniority. For example, team leaders will need to have advanced computer, communication, and interpersonal skills. Brausch thinks that these skills will be critical for team leaders to have, and that they will more likely be found among junior rather than senior employees. Brausch is in a quandary. She asks for your responses to the following questions:

1. Should seniority be eliminated as an eligibility standard for bidding on jobs—meaning the two-year-plus employees would no longer have priority?
2. Should the job posting system simply be eliminated? If so, what should replace it?
3. Should a strict promotion-from-within policy be maintained? Why or why not?
4. How could career mobility paths be developed that would allow across-team movement without threatening team identity and cohesion?
5. If a new internal labor market system is to be put in place, how should it be communicated to employees?

## Succession Planning for a CEO

Lone Star Bank, based in Amarillo, is the fourth-largest bank in Texas. Its leader, Harry "Tex" Ritter, has been with the company for 30 years, the last 12 in his current position as president and CEO. The last three years have been difficult for

Lone Star, as earnings have been below average for the industry, and shareholders have grown increasingly impatient. Last month's quarterly earnings report was the proverbial last straw for the board. Particularly troublesome was Ritter's failure to invest enough of Lone Star's assets in higher-yielding investments. Though banks are carefully regulated in terms of their investment strategies, Ritter's investment strategy was conservative even for a bank.

In a meeting last week, the board decided to allow Ritter to serve out the last year of his contract and then replace him. An attractive severance package was hastily put together; when it was presented to Ritter, he agreed to its terms and conditions. Although the board feels it has made a positive step, it is unsure how to identify a successor. When they met with Ritter, he indicated that he thought the bank's senior vice president of operations, Bob Bowers, would be an able successor. Some members of the board think they should follow Ritter's suggestion because he knows the inner workings of the bank better than anyone on the board. Others are not sure what to do.

1. How should Lone Star go about finding a successor to Ritter? Should Bowers be recruited to be the next CEO?
2. How should other internal candidates be identified and recruited?
3. Does Lone Star need a succession plan for the CEO position? If so, how would you advise the board in setting up such a plan?
4. Should Lone Star have a succession plan in place for other individuals at the bank? If so, why and for whom?

## ENDNOTES

1. BMP Forum and Success Factors, *Performance and Talent Management Trend Survey 2007* (San Mateo, CA: author, 2007).
2. B. L. Connelly, L. Tihanyi, T. R. Crook, and K. A. Gangloff, "Tournament Theory: Thirty Years of Contests and Competitions," *Journal of Management*, published online Aug. 8, 2013 (doi: 10.1177/0149206313498902).
3. S. E. Seibert, G. Wang, and S. H. Courtright, "Antecedents and Consequences of Psychological and Team Empowerment in Organizations: A Meta-Analytic Review," *Journal of Applied Psychology*, 2011, 96, pp. 981–1103; C. Chuang, S. E. Jackson, and Y. Jiang, "Can Knowledge-Intensive Teamwork Be Managed? Examining the Roles of HRM Systems, Leadership, and Tacit Knowledge," *Journal of Management*, published online Mar. 13, 2013 (doi:10.1177/0149206313478189).
4. E. C. Dierdorff and E. A. Surface, "If You Pay for Skills, Will They Learn? Skill Change and Maintenance Under a Skill-Based Pay System," *Journal of Management*, 2008, 34, pp. 721–743.
5. R. Fisher and R. McPhail, "Internal Labour Markets as a Strategic Tool," *The Service Industries Journal*, Oct. 2010, pp. 1–16.
6. D. G. Collings and K. Mellahi, "Strategic Talent Management: A Review and Research Agenda," *Human Resource Management Review*, 2009, 19, pp. 304–313.

7. D. K. Ford, D. M. Truxillo, and T. N. Bauer, "Rejected but Still There: Shifting the Focus in Applicant Reactions to the Promotional Context," *International Journal of Selection and Assessment*, Dec. 2009, pp. 402–416; A. L. García-Izquierdo, S. Moscoso, and P. J. Ramos-Villagrasa, "Reactions to the Fairness of Promotion Methods: Procedural Justice and Job Satisfaction," *International Journal of Selection and Assessment*, 2012, 20, pp. 394–403.

8. E. R. Silverman, "Break Requests," *Wall Street Journal*, Aug. 1, 2000, p. B1.

9. US Office of Personnel Management, *Human Capital Assessment and Accountability Framework* (Washington, DC: author, 2005); A. Gakovic and K. Yardley, "Global Talent Management at HSBC," *Organization Development Journal*, 2007, 25, pp. 201–206; E. Frauenheim, "Talent—Management Keeping Score With HR Analytics Software," *Workforce Management*, May 21, 2007, pp. 25–33; K. Oakes, "The Emergence of Talent Management," *T + D*, Apr. 2006, pp. 21–24.

10. N. Glube, J. Huxtable, and A. Stanard, "Creating New Temporary Hire Options Through In-House Agencies," *Staffing Management Magazine*, June 2002 (*www.shrm.org*).

11. P. Lindsay, "Personnel Services: An Innovative Alternative to Temporary Staffing Problems," *IPMA-HR News*, Dec. 2003, p. 19; "Temporary or Contingent Workers," *IPMA-HR News*, June 2004, p. 7.

12. E. Goldberg, "Why You Must Build Management Capability," *Workforce Management Online*, Nov. 2007 (*www.workforce.com*); M. Toossi, "Labor Force Projections to 2014: Retiring Boomers," *Monthly Labor Review*, 2005, 128(11), pp. 25–44; P. J. Kiger, "With Baby Boomers Graying, Employers Are Urged to Act Now to Avoid Skills Shortages," *Workforce Management*, 2005, 84(13), pp. 52–54.

13. S. McBride, "In Corporate Asia, a Looming Crisis Over Succession," *Wall Street Journal*, Aug. 7, 2003, pp. A1, A6.

14. National Association of Corporate Directors, *The Role of the Board in Corporate Succession* (Washington, DC: author, 2006).

15. F. Anseel and F. Lievens, "An Examination of Strategies for Encouraging Feedback Interest After Career Assessment," *Journal of Career Development*, 2007, 33, pp. 250–268; T. F. Harrington and T. A. Harrigan, "Practice and Research in Career Counseling and Development—2005," *Career Development Quarterly*, 2006, 55, pp. 98–167.

16. T. Minton-Eversole, "Continuous Learning—in Many Forms—Remains Top Recruiting, Retention Tool," *SHRM Online Recruiting & Staffing Focus Area*, Feb. 2006 (*www.shrm.org*); Society for Human Resource Management, *2007 Job Satisfaction* (Alexandria, VA: author, 2007).

17. I. Speizer, "The State of Training and Development: More Spending, More Scrutiny," *Workforce Management*, May 22, 2006, pp. 25–26.

18. "Panic or Pass—Preparing for Your Oral Board Review," *IPMA News*, July 1995, p. 2.

19. D. J. Walsh, *Employment Law for Human Resource Practice*, 2nd ed. (Mason, OH: Thomson Higher Education, 2007), p. 207.

20. Bureau of National Affairs, *Fair Employment Practices* (Arlington, VA: author, 2007), sec. 421: 161–166.

21. Equal Employment Opportunity Commission, *Glass Ceilings: The Status of Women as Officials and Managers in the Private Sector* (Washington, DC: author, 2004).

22. Federal Glass Ceiling Commission, "Good for Business: Making Full Use of the Nation's Human Capital—Fact-Finding Report of the Federal Glass Ceiling Commission," *Daily Labor Report*, Bureau of National Affairs, Mar. 17, 1995, Special Supplement, p. S6.

23. S. Shellenbarger, "Sales Offers Women Fairer Pay, but Bias Lingers," *Wall Street Journal*, Jan. 24, 1995, p. B1.

24. Federal Glass Ceiling Commission, "Good for Business: Making Full Use of the Nation's Human Capital," p. S19.

25. P. Digh, "The Next Challenge: Holding People Accountable," *HR Magazine*, Oct. 1998, pp. 63–69; B. R. Ragins, B. Townsend, and M. Mattis, "Gender Gap in the Executive Suite: CEOs and Female Executives Report on Breaking the Glass Ceiling," *Academy of Management Executive*, 1998, 12, pp. 28–42.

26. A. Pomeroy, "Cultivating Female Leaders," *HR Magazine*, Feb. 2007, pp. 44–50.

27. K. L. Lyness and D. E. Thompson, "Climbing the Corporate Ladder: Do Male and Female Executives Follow the Same Route?" *Journal of Applied Psychology*, 2000, 85, pp. 86–101; S. J. Wells, "A Female Executive Is Hard to Find," *HR Magazine*, June 2001, pp. 40–49; S. J. Wells, "Smoothing the Way," *HR Magazine*, June 2001, pp. 52–58; S. Shellenbarger, "The XX Factor: What's Holding Women Back?" *Wall Street Journal*, May 7, 2012, pp. B7–B12; D. J. Walsh, *Employment Law for Human Resource Practice*, 4th ed. (Mason, OH: South-Western, 2013), pp. 225–234.

# The Staffing Organizations Model

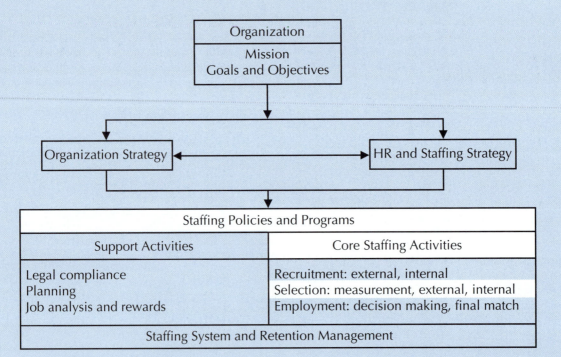

# PART FOUR

## Staffing Activities: Selection

# CHAPTER SEVEN

## Measurement

**Learning Objectives and Introduction**
    Learning Objectives
    Introduction

**Importance and Use of Measures**

**Key Concepts**
    Measurement
    Scores
    Correlation Between Scores

**Quality of Measures**
    Reliability of Measures
    Validity of Measures
    Validation of Measures in Staffing
    Validity Generalization
    Staffing Metrics and Benchmarks

**Collection of Assessment Data**
    Testing Procedures
    Acquisition of Tests and Test Manuals
    Professional Standards

**Legal Issues**
    Determining Adverse Impact
    Standardization
    Best Practices

**Summary**

**Discussion Questions**

**Ethical Issues**

**Applications**

**Endnotes**

# LEARNING OBJECTIVES AND INTRODUCTION

## Learning Objectives

- Define measurement and understand its use and importance in staffing decisions
- Understand the concept of reliability and review the different ways reliability of measures can be assessed
- Define validity and consider the relationship between reliability and validity
- Compare and contrast the two types of validation studies typically conducted
- Consider how validity generalization affects and informs validation of measures in staffing
- Review the primary ways assessment data can be collected

## Introduction

In staffing, measurement is a process used to gather and express information about people and jobs in numerical form. Measurement is critical to staffing because, as far as selection decisions are concerned, a selection decision can only be as effective as the measures on which it is based.

The first part of this chapter presents the process of measurement in staffing decisions. After showing the vital importance and uses of measurement in staffing activities, three key concepts are discussed. The first concept is that of measurement itself, along with the issues raised by it—standardization of measurement, levels of measurement, and the difference between objective and subjective measures. The second concept is that of scoring and how to express scores in ways that help in their interpretation. The final concept is that of correlations between scores, particularly as expressed by the correlation coefficient and its significance. Calculating correlations between scores is a very useful way to learn even more about the meaning of scores.

What is the quality of the measures used in staffing? How sound are they as indicators of the attributes being measured? Answers to these questions lie in the reliability and validity of the measures and the scores they yield. There are multiple ways of doing reliability and validity analysis; these methods are discussed in conjunction with numerous examples drawn from staffing situations. As these examples show, the quality of staffing decisions (e.g., who to hire or reject) depends heavily on the quality of measures and scores used as inputs to these decisions. Some organizations rely only on common staffing metrics and benchmarks—what leading organizations are doing—to measure effectiveness. Though benchmarks have their value, reliability and validity are the real keys in assessing the quality of selection measures.

An important practical concern involved in the process of measurement is the collection of assessment data. Decisions about testing procedures (who is qualified to test applicants, what information should be disclosed to applicants, and how to assess applicants with standardized procedures) need to be made. The collection of assessment data also includes the acquisition of tests and test manuals. This process will vary depending on whether paper-and-pencil or computerized selection measures are used. Finally, in the collection of assessment data, organizations need to attend to professional standards that govern their proper use.

Measurement concepts and procedures are directly involved in legal issues, particularly equal employment opportunity and affirmative action (EEO/AA) issues. This requires collection and analysis of applicant flow and stock statistics. Also reviewed are methods for determining adverse impact, standardization of measures, and best practices as suggested by the Equal Employment Opportunity Commission (EEOC).

## IMPORTANCE AND USE OF MEASURES

Measurement is one of the key ingredients for, and tools of, staffing organizations. Indeed, it is virtually impossible to have any type of systematic staffing process that does not use measures and an accompanying measurement process.

Measures are methods or techniques for describing and assessing attributes of objects that are of concern to us. Examples include tests of applicants' KSAOs (knowledge, skill, ability, and other characteristics such as personality), evaluations of employees' job performance, and applicants' ratings of their preferences for various types of job rewards. These assessments of attributes are gathered through the measurement process, which consists of (1) choosing an attribute of concern, (2) developing an operational definition of the attribute, (3) constructing a measure of the attribute (if no suitable measure is available) as it is operationally defined, and (4) using the measure to actually gauge the attribute.

The goal of the measurement process is to produce a number or score for a given attribute, which can then be used to differentiate individuals and make decisions about them. For example, applicants' scores on an ability test, employees' performance evaluation rating scores, and applicants' ratings of rewards in terms of their importance become indicators of the attribute. Information about these attributes is then used to make decisions, for example, about who to hire, who to promote, and how to reward an employee for good performance. Thus, through the measurement process, the initial attribute and its operational definition are transformed into a numerical expression of the attribute.

## KEY CONCEPTS

This section covers a series of key concepts in three major areas: measurement, scores, and correlation between scores.

## Measurement

In the preceding discussion, the essence of measurement and its importance and use in staffing were described. It is important to define the term "measurement" more formally and explore implications of that definition.

### Definition

Measurement may be defined as the process of assigning numbers to objects to represent quantities of an attribute of the objects.[1] Exhibit 7.1 depicts the general process of the use of measures in staffing, along with an example for the job of information technology analyst. The first step in measurement is to choose and define an attribute (also called a construct) to be measured. In the example, this is knowledge of programming languages. Then, a measure must be developed for the attribute so that it can be physically measured. In the example, a paper-and-pencil test is developed to measure programming knowledge, and this test is administered

**EXHIBIT 7.1**   **Use of Measures in Staffing**

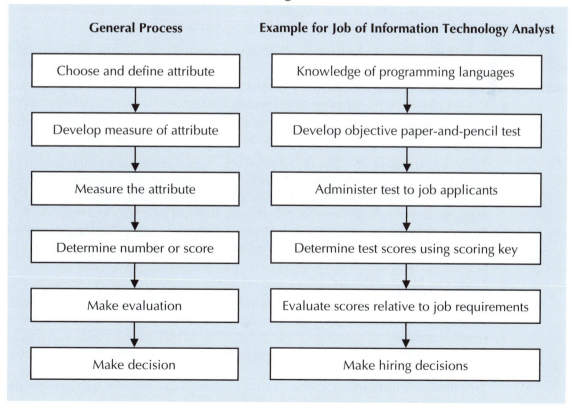

| General Process | Example for Job of Information Technology Analyst |
|---|---|
| Choose and define attribute | Knowledge of programming languages |
| Develop measure of attribute | Develop objective paper-and-pencil test |
| Measure the attribute | Administer test to job applicants |
| Determine number or score | Determine test scores using scoring key |
| Make evaluation | Evaluate scores relative to job requirements |
| Make decision | Make hiring decisions |

to applicants. Once the attribute is physically measured, numbers or scores are determined (in the example, the programming knowledge test is scored). At that point, the applicants' scores are evaluated (which scores meet the job requirements), and a selection decision can be made (e.g., hire an information technology analyst).

Of course, in practice, this textbook process is often not followed explicitly, and thus selection errors are more likely. For example, if the methods used to determine scores on an attribute are not explicitly determined and evaluated, the scores themselves may be incorrect. Similarly, if the evaluation of the scores is not systematic, each selection decision maker may put his or her own spin on the scores, thereby defeating the purpose of careful measurement. The best way to avoid these problems is for all those involved in selection decisions to go through each step of the measurement process depicted in Exhibit 7.1, apply it to the job(s) in question, and reach agreement at each step of the way.

### Standardization

The hallmark of sound measurement practice is standardization.[2] Standardization is a means of controlling the influence of outside or extraneous factors on the scores generated by the measure and ensuring that, as much as possible, the scores obtained reflect the attribute measured.

A standardized measure has three basic properties:

1. The content is identical for all objects measured (e.g., all job applicants take the same test).
2. The administration of the measure is identical for all objects (e.g., all job applicants have the same time limit on a test).
3. The rules for assigning numbers are clearly specified and agreed on in advance (e.g., a scoring key for the test is developed before it is administered).

These seemingly simple and straightforward characteristics of standardization of measures have substantial implications for the conduct of many staffing activities. These implications will become apparent throughout the remainder of this text. For example, assessment devices, such as the employment interview and letters of reference, often fail to meet the requirements for standardization, and organizations must undertake steps to make them more standardized.

### Levels of Measurement

There are varying degrees of precision in measuring attributes and in representing differences among objects in terms of attributes. Accordingly, there are different levels or scales of measurement.[3] It is common to classify any particular measure as falling into one of four levels of measurement: nominal, ordinal, interval, or ratio.

*Nominal.* With nominal scales, a given attribute is categorized, and numbers are assigned to the categories. With or without numbers, however, there is no order or level implied among the categories. The categories are merely different, and none is higher or lower than the others. For example, each job title could represent a different category, with a different number assigned to it: managers = 1, clericals = 2, sales = 3, and so forth. Clearly, the numbers do not imply any ordering among the categories (sales is not "better" or "worse" than clericals).

*Ordinal.*   With ordinal scales, objects are rank ordered according to how much of the attribute they possess. Thus, objects may be ranked from best to worst or from highest to lowest. For example, five job candidates, each of whom has been evaluated in terms of overall qualification for the job, might be rank ordered from 1 to 5, or highest to lowest, according to their job qualifications.

Though useful for making clear distinctions between objects, rank orderings represent only relative differences among objects; they do not indicate the absolute levels of the attribute. Thus, the rank ordering of the five job candidates does not indicate exactly how qualified each of them is for the job, nor are the differences in their ranks necessarily equal to the differences in their qualifications. The differences in qualifications between applicants ranked 1 and 2 may not be the same as the differences between those ranked 4 and 5. Moreover, forcing objects to be ranked creates the appearance that the differences between two objects (for example, between applicant 1 and 2) are "real" and significant, when in fact those differences may be trivial. A good example of this is annual rankings of business schools, where a switch from second to first place (and vice-versa) is touted as noteworthy, when in fact the differences between the two schools are probably not meaningful.[4]

*Interval.*   Like ordinal scales, interval scales allow us to rank order objects. However, the differences between adjacent points on the measurement scale are now equal in terms of the attribute. If an interval scale is used to rank order the five job candidates, the differences in qualifications between those ranked 1 and 2 are equal to the differences between those ranked 4 and 5.

In many instances, the level of measurement falls somewhere between an ordinal scale and an interval scale. That is, objects can be clearly rank ordered, but the differences between the ranks are not necessarily equal throughout the measurement scale. In the example of the five job candidates, the differences in qualifications between those ranked 1 and 2 might be slight compared with the differences between those ranked 4 and 5.

Unfortunately, this in-between level of measurement is characteristic of many of the measures used in staffing. Though it is not a major problem, it does signal the need for caution in interpreting the meaning of differences in scores among people.

*Ratio.*   Like interval scales, ratio scales have equal differences between scale points for the attribute being measured. In addition, ratio scales have a logical or absolute true zero point. Because of this, how much of the attribute each object possesses can be stated in absolute terms.

Normally, ratio scales are involved in counting or weighing things. Staffing has many such examples of ratio scales: Assessing how much weight a candidate can carry over some distance for physically demanding jobs such as firefighting or general construction is an example. Perhaps the most common example is counting how much previous job experience (general or specific) job candidates have had, where zero is a meaningful number (indicating no job experience).

### Objective and Subjective Measures

Frequently, staffing measures are described as either objective or subjective. The term "subjective" is often used in disparaging ways ("I can't believe how subjective that interview was; there's no way they can rate me fairly on the basis of it"). Exactly what is the difference between so-called objective and subjective measures?

The difference, in large part, pertains to the rules used to assign numbers to the attribute being assessed. With objective measures, the rules are predetermined and usually communicated and applied through some sort of scoring key or system. For example, consider a basketball game, where the total points a team receives is an objective measure. In employment contexts, most paper-and-pencil tests are considered objective. The scoring systems in subjective measures are more elusive and often involve a rater or judge who assigns the numbers. For example, consider a gymnastics competition, where the total points a team receives is a more subjective measure, depending on how the gymnasts are rated by each judge. In employment contexts, many employment interviews fall into this category, especially those wherein the interviewer has an idiosyncratic way of evaluating people's responses, one that is not known or shared by other interviewers.

In principle, any attribute can be measured objectively or subjectively, and sometimes both are used. Research shows that when an attribute is measured by both objective and subjective means, there is often relatively low agreement between scores from the two types of measures. A case in point pertains to the attribute of job performance. Performance may be measured objectively through quantity of output, and it may be measured subjectively through performance appraisal ratings, yet these two types of measures correlate only weakly with each other.[5] Undoubtedly, the raters' lack of sound scoring systems for rating job performance is a major contributor to the lack of obtained agreement.

It thus appears that whatever type of measure is used to assess attributes in staffing, serious attention should be paid to the scoring system or key. In a sense, this requires nothing more than having a firm knowledge of exactly what the organization is trying to measure. This is true for both paper-and-pencil (objective) measures and judgmental (subjective) measures, such as the employment interview. It is simply another way of emphasizing the importance of standardization in measurement.

## Scores

Measures yield numbers or scores to represent the amount of the attribute being assessed. Scores are thus the numerical indicator of the attribute. Once scores have been derived, they can be manipulated in various ways to give them even greater meaning and to better describe characteristics of the objects being scored.[6]

### Central Tendency and Variability

Assume that a group of job applicants was administered a test of their knowledge of programming languages. The test is scored using a scoring key, and each appli-cant receives a score, known as a raw score. These are shown in Exhibit 7.2.

**EXHIBIT 7.2**  **Central Tendency and Variability: Summary Statistics**

| Data | | Summary Statistics |
|---|---|---|
| **Applicant** | **Test Score (X)** | |
| A | 10 | A. Central tendency |
| B | 12 | Mean ($\overline{X}$) = 338/20 = 16.9 |
| C | 14 | Median = middle score = 17 |
| D | 14 | Mode = most frequent score = 15 |
| E | 15 | |
| F | 15 | B. Variability |
| G | 15 | Range = 10 to 24 |
| H | 15 | Standard deviation (SD) = |
| I | 15 | |
| J | 17 | $\sqrt{\dfrac{\Sigma(X-\overline{X})^2}{n-1}} = 3.52$ |
| K | 17 | |
| L | 17 | |
| M | 18 | |
| N | 18 | |
| O | 19 | |
| P | 19 | |
| Q | 19 | |
| R | 22 | |
| S | 23 | |
| T | 24 | |
| Total ($\Sigma$) = 338 | | |
| n = 20 | | |

Some features of this set of scores may be summarized through the calculation of summary statistics. These pertain to central tendency and variability in the scores and are also shown in Exhibit 7.2.

The indicators of central tendency are the mean, the median, and the mode. Since it was assumed that the data are interval level data, it is permissible to compute all three indicators of central tendency. Had the data been ordinal, the mean should not be computed. For nominal data, only the mode would be appropriate. For example, it does not make sense to compute the average of 1 = managers and 2 = clericals—only the most frequently occurring category is useful information.

The variability indicators are the range and the standard deviation. The range shows the lowest to highest actual scores for the job applicants. The standard deviation shows, in essence, the average amount of deviation of individual scores from the average score. It summarizes the amount of spread in the scores. The larger the standard deviation, the greater the variability, or spread, in the data.

## Percentiles

A percentile score for an individual is the percentage of people scoring below the individual in a distribution of scores. Refer again to Exhibit 7.2 and consider applicant C. That applicant's percentile score is in the 10th percentile ($2/20 \times 100$), meaning that 90% of the applicants scored better than applicant C. Applicant S is in the 90th percentile ($18/20 \times 100$), meaning that only 10% of the applicants scored better than applicant S.

## Standard Scores

When interpreting scores, it is natural to compare individuals' raw scores with the mean, that is, to ask whether scores are above, at, or below the mean. However, a true understanding of how well an individual did relative to the mean takes into account the amount of variability in scores around the mean (the standard deviation). That is, the calculation must be "corrected" or controlled for the amount of variability in a score distribution to accurately present how well a person scored relative to the mean. Calculation of the standard score for an individual is the way to accomplish this correction. The standard score thus answers the question, "How many standard deviations above or below the mean did a given person score?"

The formula for calculating the standard score, or Z, is as follows:

$$Z = \frac{X - \overline{X}}{SD}$$

Applicant S in Exhibit 7.2 had a raw score of 23 on the test; the mean is 16.9 and the standard deviation is 3.52. Substituting into the above formula, applicant S has a Z score of 1.7. Thus, applicant S scored about 1.7 standard deviations above the mean.

Standard scores are also useful for determining how a person performed, in a relative sense, on two or more tests. For example, assume the following data for a particular applicant:

|  | Test 1 | Test 2 |
|---|---|---|
| Raw score | 50 | 48 |
| Mean | 48 | 46 |
| SD | 2.5 | .80 |

On which test did the applicant do better? To answer that, simply calculate the applicant's standard scores on the two tests. The Z score on test 1 is .80, and the Z score on test 2 is 2.5. Thus, while the applicant got a higher raw score on test 1 than on test 2, the applicant got a higher Z score on test 2 than on test 1. Viewed in this way, it is apparent that the applicant did better on test 2, relatively speaking.

It should now be apparent that a person with a Z score of 0 scored at the mean. But what is a "high" Z score? What is a "low" Z score? When scores are normally distributed (with the mean, median, and mode all the same), the data for applicants resemble a bell curve (half the people scored above the mean, and half scored below the mean). In this case, a Z score of +1.0 means that the applicant scored in the 84th percentile (at –1.0, the applicant scored in the 16th percentile). A Z score of +2.0 means that the applicant scored in the 98th percentile (at –2.0, the applicant scored in the 2nd percentile). Thus, scoring even one standard deviation above the mean is a relatively high score.

## Correlation Between Scores

Frequently in staffing there are scores on two or more measures for a group of individuals. One common occurrence is to have scores on two (or often, more than two) KSAO measures. For example, there could be a score on the test of knowledge of programming languages and also an overall rating of the applicant's probable job success based on the employment interview. In such instances, it is logical to ask whether there is some relation between the two sets of scores. Does an increase in knowledge test scores tend to be accompanied by an increase in interview ratings? Put more simply, is there a relationship between the two measures?

As another example, an organization may have scores on a particular KSAO measure (e.g., the knowledge test) and on a measure of job performance (e.g., performance appraisal ratings) for a group of individuals. Is there a correlation between these two sets of scores? In other words, does knowing an individual's score on the knowledge test tell you something about her likely job performance? If it does, this would provide some evidence about the probable validity of the knowledge test as a predictor of job performance. This evidence would help the organization decide whether to incorporate the use of the test into the selection process for job applicants.

Investigation of the relationship between two sets of scores proceeds through the plotting of scatter diagrams and through calculation of the correlation coefficient.

## Scatter Diagrams

Assume two sets of scores for a group of people—scores on a test and scores on a measure of job performance. A scatter diagram is simply the plot of the joint distribution of the two sets of scores. Inspection of the plot provides a visual representation of the type of relationship that exists between the two sets of scores. Exhibit 7.3 provides three different scatter diagrams for the two sets of scores. Each X represents a test score (predictor) and job performance (criterion, or outcome) score combination for an individual.

Example A in Exhibit 7.3 suggests very little relationship between the two sets of scores. Example B shows a modest relationship between the scores, and example C shows a somewhat strong relationship between the two sets of scores.

## Correlation Coefficient

The relationship between two sets of scores may also be investigated through calculation of the correlation coefficient. The symbol for the correlation coefficient is r. Numerically, r values can range from $r = -1.0$ to $r = 1.0$. An r value of 0 indicates there is no relationship between the two sets of scores. The larger the absolute value of r, the stronger the relationship. So, $r = -.55$ is stronger than $r = .30$. When an r value is shown without a sign (plus or minus), the value is assumed to be positive.

The sign of the correlation coefficient is arbitrary. One could say that job satisfaction is positively related to job performance (a positive r), just as one could say that job *dis*satisfaction is negatively related to job performance (a negative r). Thus, whether r is positive or negative simply depends on how the relationship is worded (and how the measures are scored).

Naturally, the value of r bears a close resemblance to the scatter diagram. To demonstrate this, Exhibit 7.3 also shows the approximate r value for each of the three scatter diagrams. The r in example A is low ($r = .10$), the r in example B is moderate ($r = .25$), and the r in example C is high ($r = .60$).

Calculation of the correlation coefficient is straightforward, even by hand. An example of this calculation and the formula for r are shown in Exhibit 7.4. In the exhibit are two sets of scores for 20 people. The first set is the test scores for the 20 individuals in Exhibit 7.2. The second set of scores is an overall job performance rating (on a 1–5 rating scale) for these people. As can be seen from the calculation, there is a correlation of $r = .58$ between the two sets of scores. The resultant value of r succinctly summarizes both the strength of the relationship between the two sets of scores and the direction of the relationship.

While the formula for the correlation is good to know, correlations are easily calculated by a variety of computer programs, including Microsoft Excel. There, scores on each variable are placed in adjacent columns, and Excel's correlate function "(=Correl)" calculates r.

**EXHIBIT 7.3   Scatter Diagrams and Corresponding Correlations**

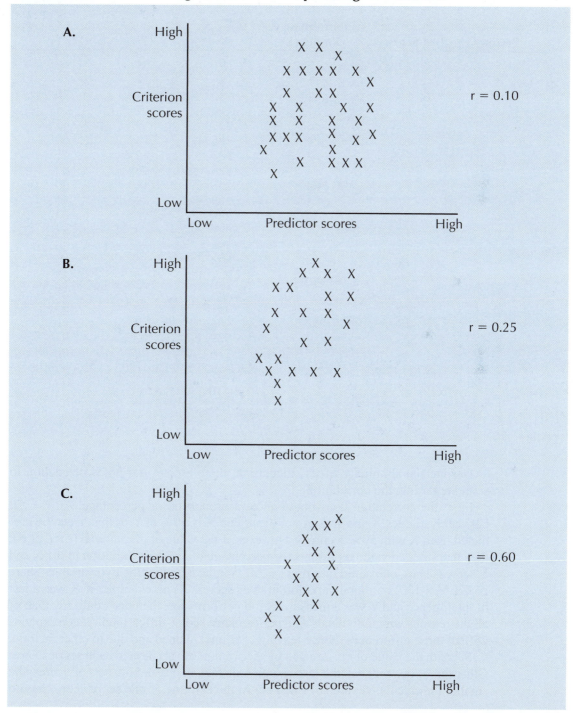

## EXHIBIT 7.4    Calculation of Product-Moment Correlation Coefficient

| Person | Test Score (X) | Performance Rating (Y) | (X²) | (Y²) | (XY) |
|--------|----------------|------------------------|------|------|------|
| A | 10 | 2 | 100 | 4 | 20 |
| B | 12 | 1 | 144 | 1 | 12 |
| C | 14 | 2 | 196 | 4 | 28 |
| D | 14 | 1 | 196 | 1 | 14 |
| E | 15 | 3 | 225 | 9 | 45 |
| F | 15 | 4 | 225 | 16 | 60 |
| G | 15 | 3 | 225 | 9 | 45 |
| H | 15 | 4 | 225 | 16 | 60 |
| I | 15 | 4 | 225 | 16 | 60 |
| J | 17 | 3 | 289 | 9 | 51 |
| K | 17 | 4 | 289 | 16 | 68 |
| L | 17 | 3 | 289 | 9 | 51 |
| M | 18 | 2 | 324 | 4 | 36 |
| N | 18 | 4 | 324 | 16 | 72 |
| O | 19 | 3 | 361 | 9 | 57 |
| P | 19 | 3 | 361 | 9 | 57 |
| Q | 19 | 5 | 361 | 25 | 95 |
| R | 22 | 3 | 484 | 9 | 66 |
| S | 23 | 4 | 529 | 16 | 92 |
| T | 24 | 5 | 576 | 25 | 120 |
| | $\Sigma X = 338$ | $\Sigma Y = 63$ | $\Sigma X^2 = 5948$ | $\Sigma Y^2 = 223$ | $\Sigma XY = 1109$ |

$$r = \frac{n\Sigma XY - (\Sigma X)(\Sigma Y)}{\sqrt{[n\Sigma X^2 - (\Sigma X)^2][n\Sigma Y^2 - (\Sigma Y)^2]}} = \frac{20(1109) - (338)(63)}{\sqrt{[20(5948) - (338)^2][20(223) - (63)^2]}} = .58$$

Despite the simplicity of its calculation, there are several notes of caution to sound regarding the correlation.

First, the correlation does not connote a proportion or percentage. An $r = .50$ between variables X and Y does not mean that X is 50% of Y or that Y can be predicted from X with 50% accuracy. However, if the value of r is squared ($r \times r$, or $r^2$), then that squared value represents the percentage of common variation in the X and Y scores. Thus, one could interpret $r = .50$ as indicating that the two variables share 25% ($.5^2 \times 100$) common variation in their scores. As an example, if X was a test of intelligence and Y was a measure of job performance, then one could say that, of all the reasons why individuals' job performance scores differ, intelligence explains 25% of those differences (hence leaving 75% unexplained and due to other factors).

Second, the value of r is affected by the amount of variation in each set of scores. Other things being equal, the less variation there is in one or both sets of scores, the smaller the calculated value of r will be. At the extreme, if one set of scores has no variation, the correlation will be r = .00 (technically, it is undefined). That is, for there to be a correlation, there must be variation in both sets of scores. The lack of variation in scores is called the problem of restriction of range.

Third, the formula used to calculate the correlation in Exhibit 7.4 is based on the assumption that there is a linear relationship between the two sets of scores. This may not always be a good assumption; something other than a straight line may best capture the true nature of the relationship between scores. For example, a new training program may initially be associated with a rapid increase in trainee performance, but repeated exposure to that program may begin to provide diminished returns. To the extent that two sets of scores are not related in a linear fashion, use of the formula for calculating the correlation will yield a value of r that understates the actual strength of the relationship.

Finally, the correlation between two variables does not imply causation between them. A correlation simply states how two variables covary or relate to each other; it says nothing about one variable necessarily causing the other one.

## Significance of the Correlation Coefficient

The statistical significance refers to the likelihood that a correlation exists in a population, based on knowledge of the actual value of r in a sample from that population. Concluding that a correlation is indeed statistically significant means that there is most likely a correlation in the population. That means if the organization were to use a selection measure based on a statistically significant correlation, the correlation is likely to be significant when used again to select another sample (e.g., future job applicants).

More formally, r is calculated in an initial group, called a sample. From this piece of information, the question arises whether to infer that there is also a correlation in the *population*. For example, one might want to know whether a correlation calculated in a sample of 200 information technology analysts would also be found in the population (all information technology analysts). To answer this, compute the t value of our correlation using the following formula,

$$t = \frac{r}{\sqrt{(1-r^2)/n-2}}$$

where r is the value of the correlation, and n is the size of the sample.

A t distribution table, which can be found in any elementary statistics book as well as online, shows the significance level of r.[7] The significance level is expressed as p < some value, for example, p < .05. This p level tells the probability of concluding that there is a correlation in the population when in fact there is not a relationship. Thus, a correlation with p < .05 means there are fewer than 5 chances in 100 of concluding that there is a relationship in the population when in fact there is not. This is a relatively small probability and usually leads to the conclusion that a correlation is indeed statistically significant.

An example might help clarify this idea. Taking our previous example of 200 information technology analysts, let's say that we found a correlation of $r = .20$ between a measure of programming language knowledge and job performance. How likely is it that we would obtain a correlation of .20 if the "true" correlation between those variables in the population was actually $r = 0$? The t value of our correlation would be 2.87, with a $p < .05$ (actually the p value would be .005). This means that if we hypothetically took 100 more different samples of 200 information technology analysts and computed the correlation in each sample, and the true correlation in the population was actually $r = 0$, we would expect to find a correlation of .20 in only half a percent (.005) of those samples. In other words, a correlation of .20 would be extremely rare, and so we conclude that the actual correlation is not $r = 0$. The correlation of $r = .20$ is deemed "statistically significant."

It is important to avoid concluding that there is a relationship in the population when in fact there is not. (Consider the ramifications of concluding that a new drug with harmful side effects drastically reduces the risk of cancer, yet in fact the drug does nothing to reduce that risk.) Therefore, one usually chooses a fairly conservative or stringent level of significance that the correlation must attain before concluding that it is significant. Typically, a standard of $p < .05$ or less (another common standard is $p < .01$) is chosen. The actual significance level (based on the t value for the correlation) is then compared with the desired significance level, and a decision is reached as to whether the correlation is statistically significant. Here are some examples:

| Desired Level | Actual Level | Conclusion About Correlation |
|:---:|:---:|:---:|
| $p < .05$ | $p < .23$ | Not significant |
| $p < .05$ | $p < .02$ | Significant |
| $p < .01$ | $p < .07$ | Not significant |
| $p < .01$ | $p < .009$ | Significant |

Although statistical significance is important in judging the usefulness of a selection measure, caution should be exercised in placing too much weight on this. With very large sample sizes, even very small correlations will be significant, and with very small samples, even strong correlations will fail to be significant. The absolute size of the correlation matters as well.

## QUALITY OF MEASURES

Measures are developed and used to gauge attributes of objects. Results of measures are expressed in the form of scores, and various manipulations may be done to them. Such manipulations lead to better understanding and interpretation of the scores, and thus the attribute represented by the scores.

In staffing, for practical reasons, the scores of individuals are treated as if they were the attribute itself rather than merely indicators of the attribute. For example, scores on a mental ability test are interpreted as being synonymous with how intelligent individuals are. Alternatively, individuals' job performance ratings from their supervisors are viewed as indicators of their true performance.

Treated in this way, scores become a major input to decision making about individuals. For example, scores on the mental ability test are used and weighted heavily to decide which job applicants will receive a job offer. Alternatively, performance ratings may serve as a key factor in deciding which individuals will be eligible for an internal staffing move, such as a promotion. In these and numerous other ways, management uses these scores to guide the conduct of staffing activities in the organization.

The quality of the decisions made and the actions taken is unlikely to be any better than the quality of the measures on which they are based. Thus, a lot is at stake in the quality of the measures used in staffing. Such concerns are best viewed in terms of reliability and validity of measures.[8]

## Reliability of Measures

Reliability of measurement refers to the consistency of measurement of an attribute.[9] A measure is reliable to the extent that it provides a consistent set of scores to represent an attribute. Rarely is perfect reliability achieved, because of the occurrence of measurement error. Reliability is thus a matter of degree.

Reliability of measurement is of concern both within a single time period in which the attribute is being measured and between time periods. Moreover, reliability is of concern for both objective and subjective measures. These two concerns help create a general framework for better understanding reliability.

The key concepts for the framework are shown in Exhibit 7.5. In the exhibit, a single attribute, "A" (e.g., knowledge of programming languages), is being measured. Scores (ranging from 1 to 5) are available for 15 individuals. A is being measured in time period 1 ($T_1$) and time period 2 ($T_2$). In each time period, A may be measured objectively, with two test items, or subjectively, with two raters. The same two items or raters are used in each time period. (In reality, more than two items or raters would probably be used to measure A, but for simplicity only two are used here.) Each test item or rater in each time period is a submeasure of A. There are thus four submeasures of A—designated $X_1$, $X_2$, $Y_1$, and $Y_2$—and four sets of scores. In terms of reliability of measurement, the concern is with the consistency or similarity in the sets of scores. This requires various comparisons of the scores.

### Comparisons Within $T_1$ or $T_2$

Consider the four sets of scores as coming from the objective measure, which used test items. Comparing sets of scores from these items in either $T_1$ or $T_2$ is called

**EXHIBIT 7.5   Framework for Reliability of Measures**

| | Scores on Attribute A | | | | | | | |
| | Objective (Test Items) | | | | Subjective (Raters) | | | |
| | Time 1 | | Time 2 | | Time 1 | | Time 2 | |
| Person | $X_1$ | $Y_1$ | $X_2$ | $Y_2$ | $X_1$ | $Y_1$ | $X_2$ | $Y_2$ |
|---|---|---|---|---|---|---|---|---|
| A | 5 | 5 | 4 | 5 | 5 | 5 | 4 | 5 |
| B | 5 | 4 | 4 | 3 | 5 | 4 | 4 | 3 |
| C | 5 | 5 | 5 | 4 | 5 | 5 | 5 | 4 |
| D | 5 | 4 | 5 | 5 | 5 | 4 | 5 | 5 |
| E | 4 | 5 | 3 | 4 | 4 | 5 | 3 | 4 |
| F | 4 | 4 | 4 | 3 | 4 | 4 | 4 | 3 |
| G | 4 | 4 | 3 | 4 | 4 | 4 | 3 | 4 |
| H | 4 | 3 | 4 | 3 | 4 | 3 | 4 | 3 |
| I | 3 | 4 | 3 | 4 | 3 | 4 | 3 | 4 |
| J | 3 | 3 | 5 | 3 | 3 | 3 | 5 | 3 |
| K | 3 | 3 | 2 | 3 | 3 | 3 | 2 | 3 |
| L | 3 | 2 | 4 | 2 | 3 | 2 | 4 | 2 |
| M | 2 | 3 | 4 | 3 | 2 | 3 | 4 | 3 |
| N | 2 | 2 | 1 | 2 | 2 | 2 | 1 | 2 |
| O | 1 | 2 | 3 | 2 | 1 | 2 | 3 | 2 |

NOTE: $X_1$ and $X_2$ are the same test item or rater; $Y_1$ and $Y_2$ are the same test item or rater. The subscript "1" refers to $T_1$, and the subscript "2" refers to $T_2$.

internal consistency reliability. The relevant comparisons are $X_1$ and $Y_1$, and $X_2$ and $Y_2$. It is hoped that the comparisons will show high similarity, because both items are intended to measure A within the same time period.

Now treat the four sets of scores as coming from the subjective measure, which relied on raters. Comparisons of these scores involve what is called interrater reliability. The relevant comparisons are the same as with the objective measure scores, namely, $X_1$ and $Y_1$, and $X_2$ and $Y_2$. Again, it is hoped that there will be high agreement between the raters, because they are focusing on a single attribute at a single moment in time.

## Comparisons Between $T_1$ and $T_2$

Comparisons of scores between time periods involve assessment of measurement stability. When scores from an objective measure are used, this is referred to as test–retest reliability. The relevant comparisons are $X_1$ and $X_2$, and $Y_1$ and $Y_2$. To the extent that A is not expected to change between $T_1$ and $T_2$, there should be high test–retest reliability.

When subjective scores are compared between $T_1$ and $T_2$, the concern is with intrarater reliability. Here, the same rater evaluates individuals in terms of A in two different time periods. To the extent that A is not expected to change, there should be high intrarater reliability.

In summary, reliability is concerned with consistency of measurement. There are multiple ways of treating reliability, depending on whether scores from a measure are being compared for consistency within or between time periods and depending on whether the scores are from objective or subjective measures. These points are summarized in Exhibit 7.6. Ways of computing agreement between scores will be covered shortly, after the concept of measurement error is explored.

## Measurement Error

Rarely will any of the comparisons among scores discussed previously yield perfect similarity or reliability. Indeed, none of the comparisons in Exhibit 7.6 visually shows complete agreement among the scores. The lack of agreement among the scores may be due to the occurrence of measurement error. This type of error represents "noise" in the measure and measurement process. Its occurrence means that the measure did not yield perfectly consistent scores, or so-called true scores, for the attribute.

The scores actually obtained from the measure thus have two components to them, a true score and measurement error. That is,

$$\text{actual score} = \text{true score} + \text{error}$$

**EXHIBIT 7.6   Summary of Types of Reliability**

|  | Compare scores within $T_1$ or $T_2$ | Compare scores between $T_1$ and $T_2$ |
|---|---|---|
| Objective measure (test items) | Internal consistency | Test–retest |
| Subjective measure (raters) | Interrater | Intrarater |

The error component of any actual score, or set of scores, represents unreliability of measurement. Unfortunately, unreliability is a fact of life for the types of measures used in staffing. To help understand why this is the case, the various types or sources of error that can occur in a staffing context must be explored. These errors may be grouped under the categories of deficiency error and contamination error.[10]

***Deficiency Error.***   Deficiency error occurs when there is failure to measure some portion or aspect of the attribute assessed. For example, if knowledge of programming languages should involve Java and our test does not have any items (or an insufficient number of items) covering this aspect, the test is deficient. As another example, if an attribute of job performance is "planning and setting work priorities" and the raters fail to rate people on that dimension during their performance appraisal, the performance measure is deficient.

Deficiency error can occur in several related ways. First, the attribute may have been inadequately defined in the first place. Thus, the test of knowledge of programming languages may fail to address Java because multiparadigm languages were never included in the initial definition of programming knowledge. Alternatively, the performance measure may fail to require raters to rate their employees on "planning and setting work priorities" because this attribute was never considered an important dimension of their work.

A second way that deficiency error occurs is in the construction of measures used to assess the attribute. Here, the attribute may be well defined and understood, but there is a failure to construct a measure that adequately gets at the totality of the attribute. This is akin to poor measurement by oversight, which happens when measures are constructed in a hurried, ad hoc fashion.

Deficiency error also occurs when the organization opts to use whatever measures are available because of ease, cost considerations, sales pitches and promotional claims, and so forth. The measures so chosen may turn out to be deficient.

***Contamination Error.***   Contamination error represents the occurrence of unwanted or undesirable influence on the measure and on individuals for whom the measure is being used. These influences muddy the scores and make them difficult to interpret.

Sources of contamination abound, as do examples of them. Several of these sources and examples are shown in Exhibit 7.7, along with some suggestions for how they might be controlled. These examples show that contamination error is multifaceted, making it difficult to minimize and control.

## Calculation of Reliability Estimates

Numerous procedures are available for calculating actual estimates of the degree of reliability of measurement.[11] The first two of these (coefficient alpha and interrater agreement) assess reliability within a single time period. The other two proce-

**EXHIBIT 7.7   Sources of Contamination Error and Suggestions for Control**

| Source of Contamination | Example | Suggestion for Control |
|---|---|---|
| Content domain | Irrelevant material on test | Define domain of test material to be covered |
| Standardization | Different time limits for same test | Have same time limits for everyone |
| Chance response tendencies | Guessing by test taker | Impossible to control in advance |
| Rater | Rater gives inflated ratings to people | Train rater in rating accuracy |
| Rating situation | Interviewees are asked different questions | Ask all interviewees the same questions |

dures (test–retest and intrarater agreement) assess reliability between time periods. Reliability scores range from 0 (indicating that there is nothing but error in the actual scores) to 1.0 (indicating that the actual scores are the "true" scores). Like the squared correlation ($r^2$), you can think of reliability estimates as the percentage of variation in a given measure that is "true" as opposed to "error."

***Coefficient Alpha.***   Coefficient alpha may be calculated in instances in which there are two or more items (or raters) for a particular attribute. Its formula is

$$\alpha = \frac{n\,(\bar{r})}{1 + \bar{r}\,(n-1)}$$

where $\bar{r}$ is the average intercorrelation among the items (raters) and n is the number of items (raters). For example, if there are five items (n = 5) and the average correlation among those five items is $\bar{r} = .80$, coefficient alpha is .95.

It can be seen from the formula and the example that coefficient alpha depends on just two things—the number of items and the amount of correlation between them. This suggests two basic strategies for increasing the internal consistency reliability of a measure—increase the number of items and increase the amount of agreement between the items (raters). It is generally recommended that coefficient alpha be at least .80 for a measure to have an acceptable degree of reliability. That means that 80% of the variation in scores is "true" variation and 20% is "error."

***Interrater Agreement.***   When raters serve as the measure, it is often convenient to talk about interrater agreement, or the amount of agreement among them. For example, if members of a group or panel interview independently rate a set of job applicants on a 1–5 scale, it is logical to ask how much they agreed with one another.

A simple way to determine this is to calculate the percentage of agreement among the raters. An example of this is shown in Exhibit 7.8.

There is no commonly accepted minimum level of interrater agreement that must be met in order to consider the raters sufficiently reliable. Normally, a fairly high level should be set—75% or higher. The more important the end use of the ratings, the greater the agreement required should be. Critical uses, such as hiring decisions, demand very high levels of reliability, well in excess of 75% agreement.

***Interrater Agreement Versus Coefficient Alpha.***  It is important to note that reliability (as assessed by coefficient alpha) and interrater agreement can be quite different. Specifically, one can have a high coefficient alpha but low agreement, and vice versa. To understand this, consider the data shown in Exhibit 7.9, which, like Exhibit 7.8, has three raters. However, instead of rating five different applicants, the three raters are rating one applicant on five different skills. Here, there are five items (skills), and the average correlation among those five items (e.g., the correlation between ratings on skill A and skill B; the correlation between ratings on skill A and skill C) is 1.0. This is the case because the ratings are proportionally consistent (although rater 1's ratings are always lower than rater 2's, they differ by the same magnitude each time). Consequently, coefficient alpha is 1.0. However, the raters do not agree at all on how much skill the applicant possesses. Rater 1's average across the five skills is 1.6, rater 2's average is 3.6, and rater 3's average is 4.6.

Now consider Exhibit 7.10. The raters exhibit perfect agreement in their assessment of the candidate. However, coefficient alpha is 0 (technically, it is undefined).

**EXHIBIT 7.8**  **Calculation of Percentage Agreement Among Raters**

| Person (ratee) | Rater 1 | Rater 2 | Rater 3 |
|:---:|:---:|:---:|:---:|
| A | 5 | 5 | 2 |
| B | 3 | 3 | 5 |
| C | 5 | 4 | 4 |
| D | 1 | 1 | 5 |
| E | 2 | 2 | 4 |

$$\% \text{ Agreement} = \frac{\# \text{ agreements}}{\# \text{ agreements} + \# \text{ disagreements}} \times 100$$

% Agreement

Rater 1 and Rater 2 = 4/5 = 80%
Rater 1 and Rater 3 = 0/5 = 0%
Rater 2 and Rater 3 = 1/5 = 20%

**EXHIBIT 7.9   High Coefficient Alpha but Low Agreement**

| Skill | Rater 1 | Rater 2 | Rater 3 |
|---|---|---|---|
| Skill A | 1 | 3 | 4 |
| Skill B | 2 | 4 | 5 |
| Skill C | 2 | 4 | 5 |
| Skill D | 1 | 3 | 4 |
| Skill E | 2 | 4 | 5 |

**EXHIBIT 7.10   Low Coefficient Alpha but High Agreement**

| Skill | Rater 1 | Rater 2 | Rater 3 |
|---|---|---|---|
| Skill A | 2 | 2 | 2 |
| Skill B | 2 | 2 | 2 |
| Skill C | 3 | 3 | 3 |
| Skill D | 2 | 2 | 2 |
| Skill E | 2 | 2 | 2 |

Why? Remember that the strength of the correlation coefficient depends on how much variation there is in the items (in this case, skills). Since there is no variation in the items (e.g., skill A is rated 2 by all three raters, as is skill B), the average correlation among the items is 0 and coefficient alpha is 0.

When assessing the reliability of scores where multiple raters are assessing candidates on multiple items, keep in mind that coefficient alpha and interrater agreement are tapping into different aspects of reliability. Therefore, it is important to consider both.

***Test–Retest Reliability.***   To assess test–retest reliability, the test scores from two different time periods are correlated through calculation of the correlation coefficient. The r may be calculated on total test scores, or a separate r may be calculated for scores on each item. The resultant r indicates the stability of measurement—the higher the r, the more stable the measure.

Interpretation of the r value is made difficult by the fact that the scores are gathered at two different points in time. Between those two time points, the attribute being measured has an opportunity to change. Interpretation of test–retest reliability thus requires some sense of how much the attribute may be expected to change, and what the appropriate time interval between tests is. Usually, for very short time intervals (hours or days), most attributes are quite stable, and a large test–retest r (r = .90 or higher) should be expected. Over longer time intervals, it is usual to expect much lower r's, depending on the attribute being measured. For example, over six months or a year, individuals' knowledge of programming languages might change. If so, there will be lower test–retest reliabilities (e.g., r = .50).

***Intrarater Agreement.*** To calculate intrarater agreement, scores that the rater assigns to the same people in two different time periods are compared. The calculation could involve computing the correlation between the two sets of scores, or it could involve using the same formula as for interrater agreement (see Exhibit 7.8).

Interpretation of intrarater agreement is made difficult by the time factor. For short time intervals between measures, a fairly high relationship is expected (e.g., r = .80, or percentage agreement = 90%). For longer time intervals, the level of reliability may reasonably be expected to be lower.

## Implications of Reliability

The degree of reliability of a measure has two implications. The first of these pertains to interpreting individuals' scores on the measure and the standard error of measurement. The second implication pertains to the effect that reliability has on the measure's validity.

***Standard Error of Measurement.*** Measures yield scores, which in turn are used as critical inputs for decision making in staffing activities. For example, in Exhibit 7.1 a test of knowledge of programming languages was developed and administered to job applicants. The applicants' scores were used as a basis for making hiring decisions.

The discussion of reliability suggests that measures and scores will usually have some amount of error in them. Hence, scores on the test of knowledge of programming languages most likely reflect both true knowledge and error. Since only a single score is obtained from each applicant, the critical issue is how accurately that particular score indicates the applicant's true level of knowledge of programming languages alone.

The standard error of measurement (SEM) addresses this issue. It provides a way to state, within limits, a person's likely score on a measure. The formula for the SEM is

$$SEM = SD_x \sqrt{1 - r_{xx}}$$

where $SD_x$ is the standard deviation of scores on the measure and $r_{xx}$ is an estimate of the measure's reliability. For example, if $SD_x = 10$ and $r_{xx} = .75$ (based on coefficient alpha), SEM = 5.

With the SEM known, the range within which any individual's true score is likely to fall can be estimated. This range is known as a confidence interval or limit. There is a 95% chance that a person's true score lies within ±2 SEM of his or her actual score. Thus, if an applicant received a score of 22 on the test of knowledge of programming languages, the applicant's true score is most likely to be within the range of 22 ± 2(5), or 12–32.

Recognition and use of the SEM allow for care in interpreting people's scores, as well as differences between individuals in terms of their scores. For example, using the preceding data, if the test score for applicant 1 is 22 and the score for applicant 2 is 19, what should be made of the difference between the two applicants? Is applicant 1 truly more knowledgeable of programming languages than applicant 2? The answer is probably not. This is because of the SEM and the large amount of overlap between the two applicants' intervals (12–32 for applicant 1, and 9–29 for applicant 2).

In short, there is not a one-to-one correspondence between actual scores and true scores. Most measures used in staffing are unreliable to some degree, meaning that small differences in scores are probably due to error of measurement and should be ignored.

***Relationship to Validity.*** The validity of a measure is defined as the degree to which it measures the attribute it is supposed to be measuring. For example, the validity of the test of knowledge of programming languages is the degree to which it measures that knowledge. There are specific ways to investigate validity, and these are discussed in the next section. Here, it simply needs to be recognized that the reliability with which an attribute is measured has direct implications for the validity of the measure.

The relationship between the reliability and the validity of a measure is

$$r_{xy} \leq \sqrt{r_{xx}}$$

where $r_{xy}$ is the validity of the measure and $r_{xx}$ is the reliability of the measure. For example, it had been assumed previously that the reliability of the test of knowledge of programming languages was $r = .75$. The validity of that test thus cannot exceed $\sqrt{.75} = 86$.

Thus, the reliability of a measure places an upper limit on the possible validity of a measure. It should be emphasized that this is only an upper limit. A highly reliable measure is not necessarily valid. Reliability does not guarantee validity; it only makes validity possible.

## Validity of Measures

The validity of a measure is defined as the degree to which it measures the attribute it is intended to measure.[12] Refer back to Exhibit 7.1, which involved the development of a test of knowledge of programming languages that was to be used in selecting job applicants. The validity of this test is the degree to which it truly measures the attribute or construct "knowledge of programming languages."

Judgments about the validity of a measure occur through the process of gathering data and evidence about the measure to assess how it was developed and whether accurate inferences can be made from scores on the measure. This process can be illustrated in terms of concepts pertaining to accuracy of measurement and accuracy of prediction. These concepts may then be used to demonstrate how validation of measures occurs in staffing.

### Accuracy of Measurement

How accurate is the test of knowledge of programming languages? This question asks for evidence about the accuracy with which the test portrays individuals' true levels of that knowledge. This is akin to asking about the degree of overlap between the attribute being measured and the actual measure of the attribute.

Exhibit 7.11 shows the concept of accuracy of measurement in Venn diagram form. The circle on the left represents the construct "knowledge of programming

**EXHIBIT 7.11** **Accuracy of Measurement**

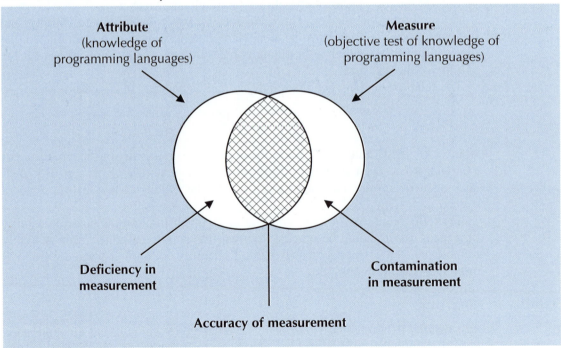

languages," and the circle on the right represents the actual test of knowledge of programming languages. The overlap between the two circles represents the degree of accuracy of measurement for the test. The greater the overlap, the greater the accuracy of measurement.

Notice that perfect overlap is not shown in Exhibit 7.11. This signifies the occurrence of measurement error with the use of the test. These errors, as indicated in the exhibit, are the errors of deficiency and contamination previously discussed.

So how does accuracy of measurement differ from reliability of measurement since both are concerned with deficiency and contamination? There is disagreement among people on this question. Generally, the difference may be thought of as follows. Reliability refers to consistency among the scores on the test, as determined by comparing scores as previously described. Accuracy of measurement goes beyond this to assess the extent to which the scores truly reflect the attribute being measured—the overlap shown in Exhibit 7.11. Accuracy requires reliability, but it also requires more by way of evidence. For example, accuracy requires knowing something about how the test was developed. Accuracy also requires some evidence concerning how test scores are influenced by other factors—for example, how do test scores change as a result of employees attending a training program devoted to providing instruction on programming languages? Accuracy thus demands greater evidence than reliability.

## Accuracy of Prediction

Measures are often developed because they provide information about people that can be used to make predictions about them. In Exhibit 7.1, the knowledge test was to be used to help make hiring decisions, which are actually predictions about which people will be successful at a job. Knowing something about the accuracy with which a test predicts future job success requires examining the relationship between scores on the test and scores on some measure of job success for a group of people.

Accuracy of prediction is illustrated in the top half of Exhibit 7.12. Where there is an actual job success outcome (criterion) to predict, the test (predictor) will be used to predict the criterion. Each person is classified as high or low on the predictor and high or low on the criterion, based on predictor and criterion scores. Individuals falling into cells A and C represent correct predictions, and individuals falling into cells B and D represent errors in prediction. Accuracy of prediction is the percentage of total correct predictions and can range from 0% to 100%.

The bottom half of Exhibit 7.12 shows an example of the determination of accuracy of prediction using a selection example. The predictor is the test of knowledge of programming languages, and the criterion is an overall measure of job performance. Scores on the predictor and criterion measures are gathered for 100 job applicants and are dichotomized into high or low scores on each. Each individual is placed into one of the four cells. The accuracy of prediction for the test is 70%.

**EXHIBIT 7.12  Accuracy of Prediction**

**A. General Illustration**

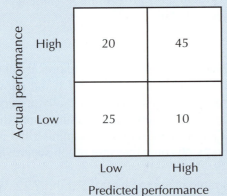

|  | | D | A |
|---|---|---|---|
| Actual criterion | High | Errors in predictions | Correct predictions |
|  | Low | C Correct predictions | B Errors in predictions |

Low    High
Predicted criterion

$$\text{Accuracy} = \frac{A+C}{A+B+C+D} \times 100$$

**B. Selection Example (n=100 job applicants)**

|  | | Low | High |
|---|---|---|---|
| Actual performance | High | 20 | 45 |
|  | Low | 25 | 10 |

Low    High
Predicted performance
(based on test scores)

$$\text{Accuracy} = \frac{45+25}{45+10+25+20} \times 100 = 70\%$$

## Validation of Measures in Staffing

In staffing, there is concern with the validity of predictors in terms of both accuracy of measurement and accuracy of prediction. It is important to have and use predictors that accurately represent the KSAOs to be measured, and those predictors need to be accurate in their predictions of job success. The validity of predictors is explored through the conduct of validation studies.

Two types of validation studies are typically conducted. The first of these is criterion-related validation, and the second is content validation. A third type of validation study, known as construct validation, involves components of reliability, criterion-related validation, and content validation. Each component is discussed separately in this book, and thus no further reference is made to construct validation.

### Criterion-Related Validation

Exhibit 7.13 shows the components of criterion-related validation and their usual sequencing.[13] The process begins with job analysis. Results of job analysis are fed

**EXHIBIT 7.13   Criterion-Related Validation**

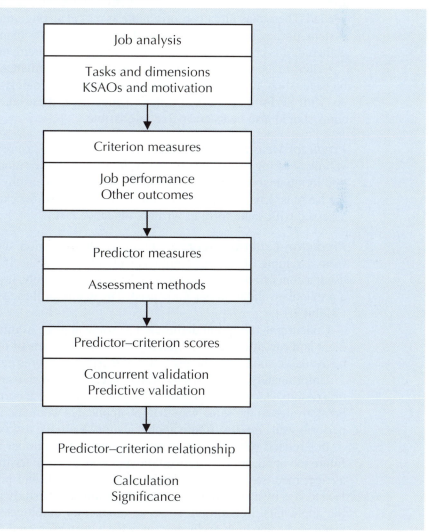

into criterion and predictor measures. Scores on the predictor and criterion are obtained for a sample of individuals; the relationship between the scores is then examined to make a judgment about the predictor's validity.

***Job Analysis.*** Job analysis is undertaken to identify and define important tasks (and broader task dimensions) of the job. The KSAOs and motivation thought to be necessary for performance of these tasks are then inferred. Results of the process of identifying tasks and underlying KSAOs are expressed in the form of the job requirements matrix. The matrix is a task × KSAO matrix; it shows the tasks required and the relevant KSAOs for each task.

***Criterion Measures.*** Measures of performance on tasks and task dimensions are needed. These may already be available as part of an ongoing performance appraisal system, or they may have to be developed. In whatever manner these measures are gathered, it is critical that they be as free from measurement error as possible.

Criterion measures need not be restricted to performance measures. Others may be used, such as measures of attendance, retention, safety, and customer service. As with performance-based criterion measures, these alternative criterion measures should also be as error-free as possible.

***Predictor Measure.*** The predictor measure is the measure whose criterion-related validity is being investigated. Ideally, it taps into one or more of the KSAOs identified in job analysis. Also, it should be the type of measure most suitable to assess the KSAOs. Knowledge of programming languages, for example, is probably best assessed with some form of written, objective test.

***Predictor–Criterion Scores.*** Predictor and criterion scores must be gathered from a sample of current employees or job applicants. If current employees are used, a concurrent validation design is used. Alternately, if job applicants are used, a predictive validation design is used. The nature of these two designs is shown in Exhibit 7.14.

Concurrent validation definitely has some appeal. Administratively, it is convenient and can often be done quickly. Moreover, results of the validation study will be available soon after the predictor and criterion scores have been gathered.

Unfortunately, some serious problems can arise with use of a concurrent validation design. One problem is that if the predictor is a test, current employees may not be motivated in the same way that job applicants would be in terms of the desire to perform well. Yet, it is future applicants for whom the test is intended to be used.

In a related vein, current employees may not be similar to, or representative of, future job applicants. Current employees may differ in terms of demographics such as age, race, sex, disability status, education level, and previous job experience. Hence, it is by no means certain that the results of the study will generalize to future job applicants. In addition, some unsatisfactory employees will have been terminated, and some high performers may have been promoted. This leads to restriction

**EXHIBIT 7.14 Concurrent and Predictive Validation Designs**

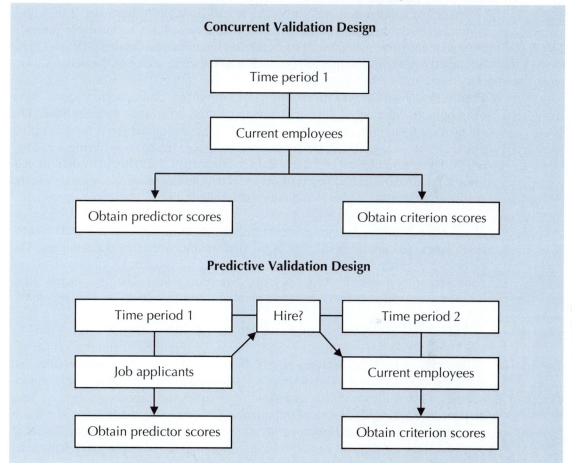

Concurrent Validation Design

Time period 1

Current employees

Obtain predictor scores          Obtain criterion scores

Predictive Validation Design

Time period 1 — Hire? — Time period 2

Job applicants          Current employees

Obtain predictor scores          Obtain criterion scores

of range on the criterion scores (i.e., most employees are high performers), which in turn will lower the correlation between the predictor and criterion scores.

Finally, current employees' predictor scores may be influenced by the amount of experience and/or success they have had in their current job. For example, scores on the test of knowledge of programming languages may reflect not only that knowledge but also how long people have been on the job and how well they have performed it. This is undesirable because one wants predictor scores to be predictive of the criterion rather than a result of it.

Predictive validation overcomes the potential limitations of concurrent validation since the predictor scores are obtained from job applicants. Applicants will be motivated to do well on the predictor, and they are more likely to be representative of future job applicants. Applicants' scores on the predictor cannot be influenced by success and/or experience on the job, because the scores are gathered prior to their being on the job.

Predictive validation is not without potential limitations, however. It is neither administratively easy nor quick. Moreover, results will not be available immediately, as some time must lapse before criterion scores can be obtained. Despite these limitations, predictive validation is considered the more sound of the two designs.

***Predictor–Criterion Relationship.***  Once predictor and criterion scores have been obtained, the correlation r, or some variation of it, must be calculated. The value of r is then referred to as the validity of the scores on the predictor. For example, if an r = .35 was found, the predictor would be referred to as having a validity of .35. Then, the practical and statistical significance of the r should be determined. Only if the r meets desired levels of practical and statistical significance should the predictor be considered valid and thus potentially usable in the selection system.

***Illustrative Study.***  A state university civil service system covering 20 institutions sought to identify predictors of job performance for clerical employees. The clerical job existed within different schools (e.g., engineering, humanities) and nonacademic departments (e.g., payroll, data processing). The goal of the study was to have a valid clerical test in two parallel forms that could be administered to job applicants in one hour.

The starting point was to conduct a job analysis, the results of which would be used as the basis for constructing the clerical tests (predictors) and the job performance ratings (criteria). Subject matter experts (SMEs) used job observation and previous job descriptions to construct a task-based questionnaire that was administered to clerical incumbents and their supervisors throughout the system. Task statements were rated in terms of importance, frequency, and essentialness (if it was essential for a newly hired employee to know how to do this task). From a statistical analysis of the ratings' means and standard deviations, 25 of the 188 task statements were retained as critical task statements. These critical task statements were the key input to the identification of key KSAOs and the dimension of job performance.

Analysis of the 25 critical task statements indicated there were five KSAO components of the job: knowledge of computer hardware and software, ability to follow instructions and prioritize tasks, knowledge and skill in responding to telephone and reception scenarios, knowledge of English language, and ability to file items in alphabetical order. A test was constructed to measure these KSAOs as follows:

- Computer hardware and software—17 questions
- Prioritize tasks—18 questions
- Route and transfer calls—14 questions
- Record messages—20 questions
- Give information on the phone—20 questions
- Correct sentences with errors—22 questions

- Identify errors in sentences—71 questions
- File documents—44 questions
- Type documents—number of questions not reported

To develop the job performance (criterion) measure, a behavioral performance rating scale (1–7 rating) was constructed for each of the nine areas, ensuring a high content correspondence between the tests and the performance criteria they sought to predict. Scores on these nine scales were summed to yield an overall performance score.

The nine tests were administered to 108 current clerical employees to obtain predictor scores. A separate score on each of the nine tests was computed, along with a total score for all tests. In addition, total scores on two short (50-question) forms of the total test were created (Form A and Form B).

Performance ratings of these 108 employees were obtained from their supervisors, who were unaware of their employees' test scores. The performance ratings were summed to form an overall performance rating. Scores on each of the nine tests, on the total test, and on Forms A and B of the test were correlated with the overall performance ratings.

Results of the concurrent validation study are shown in Exhibit 7.15. It can be seen that seven of the nine specific tests had statistically significant correlations

**EXHIBIT 7.15  Clerical Test Concurrent Validation Results**

| Test | Correlation With Overall Performance |
|---|---|
| Computer software and hardware | .37** |
| Prioritize tasks | .29* |
| Route and transfer calls | .19* |
| Record messages | .31** |
| Give information on phone | .35** |
| Correct sentences with errors | .32** |
| Identify errors in sentences | .44** |
| File documents | .22 |
| Type documents | .10 |
| Total test | .45** |
| Form A | .55** |
| Form B | .49** |

NOTE: *$p < .05$, **$p < .01$

SOURCE: Adapted from J. E. Pynes, E. J. Harrick, and D. Schaefer, "A Concurrent Validation Study Applied to a Secretarial Position in a State University Civil Service System," *Journal of Business and Psychology*, 1997, 12, pp. 3–18.

with overall performance (filing and typing did not). Total test scores were significantly correlated with overall performance, as were scores on the two short forms of the total test. The sizes of the statistically significant correlations suggest favorable practical significance of the correlations as well.

### Content Validation

Content validation differs from criterion-related validity in one important respect: no criterion measure is used in content validation. Thus, predictor scores cannot be correlated with criterion scores as a way of gathering evidence about a predictor's validity. Rather, a judgment is made about the probable correlation, had there been a criterion measure. For this reason, content validation is frequently referred to as judgmental validation.[14]

Content validation is most appropriate, and most likely to be found, in two circumstances: (1) when there are too few people to form a sample for purposes of criterion-related validation, and (2) when criterion measures are not available, or they are available but are of highly questionable quality. At an absolute minimum, an n = 30 is necessary for criterion-related validation.

Exhibit 7.16 shows the two basic steps in content validation: conducting a job analysis and choosing or developing a predictor. These steps are commented on next. Comparing the steps in content validation with those in criterion-related validation (see Exhibit 7.13) shows that the steps in content validation are part of criterion-related validation. Because of this, the two types of validation should be thought of as complementary, with content validation being a subset of criterion-related validation.

*Job Analysis.*   Like criterion-related validation, content validation begins with job analysis, which, in both cases, is undertaken to identify and define tasks and

**EXHIBIT 7.16**   **Content Validation**

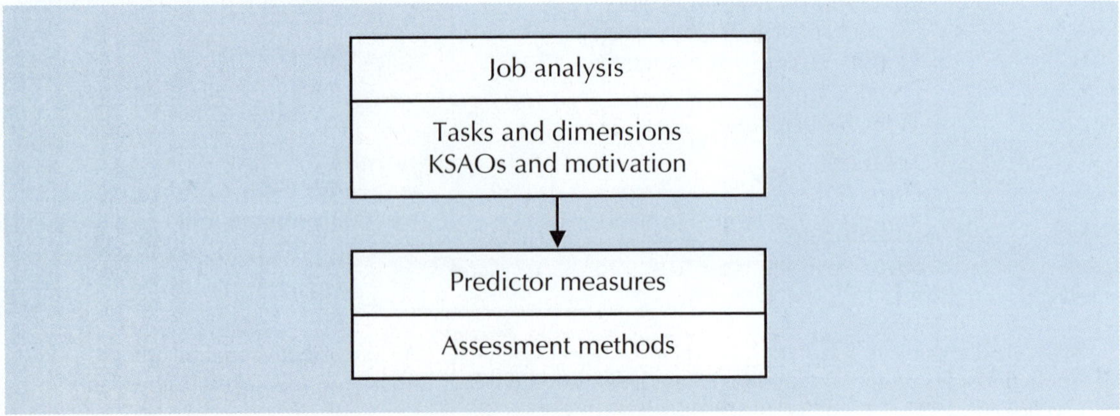

task dimensions and to infer the necessary KSAOs and motivation for those tasks. Results are expressed in the job requirements matrix.

***Predictor Measures.***   Sometimes the predictor will be one that has already been developed and is in use. An example here is a commercially available test, interviewing process, or biographical information questionnaire. Other times, such a measure will not be available. This occurs frequently in the case of job knowledge, which is usually very specific to the particular job involved in the validation.

Lacking a readily available or modifiable predictor means that the organization will have to construct its own predictors. At this point, the organization has built predictor construction into the predictor validation process. Now, content validation and the predictor development processes occur simultaneously. The organization becomes engaged in test construction, a topic beyond the scope of this book.[15]

With content validation, it is important to continually pay attention to the need for reliability of measurement and standardization of the measurement process. Though these are always matters of concern in any type of validation effort, they are of paramount importance in content validation. The reason for this is that without an empirical correlation between the predictor and the criterion, only the likely r can be judged. It is important, in forming that judgment, to pay considerable attention to reliability and standardization.

Though content validation has its benefits, including ease of administration, favorable applicant reactions to measures, and legal defensibility, it is not without drawbacks. Critics of content validation argue that, despite the transparent match between job content and measurement content, there is little empirical evidence that content validated measures actually correlate with the criteria they are supposed to predict (e.g., job performance) and thus they are not as valid as they are made out to be.[16]

***Illustrative Study.***   The Maryland Department of Transportation sought to develop a series of assessment methods for identifying supervisory potential among candidates for promotion to a first-level supervising position anywhere within the department. The content validation process and outputs are shown in Exhibit 7.17. As shown in the exhibit, job analysis was first conducted to identify and define a set of performance dimensions and then infer the KSAOs necessary for successful performance in those dimensions. Several SMEs met to develop a tentative set of task dimensions and underlying KSAOs. The underlying KSAOs were in essence general competencies required of all first-level supervisors, regardless of work unit within the department. Their results were sent to a panel of experienced human resource (HR) managers within the department for revision and finalization. Three assessment method specialists then set about developing a set of assessments that would (1) be efficiently administered at locations throughout the state, (2) be reliably scored by people at those locations, and (3) emphasize the interpersonal skills important for this job. As shown in Exhibit 7.17, five assessment methods were

---

**EXHIBIT 7.17** **Content Validation Study**

**Job Analysis: First-Level Supervisor — Maryland Department of Transportation**

Seven performance dimensions and task statements:
>    Organizing work; assigning work; monitoring work; managing consequences; counseling, efficiency reviews, and discipline; setting an example; employee development

Fourteen KSAOs and definitions:
>    Organizing; analysis and decision making; planning; communication (oral and written); delegation; work habits; carefulness; interpersonal skill; job knowledge; organizational knowledge; toughness; integrity; development of others; listening

**Predictor Measures: Five Assessment Methods**

Multiple-choice in-basket exercise
>    (assume role of new supervisor and work through in-basket on desk)

Structured panel interview
>    (predetermined questions about past experiences relevant to the KSAOs)

Presentation exercise
>    (make presentation to a simulated work group about change in their work hours)

Writing sample
>    (prepare a written reprimand for a fictitious employee)

Training and experience evaluation exercise
>    (give examples of training and work achievements relevant to certain KSAOs)

SOURCE: Adapted from M. A. Cooper, G. Kaufman, and W. Hughes, "Measuring Supervisory Potential," *IPMA News,* December 1996, pp. 8–18. Reprinted with permission of *IPMA News,* published by the International Personnel Management Association (IPMA; *www.ipma-hr.org*).

---

developed: multiple-choice in-basket exercise, structured panel interview, presentation exercise, writing sample, and training and experience evaluation exercise.

Candidates' performance on the exercises was to be evaluated by specially chosen assessors at the location where the exercises were administered. To ensure that candidates' performance was skillfully observed and reliably evaluated by the assessors, an intensive training program was developed. The program provided both a written user's manual and specific skill training.

## Validity Generalization

In the preceding discussions of validity and validation, an implicit premise is being made that validity is situation specific, and therefore validation of predictors must occur in each specific situation. All of the examples involve specific types of measures, jobs, individuals, and so forth. Nothing is said about generalizing validity across those jobs and individuals. For example, if a predictor is valid for a particular job in organization A, would it be valid for the same type of job in organization B? Or is validity specific to the particular job and organization?

The situation-specific premise is based on the following scenario, which has its origins in findings from decades of previous research. Assume that 10 criterion-related validation studies have been conducted. Each study involves various predictor measures of a common KSAO attribute (e.g., general mental ability) and various criterion measures of a common outcome attribute (e.g., job performance). The predictor will be designated $x$, and the criterion will be designated $y$. The studies are conducted in different situations (types of jobs, types of organizations), and they involve different samples (with different sample sizes [n]). In each study, the reliability of the predictor ($r_{xx}$) and the criterion ($r_{yy}$), as well as the validity coefficient ($r_{xy}$), is calculated. These results are provided in Exhibit 7.18. At first blush, the results, because of the wide range of $r_{xy}$ values, would seem to support situational specificity. These results suggest that while, on average, there seems to be some validity to $x$, the validity varies substantially from situation to situation.

The concept of validity generalization questions this premise.[17] It says that much of the variation in the $r_{xy}$ values is due to the occurrence of a number of "artifacts"— methodological and statistical differences across the studies (e.g., differences in

**EXHIBIT 7.18** **Hypothetical Validity Generalization Example**

| Study | Sample Size n | Validity $r_{xy}$ | Reliability Predictor (x) $r_{xx}$ | Reliability Criterion (y) $r_{yy}$ | Corrected Validity $r_c$ |
|---|---|---|---|---|---|
| Birch, 2013 | 454 | .41 | .94 | .94 | .44 |
| Cherry, 1990 | 120 | .19 | .66 | .76 | .27 |
| Elm, 1978 | 212 | .34 | .91 | .88 | .38 |
| Hickory, 2009 | 37 | −.21 | .96 | .90 | −.23 |
| Locust, 2000 | 92 | .12 | .52 | .70 | .20 |
| Maple, 1961 | 163 | .32 | .90 | .84 | .37 |
| Oak, 1948 | 34 | .09 | .63 | .18 | .27 |
| Palm, 2007 | 202 | .49 | .86 | .92 | .55 |
| Pine, 1984 | 278 | .27 | .80 | .82 | .33 |
| Walnut, 1971 | 199 | .18 | .72 | .71 | .25 |

reliability of $x$ and $y$). If these differences were controlled statistically, the variation in values would shrink and converge toward an estimate of the true validity of $x$. If that true r is significant (practically and statistically), one can indeed generalize validity of $x$ across situations. Validity thus is not viewed as situation specific.

Indeed, the results in the exhibit reveal that the average (weighted by sample size) uncorrected validity is $\bar{r}_{xy} = .30$, and the average (weighted by sample size) validity corrected for unreliability in the predictor and criterion is $\bar{r}_{xy} = .36$. In this example, fully two-thirds (66.62%) of the variance in the correlations was due to study artifacts (differences in sample size and differences in reliability of the predictor or the criterion). Put another way, the variability in the correlations is lower once they are corrected for artifacts, and the validities do generalize.

An enormous amount of evidence supporting the validity generalization premise has accumulated. Some experts argue that validity generalization reduces or even eliminates the need for an organization to conduct its own validation study. If validity generalization shows that a selection measure has a statistically significant and practically meaningful correlation with job performance, the reasoning goes, why go to the considerable time and expense to reinvent the wheel (to conduct a validation study when evidence clearly supports use of the measure in the first place)? There are two caveats to keep in mind in accepting this logic. First, organizations or specific jobs (for which the selection measure in question is intended) can sometimes be unusual. To the extent that the organization or job was not reflected in the validity generalization effort, the results may be inapplicable to the specific organization or job. Second, validity generalization efforts, while undoubtedly offering more evidence than a single study, are not perfect. For example, validity generalization results can be susceptible to "publication bias," where test vendors may report only statistically significant correlations. Although procedures exist for correcting this bias, they assume evidence and expertise usually not readily available to an organization.[18] Thus, as promising as validity generalization is, we think organizations, especially if they think the job in question differs from comparable organizations, may still wish to conduct validation studies of their own.

A particular form of validity generalization that has proved useful is meta-analysis. Returning to Exhibit 7.18, meta-analysis reveals that the average correlation between $x$ and $y$ (i.e., $\bar{r}_{xy}$) is $\bar{r}_{xy} = .36$, that most of the variability in the correlations is due to statistical artifacts (and not due to true substantive differences in validity across studies), and that the validity appears to generalize. Meta-analysis is very useful in comparing the relative validity of selection measures, which is precisely what we do in Chapters 8 and 9.

## Staffing Metrics and Benchmarks

For some time now, HR as a business area has sought to prove its value through the use of metrics, or quantifiable measures that demonstrate the effectiveness (or ineffectiveness) of a particular practice or procedure. Staffing is no exception. Fortunately, many of the measurement processes described in this chapter represent excellent metrics. Unfortunately, most HR managers, including many in staffing, may have limited (or no) knowledge of job analysis, validation, and measurement. The reader of this book can "show his or her stuff" by educating other organizational members about these metrics in an accessible and nonthreatening way. The result may be a more rigorous staffing process, producing higher levels of validity, higher-performing employees, and kudos for you.

Many who work in staffing are likely more familiar with another type of metric, namely, benchmarking. Benchmarking is a process where organizations evaluate their practices (in this case, staffing practices) against those used by industry leaders. Some commonly used benchmarks include cost per hire, forecasted hiring, and vacancies filled. Traditionally, most benchmarking efforts have focused on quantity of employees hired and cost. That situation is beginning to change. For example, Reuters and Dell are tracking "quality of hire," or the performance levels of those hired. Eventually, if enough organizations track such information, they can form a consortium so they can benchmark off one another's metrics for both quantity and quality.[19] More generally, the Society for Human Resource Management (SHRM) regularly offers conferences and mini-conferences on staffing that provide benchmarks of current organizational practices.

Such benchmarks can be a useful means of measuring important aspects of staffing methods or the entire staffing process. However, they are no substitute for the other measurement principles described in this chapter, including reliability and validity. Reliability, validity, utility, and measurement principles are more enduring, and more fundamental, metrics of staffing effectiveness.

## COLLECTION OF ASSESSMENT DATA

In staffing decisions, the process of measurement is put into practice by collecting assessment data on external or internal applicants. To this point in this chapter, we have discussed how selection measures can be evaluated. To be sure, thorough evaluation of selection measures is important. Selection decision makers must be knowledgeable about how to use the assessment data that have been collected; otherwise, the potential value of the data will lie dormant. On the other hand, to put these somewhat theoretical concepts to use in practice, selection decision makers must know how to collect the assessment data. Otherwise, the decision maker may find himself or herself in the unenviable "big hat, no cattle" situation—knowing how to analyze and evaluate assessment data but not knowing where to find the data in the first place.

In collecting assessment data, if a predictor is purchased, support services are needed. Consulting firms and test publishers can provide support for scoring of tests. Also necessary is legal support to ensure compliance with laws and regulations.

Validity studies are important to ensure the effectiveness of the measures. Training on how to administer the predictor is also needed.

Beyond these general principles, which apply no matter what assessment data are collected, there is other information that the selection decision maker must know about the tangible process of collecting assessment data. Collection of data with respect to testing procedures, tests and test manuals, and professional standards is discussed.

## Testing Procedures

Regardless of whether paper-and-pencil or computerized tests are given, certain guidelines need to be kept in mind.

### Qualification

Predictors cannot always be purchased by any firm that wants to use them; many test publishers require the purchaser to have certain expertise to use the test properly. For example, they may want the user to hold a PhD in a field of study related to the test and its use. For smaller organizations, this means hiring the consulting services of a specialist to use a particular test.

### Security

Care must be taken to ensure that correct answers for predictors are not shared with job applicants in advance of administration of the predictor. Any person who has access to the predictor answers should be fully trained and should sign a predictor security agreement. In addition, applicants should be instructed not to share information about the test with fellow applicants. Alternative forms of the test should be considered if the security of the test is in question.

Not only should the predictor itself be kept secure, but also the results of the predictor in order to ensure the privacy of the individual. The results of the predictor should be used only for the intended purposes and by persons qualified to interpret them. Though feedback can be given to the candidate concerning the results, the individual should not be given a copy of the predictor or the scoring key.

### Standardization

Finally, it is imperative that all applicants be assessed with standardized procedures. This means that not only should the same or a psychometrically equivalent predictor be used, but individuals should take the test under the same circumstances. The purpose of the predictor should be explained to applicants, and they should be put at ease, held to the same time requirements to complete the predictor, and take the predictor in the same location.

### Internet-Based Test Administration

Increasingly, selection measures are being administered on the Internet. For example, job applicants for hourly positions at Kmart, Albertson's, and the Sports Authority take an electronic assessment at in-store kiosks. The test vendor, Unicru, forwards the test scores on to selection decision makers. Some organizations may develop their own tests and administer them online.

In general, research suggests that web-based tests work as well as paper-and-pencil tests, as long as special care is taken to ensure that the actual applicant is the test taker and that the tests are validated in the same manner as other selection measures. Some organizations, however, in their rush to use such tests, fail to validate them. The results can be disastrous. The Transportation Security Administration (TSA) has been criticized for its "inane" online test. Many questions on the test were obvious to a grade-school student. For example, one question was: Why is it important to screen bags for improvised explosive devices (IEDs)?

    a. The IED batteries could *leak and damage* other passenger bags.
    b. The wires in the IED could *cause a short* to the aircraft wires.
    c. IEDs can cause *loss of lives*, property and aircraft.
    d. The *ticking timer* could worry other passengers.

Obviously, the correct answer is "c." The TSA farmed out the test to a vendor without asking for validation evidence. The TSA's justification was, "We administered the test the way we were told to [by the vendor]." Thus, Internet-based testing can work well and has many advantages, but organizations need to ensure that the tests are rigorously developed and validated.[20]

## Acquisition of Tests and Test Manuals

The process of acquiring tests and test manuals, whether digital versions or print versions, requires some start-up costs in terms of the time and effort required to contact test publishers. Once the selection decision maker is on an e-mail or mailing list, however, he or she can stay up to date on the latest developments.

Publishers of selection tests include Wonderlic, Consulting Psychologists Press, Institute for Personality and Ability Testing, Psychological Assessment Resources, Hogan Assessment Systems, and Psychological Services, Inc. All these organizations have information on their websites that describes the products available for purchase.

Most publishers provide sample copies of the tests and a user's manual that selection decision makers may consult before purchasing the test. Test costs vary widely depending on the test and the number of times the test is given. One test that can be scored by the selection decision maker, for example, costs $100 for testing 25 applicants and $200 for testing 100 applicants. Another test that comes with a scoring system and interpretive report costs from $25 each for testing 5 applicants to $17 each for testing 100 applicants. Discounts are thus available for testing larger numbers of applicants.

Any test worth using will be accompanied by a professional user's manual (whether in print or online). This manual should describe the development and validation of the test, including validity evidence in selection contexts. A test manual should also include administration instructions, scoring instructions or information, interpretation information, and normative data. All of this information is crucial to make sure that the test is appropriate and that it is used in an appropriate (valid, legal) manner. Avoid using a test that has no professional manual, as it is unlikely to have been validated. Using a test without a proven track record is akin to hiring an applicant sight unseen. The *Wonderlic Personnel Test User's Manual* is an excellent example of a professional user's manual. It contains information about various forms of the *Wonderlic Personnel Test* (see Chapter 9), how to administer the test and interpret and use the scores, validity and fairness of the test, and various norms by age, race, gender, and so on. The SHRM has launched the SHRM Testing Center, whereby SHRM members can review and receive discounts on more than 200 web-based tests.[21]

## Professional Standards

Revised in 2003 by the Society for Industrial and Organizational Psychology (SIOP) and approved by the American Psychological Association (APA), *Principles for the Validation and Use of Personnel Selection Procedures* is a guidebook that provides testing standards for use in selection decisions. It covers test choice, development, evaluation, and use of personnel selection procedures in employment settings. Specific topics covered include the various ways selection measures should be validated, how to conduct validation studies, which sources can be used to determine validity, generalizing validation evidence from one source to another, test fairness and bias, how to understand worker requirements, data collection for validity studies, ways in which validity information can be analyzed, the appropriate uses of selection measures, and an administration guide.

*Principles* was developed by many of the world's leading experts on selection, and therefore any selection decision maker would be well advised to consult this important document, which is written in practical, nontechnical language. This guidebook is free and can be ordered from SIOP by visiting its website.

A related set of standards has been promulgated by the APA. Formulated by the Joint Committee on Testing Practices, *The Rights and Responsibilities of Test Takers: Guidelines and Expectations* enumerates 10 rights and 10 responsibilities of test takers. One of the rights is for the applicant to be treated with courtesy, respect, and impartiality. Another right is to receive prior explanation for the purpose(s) of the testing. One responsibility is to follow the test instructions as given. In addition to enumerating test-taker rights and responsibilities, the document also provides guidelines for organizations administering the tests. For example, the standards stipulate that organizations should inform test takers about the purpose of the test. Organizations testing applicants should consult these guidelines to ensure that these rights are provided wherever possible.

## LEGAL ISSUES

Staffing laws and regulations, particularly EEO/AA laws and regulations, place great reliance on the use of measurement concepts and processes. Three key topics are determining adverse impact, standardization of measurement, and best practices suggested by the EEOC.

## Determining Adverse Impact

In Chapter 2, adverse (disparate) impact was introduced as a way of determining whether staffing practices were having potentially illegal impacts on individuals because of race, sex, and so forth. Such a determination requires the compilation and analysis of statistical evidence, primarily applicant flow and applicant stock statistics.

### Applicant Flow Statistics

Applicant flow statistical analysis requires the calculation of selection rates (proportions or percentages of applicants hired) for groups and the subsequent comparison of those rates to determine whether they are significantly different from one another. This may be illustrated by taking the example from Exhibit 2.5:

|       | Applicants | Hires | Selection Rate |
|-------|-----------|-------|----------------|
| Men   | 50        | 25    | .50 or 50%     |
| Women | 45        | 5     | .11 or 11%     |

This example shows a sizable difference in selection rates between men and women (.50 as opposed to .11). Does this difference indicate adverse impact? The Uniform Guidelines on Employee Selection Procedures (UGESP) speak directly to this question. Several points need to be made regarding the determination of disparate impact analysis.

First, the UGESP require the organization to keep records that will permit calculation of such selection rates, also referred to as applicant flow statistics. These statistics are the primary vehicle by which compliance with the law (Civil Rights Act) is judged.

Second, the UGESP require calculation of selection rates (1) for each job category, (2) for both external and internal selection decisions, (3) for each step in the selection process, and (4) by race and sex of applicants. To meet this requirement, the organization must keep detailed records of its staffing activities and decisions. Such record keeping should be built directly into the organization's staffing system routines.

Third, comparisons of selection rates among groups in a job category for purposes of compliance determination should be based on the 80% rule in the UGESP, which states that "a selection rate for any race, sex or ethnic group which is less than four-fifths (4/5) (or eighty percent) of the rate for the group with the highest rate will generally be regarded by federal enforcement agencies as evidence of adverse impact, while a greater than four-fifths rate will generally not be regarded by federal enforcement agencies as evidence of adverse impact."

If this rule is applied to the previous example, the group with the highest selection rate is men (.50). The rate for women should be within 80% of this rate, or .40 (.50 × .80 = .40). Since the actual rate for women is .11, this suggests the occurrence of adverse impact.

Fourth, the 80% rule is truly only a guideline. Note the use of the word "generally" in the rule with regard to differences in selection rates. Also, the 80% rule provides for other exceptions, based on sample size considerations and issues surrounding statistical and practical significance of difference in selection rates. Moreover, there are many other technical measurement and legal issues in determining whether adverse impact is occurring. Examples include deciding exactly who is considered an applicant and whether it is meaningful to pool applicant counts for different minority groups into a "total minority" group. Best-practice recommendations for handling such issues are available.[22]

## Applicant Stock Statistics

Applicant stock statistics require the calculation of the percentages of women and minorities in two areas: (1) employed and (2) available for employment in the population. These percentages are compared in order to identify disparities. This is referred to as utilization analysis.

To illustrate, the example from Exhibit 2.5 is shown here:

|  | Employed | Availability |
|---|---|---|
| Nonminority | 90% | 70% |
| Minority | 10% | 30% |

It can be seen that 10% of employees are minorities, whereas their availability is 30%. A comparison of these two percentages suggests an underutilization of minorities.

Utilization analysis of this sort is an integral part of not only compliance assessment but also affirmative action plans (AAPs). Indeed, utilization analysis is the starting point for the development of AAPs. This may be illustrated by reference to the Affirmative Action Programs Regulations.

The regulations require the organization to conduct a formal utilization analysis of its workforce. That analysis must be (1) conducted by job group and (2) done separately for women and minorities. Though calculation of the numbers and percentages of persons employed is relatively straightforward, determination of their availability is not. The regulations require that the availabilities take into account at least the following factors: (1) the percentage of women or minorities with requisite skills in the recruitment area, and (2) the percentage of women or minorities among those promotable, transferable, and trainable within the organization. Accurate measurement and/or estimation of availabilities that take into account these factors is difficult.

Despite these measurement problems, the regulations require comparison of the percentages of women and minorities employed with their availability. When the percentage of minorities or women in a job group is less than would reasonably be expected given their availability, underutilization exists and placement (hiring and promotion) goals must be set. Thus, the organization must exercise considerable discretion in the determination of adverse impact through the use of applicant stock statistics. It would be wise to seek technical and/or legal assistance for conducting utilization analysis (see also "Affirmative Action Plans" in Chapter 3).

## Standardization

A lack of consistency in treatment of applicants is one of the major factors contributing to the occurrence of discrimination in staffing. This is partly due to a lack of standardization in measurement, in terms of both what is measured and how it is evaluated or scored.

An example of inconsistency in what is measured is that the type of background information required of minority applicants may differ from that required of nonminority applicants. Minority applicants may be asked about credit ratings and criminal conviction records, while nonminority applicants are not. Alternatively, the type of interview questions asked of male applicants may be different from those asked of female applicants.

Even if information is consistently gathered from all applicants, it may not be evaluated the same for all applicants. A male applicant who has a history of holding several different jobs may be viewed as a career builder, while a female with the same history may be evaluated as an unstable job-hopper. In essence, different scoring keys are being used for men and women applicants.

Reducing, and hopefully eliminating, such inconsistency requires a straightforward application of the three properties of standardized measures discussed previously. Through standardization of measurement comes consistent treatment of applicants and, with it, the possibility of lessened adverse impact.

## Best Practices

Based on its long and in-depth involvement in measurement and selection procedures, the EEOC provides guidance to employers in the form of several best practices for testing and selection.[23] These practices apply to a wide range of tests and selection procedures, including cognitive and physical ability tests, sample job tasks, medical inquiries and physical exams, personality and integrity tests, criminal and credit background checks, performance appraisals, and English proficiency tests. The best practices are the following:

- Employers should administer tests and other selection procedures without regard to race, color, national origin, sex, religion, age (40 or older), or disability.
- Employers should ensure that employment tests and other selection procedures are properly validated for the positions and purposes for which they are used. The test or selection procedure must be job related and its results appropriate for the employer's purpose. While a test vendor's documentation supporting the validity of a test may be helpful, the employer is still responsible for ensuring that its tests are valid under the UGESP (discussed in Chapter 9).
- If a selection procedure screens out a protected group, the employer should determine whether there is an equally effective alternative selection procedure that has less adverse impact and, if so, adopt the alternative procedure. For example, if the selection procedure is a test, the employer should determine whether another test would predict job performance but not disproportionately exclude the protected group.
- To ensure that a test or selection procedure remains predictive of success in a job, employers should keep abreast of changes in job requirements and should update the test specifications or selection procedures accordingly.
- Employers should ensure that tests and selection procedures are not adopted casually by managers who know little about these processes. A test or selection procedure can be an effective management tool, but no test or selection procedure should be implemented without an understanding of its effectiveness and limitations for the organization, its appropriateness for a specific job, and whether it can be appropriately administered and scored.

Note that these best practices apply to virtually all selection procedures or tools, not just tests. They emphasize the need for fair administration of these tools, the importance of the procedures being job related, usage of alternative valid selection procedures that have less adverse impact, and the updating of job requirements (KSAOs) and selection tools. In addition, casual usage of selection tools by uninformed managers is to be avoided.

## SUMMARY

Measurement, defined as the process of using rules to assign numbers to objects to represent quantities of an attribute of the objects, is an integral part of the foundation of staffing activities. Standardization of the measurement process is sought. This applies to each of the four levels of measurement: nominal, ordinal, interval, and ratio. Standardization is also sought for both objective and subjective measures.

Measures yield scores that represent the amount of the attribute being measured. Scores are manipulated in various ways to aid in their interpretation. Typical manipulations involve central tendency and variability, percentiles, and standard scores. Scores are also correlated to learn about the strength and direction of the relationship between two attributes. The significance of the resultant correlation coefficient is then assessed.

The quality of measures involves issues of reliability and validity. Reliability refers to consistency of measurement, both at a moment in time and between time periods. Various procedures are used to estimate reliability, including coefficient alpha, interrater and intrarater agreement, and test–retest. Reliability places an upper limit on the validity of a measure.

Validity refers to accuracy of measurement and accuracy of prediction, as reflected by the scores obtained from a measure. Criterion-related and content validation studies are conducted to help learn about the validity of a measure. In criterion-related validation, scores on a predictor (KSAO) measure are correlated with scores on a criterion (HR outcome) measure. In content validation, there is no criterion measure, so judgments are made about the content of a predictor relative to the HR outcome it is seeking to predict. Traditionally, results of validation studies were treated as situation specific, meaning that the organization ideally should conduct a new and separate validation study for any predictor in any situation in which the predictor is to be used. Recently, however, studies have suggested that the validity of predictors may generalize across situations, meaning that the requirement of conducting costly and time-consuming validation studies in each specific situation could be relaxed. Staffing metrics such as cost per hire and benchmarks, representing how leading organizations staff positions, can be useful measures, but they are not substitutes for reliability and validity.

Various practical aspects of the collection of assessment data were described. Decisions about testing procedures and the acquisition of tests and test manuals require the attention of organizational decision makers. The collection of assessment data and the acquisition of tests and test manuals vary depending on whether paper-and-pencil or computerized selection measures are used. Finally, organizations need to attend to professional standards that govern the proper use of the collection of assessment data.

Measurement is also said to be an integral part of an organization's EEO/AA compliance activities. When adverse impact is found, changes in measurement practices may be legally necessary. These changes will involve movement toward standardization of measurement and the methods for determining adverse impact.

## DISCUSSION QUESTIONS

1. Imagine and describe a staffing system for a job in which no measures are used.
2. Describe how you might go about determining scores for applicants' responses to (a) interview questions, (b) letters of recommendation, and (c) questions about previous work experience.
3. Give examples of when you would want the following for a written job knowledge test: (a) a low coefficient alpha (e.g., $\alpha = .35$) and (b) a low test–retest reliability.
4. Assume you gave a general ability test, measuring both verbal and computational skills, to a group of applicants for a specific job. Also assume that because of severe hiring pressures, you hired all of the applicants, regardless of their test scores. How would you investigate the criterion-related validity of the test?
5. Using the same example as in question four, how would you go about investigating the content validity of the test?
6. What information does a selection decision maker need to collect in making staffing decisions? What are the ways in which this information can be collected?

## ETHICAL ISSUES

1. Do individuals making staffing decisions have an ethical responsibility to know measurement issues? Why or why not?
2. Is it unethical for an employer to use a selection measure that has high empirical validity but lacks content validity? Explain.

## APPLICATIONS

### Evaluation of Two New Assessment Methods for Selecting Telephone Customer Service Representatives

The Phonemin Company is a distributor of men's and women's casual clothing. It sells exclusively through its merchandise catalog, which is published four times per year to coincide with seasonal changes in customers' apparel tastes. Customers may order merchandise from the catalog via mail or over the phone. Currently,

70% of orders are phone orders, and the organization expects this to increase to 85% within the next few years.

The success of the organization is obviously very dependent on the success of the telephone ordering system and the customer service representatives (CSRs) who staff the system. There are currently 185 CSRs; that number should increase to about 225 CSRs to handle the anticipated growth in phone order sales. Though the CSRs are trained to use standardized methods and procedures for handling phone orders, there are still seemingly large differences among them in their job performance. CSR performance is routinely measured in terms of error rate, speed of order taking, and customer complaints. The top 25% and lowest 25% of performers on each of these measures differ by a factor of at least three (i.e., the error rate of the bottom group is three times as high as that of the top group). Strategically, the organization knows that it could substantially enhance CSR performance (and ultimately sales) if it could improve its staffing "batting average" by more accurately identifying and hiring new CSRs who are likely to be top performers.

The current staffing system for CSRs is straightforward. Applicants are recruited through a combination of employee referrals and newspaper ads. Because turnover among CSRs is so high (50% annually), recruitment is a continuous process at the organization. Applicants complete a standard application blank, which asks for information about education and previous work experience. The information is reviewed by the staffing specialist in the HR department. Only obvious misfits are rejected at this point; the others (95%) are asked to have an interview with the specialist. The interview lasts 20–30 minutes, and at the conclusion the applicant is either rejected or offered a job. Due to the tightness of the labor market and the constant presence of vacancies to be filled, 90% of the interviewees receive job offers. Most of those offers (95%) are accepted, and the new hires attend a one-week training program before being placed on the job.

The organization has decided to investigate the possibilities of increasing CSR effectiveness through sounder staffing practices. In particular, it is not pleased with its current methods of assessing job applicants; it feels that neither the application blank nor the interview provides an accurate and in-depth assessment of the applicant KSAOs that are truly needed to be an effective CSR. Consequently, it engaged the services of a consulting firm that offers various methods of KSAO assessment, along with validation and installation services. In cooperation with the HR staffing specialist, the consulting firm conducted the following study for the organization.

A special job analysis led to the identification of several specific KSAOs likely to be necessary for successful performance as a CSR. Three of these (clerical speed, clerical accuracy, and interpersonal skills) were singled out for further consideration because of their seemingly high impact on job performance. Two new methods of assessment provided by the consulting firm were chosen for experimentation. The first is a paper-and-pencil clerical test assessing clerical speed and accuracy. It contains 50 items and has a 30-minute time limit. The second is a brief work sample that could be administered as part of the interview process. In the work sample, the applicant must respond to four different phone calls: a customer who is irate about an out-of-stock item, a customer who wants more product information about an item than was provided in the catalog, a customer who wants to change an order placed yesterday, and a customer who has a routine order to place. Using a 1–5 rating scale, the interviewer rates the applicant on tactfulness (T) and concern for customers (C). The interviewer is provided with a rating manual containing examples of exceptional (5), average (3), and unacceptable (1) responses by the applicant.

A random sample of 50 current CSRs were chosen to participate in the study. At Time 1 they were administered the clerical test and the work sample; performance data were also gathered from company records for error rate (number of errors per 100 orders), speed (number of orders filled per hour), and customer complaints (number of complaints per week). At Time 2, one week later, the clerical test and the work sample were readministered to the CSRs. A member of the consulting firm sat in on all the interviews and served as a second rater of performance on the work sample at Time 1 and Time 2. It is expected that the clerical test and work sample will have positive correlations with speed and negative correlations with error rate and customer complaints.

### Results for Clerical Test

|                          | Time 1 | Time 2 |
|--------------------------|--------|--------|
| Mean score               | 31.61  | 31.22  |
| Standard deviation       | 4.70   | 5.11   |
| Coefficient alpha        | .85    | .86    |
| Test–retest r            |        | .92*   |
| r with error rate        | −.31*  | −.37*  |
| r with speed             | .41*   | .39*   |
| r with complaints        | −.11   | −.08   |
| r with work sample (T)   | .21    | .17    |
| r with work sample (C)   | .07    | .15    |

### Results for Work Sample (T)

|                          | Time 1 | Time 2 |
|--------------------------|--------|--------|
| Mean score               | 3.15   | 3.11   |
| Standard deviation       | .93    | 1.01   |
| % agreement (raters)     | 88%    | 79%    |
| r with work sample (C)   | .81*   | .77*   |
| r with error rate        | −.13   | −.12   |
| r with speed             | .11    | .15    |
| r with complaints        | −.37*  | −.35*  |

**Results for Work Sample (C)**

|  | Time 1 | Time 2 |
|---|---|---|
| Mean score | 2.91 | 3.07 |
| Standard deviation | .99 | 1.10 |
| % agreement (raters) | 80% | 82% |
| r with work sample (T) | .81* | .77* |
| r with error rate | −.04 | −.11 |
| r with speed | .15 | .14 |
| r with complaints | −.40* | −.31* |

(Note: * means that r was significant at p < .05)

After reading the description of the study and observing the results above,

1. How do you interpret the reliability results for the clerical test and work sample? Are they favorable enough for Phonemin to consider using them "for keeps" in selecting new job applicants?
2. How do you interpret the validity results for the clerical test and work sample? Are they favorable enough for Phonemin to consider using them "for keeps" in selecting new job applicants?
3. What limitations in the above study should be kept in mind when interpreting the results and deciding whether to use the clerical test and work sample?

## Conducting Empirical Validation and Adverse Impact Analysis

Yellow Blaze Candle Shops provides a full line of various types of candles and accessories such as candleholders. Yellow Blaze has 150 shops in shopping malls and strip malls throughout the country. Over 600 salespeople staff these stores, each of which has a full-time manager. Staffing the manager's position, by policy, must occur by promotion from within the sales ranks. The organization is interested in improving its identification of salespeople most likely to be successful store managers. It has developed a special technique for assessing and rating the suitability of salespeople for the manager's job.

To experiment with this technique, the regional HR department representative reviewed and rated the promotion suitability of each store's salespeople. They reviewed sales results, customer service orientation, and knowledge of store operations for each salesperson and then assigned a 1–3 promotion suitability rating (1 = not suitable, 2 = may be suitable, 3 = definitely suitable) on each of these three factors. Customer service orientation was rated based on supervisor and co-worker observations of work behavior. These ratings incorporated evaluations of how often salespeople asked customers how they could help, how effectively salespeople were able to suggest products that matched customer requests, and how well salespeople ensured that customers were happy with their intended purchases at the end of the encounter. In most cases, ratings of customer service orientation were similar across managers and assistant managers, but there were some discrepancies. Knowledge of store operations was evaluated based on a standardized exam, consisting of a variety of questions related to facts ranging from managerial practices and procedures to refund and exchange policies to record-keeping requirements. A total promotion suitability (PS) score, ranging from 3 to 9, was then computed for each salesperson.

The PS scores were gathered for all salespeople but were not formally used in promotion decisions. Over the past year, 30 salespeople were promoted to store manager. Now it is time for the organization to preliminarily investigate the validity of the PS scores and see whether their use results in adverse impact against women or minorities. Each store manager's annual overall performance appraisal rating, ranging from 1 (low performance) to 5 (high performance), was used as the criterion measure in the validation study. The following data were available for analysis:

| Employee ID | PS Score | Performance Rating | Sex M/F | Minority Status (M = Minority, NM = Nonminority) |
|---|---|---|---|---|
| 11 | 9 | 5 | M | NM |
| 12 | 9 | 5 | F | NM |
| 13 | 9 | 1 | F | NM |
| 14 | 9 | 5 | M | M |
| 15 | 8 | 4 | F | M |
| 16 | 8 | 5 | F | M |
| 17 | 8 | 4 | M | NM |
| 18 | 8 | 5 | M | NM |
| 19 | 8 | 3 | F | NM |
| 20 | 8 | 4 | M | NM |
| 21 | 7 | 5 | F | M |
| 22 | 7 | 3 | M | M |
| 23 | 7 | 4 | M | NM |
| 24 | 7 | 3 | F | NM |
| 25 | 7 | 3 | F | NM |
| 26 | 7 | 4 | M | NM |
| 27 | 7 | 5 | M | M |
| 28 | 6 | 4 | F | NM |
| 29 | 6 | 4 | M | NM |
| 30 | 6 | 2 | F | M |
| 31 | 6 | 3 | F | NM |
| 32 | 6 | 3 | M | NM |

| Employee ID | PS Score | Performance Rating | Sex M/F | Minority Status (M = Minority, NM = Nonminority) |
|---|---|---|---|---|
| 33 | 6 | 5 | M | NM |
| 34 | 6 | 5 | F | NM |
| 35 | 5 | 3 | M | NM |
| 36 | 5 | 3 | F | M |
| 37 | 5 | 2 | M | M |
| 38 | 4 | 2 | F | NM |
| 39 | 4 | 1 | M | NM |
| 40 | 3 | 4 | F | NM |

Using the data above, calculate:

1. Average PS scores for the whole sample, males, females, nonminorities, and minorities.
2. The correlation between PS scores and performance ratings, and its statistical significance ($r = .37$ or higher is needed for significance at $p < .05$).
3. Adverse impact (selection rate) statistics for males and females, and nonminorities and minorities. Use a PS score of 7 or higher as a hypothetical passing score (the score that might be used to determine who will or will not be promoted).
4. Average performance rating scores for the whole sample, males, females, nonminorities, and minorities. For each group, evaluate whether the performance rating scores are different for subgroups of employees. Also evaluate if the magnitude of these differences is sizable enough to warrant concern for Yellow Blaze.

Using the data, results, and description of the study, answer the following questions:

1. Is the PS score a valid predictor of performance as a store manager? Do you see any potential reasons why either the customer service orientation or knowledge of store operations measures might be problematic? In answering, consider issues related to reliability and validity.
2. With a cut score of 7 on the PS, would its use lead to adverse impact against women? Against minorities? If there is adverse impact, does the validity evidence justify use of the PS anyway?
3. What limitations do you see in the current study design? Do you think that the conclusions you would reach based on this sample of individuals who were promoted to store manager would generalize to the population of all salespeople who are being evaluated for promotion potential? Do you think

that the method of rating performance is sufficient as a criterion, and if so, why? If not, what additional steps would you take to ensure that performance is measured adequately?

4. Would you recommend that Yellow Blaze use the PS score in making future promotion decisions? Why or why not? If you do think the company should use the PS score system, can you think of anything they could do to make these measures even better than they are already? If you do not think the PS score system should be used, can you think of any ways that this system might be improved?

5. One employee has raised questions regarding whether the performance ratings themselves are biased. This employee has not made a formal legal complaint against Yellow Blaze yet, but the organization wants to evaluate whether there is reason for concern. Based on the calculations you made regarding the differences for performance evaluation ratings for women relative to men, and for minorities relative to non-minorities, do you believe that there is reason for the organization to be concerned regarding this issue? In other words, do the data suggest that there is, in fact, a substantial difference in performance evaluation ratings for different groups of employees? How should the organization respond to this individual employee's concerns?

# ENDNOTES

1. E. F. Stone, *Research Methods in Organizational Behavior* (Santa Monica, CA: Goodyear, 1978), pp. 35–36.

2. F. G. Brown, *Principles of Educational and Psychological Testing* (Hinsdale, IL: Dryden, 1970), pp. 38–45.

3. Stone, *Research Methods in Organizational Behavior*, pp. 36–40.

4. F. P. Morgeson and J. D. Nahrgang, "Same as It Ever Was: Recognizing Stability in the Business-Week Rankings," *Academy of Management Learning & Education*, 2005, 7, pp. 26–41.

5. W. H. Bommer, J. L. Johnson, G. A. Rich, P. M. Podsakoff, and S. B. McKenzie, "On the Interchangeability of Objective and Subjective Measures of Employee Performance: A Meta-Analysis," *Personnel Psychology*, 1995, 48, pp. 587–606; R. L. Heneman, "The Relationship Between Supervisory Ratings and Results-Oriented Measures of Performance: A Meta-Analysis," *Personnel Psychology*, 1986, 39, pp. 811–826.

6. This section draws on Brown, *Principles of Educational and Psychological Testing*, pp. 158–197; L. J. Cronbach, *Essentials of Psychological Testing*, 4th ed. (New York: Harper and Row, 1984), pp. 81–120; N. W. Schmitt and R. J. Klimoski, *Research Methods in Human Resources Management* (Cincinnati, OH: South-Western, 1991), pp. 41–87.

7. J. T. McClave and P. G. Benson, *Statistics for Business and Economics*, 3rd ed. (San Francisco: Dellan, 1985); see "t Table" (*www.sjsu.edu/faculty/gerstman/StatPrimer/t-table.pdf*).

8. For an excellent review, see Schmitt and Klimoski, *Research Methods in Human Resources Management*, pp. 88–114.

9. This section draws on E. G. Carmines and R. A. Zeller, *Reliability and Validity Assessment* (Beverly Hills, CA: Sage, 1979).

10. D. P. Schwab, *Research Methods for Organizational Studies* (New York: Routledge, 2011).

11. Carmines and Zeller, *Reliability and Validity Assessment*; J. M. Cortina, "What Is Coefficient Alpha? An Examination of Theory and Application," *Journal of Applied Psychology*, 1993, 78, pp. 98–104; Schmitt and Klimoski, *Research Methods in Human Resources Management*, pp. 89–100.

12. This section draws on R. D. Arvey, "Constructs and Construct Validation," *Human Performance*, 1992, 5, pp. 59–69; W. F. Cascio, *Applied Psychology in Personnel Management*, 4th ed. (Englewood Cliffs, NJ: Prentice-Hall, 1991), pp. 149–170; H. G. Heneman III, D. P. Schwab, J. A. Fossum, and L. Dyer, *Personnel/Human Resource Management*, 4th ed. (Homewood, IL: Irwin, 1989), pp. 300–329; N. Schmitt and F. J. Landy, "The Concept of Validity," in N. Schmitt, W. C. Borman, and Associates (eds.), *Personnel Selection in Organizations* (San Francisco: Jossey-Bass, 1993), pp. 275–309; Schwab, "Construct Validity in Organization Behavior"; S. Messick, "Validity of Psychological Assessment," *American Psychologist*, Sept. 1995, pp. 741–749.

13. Heneman, Schwab, Fossum, and Dyer, *Personnel/Human Resource Management*, pp. 300–310.

14. I. L. Goldstein, S. Zedeck, and B. Schneider, "An Exploration of the Job Analysis-Content Validity Process," in Schmitt, Borman, and Associates, *Personnel Selection in Organizations*, pp. 3–34; Heneman, Schwab, Fossum, and Dyer, *Personnel/Human Resource Management*, pp. 311–315; D. A. Joiner, *Content Valid Testing for Supervisory and Management Jobs: A Practical/Common Sense Approach* (Alexandria, VA: International Personnel Management Association, 1987); P. R. Sackett and R. D. Arvey, "Selection in Small N Settings," in Schmitt, Borman, and Associates, *Personnel Selection in Organizations*, pp. 418–447.

15. R. S. Barrett, "Content Validation Form," *Public Personnel Management*, 1992, 21, pp. 41–52; E. E. Ghiselli, J. P. Campbell, and S. Zedeck, *Measurement Theory for the Behavioral Sciences* (San Francisco: W. H. Freeman, 1981).

16. K. R. Murphy, "Content Validation Is Useful for Many Things, But Validity Isn't One of Them," *Industrial and Organizational Psychology,* 2009, 2, pp. 453–464.

17. F. Schmidt and J. Hunter, "History, Development, Evolution, and Impact of Validity Generalization and Meta-Analysis Methods, 1975–2001," in K. R. Murphy (ed.), *Validity Generalization: A Critical Review* (Mahwah, NJ: Erlbaum, 2003), pp. 31–65; K. R. Murphy, "Synthetic Validity: A Great Idea Whose Time Never Came," *Industrial and Organizational Psychology*, 2010, 3(3), pp. 356–359; K. R. Murphy, "Validity, Validation and Values," *Academy of Management Annals*, 2009, 3, pp. 421–461.

18. S. Kepes, G. C. Banks, M. McDaniel, and D. L. Whetzel, "Publication Bias in the Organizational Sciences, *Organizational Research Methods*, 2012, 15, pp. 624–662.

19. C. Winkler, "Quality Check: Better Metrics Improve HR's Ability to Measure—and Manage—the Quality of Hires," *HR Magazine*, May 2007, pp. 93–98; Society for Human Resource Management, *SHRM Human Capital Benchmarking Study* (Alexandria, VA: author, 2005).

20. J. A. Naglieri, F. Drasgow, M. Schmit, L. Handler, A. Prifitera, A. Margolis, and R. Velasquez, "Psychological Testing on the Internet," *American Psychologist*, Apr. 2004, 59, pp. 150–162; R. E. Ployhart, J. A. Weekley, B. C. Holtz, and C. Kemp, "Web-Based and Paper-and-Pencil Testing of Applicants in a Proctored Setting: Are Personality, Biodata, and Situational Judgment Tests Comparable?" *Personnel Psychology*, 2003, 56, pp. 733–752; S. Power, "Federal Official Faults TSA Screener Testing as 'Inane,'" *Wall Street Journal*, Oct. 9, 2003, pp. B1–B2.

21. See the Society for Human Resource Management Testing Center (*www.shrm.org/TemplatesTools/AssessmentResources/SHRMTestingCenter/Pages/index.aspx*).

22. D. B. Cohen, M. G. Aamodt, and E. M. Dunleavy, "Technical Advisory Committee Report on Best Practices in Adverse Impact Analysis," *Center for Corporate Equality*, 2010 (*www.cceq.org*), accessed 10/5/10.

23. Equal Employment Opportunity Commission, "Employment Tests and Selection Procedures," 2010 (*www.eeoc.gov/policy/docs/factemployment_procedures.html*), accessed 7/26/13.

# CHAPTER EIGHT

## External Selection I

**Learning Objectives and Introduction**
Learning Objectives
Introduction

**Preliminary Issues**
The Logic of Prediction
The Nature of Predictors
Development of the Selection Plan
Selection Sequence

**Initial Assessment Methods**
Résumés and Cover Letters
Application Blanks
Biographical Information
Reference and Background Checks
Initial Interview
Choice of Initial Assessment Methods

**Legal Issues**
Disclaimers
Reference Checks
Background Checks: Credit and Criminal
Preemployment Inquiries
Bona Fide Occupational Qualifications

**Summary**

**Discussion Questions**

**Ethical Issues**

**Applications**

**Endnotes**

# LEARNING OBJECTIVES AND INTRODUCTION

## Learning Objectives

- Understand how the logic of prediction guides the selection process
- Review the nature of predictors—how selection measures differ
- Understand the process involved in developing a selection plan, and the selection sequence
- Learn about initial assessment methods and understand how these methods are optimally used in organizations
- Evaluate the relative effectiveness of initial assessment methods to determine which work best, and why
- Review the legal issues involved in the use of initial assessment methods, and understand how legal problems can be avoided

## Introduction

External selection—one of the more practically important and heavily researched areas of staffing—refers to the assessment and evaluation of external job applicants. A variety of assessment methods are used. Preliminary issues that guide the use of these assessment methods will be discussed. These issues include the logic of prediction, the nature of predictors, development of the selection plan, and the selection sequence.

Initial assessment methods are used to select candidates from among the initial job applicants. Those methods that will be reviewed are résumés and cover letters, application blanks, biographical information, letters of recommendation, reference and background checks, and initial interviews. The factors that should guide the choice of initial assessment methods will be reviewed. These include frequency of use, cost, reliability, validity, utility, applicant reactions, and adverse impact.

The use of assessment methods requires a firm understanding of legal issues—including the use of disclaimers and the legal complexities surrounding reference and background checks. The most important of these details will be reviewed. Finally, bona fide occupational qualifications (BFOQs) are particularly relevant to initial assessment because such qualifications are usually assessed during the initial stages of selection. The legal issues involved in establishing such qualifications will be reviewed.

# PRELIMINARY ISSUES

Many times, selection is equated with one event, namely, the interview. Nothing could be further from the truth if the best possible person/job match is to be made. For this to be achieved, a series of well-thought-out activities needs to take place.

Hence, selection is a process rather than an event. It is guided by a logic that determines the steps that need to be taken. The logic applies to all predictors that might be used, even though they differ in terms of several characteristics. Actual implementation of the logic of prediction requires that predictors be chosen through development of a selection plan. Implementation also requires creation of a selection sequence, which is an orderly flow of people through the stages of applicant, candidate, finalist, and offer receiver.

## The Logic of Prediction

In Chapter 1, the selection component of staffing was defined as the process of assessing and evaluating people for purposes of determining the likely fit between the person and the job. This process is based on the logic of prediction, which holds that indicators of a person's degree of success in past situations should be predictive of how successful he or she will likely be in new situations. Application of this logic to selection is illustrated in Exhibit 8.1.

A person's knowledge, skills, abilities, and other characteristics (KSAOs) and motivation are the product of experiences of past job, current job, and nonjob situations. During selection, the organization identifies, assesses, and evaluates samples of these KSAOs (presumably) most relevant to the new situation or job, as well as motivation. The results constitute the person's overall qualifications for the new situation or job. These qualifications are then used to predict how successful the person is likely to be in that new situation or job regarding the human resource (HR) outcomes. The logic of prediction works in practice if the organization accurately identifies and measures qualifications relative to job requirements, and if those qualifications remain stable over time so that the person carries them over to the new job.

The logic of prediction shown in Exhibit 8.1 demonstrates how critical it is to carefully scrutinize the applicant's past situation when making selection decisions.

**EXHIBIT 8.1   The Logic of Prediction**

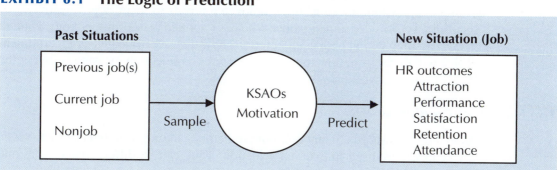

For example, in selecting someone for a police officer position, the success of the applicant in a previous security guard position might be considered a relevant predictor of the likelihood that the applicant will succeed in the police officer position. Alternatively, the fact that the person was previously successful as a homemaker might be viewed as totally irrelevant. Surprisingly, considering the homemaker role to be irrelevant might well be an incorrect assessment. Research shows that there is a close correspondence between the role of homemaker and the police officer position. Specifically, thorough job analysis showed that both jobs rely heavily on troubleshooting and emergency handling skills. Hence, in the absence of a sound job analysis, many qualified applicants may inadvertently be overlooked even though they have some of the characteristics needed to perform the job. Nonjob experience in the home, in the community, and in other institutions may be as valuable as or more valuable than previous employment experiences.

Job titles such as homemaker are not nearly specific enough for making selection decisions. Similarly, the fact that someone has a certain number of years of experience usually does not provide sufficient detail to make selection decisions. What counts, and what is revealed through job analysis, are the specific types of experiences required and the level of successfulness at each. Similarly, whether someone was paid for employment is not relevant. What counts is the quality of the experience as it relates to success in the new job. In short, the logic of prediction indicates that a point-to-point comparison needs to be made between requirements of the job to be filled and the qualifications applicants have acquired from a variety of past situations.

The logic of prediction is important to not only selection but also recruitment. One study showed that applicant reactions to selection procedures were determined in part by the job relatedness of the selection procedure. If applicants see the selection process as job related, which should occur if the logic of prediction is used, they are more likely to view the selection process as fair.[1] Applicants who view the selection procedure as fair are more likely to accept a job offer and/or encourage others to apply for a job in the organization.

Finally, the logic of prediction means separating recruitment from selection. For example, many organizations use employee referrals to identify prospective hires (recruitment), to select among those who have applied (selection), or both. Though there is nothing wrong with using referrals, how they are evaluated as a recruitment device will differ from how they are evaluated as a selection measure (often in the form of references).

## The Nature of Predictors

As will be seen shortly, many types of predictors, ranging from interviews to reference checks, are used in external selection. They can be differentiated from one another in terms of content and form.

## Content

The substance or content of what is being assessed with a predictor varies considerably and may range from a sign to a sample to a criterion.[2] A sign is a predisposition of the person that is thought to relate to performance on the job. Personality as a predictor is a good example here. If personality is used as a predictor, the prediction is that someone with a certain personality (e.g., abrasive) will demonstrate certain behaviors (e.g., rude to customers) leading to certain results on the job (e.g., failure to make a sale). As can be seen, a sign is very distant from actual on-the-job results. A sample is closer than a sign to actual on-the-job results. Observing a set of interactions between a sales applicant and a customer to see if a sale is made is an example of a sample. The criterion is very close to the actual job performance, such as sales during a probationary period for a new employee.

## Form

The form or design of the predictor may vary along several different lines.

***Speed Versus Power.*** A person's score on some predictors is based on the number of responses completed within a certain time frame, for example, the number of bench presses an individual completes in a given period of time. This is known as a speed test. A power test, on the other hand, presents individuals with items of increasing difficulty. For example, a power test of numerical ability may begin with addition and subtraction, move on to multiplication and division, and conclude with complex problem-solving questions. A speed test is used when speed of work is an important part of the job, and a power test is used when the correctness of the response is essential to the job. Of course, some tests (see the *Wonderlic Personnel Test* in Chapter 9) can be both speed and power tests, in which case few individuals would finish.

***Paper and Pencil Versus Performance.*** Many predictors are of the paper-and-pencil variety; applicants are required to fill out a form, write an answer, or complete multiple-choice items (the term "paper-and-pencil" is used loosely here given that many predictors are assessed electronically). Other predictors are performance tests, where the applicant is asked to manipulate an object or equipment. Paper-and-pencil tests are frequently used when psychological abilities are required to perform the job; performance tests are used when physical and social skills are required to perform the job. Although many organizations may use one or the other, some use both, as when NFL recruits are timed in the 40-yard dash (a performance test) and also given an intelligence test (a paper-and-pencil test).

***Objective Versus Essay.*** An objective paper-and-pencil predictor uses either multiple-choice questions or true/false questions. These tests should be used to measure knowledge in specific areas. Another form of a predictor is an essay, where the respondent provides a written answer. Essays are best used to assess written communication, problem-solving, and analytical skills.[3]

***Oral Versus Written Versus Computer.***   Responses to predictor questions can be spoken, written, or entered into a computer or other electronic communication device. When conducting interviews, some organizations listen to oral responses (either in person or through videoconferencing), read written responses, or read computer printouts of typed-in responses to assess applicants. As with all predictors, the appropriate form depends on the nature of the job. If the job requires a high level of verbal skill, oral responses should be solicited. If the job requires a large amount of writing, written responses should be required. If the job requires constant interaction with the computer, applicants should use a computer to enter their responses.[4]

## Development of the Selection Plan

To translate the results of a job analysis into the actual predictors to be used for selection, a selection plan must be developed. A selection plan describes which predictor(s) will be used to assess the KSAOs required to perform the job. The recommended format for a selection plan, and an example of such a plan for the job of secretary, is shown in Exhibit 8.2. A selection plan can be established in three steps. First, the KSAOs are written in the left-hand column. This list comes directly from the job requirements matrix. Second, for each KSAO, a "yes" or "no" is written to show whether it needs to be assessed in the selection process. Sometimes the answer is no because the applicant will acquire the KSAO once on the job (e.g., knowledge of company policies and procedures). Third, possible methods of assessment are listed for the required KSAOs, and the specific method to be used for each is indicated.

## Selection Sequence

Usually, a series of decisions are made about job applicants before they are selected. These decisions are depicted in Exhibit 8.3. The first decision is whether initial applicants who have applied for the job become candidates or are rejected. A candidate is someone who possesses the minimum qualifications to be considered for further assessment but has not yet received an offer.

Initial assessment methods are used to choose candidates (these will be discussed later in this chapter). The second decision is to determine which candidates become finalists. A finalist is someone who meets all the minimum qualifications and whom the organization considers fully qualified for the job. Substantive assessment methods, discussed in Chapter 9, are used to select finalists. The third decision is to determine which finalist receives the job offer. Offer receivers are those finalists to whom the organization extends an offer of employment. Discretionary methods, also discussed in Chapter 9, are used to

**EXHIBIT 8.2**  **Selection Plan Format and Example for Secretarial Position**

| Major KSAO Category | Necessary for Selection? (Y/N) | Method of Assessment | | | | | | | | |
|---|---|---|---|---|---|---|---|---|---|---|
| | | WP | CT | DB | LTR | TEF | ML | EM | TM | IRV |
| 1. Ability to follow oral directions/listening skills | Y | | | X | | | | | X | |
| 2. Ability to read and understand manuals and guidelines | Y | X | X | X | X | X | X | X | | |
| 3. Ability to perform basic arithmetic operations | Y | | | X | | X | | | | |
| 4. Ability to organize | Y | | | X | | X | X | | | |
| 5. Judgments/priority-setting/decision-making ability | Y | | | X | | X | | | | |
| 6. Oral communication skills | Y | | | | | | | | | X |
| 7. Written communication skills | Y | | X | | X | | | X | X | |
| 8. Interpersonal skills | Y | | X | | X | | | | | X |
| 9. Typing skills | Y | X | | | | | | | | |
| 10. Knowledge of company policies and procedures | N | | | | | | | | | |
| 11. Knowledge of basic personal computer operations | Y | X | X | X | X | X | | X | | |
| 12. Knowledge of how to use basic office machines | N | | | | | | | | | |
| 13. Flexibility in dealing with changing job demands | Y | | | | | | X | X | X | |
| 14. Knowledge of computer software | Y | X | X | X | X | X | X | X | | |
| 15. Ability to attend to detail and accuracy | Y | X | X | X | X | X | X | X | X | |

WP = Word processing test, CT = Correction test, DB = Database exam, LTR = Letter, TEF = Travel expense form, ML = Mail log, EM = Electronic mail messages, TM = Telephone messages, and IRV = Interview.

SOURCE: Adapted from N. Schmitt, S. Gilliland, R. S. Landis, and D. Devine, "Computer-Based Testing Applied to Selection of Secretarial Positions," *Personnel Psychology*, 1993, 46, pp. 149–165.

**EXHIBIT 8.3** **Assessment Methods by Applicant Flow Stage**

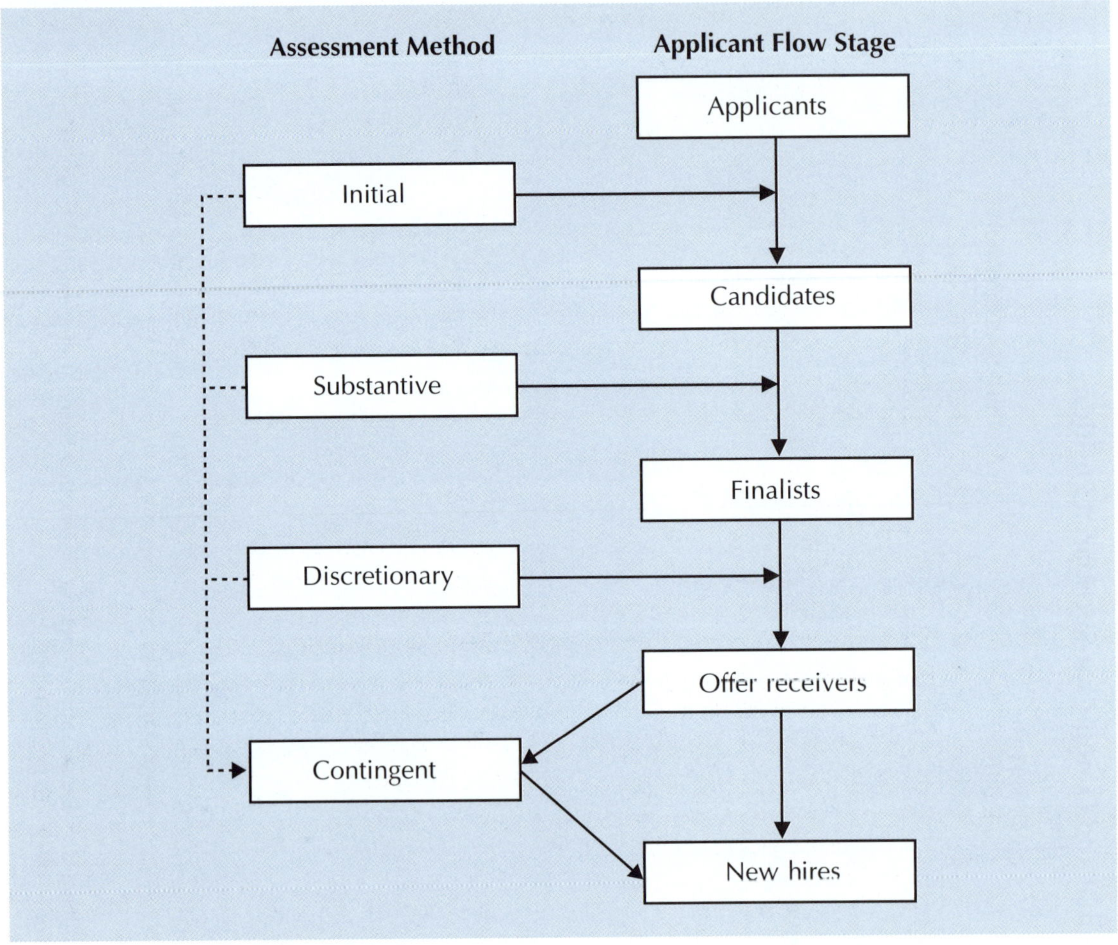

select these individuals. Contingent methods are sometimes used, meaning the job offer is subject to certain qualifications, such as the offer receiver passing a medical exam or drug test. Use of contingent methods, in particular drug testing and medical exams, will be reviewed in Chapter 9. Finally, some offer receivers become new hires when they decide to join the organization.

## INITIAL ASSESSMENT METHODS

Initial assessment methods, also referred to as preemployment inquiries, are used to minimize the costs associated with substantive assessment methods by reducing the number of people assessed. Predictors typically used to screen candidates from applicants include application blanks, biographical information, reference reports, and initial interviews. Each of these initial assessment methods will be described in turn. Using meta-analysis results, the average validity (i.e., $\bar{r}$) of each method is also provided if possible. Then, a general evaluation is presented to help guide decisions about which initial assessment methods to use.

## Résumés and Cover Letters

The first introduction of the applicant to the organization is often a cover letter and résumé. The applicant controls the introduction concerning the amount, type, and accuracy of information provided. As a result, résumés and cover letters always need to be verified with other predictors, such as background checks, to ensure that there are accurate and complete data across all job applicants with which to make informed selection decisions.

One major issue with résumés as a selection tool is the volume that organizations must process. Some organizations make few provisions for how to file and organize résumés as they filter in, and for how to store them once a hiring decision is made. Most organizations are well advised to produce and maintain an electronic copy of résumés received, both to ease sharing of information among selection decision makers and to track applicants should any questions (legal or otherwise) arise once the applicant is hired.

Employers can outsource résumé collection to résumé-tracking services. Many services not only scan résumés but also score them and place a percentage next to the applicant's name that reflects the number of criteria his or her résumé meets. Though such methods have powerful time- and cost-saving advantages, there are disadvantages, such as rejection of résumés that the software could not read (e.g., those on colored paper or that use special formatting like bullets) and applicants who try to beat the system by loading their résumés with every conceivable skill that appears in the advertisement. Despite these drawbacks, the efficiencies of such services make them particularly attractive for organizations facing large volumes of résumés.

The vast majority of large employers, and even many medium-size employers, encourage submission of résumés via e-mail or through online forms on the organization's website. For example, on the Toys "R" Us website, applicants can search an online database for openings and then apply either by completing an online form or, for managerial positions, by attaching their résumé to an e-mail message.

Even if applicants submit an electronic résumé to an employer, they need to make sure it is electronically scan-ready. This means applicants should avoid unusual fonts and formatting. With today's résumés, form definitely should follow function. In addition, applicants should stick to the relevant information. When law school graduate Brian Zulbert e-mailed his résumé to potential firms, he attached a picture of himself wearing a t-shirt and showing off his defined biceps. He also posted a shirtless picture of himself on Facebook with the joke to hire him as a lawyer rather than as an escort. Needless to say, the story went viral, with Zulbert drawing laughs from some but scorn from others.[5]

Finally, applicants should use nouns to describe noteworthy aspects of their background ("nonprofit," "3.75 GPA," "environmental science experience," etc.), as opposed to the traditional emphasis on action verbs ("managed," "guided," etc.), because nouns are more likely to be identified as keywords in scanning software. If the résumé is likely to be scanned, the applicant should build it around such keywords that will be the focus of the scan.

### Video Résumés

Video résumés are getting considerable attention in the business press. Sites like *SparkHire.com* help applicants put together video résumés where the applicants talk about their qualifications directly to the camera or in a simulated interview. Jared McKinney, a graduate of Brigham Young University, used the program *Screenr* to create a video résumé in which he discusses his past experiences and gives employers an idea of his personality. He eventually landed a job at a social media firm in Utah, which mentioned the quality of his résumé during his face-to-face interview.[6]

While the topic of video résumés is fashionable, few employers have any experience with them, and there is no research on their effectiveness. Although a survey indicated that many hiring managers would view a video résumé, a majority (58%) of those admitted they would do so out of "sheer curiosity." As one career advisor noted, "Most employers don't have much direct familiarity with them yet. Folks are still trying to figure out where the video résumé falls in the calculus in applicant selection." Some employers refuse to view video résumés for fear of introducing subjective biasing factors (appearance, race, or a disability) into their decisions. Some job applicants have submitted video résumés only to be the subject of ridicule by their potential employers. Aleksey Vayner, a finance major at Yale, sent a video résumé to bank giant UBS, only to have it posted on blogs and be mocked by others.[7]

While video résumés could be considered to fall on the more elaborate end of the résumé spectrum, on the more simplistic end of that spectrum is the tweet. Some technology and marketing firms are avoiding the traditional résumé and instead asking applicants to "tweet" their qualifications via the social networking site Twitter. Because they are more concerned with how the applicant communicates electronically rather than on paper or face-to-face, these employers argue that tweets (short texts up to 140 characters) reveal the applicant's technological savvy.[8]

Thus, while these alternative résumé formats are receiving a lot of attention in the press, it remains to be seen whether they will be a fad or the wave of the future.

### Résumé Issues

Résumés have the advantage of allowing the applicant to control information presented to employers. In evaluating résumés, employers should be aware of fabrications and distortions. Applicants, meanwhile, will want to know how to get their résumés noticed. We consider each of these issues and how to address them below.

***Résumé Fabrications and Distortions.*** Because résumés are prepared by applicants and follow no set-in-stone form, and because applicants want to present themselves in a favorable light, distortions are a significant problem. David J. Edmondson, CEO of RadioShack, was fired after a newspaper investigation revealed that he padded his résumé with two degrees he never earned, from a university he never attended. In addition, MIT dean Marilee Jones resigned after it was discovered that she never received the undergraduate or master's degrees she claimed on her résumé. Edmondson and Jones are not alone. In any given year, it seems the career of some CEO, athletic coach, or public official is derailed by a false statement the individual made on his or her résumé—often years ago. Resume-Doctor, an online company that assists applicants in preparing résumés, checked the accuracy of applicants' résumés posted on its website and found that nearly half (42.7%) had "significant inaccuracies." A background checking agency found that 56% of résumés contained a falsehood of some kind.[9]

Like the truth, résumés come in various degrees of accuracy, ranging from small, unintentional mistakes to outright fabrications. Some degree of what we might call "fudging" is commonplace. For example, Ellie Strauss's two more recent full-time jobs lasted less than six months. Ellie represented these as freelance jobs, under the heading "Senior Project Manager," to make them look like contract positions. Some might call this deception. Others might call it creative marketing or tailoring. Whatever you call it, résumé padding happens a lot. According to one survey, the three biggest areas of distortion or misinformation are the following:[10]

1. Inflated titles
2. Inaccurate dates to cover up job-hopping or employment gaps
3. Half-finished degrees, inflated education, or "purchased" degrees

The best way to combat résumé fraud or fudging is to conduct careful background checks. In addition, applying a "smell" test to any suspicious information is a wise policy. For example, in light of the false information submitted by coaches, colleges are scrutinizing résumés much more closely. On the University of Louisville's athletic department application forms, a warning has been inserted: "If a discrepancy is found after the background check, the employee is subject to dismissal." In short, the best protection against résumé fraud is for the hiring organization to do its homework.[11]

***Getting a Résumé Noticed.*** The conscientious job seeker may wonder how to best prepare a résumé. Although there are as many theories on the ingredients of a perfect résumé as there are résumé readers, a few general guidelines may be helpful. First, realize that typos and other minor mistakes can kill your chances. A survey revealed that 84% of hiring managers exclude from further consideration applicants with two typographical errors on their résumé; 47% of these managers exclude applicants with just a single error. Second, customize your résumé to the position if at all possible (try to address how your background, skills, and accomplishments fit the specific job requirements). Third, although résumés are getting somewhat longer, recognize that brevity is highly valued among hiring managers—many will not read résumés that are longer than two pages, and some will not read those that are longer than a page. Fourth, as we noted above, be factual and truthful. Where judgment is required, err on the side of accuracy. As one expert put it, "People are lying when they don't have to." Most hiring managers understand that no résumé is perfect. Even if being truthful hurts you in the short run, better to pay the price now rather than later, when you might have an entire career at stake. Finally, though taking care to be truthful, a résumé is no time to underplay your accomplishments. Do not just list your job duties; identify your accomplishments as well. Consider your impact on your division or group: What would not have happened had you not been there? What are you proudest of? Can you identify your own strengths from your performance review? Did you demonstrate skills during college that you might describe? The global head of recruiting for Accenture says he looks for evidence of teamwork skills in hiring: "I'd have to put the ability to work in a team environment toward the very top of what we look for," he says. Since most college students do some of their work in teams, why not list that as a skill acquired.[12]

***Evaluation.***   Almost no research exists on the validity and reliability of résumés and cover letters. There is also very little information on their costs or adverse impact. Regarding their validity, a review did indicate relatively low validity for applicant self-reports of grades, class standing, and test scores, but this does not address other information—such as self-reported work experience—often provided in applications and résumés. Regarding adverse impact, one study conducted in the Netherlands found that résumés with the common Arabic name "Mohammed" were four times as likely to be rejected as résumés with the common Dutch name "Henk." Moreover, résumés with female Arabic names were especially likely to be rejected when a high-status job was at stake. These situations are unfortunate given the pervasive use of résumés and cover letters in certain types of jobs, especially entry-level management, professional, and technical positions. Thus, organizations using résumés and cover letters in selection should carefully evaluate their effectiveness and make sure to independently verify information they are using in hiring decisions.[13]

## Application Blanks

Most application blanks request in written form the applicant's background concerning educational experiences, training, and job experiences. This information is often on the résumé as well and may seem unnecessarily duplicated. This is not the case. An application can be used to verify the data presented on the résumé and can also be used to obtain data omitted on the résumé, such as employment dates. The major advantage of application blanks over résumés is that the organization, rather than the applicant, dictates what information is presented. As a result, information critical to success on the job is less likely to be omitted by the applicant or overlooked by the reviewer of the résumé. The major issue with application blanks is to make sure that information requested is critical to job success, following the logic of prediction discussed earlier.

A sample application blank is provided in Exhibit 8.4. As with most application blanks, the major sections are personal information, employment desired, educational background, special interests and abilities, work experience, and suggested references. The only information sought from the application blank should be KSAOs that can be demonstrated as relevant to the job. This not only avoids wasting the organization's and the applicant's time but also protects the employer from charges of unfair discrimination (see "Legal Issues" at the end of this chapter). Note the disclaimer statement at the bottom of the application blank. It provides certain legal protections to the organization, which are discussed in "Legal Issues." Asking applicants to sign a disclaimer may also decrease the incentive to distort or falsify information.

## Educational Requirements

Special care needs to be taken in wording items on an application blank when soliciting information about educational experiences and performance.[14] Following are several particularly important areas pertaining to educational requirement information on application blanks.

*Level of Education.*   Level of education or degree is one element of educational performance used to predict job performance. Often, level of education is measured by the attainment of a degree. Despite its pervasive use, it is not clear that level of education is a truly useful selection measure. Some economists and sociologists question its importance, and a meta-analysis suggested that the correlation between education and task performance was relatively small (across all measures of task performance, $\bar{r}_{xy} = .10$).[15]

The recent economic downturn that left many unemployed, coupled with the rising cost of college tuition, has left many questioning the value of a college degree. "Is college worth it?" asks author and former US secretary of education Warren Bennett. Critics argue that the traditional path of going to a "bricks and mortar" college or university and earning a degree is no longer as useful. Instead, they argue that massive open online courses can educate people at a much cheaper cost, and that education is more about a mind-set rather than a four-year program. They also point to famous billionaires such as Mark Zuckerberg and Bill Gates, both of whom dropped out of college. As Mike Hagen, who dropped out of Princeton in 2006 and started a mobile app, noted, in Silicon Valley, eschewing college is "almost a

**EXHIBIT 8.4   Application for Employment**

**PERSONAL INFORMATION**

DATE _____

SOCIAL SECURITY
NUMBER _____

NAME _____
　　　　　　LAST　　　　　　　　FIRST　　　　　　　MIDDLE

PRESENT ADDRESS _____
　　　　　　　　　STREET　　　　　　　CITY　　　　　　STATE　　　　　ZIP

PERMANENT ADDRESS _____
　　　　　　　　　　STREET　　　　　　　CITY　　　　　STATE　　　　　ZIP

PHONE NO. _____　　ARE YOU 18 YEARS OR OLDER?　　Yes ☐　　No ☐

ARE YOU PREVENTED FROM LAWFULLY BECOMING EMPLOYED
IN THIS COUNTRY BECAUSE OF VISA OR IMMIGRATION STATUS?　　Yes ☐　　No ☐

**EMPLOYMENT DESIRED**

POSITION _____　DATE YOU
　　　　　　　　　　　CAN START _____　SALARY
　　　　　　　　　　　　　　　　　　　　　　DESIRED _____

ARE YOU EMPLOYED NOW? _____　IF SO MAY WE INQUIRE
　　　　　　　　　　　　　　　　　　OF YOUR PRESENT EMPLOYER? _____

APPLIED TO THIS COMPANY BEFORE? _____　WHERE? _____　WHEN? _____

REFERRED BY _____

**EDUCATION**

| | NAME AND LOCATION | NO. OF YEARS ATTENDED | DID YOU GRADUATE? | SUBJECTS STUDIED |
|---|---|---|---|---|
| GRAMMAR SCHOOL | | | | |
| HIGH SCHOOL (GED) | | | | |
| COLLEGE | | | | |
| OTHER | | | | |

**EXHIBIT 8.4**   **Continued**

**GENERAL**

SUBJECTS OF SPECIAL STUDY

SPECIAL SKILLS

ACTIVITIES (CIVIC, ATHLETIC, ETC.)

| U.S. MILITARY SERVICE | RANK | PRESENT MEMBERSHIP IN NATIONAL GUARD OR RESERVES |
|---|---|---|

**FORMER EMPLOYERS** (LIST BELOW LAST 3 EMPLOYERS, STARTING WITH THE LAST ONE FIRST)

| | DATE | NAME & ADDRESS | SALARY | POSITION | REASON FOR LEAVING |
|---|---|---|---|---|---|
| FROM | | | | | |
| TO | | | | | |
| FROM | | | | | |
| TO | | | | | |
| FROM | | | | | |
| TO | | | | | |

**REFERENCES** (GIVE THE NAMES OF 3 PERSONS NOT RELATED TO YOU)

| | NAME | ADDRESS | BUSINESS | YEARS ACQUAINTED |
|---|---|---|---|---|
| 1 | | | | |
| 2 | | | | |
| 3 | | | | |

"I certify that all the information submitted by me on this application is true and complete, and I understand that if any false information, omissions, or misrepresentations are discovered, my application may be rejected and, if I am employed, my employment may be terminated at any time. In consideration of my employment, I agree to conform to the company's rules and regulations, and I agree that my employment and compensation can be terminated, with or without cause, and with or without notice, at any time, at either my or the company's option. I also understand and agree that the terms and conditions of my employment may be changed, with or without cause, and with or without notice, at any time by the company. I understand that no company representative, other than its president, and only when in writing and signed by the president, has any authority to enter into any agreement for employment for any specific period of time, or to make any agreement contrary to the foregoing."

| DATE | SIGNATURE |
|---|---|

badge of honor" because individuals are more freethinking and risk-taking. Proponents of degrees counter with data that the educated earn far more in their lifetime than those without degrees, and thus the Zuckerbergs and the Gateses of the world are the exception, rather than the norm. They also argue that an education derived solely from virtual classrooms would be devoid of the interpersonal experiences and critical thinking that take place in more traditional classrooms. Although decrying higher education may simply be the current fashion, it is likely that changes in higher education are on the horizon, and definitions of "level of education" may be altered as a result of those changes.[16]

***Grade Point Average.***    Classroom grades are measured using a grade point average (GPA). Care should be exercised in the interpretation of GPA information. For example, a GPA in one's major in college may be different (usually higher) from one's GPA for all classes. Grades also vary widely by field (e.g., grades in engineering tend to be lower than in other fields). Further, a GPA of 3.5 may be good at one school but not at another. Research suggests that the validity of GPA in predicting job performance may be as high as the mid .30s. College grades are no more valid than high school grades, and grades are most valid in predicting early job performance. Although there is variability from employer to employer, evidence indicates that GPA does not play a large role in most recruiters' evaluations. GPAs tend to have adverse impact against minorities, and, as with all selection measures with adverse impact, the validity evidence must be balanced against adverse impact implications.[17]

***Quality of School.***    Much has been said and written about the quality of various educational programs. For example, *U.S. News and World Report* annually publishes the results of a survey showing ratings of school quality (or prestige, depending on the faith you have in such ratings).[18]

Graduates from prestigious universities are commanding wage premiums for MBA degrees in particular, but also educational degrees in general. Sixty percent of corporate recruiters cite the reputation of the school as the top reason for recruiting at a particular university. As one article concluded, "It's not necessarily what you learn in an MBA program, but where you learn it."[19]

***Major Field of Study.***    The more specialized the knowledge requirements of a particular position, the more important an applicant's major field of study is likely to be as a predictor. An English major may do very well as an editor but may be unsuccessful as a physician. It should also be noted that choice of major does not guarantee that a certain number or type of classes have been taken. The number and type of classes needed for a major or minor vary from school to school and need to be carefully scrutinized to ensure comparability across majors. The relationship between field of study and job performance is very difficult to assess; therefore, no conclusive validity evidence is available.

*Extracurricular Activities.* The usefulness of extracurricular activities as a predictor depends on the job. Being a field hockey player may have little relevance to being a successful manager. However, being elected captain of a hockey team may indeed be a sign of leadership qualities needed to be a successful manager. Information about extracurricular activities taken from an application blank must be relevant to the job in question. Evidence suggests that participation in extracurricular activities demonstrates interpersonal skills, indicating that it may be more valid for jobs with a heavy social component.[20]

## Training and Experience Requirements

Many past experiences predictive of future performance do not take place in a classroom. Instead, they come from life experiences in other institutions, which, fortunately, can also be captured on an application blank. A great deal of weight is often put on training and experience requirements on the theory that actions speak louder than words. Experienced surgeons tend to make better surgeons, for example. A study found that the mortality rate of procedures was about twice as high for inexperienced surgeons as for experienced surgeons. As with other jobs, though, the benefits of experience tend to be at the low levels of experience. Beyond a certain level, added experience does not help much. The drawback of putting too much emphasis on previous work experience, however, is that the amount of experience and training an applicant has may be overstated. Additionally, applicants with high potential may be overlooked because they have not had the opportunity to gain the training or experience needed.

Various methods can be used to measure training and experience. Since training and experience information is not directly equivalent across applicants, all methods require the judgment of selection decision makers. These decision makers render judgments about how to classify and weight different levels of experience. An approach termed the "behavioral consistency method" has shown the highest degree of validity because it focuses on determining the quality of an applicant's previous training and experience. One of the means by which the behavioral consistency method determines quality is by asking applicants to complete a supplemental application wherein they describe their most significant accomplishments relative to a list of key job behaviors. Due to their involved nature, however, behavioral consistency ratings are time-consuming and expensive to administer, and they require the applicant to possess some degree of analytical ability and writing skills. Thus, the choice of weighting methods rests on a trade-off between accuracy and ease and cost of administration.[21]

## Licensing, Certification, and Job Knowledge

Many professions and occupations require or encourage people to demonstrate mastery of a certain body of knowledge. Such mastery is commonly measured by two distinct methods: licensure and certification. A license is required of people by law to perform an activity, whereas a certification is voluntary in the sense that it is not mandated by law (though an individual employer may require it). The purpose of a license is to protect the public interest, whereas the purpose of a certification is to identify an individual who has met a minimum standard of proficiency. Licensing exams and certification exams are usually developed by SMEs in conjunction with testing specialists. Licensure and certification are to be distinguished from job knowledge tests. While licensure and certification demonstrate mastery of a general body of knowledge applicable to many organizations, job knowledge tests assess a specific body of knowledge within a particular organization. Job knowledge tests are usually used in the public sector as an initial screening device. In the private sector, they are used primarily for promotion purposes. Although mentioned here, job knowledge tests will be covered in detail in Chapter 9.

The actual use of licensing and certification requirements depends on whether they are used as an initial or a contingent assessment method. As an initial method, licensing and certification requirements are used to eliminate applicants who fail to possess these credentials. For example, a car repair shop electing to hire only certified mechanics might initially screen out individuals who fail to have the proper certification. When licensing and certification requirements are used as a contingent method, the selection process proceeds on the assumption that the applicant has the requisite credentials (or will have them by the time of hire). This is then verified after an initial offer decision has been made. For example, rather than verifying that each applicant for a nursing position possesses a valid state license, a hospital may assess applicants on the assumption that they have a valid license and then verify this assumption after a contingent job offer has been made. Thus, the difference between using licensing and certification requirements as initial or contingent assessment methods depends on when the information is considered in the selection process.

Increasingly, organizations are using voluntary professional certification as a method of verifying competence in various occupations. There are more than 1,000 professional certifications. Most of these voluntary certifications are issued on the basis of experience and education. The vast majority of certifications also require examinations.

There are several practical problems or limitations in using licensing and certification requirements in selection. First, one cannot assume that simply because an applicant has a license or certification he or she is qualified for the position. That assumption places full confidence in the licensing and certification standards of the professional organization. Licensing and certification requirements vary greatly in their rigor, and one should not accept on faith that the fulfillment of those requirements ensures professional competency. Moreover, even if the requirements did perfectly measure professional competence, because licenses and certifications are issued to those passing some minimum threshold, they do not discriminate between the minimally qualified and the exceptionally well qualified. In other words, licenses and certifications are like considering an applicant's college degree without looking at the applicant's GPA.

A second difficulty with licensing and certification requirements is that, as with job titles, there has been significant proliferation. This is particularly true with certifications. For example, among financial advisors are certified financial planners (CFPs), certified financial analysts (CFAs), certified investment management analysts (CIMAs), chartered financial consultants (ChFCs), chartered retirement planning counselors (CRPCs), and so forth. Indeed, more than 100 such titles are used by financial professionals. No central regulator monitors these titles, and the growth in financial services certifications seems to have done little to prevent the myriad mistakes and malfeasances that contributed to the recent financial crisis that decimated Wall Street and Main Street alike. If selection decision makers wish to require certification, they need to research the types and meanings of certifications that may exist for a job.

Finally, there are practice effects with repeated tries at a licensing or certification exam, and these effects may be quite strong. One study of medical professionals found that for one certification exam, second-time examinees improved their scores by .79 standard deviations. For another exam, the average gain was .48 standard deviations. Translating the gain from the first exam (.79SD) into a standard normal distribution, this would mean that someone who scored at the 34th percentile the first time out would be expected to score at the 66th percentile on the second try. For the second exam (.48SD), the improvement would be from the 34th percentile to the 53rd percentile. Unlike some standardized tests, where scores may be reported for each time the test is taken, there generally is no way for a selection decision maker to know how many times an applicant has taken a licensing or certification exam (nor can one determine a test taker's exact score).

We are not arguing that selection decision makers should ignore licensing and certification requirements. They are important—even necessary—for many jobs. However, selection decision makers need to be informed consumers for those areas where they require licensure and certification, and supplement licensure and certification with other information to ascertain knowledge and competency.[22]

## Weighted Application Blanks

Not all of the information contained on an application blank is of equal value to the organization in making selection decisions. Depending on the organization and job, some information predicts success on the job better than other information. Procedures have been developed that help weight application blank information by the degree to which the information differentiates between high- and low-performing individuals.[23] This scoring methodology is referred to as a weighted application blank and is useful not only in making selection decisions but also in developing application blanks. The statistical procedures involved help the organization discern which items should be retained for use in the application blank and which should be excluded, depending on how well they predict performance.

## Evaluation of Application Blanks

Evidence suggests that scored evaluations of the unweighted application blank are not particularly valid predictors of job performance (average validity ranges from $\bar{r} = .10$ to $\bar{r} = .20$).[24] This is not surprising given the rudimentary information collected in application blanks. Another factor that may undermine the validity of application blanks is distortion. Evidence suggests that about one-third of the investigations into the backgrounds of applicants suggested that misrepresentation occurred on the application blank. Subsequent studies have suggested that the most common questions that are misrepresented include previous salary, education, tenure on previous job, and reasons for leaving previous job. Some individuals even go beyond misrepresentation to outright invention. One study revealed that 15% of supposedly previous employers of applicants indicated that the individual had never worked for them.[25] Thus, as with résumés, application information that is weighted heavily in selection decisions should be verified.

The validity evidence for weighted application blanks is much more positive.[26] In a sense, this would almost have to be true since items in the weighted application blank are scored and weighted according to their ability to predict job performance. Thus, as long as *some* of the items are predictive, the scoring and weighting schemes embedded in the weighted application blank will ensure that the overall score is predictive. Because the process used to develop the weighted application blank is time-consuming and expensive, more cost-benefit studies need to be conducted. Is the validity worth the cost? Unfortunately, there is little recent research on the weighted application blank, so answering this question is difficult.

The relatively poor validity of unweighted application blanks also should not be taken as an indication that they are useless in selection decisions. Unweighted application blanks are a very inexpensive means of collecting basic information on job applicants. Most organizations use unweighted application blanks only for initial screening decisions (to rule out applicants who are obviously unqualified for the job). As long as application blanks are used in this context (and not relied on to a significant degree in making substantive hiring decisions), they can be useful for making initial decisions about applicants. Thus, it is not necessarily appropriate to condemn unweighted application blanks based on a criterion for which they are rarely used.

## Biographical Information

Biographical information, often called biodata, is personal history information on an applicant's background and interests. Results from a biodata survey provide a general description of a person's life history. The principal assumption behind the use of biodata is the axiom "The best predictor of future behavior is past behavior." These past behaviors may reflect ability or motivation.

Like application blanks, biographical information blanks ask applicants to report on their background. Responses to both of these questionnaires can provide useful information in making initial selection decisions about applicants. Unlike application blanks, however, biographical information can also be fruitfully used for substantive selection decisions. In fact, if scores on a biodata inventory are predictive of subsequent job performance (which, as we will see, is often the case), it may be somewhat limiting to use biodata scores only for initial assessment decisions. Thus, although biographical information is as much a substantive assessment method as it is an initial assessment method, because it shares many similarities with application blanks, we have included it in this section. Nevertheless, it should also be considered in deliberations about which substantive assessment methods are to be used.

Biographical information has some similarities to background tests (see the section on reference and background checks). Biodata and background checks are similar in that both look into an applicant's past. However, the two types of selection methods differ in their general purpose and measurement. First, whereas a background check is often used to turn up any "buried bones" in an applicant's background, biodata is used to predict future performance. Second, whereas reference checks are conducted through checks of records and conversations with references, biodata information is collected by survey. Thus, biodata inventories and background checks are distinct methods of selection that must be considered separately.

The type of biographical information collected varies a great deal from inventory to inventory and often depends on the job. For example, a biographical survey for executives might focus on career aspirations, accomplishments, and disappointments. A survey for blue-collar workers might focus on training and work experience. A biodata inventory for federal government workers might focus on school and educational experiences, work history, skills, and interpersonal relations. As can be seen from these examples, most biodata surveys consider individual accomplishments, group accomplishments, disappointing experiences, and stressful situations.[27] The domains in which these attributes are studied often vary from job to job but can range from childhood experiences to educational or early work experiences to current hobbies or family relations.

## Measures

Typically, biographical information is collected in a questionnaire that applicants complete. Exhibit 8.5 provides example biodata items. As can be seen, the items are quite diverse. It has been suggested that each biodata item can be classified according to 10 criteria:

- *History* (does the item describe an event that occurred in the past or a future or hypothetical event?)
- *Externality* (does the item address an observable event or an internal event such as values or judgments?)
- *Objectivity* (does the item focus on reporting factual information or subjective interpretations?)
- *Firsthandedness* (does the item seek information that is directly available to the applicant rather than an evaluation of the applicant's behavior by others?)

**EXHIBIT 8.5   Examples of Biodata Items**

1. In college, my grade point average was:
   a. I did not go to college or completed less than two years
   b. Less than 2.50
   c. 2.50 to 3.00
   d. 3.00 to 3.50
   e. 3.50 to 4.00

2. In the past five years, the number of different jobs I have held is:
   a. More than five
   b. Three to five
   c. Two
   d. One
   e. None

3. The kind of supervision I like best is:
   a. Very close supervision
   b. Fairly close supervision
   c. Moderate supervision
   d. Minimal supervision
   e. No supervision

4. When you are angry, which of the following behaviors most often describes your reaction:
   a. Reflect on the situation for a bit
   b. Talk to a friend or spouse
   c. Exercise or take a walk
   d. Physically release the anger on something
   e. Just try to forget about it

5. Over the past three years, how much have you enjoyed each of the following (use the scale at right):
   a. _____ Reading                     1 = Very much
   b. _____ Watching TV                 2 = Some
   c. _____ Home improvements           3 = Very little
   d. _____ Music                       4 = Not at all
   e. _____ Outdoor recreation

6. In most ways is your life close to ideal?
   a. Yes
   b. No
   c. Undecided or neutral

- *Discreteness* (does the item pertain to a single, unique behavior or a simple count of events as opposed to summary responses?)
- *Verifiability* (can the accuracy of the response to the item be confirmed?)
- *Controllability* (does the item address an event that the applicant controlled?)
- *Equal accessibility* (are the events or experiences expressed in the item equally accessible to all applicants?)
- *Job relevance* (does the item solicit information closely tied to the job?)
- *Invasiveness* (is the item sensitive to the applicant's right to privacy?)[28]

Most selection tests simply score items in a predetermined manner and add the scores to arrive at a total score. These total scores form the basis of selection decisions made about applicants. With most biodata inventories, the process of making decisions based on responses to items is considerably more complex. Essentially, the development of a biodata inventory is a bit of a fishing expedition where current employees are given many items to complete and the inventory used for future hiring decisions is based on those items—and the specific responses within items or questions—that seem to discriminate between high performers and low performers.

Google developed its biodata inventory by first asking its employees 300 questions and then correlating employee responses to their job performance. Once it isolated items that predicted the job performance of current employees, Google asked applicants a smaller set of questions that ranged from the age when an applicant first got excited about computers to whether the applicant has ever turned a profit at his or her own side business.[29]

## Evaluation of Biodata

Research conducted on the reliability and validity of biodata is quite positive.[30] Responses tend to be fairly reliable (test–retest coefficients range from .60 to .90). More important, past research suggests that biodata inventories are valid predictors of job performance. A number of meta-analyses have been conducted, and the average validity has ranged from $\bar{r}_{xy} = .32$ to $\bar{r}_{xy} = .37$.[31]

In addition to job performance, biodata scores appear to predict turnover (individuals with a past history of job changes are more likely to turn over) and student academic performance (biodata scores of incoming college freshmen predicted their subsequent college GPAs).[32]

Despite the quite positive validity evidence, biodata does have some important limitations. First, because biodata inventories are developed and scored on the basis of a particular job and sample, it has commonly been argued that the validity of a particular inventory in one organization is unlikely to generalize to another organization. Although this issue has not been conclusively resolved in the literature, prudent practice would suggest that organizations regularly validate their biodata inventory.[33]

Second, there is some concern about faking. Not only might applicants be motivated to fake their responses to biodata questions, but also many responses are impossible to verify (e.g., "Did you collect coins or stamps as a child?"). Research also suggests, though, that faking can be reduced through several strategies: (1) use items that are more objective and verifiable, (2) simply warn applicants against faking, and (3) ask applicants to elaborate upon and justify their responses; for example, if applicants are asked, "In the past year, how often have you read about new marketing strategies?" (1 = never, 5 = very often), they would receive a follow-up question to elaborate on their response: "If you answered 2, 3, 4, or 5, briefly list the strategies and the sources that you read." Although this elaboration technique has been shown to correlate with applicants' verbal ability, the correlation appears to be small enough such that the biodata questions do not become a test of cognitive ability.[34]

Third, applicants and managers do not react positively to biodata. The inventories often comprise more than 100 items, and most research suggests that applicants do not see the questions as job related. Neither, apparently, do HR managers. A survey of 255 HR professionals revealed that, among various selection measures, biodata beat only a "personal hunch" in terms of its perceived validity. Those hunches may also spill over into how the biodata inventory is scored. In some cases, employers may use a rational scoring scheme, whereby they give more weight to items they believe correlate more strongly with job performance and less weight to items they believe correlate less strongly with job performance. In other cases, employers may use an empirical scoring scheme, whereby weighting of items is determined by estimated validities found in previous research. A purely rational scoring scheme is likely to generate the lowest validity for a biodata inventory, while a blend of rational and empirical scoring is likely to generate the highest validity.[35]

Despite these limitations, it is important to keep in mind that biodata can have impressive validity and that its use is appropriate when it is carefully validated and when the aforementioned limitations are addressed.

## Reference and Background Checks

Background information about job applicants can come not only from the applicant but also from people familiar with the applicant (e.g., employers, creditors, and neighbors). Organizations often solicit this information on their own or use the services of agencies that specialize in investigating applicants. Background information solicited from others consists of letters of recommendation, reference checks, and background checks.

### Letters of Recommendation

A very common reference check in some settings (e.g., academic institutions) is to ask applicants to have letters of recommendation written for them. There are two major problems with this approach. First, these letters may do little to help the organization discern the more qualified applicants from the less qualified applicants. The reason for this is that only very poor applicants are unable to arrange for positive letters about their accomplishments. Second, most letters are not structured or standardized, meaning the data the organization receives from the letter writers are not consistent across organizations. For example, a letter about one applicant may concern the applicant's educational qualifications, whereas a letter about another applicant may focus on work experience. Comparing the qualifications of applicants A and B under these circumstances is like comparing apples and oranges.

The problem with letters of recommendation is demonstrated dramatically in one study that showed there was a stronger correlation between two letters written by one person for two applicants than between two people writing letters for the same person.[36] This finding indicates that letters of recommendation have more to do with the letter writer than with the person being written about. In fact, one study revealed that letter writers who had a dispositional tendency to be positive wrote consistently more favorable letters than letter writers with a tendency to be critical or negative.[37]

In addition, a surprising number of letters of recommendation are written by the applicants themselves. Regarding graduate school admissions, the Association of International Graduate Admissions Consultants discovered that a whopping 38% of applicants were asked by their recommenders to write their own letters, which the recommenders would then later sign. And some applicants have confessed to bypassing their recommender altogether, especially if the recommender was not fluent in English.[38]

Such problems indicate that organizations should downplay the weight given to letters unless a great deal of credibility and accountability can be attached to the letter writer's comments. In addition, a structured form should be provided so that each writer provides the same information about each applicant.

Another way to improve on letters of recommendation is to use a standardized scoring key, as shown in Exhibit 8.6. With this method, categories of KSAOs are established and become the scoring key (shown at the bottom of the exhibit). The adjectives in the letter are underlined and classified into the appropriate category. The number of adjectives used in each category constitutes the applicant's score.

## Reference Checks

With reference checking, a spot check is made on the applicant's background. Usually the person contacted is the immediate supervisor of the applicant or is in the HR department of current or previous organizations with which the applicant has had contact. Surveys reveal that 96% of organizations conduct reference checks. A roughly equal number conduct the checks in-house (by HR) versus a third-party vendor. The most common information sought is on criminal background and verification of employment eligibility, former employers, dates of previous employment,

**EXHIBIT 8.6   Scoring Letters of Recommendation**

Dear Personnel Director:

Mr. John Anderson asked that I write this letter in support of his application as assistant manager and I am pleased to do so. I have known John for six years as he was my assistant in the accounting department.

John always had his work completed <u>accurately</u> and <u>promptly</u>. In his years here, he <u>never missed a deadline</u>. He is very <u>detail</u> oriented, <u>alert</u> in finding errors, and <u>methodical</u> in his problem-solving approach. Interpersonally, John is a very <u>friendly</u> and <u>helpful</u> person.

I have great confidence in John's ability. If you desire more information, please let me know.

MA  0        CC  2        DR  6        U  0        V  0

Dear Personnel Director:

Mr. John Anderson asked that I write this letter in support of his application as assistant manager and I am pleased to do so. I have known John for six years as he was my assistant in the accounting department.

John was one of the most <u>popular</u> employees in our agency as he is a <u>friendly</u>, <u>outgoing, sociable</u> individual. He has a great sense of <u>humor</u>, is <u>poised</u>, and is very <u>helpful</u>. In completing his work, he is <u>independent</u>, <u>energetic</u>, and <u>industrious</u>.

I have great confidence in John's ability. If you desire more information, please let me know.

MA  0        CC  2        DR  0        U  5        V  3

*Key   MA = mental ability*
*CC = consideration-cooperation*
*DR = dependability-reliability*
*U = urbanity*
*V = vigor*

SOURCE: M. G. Aumodt, D. A. Bryan, and A. J. Whitcomb, "Predicting Performance With Letters of Recommendation," *Public Personnel Management*, 1993, 22, pp. 81–90. Reprinted with permission of *Public Personnel Management*, published by the International Personnel Management Association.

and former job titles.[39] Exhibit 8.7 provides a sample reference request. Although this reference request was developed for checking references by mail, the questions contained in the request could easily be adapted for use in checking references via telephone.

Both of the problems that occur with letters of recommendation occur with reference checks as well. An even more significant concern, however, is the reluctance of organizations to give out the requested information because they fear a lawsuit on the grounds of invasion of privacy or defamation of character. Recall that the

**EXHIBIT 8.7**   **Sample Reference Request**

### TO BE COMPLETED BY APPLICANT

NAME (PRINT): _____   SOCIAL SEC. NUMBER: _____

I have made application for employment at this company. I request and authorize you to release all information requested below concerning my employment record, reason for leaving your employ, or my education. I hereby release my personal references, my former employers and schools, and all individuals connected therewith, from all liability for any damage whatsoever for furnishing this information.

SIGNATURE _____   DATE _____

**SCHOOL REFERENCE**
DATES ATTENDED
FROM: _____   TO: _____   GRADUATED?   YES☐   NO ☐
DEGREE AWARDED: _____

**EMPLOYMENT REFERENCE**
POSITION HELD: _____   EMPLOYMENT DATES: _____

IMMEDIATE SUPERVISOR'S NAME _____

REASON FOR LEAVING   DISCHARGED ☐   RESIGNED ☐   LAID OFF ☐

**FORMER EMPLOYER OR SCHOOL—Please complete the following. Thank you.**

IS THE ABOVE INFORMATION CORRECT?   YES ☐   NO ☐

If not, give correct information: _____
_____

PLEASE CHECK

|  | EXCEL. | GOOD | FAIR | POOR | COMMENTS: |
|---|---|---|---|---|---|
| ATTITUDE | ___ | ___ | ___ | ___ | |
| QUALITY OF WORK | ___ | ___ | ___ | ___ | |
| COOPERATION | ___ | ___ | ___ | ___ | |
| ATTENDANCE | ___ | ___ | ___ | ___ | |

WOULD YOU RECOMMEND FOR EMPLOYMENT?   YES ☐   NO ☐

ADDITIONAL COMMENTS
_____
_____

survey results reported above indicated that 96% of employers always check references. The same survey indicated that 93% of employers refuse to provide reference information for fear of being sued. As one executive stated, "There's a dire need for better reference information but fear of litigation keeps employers from providing much more than name, rank, and serial number."[40] As a result of employers' reluctance to provide reference information, reference checkers claim to receive inadequate information roughly half of the time. To a large degree, this concern over providing even rudimentary reference information is excessive—less than 3% of employers have had legal problems with reference checks (see "Legal Issues" at the end of this chapter). If every organization refused to provide useful reference information, a potentially important source of applicant information could lose its value.

Most reference checking is still done over the telephone, but there is evidence that this situation is changing. Increasingly, employers are mining networking websites such as Facebook, MySpace, and LinkedIn not only to find out more about an applicant but also to locate references to contact. T-Mobile, for example, regularly mines "public" information on applicants' profile pages. These networking websites have "changed everything" about how T-Mobile conducts reference checks, according to one hiring manager.[41] No matter the source or method used to gather the information, it is critical that the questions be job related and that the same information is asked about all applicants. When properly structured and job relevant, references can have moderate levels of validity.[42]

## Background Checks

How would you feel if you found out that the organization you are hoping to join was investigating your traffic record and moral character? How would you feel if an organization did *not* investigate the backgrounds of guards to be selected for the gun storage depot of the US military base near your home? More and more organizations are thoroughly checking applicants' backgrounds even when security is not a particular issue.

Although background checking may seem to be a very invasive procedure, such checks have increased dramatically in the past 10 years. A recent survey indicated that nearly three in four organizations now perform background checks, a percentage that has steadily increased over time.[43] There are several reasons for this. First, after the September 11, 2001, terrorist attacks, more organizations became concerned about security issues. Second, some ethical lapses, and many instances of workplace violence, might be avoided by background checks. For example, consider the case of Wal-Mart. In two separate incidents in South Carolina, Wal-Mart employees were accused of sexually assaulting young girls. Both of the accused employees had past criminal convictions for sexually related offenses. In response, Wal-Mart instituted criminal background checks on all of its employees.[44] A third reason behind the growing use of background checks is legal protection against responsibility for malfeasance, and defense against claims of negligent hiring (which we review under "Reference Checks" in "Legal Issues" at the end of the chapter).

A fourth, and perhaps the most important, reason underlying the increasing use of background checks is technological. As public records have become more accessible, both legally (with so-called Sunshine laws) and practically (many local and state governments post criminal records online), and as credit checking has increased, it has become far easier to perform background checks. Moreover, scores of organizations now provide background checks, with the fee determined by the scope of information desired. Bed Bath & Beyond uses Sterling to conduct its background checks, FedEx uses Infomart, and Jackson Hewitt uses IdentityPi. com. Other large background checking services include USIS, ChoicePoint, ADP, and First Advantage. Background checks cost anywhere from $5 to $1,000 per hire, depending on the type of position and the information sought. Most background checks cost around $25 per applicant.

Background checks identify more problems than one might think. Additionally, the consequences of failing to conduct a background check are quite serious. In many cases, subsequent malfeasance could have been prevented by a background check. Take, for example, Nick Leeson, the "rogue trader" responsible for the demise of Barings Bank. Britain's Securities and Futures Authority had discovered that Leeson lied on his application regarding a civil court judgment of unpaid debts. When hiring Leeson, Barings's Singapore branch never checked into his credit history, nor was his history discovered by the Singapore stock exchange. At Barings's Singapore office, Leeson made unauthorized speculative trades and creatively hid his mounting losses. The losses eventually accumulated to $1.3 billion, bankrupting the oldest bank in London.[45]

In many industries, the percentage of applicants identified to have some problem (e.g., a criminal record or a discrepancy in past employment or education) is surprisingly high. According to one source, more than half (51.7%) of the applicants in the nonprofit industry had significant discrepancies between their self-reported and their actual employment history, and nearly half (48.9%) of the applicants in the construction industry had a major motor vehicle violation (involving license suspension).[46]

Background checks do have limitations. First, the records can be wrong or misinterpreted. For example, sometimes peoples' identities can be mixed up. Unless someone has an unusual name, there are probably many others in the population with the same name. Sometimes the records contain misleading information. Johnnie Ulrigg was denied a job in Missoula, Montana, because his background check turned up a list of probation violations. He later learned that several counties in the state list failure to pay a traffic ticket as a probation violation. It took Ulrigg two years to clear his record. Second, because background checks have become more commonplace, they can place a seemingly permanent bar on the reemployment of reformed criminals. Peter Demain was sentenced to six years for possessing 21 pounds of marijuana. While in prison, he was so adept in the prison kitchen that he quickly rose to head baker. Once out of prison, though, Demain was unable to find a job at bagel shops, coffeehouses, grocery stores, and bakeries. Is it fair for reformed criminals, no matter how long ago or the nature of the offense, to be banned from employment?[47] Such questions are difficult to answer.

Finally, many labor unions have historically resisted background checking. In 2007, Major League Baseball owners clashed with the Umpires Union about background checks.[48] Conversely, in 2010, the Air Line Pilots Association, which represents UPS pilots, backed increased use of background checks.[49]

One way to ameliorate some of these problems is to limit background checks to information that is job related (it may be difficult to establish that a spotty credit history is important to jobs that mostly involve manual labor) and to use multiple sources to verify problems for exclusionary information (i.e., if an applicant is to be excluded because of what a background check uncovered, it would be prudent to independently verify the information).

### Evaluation of Recommendations, References, and Background Checks

The empirical data that exist suggest that the validity of reference checks is low to moderate. A meta-analysis of a number of studies revealed that the validity coefficients of reference data ranged from $\bar{r} = .16$ to $\bar{r} = .26$. Another study suggested that when reference reports are structured (the same questions were asked about every applicant), their validity was $\bar{r} = .25$. To some degree, the validity depends on who is providing the information. If it is the personnel officer, a coworker, a relative, or even the applicant himself or herself, the information is not very valid. On the other hand, reference reports from supervisors and acquaintances are somewhat more valid. The information from personnel officers may be less valid because they are less knowledgeable about the applicant (their past employee); the reports of coworkers and relatives are likely less valid because these individuals are positively biased toward the applicant.

Although references do not have high validity, we need to take a cost-benefit approach. In general, the quality of the information may be low, but in the few cases where reference information changes a decision, the payoff can be significant. An executive with the US Postal Service once told one of the authors that many of the acts of violence by Postal Service employees would have been avoided if a thorough background check had been conducted. Thus, since references are a relatively cheap method of collecting information on applicants, screening out the occasional unstable applicants or, in a few cases, learning something new and important about an applicant may make reference checks a good investment. As with unweighted application blanks, using reference checks requires employers to turn elsewhere to obtain suitable information for making final decisions about applicants.

Finally, because they are difficult to quantify, we do not have validity evidence for letters of recommendation and background checks. The one exception is the credit score, as a recent study found that those with higher credit scores were more conscientious and were rated as higher performers ($r = .57$) and "good organizational citizens" ($r = .30$) by their supervisors. Although these are subjective assessments, they do suggest that credit scores as one form of background check have validity. Overall, despite a general lack of evidence, letters of recommendation and background checks likely possess some utility.[50]

## Initial Interview

The initial interview occurs very early in the initial assessment process and is often the applicant's first personal contact with the organization and its staffing system. At this point, applicants are relatively undifferentiated to the organization in terms of KSAOs. The initial interview begins the process of necessary differentiation, a sort of "rough cut."

The purpose of the initial interview is, and should be, to screen out the most obvious cases of person/job mismatches. To do this, the interview should focus on an assessment of KSAOs that are absolute requirements for the applicant. Examples of such minimum levels of qualifications for the job include certification and licensure requirements and necessary (not just preferred) training and experience requirements.

These assessments may be made from information gathered from written means (e.g., application blank or résumé) and from the interview. Care should be taken to ensure that the interviewer focuses only on this information as a basis for decision making. Evaluations of personal characteristics of the applicant (e.g., race or sex), as well as judgments about an applicant's personality (e.g., "She seems very outgoing and just right for this job"), are to be avoided. However, that may be easier said than done. One study found that applicants with facial stigmas were rated lower by interviewers, who were distracted by the stigma and recalled fewer details about the interview compared to applicants without a facial stigma.[51] Indeed, to avoid evaluations of personal characteristics, some organizations (e.g., civil service agencies) have eliminated the initial interview altogether and make the initial assessment from the written information provided by the applicant.

One of the limitations of the initial interview is that it is perhaps the most expensive method of initial assessment. One way to reduce costs dramatically is to conduct video or computer interviews, which we cover next.

### Video and Computer Interviews

With the growth of videoconferencing software, it is increasingly easy—and inexpensive—to conduct initial screening interviews from any two locations with Internet access. As long as both parties have their computers connected to the Internet, the conversation is free. Skype, which has more than 500 million registered accounts, has become a common platform for conducting computer-based initial interviews.

Larger companies often use a more customized platform to conduct initial interviews. HireVue, a Salt Lake City online video interview company, counts Dish Network, CDW, and Oracle among its customers. The advantage of providers such as HireVue, or competitors such as GreenJobInterview.com, is that they allow interviews to be securely stored, shared with others in the organization, and accompanied by ratings and comments.[52]

One of the advantages of video-based interviews is that they can dramatically lower the cost of initial interviews. This is particularly true for employers that wish to interview only a few applicants at a given location. Another advantage is that the interviews can be arranged on short notice (no travel and no schedule rearrangements). Of course, disadvantages of these interviews are that they do not permit face-to-face contact and that the quality of the video connection can, at times, be poor. The effects of these limitations on validity and applicant reactions are unknown.

Another form of video interviews takes the process a step further. Computer-based interviews utilize software that asks applicants questions (e.g., "Have you ever been terminated for stealing?") or presents realistic scenarios (e.g., an irate customer on the screen) while recording applicants' responses. These responses are forwarded to selection decision makers for use in initial screening. The software can also be configured to inform applicants about job duties and requirements. It can even track how long it takes an applicant to answer each question. Retailers are beginning to use computerized interviews on-site, where applicants walk into a store, enter a kiosk, and submit information about their work habits and experiences. As before, though, the accuracy of these high-tech interviews as compared with the old standby, the person-to-person variety, is unclear. The same holds true for how applicants will react to these relatively impersonal methods.

### Evaluation of Initial Interview

Whether high-tech or traditional, the interview has benefits and limitations. Nearly all of the research evaluating the interview in selection has considered it a substantive method (see "Structured Interview" in Chapter 9). Thus, there is little evidence about the usefulness of the initial interview. However, organizations using the initial interview in selection are likely to find it more useful by following a few guidelines:

1. Ask questions that assess the most basic KSAOs identified by job analysis. This requires separating what is required from what is preferred.
2. Stick to basic, qualifying questions suitable for making rough cuts (e.g., "Have you completed the minimum certification requirements to qualify for this job?") rather than subtle, subjective questions more suitable for substantive decisions (e.g., "How would this job fit within your overall career goals?"). Remember, the purpose of the initial interview is closer to cutting with a saw than operating with a scalpel. Ask only the most fundamental questions now, and leave the fine-tuning for later.
3. Keep interviews brief. Most interviewers make up their minds quickly, and given the limited usefulness and the type of information collected, a long interview (e.g., 45–60 minutes) is unlikely to add much over a shorter one (15–30 minutes).

4. As with all interviews, ask all of the applicants the same questions and monitor equal employment opportunity (EEO) compliance.

## Choice of Initial Assessment Methods

As described, a wide range of initial assessment methods are available to organizations to help reduce the applicant pool to bona fide candidates. A range of formats is available as well. Fortunately, with so many choices available to organizations, research results are available to help guide choices of methods to use. This research has been reviewed many times and is summarized in Exhibit 8.8. In the exhibit, each initial assessment method is rated according to several criteria. Each of these criteria will be discussed in turn.

### Use

Use refers to how frequently the surveyed organizations use each predictor. Use is probably an overused criterion in deciding which selection measures to adopt. Benchmarking—basing HR decisions on what other companies are doing—is a predominant method of decision making in all areas of HR, including staffing. However, is this a good way to make decisions about selection methods? Although it is always comforting to do what other organizations are doing, relying on information from other organizations assumes that they know what they are doing. Just because many organizations use a selection measure does not necessarily make it a good idea for a particular organization. Circumstances differ from organization to organization. In addition, at a time when many organizations are trying to differentiate themselves from their competitors, innovation in selection, rather than imitation, may be more effective in acquiring a talented workforce.

Perhaps more important, many organizational decision makers (and HR consultants) either lack knowledge about the latest findings in HR research or have decided that such findings are not applicable to their organization. It is also difficult to determine whether a successful organization that uses a particular selection method is successful because it uses this method or because of some other reason. Thus, from a research standpoint, there may be a real strategic advantage in relying on "effectiveness" criteria (e.g., validity, utility, and adverse impact) rather than worrying about the practices of other organizations.

Another reason to have a healthy degree of skepticism about the use criterion is that there is a severe lack of timely and broad surveys of selection practices (i.e., coverage of many industries and regions in the United States). The Bureau of National Affairs (BNA) has conducted broad surveys of selection practices, but the most recent was in 1988. Other surveys of selection practices are available, but they generally cover only a single selection practice (e.g., drug testing) or lack adequate scope or breadth. In providing conclusions about the use of various selection methods in organizations, we are forced to make judgment calls concerning which survey to rely on. In the case of some selection measures (e.g., application blanks),

**EXHIBIT 8.8** **Evaluation of Initial Assessment Methods**

| Predictor | Use | Cost | Reliability | Validity | Utility | Applicant Reactions | Adverse Impact |
|---|---|---|---|---|---|---|---|
| Level of education | High | Low | Moderate | Low | Low | ? | Moderate |
| Grade point average | Moderate | Low | Moderate | Moderate | ? | ? | ? |
| Quality of school | ? | Low | Moderate | Low | ? | ? | Moderate |
| Major field of study | ? | Low | Moderate | Moderate | ? | ? | ? |
| Extracurricular activity | ? | Low | Moderate | Moderate | ? | ? | ? |
| Training and experience | High | Low | High | Moderate | Moderate | ? | Moderate |
| Licensing and certification | Moderate | Low | ? | ? | ? | ? | ? |
| Weighted application blanks | Low | Moderate | Moderate | Moderate | Moderate | ? | ? |
| Biographical data | Low | High | High | High | High | Negative | Moderate |
| Letters of recommendation | Moderate | Low | ? | Low | ? | ? | ? |
| Reference check | High | Moderate | Low | Low | Moderate | Mixed | Low |
| Background check | Moderate | High | ? | ? | ? | Mixed | Moderate |
| Résumé and cover letter | Moderate | Low | Moderate | ? | ? | Moderate | ? |
| Initial interview | High | Moderate | Low | Low | ? | Positive | Moderate |

there is little reason to believe the BNA figures have changed much. With other predictors, the use figures have shown a fair degree of volatility and change from year to year. Thus, in classifying the use of assessment methods, we rely on the most recent surveys that achieve some degree of breadth. For purposes of classifying the predictors, high use refers to use by more than two-thirds of organizations, moderate is use by one-third to two-thirds of organizations, and low use refers to use by less than one-third of organizations.

Now that we have issued these caveats about the use criterion, Exhibit 8.8 reveals clear differences in the use of various methods of initial assessment. The most frequently used methods of initial assessment are education level, training and experience, reference checks, and initial interview. These methods are considered, to some degree, in selection decisions for most types of positions. Grade point average, licensing and certification requirements, letters of recommendation, background checks, and résumés and cover letters have moderate levels of use. All of these methods are widely used in filling some types of positions but infrequently used in filling many others. The least widely used initial assessment methods are weighted application blanks and biographical information. It is relatively unusual for organizations to use these methods for initial screening decisions. There are no reliable figures on the use of quality of school, major field of study, and extracurricular activity in initial selection decisions; thus, their use could not be estimated.

## Cost

Cost refers to expenses incurred in using the predictor. Although most of the initial assessment methods may seem relatively cost-free since the applicant provides the information on his or her own time, this is not entirely accurate. For most initial assessment methods, the major cost associated with each selection measure is administration. Consider an application blank. It is true that applicants complete application blanks on their own time, but someone must be present to hand out applications (or guide applicants to relevant websites), answer inquiries in person and over the phone about possible openings, and collect, sort, and forward applications to the appropriate person. Then the selection decision maker must read each application, perhaps make notes about an applicant, weed out the clearly unacceptable applicants, and then make decisions about candidates. Thus, even for the least expensive methods of initial assessment, costs associated with their use are far from trivial.

On the other hand, utility research has suggested that costs do not play a large part in evaluating the financial benefit of using particular selection methods. This becomes readily apparent when one considers the costs of hiring a poor performer. For example, a secretary who performs one standard deviation below average (16th percentile, if performance is normally distributed) may cost the organization $8,000 in lost productivity per year. This person is likely to remain on the job for more than one year, multiplying the costs. Considered in this light, spending an extra few hundred dollars to accurately identify good secretaries is an excellent investment. Thus, although costs need to be considered in evaluating assessment methods, more consideration should be given to the fact that valid selection measures pay off handsomely and will return many times their cost.

As can be seen in Exhibit 8.8, the least costly initial assessment methods include information that can be obtained from application blanks (level of education, grade point average, quality of school, major field of study, extracurricular activity, training and experience, and licensing and certification) and information provided by the applicant (letters of recommendation, résumés, and cover letters). Initial assessment methods of moderate cost include weighted application blanks, reference checks, and initial interviews. Biographical information and background checks are relatively expensive assessment methods.

## Reliability

Reliability refers to consistency of measurement. As was noted in Chapter 7, reliability is a requirement for validity, so it would be very difficult for a predictor with low reliability to have high validity. Similarly, it is unlikely that a valid predictor would have low reliability. Unfortunately, the reliability information on many initial assessment methods is lacking in the literature. However, given the frequency with which individuals distort their résumés, it is probably reasonable to infer that applicant-supplied information in application blanks and résumés is of moderate reliability. The reliability of reference checks appears to be relatively low. In terms of training and experience evaluations, while distortion can occur if the applicant supplies training and experience information, interrater agreement in evaluating this information is quite high.[53] Biographical information also generally has high reliability. The initial interview, like most unstructured interviews, probably has a relatively low level of reliability.

## Validity

Validity refers to the strength of the relationship between the predictor and job performance. Low validity ranges from about .00 to .15, moderate validity ranges from about .16 to .30, and high validity is .31 and above. As might be expected, most initial assessment methods have moderate to low validity because they are used only for making rough cuts among applicants rather than for final decisions. Perhaps the two most valid initial assessment methods are biodata and training and experience requirements; their validity can range from moderate to high.

## Utility

Utility refers to the monetary return associated with using the predictor, relative to its cost. According to researchers and decision makers, when comparing the utility of selection methods, validity appears to be the most important consideration.[54] In short, it would be very unusual for a valid selection method to have low utility. Thus, as can be seen in Exhibit 8.8, high, moderate, and low validities tend to directly correspond to high, moderate, and low utility values, respectively. Question marks predominate this column in the exhibit because relatively few studies have directly investigated the utility of these methods. However, based on the argument that validity should be directly related to utility, it is likely that high validity methods will also realize large financial benefits to organizations that choose to use them. Research does indicate that training and experience requirements have moderate (or even high) levels of utility, and reference checks have moderate levels of utility.

### Applicant Reactions

Applicant reactions refers to how favorably individuals feel about a given selection practice. Applicant reactions has been suggested as an important criterion because applicants who feel positively about selection methods and the selection process might be more inclined to join or recommend an organization, and they have more positive attitudes toward the organization once hired. Some have argued, however, that evidence suggesting that applicant reactions matter is scarce. One review concluded, "Evidence for a relationship between applicant perceptions and actual behavioral outcomes was meager and disappointing."[55]

Research suggests that whatever their centrality to the selection process, selection measures that are perceived as job related, that present applicants with an opportunity to perform, that are administered consistently, and that provide applicants with feedback about their performance are likely to generate favorable applicant reactions. Moreover, a meta-analysis of 26 studies revealed that explanations justifying the use of selection measures shape applicant perceptions of fairness of the selection process and their affective reactions to the organization.[56] Although research on applicants' reactions to specific selection procedures is lacking, evidence has been accumulating and suggests that applicants react more positively to some initial assessment methods, such as interviews, résumés, and reference checks, than to others, such as biodata or background checks.[57]

### Adverse Impact

Adverse impact refers to the possibility that a disproportionate number of protected-class members may be rejected using this predictor. Several initial assessment methods have moderate degrees of adverse impact against women and/or minorities, including level of education, quality of school, training and experience, biographical information, and the initial interview. Reference and background checks appear to have moderate adverse impact.

## LEGAL ISSUES

Initial assessment methods are subject to numerous laws, regulations, and other legal considerations. Five major matters of concern pertain to using disclaimers, conducting reference checks, conducting background (credit and criminal) checks, making preemployment inquiries, and making BFOQ claims.

# Disclaimers

During the initial stages of contact with job applicants, it is important for the organization to protect itself legally by clearly identifying rights it wants to maintain. This involves the use of disclaimers. Disclaimers are statements (usually written) that provide or confer explicit rights to the employer as part of the employment contract and that are shown to job applicants. The organization needs to decide (or reevaluate) which rights it wants to retain and how these will be communicated to job applicants.

Three areas of rights are usually suggested for possible inclusion in a disclaimer policy: (1) employment-at-will (right to terminate the employment relationship at any time, for any reason), (2) verification consent (right to verify information provided by the applicant), and (3) false statement warning (right to not hire, terminate, or discipline prospective employee for providing false information to the employer). An example of a disclaimer statement covering these three areas is shown at the bottom of the application blank in Exhibit 8.4. Disclaimer language must be clear, understandable, and conspicuous to the applicant or employee.[58]

# Reference Checks

Reference checking creates a legal quagmire for organizations. Current or former employers of the job applicant may be reluctant to provide a reference (especially one with negative information about the applicant) because they fear the applicant may file a defamation suit against them. On the other hand, failure to conduct a reference check opens up the organization to the possibility of a negligent hiring suit. To deal with such problems and obtain thorough, accurate information, the following suggestions are offered.

First, gather as much information as possible directly from the applicant, along with a verification consent. This will minimize the use of reference providers and the information demands on them.

Second, be sure to obtain written authorization from the applicant to check references. The applicant should sign a blanket consent form for this purpose. In addition, the organization could prepare a request-for-reference form that the applicant would give to the person(s) being asked to provide a reference (see Exhibit 8.7).

Third, specify the type of information being requested and obtain the information in writing. The information should be specific, factual, and job related in content; do not seek health or disability information.

Fourth, be wary of (or even prohibit) information obtained from online social networking websites; information provided about applicants by other individuals on these sites should not be treated as a reference. Questions about accuracy, job-relatedness, and confidentiality abound for such information. Also, develop a policy about whether your own employees can make recommendations about their current or former colleagues on these sites.

Fifth, limit access to reference information to those making selection decisions.

Finally, check relevant state laws about permissible and impermissible reference-check practices. Also, determine whether your organization is covered by state reference immunity laws, which provide some degree of immunity from civil liability to organizations that in good faith provide information about the job performance and professional conduct of former or current employees. Organizations in these states (currently 39) may be more willing to request and provide reference information.[59]

## Background Checks: Credit and Criminal

### Credit Checks

The first legal requirement for the organization is to comply with the federal Fair Credit Reporting Act (FCRA; see Chapter 2). The FCRA governs the gathering and use of background information on applicants and employees. Its requirements apply to both consumer reports and investigative consumer reports. Consumer reports are prepared from accessible databases by a consumer reporting agency and bear on the person's creditworthiness and standing, character, general reputation, personal information, and mode of living. Investigative consumer reports are a subset of consumer reports; they obtain information about the applicant's or employee's general reputation, character, personal characteristics, and mode of living via personal interviews with friends, neighbors, or business associates.

Before obtaining a consumer report, the organization must (1) give the applicant clear notice in writing that a report may be obtained and used in hiring or promotion procedures, and (2) obtain the applicant's written authorization to seek the report. These notification requirements do not apply to an organization conducting a third-party investigation of suspected employee misconduct. The consumer reporting agency may not furnish a consumer report to the organization unless the organization certifies to the agency that it has given the required notice and received authorization. Before taking any adverse action, such as denial of employment, based in whole or part on the report received, the organization must wait a reasonable amount of time and then provide the applicant with a copy of the report and a written description of his or her consumer rights put forth by the Consumer Financial Protection Bureau. After taking an adverse action, the organization must (1) notify (by written, oral, or electronic means) the applicant of the adverse action, (2) provide the name, address, and phone number of the consumer reporting agency to the applicant, and (3) provide notice of the applicant's right to obtain a free copy of the report from the agency and to dispute the accuracy and completeness of the report. The organization is not required to inform the applicant which information in the report led to the adverse action, but it must inform the applicant that the agency had no part in the decision.

Another legal requirement for the organization is to comply with the state and local laws that govern background checks. This should include the state/locale in which the individual being investigated resides, the reporting agency conducts business, and the requesting organization is incorporated and conducts business.[60]

Credit checking is coming under heightened legal scrutiny and likely regulation. Reasons for this include (1) credit report errors, (2) blanket usage of hiring bars for applicants with credit problems, regardless of type of job and job requirements, (3) lack of evidence supporting credit checks as a valid predictor of job performance or theft and embezzlement, and (4) possible adverse impact, especially against minorities.

Several suggestions are offered for navigating these difficult legal waters. Do credit checks only for jobs with financial and legal responsibilities, such as tellers, auditors, senior executives, and law enforcement. Be able to explain for each of these jobs exactly why a credit check is necessary, and allow applicants to explain any unfavorable credit information. Be sure to watch for the development of new credit checking laws and regulations, especially at the state level. The Illinois Employer Credit Privacy Act, for example, prohibits employers from inquiring about or using a credit history or report from applicants and employees, except for certain positions.[61] Finally, remember to comply with the provisions of the FCRA.

### Criminal Checks

Criminal background checks are generally an attempt to head off potential problems of workplace violence, theft, fraud, and negligent hiring. The collection and use of criminal history (arrest and conviction) information is governed by numerous laws and regulations. The need for these protections is the result of several factors: disparate treatment and impact against minorities (especially African Americans and Hispanics) in screening decisions based on the information, the questionable relevance and validity of criminal information for many jobs, use of blanket "no felons" hiring practices, and the inaccuracy of criminal history information in databases and elsewhere.

If the organization uses a third-party vendor to conduct criminal background checks, the vendor must comply with the requirements of the FCRA described above. The organization should carefully choose vendors whose practices are in compliance, and it should be wary of vendors that promise to provide "instant check" services, since such rapid service might well violate the FCRA.

The lines between permissible and impermissible practices differ for arrest and conviction information. It is important to keep in mind that an arrest does not establish that criminal conduct has occurred. Because of this, state and local preemployment inquiry laws and regulations generally prohibit collection and use of arrest information, as does the EEOC guidance on preemployment inquiries (discussed below). Moreover, additional EEOC guidance on arrest and conviction records says that an exclusion of an applicant with an arrest record likely violates the FCRA because it is not job related and consistent with business necessity (unless the employer can provide fact-based evidence to the contrary).

For collection and use of conviction information, a more complicated picture emerges. Since a conviction indicates criminal misconduct has occurred, the nature of the misconduct might be relevant to the applicant's suitability for the job. State and local laws often allow collection and use of conviction information if it is job related.

The EEOC enforcement guidance on arrest and conviction records has several provisions about conviction records. It warns that collection and use of conviction records could result in disparate treatment, in which case the organization must be prepared to either defend the impact as job related and consistent with business necessity or take steps to eliminate its occurrence.

For disparate impact, in particular, the guidance says there are two ways to meet this defense requirement. The first defense is providing validation evidence about the criminal history screening procedure. That evidence must be collected in accordance with the Uniform Guidelines on Employee Selection Procedures (see Chapter 9). The evidence must show that the screening procedure is predictive of important employment outcomes, such as job performance or theft.

The second defense is for the organization to have a targeted screening procedure. The procedure must consider three factors in showing how specific criminal conduct may be linked to important employment outcomes for a specific position:

1. The nature and severity of the offense or conduct
2. The time that has passed since the offense, conduct, or sentence completion
3. The nature of the job held or sought

Moreover, in the procedure, the organization must conduct an individualized assessment for those who may be rejected for the job. In that assessment, the organization should:

1. Inform the person that he or she may be rejected because of previous criminal conduct
2. Provide the person an opportunity to show why that rejection should not apply to his or her case
3. Consider whether the information provided by the individual shows that the rejection policy as applied is not job related and consistent with business necessity

If the individual does not provide the requested information, the organization may go ahead and make its hiring decision without it.

Finally, the enforcement guidelines do not preempt federal restrictions on hiring persons with convictions for certain jobs (e.g., airport security screener, law enforcement officer, child care worker, bank employee, or port worker). They also do not preempt federal occupation and licensing requirements.

States also place restrictions on criminal check usage. Pennsylvania allows refusal to hire only when the job is related to the crime. In New York, refusal to hire must take into account job responsibilities, time since the crime was committed, applicant's age at the time of the crime, and seriousness of the offense. There may also be exemptions for arrest/conviction usage. Washington, for example, exempts law enforcement agencies, state agencies, school districts, and organizations that have a direct responsibility for the supervision, care, or treatment of children, mentally ill persons, or other vulnerable adults.[62]

## Preemployment Inquiries

The term "preemployment inquiry" (PI), as used here, pertains to both content and method of assessment. Regarding content, PI refers to applicants' personal and background data. These data cover such areas as demographics (race, color, religion, sex, national origin, and age), physical characteristics (disability, height, and weight), family and associates, residence, economic status, and education. The information could be gathered by any method; most frequently, it is gathered with an initial assessment method, particularly the application blank, biodata questionnaire, or preliminary interview. At times, PIs may also occur as part of an unstructured interview.

PIs have been singled out for particular legal (equal employment opportunity and affirmative action [EEO/AA]) attention at both the federal and state levels. The reason for this is that PIs have great potential for use in a discriminatory manner early on in the selection process. Moreover, research continually finds that organizations make inappropriate and illegal PIs. One study, for example, found that out of 48 categories of application blank items, employers used an average of 5.4 inadvisable items on their application blanks for customer service jobs.[63] It is thus critical to understand the laws and regulations surrounding the use of PIs.

### Federal Laws and Regulations

The laws and their interpretation indicate that it is illegal to use PI information that has a disparate impact based on a protected characteristic (race, color, etc.), unless such disparate impact can be shown to be job related and consistent with business necessity. The emphasis here is on the potentially illegal use of the information rather than on its collection per se.

***EEOC Guide to Preemployment Inquiries.*** The EEOC guide provides the principles given above, along with specific guidance (dos and don'ts) on PIs regarding race, color, religion, sex, national origin, age, height and weight, marital status, number of children, provisions for child care, English language skill, educational requirements, friends or relatives working for the employer, arrest records, conviction records, discharge from military service, citizenship, economic status, and availability for work on weekends or holidays.

***Americans With Disabilities Act Regulations.*** There appears to be a fine line between permissible and impermissible information that may be gathered, and between appropriate and inappropriate methods for gathering it, under the Americans With Disabilities Act (ADA). To help employers, the EEOC has developed specific enforcement guidance on these matters.

The general thrust of the guidance is that the organization may not ask disability-related questions and may not conduct medical examinations until after it makes a conditional job offer to a person. Once that offer is made, however, the organization may ask disability-related questions and conduct medical examinations so long as this is done for all entering employees in the job category. When such questions or exams screen out a person with a disability, the reason for rejection must be job related and consistent with business necessity. A person who provides a direct threat of substantial harm to himself, herself, or others may be rejected for safety reasons. We will have more to say about the legality of medical examinations in the next chapter.

More specific guidance is provided for the pre-offer stage as follows. Disability-related questions cannot be asked, meaning questions that (1) inquire whether a person has a disability, (2) are likely to elicit information about a disability, or (3) are closely related to asking about a disability. Along with these general prohibitions, it is impermissible to ask applicants whether they will need reasonable accommodation to perform the functions of the job or can perform major life activities (e.g., lifting, walking), to ask about lawful use of drugs, to ask about workers' compensation history, or to ask third parties (e.g., former employers, references) questions that cannot be asked of the applicant.

Alternatively, before the offer is made, it is permissible to ask:

- Whether the applicant can perform the job, with or without reasonable accommodation
- Whether the applicant can meet the organization's attendance requirement
- Whether the applicant will need reasonable accommodation for the hiring process (unless there is an obvious disability or the applicant discloses a disability)
- The applicant to provide documentation of a disability if requesting reasonable accommodation for the hiring process
- The applicant to describe or demonstrate how he or she would perform the job (including any needed reasonable accommodation)
- The applicant for certifications and licenses
- About the applicant's current illegal use of drugs (but not past addiction)
- About the applicant's drinking habits (but not alcoholism)

### State Laws and Regulations

There is a vast cache of state laws and regulations pertaining to PIs.[64] These requirements vary substantially among the states and are often more stringent and inclusive than federal laws and regulations. The organization thus must become familiar with and adhere to the laws for each state in which it is located.

An example of Ohio state law regarding PIs is shown in Exhibit 8.9. Notice how the example points out both lawful and unlawful ways of gathering PI information.

**EXHIBIT 8.9**    **Ohio Employment Guide—Questioning Applicants**

| Inquiry | Lawful | Unlawful |
|---|---|---|
| Name | Name | Inquiry into any title that would indicate race, color, religion, sex, national origin, disability, age, or ancestry |
| Address | Inquiry into place and length of time at current address | Inquiry into any foreign addresses that would indicate national origin |
| Age | Any inquiry limited to establishing that applicant meets any minimum age requirement that may be established by law | A. Requirement of birth certificate or baptismal record<br>B. Any inquiry that would reveal the date of high school graduation<br>C. Any other inquiry that would reveal whether applicant is at least 40 years of age |
| Race, color, religion | | Any inquiry that would indicate applicant's race, color, or religion |
| Sex | | Any inquiry that would indicate the applicant's sex |
| Height and weight | Inquiries as to a person's ability to perform actual job duties and responsibilities | A requirement of a certain height or weight, unless the employer can show that no employee with the ineligible height or weight could do the work |
| Birthplace, national origin, ancestry | | A. Any inquiry into place of birth<br>B. Any inquiry into place of birth of parents, grandparents, or spouse<br>C. Any other inquiry into national origin or ancestry |
| Citizenship | A. Whether a US citizen<br>B. If not, whether applicant intends to become one<br>C. If US residence is legal<br>D. If spouse is citizen<br>E. A requirement of proof of citizenship after hire<br>F. Any other requirement mandated by the Immigration Reform and Control Act of 1986, as amended | A. Any inquiry that would indicate whether the applicant is native-born or naturalized<br>B. A requirement of proof of citizenship before hire<br>C. Any inquiry that would indicate whether the applicant's parents or spouse are native-born or naturalized |

**EXHIBIT 8.9   Continued**

| Inquiry | Lawful | Unlawful |
|---|---|---|
| Disability | Inquiries necessary to determine applicant's ability to substantially perform a specific job without significant hazard | A. Any inquiry into past or current medical conditions<br>B. Any inquiry into workers' compensation or similar claims |
| Work schedule | Inquiry into the job applicant's willingness to work a required schedule | Any inquiry into the job applicant's willingness to work any particular religious holidays |
| References | General, personal, and work references that do not reveal the race, color, religion, sex, national origin, disability, ancestry, or age of the applicant | Request for references specifically from clergy or any other persons that might reflect the race, color, religion, sex, national origin, disability, ancestry, or age of the applicant |
| Organizations | Inquiry into membership in organizations excluding those that reveal the race, color, religion, sex, national origin, disability, ancestry, or age of its members | Inquiry into every club and organization where membership is held, including those that reveal the race, color, religion, sex, national origin, disability, ancestry, or age of its members. |
| Other | Any questions required to reveal qualifications for the job for which the applicant applied | Any non-job-related inquiry that may elicit information concerning race, color, religion, sex, national origin, disability, age, or ancestry of applicant |

SOURCE: Ohio Civil Rights Commission, 2013.
NOTE: The above is not a complete definition of what can and cannot be asked of applicants. It attempts to answer the questions most frequently asked concerning the law.

## Bona Fide Occupational Qualifications

Title VII of the Civil Rights Act explicitly permits discrimination on the basis of sex, religion, or national origin (but not race or color) if it can be shown to be a BFOQ "reasonably necessary to the normal operation" of the business. The Age Discrimination in Employment Act (ADEA) contains a similar provision regarding age. These provisions thus permit outright rejection of applicants because of their sex, religion, national origin, or age, as long as the rejection can be justified under the "reasonably necessary" standard. Exactly how have BFOQ claims by employers fared? When are BFOQ claims upheld as legitimate? Several points are relevant to understanding the BFOQ issue.

The burden of proof is on the employer to justify any BFOQ claim, and it is clear that the BFOQ exception is to be narrowly construed. Thus, it does not apply to the following:[65]

- Refusing to hire women because of a presumed difference in comparative HR outcomes (e.g., women are lower performers, have higher turnover rates)
- Refusing to hire women because of personal characteristic stereotypes (e.g., women are less aggressive than men)
- Refusing to hire women because of the preferences of others (customers or fellow workers)

To amplify on the above points, an analysis of BFOQ claims involving sex reveals four types of justifications usually presented by the employer: (1) inability to perform the work, (2) personal contact with others that requires the same sex, (3) customers' preference for dealing with one sex, and (4) pregnancy or fertility protection concerns.[66]

### Inability to Perform

The general employer claim here is that one gender (usually women) is unable to perform the job due to job requirements such as lifting heavy weights, being of a minimum height, or working long hours. The employer must be able to show that the inability holds for most, if not all, members of the gender. Moreover, if it is possible to test the required abilities for each person, then that must be done rather than having a blanket exclusion from the job based on sex.

### Same-Sex Personal Contact

Due to a job requirement of close personal contact with other people, the employer may claim that employees must be the same sex as those people with whom they have contact. This claim has often been made, but not always successfully defended, for the job of prison guard. Much will depend on an analysis of just how inhospitable and dangerous the work environment is (e.g., minimum security versus maximum security prisons). Same-sex personal conflict claims have been successfully made for situations involving personal hygiene, health care, and rape victims. In short, the permissibility of these claims depends on a very specific analysis of the job requirements matrix (including the job context portion).

### Customer Preference

Organizations may argue that customers prefer members of one sex, and this preference must be honored in order to serve and maintain the continued patronage of the customer. This claim might occur, for example, for the job of salesperson in women's sportswear. Another example, involving religion, is a refusal to hire people who wear turbans or hijabs, due to a fear that customers will not want to interact with them. Usually, customer preference claims cannot be successfully defended by the employer.

### Pregnancy or Fertility

Exclusion of pregnant applicants could be a valid BFOQ claim, particularly in jobs where the risk of sudden incapacitation due to pregnancy poses threats to public safety (e.g., airline attendant). A threat to fertility of either sex generally cannot be used as a basis for sustaining a BFOQ claim. For example, an employer's fetal protection policy that excluded women from jobs involving exposure to lead in the manufacture of batteries was held to not be a permissible BFOQ.[67]

The discussion and examples here should make clear that BFOQ claims involve complex situations and considerations. The organization should remember that the burden of proof is on it to defend BFOQ claims. BFOQ provisions in the law are and continue to be construed very narrowly. The employer thus must have an overwhelming preponderance of argument and evidence on its side in order to make and successfully defend a BFOQ claim.

## SUMMARY

This chapter reviewed the processes involved in external selection and focused specifically on methods of initial assessment. Before candidates are assessed, it is important to base assessment methods on the logic of prediction and to use selection plans. The logic of prediction focuses on the requisite correspondence between elements in applicants' past situations and KSAOs critical to success on the job applied for. The selection plan involves the process of detailing the required KSAOs and indicating which selection methods will be used to assess each KSAO. The selection sequence is the means by which the selection process is used to narrow down the initial applicant pool to candidates, then finalists, and, eventually, job offer receivers.

Initial assessment methods are used during the early stages of the selection sequence to reduce the applicant pool to candidates for further assessment. The methods of initial assessment were reviewed in some detail; they include résumés and cover letters, application blanks, biographical data, letters of recommendation, reference and background checks, and initial interviews. Initial assessment methods differ widely in their usefulness. The means by which these methods can be evaluated for potential use include frequency of use, cost, reliability, validity, utility, applicant reactions, and adverse impact.

Legal issues need to be considered in making initial assessments about applicants. The use of disclaimers as a protective mechanism is critical. Also, three areas of initial assessment that require special attention are reference and background checking, PIs, and BFOQs.

## DISCUSSION QUESTIONS

1. A selection plan describes the predictor(s) that will be used to assess the KSAOs required to perform the job. What are the three steps to follow in establishing a selection plan?
2. In what ways are the following three initial assessment methods similar and in what ways are they different: application blanks, biographical information, and reference and background checks?
3. Describe the criteria by which initial assessment methods are evaluated. Are some of these criteria more important than others?
4. Some methods of initial assessment appear to be more useful than others. If you were starting your own business, which initial assessment methods would you use and why?
5. How can organizations avoid legal difficulties in the use of preemployment inquiries in initial selection decisions?

## ETHICAL ISSUES

1. Is it wrong to pad one's résumé with information that, while not an outright lie, is an enhancement? For example, would it be wrong to term one's job "maintenance coordinator" when in fact one simply emptied garbage cans?
2. Do you think employers have a right to check into applicants' backgrounds? Even if there is no suspicion of misbehavior? Even if the job poses no security or sensitivity risks? Even if the background check includes driving offenses and credit histories?

## APPLICATIONS

### Reference Reports and Initial Assessment in a Start-Up Company

Stanley Jausneister owns a small high-tech start-up company called BioServer-Systems (BSS). Stanley's company specializes in selling web server space to clients. The server space that Stanley markets runs from a network of personal computers. This networked configuration allows BSS to manage its server space more efficiently and provides greater flexibility to its customers, who often want weekly or even daily updates of their websites. The other innovation Stanley brought to BSS is special security encryption software protocols that make the BSS server space nearly impossible for hackers to access. This flexibility is particularly attractive to organizations that need to manage large, security-protected databases with multiple points of access. Stanley has even been contacted by the government, which is interested in using BSS's systems for some of its classified intelligence.

Due to its niche, BSS has experienced rapid growth. In the past year, BSS hired 12 programmers and 2 marketers, as well as a general manager, an HR manager, and other support personnel. Before starting BSS, Stanley was a manager with a large pharmaceutical firm. Because of his industry connections, most of BSS's business has been with drug and chemical companies.

Yesterday, Stanley received a phone call from Lee Rogers, head of biotechnology for Mercelle-Poulet, one of BSS's largest customers. Lee is an old friend, and he was one of BSS's first customers. Lee had called to express concern about BSS's security. One area of Mercelle-Poulet's biotech division is responsible for research and development on vaccines for various bioterrorist weapons such as anthrax and the plague. Because the research and development on these vaccines require the company to develop cultures of the biological weapons themselves, Lee has used BSS to house information for this area. A great deal of sensitive information is housed on BSS's servers, including in some cases the formulas used in developing the cultures.

Despite the sensitivity of the information on BSS's servers, given BSS's advanced software, Stanley was very surprised to hear Lee's concern about security. "It's not your software that worries me," Lee commented, "it's the people running it." Lee explained that last week a Mercelle-Poulet researcher was arrested for attempting to sell certain cultures to an overseas client. This individual had been dismissed from a previous pharmaceutical company for unethical behavior, but this information did not surface during the individual's background check. This incident not only caused Lee to reexamine Mercelle-Poulet's background checks, but also made him think of BSS, as certain BSS employees have access to Mercelle-Poulet's information.

Instantly after hearing Lee's concern, Stanley realized he had a problem. Like many small employers, BSS did not do thorough background checks on its employees. It assumed that the information provided on the application was accurate and generally only called the applicant's previous employer (often with ineffective results). Stanley realized he needed to do more, not only to keep Lee's business but also to protect his company and customers.

1. What sort of background testing should BSS conduct on its applicants?
2. Is there any information BSS should avoid obtaining for legal or EEO reasons?

3. How can BSS know that its background testing programs are effective?

4. In the past, BSS has used the following initial assessment methods: application blank, interviews with Stanley and other BSS managers, and a follow-up with the applicant's former employer. Beyond changes to its background testing program, would you suggest any other alterations to BSS's initial assessment process?

## Developing a Lawful Application Blank

Consolidated Trucking Corporation, Inc. (CTCI) is a rapidly growing short-haul (local) firm within the greater Columbus, Ohio, area. It has grown primarily through the acquisitions of numerous small, family-owned trucking companies. Currently it has a fleet of 150 trucks and over 250 full-time drivers. Most of the drivers were hired initially by the firms that CTCI acquired, and they accepted generous offers to become members of the CTCI team. CTCI's expansion plans are very ambitious, but they will be fulfilled primarily from internal growth rather than additional acquisitions. Consequently, CTCI is now faced with the need to develop an external staffing system that will be geared up to hire 75 new truckers within the next two years.

Terry Tailgater is a former truck driver for CTCI who was promoted to truck maintenance supervisor, a position he has held for the past five years. Once CTCI's internal expansion plans were finalized, the firm's HR director (and sole member of the HR department), Harold Hornblower, decided he needed a new person to handle staffing and employment law duties. Harold promoted Terry Tailgater to the job of staffing manager. One of Terry's major assignments was to develop a new staffing system for truck drivers.

One of the first projects Terry undertook was to develop a new, standardized application blank for the job of truck driver. To do this, Terry looked at the many different application blanks the current drivers had completed for their former companies. (These records were given to CTCI at the time of acquisition.) The application blanks showed that a large amount of information was requested and that the specific information sought varied among the application forms. Terry scanned the various forms and made a list of all the questions the forms contained. He then decided to evaluate each question in terms of its probable lawfulness under federal and state (Ohio) laws. Terry wanted to identify and use only lawful questions on the new form he is developing.

Following is the list of questions Terry developed, along with columns labeled "probably lawful" and "probably unlawful." Assume that you are Terry and are deciding on the lawfulness of each question. Place a check mark in the appropriate column for each question and prepare a justification for its mark as "probably lawful" or "probably unlawful."

| Questions Terry Is Considering Including on Application Blank | | |
| --- | --- | --- |
| **Question About** | **Probably Lawful** | **Probably Unlawful** |
| Birthplace | ___ | ___ |
| Previous arrests | ___ | ___ |
| Previous felony convictions | ___ | ___ |
| Distance between work and residence | ___ | ___ |
| Domestic responsibilities | ___ | ___ |
| Height | ___ | ___ |
| Weight | ___ | ___ |
| Previous work experience | ___ | ___ |
| Educational attainment | ___ | ___ |
| Favorite high school subjects | ___ | ___ |
| Grade point average | ___ | ___ |
| Received workers' compensation in past | ___ | ___ |
| Currently receiving workers' compensation | ___ | ___ |
| Child care arrangements | ___ | ___ |
| Length of time on previous job | ___ | ___ |
| Reason for leaving previous job | ___ | ___ |
| Age | ___ | ___ |
| Sex | ___ | ___ |
| Home ownership | ___ | ___ |
| Any current medical problems | ___ | ___ |
| History of mental illness | ___ | ___ |
| OK to seek references from previous employer? | ___ | ___ |
| Have you provided complete/truthful information? | ___ | ___ |
| Native language | ___ | ___ |
| Willing to work on Easter and Christmas | ___ | ___ |
| Get recommendation from pastor/priest | ___ | ___ |

## ENDNOTES

1. J. W. Smither, R. R. Reilly, R. E. Millsap, K. Pearlman, and R. W. Stoffey, "Applicant Reactions to Selection Procedures," *Personnel Psychology*, 1993, 46, pp. 49–76.
2. P. F. Wernimont and J. P. Campbell, "Signs, Samples, and Criteria," *Journal of Applied Psychology*, 1968, 52, pp. 372–376.
3. State of Wisconsin, Chapter 134, *Evaluating Job Content for Selection*, Undated.

4. State of Wisconsin, *Evaluating Job Content for Selection*.

5. M. Singletary, "Beefing Up a Resume," *Washington Post*, Aug. 1, 2013 (*http://articles.washington post.com/2013-08-01/business/40936834_1_social-media-careerbuilder-job-market*).

6. V. Luckerson, "Finding a Job in 2012: Real-Life Success Stories," *Time*, June 21, 2012 (*http://business.time.com/2012/06/21/finding-a-job-in-2012-real-life-success-stories/*).

7. A. Ellin, "Lights! Camera! It's Time to Make a Résumé," *New York Times*, Apr. 21, 2007, pp. B1, B6; K. Gurchiek, "Video Résumé Use Rises, but So Do Big Questions," *SHRM Online*, Apr. 12, 2007, pp. 1–2; M. J. de la Merced, "Student's Video Résumé Gets Attention (Some of It Unwanted)," *New York Times*, Oct. 21, 2006, pp. B1, B6.

8. B. Horovitz, "Tweet for This Job—and It Could Be Yours; Resumes? No Need Apply for Some Firms," *USA Today*, Feb. 18, 2013, p. 3A.

9. R. Strauss, "When the Résumé Is Not to Be Believed," *New York Times*, Sept. 12, 2006, p. 2; K. J. Winstein and D. Golden, "MIT Admissions Dean Lies on Résumé in 1979, Quits," *New York Times*, Apr. 27, 2007, pp. B1, B2; M. Villano, "Served as King of England, Said the Résumé," *New York Times*, Mar. 19, 2006, p. BU9.

10. "Resume Fraud," *Gainesville Sun*, Mar. 5, 2006, pp. 5G, 6G.

11. "Getting Jail Time for This Resume Lie?" *Netscape Careers & Jobs*, Mar. 18, 2004 (*www.channels.netscape.com/ns/careers*); "Lying on Your Resume," *Netscape Careers & Jobs*, Mar. 18, 2004 (*www.channels.netscape.com/ns/careers*); K. Maher, "The Jungle," *Wall Street Journal*, May 6, 2003, p. B5; E. Stanton, "If a Résumé Lies, Truth Can Loom Large," *Wall Street Journal*, Dec. 29, 2002, p. B48; T. Weir, "Colleges Give Coaches' Résumés Closer Look," *USA Today*, May 28, 2002, p. C1.

12. "Survey Finds a Single Resume Typo Can Ruin Job Prospects," *IPMA-HR Bulletin*, Sept. 15, 2006, p. 1; C. Soltis, "Eagle-Eyed Employers Scour Résumés for Little White Lies," *Wall Street Journal*, Mar. 21, 2006, p. B7; D. Mattioli, "Standing Out in a Sea of CVs," *Wall Street Journal*, Jan. 16, 2007, p. B8; D. Mattioli, "Hard Sell on 'Soft' Skills Can Primp a Resume," *Wall Street Journal*, May 15, 2007, p. B6.

13. N. R. Kuncel, M. Credé, and L. L. Thomas, "The Validity of Self-Reported Grade Point Averages, Class Ranks, and Test Scores: A Meta-Analysis and Review of the Literature," *Review of Educational Research*, 2005, 75, pp. 63–82; E. Derous, A. M. Ryan, and H. D. Nguyen, "Multiple Categorization in Resume Screening: Examining Effects on Hiring Discrimination Against Arab Applicants in Field and Lab Settings," *Journal of Organizational Behavior*, 2012, 33, pp. 544–570.

14. A. Howard, "College Experiences and Managerial Performance," *Journal of Applied Psychology*, 1986, 71, pp. 530–552; R. Merritt-Halston and K. N. Wexley, "Educational Requirements: Legality and Validity," *Personnel Psychology*, 1983, 36, pp. 743–753.

15. C. Murray, *Real Education: Four Simple Truths for Bringing America's Schools Back to Reality* (New York: Crown Forum, 2008); T.W.H. Ng and D. C. Feldman, "How Broadly Does Education Contribute to Job Performance?" *Personnel Psychology*, 2009, 62, pp. 89–134.

16. W. J. Bennett and D. Wilezol, *Is College Worth It? A Former United States Secretary of Education and a Liberal Arts Graduate Expose the Broken Promise of Higher Education* (Nashville, TN: Thomas Nelson, 2013); D. Matthews, "Going to College Is Worth It—Even if You Drop Out," *Washington Post,* June 10, 2013 (*www.washingtonpost.com/blogs/wonkblog/wp/2013/06/10/going-to-college-is-worth-it-even-if-you-drop-out/*); A. Williams, "Saying No to College," *New York Times*, Nov. 30, 2012 (*www.nytimes.com/2012/12/02/fashion/saying-no-to-college.html?pagewanted=all&_r=0*), accessed 8/9/2013.

17. A. E. McKinney, K. D. Carlson, R. L. Meachum, N. C. D'Angelo, and M. L. Connerley, "Recruiters' Use of GPA in Initial Screening Decisions: Higher GPAs Don't Always Make the

Cut," *Personnel Psychology*, 2003, 56, pp. 823–845; P. L. Roth, C. A. BeVier, F. S. Switzer, and J. S. Schippman, "Meta-Analyzing the Relationship Between Grades and Job Performance," *Journal of Applied Psychology*, 1996, 81, pp. 548–556; P. L. Roth and P. Bobko, "College Grade Point Average as a Personnel Selection Device: Ethnic Group Differences and Potential Adverse Impact," *Journal of Applied Psychology*, 2000, 85, pp. 399–406.

18. F. P. Morgeson and J. D. Nahrgang, "Same as It Ever Was: Recognizing Stability in the *Business-Week* Rankings," *Academy of Management Learning & Education*, 2008, 7, pp. 26–41.

19. S. Jaschik, "The B-School Hierarchy," *New York Times*, Apr. 25, 2004, pp. 36–40; J. Merritt, "What's an MBA Really Worth?" *BusinessWeek*, Sept. 22, 2003, pp. 90–102; J. Pfeffer and C. T. Fong, "The End of Business Schools? Less Success Than Meets the Eye," *Academy of Management Learning & Education*, 2002, 1(1), pp. 78–95.

20. R. S. Robin, W. H. Bommer, and T. T. Baldwin, "Using Extracurricular Activity as an Indicator of Interpersonal Skill: Prudent Evaluation or Recruiting Malpractice?" *Human Resource Management*, 2002, 41(4), pp. 441–454.

21. R. A. Ash, "A Comparative Study of Behavioral Consistency and Holistic Judgment Methods of Job Applicant Training and Work Experience Evaluation," *Public Personnel Management*, 1984, 13, pp. 157–172; M. A. McDaniel, F. L. Schmidt, and J. E. Hunter, "A Meta-Analysis of the Validity of Methods for Rating Training and Experience in Personnel Selection," *Personnel Psychology*, 1988, 41, pp. 283–314; R. Tomsho, "Busy Surgeons Are Good for Patients," *Wall Street Journal*, Nov. 28, 2003, p. B3.

22. M. R. Raymond, S. Neustel, and D. Anderson, "Retest Effects on Identical and Parallel Forms in Certification and Licensure Testing," *Personnel Psychology*, 2007, 60, pp. 367–396; J. D. Opdyke, "'Wait, Let Me Call My ChFC,'" *Wall Street Journal*, Jan. 28, 2006, pp. B1, B3; J. McKillip and J. Owens, "Voluntary Professional Certifications: Requirements and Validation Activities," *The Industrial-Organizational Psychologist*, July 2000, pp. 50–57.

23. G. W. England, *Development and Use of Weighted Application Blanks* (Dubuque, IA: William C. Brown, 1961).

24. J. E. Hunter and R. F. Hunter, "Validity and Utility of Alternative Predictors of Job Performance," *Psychological Bulletin*, 1984, 96, pp. 72–98.

25. I. L. Goldstein, "The Application Blank: How Honest Are the Responses?" *Journal of Applied Psychology*, 1974, 59, pp. 491–494.

26. G. W. England, *Development and Use of Weighted Application Blanks*, rev. ed. (Minneapolis: University of Minnesota Industrial Relations Center, 1971).

27. C. J. Russell, J. Mattson, S. E. Devlin, and D. Atwater, "Predictive Validity of Biodata Items Generated From Retrospective Life Experience Essays," *Journal of Applied Psychology*, 1990, 75, pp. 569–580.

28. F. A. Mael, "A Conceptual Rationale for the Domain and Attributes of Biodata Items," *Personnel Psychology*, 1991, 44, pp. 763–792.

29. S. Hansell, "Google Answer to Filling Jobs Is an Algorithm," *New York Times*, Jan. 3, 2007, pp. A1, C9.

30. J. S. Breaugh, "The Use of Biodata for Employee Selection: Past Research and Future Directions," *Human Resource Management Review*, 2009, 19, pp. 219–231; C. M. Harold, L. A. McFarland, and J. A. Weekley, "The Validity of Verifiable and Non-verifiable Biodata Items: An Examination Across Applicants and Incumbents," *International Journal of Selection and Assessment*, 2006, 14, pp. 336–346.

31. J. E. Hunter and R. F. Hunter, "Validity and Utility of Alternative Predictors of Job Performance"; R. R. Reilly and G. T. Chao, "Validity and Fairness of Some Alternative Selection Procedures," *Personnel Psychology*, 1982, 35, pp. 1–62.

32. J. B. Becton, M. C. Matthews, D. L. Hartley, and D. H. Whitaker, "Using Biodata to Predict Turnover, Organizational Commitment, and Job Performance in Healthcare," *International Journal of Selection and Assessment*, 2009, 17, pp. 189–202; N. Schmitt, J. Keeney, F. L. Oswald, T. J. Pleskac, A. Q. Billington, R. Sinha, and M. Zorzie, "Prediction of 4-Year College Student Performance Using Cognitive and Noncognitive Predictors and the Impact on Demographic Status of Admitted Students," *Journal of Applied Psychology*, 2009, 94, pp. 1479–1497.

33. K. D. Carlson, S. Sculten, F. L. Schmidt, H. Rothstein, and F. Erwin, "Generalizable Biographical Data Validity Can Be Achieved Without Multi-Organizational Development and Keying," *Personnel Psychology*, 1999, 52, pp. 731–755; Breaugh, "The Use of Biodata for Employee Selection: Past Research and Future Directions."

34. N. Schmitt, F. L. Oswald, B. H. Kim, M. A. Gillespie, L. J. Ramsay, and T. Yoo, "Impact of Elaboration on Socially Desirable Responding and the Validity of Biodata Measures," *Journal of Applied Psychology*, 2003, 88, pp. 979–988; J. Levashina, F. P. Morgeson, and M. A. Campion, "Tell Me Some More: Exploring How Verbal Ability and Item Verifiability Influence Responses to Biodata Questions in a High-Stakes Selection Context," *Personnel Psychology*, 2012, 65, pp. 359–383.

35. N. Anderson, J. F. Salgado, and U. R. Hülsheger, "Applicant Reactions in Selection: Comprehensive Meta-Analysis Into Reaction Generalization Versus Situational Specificity," *International Journal of Selection and Assessment*, 2010, 18, pp. 291–304; A. Furnham, "HR Professionals' Beliefs About, and Knowledge of, Assessment Techniques and Psychometric Tests," *International Journal of Selection and Assessment*, 2008, 16, pp. 300–305; J. M. Cucina, P. M. Caputo, H. F. Thibodeaux, and C. N. MaClane, "Unlocking the Key to Biodata Scoring: A Comparison of Empirical, Rational, and Hybrid Approaches at Different Sample Sizes," *Personnel Psychology*, 2012, 65, pp. 385–428.

36. J. C. Baxter, B. Brock, P. C. Hill, and R. M. Rozelle, "Letters of Recommendation: A Question of Value," *Journal of Applied Psychology*, 1981, 66, pp. 296–301.

37. T. A. Judge and C. A. Higgins, "Affective Disposition and the Letter of Reference," *Organizational Behavior and Human Decision Processes*, 1998, 75, pp. 207–221.

38. L. Everitt, "Why MBAs Are Writing Their Own Recommendation Letters," *Fortune*, July 15, 2013 (*http://management.fortune.cnn.com/2013/07/15/mba-recommendation-letters/*), accessed 8/9/2013.

39. M. E. Burke, "2004 Reference Check and Background Testing," *Society for Human Resource Management*, 2005; P. J. Taylor, K. Pajo, G. W. Cheung, and P. Stringfield, "Dimensionality and Validity of a Structured Telephone Reference Check Procedure," *Personnel Psychology*, 2004, 57, pp. 745–772.

40. J. Click, "SJRM Survey Highlights Dilemmas of Reference Checks," *HR News*, July 1995, p. 13.

41. A. Athavaley, "Job References You Can't Control," *Wall Street Journal*, Sept. 27, 2007, pp. D1, D2.

42. Taylor et al., "Dimensionality and Validity of a Structured Telephone Reference Check Procedure."

43. S. Hananel, "Some Job-Screening Tactics Challenged as Illegal," *MSNBC*, Oct. 12, 2010 (*www.msnbc.msn.com/id/38664839*), accessed 1/28/11.

44. A. Zimmerman, "Wal-Mart to Probe Job Applicants," *Wall Street Journal*, Aug. 12, 2004, pp. A3, B6.

45. H. Drummond, *The Dynamics of Organizational Collapse: The Case of Barings Bank* (London: Routledge, 2007).

46. "Employers Increase Use of Background Checks," *USA Today*, Apr. 26, 2007, p. 1B; T. Minton-Eversole, "More Background Screening Yields More 'Red Tape,'" *SHRM News*, July 2007, pp. 1–5.

47. K. Maher, "The Jungle," *Wall Street Journal*, Jan. 20, 2004, p. B8; A. Zimmerman and K. Stringer, "As Background Checks Proliferate, Ex-Cons Face Jobs Lock," *Wall Street Journal*, Aug. 26, 2004, pp. B1, B3.

48. L. Schwarz, "Baseball and Umpires Clash Over Background Checks," *New York Times*, Aug. 7, 2007, p. C15.

49. A. Levin, "Unions: Safety Bar Set Lower for Cargo Planes," *USA Today*, Nov. 5, 2010, p. 1A.

50. J. B. Bernerth, S. G. Taylor, H. J. Walker, and D. S. Whitman, "An Empirical Investigation of Dispositional Antecedents and Performance-Related Outcomes of Credit Scores," *Journal of Applied Psychology*, 2012, 97, pp. 469–478.

51. J. M. Madera and M. R. Hebl, "Discrimination Against Facially Stigmatized Applicants in Interviews: An Eye-Tracking and Face-to-Face Investigation," *Journal of Applied Psychology*, 2012, 97, pp. 317–330.

52. M. Harding, "Companies Turning to Web Conferencing for Employment Interviews," *Pittsburgh Tribune Review*, Apr. 20, 2010, p. 1.

53. R. A. Ash and E. L. Levine, "Job Applicant Training and Work Experience Evaluation: An Empirical Comparison of Four Methods," *Journal of Applied Psychology*, 1985, 70, pp. 572–576.

54. G. P. Latham and G. Whyte, "The Futility of Utility Analysis," *Personnel Psychology*, 1994, 47, pp. 31–46.

55. P. R. Sackett and F. Lievens, "Personnel Selection," *Annual Review of Psychology*, 2008, 59, pp. 419–450; U. R. Hülsheger and N. Anderson, "Applicant Perspectives in Selection: Going Beyond Preference Reactions," *International Journal of Selection and Assessment*, 2009, 17, pp. 335–345; F. P. Morgeson and A. M. Ryan, "Reacting to Applicant Perspectives Research: What's Next?" *International Journal of Selection and Assessment*, 2009, 17, pp. 431–437.

56. J. P. Hausknecht, D. V. Day, and S. C. Thomas, "Applicant Reactions to Selection Procedures: An Updated Model and Meta-Analysis," *Personnel Psychology*, 2004, 57, pp. 639–683; D. M. Truxillo, T. E. Bodner, M. Bertolino, T. N. Bauer, and C. A. Yonce, "Effects of Explanations on Applicant Reactions: A Meta-Analytic Review," *International Journal of Selection and Assessment*, 2009, 17, pp. 346–361.

57. Anderson, Salgado, and Hülsheger, "Applicant Reactions in Selection: Comprehensive Meta-Analysis Into Reaction Generalization Versus Situational Specificity."

58. G. P. Panaro, *Employment Law Manual*, 2nd ed. (Boston: Warren Gorham Lamont, 1993), pp. 1-29 to 1-42; M. G. Danaher, "Handbook Disclaimer Dissected," *HR Magazine*, Feb. 2007, p. 116; D. J. Walsh, *Employment Law for Human Resource Practice*, 4th ed. (Mason, OH: South-Western, Cengage Learning, 2012), pp. 634–636.

59. J. E. Bahls, "Available Upon Request," *HR Magazine Focus*, Jan. 1999, p. 206; Panaro, *Employment Law Manual*, pp. 2-101 to 2-106; M. E. Burke and L. A. Weatherly, *Getting to Know the Candidate: Providing Reference Checks* (Alexandria, VA: Society for Human Resource Management, 2005); S. Z. Hable, "The Trouble With Online References," *Workforce Management Online*, Feb. 2010 (*www.workforce.com/articles/the-trouble-with-online-references*), accessed 6/22/10; L. S. Rosen, *The Safe Hiring Manual*, 2nd ed. (Tempe, AZ: 13RP Publications, 2012), pp. 173–192.

60. T. B. Stivarius, J. Skonberg, R. Fliegel, R. Blumberg, R. Jones, and K. Mones, "Background Checks: Four Steps to Basic Compliance in a Multistate Environment," *Legal Report*, Society for Human Resource Management, Mar.–Apr. 2003.

61. K. McNamera, "Bad Credit Derails Job Search," *Wall Street Journal*, Mar. 16, 2010, p. D6; R. Maurer, "Federal Lawmakers, Enforcers Set Sights on Background Screening," Society for Human Resource Management, March 9, 2010 (*www.shrm.org/LegalIssues/FederalResources/Pages/BackgroundScreening.aspx*); Employment Screening Resources, *ESR Newsletter and Legal Update*, Oct. 2009, pp. 1–2; Employment Screening Resources, *ESR Newsletter and Legal Update*, Aug. 2010, pp. 1–2.

62. F. Hansen, "Burden of Proof," *Workforce Management*, Feb. 2010, pp. 27–33; F. Hansen, "Blaming Clients in Background Check Lawsuits," *Workforce Management*, July 2010, pp. 8–9; J. Greenwald, "Ex-Convicts in Workforce Pose Liability Problems," *Workforce Management Online*, Sept. 13, 2009 (*www.businessinsurance.com/article/20090913/ISSUE01/309139995#*), accessed 3/12/10.

63. J. C. Wallace and S. J. Vadanovich, "Personal Application Blanks: Persistence and Knowledge of Legally Inadvisable Application Blank Items," *Public Personnel Management*, 2004, 33, pp. 331–349.

64. Bureau of National Affairs, *Fair Employment Practices* (Washington, DC: author, periodically updated), 454: whole section.

65. Bureau of National Affairs, *Fair Employment Practices*, sec. 421:352–356.

66. N. J. Sedmak and M. D. Levin-Epstein, *Primer on Equal Employment Opportunity* (Washington, DC: Bureau of National Affairs, 1991), pp. 36–40.

67. Bureau of National Affairs, *Fair Employment Practices,* sec. 405:6941–6943.

# CHAPTER NINE

## External Selection II

## LEARNING OBJECTIVES AND INTRODUCTION

### Learning Objectives

- Distinguish among initial, substantive, and contingent selection
- Review the advantages and disadvantages of personality and cognitive ability tests
- Compare and contrast work sample and situational judgment tests
- Understand the advantages of structured interviews and how interviews can be structured
- Review the logic behind contingent assessment methods and how they are administrated
- Understand the ways in which substantive and contingent assessment methods are subject to various legal rules and restrictions

### Introduction

The previous chapter reviewed preliminary issues surrounding external staffing decisions made in organizations, including the use of initial assessment methods. This chapter continues the discussion of external selection by discussing in some detail substantive assessment methods. The use of discretionary and contingent assessment methods, collection of assessment data, and legal issues will also be considered. In a real sense, substantive and contingent assessment are the heart of staffing decisions. This is because substantive and contingent selection are the highlight of actual hiring decisions. Done well, the stage is set for effective organizational staffing. Done poorly, it is difficult, if not impossible, to staff successfully.

Whereas initial assessment methods are used to reduce the applicant pool to candidates, substantive assessment methods are used to reduce the candidate pool to finalists for the job. Thus, the use of substantive methods is often more involved than the use of initial methods. Numerous substantive assessment methods will be discussed in depth, including various tests (personality, ability, emotional intelligence, performance/work samples, situational judgment, and integrity); interest, values, and preference inventories; structured interviews; and assessment for team environments. The average validity (i.e., $\bar{r}_{xy}$) of each method and the criteria used to choose among methods will be reviewed.

Discretionary assessment methods are used in some circumstances to separate those who receive job offers from the list of finalists. The applicant characteristics that are assessed when using discretionary methods are sometimes very subjective. Several of the characteristics most commonly assessed by discretionary methods will be reviewed.

Contingent assessment methods are used to make sure that tentative offer recipients meet certain qualifications for the job. Although any assessment method can be used as a contingent method (e.g., licensing/certification requirements, background checks), drug tests and medical exams are perhaps the two most common methods. These procedures will be reviewed.

All forms of assessment decisions require the collection of assessment data. The procedures used to make sure this process is properly conducted will be reviewed. In particular, several issues will be discussed, including support services, training requirements in using various predictors, maintaining security and confidentiality, and the importance of standardized procedures.

Finally, many important legal issues surround the use of substantive, discretionary, and contingent methods of selection. The most important of these issues will be reviewed. Particular attention will be given to the Uniform Guidelines on Employee Selection Procedures (UGESP) and staffing requirements under the Americans With Disabilities Act (ADA).

## SUBSTANTIVE ASSESSMENT METHODS

Organizations use initial assessment methods to make rough cuts among applicants, weeding out the obviously unqualified. Conversely, substantive assessment methods are used to make more precise decisions about applicants. Generally speaking, these methods are used to answer the following question: Among those who meet the minimum qualifications for the job, who are the most likely to be high performers if hired? In other words, these methods are used to predict which applicants, if hired, will be the best performers. For that reason, the validity of substantive assessment methods is critical. Moreover, because substantive methods are used to make fine distinctions among applicants, the nature of their use is somewhat more involved than that of initial assessment methods. Like initial assessment methods, substantive assessment methods are developed using the logic of prediction outlined in Exhibit 8.1 and the selection plan shown in Exhibit 8.2. Predictors typically used to select finalists from the candidate pool include personality tests; ability tests; emotional intelligence tests; performance tests and work samples; situational judgment tests; integrity tests; interest, values, and preference inventories; structured interviews; and team assessments. Each of these predictors is described next in some detail.

### Personality Tests

At one time, personality tests were not perceived as a valid selection method.[1] Today, however, most researchers reach much more positive conclusions about the role of personality tests in predicting job performance.[2] Mainly, this is due to the widespread acceptance of a major taxonomy of personality, often called the Big Five. The Big Five are used to describe behavioral (as opposed to emotional or cognitive) traits that may capture up to 75% of an individual's personality.

The Big Five factors are *extraversion* (tendency to be sociable, assertive, active, upbeat, and talkative), *agreeableness* (tendency to be altruistic, trusting, sympathetic, and cooperative), *conscientiousness* (tendency to be purposeful, determined, dependable, and attentive to detail), *emotional stability* (tendency to be calm, optimistic, and well adjusted), and *openness to experience* (tendency to be imaginative, attentive to inner feelings, intellectually curious, and independent). The Big Five are very stable over time, and evidence suggests that roughly 50% of the variance in the Big Five traits appears to be inherited.[3]

## Measures of Personality

Although personality can be measured in many ways, for personnel selection, the most common measures are self-report surveys. Several survey measures of the Big Five traits are used in selection. The *International Personality Item Pool* (IPIP), which can be found online and used freely, contains several Big Five measures. Exhibit 9.1 provides sample items from the IPIP. The *Personal Characteristics Inventory* (PCI) is a self-report measure of the Big Five that asks applicants to report their agreement or disagreement (using a "strongly disagree" to "strongly agree" scale) with 150 sentences.[4] The measure takes about 30 minutes to complete and has a fifth- to sixth-grade reading level. Another commonly used measure of the Big Five is the *NEO Personality Inventory* (NEO), of which there are several versions that have been translated into numerous languages.[5] A third alternative is the *Hogan Personality Inventory* (HPI), which is also based on the Big Five typology. Responses to the HPI can be scored to yield measures of employee reliability and service orientation.[6] All of these measures have shown validity in predicting job performance in various occupations.

Traditionally, personality tests were administered to applicants on-site, with a paper-and-pencil survey. Nowadays, many surveys are administered online, which is cheaper for the organization and more convenient for the applicant. However, because most online testing is unmonitored, there are three potential problems: (1) test security might be compromised (e.g., test items posted on a blog), (2) applicants may find it easier to cheat or be more motivated to cheat online, and (3) applicants may not tolerate long online personality tests. There are no silver bullet remedies to these problems. Because each of these problems is less of an issue with paper-and-pencil tests, organizations may be well advised to use that format where feasible. That being said, even when these problems are avoided with a paper-and-pencil test, online reporting of items can still be an issue. For example, the Internet is rife with posts and blogs about Wal-Mart's preemployment test, which includes personality questions. Some posts include the items themselves, whereas others provide tips on how to "game" the test. Thus, even when companies attempt to keep their personality inventories as private as possible, word often leaks out.[7]

Where traditional paper-and-pencil personality testing is infeasible, several steps can be taken to ameliorate the problems with online testing. First, experts

---

**EXHIBIT 9.1    Sample Items Measuring Big Five Personality Dimensions**

*Please rate how accurately each statement describes you on a scale from 1="to no extent" to 5="to a very great extent."*

**Extraversion**

Am quiet around strangers. (reverse-scored)

Take charge.

Am skilled in handling social situations.

**Agreeableness**

Have a soft heart.

Insult people. (reverse-scored)

Have a good word for everyone.

**Conscientiousness**

Am always prepared.

Pay attention to details.

Am exacting in my work.

**Emotional Stability**

Am relaxed most of the time.

Seldom feel blue.

Have frequent mood swings. (reverse-scored)

**Openness to Experience**

Have a vivid imagination.

Love to think up new ways of doing things.

Try to avoid complex people. (reverse-scored)

Source: *International Personality Item Pool (ipip.ori.org).*

recommend keeping online personality tests as brief as possible. If the test takes more than 20 minutes, applicants may grow impatient. Second, it is important to assign applicants identification codes, to collect basic background data, and to break the test into sections. These steps increase accountability (lessening the odds of faking) and ensure that if the applicant loses the Internet connection while taking the test, the portions completed will not be lost. Third, strategies (which we discuss shortly) designed to reduce faking by applicants should be implemented. These steps are especially important for online testing. Finally, many experts recommend the use of "item banking" (variation in specific items used to measure each trait) to enhance test security; to further reduce faking, inform test takers that their online scores will be verified with a paper-and-pencil test should they advance in the selection process.[8]

## Evaluation of Personality Tests

Many comprehensive reviews of the validity of personality tests have been published. Nearly all of the recent reviews focus on the validity of the Big Five.[9] Although there are some inconsistencies across reviews, the results can be summarized in Exhibit 9.2. As the exhibit shows, each of the Big Five traits has advantages and disadvantages. However, the traits differ in the degree to which they are a mixed blessing. Specifically, whereas the disadvantages of agreeableness and openness appear to offset their advantages, the advantages of conscientiousness, emotional stability, and, to some degree, extraversion outweigh the disadvantages. These three traits also happen to have the strongest correlates with overall job performance. Conscientiousness and emotional stability, in particular, appear to be useful across a wide range of jobs. Thus, in general, the personality traits of

**EXHIBIT 9.2   Implications of Big Five Personality Traits at Work**

| Big Five Trait | Advantages | Disadvantages |
|---|---|---|
| Conscientiousness | • Better overall job performers<br>• Higher levels of job satisfaction<br>• More likely to emerge as leaders<br>• Fewer "deviant" work behaviors<br>• Higher retention (lower turnover) | • Lower adaptability |
| Emotional stability | • Better overall job performers<br>• Higher levels of job satisfaction<br>• More effective leaders<br>• Higher retention (lower turnover) | • Less able to identify threats<br>• More likely to engage in high-risk behaviors |
| Extraversion | • Perform better in sales<br>• More likely to emerge as leaders<br>• Higher levels of job satisfaction | • Higher absenteeism<br>• More accidents |
| Agreeableness | • More valued as team members<br>• More "helping" behaviors<br>• Fewer "deviant" work behaviors | • Lower career success<br>• Less able to cope with conflict<br>• Give more lenient ratings |
| Openness | • Higher creativity<br>• More effective leaders<br>• More adaptable | • Less committed to employer<br>• More "deviant" work behaviors<br>• More accidents |

conscientiousness, emotional stability, and extraversion—in that order—appear to be the most useful for selection contexts. Of course, in certain situations—such as where adaptability or creativity may be highly valued, or where cooperative relations are crucial—openness and agreeableness may be important to assess as well.

Today there is widespread acceptance regarding the validity and utility of personality tests in personnel selection. This does not mean that the area is free of its critics, however. Some researchers have argued that personality traits are not useful selection tools.[10] Here we evaluate three of the most important criticisms of the use of personality tests in selection decisions: the validities are trivial, faking undermines their usefulness, and applicants react negatively to them.

*Trivial Validities.* One set of critics has argued that the validities of personality traits are so small as to border on the trivial, rendering them of limited usefulness as selection devices. These researchers noted, "Why are we now suddenly looking at personality as a valid predictor of job performance when the validities still haven't changed and are still close to zero?"[11] While this is an extreme position, it does contain a grain of truth: the validities are far from perfect. For example, our best estimate of the validity of conscientiousness in predicting overall job performance is $\bar{r}_{xy} = .24$. By no means would this be labeled a strong validity (though, in fairness, we are not aware of any personality researchers who have done so). Does this mean that the validity of personality measures, though, are trivial? We do not believe so, for five reasons.

First, because applicants can complete an entire Big Five inventory in less than 30 minutes in most selection situations, the entire Big Five framework is used, or at least more than a single trait is assessed. In addition, the Big Five traits do not correlate very highly with each other, so knowing a person's level of one trait (for example, conscientiousness) tells you little about their level of another trait (for example, extraversion). Therefore, it is important to look at the multiple correlations between the set of Big Five traits and criteria such as job performance. For example, the multiple correlations between the Big Five and criteria such as overall job performance and leadership is roughly $r = .50$. This is hardly trivial.[12]

Second, as with any selection measure, one can find situations in which a personality trait does not predict job performance. Even though personality tests generalize across jobs, this does not mean they will work in every case. Moreover, the times when they do work and the times when they don't are counterintuitive. For example, evidence suggests that conscientiousness and positive self-concept work well in predicting player success in the NFL but not so well in predicting the performance of police officers.[13] Organizations need to perform their own validation studies to ensure that the tests work as hoped. In general, personality is more predictive of performance in jobs that have substantial autonomy, meaning that individuals have discretion in deciding how—and how well—to do their work.[14]

Third, the Big Five do not exhaust the set of potentially relevant personality traits. Research suggests, for example, that a trait termed proactive personality (degree to which people take action) predicts performance and career success, even controlling for the Big Five traits.[15] Another trait, termed core self-evaluations (a reflection of individuals' self-confidence and self-worth), has also been linked to job performance. The Core Self-Evaluations Scale is shown in Exhibit 9.3. Research indicates that core self-evaluations are predictive of job performance, and the Core Self-Evaluations Scale appears to have validity equivalent to that of conscientiousness. A further advantage of this measure is that it is nonproprietary (free).[16]

Fourth, personality is not intended to be a stand-alone selection tool. In nearly all cases, it is part of a selection battery consisting of other substantive selection measures. No reasonable person would recommend that applicants be hired solely based on scores on a personality test. But by the same token, personality measures do appear to add to the validity of other selection measures.[17]

Recent studies suggest that personality validities may be nonlinear. One study found that in two samples, the validities of conscientiousness and emotional stabil-

---

**EXHIBIT 9.3**   **The Core Self-Evaluations Scale**

*Instructions*: Below are several statements about you with which you may agree or disagree. Using the response scale below, indicate your agreement or disagreement with each item by placing the appropriate number on the line preceding that item.

| 1 | 2 | 3 | 4 | 5 |
|---|---|---|---|---|
| Strongly Disagree | Disagree | Neutral | Agree | Strongly Agree |

1. _____I am confident I get the success I deserve in life.
2. _____Sometimes I feel depressed. (r)
3. _____When I try, I generally succeed.
4. _____Sometimes when I fail, I feel worthless. (r)
5. _____I complete tasks successfully.
6. _____Sometimes I do not feel in control of my work. (r)
7. _____Overall, I am satisfied with myself.
8. _____I am filled with doubts about my competence. (r)
9. _____I determine what will happen in my life.
10. _____I do not feel in control of my success in my career. (r)
11. _____I am capable of coping with most of my problems.
12. _____There are times when things look pretty bleak and hopeless to me. (r)

Note: r = reverse-scored (for these items, 5 is scored 1, 4 is scored 2, 2 is scored 4, and 1 is scored 5).

Source: T. A. Judge, A. Erez, J. E. Bono, and C. J. Thoresen, "The Core Self-Evaluations Scale: Development of a Measure," *Personnel Psychology*, 2003, 56, pp. 303–331.

ity in predicting job performance were nonlinear, such that there were diminishing returns to increasing levels of these traits (extremely conscientious employees do not necessarily perform better than highly conscientious employees). Thus, correlation coefficients (which assume linearity) may understate the true validity of personality tests. Practically, when choosing between two applicants, it may make sense to consider where they are on the distribution of each trait.[18]

Finally, there is evidence that the validities of the Big Five may be improved by contextualizing the measures. Most personality inventories ask about behaviors in general, ignoring the context in which those behaviors occur. Researchers argue that tailoring items to ask about behaviors specific to the workplace, or asking applicants to report on how they behave at work only, will strengthen the validities of the Big Five. A recent meta-analysis found support for this notion, demonstrating that the validities of each of the Big Five traits increased when the measures were contextualized. Specifically, for four of the Big Five traits—extraversion, agreeableness, emotional stability, and openness to experience—the validity of contextualized measures was twice as high compared to more traditional, decontextualized measures. Although measures of conscientiousness specific to the workplace also improved validities, those improvements were not as strong as the others, presumably because traditional measures of conscientiousness already reference people's work behaviors.[19]

*Faking.* Another frequent criticism of personality measures is that they are "fakeable," meaning applicants will distort their responses to increase their odds of being hired. This concern is apparent when one considers personality items (see Exhibits 9.1 and 9.3) and the nature of the traits. Few individuals would want to describe themselves as disagreeable, neurotic, unconscientious, and unconfident. Furthermore, since answers to these questions are nearly impossible to verify (e.g., imagine trying to verify whether an applicant prefers reading a book to watching television), the possibility of "faking good" is quite real. This then leads to the perverse outcome that the applicants most likely to be hired are those who enhanced their responses (faked) the most.

There is a voluminous literature on faking. The results of this literature can be summarized as follows. First, there is little doubt that some faking or enhancement does occur. Studies suggest that applicants consistently score higher on socially desirable personality traits (like conscientiousness, emotional stability, and agreeableness) than do current employees (in most situations, there is no reason to believe that applicants should score more favorably on personality tests than employees—if anything, the reverse would be expected). Also, when individuals are informed that their scores matter (might be used in selection decisions), their scores on personality tests increase.[20]

But what is the outcome of this enhancement? Does the fact that some applicants fake their responses destroy the validity of personality measures in selection? Interestingly, the answer to this question appears to be quite clearly no. In short, though applicants do try to look good by enhancing their responses to personality tests, it seems clear that such enhancement does not significantly detract from the validity of the tests. Why might this be the case? Evidence suggests that socially desirable responding, or presenting oneself in a favorable light, does not end once someone takes a job. Therefore, the same tendencies that cause someone to present himself or herself in a somewhat favorable light on a personality test also help him or her do better on the job. As an example, consider the job of customer service representative. An individual in that occupation needs to be able to assess a customer's needs, deal with potential problems, and interact with that customer in a way that will result in the customer being satisfied. An employee who is able to assess a situation and determine the socially desirable response should be more adept at achieving customer satisfaction than an employee who is less skilled in this area. Thus, socially desirable responding may very well be desired in many cases.[21]

Because faking does not appear to undermine personality validities, some of the proposed solutions to faking may be unnecessary or may cause more problems than they solve. For example, some have proposed correcting applicant scores for faking. However, the literature is quite clear that such corrections do not improve the validity of personality measures.[22] Another proposed solution—using forced-choice personality measures, where applicants must evaluate themselves as either, say, conscientious or emotionally stable—also appears to be fraught with considerable problems.[23] A third possible method of reducing faking involves warning applicants that their scores will be verified. Typically, this warning is presented to applicants prior to completing a given inventory. However, one recent study tried an approach whereby applicants who were suspected of faking were given a warning *during* the testing process. "Fakers" were detected based on whether they endorsed bogus statements and whether their scores on an impression management scale were well above the norm. Although the warning message reduced subsequent faking, it also increased perceptions of testing unfairness. There is also recent evidence that fakers attend visually more to the extreme ends of response options on personality inventories (e.g., "strongly disagree" and "strongly agree"); however, detection of this requires eye-tracking software and thus is likely to be impractical for many organizations. Overall, while there are pros and cons to warning applicants against faking, studies have shown that such warnings can reduce faking (by as much as 30%) without undermining validities.[24]

A final possibility is to use other reports of personality. One might have individuals who have worked with an applicant report on the applicant's personality. The upside of observer reports appears to be noteworthy in that most research suggests that observer ratings of personality outperform self-reports when predicting job performance.[25] If one is using observer reports of personality, however, it is important to attend to information security concerns. One should ensure that the observer nominated by the applicant actually completes the assessment and that the observer is asked to be objective in the assessment. In addition, to the extent possible, multiple observer ratings should be used, as it greatly improves reliability and, thus, validity.

***Negative Applicant Reactions.*** It is important to evaluate personality tests not only in terms of their validity but also in terms of the applicant's perspective. From an applicant's standpoint, the subjective and personal nature of the questions asked in these tests may raise questions about their validity and concerns about invasiveness. In fact, the available evidence concerning applicants' perceptions of personality tests suggests that they are viewed relatively negatively compared with other selection measures. To some degree, applicants who react the most negatively are those who believe they have scored the worst.[26] In general, though, applicants do not perceive personality measures to be as face-valid as other selection measures. Thus, while personality tests—when used properly—do have validity, this validity does not seem to translate into favorable applicant perceptions. More research is needed into the ways that these tests could be made more acceptable to applicants.

## Ability Tests

Ability tests are measures that assess an individual's capacity to function in a certain way. There are two major types of ability tests: aptitude and achievement. Aptitude tests look at a person's innate capacity to function, whereas achievement tests assess a person's learned capacity to function. In practice, these types of abilities are often difficult to separate. Thus, it is not clear that this is a productive, practical distinction for ability tests used in selection.

Surveys reveal that between 15% and 20% of organizations use some sort of ability test in selection decisions, although there is reason to believe that use is increasing.[27] Organizations that use ability tests do so because they assume the tests assess a key determinant of employee performance. Without a certain level of ability, innate or learned, performance is unlikely to be acceptable, regardless of motivation. Someone may try extremely hard to do well in a very difficult class (e.g., calculus) but will not succeed unless he or she has the ability to do so (e.g., mathematical aptitude).

There are four major classes of ability tests: cognitive, psychomotor, physical, and sensory/perceptual.[28] As these ability tests are quite distinct, each will be considered separately below. Because most of the research attention—and public controversy—has focused on cognitive ability tests, they are discussed in considerable detail.

### Cognitive Ability Tests

Cognitive ability tests refer to measures that assess abilities involved in thinking (including perception), memory, reasoning, verbal and mathematical abilities, and the expression of ideas. Is cognitive ability a general construct or does it have a number of specific aspects? Research shows that measures of specific cognitive abilities, such as verbal, quantitative, reasoning, and so on, appear to reflect general intelligence (sometimes referred to as GMA [general mental ability], IQ, or "g").[29] One of the facts that best illustrate this finding is the relatively high correlations among scores on measures of specific facets of intelligence. Someone who scores well on a measure of one specific ability is more likely to score well on measures of other specific abilities. In other words, general intelligence causes individuals to have similar scores on measures of specific abilities.

***Measures of Cognitive Ability.*** Many cognitive ability tests measure both specific cognitive abilities and general mental ability. Many test publishers offer an array of tests. The Psychological Corporation sells the *Employee Aptitude Survey*, a test of 10 specific cognitive abilities (e.g., verbal comprehension, numerical ability, numerical and verbal reasoning, and word fluency). Each of these specific tests is sold separately and takes no more than five minutes to administer to applicants. Each of the 10 specific tests is sold in packages of 25 for about $44 per package. The Psychological Corporation also sells the *Wonderlic Personnel Test*, perhaps the most widely used test of general mental ability for selection decisions. The Wonderlic is a 12-minute, 50-item test. Items range in type from spatial relations to numerical problems to analogies. Exhibit 9.4 provides examples of items from one of the Wonderlic forms. In addition to being a speed (timed) test, the Wonderlic is also a power test—the items get harder as the test progresses (very few individuals complete all 50 items). The Wonderlic has been administered to more than 2.5 million applicants, and normative data are available from a database of more than 450,000 individuals. One prominent organization that has used the Wonderlic for more than 30 years is the National Football League (NFL). Each year, potential recruits are given the Wonderlic, and although scores are supposed to be kept confidential, they inevitably are leaked to the press. Much is then made about top prospects who "bomb" the Wonderlic versus those who "ace" it, although it seems that players' scores often do not play a major role in their eventual draft position.[30] Cost of the Wonderlic ranges from about $1.50 to $3.50 per applicant, depending on whether the organization scores the test itself. Costs of other cognitive ability tests are similar. Although cognitive ability tests are not entirely costless, they are among the least expensive of any substantive assessment method.

There are many other tests and test publishers in addition to those reviewed above. Before deciding which test to use, organizations should seek out a reputable testing firm. An association of test publishers has been formed with bylaws to help ensure this process.[31] It is also advisable to seek out the advice of researchers or testing specialists, many of whom are members of the American Psychological Association or the American Psychological Society.

***Evaluation of Cognitive Ability Tests.*** The findings regarding general intelligence have had profound implications for personnel selection. A number of meta-analyses have been conducted on the validity of cognitive ability tests.

---

**EXHIBIT 9.4**   **Sample Cognitive Ability Test Items**

Look at the row of numbers below. What number should come next?

8         4         2         1         1/2         1/4         ?

Assume the first 2 statements are true. Is the final one: (1) true, (2) false, (3) not certain?

  The boy plays baseball. All baseball players wear hats. The boy wears a hat.

One of the numbered figures in the following drawing is most different from the others. What is the number in that drawing?

A train travels 20 feet in 1/5 second. At this same speed, how many feet will it travel in three seconds?

How many of the six pairs of items listed below are exact duplicates?

|           |           |
|-----------|-----------|
| 3421      | 1243      |
| 21212     | 21212     |
| 558956    | 558956    |
| 10120210  | 10120210  |
| 612986896 | 612986896 |
| 356471201 | 356571201 |

The hours of daylight and darkness in SEPTEMBER are nearest equal to the hours of daylight and darkness in

   (1) June         (2) March         (3) May         (4) November

SOURCE: Reprinted with permission from C. F. Wonderlic Personnel Test, *1992 Catalog: Employment Tests, Forms, and Procedures* (Libertyville, IL: author, 1992).

Although the validities found in these studies have fluctuated to some extent, the most comprehensive reviews have estimated the "true" validity of measures of general cognitive ability to be roughly $\bar{r}_{xy} = .50$.[32] The conclusions from these meta-analyses are dramatic:

1. Cognitive ability tests are among the most valid, if not *the* most valid, methods of selection.

2. Cognitive ability tests appear to generalize across all organizations, all job types, and all types of applicants; thus, they are likely to be valid in virtually any selection context.

3. Organizations using cognitive ability tests in selection enjoy large economic gains compared with organizations that do not use them.

4. Cognitive ability tests appear to generalize across cultures, with validities in Europe at least as high as those in the United States.

5. Beyond job performance, cognitive ability predicts other important criteria, including health-conscious behaviors (such as exercise), occupational prestige, income, steeper career success trajectories, and lower turnover.[33]

These conclusions are not simply esoteric speculations from the ivory tower. They are based on hundreds of studies of hundreds of organizations employing hundreds of thousands of workers. Thus, whether an organization is selecting engineers, customer service representatives, or meat cutters, general mental ability is likely the single most valid method of selecting among applicants. A large-scale quantitative review of the literature suggested relatively high average validities for many occupational groups:[34]

Manager, $\bar{r}_{xy} = .53$
Clerk, $\bar{r}_{xy} = .54$
Salesperson, $\bar{r}_{xy} = .61$
Protective professional, $\bar{r}_{xy} = .42$
Service worker, $\bar{r}_{xy} = .48$
Trades and crafts, $\bar{r}_{xy} = .46$
Elementary industrial worker, $\bar{r}_{xy} = .37$
Vehicle operator, $\bar{r}_{xy} = .28$
Sales clerk, $\bar{r}_{xy} = .27$

These results show that cognitive ability tests have some degree of validity for all types of jobs. The validity is particularly high for complex jobs (e.g., manager, engineer), but even for simple jobs the validity is positive. The same review also revealed that cognitive ability tests have very high degrees of validity in predicting training success—$\bar{r}_{xy} = .37$ for vehicle operators to $\bar{r}_{xy} = .87$ for protective professionals. This is due to the substantial learning component of training and the obvious fact that smart people learn more and adapt more readily to changing job conditions.[35]

Whereas cognitive ability tests are more valid for jobs of medium complexity (e.g., police officers, salespeople) and high complexity (e.g., computer programmers, pilots), they are even valid for jobs of relatively low complexity (e.g., bus driver, factory worker). Why are cognitive ability tests predictive even for relatively simple jobs where intelligence would not appear to be an important attribute? The fact is that some degree of intelligence is important for *any* type of job.

Why do cognitive ability tests work so well in predicting job performance? Research has shown that most of the effect of cognitive ability tests is because intelligent employees learn more on the job and thus have greater job knowledge. As we noted earlier, evidence also suggests that intelligent employees adapt better to changing job conditions, an important skill in many workplaces.[36]

Another important issue in understanding the validity of cognitive ability tests is the nature of specific versus general abilities. Historically, evidence has suggested that specific abilities add little to the prediction of job performance beyond the general factor. More recently, however, this conclusion has been challenged. Researchers in one study argued that specific abilities are sometimes more important than GMA, and another research study suggested that specific cognitive abilities may matter to certain narrow criteria (e.g., perceptual accuracy may predict the degree to which an editor spots errors).[37] Thus, while GMA is the most important predictor of job performance in nearly every situation, there may be situations in which specific abilities are important.

***Potential Limitations.*** If cognitive ability tests are so valid and cheap, why don't more organizations use them? One of the main reasons is concern over the adverse impact and fairness of these tests. In terms of adverse impact, regardless of the type of measure used, cognitive ability tests have severe adverse impact against minorities. Specifically, blacks on average have scored 1 standard deviation below whites, and Hispanics on average have scored .72 standard deviation below whites. This means that only 10% of blacks have scored above the average score for whites.[38] Historically, this led to close scrutiny—and sometimes rejection—of cognitive ability tests by the courts. The issue of fairness of cognitive ability tests has been hotly debated and heavily researched. One way to think of fairness is in terms of accuracy of prediction of a test. If a test predicts job performance with equal accuracy for two groups, such as whites and blacks, then most people would say the test is fair. The problem is that even though the test is equally accurate for both groups, the average test score may be different between the two groups. When this happens, use of the test will cause some degree of adverse impact. This causes a dilemma: Should the organization use the test because it is an accurate and unbiased predictor, or should it not be used because it would cause adverse impact?

Research shows that cognitive ability tests are equally accurate predictors of job performance for various racial and ethnic groups.[39] But research also shows that blacks and Hispanics score lower on such tests than whites. Thus, the dilemma noted above is a real one for the organization. It must decide whether to (1) use the cognitive ability test and experience the positive benefits of using an accurate predictor, (2) not use the cognitive ability test, to avoid adverse impact, and substitute a different measure that has less adverse impact, or (3) use the cognitive ability test in conjunction with other predictors that do not have adverse impact, thus lessening adverse impact overall. Unfortunately, current research does not offer clear guidance on which approach is best. Research suggests that while using other selection measures in conjunction with cognitive ability tests reduces the adverse impact of cognitive ability tests, it by no means eliminates it.[40]

Although the apparent trade-off between diversity and validity is not likely to disappear anytime soon, there have been three positive developments in the cognitive ability testing area. First, one study suggests that tests constructed in an open-ended manner—where the test taker writes in a response—reduce differences in test scores between blacks and whites by 39% while producing equivalent levels of validity, compared with traditional multiple-choice tests. Evidence suggests that open-ended tests reduce group differences because they generate more positive reactions from minority test takers (minority test takers are more likely to see open-ended tests as fair and are more motivated to do well on them). Second, some research suggests the negative effects of cognitive ability testing on diversity can be mitigated by recruiting—by targeted recruiting not only for diversity but also for cognitive ability and personality (e.g., by announcing in recruiting materials that one is looking for smart, diverse, and conscientious applicants).[41] Finally, some evidence suggests that the gap in test scores between whites and blacks is narrowing, perhaps by as much as 10%. Though controversy exists over this issue, if it is true, it would mean that future employers may still face a validity-diversity trade-off, but one that is less severe.[42]

Another aspect of using cognitive ability tests in selection is concern over applicant reactions. Research on how applicants react to cognitive ability tests is scant and somewhat mixed. One study suggested that 88% of applicants for managerial positions perceived the Wonderlic as job related.[43] Another study, however, demonstrated that applicants thought companies had little need for information obtained from a cognitive ability test.[44] Perhaps one explanation for these conflicting findings is the nature of the test. One study characterized eight cognitive ability tests as either concrete (vocabulary, mathematical word problems) or abstract (letter sets, quantitative comparisons) and found that concrete cognitive ability test items were viewed as job related while abstract test items were not.[45] Thus, while applicants may have mixed reactions to cognitive ability tests, concrete items are less likely to be objectionable. In general, applicants perceive cognitive ability tests to be more valid than personality tests but less valid than interviews or work samples.[46]

**Conclusion.**   In sum, cognitive ability tests are one of the most valid selection measures across jobs; they also predict both learning and training success and retention.[47] But they also have some troubling side effects, notably that applicants aren't wild about the tests and that the tests have substantial adverse impact against minorities.

A survey of 703 members of the main professional association in which cognitive ability tests are used generated some interesting findings. Among the experts, there were several areas of consensus:[48]

1. Cognitive ability is measured reasonably well by standardized tests.
2. General cognitive ability will become increasingly important in selection as jobs become more complex.
3. The predictive validity of cognitive ability tests depends on how performance is defined and measured.

4. The complex nature of job performance means that cognitive ability tests need to be supplemented with other selection measures.

5. There is more to intelligence than what is measured by a standard cognitive ability test.

Given such prominent advantages and disadvantages, cognitive ability tests are here to stay, as is the controversy over their use.

## Other Types of Ability Tests

Following the earlier classification of abilities into cognitive, psychomotor, physical, and sensory/perceptual, and having just reviewed cognitive ability tests, we now consider the other types of ability tests.

*Psychomotor Ability Tests.* Psychomotor ability tests measure the correlation of thought with bodily movement. Involved here are processes such as reaction time, arm-hand steadiness, control precision, and manual and digit dexterity. An example of testing for psychomotor abilities is the test used by the city of Columbus, Ohio, to select firefighters. The test mimics coupling a hose to a fire hydrant, and it requires a certain level of processing with psychomotor abilities to achieve a passing score. Some tests of mechanical ability are psychomotor tests. The *MacQuarrie Test for Mechanical Ability* is a 30-minute test that measures manual dexterity. Seven subtests require tracing, tapping, dotting, copying, and so on.

*Physical Abilities Tests.* Physical abilities tests measure muscular strength, cardiovascular endurance, and movement quality.[49] An example of a test that requires all three is the test given to firefighters in the city of Milwaukee, Wisconsin. The test measures upper-body strength (bench press, a lat pulldown, and grip strength pressure), abdominal strength (sit-ups), aerobic endurance (five-minute step tests), and physical mobility (roof ladder placement).[50]

Physical abilities tests are becoming increasingly common to screen out individuals susceptible to repetitive stress injuries, such as carpal tunnel syndrome. Physical abilities tests may also be necessary for equal employment opportunity (EEO) reasons.[51] Although female applicants typically score 1.5 standard deviations lower than male applicants on a physical abilities test, the distributions of scores for male and female applicants overlap considerably. Therefore, all applicants must be given a chance to pass requirements and not be judged as a class. Another reason to use physical abilities tests for appropriate jobs is to avoid injuries on the job. Well-designed tests will screen out applicants who have applied for positions that are poorly suited to their physical abilities. Thus, fewer injuries should result. In fact, one study using a concurrent validation approach on a sample of railroad workers found that 57% of all injury costs were due to the 26% of current employees who failed the physical abilities test.[52]

When carefully conducted for appropriate jobs, physical abilities tests can be highly valid. One comprehensive study reported average validities of $\bar{r} = .39$ for warehouse workers to $\bar{r} = .87$ for enlisted army men.[53] Applicant reactions to these sorts of tests are unknown.

***Sensory/Perceptual Abilities Tests.*** Sensory/perceptual abilities tests assess the ability to detect and recognize environmental stimuli. An example of a sensory/perceptual ability test is a flight simulator used as part of the assessment process for airline pilots. Some tests of mechanical and clerical ability can be considered measures of sensory/perceptual ability, although they take on characteristics of cognitive ability tests. For example, the most commonly used mechanical ability test is the *Bennett Mechanical Comprehension Test*, which contains 68 items that measure an applicant's knowledge of the relationship between physical forces and mechanical objects (e.g., how a pulley operates, how gears function). In terms of clerical tests, the most widely known is the *Minnesota Clerical Test*. This timed test consists of 200 items in which the applicant is asked to compare names or numbers to identify matching elements. For example, an applicant might be asked (needing to work under time constraints) to check the pairs of numbers in the following list for the set that is the same:

109485_____104985
456836_____456836
356823_____536823
890940_____890904
205837_____205834

These tests of mechanical and clerical ability and others like them have reliability and validity data available that suggest they are valid predictors of performance within their specific area.[54] The degree to which these tests add validity over general intelligence, however, is not known.

***Job Knowledge Tests.*** Job knowledge tests attempt to directly assess an applicant's ability to comprehend job requirements. Although generally not marketed as cognitive ability tests per se, not surprisingly, job knowledge test scores tend to correlate highly with cognitive ability test scores.

Job knowledge tests can be of two kinds. One type asks questions that directly assess knowledge of the duties involved in a particular job. For example, an item from a job knowledge test for an oncology nurse might be, "Describe the five oncological emergencies in cancer patients." The other type of job knowledge test focuses on the level of experience with, and corresponding knowledge about, critical job tasks and tools/processes necessary to perform the job. The state of Wisconsin uses the *Objective Inventory Questionnaire* to evaluate applicants based on their experience with tasks, duties, tools, technologies, and equipment that are relevant to a particular job.[55]

There has been less research on the validity of job knowledge tests than on other ability tests. One study, however, provided relatively strong support for the validity of job knowledge tests. A meta-analytic review of 502 studies indicated that the "true" validity of job knowledge tests in predicting job performance is .45. These validities were found to be higher for complex jobs and when job and test content were similar.[56]

## Emotional Intelligence Tests

Increasingly, researchers argue that measures of cognitive intelligence miss an important piece of the abilities puzzle, namely, social or emotional intelligence. More and more, organizations are using measures of emotional intelligence (EI) in selection decisions. We consider EI by answering four questions: (1) What is EI? (2) How is EI measured? (3) How valid is EI? and (4) What are the criticisms of EI?

### What Is Emotional Intelligence?

One of the most prominent EI researchers defines EI as "the ability to monitor one's own and others' feelings, to discriminate among them, and to use this information to guide one's thinking and action."[57] Thus, EI may be broken down into the following components:

- *Self-awareness:* Good at recognizing and understanding one's own emotions
- *Other awareness:* Good at recognizing and understanding others' emotions
- *Emotion regulation:* Good at making use of or managing this awareness

It is not hard to understand that this concept is important. Wouldn't nearly every employee be more effective if he or she could readily sense what he or she was feeling (and why), sense what others were feeling, and manage his or her own (and others') emotions?

### How Is Emotional Intelligence Measured?

Although there are many variants, EI has mainly been measured in two ways. First, some EI measures are very similar to items contained in a personality test, and, indeed, one review found that such EI items are strongly related to personality, especially to emotional stability and conscientiousness. Second, other EI measures are more ability-focused. For example, some measures involve describing the emotional qualities of certain sounds and images. While these measures bear less similarity to personality measures, they have been criticized for having poor reliability and for their content validity (one measure asks test takers to identify the emotions of colors). Somewhat troubling is the fact that the two types of measures do not appear to assess the same construct. One review revealed that personality-like and ability measures only correlated r = .14.[58]

Of the two types of EI measures, the former—the personality-like variety—is more common. Exhibit 9.5 contains items from a nonproprietary (i.e., free) personality-like EI measure.

**EXHIBIT 9.5** Sample Items Measuring Emotional Intelligence

**Self-awareness**

Generally, I find it difficult to know exactly what emotion I'm feeling.

I'm generally aware of my emotions as I experience them.

**Other awareness**

I often find it difficult to see things from another person's viewpoint.

I'm normally able to "get into someone's shoes" and experience their emotions.

**Emotion regulation**

I usually find it difficult to regulate my emotions.

I'm usually able to influence the way other people feel.

SOURCE: A. Cooper and K. V. Petrides, "A Psychometric Analysis of the Trait Emotional Intelligence Questionnaire—Short Form (TEIQue-SF) Using Item Response Theory," *Journal of Personality Assessment*, 2010, 92(5), pp. 449–457.

### How Valid Is Emotional Intelligence?

Evidence suggests that EI is modestly related to job performance. A meta-analysis suggested that of the various dimensions of EI, emotion regulation had the highest correlation with job performance, $\bar{r}_{xy} = .18$. This same study found that once individual differences related to EI (cognitive ability, conscientiousness, and emotional stability) were controlled, the relationship between emotion recognition and job performance dropped to .08.[59] Thus, one could conclude that EI has a relatively small and unique effect on job performance, though the effects may be higher with some measures of EI and in certain situations (e.g., jobs that are emotionally demanding). Some recent evidence suggests that the emotional regulation aspect of EI may be the most critical, as it showed a stronger unique effect on behaviors such as job performance, "citizenship" behaviors like helping, and "deviant" behaviors like harming (those with greater emotion regulation ability performed fewer deviant behaviors), even after cognitive ability and personality were controlled. The general EI measure, however, exhibited a smaller unique effect. The greater importance of emotion regulation, compared to emotion awareness, may be due to the increase in customer service occupations and interpersonal interactions in general, as organizations have moved to more team-based structures, where it has become more critical to be able to control and influence one's emotional responses toward others.[60]

### What Are the Criticisms of Emotional Intelligence?

It's safe to say that EI has proved to be a controversial measure—many criticisms have been offered.[61] First, many researchers have focused on measuring EI, or seeing how well EI predicts performance (often to disappointing effect), without paying sufficient attention to what EI might uniquely predict. To understand this, one has to work from the criterion backward. Shouldn't EI better predict empathetic behavior on the part of social workers than predict whether a bank teller's cash drawer will balance?[62] Second, for many researchers, it is not clear what EI is. Is it really a form of intelligence? Most of us would not think that being self-aware or sensitive to others' emotions is a matter of intellect. Beyond this definitional ambiguity, different EI researchers have studied a dizzying array of concepts—including emotion recognition, self-awareness, empathy, self-control, interpersonal skills, stress management, well-being, and self-discipline. One reviewer noted, "The concept of EI has now become so broad and the components so variegated that . . . it is no longer even an intelligible concept."[63] Finally, some critics argue that because EI is so closely related to intelligence and personality, once you control for these factors, EI has nothing unique to offer. We noted earlier evidence showing that controlling for personality and cognitive ability does indeed detract from the validity of EI.[64]

Still, among consulting firms and in the popular press, EI is wildly popular. For example, one organization's promotional materials for an EI measure claimed, "EI accounts for more than 85 percent of star performance in top leaders."[65] To say the least, it is hard to validate this statement with the research literature.

### Summary

Although few would deny that emotional awareness and regulation are important for many jobs, EI has proved hard to measure in a way that is valid. Weighing the arguments for and against EI, it is still too early to tell whether the concept is useful. It *is* clear, though, that more and more organizations are using EI measures in selection decisions. If an organization wishes to use an EI measure in selection decisions, we urge a certain amount of caution. At the very least, it should be restricted to jobs with exceptional emotional demands, and the construct and empirical validity of the EI measure used should be investigated before it is used in actual selection decisions.

## Performance Tests and Work Samples

Performance tests are mechanisms to assess actual performance rather than underlying capacity or disposition. As such, they are more akin to samples rather than signs of work performance. For example, Chrysler asks applicants for its assembly-line jobs to try assembling auto parts, and applicants for executive-level positions undergo a "day in the life" simulation in which they play the role of plant manager, a process that has been followed by Hyundai and Mitsubishi.[66] Exhibit 9.6 provides examples of performance tests and work samples for a variety of jobs. As can be seen in the exhibit, the potential uses of these selection measures are quite broad in terms of job content and skill level.

**EXHIBIT 9.6** **Examples of Performance Tests and Work Samples**

**Professor**
  Teaching a class while on a campus interview
  Presenting research while on a campus interview
**Mechanic**
  Repairing a particular problem on a car
  Reading a blueprint
**Clerical Worker**
  Typing test
  Proofreading
**Cashier**
  Operating a cash register
  Counting money and totaling a balance sheet
**Manager**
  Performing a group problem-solving exercise
  Reacting to memos and letters
**Airline Pilot**
  Pilot simulator
  Rudder control test
**Taxicab Driver**
  Driving test
  Street knowledge test
**TV Repair Person**
  Repairing a broken television
  Finger and tweezer dexterity test
**Police Officer**
  Check police reports for errors
  Shooting accuracy test
**Computer Programmer**
  Programming and debugging test
  Hardware replacement test

## Types of Tests

***Performance Test Versus Work Sample.*** A performance test measures what the person actually does on the job. The best examples of performance tests are internships, job tryouts, and probationary periods. Although probationary periods have their uses when one cannot be completely confident in an applicant's ability to perform a job, they are no substitute for a valid prehire selection process. Discharging a probationary employee and finding a replacement is expensive and has numerous legal issues.[67] A work sample is designed to capture parts of the job, for example, a drill press test for machine operators and a programming test for computer programmers.[68] A performance test is more costly to develop than a work sample, but it is usually a better predictor of job performance.

***Motor Versus Verbal Work Samples.*** A motor work sample test involves the physical manipulation of things. Examples include a driving test and a clothes-making test. A verbal work sample test involves a problem situation requiring language skills and interaction with people. Examples include role-playing tests that simulate contact with customers, and an English test for foreign teaching assistants.

***High- Versus Low-Fidelity Tests.*** A high-fidelity test uses realistic equipment and scenarios to simulate the actual tasks of the job. Therefore, it elicits actual responses encountered in performing the task.[69] A good example of a high-fidelity test is one used in the petroleum industry to select truck drivers. The test is performed on a computer and mimics all the steps taken to load and unload fuel from a tanker to a fuel reservoir at a service station.[70] It is not a test of perfect high fidelity, because fuel is not actually unloaded. It is, however, a much safer test because the dangerous process of fuel transfer is simulated rather than performed.

A low-fidelity test simulates the task in a written or verbal description and elicits a written or verbal response rather than an actual response. An example of a low-fidelity test is describing a work situation to job applicants and asking them what they would do in that particular situation. In one study, seven organizations in the telecommunications industry used a written low-fidelity test for the position of manager.[71] Low-fidelity work samples bear many similarities to some types of structured interviews, and in some cases they may be indistinguishable (see "Structured Interview" section).

Work sample tests are becoming more innovative and are increasingly being used for customer service positions. For example, Aon Consulting has developed a web-based simulation called REPeValuator in which applicants assume the role of a customer service specialist. In the simulation, the applicant takes phone calls, participates in Internet chat, and responds to e-mails. The test takes 30 minutes to complete and costs $20 per applicant. The test provides scores on rapport, problem solving, communication, empathy, and listening skills.[72] Another interesting work sample test resembles a job tryout, except that the applicant is not hired or compensated. One small business took a promising applicant on a sales call. In this case, although the applicant looked perfect on paper, the sales call revealed troubling aspects to the applicant's behavior and she wasn't hired.[73] Finally, some technology organizations are hosting "coding competitions" at colleges, where in return for a hefty prize (first-place awards can be as high as $50,000) and a job offer, students can try to develop software or solve a programming problem. The organization gets a chance to spread its brand name and a crack at hiring the best applicants, who have just proved themselves.[74]

***Computer Interaction Performance Tests Versus Paper-and-Pencil Tests.***   As with ability testing, the computer has made it possible to measure aspects of work that are not possible to measure with a paper-and-pencil test. The computer can capture the complex and dynamic nature of work. This is especially true in work where perceptual and motor performance are required.

An example of how the computer can be used to capture the dynamic nature of service work comes from Suntrust Bank. Suntrust has applicants perform some of the same tasks its tellers perform, such as looking up account information and entering customer data. The candidates' reactions to the scenarios, both mental (e.g., comprehension, coding, and calculation) and motor (e.g., typing speed and accuracy), are assessed.[75]

## Evaluation

Research indicates that performance or work sample tests have a high degree of validity in predicting job performance. One meta-analysis of a large number of studies suggested that the average validity was $\bar{r} = .54$ in predicting job performance.[76] Because performance tests measure the entire job and work samples measure part of the job, they also have a high degree of content validity. Thus, when one considers the high degree of empirical and content validity, work samples are perhaps the most valid method of selection for many types of jobs.

Performance tests and work samples have other advantages as well. Research indicates that these measures are widely accepted by applicants as being job related. One study found that no applicants complained about performance tests but that 10%–20% complained about other selection procedures.[77] A study of American workers in a Japanese automotive plant concluded that work sample tests are best able to accommodate cross-cultural values and therefore are well suited for selecting applicants in international joint ventures. Another possible advantage of performance tests and work samples is that they have low degrees of adverse impact, though some evidence suggests that they may have more adverse impact than is commonly thought.[78]

Work samples do have several limitations. The costs of the realism embedded in work samples are high. The closer a predictor comes to simulating actual job performance, the more expensive it becomes to use it. Actually having people perform the job, as with an internship, may require paying a wage. Using videos and computers adds costs as well. As a result, performance tests and work samples are among the most expensive means of selecting workers; their costs are amplified when one considers the lack of generalizability of such measures. Probably more than any other selection method, performance tests and work samples are tied to the specific job at hand. This means that a different test, based on a thorough analysis of the job, will need to be developed for each job. While their validity may well be worth the cost, in some circumstances the costs of work samples may be prohibitive. One means of mitigating the administrative expense associated with performance tests or work samples is to use a two-stage selection process whereby the full set of applicants is reduced using relatively inexpensive tests (e.g., cognitive ability tests and personality inventories). Once the initial cut is made, performance tests or work samples can be administered to the smaller group of applicants who demonstrated minimum competency levels on the first-round tests.[79]

Finally, most performance tests and work samples assume that the applicant already possesses the knowledge, skill, ability, and other characteristics (KSAOs) necessary to do the job. If substantial training is involved, applicants will not be able to perform the work sample effectively, even though with adequate training they could be high performers. In such situations, work samples simply will not be feasible.

## Situational Judgment Tests

A hybrid selection procedure that takes on some of the characteristics of an ability test (especially a job knowledge test) and some of the aspects of a work sample is the situational judgment test. These tests place applicants in hypothetical job-related situations where they are asked to choose a course of action from several alternatives. For example, applicants for a 911 operator position may listen to a series of phone calls and then are asked to choose the best response from a series of multiple-choice alternatives. Or, individuals applying to be a member of a project team may be confronted with a scenario in which the team is in conflict and the applicant must choose a method to resolve the conflict. Exhibit 9.7 provides two examples of situational judgment test items.

As one can see, situational judgment tests are very similar to job knowledge tests and work samples, so much so that the main differentiation in the type of situational judgment test reflects whether the test assesses knowledge (more similar to job knowledge tests) or behavioral tendency (more similar to work samples). Situational judgment tests can also be distinguished from job knowledge tests and work samples. A job knowledge test more explicitly taps the content of the job (areas that applicants are expected to know immediately upon hire), whereas situational judgment tests are more likely to deal with future hypothetical job situations. Furthermore, job knowledge tests are less "holistic" than situational judgment tests in that the latter are more likely to include video clips and other more realistic material. Situational judgment tests differ from work samples in that the former presents applicants with multiple-choice responses to the scenarios, whereas in the latter, applicants actually engage in behavior that is observed by others.

The principal argument in favor of situational judgment tests is to capture the validity of work samples and cognitive ability tests in a way that is cheaper than work samples and that has less adverse impact than cognitive ability tests. How

---

**EXHIBIT 9.7** **Examples of Situational Judgment Test Items**

**Retail Industry Manager**
You are the assistant manager of a large department store. One weekend day while you are in charge of the store, a customer seeks to return a pair of tennis shoes. The employee in charge of the customer service department has refused to accept the return. The customer has asked to speak to the manager, and so the employee has paged you. Upon meeting the customer—who is clearly agitated—you learn that the customer does not have a receipt, and, moreover, you see that the shoes are clearly well worn. When you ask the customer why she is returning the shoes, she tells you that she has bought many pairs of shoes from your store, and in the past they have "held up much better over time than these." You recognize the shoes as a brand that your store has stocked, so you have no reason to believe the customer is lying when she says that she bought them from your store. Still, the shoes have clearly been worn for a long time. Should you:
   a. Issue a refund to the customer
   b. Check with your boss—the store manager—when he is at the store on Monday
   c. Deny a refund to the customer, explaining that the shoes are simply too worn to be returned
   d. Inform the customer of the current sale prices on comparable tennis shoes

**Park Ranger**
You are a park ranger with the National Park Service, stationed in Yellowstone National Park. One of your current duties is to scout some of the park's more obscure trails to look for signs of lost hikers, to detect any malfeasance, and to inspect the conditions of the trails. It is mid-September, and you're inspecting one of the more remote trails in the Mount Washburn area to determine whether it should be closed for the season. When you first set out on your hike, the forecast called for only a slight chance of snow, but midway through your hike, an early fall blizzard struck. For a time you persisted on, but later you took refuge under a large lodgepole pine tree. Although the storm is now abating, it is near dark. Which of the following would be your best course of action?
   a. Stay put until help comes
   b. Reverse course and hike back to the ranger station
   c. Once the clouds clear, locate the North Star, and hike north to the nearest ranger station
   d. Use your matches to build a fire, and hike back in the morning

---

well are these aims achieved? A meta-analysis of the validity of situational judgment tests indicated that such tests are reasonably valid correlates of job performance ($\bar{r}_{xy} = .26$).[80] One study of medical students showed that a situational judgment test on interpersonal skills predicted internship performance seven years later and job performance nine years later.[81] Research also suggests that situational judgment tests have less (but not zero) adverse impact against minorities.[82]

Furthermore, video-based situational judgment tests appear to generate positive applicant reactions.[83]

One possible limitation of situational judgment tests is that while they are easier to administer than work sample tests, and have less adverse impact and more positive applicant reactions than cognitive ability tests, they are not as valid as work sample tests or job knowledge tests. Moreover, because situational judgment tests are generally significantly correlated with cognitive ability ($\bar{r}_{xy} = .32$) and personality (especially conscientiousness, $\bar{r}_{xy} = .27$), there is reason to worry about whether they have incremental validity beyond cognitive ability and personality. Some studies have shown that they do.[84] However, other studies have shown little or no incremental validity.[85] In the aforementioned meta-analysis, the average incremental validity contributed by situational judgment tests over cognitive ability and personality tests was only $\Delta r = .02$. As the authors note, this is not the last word on the incremental validity of situational judgment tests. However, given the recent attention focused on situational judgment tests, one might well wonder, "Where's the beef?"

If situational judgment tests are used, three important decisions must be made. First, there is the issue of format. The two main formats of situational judgment tests are written and video. With video tests, applicants first view a video clip that typically involves a role-play episode (e.g., an employee whom the applicant is assumed to supervise asks for advice about a personal matter) and then are asked to choose from a list of responses. Some evidence suggests that video-based situational judgment tests have less adverse impact than written ones and may have higher levels of incremental validity.[86]

Second, there is the issue of scoring. Although general scoring schemes are often developed so that responses can be quickly recorded and scores computed, care needs to be taken in developing the scoring scheme. Generally, the more knowledge the scorer has about the specific requirements of the job, the more valid the situational judgment test scores will be.[87]

Finally, the third issue is which constructs should be measured. Of course, job analysis should be the guide here: constructs that job analysis has suggested are important in order to perform the job should be assessed. More generally, research indicates that some constructs measured by situational judgment tests appear to be more valid than others. Specifically, research indicates that situational judgment tests that measure leadership, personal initiative, and teamwork tend to predict job performance best. That may be because these constructs are not well measured by other means (i.e., situational judgment tests measure these important aspects distinctly well).[88]

## Integrity Tests

When asked to identify the qualities desired in ideal job applicants, employers routinely put honesty and integrity at the top of their list. In a survey, college recruiters were asked to rate the importance of various skills/qualities in job candidates on a 1 = *not important* to 5 = *extremely important* scale. The following skills/qualities were the six most highly rated:[89]

| | |
|---|---|
| 1. Honesty/integrity | 4.7 |
| 2. Communication skills (oral and written) | 4.7 |
| 3. Interpersonal skills (relates well to others) | 4.5 |
| 4. Motivation/initiative | 4.5 |
| 5. Strong work ethic | 4.5 |
| 6. Teamwork skills | 4.5 |

Clearly, integrity is an important quality in applicants; integrity tests are designed to tap this important attribute.

Integrity tests are paper-and-pencil or computerized tests that attempt to assess an applicant's honesty and moral character. They are alternatives to other methods—such as polygraph (so-called lie detector) tests or interviewer evaluations—that attempt to ascertain an applicant's honesty and morality. For most employers, polygraph tests are prohibited by law. Even if they were legal, polygraphs are so invasive that negative applicant reactions would weigh against their use in most situations. Interviewer evaluations of applicant integrity are, of course, not illegal, but they are unreliable as a method of detecting dishonesty, as dishonesty is very hard to detect. Even experts such as FBI agents, judges, and psychologists scarcely perform above chance in detecting lying. A review of 108 studies revealed that people detect lies at a rate that is only 4.2% better than chance.[90] For these reasons, integrity tests are seen as a superior alternative to polygraph tests and interviews, and indeed the use of integrity tests in selection decisions has grown dramatically in the past decade. The tests are especially likely to be used where theft, safety, or malfeasance is an important concern. For example, retail organizations lose an estimated $19 billion per year to employee theft, and it might surprise you to learn that theft due to employees accounts for roughly half (46.8%) of all inventory shrinkage—much greater than that attributed to shoplifting (31.6%).[91] The promise of integrity testing is that it will weed out those most prone to these counterproductive work behaviors.[92]

### Measures

There are two major types of integrity tests: clear purpose (sometimes called overt) and general purpose (sometimes called veiled purpose or personality-oriented). Exhibit 9.8 provides examples of items from both types of measures. Clear purpose tests directly assess employee attitudes toward theft. Such tests often consist of two sections: (1) questions of antitheft attitudes (see items 1 and 2 in Exhibit 9.8), and (2) questions about the frequency and degree of involvement in theft or other counterproductive activities (see items 3 and 4 in Exhibit 9.8).[93] General or veiled purpose integrity tests assess employee personality with the idea that personality

---

**EXHIBIT 9.8** **Sample Integrity Test Questions**

**Clear Purpose or Overt Test Questions**

1. Do you think most people would cheat if they thought they could get away with it?
2. Do you believe a person has a right to steal from an employer if he or she is unfairly treated?
3. Did you ever write a check knowing there was not enough money in your bank account?
4. Have you ever stolen anything?

**Veiled Purpose or Personality-Based Test Questions**

5. Would you rather go to a party than read a newspaper?
6. How often do you blush?
7. Do you almost always make your bed?
8. Do you like to take chances?

---

influences dishonest behavior (see items 5–8 in Exhibit 9.8). The most commonly used clear purpose or overt integrity tests are the *Personnel Selection Inventory*, the *Reid Report*, and the *Stanton Survey*. The most commonly used general or veiled purpose tests are the *Personnel Reaction Blank*, the *PDI Employment Survey*, and the *Reliability Scale of the Hogan Employment Inventory*.[94]

Some have suggested that integrity represents a sixth personality factor, something unique from the Big Five traits.[95] However, most researchers believe that scores on integrity tests reflect a broad or "compound" personality trait that is a combination of several Big Five personality traits. Specifically, integrity test scores appear to reflect conscientiousness, agreeableness, and emotional stability.[96] Regardless of which aspects of personality integrity tests measure, it appears that they predict workplace deviance or counterproductive behaviors better than any of the individual Big Five traits.

### Validity of Integrity Tests

Over the years, several meta-analyses have been published attempting to discern the validity of integrity tests. One major meta-analysis of more than 500,000 people and more than 650 individual studies suggests that integrity tests have surprising levels of validity.[97] The principal findings from this study are the following:

1. Both clear and general purpose integrity tests are valid predictors of counterproductive behaviors (actual and admitted theft, dismissals for theft, illegal activities, absenteeism, tardiness, and workplace violence). The average

validity for clear purpose measures ($\bar{r}$ = .55) was higher than for general purpose ($\bar{r}$ = .32).

2. Both clear and general purpose tests are valid predictors of job performance ($\bar{r}$ = .33 and $\bar{r}$ = .35, respectively).

3. Limiting the analysis to estimates using a predictive validation design and actual detection of theft lowers the validity to $\bar{r}$ = .13.

4. Integrity tests have no adverse impact against women or minorities and are relatively uncorrelated with intelligence. Thus, integrity tests demonstrate incremental validity over cognitive ability tests and reduce the adverse impact of cognitive ability tests.

However, a more recent meta-analysis has called into question the validity of integrity tests. Using a smaller number of studies (104, to be exact), the study found that the overall average validities of integrity tests in predicting a variety of work-related outcomes are much lower than the validities in previous meta-analytic findings. For example, the average validity was $\bar{r}$ = .15 for job performance, $\bar{r}$ = .32 for counterproductive behaviors, and $\bar{r}$ = .09 for turnover. Interestingly, the study found that validities were stronger when they came from studies authored by publishers of integrity tests.[98]

So, you might ask, "Which results should I trust?" On the one hand, the meta-analysis with the weaker validities drew from more recent studies, in which case its results should be trusted more. On the other hand, the meta-analysis with the stronger validities was based on a larger number of studies, in which case its results should be trusted more. In any event, although it is clear that integrity tests do have some validity, the jury is still out on the strength of that validity. Although organizations would likely benefit from using integrity tests for a wide array of jobs, given the conflicting findings reviewed above, those who do so should consider conducting their own validation studies.

## Criticisms and Concerns

*Faking.* One of the most significant concerns with the use of integrity tests is the obvious possibility that applicants might fake their responses. Consider answering the questions in Exhibit 9.8. Now consider answering these questions in the context of applying for a job that you want. It seems more than plausible that applicants might distort their responses in such a context (particularly given that most of the answers would be impossible to verify). This possibility becomes a real concern when one considers the prospect that the individuals most likely to "fake good" (people behaving dishonestly) are exactly the type of applicants organizations would want to weed out.

Embedded within the issue of faking are three questions: (1) Can integrity tests be faked? (2) Do applicants fake or enhance their responses to integrity tests? and (3) Does faking harm the validity of the tests, such that a "perverse inversion" occurs where those who get high scores are those who have the least integrity (fake the most)?

First, it is clear that applicants can fake their scores when instructed or otherwise sufficiently motivated to do so, just as they can with personality tests. Studies that compare individuals who are asked to respond honestly with those who are told to "fake good" reveal that, unsurprisingly, integrity test scores in the "fake condition" situation are higher.

Second, a problem with interpreting whether applicants *can* fake is that it does not tell us whether they indeed *do* fake. After all, job applicants certainly are not told to "fake good" when completing employment tests, and many applicants may not purposely enhance their responses out of moral reasons (they feel it would be wrong to enhance) or practical reasons (they believe enhancements would be detected). Unfortunately, there is much less evidence on this second question. As one review noted, "A generally unanswered question is whether job applicants actually do fake on integrity tests."[99]

Finally, in terms of whether faking matters, if faking was pervasive, integrity test scores would either have no validity in predicting performance from applicant scores or have *negative* validity (honest applicants reporting worse scores than dishonest applicants). The fact that validity was positive for applicant samples suggests that if faking does occur, it does not severely impair the predictive validity of integrity tests. It has been suggested that dishonest applicants do not fake more than honest applicants do, because they believe that everyone is dishonest and therefore they are reporting only what everyone else already does. No matter what the reason, it does seem clear that if faking is a problem, it is not sufficient enough to undermine the validity of the tests.

***Misclassification and Stigmatization.*** Some object to integrity tests because of applicants being misclassified as dishonest.[100] In a sense, this is an odd objection in that all selection procedures involve misclassification of individuals because all selection methods are imperfect (having validities less than 1.0). We think the larger issue is the possible stigmatization of applicants who are thought to be dishonest due to their test scores. These problems can be avoided with proper procedures for maintaining the security and confidentiality of test scores (which, of course, should be done in any case).

***Negative Applicant Reactions.*** A meta-analysis compared applicant reactions to 10 selection procedures, including interviews, work samples, cognitive ability tests, and integrity tests. The results revealed that applicants react negatively to integrity tests—indeed, they rated integrity tests lower than all other methods except graphology (handwriting analysis).[101] It is likely that applicants react quite differently to various kinds of integrity test questions, and that applicants' negative reactions might be mollified with explanations and administrative instructions. Unfortunately, there is little published research on these issues.

## Interest, Values, and Preference Inventories

Interest, values, and preference inventories attempt to assess the activities individuals prefer to do both on and off the job. This is in comparison with predictors that measure whether the person can do the job. However, just because a person can do a job does not guarantee success on the job. If the person does not want to do the job, that individual will fail, regardless of ability. Although interests seem important, they have not been used very much in human resource (HR) selection.

Standardized tests of interests, values, and preferences are available. Many of these measure vocational interests (e.g., the type of career that would motivate and satisfy someone) rather than organizational interests (e.g., the type of job or organization that would motivate and satisfy someone). The two most widely used interest inventories are the *Strong Vocational Interest Blank* (SVIB) and the *Myers-Briggs Type Inventory* (MBTI). Rather than classify individuals along continuous dimensions (e.g., someone is more or less conscientious than another), both the SVIB and the MBTI classify individuals into distinct categories based on their responses to the survey. With the MBTI, individuals are classified into 16 types that have been found to be related to the Big Five personality characteristics discussed earlier.[102] Example interest inventory items are provided in Exhibit 9.9. The SVIB classifies individuals into six categories (realistic, investigative, artistic, social, enterprising, and conventional) that match jobs that are characterized in a corresponding manner. Both of these inventories are used extensively in career counseling in high school, college, and trade schools.

Past research has suggested that interest inventories are not valid predictors of job performance. In this research, the average validity of interest inventories in predicting job performance was estimated to be roughly $\bar{r}_{xy} = .10$. However, a more recent review of more than 400 studies suggested more positive conclusions.[103] Specifically, vocational interests organized by Holland's six occupational types (realistic, investigative, artistic, social, enterprising, and conventional) predicted various criteria (investigative scores were positively related to task performance; artistic scores negatively so), though these validities were not strong (less than .20 in all cases).

Even if interest inventories are modest predictors of performance, this does not mean that they are invalid for all purposes. Research clearly suggests that when individuals' interests match those of their occupation, they are happier with their jobs and are more likely to remain in their chosen occupation.[104] Thus, although interest inventories fail to predict job performance, they do predict occupational choices and job satisfaction levels. Undoubtedly, one of the reasons why vocational interests are poorly related to job performance is because the interests are tied to the occupation rather than the organization or the job.

Research suggests that while interest inventories play an important role in vocational choice, their role in organizational selection decisions is limited. However, a more promising way of considering the role of interests and values in the staffing process is to focus on person/organization fit.[105] As was discussed in Chapter 1,

## EXHIBIT 9.9  Sample Items From Interest Inventory

1. Are you usually:
   (a) A person who loves parties
   (b) A person who prefers to curl up with a good book?

2. Would you prefer to:
   (a) Run for president
   (b) Fix a car?

3. Is it a higher compliment to be called:
   (a) A compassionate person
   (b) A responsible person?

4. Would you rather be considered:
   (a) Someone with much intuition
   (b) Someone guided by logic and reason?

5. Do you more often:
   (a) Do things on the spur of the moment
   (b) Plan out all activities carefully in advance?

6. Do you usually get along better with:
   (a) Artistic people
   (b) Realistic people?

7. With which statement do you most agree?
   (a) Learn what you are, and be such.
   (b) Ah, but a man's reach should exceed his grasp, or what's a heaven for?

8. At parties and social gatherings, do you more often:
   (a) Introduce others
   (b) Get introduced?

person/organization fit argues that it is not the applicant's characteristics alone that influence performance but rather the interaction between the applicant's characteristics and those of the organization. For example, an individual with a strong interest in social relations at work may perform well in an organization that emphasizes cooperation and teamwork, but the same individual might do poorly in an organization whose culture is characterized by independence or rugged individualism. Thus, interest and value inventories may be more valid when they consider the match between applicant values and organizational values (person/organization fit).[106]

## Structured Interview

The structured interview is a very standardized, job-related method of assessment. It requires careful and thorough construction, as described in the sections that follow. It is instructive to compare the structured job interview with an unstructured or psychological interview. This comparison will serve to highlight the differences between the two.

A typical unstructured interview has the following characteristics:

- It is often unplanned, informal, and quick, and the interviewer often spends little time preparing for it.
- Rather than being based on the requirements of the job, questions are based on interviewer "hunches" or "pet questions" in order to psychologically diagnose applicant suitability.
- It consists of casual, open-ended, or subjective questioning (e.g., "Tell me a little bit about yourself").
- It has obtuse questions (e.g., "What type of animal would you most like to be, and why?").
- It has highly speculative questions (e.g., "Where do you see yourself 10 years from now?").
- The interviewer makes a quick, and final, evaluation of the candidate (often in the first couple of minutes).

Despite its continued prevalence—it remains the most widely used substantive selection procedure—research shows that organizations clearly pay a price for using the unstructured interview, namely, lower reliability and validity.[107] Interviewers using the unstructured interview are unable to agree among themselves in their evaluation of job candidates and cannot predict the job success of candidates with any degree of consistent accuracy.

Over the years, research has unraveled the reasons why the unstructured interview does not work well and what factors need to be changed to improve reliability and validity. Sources of error or bias in the unstructured interview include the following:[108]

- Reliability of the unstructured interview is relatively low. Interviewers base their evaluations on different factors, have different hiring standards, and differ in the degree to which their actual selection criteria match their intended criteria.
- Applicant physical attractiveness has consistently been shown to predict interviewer evaluations.
- Negative information receives more weight than positive information in the interview. Research suggests it takes more than twice as much positive information as negative information to change an interviewer's initial impression of an applicant. As a result, the unstructured interview has been labeled a "search for negative evidence."
- Interviewers tend to make snap decisions—people's first impressions form after only 1/10 of one second, and the majority of interviewers make their decisions after the first few minutes of the interview.

- Interviewers place weight on superficial background characteristics such as names and the presence of accents. One study found that when responding to actual employment ads in Boston and Chicago, fictitious applicants with the first names of Allison and Brad were twice as likely to receive interview invitations than individuals with the first names of Kenya and Hakim, even though the résumés were otherwise identical.
- Evaluations from unstructured interviews are particularly affected by applicant impression management and nonverbal behavior.
- Similarity effects—where applicants who are similar to the interviewer with respect to race, gender, or other characteristics receive higher ratings—also exist.
- Poor recall by interviewers often plagues unstructured interviews. One study demonstrated this by giving managers an exam based on factual information after watching a 20-minute videotaped interview. Some managers got all 20 questions correct, but the average manager got only half right.

Thus, the unstructured interview is not very valid, and research has identified the reasons why. So why is it so prevalent? Individuals often believe that they are better at "people-reading" than they actually are, and thus are unaware of the biases that distort evaluations during unstructured interviews. Interviewers also are often not trained. In addition, the unstructured interview requires little advance preparation or much work afterward—a conversation with an applicant takes place and an evaluation is made. Organizations can overcome these limitations by using a structured interview, which attempts to eliminate the biases inherent in unstructured formats by standardizing the process.

## Characteristics of Structured Interviews

There are numerous hallmarks of structured interviews. Some of the more prominent characteristics are the following: (1) questions are based on job analysis, (2) the same questions are asked of each candidate, (3) the response to each question is numerically evaluated, (4) detailed anchored rating scales are used to score each response, and (5) detailed notes are taken, particularly focusing on interviewees' behaviors.[109]

There are two principal types of structured interviews: situational and experience based. Situational interviews assess an applicant's ability to project what his or her behavior would be in future hypothetical situations.[110] The assumption behind the use of the situational interview is that the goals or intentions individuals set for themselves are good predictors of what they will do in the future.

Experience-based or job-related interviews assess past behaviors that are linked to the prospective job. The assumption behind the use of experience-based interviews is the same as that for the use of biodata: past behavior is a good predictor of future behavior. It is assumed that applicants who are likely to succeed have demonstrated success with past job experiences similar to the experiences they would encounter in the prospective job. An example of an experience-based interview is the *Patterned Behavior Description Interview*, which collects four types of experiential information during the interview: (1) credentials (objective verifiable information about past experiences and accomplishments), (2) experience descriptions (descriptions of applicant's normal job duties, capabilities, and responsibilities), (3) opinions (applicant's thoughts about his or her strengths, weaknesses, and self-perceptions), and (4) behavior descriptions (detailed accounts of actual events from the applicant's job and life experiences).[111]

Situational and experience-based interviews have many similarities. Generally, both are based on the critical incidents approach to job analysis, where job behaviors especially important to (as opposed to typically descriptive of) job performance are considered. In addition, both approaches attempt to assess applicant *behaviors* rather than feelings, motives, values, or other psychological states. Finally, both methods have substantial reliability and validity evidence in their favor.

On the other hand, situational and experience-based interviews have important differences. The most obvious difference is that situational interviews are future oriented ("what *would* you do if?"), whereas experience-based interviews are past oriented ("what *did* you do when?"). Also, situational interviews are more standardized in that they ask the same questions of all applicants, while many experience-based interviews place an emphasis on discretionary probing based on responses to particular questions. Presently, there is little basis to guide decisions about which of these two types of structured interviews should be adopted. However, one factor to consider is that experience-based interviews may only be relevant for individuals who have had significant job experience. It does not make much sense to ask applicants what they did in a particular situation if they have never been in that situation. Another relevant factor is complexity of the job. Situational interviews fare worse than experience-based interviews when the job is complex. This may be because it is hard to simulate the nature of complex jobs.

***Structured Video Interviews.***    Although structured interviews help reduce some of the biases that may arise from unstructured interviews, applicant responses still may be shaped in subtle ways by the manner in which the interviewer behaves (e.g., looking bored or uninterested versus enthusiastic, elaborating upon an applicant's response versus saying nothing at all). Some organizations are abandoning face-to-face interaction altogether by presenting applicants with a scripted set of questions and recording their responses for later scoring. HireVue, whose clients include Nike, Hasbro, and Starbucks, conducts 12-minute interviews consisting of one practice question and four actual questions. Applicants are given 30 seconds to read each question and consider their response, which is limited to about 3 minutes. HireVue provides a set of "stock" questions (e.g., "Tell us about a time you had to cope with a high-pressure or stressful work situation"), or companies can provide their own questions. The recorded interviews are then stored and shared among employers who eventually rate the answers to each question. Although recorded interviews such as these offer a number of benefits to organizations, including increased efficiency and greater standardization across interviews, it is unclear how applicants view them. On the one hand, it may be easier for job hunters—especially those who are already employed—to squeeze in interviews after normal work hours. On the other hand, applicants may view the organization as impersonal, and the lack of face-to-face interaction, as well as an onsite visit, may make it difficult to assess person/organization fit. Thus, organizations might be better off using these types of interviews as initial, rather than final, screens.[112]

## Evaluation

Traditionally, the employment interview was thought to have a low degree of validity. Recently, however, evidence for the validity of interviews (especially those that are structured) has been much more positive. In fact, one study found that it took three to four unstructured interviews to achieve the same validity as a single structured interview, which is a huge difference in time and resources.[113] In addition, meta-analyses have suggested the following conclusions:[114]

1. The average validity of interviews is $\bar{r} = .37$.
2. Structured interviews are more valid ($\bar{r} = .31$) than unstructured interviews ($\bar{r} = .23$).
3. The literature on whether situational or experience-based interviews are more valid is not consistent. The largest meta-analysis found that situational interviews were more valid ($\bar{r} = .35$) than experience-based interviews ($\bar{r} = .28$). However, a more recent meta-analysis found the opposite.
4. Panel interviews may be *less* valid ($\bar{r} = .22$) than individual interviews ($\bar{r} = .31$).

Given the advantages of structured interviews, their lack of use is perplexing—whereas 99% of organizations indicate they use the interview in selection, only slightly more than half (55%) claim to use a structured interview. As one review concluded, "Structured interviews are infrequently used in practice." Like all of us, selection decision makers show considerable inertia and continue to use the unstructured interview because they always have, and because they favor expediency over quality. Thus, a cycle of past practice generating continued use needs to be broken by changing the climate. The best way to do this is to educate decision makers about the benefits of structured interviews.[115]

Applicants tend to react very favorably to the interview, whether it is structured or not. Research suggests that most applicants believe the interview is an essential component of the selection process, and most view the interview as the most suitable measure of relevant abilities. As a result, applicants have rated the interview as more job related than any other selection procedure.[116]

The interview appears to have moderate adverse impact against minorities—more than personality tests but considerably less than cognitive ability tests.[117]

Structuring an interview requires that organizations follow a systematic and standardized process. For illustration purposes, we describe development of a situational interview.

## Constructing a Structured Interview

The structured interview, by design and conduct, standardizes and controls for sources of influence on the interview process and the interviewer. The goal is to improve interview reliability and validity beyond that of the unstructured interview. Research shows that this goal can be achieved; doing so requires following each of these steps: consult the job requirements matrix, develop the selection plan, develop the structured interview plan, select and train interviewers, and evaluate effectiveness. Each of these steps is elaborated on next.

## The Job Requirements Matrix and Selection Plan

The starting point for the structured interview is the job requirements matrix. It identifies the tasks and KSAOs that define the job requirements around which the structured interview is constructed and conducted.

Because the selection plan flows from the KSAOs identified in the job requirements matrix, it helps identify which KSAOs are necessary to assess during selection and whether the structured interview is the preferred method of assessing them.

**Is the KSAO Necessary?**   The candidate must bring some KSAOs to the job, and others can be acquired on the job (through training and/or job experience). The bring-it/acquire-it decision must be made for each KSAO, and it should be guided by the importance indicator(s) for the KSAOs in the job requirements matrix.

**Is the Structured Interview the Preferred Method?**   Several factors should be considered when determining whether the structured interview is the preferred method of assessing each KSAO necessary for selection. The structured interview is probably best suited for assessing the more interpersonal or face-to-face skills and abilities, such as communication and interpersonal skills.

An example of a selection plan for the job of sales associate in a retail clothing store is shown in Exhibit 9.10. While there were five task dimensions for the job in the job requirements matrix (customer service, use of machines, use of customer service outlets, sales and departmental procedures, and cleaning and maintenance), the selection plan shows only the dimension of customer service.

Note in the exhibit that the customer service dimension has several required KSAOs. However, only some of these will be assessed during selection, and only some of those will be assessed by the structured interview. The method of assessment is thus carefully targeted to the KSAO to be assessed.

**EXHIBIT 9.10** **Partial Selection Plan for Job of Retail Store Sales Associate**

**Task Dimension: Customer Service**

| KSAO | Necessary for Selection? | Method of Assessment |
| --- | --- | --- |
| 1. Ability to make customer feel welcome ............... | Yes | Interview |
| 2. Knowledge of merchandise to be sold ................. | Yes | Written test |
| 3. Knowledge of location of merchandise in store .... | No | None |
| 4. Skill in being cordial with customers ................... | Yes | Interview |
| 5. Ability to create and convey ideas to customers ... | Yes | Interview |

### The Structured Interview Plan

Development of the structured interview plan proceeds along three sequential steps: construction of interview questions, construction of benchmark responses for the questions, and weighting of the importance of the questions. The output of this process for the sales associate job is shown in Exhibit 9.11 and is referred to in the discussion that follows.

*Constructing Questions.* One or more questions must be constructed for each KSAO targeted for assessment by the structured interview. Care must be taken to ensure that the questions reflect a sampling of the candidate's behavior, as revealed by past situations (behavioral description) or what the candidate reports would be his or her behavior in future situations (situational). The questions ask, in essence, "What did you do in this situation?" and "What would you do if you were in this situation?"

The key to constructing both types of questions is to create a scenario relevant to the KSAO in question and ask the candidate to respond to it by way of answering a question. If one plans to consider applicants with limited prior experience, future-oriented or situational questions should be favored over behavioral description questions, since not all applicants will have been in the situation previously.

Exhibit 9.11 shows three questions for the KSAOs to be assessed by the interview, as determined by the initial selection plan for the job of sales associate in a retail store. As can be seen, all three questions present very specific situations that a sales associate is likely to encounter. The content of all three questions is clearly job relevant, a logical outgrowth of the process that began with the development of the job requirements matrix.

*Developing Benchmark Responses and Rating Scales.* The interviewer must somehow evaluate or judge the quality of the candidate's responses to the

**EXHIBIT 9.11** Structured Interview Questions, Benchmark Responses, Rating Scale, and Question Weights

**Job: Sales Associate**
**Task Dimension: Customer Service**

| | Rating Scale | | | | | Rating | × | Weight | = Score |
|---|---|---|---|---|---|---|---|---|---|
| | 1 | 2 | 3 | 4 | 5 | | | | |
| **Question No. One (KSAO 1)**<br>A customer walks into the store. No other salespeople are around to help the person, and you are busy arranging merchandise. What would you do if you were in this situation? | Keep on arranging merchandise | | Keep working, but greet customer | | Stop working, greet customer, offer to provide assistance | 5 | | 1 | 5 |
| **Question No. Two (KSAO 4)**<br>A customer is in the fitting room and asks you to bring her some shirts to try on. You do so, but by accident bring the wrong size. The customer becomes irate and starts shouting at you. What would you do if you were in this situation? | Tell customer to "keep her cool" | | Go get correct size | | Apologize, go get correct size | 3 | | 1 | 3 |
| **Question No. Three (KSAO 5)**<br>A customer is shopping for the "right" shirt for her 17-year-old granddaughter. She asks you to show her shirts that you think would be "right" for her. You do this, but the customer doesn't like any of them. What would you do if you were in this situation? | Tell customer to go look elsewhere | | Explain why you think your choices are good ones | | Explain your choices, suggest gift certificate as alternative | 5 | | 2 | 10 |
| | | | | | | | | | 18 |

interview questions. Prior development of benchmark responses and corresponding rating scales will provide firm guidance to the interviewer in doing this task. Benchmark responses represent qualitative examples of the types of candidate responses that the interviewer may encounter. They are located on a rating scale (usually 1–5 or 1–7 rating scale points) to represent the level or "goodness" of the response.

Exhibit 9.11 contains benchmark responses, positioned on a 1–5 rating scale, for each of the three interview questions. Note that all the responses are quite specific and that some answers are better than others. These responses represent judgments on the part of the organization as to the desirability of behaviors its employees could engage in.

***Weighting Responses.*** Each candidate will receive a total score for the structured interview. It thus must be decided whether each question is of equal importance in contributing to the total score. If so, the candidate's total interview score is simply the sum of the scores on the individual rating scales. If some questions are more important than others in assessing candidates, those questions receive greater weight. The more important the question, the greater its weight relative to the other questions.

Exhibit 9.11 shows the weighting decided on for the three interview questions. The first two questions receive a weight of 1, and the third question receives a weight of 2. The candidate's assigned ratings are multiplied by their weights and then summed to determine a total score for this particular task dimension. In the exhibit, the candidate receives a score of 18 (5 + 3 + 10 = 18) for customer service. The candidate's total interview score would be the sum of the scores on all the dimensions.

### Selection and Training of Interviewers

Some interviewers are more accurate in their judgments than others. In fact, several studies have found significant differences in interviewer validity and that even in structured interviews many interviewers form lasting early impressions.[118] Thus, rather than asking, "How valid is the interview?" it might be more appropriate to ask, "Who is a valid interviewer?" Answering this question requires selecting interviewers with characteristics that will enable them to make accurate decisions about applicants. Little research is available regarding the factors that should guide selection of interviewers. Perhaps not surprisingly, cognitive ability has been linked to accuracy in evaluating others. It would also be possible to design an interview simulation where prospective interviewers are asked to analyze jobs to determine applicant KSAOs, preview applications, conduct hypothetical interviews, and evaluate applicants.

Interviewers will probably need training in the structured interview process, as it may be quite different from what they have encountered and/or used. Training is a way of introducing them to the process, and it is another means of increasing the validity of structured interviews. Logical program content areas to be covered as part of the training are the following:

- Problems with the unstructured interview
- Advantages of the structured interview
- Development of the structured interview
- Use of note taking and elimination of rating errors
- Actual practice in conducting the structured interview

Research on whether interviewer training works is inconsistent. One review concluded that the evidence regarding the ability of training programs to reduce rating errors showed that these programs "have achieved at best mixed results."[119] However, a more recent study revealed that an interviewer training program was effective, in no small part because it increased the degree to which a structured format was followed.[120] Given that interviewers tend not to use structured formats, this is a key advantage.

### Evaluating Effectiveness

As with any assessment device, there is a constant need to learn more about the reliability, validity, and utility of the structured interview. This is particularly so because of the complexity of the interview process. Thus, evaluation of the structured interview's effectiveness should be built into the process.

### Selection for Team Environments

Decades ago, when companies such as W. L. Gore and General Foods used work teams, it was news. Nowadays, of course, teams are pervasive. One of the main reasons organizations have turned to teams is that they feel teams are more flexible and responsive to changing events. They may also believe that teams operate more efficiently than individuals working alone. Alternatively, they may wish to make teamwork part of their culture as a way to democratize themselves and increase employee motivation.[121]

There are as many types of teams as there are configurations of individuals. However, teams can be clustered into four categories:[122] (1) problem-solving teams, or teams where members share ideas or offer suggestions on how work processes can be improved (though they rarely have the authority to unilaterally implement any of their suggested actions), (2) self-managed work teams, where groups of typically 10–15 employees perform highly related or interdependent jobs and take on many of the responsibilities of their former supervisors, (3) cross-functional teams, or teams made up of employees from roughly the same hierarchical level but different work areas or functions, and (4) virtual teams, or teams that use computers to tie together physically dispersed members in order to achieve a common goal or work on a single project.

No matter the reason for the existence of teams, or the type of team involved, teamwork means revisiting the way work is done in an organization, which necessarily affects how positions are staffed.

The first step in understanding the proper steps for selection in team-based environments is to understand the requirements of the job. This involves determining the knowledge, skills, and abilities (KSAs) required for teamwork. For example, to be effective in a teamwork assignment, an employee may need to demonstrate *interpersonal KSAs* (consisting of conflict resolution, collaborative problem solving, and communication KSAs) and *self-management KSAs* (consisting of goal setting and performance management KSAs, and planning and task coordination KSAs).

One means of incorporating team-based KSAs into the existing selection process has been developed.[123] Exhibit 9.12 provides some sample items from the 35-item test. This test has been validated against three criteria (teamwork performance, technical performance, and overall performance) in two studies.[124] The teamwork test showed substantial validity in predicting teamwork and overall performance in one of the studies, but no validity in predicting any of the criteria in the other study. (It is not clear why the teamwork test worked well in one study but not in the other.) It should be noted that tests are not the only method of measuring teamwork KSAs. Other methods of assessment that some leading companies have used in selecting team members include structured interviews, assessment centers, personality tests, and biographical inventories.[125] For example, one research study developed and validated a situational judgment test to assess team role orientation. One scenario from the situational judgment test is paraphrased below:

> Assume the role of a sales team member at a bookstore. The bookstore has been experiencing rapidly declining sales, and the team was tasked with finding solutions to the problem. During the meeting, the discussion became heated when one team member blamed the problem on the two new sales representatives. One of the new sales representatives reacted angrily to the accusation and made accusations of his own. The other new sales representative simply stared at the floor. How would you respond?

Applicants choose one of four responses, the best of which was: "Remind the two sales reps that personal attacks are not appropriate and that the team should focus on the future solutions." This study revealed that scores on the test were correlated r = .30 with team role performance in a sample of 82 production and maintenance teams.[126]

Another important decision in team member selection is who should make the hiring decisions. In many cases, team assessments are made by members of the self-directed work team in deciding who becomes a member of the group. An example of an organization following this procedure is South Bend, Indiana–based I/N Tek, a billion-dollar steel-finishing mill established in a joint venture between the United States' Inland Steel and Japan's Nippon Steel. Employees in

---

**EXHIBIT 9.12** **Example Items Assessing Teamwork KSAs**

1. Suppose that you find yourself in an argument with several coworkers about who should do a very disagreeable but routine task. Which of the following would likely be the most effective way to resolve this situation?
   A. Have your supervisor decide, because this would avoid any personal bias.
   B. Arrange for a rotating schedule so everyone shares the chore.
   C. Let the workers who show up earliest choose on a first-come, first-served basis.
   D. Randomly assign a person to do the task and don't change it.

2. Your team wants to improve the quality and flow of the conversations among its members. Your team should:
   A. Use comments that build on and connect to what others have said.
   B. Set up a specific order for everyone to speak and then follow it.
   C. Let team members with more to say determine the direction and topic of conversation.
   D. Do all of the above.

3. Suppose you are presented with the following types of goals. You are asked to pick one for your team to work on. Which would you choose?
   A. An easy goal to ensure the team reaches it, thus creating a feeling of success.
   B. A goal of average difficulty so the team will be somewhat challenged, but successful without too much effort.
   C. A difficult and challenging goal that will stretch the team to perform at a high level, but attainable so that effort will not be seen as futile.
   D. A very difficult, or even impossible goal so that even if the team falls short, it will at least have a very high target to aim for.

SOURCE: M. J. Stevens and M. A. Campion, "The Knowledge, Skill, and Ability Requirements for Teamwork: Implications for Human Resource Management," *Journal of Management*, 1994, 20, pp. 503–530. With permission from Elsevier Science.

self-directed work teams, along with managers and HR professionals, interview candidates as a final step in the selection process. This approach is felt to lead to greater satisfaction with the results of the hiring process because employees have a say in which person is selected to be part of the team.[127]

Thus, staffing processes and methods in team environments require modifications from the traditional approaches to selection. Before organizations go to the trouble and expense of modifying these procedures, however, it would be wise to examine whether the team initiatives are likely to be successful. Many teams fail because they are implemented as an isolated practice.[128] Thus, before overhauling selection practices in an effort to build teams, care must be taken to ensure the proper context for these environments in the first place.

# Choice of Substantive Assessment Methods

As with the choice of initial assessment methods, a large amount of research has been conducted on substantive assessment methods that can help guide organizations in the appropriate methods to use. Reviews of this research, using the same criteria that were used to evaluate initial assessment methods, are shown in Exhibit 9.13. Specifically, the criteria are use, cost, reliability, validity, utility, applicant reactions, and adverse impact.

## Use

As can be seen in Exhibit 9.13, there are no widely used (at least two-thirds of all organizations) substantive assessment methods. Structured interviews, emotional intelligence tests, and performance tests and work samples have moderate degrees of use. The other substantive methods are only occasionally or infrequently used by organizations.

## Cost

The costs of substantive assessment methods vary widely. Some methods can be purchased from vendors quite inexpensively (personality tests; ability tests; emotional intelligence tests; interest, values, and preference inventories; integrity tests)—often for less than $2 per applicant. (Of course, the costs of administering and scoring the tests must be factored in.) Some methods, such as team assessments, can vary in price depending on whether the organization develops the measure itself or purchases it from a vendor. Other methods, such as structured interviews, performance tests and work samples, and situational judgment tests, generally require extensive time and resources to develop; thus, these measures are the most expensive of the substantive assessment methods.

## Reliability

The reliability of all the substantive assessment methods is moderate or high. This is because many of these methods have undergone extensive development efforts by vendors. However, whether an organization purchases an assessment tool from a vendor or develops it independently, the reliability of the method must be investigated. Just because a vendor claims a method is reliable does not necessarily mean it will be so within a particular organization.

## Validity

Like cost, the validity of substantive assessment methods varies a great deal. Some methods, such as interest, values, and preference inventories, have demonstrated little validity in past research. As was noted when reviewing these measures, however, steps can be taken to increase their validity. Emotional intelligence tests also have relatively low validity, though there is reason to believe the tests are

**EXHIBIT 9.13** **Evaluation of Substantive Assessment Methods**

| Predictors | Use | Cost | Reliability | Validity | Utility | Applicant Reactions | Adverse Impact |
|---|---|---|---|---|---|---|---|
| Personality tests | Low | Low | High | Moderate | ? | Negative | Low |
| Ability tests | Low | Low | High | High | High | Negative | High |
| Emotional intelligence tests | Moderate | Low | High | Low | ? | ? | Low |
| Performance tests and work samples | Moderate | High | High | High | High | Positive | Low |
| Situational judgment tests | Low | High | Moderate | Moderate | ? | Positive | Moderate |
| Integrity tests | Low | Low | High | High | High | Negative | Low |
| Interest, values, and preference inventories | Low | Low | High | Low | ? | ? | Low |
| Structured interviews | Moderate | High | Moderate | High | ? | Positive | Mixed |
| Team assessments | Low | Moderate | ? | ? | ? | Positive | ? |

improving. Some methods, such as personality tests and structured interviews, have at least moderate levels of validity. Some structured interviews have high levels of validity, but the degree to which they add validity beyond cognitive ability tests remains in question. Ability tests, performance tests, and work samples have high levels of validity. Integrity tests appear to range from low to moderately high predictors of job performance; their validity in predicting other important job behaviors (counterproductive work behaviors) appears to be stronger.

## Utility

As with initial assessment methods, the utility of most substantive assessment methods is unknown. A great deal of research has shown that the utility of ability tests (in particular, cognitive ability tests) is quite high. Performance tests, work samples, and integrity tests also appear to have high levels of utility.

## Applicant Reactions

Research is just beginning to emerge concerning applicant reactions to substantive assessment methods. From the limited research that has been conducted, however, applicants' reactions to substantive assessment methods appear to depend on the particular method. Relatively abstract methods that require an applicant to answer questions not directly tied to the job (i.e., questions on personality tests, most ability tests, and integrity tests) seem to generate negative reactions from applicants. Thus, research tends to suggest that applicants view personality, ability, and integrity tests unfavorably. Methods that are manifestly related to the job for which applicants are applying appear to generate positive reactions. Thus, research suggests that applicants view performance tests, work samples, and structured interviews favorably. Little is known for how applicants react to emotional intelligence tests.

## Adverse Impact

A considerable amount of research has been conducted on adverse impact of some substantive assessment methods. In particular, research suggests that personality tests, emotional intelligence tests, performance tests and work samples, and integrity tests have little adverse impact against women or minorities. In the past, interest, values, and preference inventories had substantial adverse impact against women, but this problem has been corrected. Conversely, ability tests have a high degree of adverse impact. In particular, cognitive ability tests have substantial adverse impact against minorities, while physical ability tests have significant adverse impact against women. The adverse impact of structured interviews was denoted as mixed. Furthermore, since even structured interviews have an element of subjectivity to them, the potential always exists for interviewer bias to enter into the process.

A comparison of Exhibits 8.8 and 9.13 is instructive. In general, both the validity and the cost of substantive assessment procedures are higher than those of initial assessment procedures. As with the initial assessment procedures, the economic and social impacts of substantive assessment procedures are not well understood. Many initial assessment methods are widely used, whereas most substantive assessment methods have moderate or low degrees of use. Thus, many organizations rely on initial assessment methods to make substantive assessment decisions. This is unfortunate, because, with the exception of biographical data, the validity of substantive assessment methods is higher. This is especially true of the initial interview relative to the structured interview. At a minimum, organizations need to supplement the initial interview with structured interviews. Better yet, organizations should strongly consider using ability, performance, personality, and work sample tests along with either interview.

## DISCRETIONARY ASSESSMENT METHODS

Discretionary assessment methods are used to separate those who receive job offers from the list of finalists. Sometimes discretionary methods are not used, because all finalists may receive job offers. When used, discretionary assessment methods are typically highly subjective and rely heavily on the intuition of the decision maker. Thus, factors other than KSAOs may be assessed. Organizations intent on maintaining strong cultures may wish to consider assessing the person/organization match at this stage of the selection process.

Another interesting method of discretionary assessment that focuses on person/organization match is the selection of people based on their likely organizational citizenship behavior.[129] With this approach, finalists not only must fulfill all the requirements of the job but also are expected to fulfill some roles outside the requirements of the job, called organizational citizenship behaviors. These behaviors include things like doing extra work, helping others at work, covering for a sick coworker, and being courteous.

Discretionary assessments should involve use of the organization's staffing philosophy regarding equal employment opportunity and affirmative action (EEO/AA) commitments. Here, the commitment may be to enhance the representation of minorities and women in the organization's workforce, either voluntarily or as part of an organization's affirmative action plans and programs (AAPs). At this point in the selection process, the demographic characteristics of the finalists may be given weight in determining which applicant will receive the job offer. Regardless of how the organization chooses to make its discretionary assessments, they should never be used without being preceded by initial and substantive methods.

## CONTINGENT ASSESSMENT METHODS

As was shown in Exhibit 8.3, contingent methods are not always used, depending on the nature of the job and legal mandates. Virtually any selection method can be used as a contingent method. For example, a health clinic may verify that an applicant for a nursing position possesses a valid license after a tentative offer has been made. Similarly, a defense contractor may perform a security clearance check on applicants once initial, substantive, and discretionary methods have been exhausted. While these methods may be used as initial or contingent methods, depending on the preferences of the organization, two selection methods, drug testing and medical exams, should be used exclusively as contingent assessment methods for legal compliance. When drug testing and medical exams are used, considerable care must be taken in their administration and evaluation.

## Drug Testing

More than 70% of substance abusers hold jobs, and substance abuse has been identified as a major cause of workplace violence, accidents, and absenteeism and increased health care costs. A workplace study revealed that the average drug user was 3.6 times more likely to be involved in an accident, received 3 times the average level of sick benefits, was 5 times more likely to file a workers' compensation claim, and missed 10 times as many work days as nonusers.[130] One comprehensive study found that over an 11-year period, approximately 50 train accidents were attributed to workers under the influence of drugs or alcohol. These accidents resulted in 37 people killed, 80 injured, and the destruction of property valued at $34 million. A National Transportation Safety Board study found that 31% of all fatal truck accidents were due to alcohol or drugs.[131]

As a result of the manifold problems caused by drug use, many employers have drug-testing programs to screen out drug users. A survey of over 600 organizations by the Society for Human Resource Management found that 57% conducted pre-employment drug testing on all job candidates. In contrast, only 36% of organizations reported that they conduct drug tests on their current employees. Drug testing was more likely in larger organizations (those employing more than 2,500 employees) and in publicly owned, for-profit organizations. On average, each drug test cost the company between $30 and $40.[132] These figures are much less than they were in 1996, when drug testing peaked and 81% of employers screened workers and applicants.[133]

One of the reasons drug testing has declined is shown in Exhibit 9.14: drug tests do not catch many people.[134] Far and away, the highest positive test rate is for marijuana, and it is only 2.54%—meaning that only 2.54% of applicants tested positive for marijuana. Overall, only 3.8% tested positive (the positive results in the exhibit add up to more than 3.8% because some applicants tested positive for more than one drug). The 3.8% positive rate means that if an organization tested 100 applicants, only about 4 would fail the test (i.e., test positive). The positive rate has dropped over time—indeed, the largest provider of employer drug testing says that positive tests are at a 17-year low. The decline is probably due to a combination of factors, including lower drug use in the population and the deterrent effect of the drug tests themselves (if an individual has used drugs recently and is aware that the

**EXHIBIT 9.14  Percentage of Applicants Testing Positive by Drug Category**

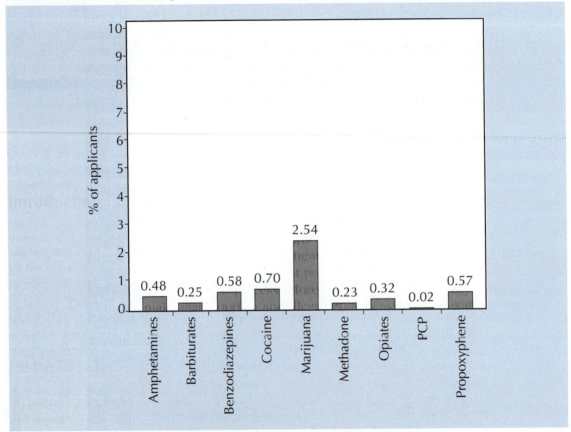

SOURCE: *Amphetamines Use Declined Significantly Among U.S. Workers in 2005, According to Quest Diagnostics' Drug Testing Index*, Quest Diagnostics Incorporated, 2006.

organization tests for drugs, he or she will not apply). It may also reflect applicants "gaming" the tests (diluting, adulterating, or substituting samples); though, as we note shortly, if properly conducted, drug tests are difficult to fake.

### Types of Tests

A variety of tests may be used to ascertain substance abuse. The major categories of tests are the following:[135]

1. *Body fluids.* Both urine and blood tests can be used. Urine tests are by far the most frequently used method of detecting substance abuse. There are different types of measures for each test. For example, urine samples can be measured using the enzyme-multiplied immunoassay technique or the gas

chromatography/spectrometry technique. The latest innovation in drug testing uses a strip that is dipped into a urine sample (similar to a home pregnancy test), allowing organizations to test applicants and receive results on the spot.

2. *Hair analysis*. Samples of hair are analyzed using the same techniques as those used to measure urine samples. Chemicals remain in the hair as it grows, so it can provide a longer record of drug use. Hair analysis is more expensive than urinalysis.

3. *Pupillary reaction test*. The reaction of the pupil to light is assessed. The pupils will react differently when the applicant is under the influence of drugs than when the applicant is drug-free.

4. *Performance tests*. Hand-eye coordination is assessed to see if there is impairment compared with the standard drug-free reactions. One of the limitations of performance tests in a selection context is that there may be no feasible means of establishing a baseline against which performance is compared. Thus, performance tests are usually more suitable for testing employees than applicants.

5. *Integrity test*. Many integrity tests contain a section with 20 or so items that ask applicants about past and present drug use (e.g., "I only drink at work when things get stressful") as well as attitudes toward drug use (e.g., "How often do you think the average employee smokes marijuana on the job?"). Of course, such tests are susceptible to denial or deliberate falsification.

## Administration

For the results of drug tests to be accurate, precautions must be taken in their administration. When collecting samples to be tested, care must be exercised to ensure that the sample is authentic and not contaminated. The US Department of Health and Human Services has established specific guidelines that must be followed by federal agencies (and are good guidelines to follow in the private sector as well).[136]

The testing itself must be carefully administered. Large labs process thousands of samples each day. Hence, human error can occur in the detection process. In addition, false-positive results can be generated due to cross-reactions. This means that a common compound (e.g., poppy seeds) may interact with the antibodies and mistakenly identify a person as a substance abuser. Prescription medications may also affect drug-test results. One new complicating factor in evaluating drug-test results is the use of adulterants that mask the detection of certain drugs in the system. Although most adulterants can be tested, not all are easily detected, and many firms are unaware they can ask drug companies to test for adulterants.

For the testing to be carefully administered, two steps need to be taken. First, care must be taken in the selection of a reputable drug-testing firm. Various certification programs, such as the College of American Pathologists and the National

Institute for Drug Abuse (NIDA), exist to ensure that accurate procedures are followed. More than 50 drug-testing laboratories have been certified by NIDA. Second, positive drug tests should always be verified by a second test to ensure reliability.

What does a well-conducted drug-testing program look like?[137] Samples are first submitted to screening tests, which are relatively inexpensive ($30–$40 per applicant) but yield many false positives (test indicates drug use when none occurred) due to the cross-reactions described above. Confirmatory tests are then used, which are extremely accurate but more expensive. Error rates for confirmatory tests with reputable labs are very low. To avoid false positives, most organizations have nonzero cutoff levels for most drugs. Thus, if a mistake does occur, it is much more likely to be a false negative (testing negative when in fact drug use did occur) than a false positive. Thus, some applicants who occasionally use drugs may pass a test, but it is very rare for an individual who has never used drugs to fail the test—assuming the two-step process described above is followed. Exhibit 9.15 outlines the steps involved in a well-designed drug-testing program. In this example:

- Applicants are advised in advance of testing.
- All applicants are screened by urine testing.
- Prescreening is done in-house; positives are referred to an independent lab.

**EXHIBIT 9.15   Example of an Organizational Drug-Testing Program**

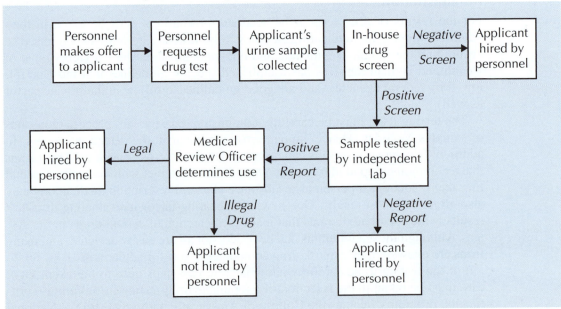

- A strict chain of custody is followed.
- Verified positive applicants are disqualified.
- Disqualified applicants cannot reapply for two years.

## The Other Drugs: Smoking and Alcohol

Increasingly, employers are banning smokers from hiring consideration. World-renowned Cleveland Clinic, for example, now bans hiring of smokers. (About half of US states prohibit rejecting applicants on the basis of smoking.) Union Pacific, a railroad that operates in 23 states, screens job candidates for smoking not by a nicotine test but by another method. "We will not process applications of people who indicate they are smokers," commented Kathryn Blackwell, a Union Pacific manager. Because smoking has been linked to higher health care costs, increased accident claims, and absenteeism, such policies may be justified. On the other hand, employers need to have arguments and evidence to support such policies: you have to "make the business case," as one expert noted. Thus, regardless of how smokers are screened out, employers that do so need to ensure that their policies comply with federal, state, and local regulations.[138]

As for alcohol, few employers test applicants for alcohol use for two reasons. First, because alcohol use is legal, and far more socially accepted than use of other mood-altering drugs, most employers have no desire to test applicants for alcohol; doing so would exclude large numbers of applicants. A second reason alcohol testing is infrequently used is because alcohol remains in the system for only a day. Some organizations that do test for alcohol use a test called EtG. The advantage of this test is that rather than scanning for the presence of alcohol, EtG scans for a by-product of the metabolization of alcohol, ethyl glucuronide, which remains in the system for about 80 hours. To date, the only organizations using the EtG test are those that prohibit or restrict alcohol use in certain jobs (e.g., some health care positions, transportation jobs), and those that have applicants who have had former alcohol problems but now claim to be sober.[139]

## Evaluation

It is commonly believed that drug testing results in a large number of false positives. Nevertheless, if the proper procedures are followed, drug-test results are extremely accurate and error rates are very low. Accuracy of the test, however, is not the same as its validity in predicting important job criteria. The most accurate drug test in the world will be a poor investment if it cannot be established that substance abuse is related to employee behaviors such as accidents, absenteeism, tardiness, impaired job performance, and so on.

Although more research on the validity of drug-testing programs is needed, some organizations are conducting research on the deleterious effects of substance abuse. The US Postal Service conducted an evaluation of its drug-testing program using applicants who applied for positions in 21 sites over a six-month period.[140] A quality control process revealed that the drug-testing program was 100% accurate (zero false positives and false negatives). Ten percent of applicants tested positive for drug use (for the purposes of the study, applicants were hired without regard to their test scores). Of those positive tests, 65% were for marijuana, 24% were for cocaine, and 11% were for other drugs. The evaluation revealed higher absenteeism for drug users and higher dismissal rates for cocaine users. Drug use was not related to accidents or injuries. A cost-benefit analysis suggested that full implementation of the program would save the Postal Service several million dollars per year in lower absenteeism and turnover rates.

The validity of performance and psychological drug tests is not well established. As with integrity tests, a major concern is faking, but an advantage of psychological drug tests is that applicants are likely to perceive them as less intrusive. Of those organizations that drug test, few rely on physical or psychological tests.

In considering the validity of drug tests, one should not assume that the logical criterion against which the tests are validated is job performance. Typically, the criterion of job performance is central to evaluating the validity of most selection measures, yet drug tests have not been validated against job performance. Thus, it is far from clear that drug tests do a good job of discerning good performers from poor performers. Drug tests do appear to predict other work behaviors, however, including absenteeism, accidents, and other counterproductive behavior. For the purposes for which they are suited, then, validity of drug tests can be concluded to be high.

Finally, as with other assessment methods, two other criteria against which drug testing should be evaluated are adverse impact and applicant reactions. The adverse impact of drug testing is not universally accepted, but the Postal Service study indicated that drug-testing programs have a moderate to high degree of adverse impact against black and Hispanic applicants. Research on applicant reactions to drug tests shows that if applicants perceive a need for drug testing, they are more likely to find such a program acceptable.[141] Thus, organizations that do a good job explaining the reasons for the tests to applicants are more likely to find that applicants react favorably to the program.

## Recommendations for Effective Drug-Testing Programs

Though drug testing may have peaked, it is likely to continue as one of the most commonly used selection methods, especially among large employers. In an effort to make organizations' drug-testing programs as accurate and effective as possible, six recommendations are outlined as follows:

1. Emphasize drug testing in safety-sensitive jobs as well as in positions where the link between substance abuse and negative outcomes (e.g., as was the case with the Postal Service study described earlier) has been documented.
2. Use only reputable testing laboratories, and ensure that strict chain of custody is maintained.

3. Ask applicants for their consent and inform them of test results; provide rejected applicants an opportunity to appeal.

4. Use retesting to validate positive samples from the initial screening test.

5. Ensure that proper procedures are followed to maintain the applicant's right to privacy.

6. Review the program and validate the results against relevant criteria (accidents, absenteeism, turnover, and job performance); conduct a cost-benefit analysis of the program, as a very small number of detections may cause the program to have low utility.

## Medical Exams

Medical exams are often used to identify potential health risks in job candidates. Care must be taken to ensure that medical exams are used only when there is a compelling reason to do so. This is to ensure that individuals with disabilities unrelated to job performance are not screened out. Because of these sorts of potential abuses, the use of medical exams is strictly regulated by the ADA (discussed later in this chapter).

Although many organizations use medical exams, they are not particularly valid, because the procedures performed vary from doctor to doctor.[142] Also, medical exams are not always job related.[143] Finally, the emphasis is usually on short-term rather than long-term health. One way to make medical exams more reliable, and therefore more valid, is to ensure that the exam is based on job-related medical standards (i.e., the exam focuses on the specific diseases and health conditions that prohibit adequate functioning on specific jobs or clusters of tasks). Such an approach should improve not only content validity (because it is job related) but also reliability because it standardizes the diagnosis across physicians.

## LEGAL ISSUES

This section discusses three major legal issues. The first of these is the UGESP, a document that addresses the need to determine whether a selection procedure is causing adverse impact, and if so, the validation requirements for the procedure. The second issue is selection in conformance with the ADA as pertains to reasonable accommodation to job applicants and the use of medical tests. The final issue is that of drug testing for job applicants.

## Uniform Guidelines on Employee Selection Procedures

The UGESP are a comprehensive set of federal regulations specifying requirements for the selection systems of organizations covered under the Civil Rights Acts and under E.O. 11246. There are four major sections to the UGESP, namely, general principles, technical standards, documentation of impact and validity evidence, and definitions of terms. Each of these sections is summarized next. An excellent review of the UGESP in terms of court cases and examples of acceptable and unacceptable practices is available and should be consulted. The organization should also consult research that reviews how the UGESP have been interpreted, criticized, and used since their passage.[144]

## General Principles

1. *Summary.* The organization must keep records that allow it to determine whether its selection procedures are causing adverse impact in employment decisions. If no adverse impact is found, the remaining provisions of the UGESP generally do not apply. If adverse impact is found, the organization must either validate the selection procedure(s) causing the adverse impact or take steps to eliminate the adverse impact (such as stopping use of the procedure or using an alternate selection procedure that has less adverse impact).

2. *Scope.* The scope of the UGESP is very broad in that the guidelines apply to selection procedures used as the basis for any employment decisions. Employment decisions include hiring, promotion, demotion, and retention. A selection procedure is defined as "any measure, combination of measures, or procedure used as a basis for any employment decision." The procedures include "the full range of assessment techniques from traditional paper-and-pencil tests, performance tests, training programs, or probationary periods and physical, educational, and work experience requirements through informal or casual interviews and unscored application forms."

3. *Discrimination defined.* In general, any selection procedure that has an adverse impact is discriminatory unless it has been shown to be valid. There is a separate section for procedures that have not been validated.

4. *Suitable alternative selection procedures.* When a selection procedure has adverse impact, consideration should be given to the use of any suitable alternative selection procedures that may have less adverse impact.

5. *Information on adverse impact.* The organization must keep impact records by race, sex, and ethnic group for each of the job categories shown on the EEO-1 form (see Chapter 13).

6. *Evaluation of selection rates.* For each job or job category, the organization should evaluate the results, also known as the "bottom line," of the total selection process. The purpose of the evaluation is to determine whether there are differences in selection rates that indicate adverse impact. If adverse impact is not found, the organization usually does not have to take additional compliance steps, such as validation of each step in the selection process. If overall adverse impact is found, the individual components of the selection process should be evaluated for adverse impact.

7. *Adverse impact and the four-fifths rule.* To determine whether adverse impact is occurring, the organization should compute and compare selection rates for race, sex, and ethnic groups. A selection rate that is less than four-fifths (or 80%) of the rate for the group with the highest rate is generally regarded as evidence of adverse impact. There are exceptions to this general rule, based on sample size (small sample) considerations and on the extent to which the organization's recruitment practices have discouraged applicants disproportionately on grounds of race, sex, or ethnic group.

8. *General standards for validity studies.* There are three types of acceptable validity studies: criterion related, content, and construct. Numerous provisions pertain to standards governing these validity studies, as well as the appropriate use of selection procedures.

9. *Procedures that have not been validated.* This section discusses the use of alternative selection procedures to eliminate adverse impact. It also discusses instances in which validation studies cannot or need not be performed.

10. *Affirmative action.* Use of validated selection procedures does not relieve the employer of any affirmative action obligation it may have. The employer is encouraged to adopt and implement voluntary AAPs.

## Technical Standards

This section contains a lengthy specification of the minimum technical standards that should be met when conducting a validation study. Separate standards are given for each of the three types of validity (criterion-related, content, construct) studies.

## Documentation of Impact and Validity Evidence

For each job or job category, the employer is required to keep detailed records on adverse impact and, where adverse impact is found, evidence of validity. Detailed record-keeping requirements are provided.

There are two important exceptions to these general requirements. First, a small employer (fewer than 100 employees) does not have to keep separate records for each job category, but only for its total selection process across all jobs. Second, records for race or national origin do not have to be kept for groups constituting less than 2% of the labor force in the relevant labor area.

## Definitions

This section defines terms (25 total) used throughout the UGESP.

## Summary

The UGESP make substantial demands on an organization and its staffing systems. Those demands exist to ensure organizational awareness of the possibility of adverse impact in employment decisions. When adverse impact is found, the

UGESP provide mechanisms (requirements) for coping with it. The UGESP thus should occupy a prominent place in any covered organization's EEO/AA policies and practices.

## Selection Under the Americans With Disabilities Act

The ADA, as interpreted by the Equal Employment Opportunity Commission (EEOC), creates substantial requirements and suggestions for compliance pertaining to external selection.[145] The general nature of these is identified and commented on next.

### General Principles

Two major, overarching principles pertain to selection. The first principle is that it is unlawful to screen out individuals with disabilities, unless the selection procedure is job related and consistent with business necessity. The second principle is that a selection procedure must accurately reflect the KSAOs being measured, and not impaired sensory, manual, or speaking skills, unless those impaired skills are the ones being measured by the procedure.

The first principle is obviously very similar to principles governing selection generally under federal laws and regulations. The second principle is important because it cautions the organization to be sure that its selection procedures do not inadvertently and unnecessarily screen out applicants with disabilities.

### Access to Job Application Process

The organization's job application process must be accessible to individuals with disabilities. Reasonable accommodation must be provided to enable all persons to apply, and applicants should be provided assistance (if needed) in completing the application process. Applicants should also be told about the nature and content of the selection process. This allows them to request reasonable accommodation to testing, if needed, in advance.

### Reasonable Accommodation to Testing

In general, the organization may use any kind of test in assessing job applicants. These tests must be administered consistently to all job applicants for any particular job.

A very important provision of testing pertains to the requirement to provide reasonable accommodation if requested by an applicant to take the test. The purpose of this requirement is to ensure that the test accurately reflects the KSAO being measured, rather than an impairment of the applicant. Reasonable accommodation, however, is not required for a person with an impaired skill if the purpose of that test is to measure that skill. For example, the organization does not have to provide reasonable accommodation on a manual dexterity test to a person with arthritis in the fingers and hands if the purpose of the test is to measure manual dexterity.

Numerous types of reasonable accommodation can be made, and there is organizational experience and research in providing reasonable accommodation.[146] Examples include substituting an oral test for a written one (or vice versa); providing extra time to complete a test; scheduling rest breaks during a test; administering tests in large print, in Braille, or by reader; and using assistive technologies to adapt computers, such as a special mouse or screen magnifier.

### Inquiries About Disabilities

Virtually all assessment tools and questions are affected by the ADA. A summary of permissible and impermissible practices is shown in Exhibit 9.16. Note that permissibility depends on the assessment tool, whether the tool is being used for an external applicant or employee, and whether the tool is being used prehire (like most selection procedures) or after a conditional offer has been made. Also note the many stipulations governing usage. Another useful source of information is "Job Applicants and the Americans With Disabilities Act."

### Medical Examinations: Job Applicants

Substantial regulations surround medical exams, both before and after a job offer. Prior to the offer, the organization may not make medical inquiries or require medical exams of an applicant. The job offer, however, may be conditional, pending the results of a medical exam.

Postoffer, the organization may conduct a medical exam. The exam must be given to all applicants for a particular job, not just individuals with a known or suspected disability. Whereas the content of the exam is not restricted to being only job related, the reasons for rejecting an applicant on the basis of the exam must be job related. A person may also be rejected if exam results indicate a direct threat to the health and safety of the applicant or others such as employees or customers. This rejection must be based on reasonable medical judgment, not a simple judgment that the applicant might or could cause harm. Each applicant must be assessed individually in order to determine whether an impairment creates a significant risk of harm and cannot be accommodated through reasonable means. Results of medical exams are to be kept confidential, held separate from the employee's personnel file, and released only under very specific circumstances.

It may be difficult to determine whether something is a medical examination and thus subject to the above requirements surrounding its use. The EEOC defines a medical examination as "a procedure or test that seeks information about an individual's physical or mental impairments or health."[147] The following factors are suggestive of a selection procedure that would be considered a medical examination:

- It is administered by a health care professional and/or someone trained by such a professional.
- It is designed to reveal an impairment of physical or mental health.

**EXHIBIT 9.16** **Inquiries About Disabilities**

## What Inquiries Can Be Made About Disabilities?

| Type | External Applicants (Pre-Offer Stage) | External Applicants (Post-Conditional Offer Stage) | Employees |
|---|---|---|---|
| AA data (self-ID and requests) | Yes | Yes | Yes |
| Physical exam | No | Yes (C, D) | Yes (B, E) |
| Psychological exam | No | Yes (C, D) | Yes (B, E) |
| Health questionnaire | No | Yes (C, D) | Yes (B, E) |
| Work comp history | No | Yes (C, D) | Yes (B, E) |
| Physical agility test | Yes (A, C) | Yes (A, C) | Yes (A, C) |
| Drug test | Yes | Yes | Yes |
| Alcohol test | No | Yes (B, D) | Yes (B, E) |
| **Specific questions (oral and written)** | | | |
| About existence of a disability, its nature | Yes | Yes (A, C) | Yes (B, E) |
| About ability to perform job-related functions (essential and nonessential) | Yes | Yes | Yes |
| About smoking (but not allergic to it) | Yes | Yes | Yes |
| About history of illegal drug use | No | Yes (B, D) | Yes (B, E) |
| **Specific requests** | | | |
| Describe how you would perform job-related functions (essential and nonessential) with or without reasonable accommodation | Yes (D, F) | Yes (C, D) | Yes (B, E) |
| Provide evidence of not currently using drugs | Yes | Yes | Yes |

A. If given to all similarly situated applicants/employees
B. If job related and consistent with business necessity
C. If only job-related criteria consistent with business necessity are used afterwards to screen out/ exclude the applicant, at which point reasonable accommodation must be considered
D. If all entering employees in the same job category are subjected to it and subjected to same qualification standard
E. But only for the following purposes:
   a. To determine fitness for duty (still qualified or still able to perform essential functions)
   b. To determine reasonable accommodation
   c. To meet requirements imposed by federal, state, or local law (DOT, OSHA, EPA, etc.)
   d. To determine direct threat
F. Can be requested of a particular individual if the disability is known and may interfere with or prevent performance of a job-related function

SOURCE: S. K. Willman, "Tips for Minimizing Abuses Under the Americans With Disabilities Act," *Legal Report*, Society for Human Resource Management, Jan.–Feb. 2003, p. 8. Used with permission.

- It is invasive (e.g., requires drawing blood, urine, or breath).
- It measures the applicant's physiological responses to performing a task.
- It is normally given in a medical setting and/or medical equipment is used.
- It tests for alcohol consumption.

Though closely allied with medical examinations, several types of tests fall outside the bounds of medical examinations; these may be used preoffer. These include physical agility tests, physical fitness tests, vision tests, drug tests for current illegal use of controlled substances, and tests that measure honesty, tastes, and habits.

A gray area involves the use of psychological tests, such as personality tests. They are considered medical if they lead to identifying a medically recognized mental disorder or impairment, such as those in the American Psychiatric Association's *Diagnostic and Statistical Manual of Mental Disorders*. Future regulations and court rulings may help clarify which types of psychological tests are medical exams.

## Medical Examinations: Current Employees

This enforcement guidance applies to employees generally, not just employees with disabilities.[148] An employee who applies for a new (different) job with the same employer should be treated as an applicant for a new job and thus subject to the provisions described above for job applicants. An individual is not an applicant where she or he is entitled to another position with the same employer (e.g., because of seniority or satisfactory performance in her or his current position) or when returning to a regular job after being on temporary assignment in another job. Instead, these individuals are considered employees.

For employees, the employer may make disability-related inquiries and require medical examinations only if they are job related and consistent with business necessity. Any information obtained, or voluntarily provided by the employee, is a confidential medical record. The record may only be shared in limited circumstances with managers, supervisors, first aid and safety personnel, and government officials investigating ADA compliance. Generally, a disability-related inquiry or medical examination is job related and consistent with business necessity when the employer has a reasonable belief, based on objective evidence, that (1) an employee's ability to perform essential job functions will be impaired by a medical condition or (2) an employee will pose a direct threat due to a medical condition.

A medical examination for employees is defined the same way as for job applicants. Examples of disability-related inquiries include the following:

- Asking an employee whether she or he was disabled (or ever had a disability) or how she or he became disabled, or asking about the nature or severity of an employee's disability

- Asking an employee to provide medical documentation regarding her or his disability
- Asking an employee's coworkers, family members, doctor, or another person about the employee's disability
- Asking about an employee's genetic information
- Asking about an employee's prior workers' compensation history
- Asking if an employee is taking any medication or drugs or has done so in the past
- Asking an employee broad information that is likely to elicit information about a disability

### Drug Testing

Drug testing is permitted to detect the use of illegal drugs. The law, however, is neutral as to its encouragement.

### UGESP

The UGESP do not apply to the ADA or its regulations. This means that the guidance and requirements for employers' selection systems under the Civil Rights Act may or may not be the same as those required for compliance with the ADA.

## Drug Testing

Drug testing is surrounded by an amalgam of laws and regulations at the federal and state levels. Special law for the Department of Transportation requires alcohol and drug testing for transportation workers in safety-sensitive jobs.[149] The organization should seek legal and medical advice to determine whether it should do drug testing and, if so, what the nature of the drug-testing program should be. Beyond that, the organization should require and administer drug tests on a contingency (postoffer) basis only, to avoid the possibility of obtaining and using medical information illegally. For example, positive drug test results may occur because of the presence of a legal drug, and using these results preoffer to reject a person would be a violation of the ADA.

## SUMMARY

This chapter continued the discussion of proper methods and processes to be used in external selection. Specifically, substantive, discretionary, and contingent assessment methods were discussed, as well as collection of assessment data and pertinent legal issues.

Most of the chapter discussed various substantive methods, which are used to separate finalists from candidates. Like initial assessment methods, substantive assessment methods should always be based on the logic of prediction and the use of selection plans. The substantive methods that were reviewed include personality tests; ability tests; emotional intelligence tests; performance tests and work samples; situational judgment tests; integrity tests; interest, values, and preference inventories; structured interviews; and assessment for team environments. As with initial assessment methods, the criteria used to evaluate the effectiveness of substantive assessment methods are frequency of use, cost, reliability, validity, utility, applicant reactions, and adverse impact. In general, substantive assessment methods show a marked improvement in reliability and validity over initial assessment methods. This is probably due to the stronger relationship between the sampling of the applicant's previous situations and the requirements for success on the job.

Discretionary selection methods are somewhat less formal and more subjective than other selection methods. When discretionary methods are used, two judgments are important: will the applicant be a good organization "citizen," and do the values and goals of this applicant match those of the organization?

Though discretionary methods are subjective, contingent assessment methods typically involve decisions about whether applicants meet certain objective requirements for the job. The two most common contingent methods are drug testing and medical exams. Particularly in the case of drug testing, the use of contingent methods is relatively complex from an administrative and legal standpoint.

Regardless of predictor type, attention must be given to the proper collection and use of predictor information. In particular, support services need to be established, administrators with the appropriate credentials need to be hired, data need to be kept private and confidential, and administration procedures must be standardized.

Along with administrative issues, legal issues need to be considered as well. Particular attention must be paid to regulations that govern permissible activities by organizations. Regulations include those in the UGESP and the ADA.

## DISCUSSION QUESTIONS

1. Describe the similarities and differences between personality tests and integrity tests. When is each warranted in the selection process?

2. How would you advise an organization considering adopting a cognitive ability test for selection?

3. Describe the structured interview. What are the characteristics of structured interviews that improve on the shortcomings of unstructured interviews?

4. What are the most common discretionary and contingent assessment methods? What are the similarities and differences between the use of these two methods?

5. What is the best way to collect and use drug-testing data in selection decisions?

6. How should organizations apply the general principles of the UGESP to practical selection decisions?

## ETHICAL ISSUES

1. Do you think it's unethical for employers to select applicants on the basis of measures such as "Dislike loud music" and "Enjoy wild flights of fancy" even if the scales that such items measure have been shown to predict job performance? Explain.

2. Cognitive ability tests are one of the best predictors of job performance, yet they have substantial adverse impact against minorities. Do you think it's fair to use such tests? Why or why not?

## APPLICATIONS

### Assessment Methods for the Job of Human Resources Director

Nairduwel, Inoalot, and Imslo (NII) is a law firm specializing in business law. Among other areas, it deals in equal employment opportunity law, business litigation, and workplace torts. The firm has more than 50 partners and approximately 120 employees. It does business in three states and has law offices in two major metropolitan areas. The firm has no federal contracts.

NII plans to expand into two additional states with two major metropolitan areas. One of the primary challenges accompanying this ambitious expansion plan is how to staff, train, and compensate the individuals who will fill the positions in the new offices. Accordingly, the firm wishes to hire an HR director to oversee the recruitment, selection, training, performance appraisal, and compensation activities accompanying the business expansion, as well as supervise the HR activities in the existing NII offices. The newly created job description for the HR director is listed in the accompanying exhibit.

The firm wishes to design and then use a selection system for assessing applicants that will achieve two objectives: (1) create a valid and useful system that will do a good job of matching applicant KSAOs to job requirements, and (2) be in compliance with all relevant federal and state employment laws.

The firm is considering numerous selection techniques for possible use. For each method listed below, decide whether you would or would not use it in the selection process and state why.

1. A job knowledge test specifically designed for HR professionals that focuses on an applicant's general knowledge of HR management

2. A medical examination and drug test at the beginning of the selection process in order to determine if applicants are able to cope with the high level of stress and frequent travel requirements of the job and are drug-free

3. A paper-and-pencil integrity test

4. A structured behavioral interview that would be specially designed for use in filling only this job

5. A general cognitive ability test

6. Personal Characteristics Inventory

7. A set of interview questions that the firm typically uses for filling any position:

   a. Tell me about a problem you solved on a previous job.

   b. Do you have any physical impairments that would make it difficult for you to travel on business?

   c. Have you ever been tested for AIDS?

   d. Are you currently unemployed, and if so, why?

   e. This position requires fresh ideas and energy. Do you think you have those qualities?

   f. What is your definition of success?

   g. What kind of sports do you like?

   h. How well do you work under pressure? Give me some examples.

**Exhibit**

**Job Description for Human Resources Director**

## JOB SUMMARY

Performs responsible administrative work managing personnel activities. Work involves responsibility for the planning and administration of HRM programs, including recruitment, selection, evaluation, appointment, promotion, compensation, and recommended change of status of employees, and a system of communication for disseminating information to workers. Works under general supervision, exercising initiative and independent judgment in the performance of assigned tasks.

## TASKS

1. Participates in overall planning and policy making to provide effective and uniform personnel services.

2. Communicates policy through organization levels by bulletin, meetings, and personal contact.

3. Supervises recruitment and screening of job applicants to fill vacancies. Supervises interviewing of applicants, evaluation of qualifications, and classification of applications.

4. Supervises administration of tests to applicants.

5. Confers with supervisors on personnel matters, including placement problems, retention or release of probationary employees, transfers, demotions, and dismissals of permanent employees.

6. Initiates personnel training activities and coordinates these activities with work of officials and supervisors.

7. Establishes effective service rating system and trains unit supervisors in making employee evaluations.

8. Supervises maintenance of employee personnel files.

9. Supervises a group of employees directly and through subordinates.

10. Performs related work as assigned.

## JOB SPECIFICATIONS

1. *Experience and Training*

   Should have considerable experience in area of HRM administration. Six years minimum.

2. *Education*

   Graduation from a four-year college or university, with major work in human resources, business administration, or industrial psychology. Master's degree in one of these areas is preferable.

3. *Knowledge, Skills, and Abilities*

   Considerable knowledge of principles and practices of HRM, including staffing, compensation, training, and performance evaluation.

4. *Responsibility*

   Supervises the human resource activities of six office managers, one clerk, and one assistant.

## Choosing Among Finalists for the Job of Human Resources Director

Assume that NII, after weighing its options, decided to use the following selection methods to assess applicants for the HR director job: résumé, cognitive ability test,

**Exhibit**

**Results of Assessment of Finalists for Human Resources Director Position**

|  | Finalist 1—<br>Lola Vega | Finalist 2—<br>Sam Fein | Finalist 3—<br>Shawanda Jackson |
|---|---|---|---|
| Résumé | GPA 3.9/Cornell University<br>B.S. Human Resource Mgmt.<br>5 years' experience in HRM<br>• 4 years in recruiting | GPA 2.8/SUNY Binghamton<br>B.B.A. Finance<br>20 years' experience in HRM<br>• Numerous HR assignments<br>• Certified HR professional | GPA 3.2/Auburn University<br>B.B.A. Business and English<br>8 years' experience in HRM<br>• 3 years HR generalist<br>• 4 years compensation analyst |
|  | No supervisory experience | 15 years' supervisory experience | 5 years' supervisory experience |
| Cognitive ability test | 90% correct | 78% correct | 84% correct |
| Knowledge test | 94% correct | 98% correct | 91% correct |
| Structured int. (out of 100 pts.) | 85 | 68 | 75 |
| Question (f) | Ability to influence others | To do things you want to do | Promotions and earnings |
| Question (g) | Golf, shuffleboard | Spectator sports | Basketball, tennis |

job knowledge test, structured interview, and questions (f) and (g) from the list of generic interview questions.

NII advertised for the position extensively, and out of a pool of 23 initial applicants, it was able to come up with a list of three finalists. Shown in the accompanying exhibit are the results from the assessment of the three finalists using these selection methods. In addition, information from an earlier résumé screen is included for possible consideration. For each finalist, decide whether you would hire the person and why.

## ENDNOTES

1. L. M. Hough, "The 'Big Five' Personality Variables—Construct Confusion: Description Versus Prediction," *Human Performance*, 1992, 5, pp. 139–155.
2. D. S. Ones, S. Dilchert, C. Viswesvaran, and T. A. Judge, "In Support of Personality Assessments in Organizational Settings," *Personnel Psychology*, 2007, 60, pp. 995–1027.
3. P. T. Costa, Jr., and R. R. McCrae, "Four Ways Five Factors Are Basic," *Personality and Individual Differences*, 1992, 13, pp. 653–665.
4. M. K. Mount and M. R. Barrick, *Manual for the Personal Characteristics Inventory* (Iowa City, IA: authors, 1995).
5. P. T. Costa, Jr., and R. R. McCrae, *Revised NEO Personality Inventory (NEO-PI-R) and NEO Five-Factor Inventory (NEO-FFI) Professional Manual* (Odessa, FL: Psychological Assessment Resources, 1992).
6. J. Hogan and R. Hogan, "How to Measure Employee Reliability," *Journal of Applied Psychology*, 1989, 74, pp. 273–279.
7. See, for example, A. Doyle, "WalMart Job Application: WalMart Job Application and Pre-Employment Assessment Test," (*www.jobsearch.about.com/od/jobapplications/a/walmartapp.htm*), accessed 8/11/13.
8. N. T. Tippins, J. Beaty, F. Drasgow, W. M. Gibson, K. Pearlman, D. O. Segall, and W. Shepherd, "Unproctored Internet Testing in Employment Settings," *Personnel Psychology*, 2006, 59, pp. 189–225; S. Overman, "Online Screening Saves Time and Money," *Staffing Management*, July–Sept. 2005, pp. 18–22.
9. Exhibit 9.2 and the review here are based on C. M. Berry, D. S. Ones, and P. R. Sackett, "Interpersonal Deviance, Organizational Deviance, and Their Common Correlates: A Review and Meta-Analysis," *Journal of Applied Psychology*, 2007, 92, pp. 410–424; C. Viswesvaran, J. Deller, and D. S. Ones, "Personality Measures in Personnel Selection: Some New Contributions," *International Journal of Selection and Assessment*, 2007, 15, pp. 354–358; N. M. Dudley, K. A. Orvis, J. E. Lebiecki, and J. M. Cortina, "A Meta-Analytic Investigation of Conscientiousness in the Prediction of Job Performance: Examining the Intercorrelations and the Incremental Validity of Narrow Traits," *Journal of Applied Psychology*, 2006, 91, pp. 40–57; D. S. Ones, C. Viswesvaran, and S. Dilchert, "Personality at Work: Raising Awareness and Correcting Misconceptions," *Human Performance*, 2005, 18, pp. 389–404; M. G. Rothstein and R. D. Goffin, "The Use of Personality Measures in Personnel Selection: What Does Current Research Support?" *Human Resource Management Review*, 2006, 16, pp. 155–180; J. A. Shaffer and B. E. Postlethwaite, "A Matter of Context: A Meta-Analytic Investigation of the Relative Validity of Contextualized and Noncontextualized Personality Measures," *Personnel Psychology*, 2012, 65, pp. 445–494.
10. For a review of these criticisms and responses to them, see F. P. Morgeson, M. A. Campion, R. L. Dipboye, J. R. Hollenbeck, K. Murphy, and N. Schmitt, "Reconsidering the Use of Personality Tests in Personnel Selection Contexts," *Personnel Psychology*, 2007, 60, pp. 683–729; Ones, Dilchert, Viswesvaran, and Judge, "In Support of Personality Assessment in Organizational Settings"; R. P. Tett and N. D. Christiansen, "Personality Tests at the Crossroads: A Response to Morgeson, Campion, Dipboye, Hollenbeck, Murphy, and Schmitt (2007)," *Personnel Psychology*, 2007, 60, pp. 967–993.
11. Morgeson et al., "Reconsidering the Use of Personality Tests in Personnel Selection Contexts," p. 694.
12. Ones, Dilchert, Viswesvaran, and Judge, "In Support of Personality Assessment in Organizational Settings"; M. R. Barrick, M. K. Mount, and T. A. Judge, "Personality and Performance at

the Beginning of the New Millennium: What Do We Know and Where Do We Go Next?" *International Journal of Selection & Assessment*, 2001, 9, pp. 9–30.

13. G. V. Barrett, R. F. Miguel, J. M. Hurd, S. B. Lueke, and J. A. Tan, "Practical Issues in the Use of Personality Tests in Police Selection," *Public Personnel Management*, 2003, 32, pp. 497–517; V. M. Mallozzi, "This Expert in Scouting Athletes Doesn't Need to See Them Play," *New York Times*, Apr. 25, 2004, pp. SP3, SP7.

14. M. R. Barrick and M. K. Mount, "Autonomy as a Moderator of the Relationships Between the Big Five Personality Dimensions and Job Performance," *Journal of Applied Psychology*, 1993, 78, pp. 111–118.

15. D. Chan, "Interactive Effects of Situational Judgment Effectiveness and Proactive Personality on Work Perceptions and Work Outcomes," *Journal of Applied Psychology*, 2006, 91, pp. 475–481; J. A. Thompson, "Proactive Personality and Job Performance: A Social Capital Perspective," *Journal of Applied Psychology*, 2005, 90, pp. 1011–1017; S. E. Seibert, M. L. Kraimer, and J. M. Crant, "What Do Proactive People Do? A Longitudinal Model Linking Proactive Personality and Career Success," *Personnel Psychology*, 2001, 54, pp. 845–874.

16. T. A. Judge and J. E. Bono, "Relationship of Core Self-Evaluations Traits—Self-Esteem, Generalized Self-Efficacy, Locus of Control, and Emotional Stability—With Job Satisfaction and Job Performance: A Meta-Analysis," *Journal of Applied Psychology*, 2001, 86, pp. 80–92; T. A. Judge, A. Erez, J. E. Bono, and C. J. Thoresen, "The Core Self-Evaluations Scale: Development of a Measure," *Personnel Psychology*, 2003, 56, pp. 303–331.

17. S. A. Birkeland, T. M. Manson, J. L. Kisamore, M. T. Brannick, and M. A. Smith, "A Meta-Analytic Investigation of Job Applicant Faking on Personality Measures," *International Journal of Selection and Assessment*, 2006, 14, pp. 317–335; S. Stark, O. S. Chernyshenko, and F. Drasgow, "Examining Assumptions About Item Responding in Personality Assessment: Should Ideal Point Methods Be Considered for Scale Development and Scoring?" *Journal of Applied Psychology*, 2006, 91, pp. 25–39.

18. H. Le, I. Oh, S. B. Robbins, R. Ilies, E. Holland, and P. Westrick, "Too Much of a Good Thing: Curvilinear Relationships Between Personality Traits and Job Performance," *Journal of Applied Psychology*, 2011, 96, pp. 113–133; D. L. Whetzel, M. A. McDaniel, A. P. Yost, and N. Kim, "Linearity of Personality-Performance Relationships: A Large-Scale Examination," *International Journal of Selection and Assessment*, 2010, 18(3), pp. 310–320.

19. Shaffer and Postlethwaite, "A Matter of Context: A Meta-Analytic Investigation of the Relative Validity of Contextualized and Noncontextualized Personality Measures."

20. Rothstein and Goffin, "The Use of Personality Measures in Personnel Selection: What Does Current Research Support?"

21. J. E. Ellingson, D. B. Smith, and P. R. Sackett, "Investigating the Influence of Social Desirability on Personality Factor Structure," *Journal of Applied Psychology*, 2001, 86, pp. 122–133; D. B. Smith and J. E. Ellingson, "Substance Versus Style: A New Look at Social Desirability in Motivating Contexts," *Journal of Applied Psychology*, 2002, 87, pp. 211–219.

22. N. Schmitt and F. L. Oswald, "The Impact of Corrections for Faking on the Validity of Noncognitive Measures in Selection Settings," *Journal of Applied Psychology*, 2006, 91, pp. 613–621.

23. E. D. Heggestad, M. Morrison, C. L. Reeve, and R. A. McCloy, "Forced-Choice Assessments of Personality for Selection: Evaluating Issues of Normative Assessment and Faking Resistance," *Journal of Applied Psychology*, 2006, 91, pp. 9–24; S. Dilchert, D. S. Ones, C. Viswesvaran, and J. Deller, "Response Distortion in Personality Measurement: Born to Deceive, yet Capable of Providing Valid Self-Assessments?" *Psychology Science*, 2006, 48, pp. 209–225.

24. S. A. Dwight and J. J. Donovan, "Do Warnings Not to Fake Reduce Faking?" *Human Performance*, 2003, 16, pp. 1–23; J. Hogan, P. Barrett, and R. Hogan, "Personality Measurement, Faking, and Employment Selection," *Journal of Applied Psychology*, 2007, 92, pp. 1270–1285; J. E. Ellingson, P. R. Sackett, and B. S. Connelly, "Personality Assessment Across Selection and Development Contexts: Insights Into Response Distortion," *Journal of Applied Psychology*, 2007, 92, pp. 386–395; E.A.J. van Hooft and M. P. Born, "Intentional Response Distortion on Personality Tests: Using Eye-Tracking to Understand Response Processes When Faking," *Journal of Applied Psychology*, 97, 2, pp. 301–316; J. Fan, D. Gao, S. A. Carroll, F. J. Lopez, T. S. Tian, and H. Meng, "Testing the Efficacy of a New Procedure for Reducing Faking on Personality Tests Within Selection Contexts," *Journal of Applied Psychology*, 97, pp. 866–880.

25. R. D. Zimmerman, M. Triana, and M. R. Barrick, "Predictive Criterion-Related Validity of Observer Ratings of Personality and Job-Related Competencies Using Multiple Raters and Multiple Performance Criteria," *Human Performance*, 2010, 23(4), pp. 361–378; C. M. Berry, P. R. Sackett, and V. Tobares, "A Meta-Analysis of Conditional Reasoning Tests of Aggression," *Personnel Psychology*, 2010, 63(2), pp. 361–384; R. E. Johnson, A. L. Tolentino, O. B. Rodopman, and E. Cho, "We (Sometimes) Know Not How We Feel: Predicting Job Performance With an Implicit Measure of Trait Affectivity," *Personnel Psychology*, 2010, 63(1), pp. 197–219; I. Oh and C. M. Berry, "The Five-Factor Model of Personality and Managerial Performance: Validity Gains Through the Use of 360 Degree Performance Ratings," *Journal of Applied Psychology*, 2009, 94(6), pp. 1498–1513.

26. J. P. Hausknecht, D. V. Day, and S. C. Thomas, "Applicant Reactions to Selection Procedures: An Updated Model and Meta-Analysis," *Personnel Psychology*, 2004, 57(3), pp. 639–683; "Workers Question Validity of Personality Tests," *Staffing Management*, Jan.–Mar. 2007, p. 11.

27. A. Wolf and A. Jenkins, "Explaining Greater Test Use for Selection: The Role of HR Professionals in a World of Expanding Regulation," *Human Resource Management Journal*, 2006, 16(2), pp. 193–213.

28. E. A. Fleishman and M. E. Reilly, *Handbook of Human Abilities* (Palo Alto, CA: Consulting Psychologists Press, 1992).

29. C. L. Reeve and N. Blacksmith, "Identifying g: A Review of Current Factor Analytic Practices in the Science of Mental Abilities," *Intelligence*, 2009, 37(5), pp. 487–494.

30. J. Schmidt, "2012 NFL Draft: The 5 Best, 5 Worst Wonderlic Scores in NFL History," *Bleacher Report*, Apr. 4, 2012 (http://bleacherreport.com/articles/1130834-nfl-draft-2012-the-5-best-and-the-5-worst-wonderlic-scores-in-nfl-history), accessed 8/12/2013.

31. C. F. Wonderlic, Jr., "Test Publishers Form Association," *Human Resource Measurements* (Supplement to the Jan. 1993 *Personnel Journal*), p. 3.

32. L. S. Gottfredson, "Societal Consequences of the g Factor in Employment," *Journal of Vocational Behavior*, 1986, 29, pp. 379–410; J. F. Salgado, N. Anderson, S. Moscoso, C. Bertua, F. de Fruyt, and J. P. Rolland, "A Meta-Analytic Study of General Mental Ability Validity for Different Occupations in the European Community," *Journal of Applied Psychology*, 2003, 88, pp. 1068–1081.

33. T. A. Judge, R. Ilies, and N. Dimotakis, "Are Health and Happiness the Product of Wisdom? The Relationship of General Mental Ability to Educational and Occupational Attainment, Health, and Well-Being," *Journal of Applied Psychology*, 2010, 95(3), pp. 454–468; M. A. Maltarich, A. J. Nyberg, and G. A. Reilly, "A Conceptual and Empirical Analysis of the Cognitive Ability–Voluntary Turnover Relationship," *Journal of Applied Psychology*, 2010, 95(6), pp. 1058–1070.

34. J. E. Hunter, "Cognitive Ability, Cognitive Aptitudes, Job Knowledge, and Job Performance," *Journal of Vocational Behavior*, 1986, 29, pp. 340–362.

35. J.W.B. Lang and P. D. Bliese, "General Mental Ability and Two Types of Adaptation to Unforeseen Change: Applying Discontinuous Growth Models to the Task-Change Paradigm," *Journal of Applied Psychology*, 2009, 94(2), pp. 411–428; M. J. Ree and J. A. Earles, "Predicting Training Success: Not Much More Than g," *Personnel Psychology*, 1991, 44, pp. 321–332.

36. Hunter, "Cognitive Ability, Cognitive Aptitudes, Job Knowledge, and Job Performance"; F. L. Schmidt and J. E. Hunter, "Development of a Causal Model of Processes Determining Job Performance," *Current Directions in Psychological Science*, 1992, 1, pp. 89–92.

37. J.W.B. Lang, M. Kersting, U. R. Hülsheger, and J. Lang, "General Mental Ability, Narrower Cognitive Abilities, and Job Performance: The Perspective of the Nested-Factors Model of Cognitive Abilities," *Personnel Psychology*, 2010, 63(3), pp. 595–640; M. K. Mount, I. Oh, and M. Burns, "Incremental Validity of Perceptual Speed and Accuracy Over General Mental Ability," *Personnel Psychology*, 2008, 61(1), pp. 113–139.

38. P. L. Roth, C. A. BeVier, P. Bobko, F. S. Switzer, and P. Tyler, "Ethnic Group Differences in Cognitive Ability in Employment and Educational Settings: A Meta-Analysis," *Personnel Psychology*, 2001, 54, pp. 297–330.

39. See P. R. Sackett and W. Shen, "Subgroup Differences on Cognitive Tests in Contexts Other Than Personnel Selection," in J. L. Outtz (ed.), *Adverse Impact: Implications for Organizational Staffing and High Stakes Selection* (New York: Routledge/Taylor & Francis, 2010), pp. 323–346; C. L. Reeve and J. E. Charles, "Survey of Opinions on the Primacy of g and Social Consequences of Ability Testing: A Comparison of Expert and Non-Expert Views," *Intelligence*, 2008, 36(6), pp. 681–688.

40. W. F. Cascio, R. Jacobs, and J. Silva, "Validity, Utility, and Adverse Impact: Practical Implications From 30 Years of Data," in Outtz (ed.), *Adverse Impact: Implications for Organizational Staffing and High Stakes Selection*, pp. 271–288; P. Bobko, P. L. Roth, and D. Potosky, "Derivation and Implications of a Meta-Analytic Matrix Incorporating Cognitive Ability, Alternative Predictors, and Job Performance," *Personnel Psychology*, 1999, 52, pp. 561–589; A. M. Ryan, R. E. Ployhart, and L. A. Friedel, "Using Personality to Reduce Adverse Impact: A Cautionary Note," *Journal of Applied Psychology*, 1998, 83, pp. 298–307; K. Mattern and B. F. Patterson, "Test of Slope and Intercept Bias in College Admissions: A Response to Aguinis, Culpepper, and Pierce," *Journal of Applied Psychology*, 2013, 98, pp. 134–147.

41. B. D. Edwards and W. Arthur, Jr., "An Examination of Factors Contributing to a Reduction in Subgroup Differences on a Constructed-Response Paper-and-Pencil Test of Scholastic Achievement," *Journal of Applied Psychology*, 2007, 92, pp. 794–801; D. A. Newman and J. S. Lyon, "Recruitment Efforts to Reduce Adverse Impact: Targeted Recruiting for Personality, Cognitive Ability, and Diversity," *Journal of Applied Psychology*, 2009, 94(2), pp. 298–317.

42. W. T. Dickens and J. R. Flynn, "Black Americans Reduce the IQ Gap," *Psychological Science*, 2006, 17, pp. 913–920; J. P. Rushton and A. R. Jensen, "The Totality of Available Evidence Shows the Race IQ Gap Still Remains," *Psychological Science*, 2006, 17, pp. 921–922. See also E. Hunt and J. Carlson, "Considerations Relating to the Study of Group Differences in Intelligence," *Perspectives on Psychological Science*, 2007, 2, pp. 194–213.

43. T. A. Judge, D. Blancero, D. M. Cable, and D. E. Johnson, "Effects of Selection Systems on Job Search Decisions," Paper presented at the Tenth Annual Conference of the Society for Industrial and Organizational Psychology, Orlando, FL, 1995.

44. S. L. Rynes and M. L. Connerley, "Applicant Reactions to Alternative Selection Procedures," *Journal of Business and Psychology*, 1993, 7, pp. 261–277.

45. Hausknecht, Day, and Thomas, "Applicant Reactions to Selection Procedures: An Updated Model and Meta-Analysis"; J. W. Smither, R. R. Reilly, R. E. Millsap, K. Pearlman, and R. W. Stoffey, "Applicant Reactions to Selection Procedures," *Personnel Psychology*, 46, pp. 49–76.

46. Hausknecht, Day, and Thomas, "Applicant Reactions to Selection Procedures: An Updated Model and Meta-Analysis."

47. S. M. Gully, S. C. Payne, and K.L.K. Koles, "The Impact of Error Training and Individual Differences on Training Outcomes: An Attribute-Treatment Interaction Perspective," *Journal of Applied Psychology*, 2002, 87, pp. 143–155; J. P. Hausknecht, C. O. Trevor, and J. L. Farr, "Retaking Ability Tests in a Selection Setting: Implications for Practice Effects, Training Performance, and Turnover," *Journal of Applied Psychology*, 2002, 87, pp. 243–254; J. F. Salgado, N. Anderson, and S. Moscoso, "International Validity Generalization of GMA and Cognitive Abilities: A European Community Meta-Analysis," *Personnel Psychology*, 2003, 56, pp. 573–605.

48. K. R. Murphy, B. E. Cronin, and A. P. Tam, "Controversy and Consensus Regarding Use of Cognitive Ability Testing in Organizations," *Journal of Applied Psychology*, 2003, 88, pp. 660–671.

49. J. Hogan, "Physical Abilities," in M. D. Dunnette and L. M. Hough (eds.), *Handbook of Industrial and Organizational Psychology*, Vol. 2 (Palo Alto, CA: Consulting Psychologists Press, 1991), pp. 753–831.

50. N. Henderson, M. W. Berry, and T. Malic, "Field Measures of Strength and Fitness Predict Firefighter Performance on Physically Demanding Tasks," *Personnel Psychology*, 2007, 60, pp. 431–473.

51. M. A. Campion, "Personnel Selection for Physically Demanding Jobs: Review and Recommendations," *Personnel Psychology*, 1987, 36, pp. 527–550.

52. T. A. Baker, "The Utility of a Physical Test in Reducing Injury Costs," Paper presented at the Ninth Annual Meeting of the Society for Industrial and Organizational Psychology, Nashville, TN, 1995.

53. B. R. Blakley, M. A. Quinones, M. S. Crawford, and I. A. Jago, "The Validity of Isometric Strength Tests," *Personnel Psychology*, 1994, 47, pp. 247–274.

54. E. E. Ghiselli, "The Validity of Aptitude Tests in Personnel Selection," *Personnel Psychology*, 1973, 61, pp. 461–467.

55. Wisconsin Department of Employment Relations, *Developing Wisconsin State Civil Service Examinations and Assessment Procedures* (Madison, WI: author, 1994).

56. D. M. Dye, M. Reck, and M. A. McDaniel, "The Validity of Job Knowledge Measures," *International Journal of Selection and Assessment*, 1993, 1, pp. 153–157.

57. P. Salovey and D. Grewal, "The Science of Emotional Intelligence," *Current Directions in Psychological Science*, 2005, 14, p. 281; J. D. Mayer, P. Salovey, and D. R. Caruso, "Emotional Intelligence: New Ability or Eclectic Traits?" *American Psychologist*, 2008, 63(6), pp. 503–517.

58. D. L. Van Rooy, D. S. Whitman, and C. Viswesvaran, "Emotional Intelligence: Additional Questions Still Unanswered," *Industrial and Organizational Psychology*, 2010, 3(2), pp. 149–153.

59. D. L. Joseph and D. A. Newman, "Emotional Intelligence: An Integrative Meta-Analysis and Cascading Model," *Journal of Applied Psychology*, 2010, 95(1), pp. 54–78.

60. D. H. Kluemper, T. DeGroot, and S. Choi, "Emotion Management Ability: Predicting Task Performance, Citizenship, and Deviance," *Journal of Management*, 2013, 39, pp. 878–905.

61. M. Zeidner, G. Matthews, and R. D. Roberts, "Emotional Intelligence in the Workplace: A Critical Review," *Applied Psychology: An International Review*, 2004, 53, pp. 371–399.

62. S. Kaplan, J. Cortina, and G. A. Ruark, "Oops . . . We Did It Again: Industrial-Organizational's Focus on Emotional Intelligence Instead of on Its Relationships to Work Outcomes," *Industrial and Organizational Psychology*, 2010, 3(2), pp. 171–177.

63. E. A. Locke, "Why Emotional Intelligence Is an Invalid Concept," *Journal of Organizational Behavior*, 2005, 26, p. 426; C. Cherniss, "Emotional Intelligence: Toward Clarification of a Concept," *Industrial and Organizational Psychology*, 2010, 3(2), pp. 110–126; S. Côté, "Taking the 'Intelligence' in Emotional Intelligence Seriously," *Industrial and Organizational Psychology*, 2010, 3(2), pp. 127–130.

64. Joseph and Newman, "Emotional Intelligence: An Integrative Meta-Analysis and Cascading Model."

65. F. J. Landy, "Some Historical and Scientific Issues Related to Research on Emotional Intelligence," *Journal of Organizational Behavior*, 2005, 26, p. 421.

66. E. White, "Walking a Mile in Another's Shoes," *Wall Street Journal*, Jan. 16, 2006, p. B3.

67. R. Miller, "The Legal Minefield of Employment Probation," *Benefits and Compensation Solutions*, 1998, 21, pp. 40–43.

68. J. J. Asher and J. A. Sciarrino, "Realistic Work Sample Tests: A Review," *Personnel Psychology*, 1974, 27, pp. 519–533.

69. S. J. Motowidlo, M. D. Dunnette, and G. W. Carter, "An Alternative Selection Procedure: The Low-Fidelity Simulation," *Journal of Applied Psychology*, 1990, 75, pp. 640–647.

70. W. Arthur, Jr., G. V. Barrett, and D. Doverspike, "Validation of an Information Processing-Based Test Battery Among Petroleum-Product Transport Drivers," *Journal of Applied Psychology*, 1990, 75, pp. 621–628.

71. Motowidlo, Dunnette, and Carter, "An Alternative Selection Procedure: A Low-Fidelity Simulation."

72. "Making a Difference in Customer Service," *IPMA News*, May 2002, pp. 8–9.

73. P. Thomas, "Not Sure of a New Hire? Put Her to a Road Test," *Wall Street Journal*, Jan. 2003, p. B7.

74. S. Greengard, "Cracking the Hiring Code," *Workforce Management*, June 2004 (*www.workforce.com/articles/15333*).

75. C. Winkler, "Job Tryouts Go Virtual," *HR Magazine*, Sept. 2006, pp. 131–134.

76. J. E. Hunter and R. F. Hunter, "Validity and Utility of Alternative Predictors of Job Performance," *Psychological Bulletin*, 1984, 96, pp. 72–98.

77. W. Cascio and W. Phillips, "Performance Testing: A Rose Among Thorns?" *Personnel Psychology*, 1979, 32, pp. 751–766.

78. P. Bobko, P. L. Roth, and M. A. Buster, "Work Sample Tests and Expected Reduction in Adverse Impact: A Cautionary Note," *International Journal of Selection and Assessment*, 2005, 13, pp. 1–24.

79. K. A. Hanisch and C. L. Hulin, "Two-Stage Sequential Selection Procedures Using Ability and Training Performance: Incremental Validity of Behavioral Consistency Measures," *Personnel Psychology*, 1994, 47, pp. 767–785.

80. M. A. McDaniel, N. S. Hartman, D. L. Whetzel, and W. L. Grubb, "Situational Judgment Tests, Response Instructions, and Validity: A Meta-Analysis," *Personnel Psychology*, 2007, 60, pp. 63–91.

81. F. Lievens and P. R. Sackett, "The Validity of Interpersonal Skills Assessment via Situational Judgment Tests for Predicting Academic Success and Job Performance," *Journal of Applied Psychology*, 2012, 97, pp. 460–468.

82. D. L. Whetzel, M. A. McDaniel, and N. T. Nguyen, "Subgroup Differences in Situational Judgment Test Performance: A Meta-Analysis," *Human Performance*, 2008, 21, pp. 291–309.

83. F. Lievens and P. R. Sackett, "Video-Based Versus Written Situational Judgment Tests: A Comparison in Terms of Predictive Validity," *Journal of Applied Psychology*, 2006, 91, pp. 1181–1188.

84. McDaniel et al., "Situational Judgment Tests, Response Instructions, and Validity: A Meta-Analysis"; D. Chan and N. Schmitt, "Situational Judgment and Job Performance," *Human Performance*, 2002, 15, pp. 233–254; J. A. Weekley and C. Jones, "Further Studies of Situational Tests," *Personnel Psychology*, 1999, 52, pp. 679–700; J. Clevenger, G. M. Pereira, D. Wiechmann, N. Schmitt, and V. S. Harvey, "Incremental Validity of Situational Judgment Tests," *Journal of Applied Psychology*, 2001, 86, pp. 410–417.

85. M. S. O'Connell, N. S. Hartman, M. A. McDaniel, W. L. Grubb, and A. Lawrence, "Incremental Validity of Situational Judgment Tests for Task and Contextual Job Performance," *International Journal of Selection and Assessment*, 2007, 15, pp. 19–29.

86. Lievens and Sackett, "Video-Based Versus Written Situational Judgment Tests: A Comparison in Terms of Predictive Validity."

87. S. J. Motowidlo and M. E. Beier, "Differentiating Specific Job Knowledge from Implicit Trait Policies in Procedural Knowledge Measured by a Situational Judgment Test," *Journal of Applied Psychology*, 2010, 95(2), pp. 321–333.

88. M. S. Christian, B. D. Edwards, and J. C. Bradley, "Situational Judgment Tests: Constructs Assessed and a Meta-Analysis of Their Criterion-Related Validities," *Personnel Psychology*, 2010, 63(1), pp. 83–117; R. Bledow and M. Frese, "A Situational Judgment Test of Personal Initiative and Its Relationship to Performance," *Personnel Psychology*, 2009, 62(2), pp. 229–258.

89. "Employers Cite Communication Skills, Honesty/Integrity as Key for Job Candidates," *IPMA-HR Bulletin*, Mar. 23, 2007, p. 1.

90. M. G. Aamodt and H. Custer, "Who Can Best Catch a Liar? A Meta-Analysis of Individual Differences in Detecting Deception," *The Forensic Examiner*, Spring 2006, pp. 6–11.

91. R. C. Hollinger, "2006 National Retail Security Survey Final Report," Survey Research Project, University of Florida.

92. Berry, Ones, and Sackett, "Interpersonal Deviance, Organizational Deviance, and Their Common Correlates: A Review and Meta-Analysis."

93. P. R. Sackett and J. E. Wanek, "New Developments in the Use of Measures of Honesty, Integrity, Conscientiousness, Dependability, Trustworthiness, and Reliability for Personnel Selection," *Personnel Psychology*, 1996, 49, pp. 787–829.

94. C. M. Berry, P. R. Sackett, and S. Wiemann, "A Review of Recent Developments in Integrity Test Research," *Personnel Psychology*, 2007, 60, pp. 271–301.

95. B. Marcus, K. Lee, and M. C. Ashton, "Personality Dimensions Explaining Relations Between Integrity Tests and Counterproductive Behavior: Big Five, or One in Addition?" *Personnel Psychology*, 2007, 60, pp. 1–34.

96. Ones, Viswesvaran, and Dilchert, "Personality at Work: Raising Awareness and Correcting Misconceptions."

97. D. S. Ones, C. Viswesvaran, and F. L. Schmidt, "Comprehensive Meta-Analysis of Integrity Test Validities: Findings and Implications for Personnel Selection and Theories of Job Performance," *Journal of Applied Psychology* (monograph), 1993, 78, pp. 531–537.

98. C. H. Van Iddekinge, P. L. Roth, P. H. Raymark, and H. N. Odle-Dusseau, "The Criterion-Related Validity of Integrity Tests: An Updated Meta-Analysis," *Journal of Applied Psychology*, 2012, 97, pp. 499–530. For commentaries, see P. R. Sackett and N. Schmitt, "On Reconciling Conflicting Meta-Analytic Findings Regarding Integrity Test Validity," *Journal of Applied Psychology*, 2012, 97, pp. 550–556; D. S. Ones, C. Viswesvaran, and F. L. Schmidt, "Integrity Tests Predict Counterproductive Work Behaviors and Job Performance Well: Comment on Van Iddekinge, Roth, Raymark, and Odle-Dusseau (2012)," *Journal of Applied Psychology*, 2012, 97, pp. 537–542.

99. Berry, Sackett, and Wiemann, "A Review of Recent Developments in Integrity Test Research."

100. R. J. Karren and L. Zacharias, "Integrity Tests: Critical Issues," *Human Resource Management Review*, 2007, 17, pp. 221–234.

101. Hausknecht, Day, and Thomas, "Applicant Reactions to Selection Procedures: An Updated Model and Meta-Analysis."

102. R. R. McCrae and P. T. Costa, Jr., "Reinterpreting the Myers-Briggs Type Indicator From the Perspective of the Five-Factor Model of Personality," *Journal of Personality*, 1989, 57, pp. 17–40.

103. C. H. Van Iddekinge, D. J. Putka, and J. P. Campbell, "Reconsidering Vocational Interests for Personnel Selection: The Validity of an Interest-Based Selection Test in Relation to Job Knowledge, Job Performance, and Continuance Intentions," *Journal of Applied Psychology*, 2011, 96(1), pp. 13–33.

104. M. Assouline and E. I. Meir, "Meta-Analysis of the Relationship Between Congruence and Well-Being Measures," *Journal of Vocational Behavior*, 1987, 31, pp. 319–332.

105. See B. Schneider, H. W. Goldstein, and D. B. Smith, "The ASA Framework: An Update," *Personnel Psychology*, 1995, 48, pp. 747–773.

106. D. M. Cable, "The Role of Person-Organization Fit in Organizational Entry," Unpublished doctoral dissertation, Cornell University, Ithaca, NY, 1995.

107. R. W. Eder and M. Harris (eds.), *The Employment Interview Handbook* (Thousand Oaks, CA: Sage, 1999).

108. M. Hosoda, E. F. Stone-Romero, and G. Coats, "The Effects of Physical Attractiveness on Job-Related Outcomes: A Meta-Analysis of Experimental Studies," *Personnel Psychology*, 2003, 56, pp. 431–462; M. R. Barrick, J. A. Shaffer, and S. W. DeGrassi, "What You See May Not Be What You Get: Relationships Among Self-Presentation Tactics and Ratings of Interview and Job Performance," *Journal of Applied Psychology*, 2009, 94, pp. 1394–1411; "Survey Finds Employers Form Opinions of Job Interviewees Within 10 Minutes," *IPMA-HR Bulletin*, Apr. 21, 2007, p. 1; M. Bertrand and S. Mullainathan, "Are Emily and Greg More Employable Than Lakisha and Jamal? A Field Experiment on Labor Market Discrimination," *American Economic Review*, 2004, 94, pp. 991–1013; S. L. Purkiss, P. L. Perrewé, T. L. Gillespie, B. T. Mayes, and G. R. Ferris, "Implicit Sources of Bias in Employment Interview Judgments and Decisions," *Organizational Behavior and Human Decision Processes*, 2006, 101, pp. 152–167.

109. M. A. Campion, D. K. Palmer, and J. E. Campion, "A Review of Structure in the Selection Interview," *Personnel Psychology*, 1997, 50, pp. 655–702.

110. G. P. Latham, L. M. Saari, E. D. Pursell, and M. A. Campion, "The Situational Interview," *Journal of Applied Psychology*, 1980, 65, pp. 422–427; S. D. Maurer, "The Potential of the Situational Interview: Existing Research and Unresolved Issues," *Human Resource Management Review*, 1997, 7, pp. 185–201.

111. A. I. Huffcutt, J. N. Conurey, P. L. Roth, and U. Klehe, "The Impact of Job Complexity and Study Design on Situational and Behavior Description Interview Validity," *International Journal of Selection and Assessment*, 2004, 12, pp. 262–273.

112. S. Adams, "The Innovation That Could Make Most Job Interviews Obsolete," *Forbes*, Aug. 8, 2012 (*www.forbes.com/sites/susanadams/2012/08/28/the-innovation-that-could-make-most-job-interviews-obsolete/*), accessed 8/12/13.

113. F. L. Schmidt and R. D. Zimmerman, "A Counterintuitive Hypothesis About Employment Interview Validity and Some Supporting Evidence," *Journal of Applied Psychology*, 2004, 89, pp. 553–561.

114. M. A. McDaniel, D. L. Whetzel, F. L. Schmidt, and S. D. Maurer, "The Validity of Employment Interviews: A Comprehensive Review and Meta-Analysis," *Journal of Applied Psychology*, 1994, 79, pp. 599–616; Huffcutt et al., "The Impact of Job Complexity and Study Design on Situational and Behavior Description Interview Validity."

115. K. I. van der Zee, A. B. Bakker, and P. Bakker, "Why Are Structured Interviews So Rarely Used in Personnel Selection?" *Journal of Applied Psychology*, 2002, 87, pp. 176–184; F. Lievens and A. De Paepe, "An Empirical Investigation of Interviewer-Related Factors That Discourage the Use of High Structure Interviews," *Journal of Organizational Behavior*, 2004, 25, pp. 29–46; N. Smith, "Using Structured Interviews to Increase Your Organization's Hiring Investments," *HR Weekly*, Oct. 2006, pp. 1–3.

116. Hausknecht, Day, and Thomas, "Applicant Reactions to Selection Procedures: An Updated Model and Meta-Analysis."

117. A. I. Huffcutt and P. L. Roth, "Racial Group Differences in Interview Evaluations," *Journal of Applied Psychology*, 1998, 83, pp. 179–189.

118. C. H. Van Iddekinge, C. E. Sager, J. L. Burnfield, and T. S. Heffner, "The Variability of Criterion-Related Validity Estimates Among Interviewers and Interview Panels," *International Journal of Selection and Assessment*, 2006, 14, pp. 193–205; M. R. Barrick, B. W. Swider, and G. L. Stewart, "Initial Evaluations in the Interview: Relationships With Subsequent Interviewer Evaluations and Employment Offers," *Journal of Applied Psychology*, 2010, 95, pp. 1163–1172.

119. M. Harris, "Reconsidering the Employment Interview: A Review of Recent Literature and Suggestions for Future Research," *Personnel Psychology*, 1989, 42, pp. 691–726.

120. D. S. Chapman and D. I. Zweig, "Developing a Nomological Network for Interview Structure: Antecedents and Consequences of the Structured Selection Interview," *Personnel Psychology*, 2005, 58, pp. 673–702.

121. S. P. Robbins and T. A. Judge, *Organizational Behavior*, 13th ed. (Upper Saddle River, NJ: Prentice-Hall, 2008).

122. Robbins and Judge, *Organizational Behavior*.

123. M. J. Stevens and M. A. Campion, "The Knowledge, Skill, and Ability Requirements for Teamwork: Implications for Human Resource Management," *Journal of Management*, 1994, 20, pp. 503–530.

124. M. J. Stevens, "Staffing Work Teams: Testing for Individual-Level Knowledge, Skill, and Ability Requirements for Teamwork," Unpublished doctoral dissertation, Purdue University, West Lafayette, IN, 1993.

125. R. S. Wellens, W. C. Byham, and G. R. Dixon, *Inside Teams* (San Francisco: Jossey-Bass, 1995).

126. T. V. Mumford, C. H. Van Iddekinge, F. P. Morgeson, and M. A. Campion, "The Team Role Test: Development and Validation of a Team Role Knowledge Situational Judgment Test," *Journal of Applied Psychology*, 2008, 93(2), pp. 250–267.

127. S. M. Colarelli and A. L. Boos, "Sociometric and Ability-Based Assignment to Work Groups: Some Implications for Personnel Selection," *Journal of Organizational Behavior Management*, 1992, 13, pp. 187–196; M. Levinson, "When Workers Do the Hiring," *Newsweek*, June 21, 1993, p. 48.

128. B. Dumaine, "The Trouble With Teams," *Fortune*, Sept. 5, 1994, pp. 86–92.

129. W. C. Borman and S. J. Motowidlo, "Expanding the Criterion Domain to Include Elements of Contextual Performance," in N. Schmitt, W. Borman, and Associates (eds.), *Personnel Selection in Organizations* (San Francisco: Jossey-Bass, 1993), pp. 71–98.

130. "Why Worry About Drugs and Alcohol in the Workplace?" Facts for Employers, American Council for Drug Education, 2007.

131. Smithers Institute, "Drug Testing: Cost and Effect," *Cornell/Smithers Report*, Vol. 1 (Ithaca, NY: Cornell University, 1992), pp. 1–5.

132. "SHRM Poll: Drug Testing Efficacy," Society for Human Resource Management, Sept. 7, 2011 (*www.shrm.org/research/surveyfindings/articles/pages/ldrugtestingefficacy.aspx*).

133. "U.S. Corporations Reduce Levels of Medical, Drug and Psychological Testing of Employees," American Management Association, 2007 (*www.amanet.org*).

134. *Amphetamines Use Declined Significantly Among U.S. Workers in 2005, According to Quest Diagnostics' Drug Testing Index,* Quest Diagnostics Incorporated, 2006.

135. L. Paik, "Organizational Interpretations of Drug Test Results," *Law & Society Review*, Dec. 2006, pp. 1–28.

136. *Mandatory Guidelines and Proposed Revisions to Mandatory Guidelines for Federal Workplace Drug Testing Programs*, Department of Health and Human Services, Substance Abuse and Mental Health Services Administration, 2004.

137. S. Overman, "Debating Drug Test ROI," *Staffing Management*, Oct.–Dec. 2005, pp. 19–22.

138. S. Overman, "Staffing Management: Wanted: Non-Smokers," *Staffing Management*, Jan. 1, 2008 (*www.shrm.org/Publications/StaffingManagementMagazine/editorialcontent/pages/0801_tools.aspx*), accessed 1/28/2011.

139. K. Helliker, "A Test for Alcohol—and Its Flaws," *Wall Street Journal*, Aug. 12, 2006, pp. A1, A6.

140. J. Normand, S. D. Salyards, and J. J. Mahoney, "An Evaluation of Preemployment Drug Testing," *Journal of Applied Psychology*, 1990, 75, pp. 629–639.

141. J. M. Crant and T. S. Bateman, "An Experimental Test of the Impact of Drug-Testing Programs on Potential Job Applicants' Attitudes and Intentions," *Journal of Applied Psychology*, 1990, 75, pp. 127–131; K. R. Murphy, G. C. Thornton III, and D. H. Reynolds, "College Students' Attitudes Toward Employee Drug Testing Programs," *Personnel Psychology*, 1990, 43, pp. 615–631.

142. E. A. Fleishman, "Some New Frontiers in Personnel Selection Research," *Personnel Psychology*, 1988, 41, pp. 679–701.

143. M. A. Campion, "Personnel Selection for Physically Demanding Jobs: Review and Recommendations," *Personnel Psychology*, 1983, 36, pp. 527–550.

144. W. F. Cascio and H. Aquinis, "The Federal Uniform Guidelines on Employee Selection Procedures: An Update on Selected Issues," *Review of Public Personnel Administration*, 2001, 21, pp. 200–218; C. Daniel, "Separating Law and Professional Practice From Politics: The Uniform Guidelines Then and Now," *Review of Public Personnel Administration*, 2001, 21, pp. 175–184; A.I.E. Ewoh and J. S. Guseh, "The Status of the Uniform Guidelines on Employee Selection Procedures: Legal Developments and Future Prospects," *Review of Public Personnel Administration*, 2001, 21, pp. 185–199; G. P. Panaro, *Employment Law Manual*, 2nd ed. (Boston: Warren Gorham Lamont, 1993), pp. 3-28 to 3-82.

145. Equal Employment Opportunity Commission, *Technical Assistance Manual of the Employment Provisions (Title 1) of the Americans With Disabilities Act* (Washington, DC: author, 1992), pp. 51–88; J. G. Frierson, *Employer's Guide to the Americans With Disabilities Act* (Washington, DC: Bureau of National Affairs, 1992); D. L. Stone and K. L. Williams, "The Impact of the ADA on the Selection Process: Applicant and Organizational Issues," *Human Resource Management Review*, 1997, 7, pp. 203–231.

146. L. Daley, M. Dolland, J. Kraft, M. A. Nester, and R. Schneider, *Employment Testing of Persons With Disabling Conditions* (Alexandria, VA: International Personnel Management Association, 1988); L. D. Eyde, M. A. Nester, S. M. Heaton, and A. V. Nelson, *Guide for Administering Written Employment Examinations to Persons With Disabilities* (Washington, DC: US Office of Personnel Management, 1994).

147. Equal Employment Opportunity Commission, "Employment Tests and Selection Procedures" (*www.eeoc.gov/policy/docs/factemployment_procedures.html*), last modified 9/23/10.

148. Equal Employment Opportunity Commission, *Enforcement Guidance on Disability-Related Inquiries and Medical Examinations of Employees Under the Americans With Disabilities Act* (Washington, DC: author, 2001).

149. J. E. Balls, "Dealing With Drugs: Keep It Legal," *HR Magazine*, Mar. 1998, pp. 104–116; A. G. Feliu, *Primer on Employee Rights* (Washington, DC: Bureau of National Affairs, 1998), pp. 137–166.

# CHAPTER TEN

# Internal Selection

**Learning Objectives and Introduction**
Learning Objectives
Introduction

**Preliminary Issues**
The Logic of Prediction
Types of Predictors
Selection Plan

**Initial Assessment Methods**
Talent Management/Succession Systems
Peer Assessments
Self-Assessments
Managerial Sponsorship
Informal Discussions and Recommendations
Choice of Initial Assessment Methods

**Substantive Assessment Methods**
Seniority and Experience
Job Knowledge Tests
Performance Appraisal
Promotability Ratings
Assessment Centers
Interview Simulations
Promotion Panels and Review Boards
Choice of Substantive Assessment Methods

**Discretionary Assessment Methods**

**Legal Issues**
Uniform Guidelines on Employee Selection Procedures
The Glass Ceiling

**Summary**

**Discussion Questions**

**Ethical Issues**

**Applications**

**Endnotes**

# LEARNING OBJECTIVES AND INTRODUCTION

## Learning Objectives

- Compare how the logic of prediction applies to internal vs. external selection decisions
- Evaluate the relative advantages and disadvantages of the five initial assessment methods used in internal selection
- Consider the merits and pitfalls of using seniority and experience for internal selection decisions
- Describe the main features of assessment centers
- Understand the advantages and disadvantages of using assessment centers for internal selection decisions
- Evaluate the relative advantages and disadvantages of the seven substantive assessment methods used in internal selection

## Introduction

Internal selection refers to the assessment and evaluation of employees from within the organization as they move from job to job via transfer and promotion systems. Internal selection is of considerable practical value to an organization because one nearly always knows one's own employees better than external applicants, and effective internal selection decisions can motivate valued employees in any organization.

Preliminary issues we will discuss to guide the use of these assessment methods include the logic of prediction, the nature of predictors, and the development of a selection plan. Initial assessment methods are used to select candidates from among the internal applicants. Methods that will be reviewed include talent management/succession systems, peer assessments and self-assessments, managerial sponsorship, and informal discussions and recommendations. The criteria that should be used to choose among these methods will be discussed.

Substantive assessment methods are used to select finalists from among the internal candidates. Various methods will be reviewed, including seniority and experience, job knowledge tests, performance appraisals, promotability ratings, assessment centers, interview simulations, and promotion panels and review boards. The criteria used to choose among the substantive assessment methods will also be discussed.

Discretionary assessment methods are used to select offer recipients from among the finalists. The factors on which these decisions are based, such as equal employment opportunity and affirmative action (EEO/AA) concerns, whether the finalist had previously been a finalist, and second opinions about the finalist by others in the organization, will be considered.

All of these assessment methods require a large amount of data to be collected. Accordingly, attention must be given to support services; the required expertise needed to administer and interpret predictors; security, privacy, and confidentiality; and the standardization of procedures. Also, the use of internal selection methods requires a clear understanding of legal issues.

# PRELIMINARY ISSUES

## The Logic of Prediction

The logic of prediction, described in Chapter 8, is equally relevant to the case of internal selection. Specifically, indicators of internal applicants' degree of success in past situations should be predictive of their likely success in new situations. Past situations importantly include previous jobs, as well as the current one, held by the applicant with the organization. The new situation is the internal vacancy the applicant is seeking via the organization's transfer or promotion system.

There may also be similarities between internal and external selection in terms of the effectiveness of selection methods. As you may recall from Chapters 8 and 9, three of the most valid external selection measures are biographical data, cognitive ability tests, and work samples. These methods also have validity in internal selection decisions. Personality measures have been found to be a valid predictor in selecting top corporate leaders. Research indicates that cognitive ability is strongly predictive of long-term job performance and advancement. Finally, work samples are also valid predictors of advancement.[1] In this chapter we focus on processes and methods of selection that are unique to promotion and transfer decisions. However, in considering these methods and processes, it should be remembered that many of the techniques of external selection might be relevant as well.

Although the logic of prediction and the likely effectiveness of selection methods are similar for external and internal selection, in practice internal selection has several potential advantages over external selection. In particular, the data collected on internal applicants in their previous jobs often provide greater depth, relevance, and verifiability than the data collected on external applicants. This is because organizations usually have much more detailed and in-depth information about internal candidates' previous job experiences.

Along with depth and relevance, another positive aspect of the nature of predictors for internal selection is variability. Rather than simply relying on the opinion of one person as to the suitability of an internal candidate for the job, multiple assessments may be solicited from other supervisors and peers. By pooling opinions, it is possible to get a more complete and accurate picture of a candidate's qualifications.

While internal selection has important advantages over external selection, two factors can derail the logic of prediction. First, impression management and organizational politics can play important roles in who gets promoted in organizations. Although impression management also plays a role in external hiring (especially in employment interviews), internal "apple polishers" have a much greater opportunity to work their magic, with more targets for their influence and over a longer period of time, than external candidates. On this point, one recent study found that those who are politically skilled were more likely to be viewed as promotable by not only their bosses but also their peers and direct reports.[2] Thus, decision makers selecting internal candidates need to make sure they are selecting candidates for the right reasons. A second factor that can undermine the logic of prediction for internal selection is title inflation. A recent study revealed that the job responsibilities of nearly half (46%) of recently promoted executives remained roughly the same after their new titles. Although such title inflation may not be harmful, the newly promoted, with no corresponding change in pay or responsibilities, should see these "promotions" for what they are. Being given a title of "process change manager" may mean little more than words.[3]

## Types of Predictors

The distinctions made between types of predictors used in external selection are also applicable to the different types of internal predictors. One important difference to note between internal and external predictors pertains to content. There is usually greater depth and relevance to the data available on internal candidates. That is, the organization can go to its own files or managers to get reports on the applicants' previous experiences.

## Selection Plan

Often it seems that internal selection is based on "who you know" rather than on relevant knowledge, skill, ability, and other characteristics (KSAOs). Managers tend to rely heavily on the subjective opinions of previous managers who supervised the internal candidate. When asked why they rely on these subjective assessments, the answer is often, "Because the candidate has worked here for a long time, and I trust the supervisor's feel for the candidate."

Decision errors often occur when relying on subjective feelings for internal selection decisions. For example, in selecting managers to oversee engineering and scientific personnel in organizations, it is sometimes felt that those internal job candidates with the best technical skills will be the best managers. This is not always the case. Some technical wizards are poor managers and vice versa. As another example, because internal candidates have spent some time in the organization, feelings and friendships that develop over time may create barriers to effective selection. Such "feelings" about job applicants may result in lowered hiring standards for some employees, discrimination against protected-class employees, and decisions with low validity. Sound internal selection procedures need to be followed to guard against these errors. A sound job analysis will show that both technical and managerial skills need to be assessed with well-crafted predictors, while at the same time leaving irrelevant factors off the table. Therefore, it is imperative that a selection plan be used for internal as well as external selection. As described in Chapter 8, a selection plan lists the predictors to be used for assessment of each KSAO.

## INITIAL ASSESSMENT METHODS

The internal recruitment process may generate a large number of applications for vacant positions. This is especially true when an open recruitment system (where jobs are posted for employees to apply) rather than a closed recruitment system is used. Given the time and cost of rigorous selection procedures, organizations use initial assessment methods to screen out applicants who do not meet the minimum qualifications needed to become a candidate. Initial assessment methods for internal recruitment typically include the following predictors: talent management/succession systems, peer evaluations, self-assessments, managerial sponsorship, and informal discussions and recommendations. Each of these predictors will be discussed in turn, followed by a general evaluation of all predictors.

### Talent Management/Succession Systems

Most organizations have a desire to internally select, or promote from within, for both informational and motivational reasons. The reasons are, respectively, that one knows one's employees better than external applicants and that valued employees may be motivated, and retained, based on an expectation of future promotions. For example, nearly all managers at Enterprise Rent-A-Car, including its CEO, began in the company's management trainee program. Based on their performance, employees move up the ranks, from management trainee, to assistant manager, to branch manager, area and city manager, and so forth—all promoted from within.

Though internal selection is attractive to employees, a major problem for organizations, especially medium-sized and large ones, is finding out which employees have the desired skills. This is where talent management/succession systems come into play.

Talent management/succession systems—sometimes called human capital management—keep an ongoing organizational record of the skills, talents, and capabilities of an organization's employees to inform human resource (HR) decisions. Talent management/succession systems can be used to attain many goals, including performance management, recruitment needs analysis, employee development, and compensation and career management. However, one of the primary goals of such systems is to facilitate internal selection decisions by keeping an organized, up-to-date record of employee skills, talents, and capabilities.

As logical as talent management/succession systems seem, a recent survey of large multinationals revealed that less than half had such a system in place. Organizations may not use a talent management system for two reasons. First, it may be perceived as too costly. However, the cost of a talent management/succession system should be considered against the cost of not using a system: what are the costs of making selection decisions based on incomplete knowledge of the skills and capabilities of current employees? Second, the expertise to develop a system may not be available. This problem can be mitigated by working with a vendor that specializes in talent management software. According to one recent estimate, the talent management software market grew by 20% in 2012.[4] Talent management/ succession software is often integrated within a vendor's human resource informa- tion systems (HRISs). For example, the two largest HRIS providers—SAP and Oracle/Peoplesoft—include talent management systems in the HRIS packages they market to organizations.

Whether developed internally or purchased from a vendor, a good talent management/succession system includes the KSAOs held by each employee in the organization. The KSAOs are organized by skill categories such as education/ experience, intangible talents such as leadership accomplishments and potential, and ratings of managerial competencies or talents. An effective talent management/ succession system also includes the employee's current position, along with any future positions that the employee is capable of occupying. Additionally, a good tal- ent management system also summarizes the data so that a skills audit can be gen- erated to ascertain unit- or organization-wide talent shortages. Indianapolis-based pharmaceutical giant Eli Lilly does this on a quarterly basis.

One of the problems with talent management/succession systems is that they often quickly become outdated. For the system to be useful (rather than simply another bureaucratic form to complete), managers must systematically update the database with the latest skills acquired by employees. Another limitation is that the KSAOs are often rather general or generic. For a talent management/succession system to be successful, it must be specific, actively maintained and updated, aligned with an organization's strategies (so as to anticipate future talent needs), and used when internal selection decisions are made.[5]

## Peer Assessments

Assessments by peers or coworkers can be used to evaluate the promotability of an internal applicant. A variety of methods can be used, including peer ratings, peer nominations, and peer rankings.[6] Examples of all three are shown in Exhibit 10.1.

As can be seen in Exhibit 10.1, whereas peers are used to make promotion deci- sions in all three methods of peer assessments, the format of each is different. With peer ratings, readiness to be promoted is assessed using a rating scale for each peer. The person with the highest rating is deemed most promotable. Peer nominations rely on voting for the most promotable candidates. Peers receiving the greatest number of votes are the most promotable. Finally, peer rankings rely on a rank ordering of peers. Those peers with the highest rankings are the most promotable.

Peer assessments have been used extensively in the military over the years and to a lesser degree in industry. A virtue of peer assessments is that they rely on raters

---

**EXHIBIT 10.1** **Peer Assessment Methods**

**Peer Rating**

On a scale of 1–5, please rate the following employees for the position of manager as described in the job requirements matrix:

| | Not Promotable 1 | 2 | Promotable in One Year 3 | 4 | Promotable Now 5 |
|---|---|---|---|---|---|
| Jean | 1 | 2 | 3 | 4 | 5 |
| John | 1 | 2 | 3 | 4 | 5 |
| Andy | 1 | 2 | 3 | 4 | 5 |
| Herb | 1 | 2 | 3 | 4 | 5 |

**Peer Nomination**

Please place an X next to the employee who is most promotable to the position of manager as described in the job requirements matrix:

| | |
|---|---|
| Joe | _____ |
| Nishant | _____ |
| Carlos | _____ |
| Suraphon | _____ |
| Renee | _____ |

**Peer Ranking**

Please rank the following employees from the most promotable (1) to the least promotable (5) for the position of manager as described in the job requirements matrix:

| | |
|---|---|
| Ila | _____ |
| Karen | _____ |
| Phillip | _____ |
| Yi-Chan | _____ |
| Kimlang | _____ |

who presumably are very knowledgeable of the applicants' KSAOs due to their day-to-day contact with them. A possible downside to peer assessments, however, is that they may encourage friendship bias and may undermine morale in a work group by fostering a competitive environment.

Another possible problem is that the criteria by which assessments are made are not always made clear. For peer assessments to work, the KSAOs needed for successful performance in the position the peer is being considered for should be spelled out in advance. To do so, a job requirements matrix should be used. In addition, recent research on peer nominations specifically suggests that examining not only nominations received but also nominations by nominees and nominations not returned increases predictive validity by more accurately reflecting the candidate's social network. Of course, that increased accuracy comes with increased complexity and time.[7]

A probable virtue of peer assessments is that peers are more likely to feel that the decisions reached are fair since they had input into the process; thus, it is not seen as a "behind the back" maneuver by management. Peer assessments are used more often with open rather than closed systems of internal recruitment.

## Self-Assessments

Job incumbents can be asked to evaluate their own skills as a basis for determining promotability. This procedure is sometimes used with open recruitment systems. An example of this approach is shown in Exhibit 10.2. Caution must be exercised

**EXHIBIT 10.2**   **Self-Assessment Form Used for Application in Job Posting System**

### SUPPLEMENTAL QUESTIONNAIRE

This supplemental questionnaire will be the principal basis for determining whether or not you are highly qualified for this position. You may add information not identified in your SF-171 or expand on that which is identified. You should consider appropriate work experience, outside activities, awards, training, and education for each of the items listed below.

1. Knowledge of the Bureau of Indian Affairs' mission, organization, structure, policies, and functions, as they relate to real estate.
2. Knowledge of technical administrative requirements to provide technical guidance in administrative areas, such as personnel regulations, travel regulations, time and attendance requirements, budget documents, Privacy Act, Freedom of Information Act, etc.
3. Ability to work with program directors and administrative staff and ability to apply problem-solving techniques and management concepts; ability to analyze facts and problems and develop alternatives.
4. Ability to operate various computer programs and methodology in the analysis and design of automated methods for meeting the information and reporting requirements for the division.
5. Knowledge of the bureau budget process and statistical profile of all field operations that impact in the Real Estate Services program.

On a separate sheet of paper, address the above items in narrative form. Identify the vacancy announcement number across the top. Sign and date your supplemental questionnaire.

SOURCE: Department of the Interior, Bureau of Indian Affairs. Form BIA-4450 (4/22/92).

in using this process for selection, as it may raise the expectations of those rating themselves that they will be selected. As one VP of HR noted, "Some people think a lot more highly of their skills and talent" than is warranted. Employees' supervisors should encourage upward mobility (not "hoard" talent), but they also need to ensure that employees are realistic in their self-assessments.[8]

## Managerial Sponsorship

Increasingly, organizations are relying on higher-ups to identify and develop the KSAOs of those at lower levels in the organization. Historically, the higher-up has been the person's immediate supervisor. Today, however, the higher-up may be a person at a higher level of the organization who does not have direct responsibility for the person being rated. Higher-ups are sometimes labeled coaches, sponsors, or mentors, and their roles are defined in Exhibit 10.3. Some organizations have formal mentorship programs where employees are assigned coaches, sponsors, and mentors. In other organizations, these matches may naturally occur, often progressing from coach to sponsor to mentor as the relationship matures. Regardless of the formality of the relationship, these higher-ups are often given considerable influence in promotion decisions.

## EXHIBIT 10.3 Employee Advocates

### Coach

- Provides day-to-day feedback
- Diagnoses and resolves performance problems
- Creates opportunities for employees using existing training programs and career development programs

### Sponsor

- Actively promotes person for advancement opportunities
- Guides person's career rather than simply informing them of opportunities
- Creates opportunities for people in decision-making capacities to see the skills of the employee (e.g., lead a task force)

### Mentor

- Becomes personally responsible for the success of the person
- Is available to person on and off the job
- Lets person in on "insider" information
- Solicits and values person's input

SOURCE: Reprinted with permission from Dr. Janina Latack, PhD, Nelson O'Connor & Associates/ Outplacement International, Phoenix/Tucson.

Important, too, is the developmental nature of these relationships. Sponsors are in a position to not only internally select candidates to sponsor but also give these individuals valuable developmental experiences that make them viable candidates in the future. Research shows that employees working with sponsors who provide them with challenging developmental experiences earn higher promotability ratings after those experiences. Mentors, too, may provide "psychosocial" support for employees—by being a sounding board, a source of interpersonal support, or a confidante—and, indeed, this form of support may be the clearest consequence of mentoring.[9]

Research also has shown that protégés are not the only ones who benefit from mentoring relationships. Mentors do as well. A recent meta-analysis found that, compared with those not in mentoring roles, those who mentored others had higher levels of job satisfaction, commitment to the organization, and job performance. Thus, rather than a one-sided relationship, effective mentoring can be reciprocally rewarding for both parties.[10]

## Informal Discussions and Recommendations

Not all promotion decisions are made on the basis of formal HR policy and procedures. For many promotions, much or all of the decision process occurs outside normal channels, through informal discussions and recommendations. For example, Celeste Russell, vice president of HR for Good Times Entertainment, a New York home video and direct marketing company, invites employees out for coffee. "It's like a sales call," she says. Although such informal discussions are a common means of internal selection decisions, especially in small companies, they may have limited validity because they are quite subjective. Although Russell prides herself on knowing the names of employees' pets and other personal information, it seems likely that the personal and subjective nature of these conversations compromises her ability to make internal selection decisions relative to "cold and hard" data such as skills, accomplishments, abilities, and so forth. Such is the case with many, if not most, informal approaches to selection.[11]

## Choice of Initial Assessment Methods

As was discussed, there are several formal and informal methods of initial assessment available to screen internal applicants to produce a list of candidates. Research has been conducted on the effectiveness of each method, which will now be presented to help determine which initial assessment methods should be used. The reviews of this research are summarized in Exhibit 10.4.

In Exhibit 10.4, the same criteria are applied to evaluate the effectiveness of these predictors as were used to evaluate the effectiveness of predictors for external selection. Use refers to how much or often the predictor is utilized. Cost refers to expenses incurred in using the predictor. Reliability refers to the consistency of measurement. Validity refers to the strength of the relationship between the predictor

**EXHIBIT 10.4** Evaluation of Initial Assessment Methods

| Predictor | Use | Cost | Reliability | Validity | Utility | Applicant Reactions | Adverse Impact |
|---|---|---|---|---|---|---|---|
| Self-nominations | Low | Low | Moderate | Moderate | ? | Mixed | ? |
| Talent management/ succession systems | High | High | Moderate | Moderate | ? | ? | ? |
| Peer assessments | Low | Low | High | High | ? | Negative | ? |
| Managerial sponsorship | Low | Moderate | ? | ? | ? | Positive | ? |
| Informal methods | High | Low | ? | ? | ? | Mixed | ? |

and job performance. Low validity ranges from about .00 to .15, moderate validity ranges from about .16 to .30, and high validity is .31 and above. Utility refers to the monetary return, minus costs, associated with using the predictor. Adverse impact refers to the possibility that a disproportionate number of women and minorities are rejected using this predictor. Finally, applicant reactions refers to the likely impact on applicants.

Two points should be made about the effectiveness of initial internal selection methods. First, talent management/succession systems and informal methods are used extensively, suggesting that many organizations continue to rely on closed rather than open internal recruitment systems. Certainly this is a positive procedure when administrative ease is of importance. However, it must be noted that talented applicants may be overlooked in these approaches. Also, there may be a discriminatory impact on women and minorities.

The second point is that peer assessment methods are very promising in terms of reliability and validity. They are not frequently used, but more organizations should consider using them as a screening device. Perhaps this will take place as organizations continue to decentralize decision making and empower employees to make business decisions historically made only by the supervisor.

## SUBSTANTIVE ASSESSMENT METHODS

The internal applicant pool is narrowed down to candidates using the initial assessment methods. A decision as to which internal candidates will become finalists is usually made using the following substantive assessment methods: seniority and experience, job knowledge tests, performance appraisal, promotability ratings, assessment centers, interview simulations, and review boards. After each of these methods is discussed, an evaluation is made.

### Seniority and Experience

Initially, the concepts of seniority and experience may seem the same. In reality, however, they are quite different. Seniority typically refers to length of service or tenure with the organization, department, or job. For example, company seniority is measured as length of continuous employment in an organization—the difference between the present date of employment and the date of hire. Thus, seniority is a purely quantitative measure that has nothing to do with the type or quality of job experiences.

Conversely, experience generally has a broader meaning. While seniority may be one aspect of experience, experience also reflects type of experience. Two employees working at the same company for 20 years may have the same level of seniority but very different levels of experience if one of them has performed a number of different jobs, worked in different areas of the organization, and enrolled in various training programs. Thus, experience includes not only length of service in the organization or in various positions in the organization but also the kinds of activities undertaken in those positions. So, although seniority and experience are often considered synonymous, they are quite different. And as we will see in the following discussion, these differences have real implications for internal selection decisions.

## Use and Evaluation

Seniority and experience are among the most prevalent methods of internal selection. Most unionized companies place heavy reliance on seniority over other KSAOs for advancement, and most union contracts stipulate that seniority be considered in promotion decisions. Indeed, research suggests that seniority matters more to the wages and advancement of union workers than nonunion workers. In policy, nonunion organizations claim to place less weight on seniority than on other factors in making advancement decisions. In practice, however, at least one study showed that regardless of the wording in policy statements, heavy emphasis is still placed on seniority in nonunion settings. Research has shown that seniority is more likely to be used for promotions in small, unionized, and capital-intensive companies.[12]

Seniority and experience are widely used methods of internal selection for many reasons. First, organizations believe that direct experience in a job content area reflects an accumulated stock of KSAOs necessary to perform the job. In short, experience may be content valid because it reflects on-the-job experience. Second, seniority and experience information is easily obtained. Furthermore, unions believe that reliance on objective measures such as seniority and experience protects the employee from capricious treatment and favoritism. Finally, promoting experienced or senior individuals is socially acceptable because it is seen as rewarding loyalty.

Due to these reasons, moving from a seniority-based system is not easy, particularly in union environments. When former Washington, DC, mayor Adrian Fenty and former schools chancellor Michelle Rhee attempted to reduce the weight placed on seniority in teacher hiring, promotion, and pay decisions, they were met with fierce resistance from teachers and teachers' unions.[13]

In evaluating seniority and experience as methods of internal selection, it is important to return to our earlier distinction between the two concepts. A meta-analysis of 350 empirical studies revealed that seniority (organizational tenure) was rather weakly related to task performance ($\bar{r}_{xy} = .10$), helping behavior at work ($\bar{r}_{xy} = .08$), work creativity ($\bar{r}_{xy} = .06$), and work counterproductive behavior ($\bar{r}_{xy} = -.07$).[14]

As compared with seniority, evidence for the validity of experience is more positive. A large-scale review of the literature has shown that experience is moderately related to job performance.[15] Research suggests that experience is predictive of job performance in the short run but is followed by a plateau during which experience loses its ability to predict job performance. It appears that most of the effect of experience on performance is because experienced employees have greater job knowledge. However, while experience may result in increased performance due to greater job knowledge, it does not remedy performance difficulties due to low ability; initial performance deficits of low-ability employees are not remedied by increased experience over time.[16] Thus, while experience is more likely to be related to job performance than seniority, neither ranks among the most valid predictors for internal selection decisions.

Several conclusions drawn from the research evidence about the use of seniority and experience in internal selection decisions seem appropriate:

1. Experience is a more valid method of internal selection than seniority (although unionized employers may have little choice but to use seniority).
2. Experience is better suited to predict short-term rather than long-term potential.
3. Experience is more likely to be content valid if the past or present jobs are similar to the future job.
4. Employees seem to expect that promotions will go to the most senior or experienced employee, so using seniority or experience for promotions may yield positive reactions from employees.
5. Experience is unlikely to remedy initial performance difficulties of low-ability employees.

## Job Knowledge Tests

Job knowledge measures one's mastery of the concepts needed to perform certain work. Job knowledge is a complex concept that includes elements of both ability (capacity to learn) and seniority (opportunity to learn). It is usually measured with a paper-and-pencil test. To develop a paper-and-pencil test to assess job knowledge, the content domain from which test questions will be constructed must be clearly identified. For example, a job knowledge test used to select sales managers from salespeople must identify the specific knowledge necessary for being a successful sales manager.

Job knowledge tests are often used in occupations where specific job knowledge is needed immediately on the first day of the job. Accordingly, they are often used for jobs that require technical or specialized knowledge that cannot be quickly acquired or learned. Job knowledge tests are very specific to the occupation for which candidates are being selected. For example, a job knowledge test for an information technology analyst in the health care industry might ask about knowledge of specific software used in that industry, such as Epic and NextGen.

Although job knowledge is not a well-researched method of either internal or external employee selection, it holds great promise as a predictor of job performance. This is because it reflects an assessment of previous experiences of an applicant and an important KSAO, namely, cognitive ability.[17] However, it is important to distinguish between cognitive ability, which reflects learning potential, and job knowledge, which reflects what has already been learned. Job knowledge tests are also likely to be viewed favorably by candidates, so long as they see the link between the knowledge being tested and the knowledge required to perform the job.

## Performance Appraisal

One possible predictor of future job performance is past job performance. This assumes, of course, that elements of the future job are similar to those of the past job. Data on employees' previous performance are routinely collected as part of the performance appraisal process and thus available for use in internal selection.

One advantage of performance appraisals over other internal assessment methods is that they are readily available in many organizations. Another desirable feature is that they likely capture both ability and motivation. Hence, they can offer a complete look at the person's qualifications for the job. Care must be taken in using performance appraisals, because there is not always a direct correspondence between the requirements of the current job and the requirements of the position applied for. Performance appraisals should only be used as predictors when job analysis indicates a close relationship between the current job and the position applied for.

For example, performance in a highly technical position (e.g., scientist, engineer) may require certain skills (e.g., quantitative skills) that are required in both junior- and senior-level positions. Thus, using the results of the performance appraisal of the junior position is appropriate in predicting performance in the senior position. It is not, however, appropriate to use the results of the performance appraisal for the junior-level technical job to predict performance in a job requiring a different set of skills (e.g., planning, organizing, and staffing), such as that of manager.

Although there are some advantages to using performance appraisal results for internal selection, they are far from perfect predictors. They are subject to many influences that have nothing to do with the likelihood of success in a future job.[18] In addition, decision makers appear to be swayed not only by a person's level of performance but also by his or her trajectory, that is, whether the person's performance has increased or decreased over time. One recent study found that NBA players whose performance was on a positive trajectory received higher levels of compensation than those whose trajectory was not as positive—even controlling for their average level of performance. Presumably, those with positive trajectories were viewed as "rising stars," even though those views were overly optimistic. One implication is that employees viewed as rising stars, even if their initial performance is low, may be promoted more quickly than they deserve.[19]

The well-known "Peter Principle"—that individuals rise to their lowest level of incompetence—illustrates another limitation of using the performance appraisal as a method for internal staffing decisions.[20] The argument behind the Peter Principle is that if organizations promote individuals on the basis of their past performance, the only time that people stop being promoted is when they perform poorly in the job into which they were last promoted. Thus, over time, organizations will have internally staffed positions with incompetent individuals. In fact, the authors have data from a Fortune 100 company showing that less than one-fifth of the variance in an employee's current performance rating can be explained by the performance ratings of the previous three years. Thus, although past performance may have some validity in predicting future performance, the relationship may not be overly strong.

This is not to suggest that organizations should abandon using performance ratings as a factor in internal staffing decisions. Rather, the validity of using the performance appraisal as an internal selection method may depend on a number of considerations. Exhibit 10.5 provides several questions that should be asked in deciding how much weight to place on performance appraisal as a means of making internal selection decisions. Answering yes to these questions suggests that past performance may be validly used in making internal selection decisions.

If organizations do rely on performance appraisals to make internal staffing decisions, a challenge is to ensure that performance measures are interpreted similarly by raters. This is especially the case when ratings from multiple sources (e.g., supervisors, peers, and direct reports) are obtained. Recent evidence suggests that providing raters with an explicit frame of reference can increase rating accuracy. An explicit frame of reference is achieved by including definitions and specific behavioral examples of performance on the measure itself and using multiple behavioral indicators for each competency assessed. The overall goal of this approach is to reduce idiosyncratic scoring tendencies between different raters (e.g., being consistently lenient or harsh) by providing raters with an unambiguous frame of reference. For example, if "ability to work in teams" is a performance dimension being assessed, the rating scale itself would have an explicit definition of high versus low levels of performance, as well as multiple examples of behaviors exemplifying high performance.[21]

An advance over simple use of performance ratings is to review past performance records more thoroughly, including evaluating various dimensions of performance that are particularly relevant to job performance (where the dimensions are based on job analysis results). For example, a study of police officer promotions used a pool of six supervisors to score officers on four job-relevant police officer performance dimensions—supervisory-related education and experience, disciplined behavior, commendatory behavior, and reliability—with the goal of

**EXHIBIT 10.5**  **Questions to Ask in Using Performance Appraisal as a Method of Making Internal Staffing Decisions**

- Is the performance appraisal process reliable and unbiased?
- Is the present job content representative of future job content?
- Have the KSAOs required for performance in the future job(s) been acquired and demonstrated in the previous job(s)?
- Is the organizational or job environment stable such that what led to past job success will lead to future job success?

predicting future performance. Results of the study indicated that using ratings of past performance records was an effective method of promoting officers.[22] Such a method might be adapted to other positions and provide a useful means of incorporating past performance data into a more valid prediction of future potential.

## Promotability Ratings

In many organizations, an assessment of promotability (assessment of potential for a higher-level job) is made at the same time that performance appraisals are conducted. Replacement and succession planning frequently use both types of assessments (see Chapter 3).

Promotability ratings are useful not only from a selection perspective but also from a recruitment perspective. By discussing what is needed to be promotable, employee development may be encouraged as well as coupled with organizational sponsorship of the opportunities needed to develop. In turn, the development of new skills in employees increases the internal recruitment pool for promotions.

Caution must be exercised in using promotability ratings as well. If employees receive separate evaluations for purposes of performance appraisal, promotability, and pay, they may receive mixed messages. For example, it would be difficult to understand why one received an excellent performance rating and a solid pay raise, but at the same time was rated as not promotable. Care must be taken to show employees the relevant judgments being made in each assessment. In this example, it must be clearly indicated that promotion is based not only on past performance but also on skill acquisition and opportunities for advancement.

## Assessment Centers

An elaborate method of employee selection that is primarily used internally and for higher-level jobs is an assessment center. An assessment center is a collection of predictors used to forecast success. It is used for higher-level jobs because of the high costs involved in conducting the center. The assessment center can be used to select employees for lower-level jobs as well, though this is rarely done.

The theory behind assessment centers is relatively straightforward. Concern is with predicting an individual's behavior and effectiveness in critical roles, usually managerial. Since these roles require complex behavior, multiple KSAOs will predict those behaviors. Hence, there is a need to carefully identify and assess those KSAOs; multiple methods, as well as multiple assessors, will be required. The result should be higher validity than could be obtained from a single assessment method or assessor.

As with any sound selection procedure, the assessment center predictors are based on job analysis to identify KSAOs and aid in the construction of content-valid methods of assessment for those KSAOs. As a result, a selection plan must be developed when using assessment centers. An example of such a selection plan is shown in Exhibit 10.6.

**EXHIBIT 10.6**   Selection Plan for an Assessment Center

| KSAO | Writing Exercise | Speech Exercise | Analysis Problem | In-Basket Tent. | In-Basket Final | Leadership Group Discussion Management Problems | Leadership Group Discussion City Council |
|---|---|---|---|---|---|---|---|
| Oral communications | | | | | X | X | X |
| Oral presentation | | X | | | | X | |
| Written communications | X | | X | X | X | | X |
| Stress tolerance | | | | X | X | X | X |
| Leadership | | | | X | X | X | |
| Sensitivity | | | X | X | X | X | X |
| Tenacity | | | | X | X | X | |
| Risk taking | | | X | X | X | X | X |
| Initiative | | | X | X | X | X | X |
| Planning & organization | | | X | X | X | X | X |
| Management control | | | X | X | X | X | |
| Delegation | | | | X | X | | |
| Problem analysis | | | X | X | X | X | X |
| Decision making | | | X | X | X | X | X |
| Decisiveness | | | X | X | X | X | X |
| Responsiveness | | | X | X | X | X | X |

SOURCE: Department of Employment Relations, State of Wisconsin.

## Characteristics of Assessment Centers

Whereas specific characteristics vary from situation to situation, assessment centers generally have some common characteristics. Job candidates usually participate in an assessment center for a period of days rather than hours. Most assessment centers last two to three days, but some may be as long as five days. As we describe shortly, a big part of assessment centers is simulations, where employees participate in exercises and trained assessors evaluate their performance. Assessors are usually line managers, but sometimes psychologists are used as well. The average ratio of assessors to assessees ranges from 1:1 to 4:1.

The participants in the center are usually managers who are being assessed for higher-level managerial jobs. Normally, they are chosen to participate by other organization members, such as their supervisor. Often selection is based on an employee's current level of job performance.

At the conclusion of the assessment center, the participants are evaluated by the assessors. Typically, this involves the assessor examining all the information gathered about each participant. The information is then translated into a series of ratings on several dimensions of managerial jobs. Typical dimensions assessed include communications (written and oral), leadership and human relations, planning, problem solving, and decision making. In evaluating these dimensions, assessors are trained to look for critical behaviors that represent highly effective or ineffective responses to the exercise situations in which participants were placed. There may also be an overall assessment rating that represents the bottom-line evaluation for each participant. Assessment center dimensions are relatively highly correlated with one another, though evidence suggests that the dimensions do add to the prediction of performance beyond the overall score.[23] Exhibit 10.7 provides a sample rating form.

A variety of exercises are used at a center. Experts argue that the simulation is the key to an assessment center, though exactly how future performance is simulated varies from center to center.[24]

Although many assessment centers contain written tests and interviews—and thus may include some of the external selection techniques we discussed in Chapters 8 and 9—the simulation exercises are the heart of the assessment center. The most frequently used exercises are the in-basket exercise, group discussion, and case analysis. Each of these exercises will be briefly described.

***In-Basket Exercise.*** The most commonly used assessment center exercise is the in-basket (according to one study, 82% of assessment centers use it). The in-basket (sometimes called "inbox") usually contains memoranda, reports, phone messages, and letters that require a response. These materials are presented to a candidate, and he or she is asked to respond to the items by prioritizing them, drafting

**EXHIBIT 10.7    Sample Assessment Center Rating Form**

Participant Name: _____

**Personal Qualities**

    1. Energy                                   _____

    2. Risk taking                            _____

    3. Tolerance for ambiguity       _____

    4. Objectivity                           _____

    5. Reliability                           _____

**Communication Skills**

    6. Oral      _____

    7. Written      _____

    8. Persuasion      _____

**Human Relations**

    9. Teamwork      _____

    10. Flexibility      _____

    11. Awareness of social environment      _____

**Leadership Skills**

    12. Impact      _____

    13. Autonomy      _____

**Decision-Making Skills**

    14. Decisiveness      _____

    15. Organizing      _____

    16. Planning      _____

**Problem-Solving Skills**

    17. Fact finding      _____

    18. Interpreting information      _____

**Overall Assessment Rating**

Indication of potential to perform
effectively at the next level is:

    Excellent      _____

    Good      _____

    Moderate      _____

    Low      _____

responses, scheduling meetings, and so forth. It is a timed exercise, and usually the candidate has two to three hours to complete it. Even when used alone, the in-basket exercise seems to forecast ascendancy, one of the key criteria of assessment centers.[25]

***Group Discussion.*** In a group discussion, a small group of candidates is given a problem to solve. The problem is one they would likely encounter in the higher-level position for which they are applying. As the candidates work on the problem, assessors sit around the perimeter of the group and evaluate how each candidate behaves in an unstructured setting. They look for skills such as leadership and communication. Roughly 60% of assessment centers include a group discussion. Some group discussion exercises assign candidates specific roles to play; others are "leaderless" in that no one is assigned a particular role. An example of the former is where participants are part of a project team and each participant assumes a role (IT, HR, marketing, etc.). An example of the latter is a "lost in the wilderness" exercise, where a group of individuals is presented a scenario in which they are lost and have a few resources on which they can survive and find their way home. Both assigned-role and leaderless group discussions assess the skills of leadership, judgment, persuasive oral communication, teamwork, and interpersonal sensitivity.

***Case Analysis.*** Cases of actual business situations can also be presented to the candidates. Each candidate is asked to provide a written analysis of the case, describing the nature of the problem, likely causes, and recommended solutions. Not only are the written results evaluated but the candidate's oral report is scored as well. The candidates may be asked to give an oral presentation to a panel of managers and to respond to their questions, comments, and concerns. Case analyses are used in roughly half of all assessment centers.

### Validity and Effective Practices

A meta-analysis of 27 validity studies revealed that the correlation between the assessment center overall assessment rating (OAR) and job performance was reasonably positive ($\bar{r}_{xy} = .28$).[26] Another advantage of assessment centers is that they appear to have little to no adverse impact against protected groups, including women and African Americans—even when the assessors are predominantly white men. Indeed, one study of nearly 2,000 managers found that female candidates generally performed better than male candidates. However, one study found that assessment centers were more likely to have adverse impact against Hispanics. Finally, analyses based on meta-analytic data suggest that assessment centers add incremental validity over personality and cognitive ability.[27]

On the other hand, research has uncovered several problems with assessment centers. First, the construct validity of assessment center evaluations is often questioned. Research has shown that there are much stronger exercise and assessor effects than there are dimension effects, meaning that there is much higher agreement within exercises and within assessors than there is within dimensions. Recent research illuminates that reliability of assessment center ratings is a complex interaction between assessors, exercises, and dimensions and recommends separating ratings into finer categories as opposed to simply aggregating ratings into one score. However, it is unclear whether the construct validity improvements are substantial enough to warrant the increased complexity that would result from such separation.[28] In short, assessment center dimensions do not show much construct validity, calling into question the content of what is being assessed. As one reviewer of the literature noted, "Assessment centers (ACs), as they are often designed and implemented, do not work as they are intended to work and probably never will." Two reasons why dimensional effects tend to be weak are (1) halo effects in assessors' ratings (if an assessor thinks an assessee is a strong candidate, it spills over onto ratings on other dimensions), and (2) assessee behavior tends to be consistent across situations (and thus across exercises and dimensions). These pieces of evidence do not mean assessment centers utterly lack construct validity, but they do suggest that more research is needed as to what constructs are uniquely captured with assessment centers.[29]

One of the biggest limitations of assessment centers is their cost. The nature of the individualized assessment and the requirement of multiple assessors make them cost-prohibitive for many organizations. One way some organizations are mitigating the costs is through other, related assessments. For example, the organization videotapes an assessee's performance so that assessors can evaluate his or her performance when convenient. This saves coordination and travel costs. A practice that results in even greater cost savings is to use situational judgment tests, where assessees are given various exercises in written, video, or computerized form. A meta-analysis of 45 studies suggested that the validity of a situational judgment test composite score ($\bar{r}_{xy}$ = .28) was identical to the validity of assessment centers.[30]

Another way to reduce the costs of the assessment center is to use computerized assessments. One research study reported favorable results for a computerized assessment center simulation that asked assessees to prioritize information, formulate e-mail correspondences, make decisions about hypothetical simulations, and engage in strategic planning.[31] Another means of reducing costs is to use off-the-shelf assessments provided by vendors. For example, Assessment Center Exercises (AC-ESX) is a vendor that sells more than 150 assessment center exercises, including instructions on how to train assessors, administer the exercises, and score responses. The exercises include the three most common exercises noted above, as well as scheduling exercises, interview simulations, and fact-finding exercises. While using such off-the-shelf products may save money, it is critical that assessors have proper training. Without the right training, the resulting assessment or score derived from the assessment may be so scattershot as to be useless.

There is little research that has examined participant reactions to assessment centers, though professional guidelines recommend that assessee reactions be included in the process. However, it is commonly noted that assessment centers are stressful to participants, and the unfavorable feedback that often results from participation is particularly taxing to assessees. This does not mean, however, that assessment centers always or even generally generate negative reactions from assesses. It is true that assessment centers are stressful and often provide applicants with sobering feedback. Evidence also suggests, though, that assessees quickly recover from either positive or negative initial reactions from assessment center participation. It is, perhaps, more important what happens *after* the assessment center experience (whether the assessee was promoted and whether the feedback proved helpful) than what happened *during* the assessment center experience.[32]

### Assessment for Global Assignments

When assessment centers were developed, little thought was given to the prospect of using assessment data to forecast job success in a foreign environment. As globalization continues, however, organizations are increasingly promoting individuals into positions overseas. A survey indicated that 80% of midsize and large companies send professionals abroad, and many plan on increasing this percentage. Because overseas assignments present additional demands on an employee beyond the typical skills and motivations required to perform a job in the host country, staffing overseas positions presents special challenges for employers. Indeed, one study revealed that cultural factors were much more important to success in an overseas assignment than were technical skills factors. Although many competencies are important to expatriate success, such as family stability/support and language skills, the most important competency is cultural adaptability and flexibility.

One means of predicting success in overseas assignments is a personality test. For example, employees who respond positively to items such as, "It is easy for me to strike up conversations with people I do not know" or "I find it easy to put myself in other people's positions" may better navigate the challenges of overseas assignments. Personnel Decisions International developed a personality test designed to assess whether employees will be successful in overseas assignments. The company reports a positive relationship between scores on the test and success in overseas assignments. Another tool is simulations or interviews designed to simulate conditions overseas or typical challenges that arise.[33] As one can see, bringing these methods together may make the assessment process for global assignments closely resemble an assessment center.

# Interview Simulations

An interview simulation mimics the oral communication required on the job. It is sometimes used in an assessment center, but less frequently than in-baskets, leaderless group discussions, and case analysis. It is also used as a predictor separate from the assessment center. There are several different forms of interview simulations.[34]

## Role-Play

With a role-play, the job candidate is placed in a simulated situation where he or she must interact with a person at work, such as the boss, a subordinate, or a customer. The interviewer or another individual plays one role, and the job candidate plays the role of the person in the position applied for. So, for example, in selecting someone to be promoted to a supervisory level, the job candidate may be asked to role-play dealing with a difficult employee.

## Fact Finding

In a fact-finding interview, the job candidate is presented with a case or problem with incomplete information. The candidate's job is to solicit from the interviewer or a resource person the additional facts needed to resolve the case. A candidate for the position of EEO manager, for example, might be presented with a case where adverse impact is suggested. The candidate would be evaluated by the interviewer according to the data he or she solicits to confirm or disconfirm adverse impact.

## Oral Presentations

In many jobs, presentations need to be made to customers, clients, or even boards of directors. To select someone to perform this role, an oral presentation can be required. This approach would be useful, for example, to see what sort of "sales pitch" a consultant might make or to see how an executive would present his or her proposed strategic plan to a board of directors.

   Given the importance of interpersonal skills in many jobs, it is unfortunate that not many organizations use interview simulations. This is especially true with internal selection, where the organization knows whether the person has the right credentials (e.g., company experiences, education, and training) but may not know whether the person has the right interpersonal chemistry to fit in with the work group. Interview simulations allow for a systematic assessment of this chemistry rather than relying on the instinct of the interviewer. To be effective, these interviews need to be structured and evaluated according to observable behaviors identified in the job analysis as necessary for successful performance.

## Promotion Panels and Review Boards

In the public sector, it is a common practice to use a panel or board of people to review the qualifications of candidates. Frequently, a combination of both internal and external candidates are being assessed. The panel or board typically consists of job experts, HR professionals, and representatives from constituencies in the community that the board represents. Having a board such as this to hire public servants, such as school superintendents or fire and police officials, offers two advantages. First, as with assessment centers, there are multiple assessors with which to ensure a complete and accurate assessment of the candidate's qualifications. Second, by participating in the selection process, constituents are likely to be more committed to the decision reached. This buy-in is particularly important for community representatives with whom the job candidate will interact. It is hoped that by having a say in the process, they will be less likely to voice objections once the candidate is hired.

## Choice of Substantive Assessment Methods

Along with research on initial assessment methods, research has also been conducted on substantive assessment methods. The reviews of this research are summarized in Exhibit 10.8. The same criteria are applied to evaluating the effectiveness of these predictors as were used to evaluate the effectiveness of initial assessment methods.

An examination of Exhibit 10.8 indicates that there is no single best method of narrowing down the candidate list to finalists. What is suggested, however, is that some predictors are more likely to be effective than others. In particular, job knowledge tests, promotability ratings, and assessment centers have strong records in terms of reliability and validity in choosing candidates. A very promising development for internal selection is the use of job knowledge tests. The validity of these tests appears to be substantial, but unfortunately, few organizations use them for internal selection purposes.

The effectiveness of several internal selection predictors (case analysis, interview simulations, and panels and review boards) is not known at this stage. Interview simulations appear to be a promising technique for jobs requiring public contact skills. All of them need additional research. Other areas in need of additional research are the utility, applicant reactions, and adverse impact associated with all the substantive assessment methods.

## DISCRETIONARY ASSESSMENT METHODS

Discretionary methods are used to narrow down the list of finalists to those who will receive job offers. Sometimes all finalists will receive offers, but other times there may not be enough positions to fill for each finalist to receive an offer. As

**EXHIBIT 10.8**   **Evaluation of Substantive Assessment Methods**

| Predictor | Use | Cost | Reliability | Validity | Utility | Applicant Reactions | Adverse Impact |
|---|---|---|---|---|---|---|---|
| Seniority | High | Low | High | Low | ? | ? | High |
| Experience | High | Low | High | Moderate | High | Positive | Mixed |
| Job knowledge tests | Low | Moderate | High | High | ? | ? | ? |
| Performance appraisal | Moderate | Moderate | ? | Moderate | ? | ? | ? |
| Promotability ratings | Low | Low | High | High | ? | ? | ? |
| Assessment center | Low | High | High | High | High | ? | ? |
| In-basket exercise | Low | Moderate | Moderate | Moderate | High | Mixed | Mixed |
| Leaderless group discussion | Low | Low | Moderate | Moderate | ? | ? | ? |
| Case analysis | Low | Low | ? | Moderate | ? | ? | ? |
| Global assignments | High | Moderate | ? | ? | ? | ? | ? |
| Interview simulations | Low | Low | ? | ? | ? | ? | ? |
| Panels and review boards | Low | ? | ? | ? | ? | ? | ? |

with external selection, discretionary assessments are sometimes made on the basis of organizational citizenship behavior and staffing philosophy regarding EEO/AA.

Two areas of discretionary assessment differ from external selection and need to be considered in deciding job offers. First, previous finalists who do not receive job offers do not simply disappear. They may remain with the organization in hopes of securing an offer the next time the position is open. At the margin, this may be a factor in decision making because being bypassed a second time may create a disgruntled employee. As a result, a previous finalist may be given an offer over a first-time finalist, all other things being equal.

Second, multiple assessors are generally used with internal selection. That is, not only can the hiring manager's opinion be used to select who will receive a job offer but so can the opinions of others (e.g., previous manager, top management) who are knowledgeable about the candidate's profile and the requirements of the current position. As a result, in deciding which candidates will receive job offers, evaluations by people other than the hiring manager may be accorded substantial weight in the decision-making process.

## LEGAL ISSUES

From a legal perspective, methods and processes of internal selection are to be viewed in the same way as those of external selection. The laws and regulations do not distinguish between them. Consequently, most of the legal influences on internal selection have already been treated in Chapters 8 and 9. There are, however, some brief comments to be made about internal selection legal influences. Those influences are the Uniform Guidelines on Employee Selection Procedures (UGESP) and the glass ceiling.

### Uniform Guidelines on Employee Selection Procedures

The UGESP define a "selection procedure" in such a way that virtually any selection method, be it used in an external or internal context, is covered by the requirements of the UGESP. Moreover, the UGESP apply to any "employment decision," which explicitly includes promotion decisions.

When there is adverse impact in promotions, the organization is given the option of justifying it through the conduct of validation studies. These are primarily criterion-related or content validity studies. Ideally, criterion-related studies with predictive validation designs will be used, as has been partially done in the case of assessment centers. Unfortunately, this places substantial administrative and research demands on the organization that are difficult to fulfill most of the time. Consequently, content validation appears to be a better bet for validation purposes.

Many of the methods of assessment used in internal selection attempt to gauge KSAOs and behaviors directly associated with a current job that are felt to be related to success in higher-level jobs. Examples include seniority, performance appraisals, and promotability ratings. These are based on current, as well as past, job content. Validation of these methods, if legally necessary, likely occurs along content validation lines. The organization thus should pay particular and close attention to the validation and documentation requirements for content validation in the UGESP.

## The Glass Ceiling

In Chapter 6, the nature of the glass ceiling was discussed, as well as staffing steps to remove it from organizational promotion systems. Most of that discussion centered on internal recruitment and supporting activities that could be undertaken. Surprisingly, selection methods used for promotion assessment are rarely mentioned in literature on the glass ceiling.

This is a major oversight. Whereas the internal recruitment practices recommended may enhance the identification and attraction of minority and women candidates for promotion, effectively matching them to their new jobs requires applying internal selection processes and methods. The policy of the Equal Employment Opportunity Commission (EEOC) on nondiscriminatory promotions is (1) the KSAOs to be assessed must be job related and consistent with business necessity, and (2) there must be uniform and consistently applied standards across all promotion candidates.[35] How might the organization operate its internal selection system to comply with EEOC policy?

The first possibility is for greater use of selection plans. As discussed in Chapter 8, these plans lay out the KSAOs required for a job, which KSAOs are necessary to bring to the job (as opposed to being acquired on the job), and, of those necessary, the most appropriate method of assessment for each. Such a plan forces an organization to conduct job analysis, construct career ladders or KSAO lattices, and consider alternatives to many of the traditional methods of assessment used in promotion systems.

A second suggestion is for the organization to back away from use of these traditional methods of assessment as much as possible, in ways consistent with the selection plan. This means a move away from casual, subjective methods such as supervisory recommendation, typical promotability ratings, quick reviews of personnel files, and informal recommendations. In their place should be more formal, standardized, and job-related assessment methods. Examples here include assessment centers, promotion review boards or panels, and interview simulations.

A final suggestion is for the organization to pay close attention to the types of KSAOs necessary for advancement, and undertake programs to impart these KSAOs to aspiring employees. These developmental actions might include key job and committee assignments, participation in conferences and other networking opportunities, mentoring and coaching programs, and skill acquisition in formal training programs. Internal selection methods would then be used to assess proficiency on these newly acquired KSAOs, in accordance with the selection plan.

## SUMMARY

The selection of internal candidates follows a process very similar to the selection of external candidates. The logic of prediction is applied, and a selection plan is developed and implemented.

One important area where internal and external selection methods differ is in the nature of the predictor. Predictors used for internal selection tend to have greater depth and more relevance and are better suited for verification. As a result, different types of predictors are used for internal selection decisions than for external selection decisions.

Initial assessment methods are used to narrow down the applicant pool to a set of qualified candidates. Approaches used are talent management/succession systems, peer assessments, self-assessments, managerial sponsorship, and informal discussions and recommendations. Of these approaches, none is particularly strong in predicting future performance. Hence, consideration should be given to using multiple predictors to verify the accuracy of any one method. These results also point to the need to use substantive as well as initial assessment methods in making internal selection decisions.

Substantive assessment methods are used to select finalists from the list of candidates. Predictors used to make these decisions include seniority and experience, job knowledge tests, performance appraisals, promotability ratings, assessment centers, interview simulations, and panels and review boards. Of this set of predictors, job knowledge tests, promotability ratings, and assessment centers work well. Organizations need to give greater consideration to the latter three predictors to supplement traditional seniority and experience.

Although very costly, the assessment center seems to be very effective. This is because it is grounded in behavioral science theory and the logic of prediction. In particular, samples of behavior are analyzed, multiple assessors and predictors are used, and predictors are developed on the basis of job analysis.

Internal job applicants have the potential for far greater access to selection data than do external job applicants due to their physical proximity to the data. As a result, procedures must be implemented to ensure that manual and computer files with sensitive data are kept private and confidential.

Two areas of legal concern for internal selection decisions are the UGESP and the glass ceiling. In terms of the UGESP, particular care must be taken to ensure that internal selection methods are valid if adverse impact is occurring. To minimize glass ceiling effects, organizations should make greater use of selection plans and more objective internal assessment methods, as well as help impart the KSAOs necessary for advancement.

## DISCUSSION QUESTIONS

1. Explain how internal selection decisions differ from external selection decisions.
2. What are the differences among peer ratings, peer nominations, and peer rankings?
3. Explain the theory behind assessment centers.
4. Describe the three different types of interview simulations.
5. Evaluate the effectiveness of seniority, assessment centers, and job knowledge as substantive internal selection procedures.
6. What steps should be taken by an organization that is committed to shattering the glass ceiling?

## ETHICAL ISSUES

1. Given that seniority is not a particularly valid predictor of job performance, do you think it's unethical for a company to use it as a basis for promotion? Why or why not?
2. Vincent and Peter are sales associates and are up for promotion to sales manager. In the past five years, on a 1 = poor to 5 = excellent scale, Vincent's average performance rating was 4.7 and Peter's was 4.2. In an assessment center that was meant to simulate the job of sales manager, on a 1 = very poor to 10 = outstanding scale, Vincent's average score was 8.2 and Peter's was 9.2. Other things being equal, who should be promoted? Why?

## APPLICATIONS

### Changing a Promotion System

Bioglass, Inc. specializes in sales of a wide array of glass products. One area of the company, the commercial sales division (CSD), specializes in selling high-tech mirrors and microscope and photographic lenses. Sales associates in CSD are responsible for selling the glass products to corporate clients. CSD has four levels of sales associates, ranging in pay from $28,000 to $76,000 per year. There are also four levels of managerial positions; those positions range in pay from $76,000 to $110,000 per year (that's what the division president makes).

Tom Caldwell has been a very effective sales associate. He has consistently demonstrated good sales techniques in his 17 years with Bioglass and has a large and loyal client base. Over the years, Tom has risen from the lowest level of sales associate to the highest. He has proved himself successful at each stage. An entry-level management position in CSD opened up last year, and Tom was a natural candidate. Although several other candidates were considered, Tom was the clear choice for the position.

However, once in the position, Tom had a great deal of difficulty being a manager. He was not accustomed to delegating and rarely provided feedback or guidance to the people he supervised. Although he set goals for himself, he never set performance goals for his workers. Morale in Tom's group was low, and group performance suffered. The company felt that demoting Tom back to sales would be disastrous for him and present the wrong image to other employees; firing such a loyal employee was considered unacceptable. Therefore, Bioglass decided to keep Tom where he was but not consider him for future promotions. It was also considering enrolling Tom in some expensive managerial development programs to enhance his management skills.

Meanwhile, Tom's replacement, although successful at the lower three levels of sales associate positions, was having a great deal of difficulty with the large corporate contracts that the highest-level sales associates must service. Two of Tom's biggest clients had recently left Bioglass for a competitor. CSD was confused about how such a disastrous situation had developed when they seemed to make all the right decisions.

Based on this application and your reading of this chapter, answer the following questions:

1. What is the likely cause of CSD's problems?
2. How might CSD, and Bioglass more generally, make better promotion decisions in the future? Be specific.
3. In general, what role should performance appraisals play in internal selection decisions? Are there some cases in which they are more relevant than others? Explain.

## Promotion From Within at Citrus Glen

Mandarine "Mandy" Pamplemousse is vice president of HR for Citrus Glen, a juice producer based in south Florida that supplies orange and grapefruit juice to grocery stores, convenience stores, restaurants, and food processors throughout the United States. Citrus Glen has been growing rapidly over the last few years, leading Mandy to worry about how to hire and promote enough qualified individuals to staff the ever-expanding array of positions within the company.

One of the ways Mandy has been able to staff positions internally is by contracting with Staffing Systems International (SSI), a management consulting firm based in Charlotte, North Carolina. When positions open up at Citrus Glen that are appropriate to staff internally, Mandy sends a group of candidates for the position up to SSI to participate in its assessment center. The candidates return from SSI three days later, and a few days after that, SSI sends Mandy the results of the assessment with a recommendation. Though Mandy has never formally evaluated the accuracy of the promotions, she feels that the process is pretty accurate. Of course, for $5,500 per candidate, Mandy thought, it *should* be accurate.

A few days ago, Mandy was hosting Thanksgiving, and her brother-in-law, Vin Pomme, joined them. Vin is a doctoral student in industrial psychology at Ohio International University. After Thanksgiving dinner, while Mandy, Vin, and their family were relaxing on her lanai and enjoying the warm Florida sunshine, Mandy was talking to Vin about her difficulties in promoting from within and the cost of SSI's assessment process. Vin quickly realized that SSI was using an assessment center. He was also aware of research suggesting that once one takes an applicant's personality and cognitive ability into account, assessment center scores may contribute little additional validity. Given the high cost of assessment centers, he reasoned, one must wonder whether this "incremental" validity (the validity that assessment centers contribute beyond the validity provided by personality and cognitive ability tests) would prove cost effective. After Vin conveyed these impressions to Mandy, she felt that after the holidays she would reexamine Citrus Glen's internal selection processes.

## Questions

1. Drawing from concepts presented in Chapter 7 ("Measurement"), how could Mandy more formally evaluate SSI's assessment process, as well as the alternative presented to her by Vin?

2. Construct a scenario in which you think Mandy should continue her business relationship with SSI. On the other hand, if Mandy decides on an alternative assessment process, what would that process be? How would she evaluate whether that process was effective?

3. Citrus Glen has considered expanding its operations into the Caribbean and Latin America. One of Mandy's concerns is how to staff such positions. If Citrus Glen does expand its operations to different cultures, how should Mandy go about staffing such positions? Be specific.

## ENDNOTES

1. A. Howard and D. W. Bray, "Predictions of Managerial Success Over Long Periods of Time: Lessons From the Management Progress Study," in K. E. Clark and M. B. Clark (eds.), *Measures of Leadership* (West Orange, NJ: Leadership Library of America, 1990), pp. 113–130; C. J. Russell, "Selecting Top Corporate Leaders: An Example of Biographical Information," *Journal of Management*, 1990, 16, pp. 73–86; J. S. Schippman and E. P. Prien, "An Assessment of the Contributions of General Mental Ability and Personality Characteristics to Management Success," *Journal of Business and Psychology*, 1989, 3, pp. 423–437.

2. W. Gentry, D. C. Gilmore, M. L. Shuffler, and J. B. Leslie, "Political Skill as an Indicator of Promotability Among Multiple Rater Sources," *Journal of Organizational Behavior*, 2012, 33, pp. 89–104.

3. "Nearly Half of Newly-Promoted Executives Say Their Responsibilities Are Same," *IPMA-HR Bulletin*, Dec. 22, 2006, p. 1.

4. J. Bersin, "The Talent Management Software Market Continues to Explode," *Forbes*, Nov. 29, 2012 (*www.forbes.com/sites/joshbersin/2012/11/29/the-talent-management-software-market-continues-to-explode/*), accessed 8/12/13.

5. E. E. Lawler III, "Make Human Capital a Source of Competitive Advantage," *Organizational Dynamics*, 2009, 38(1), pp. 1–7; R. Burbach and T. Royle, "Talent on Demand? Talent Management in the German and Irish Subsidiaries of a US Multinational Corporation," *Personnel Review*, 2010, 39(4), pp. 414–431; A. McDonnell, R. Lamare, and P. Gunnigle, "Developing Tomorrow's Leaders—Evidence of Global Talent Management in Multinational Enterprises," *Journal of World Business*, 2010, 45(2), pp. 150–160.

6. J. J. Kane and E. E. Lawler, "Methods of Peer Assessment," *Psychological Bulletin*, 1978, 85, pp. 555–586.

7. G. Luria and Y. Kalish, "A Social Network Approach to Peer Assessment: Improving Predictive Validity," *Human Resource Management*, 2013, 52, pp. 537–560.

8. L. Grensing-Pophal, "Internal Selections," *HR Magazine*, Dec. 2006, p. 75.

9. I. E. De Pater, A.E.M. Van Vianen, M. N. Bechtoldt, and U. Klehe, "Employees' Challenging Job Experiences and Supervisors' Evaluations of Promotability," *Personnel Psychology*, 2009, 62(2), pp. 297–325; J. D. Kammeyer-Mueller and T. A. Judge, "A Quantitative Review of Mentoring Research: Test of a Model," *Journal of Vocational Behavior*, 2008, 72, pp. 269–283.

10. R. Ghosh and T. G. Reio, Jr., "Career Benefits Associated With Mentoring for Mentors: A Meta-Analysis," *Journal of Vocational Behavior*, 2013, 83, pp. 106–116.

11. C. Patton, "Standout Performers: HR Professionals Are Testing Unconventional Strategies for Finding Employees With Leadership Potential," *Human Resource Executive*, Aug. 1, 2005, pp. 46–49.

12. N. Williams, "Seniority, Experience, and Wages in the UK," *Labour Economics*, 2009, 16, pp. 272–283.

13. B. Turque, "Top Teachers Have Uneven Reach in District," *Washington Post*, November 14, 2010, pp. M1–M2.

14. T.W.H. Ng and D. C. Feldman, "Organizational Tenure and Job Performance," *Journal of Management*, 2010, 36(5), pp. 1220–1250.

15. M. A. Quinones, J. K. Ford, and M. S. Teachout, "The Relationship Between Work Experience and Job Performance: A Conceptual and Meta-Analytic Review," *Personnel Psychology*, 1995, 48, pp. 887–910; P. E. Tesluk and R. R. Jacobs, "Toward an Integrated Model of Work Experience," *Personnel Psychology*, 1998, 51, pp. 321–355.

16. F. L. Schmidt, J. E. Hunter, and A. N. Outerbridge, "Joint Relation of Experience and Ability With Job Performance: Test of Three Hypotheses," *Journal of Applied Psychology*, 1988, 73, pp. 46–57.

17. F. L. Schmidt and J. E. Hunter, "Development of a Causal Model of Processes Determining Job Performance," *Current Directions in Psychological Science*, 1992, 1, pp. 89–92.

18. K. R. Murphy and J. M. Cleveland, *Performance Appraisal: An Organizational Perspective* (Boston: Allyn and Bacon, 1991).

19. C. M. Barnes, J. Reb, and D. Ang, "More Than Just the Mean: Moving to a Dynamic View of Performance-Based Compensation," *Journal of Applied Psychology*, 2012, 97, pp. 711–718.

20. L. J. Peter and R. Hull, *The Peter Principle* (New York: William Morrow, 1969).

21. B. J. Hoffman, C. A. Gorman, C. A. Blair, J. P. Meriac, B. Overstreet, and E. K. Atchley, "Evidence for the Effectiveness of an Alternative Multisource Performance Rating Methodology," *Personnel Psychology*, 2012, 65, pp. 531–563.

22. G. C. Thornton III and D. M. Morris, "The Application of Assessment Center Technology to the Evaluation of Personnel Records," *Public Personnel Management*, 2001, 30, pp. 55–66.

23. W. Arthur, Jr., E. A. Day, T. L. McNelly, and P. S. Edens, "A Meta-Analysis of the Criterion-Related Validity of Assessment Center Dimensions," *Personnel Psychology*, 2003, 56, pp. 125–154.

24. D. A. Joiner, "Assessment Center: What's New?" *Public Personnel Management*, 2003, 31, pp. 179–185.

25. B. B. Gaugler, D. B. Rosenthal, G. C. Thornton III, and C. Bentson, "Meta-Analysis of Assessment Center Validity," *Journal of Applied Psychology*, 1987, 72, pp. 493–511.

26. E. Hermelin, F. Lievens, and I. T. Robertson, "The Validity of Assessment Centres for the Prediction of Supervisory Performance Ratings: A Meta-Analysis," *International Journal of Selection and Assessment*, 2007, 15, pp. 405–411.

27. J. P. Meriac, B. J. Hoffman, D. J. Woehr, and M. S. Fleisher, "Meta-Analysis of the Incremental Criterion-Related Validity of Dimension Ratings," *Journal of Applied Psychology*, 2008, 93(5), pp. 1042–1052; S. Dilchert and D. S. Ones, "Assessment Center Dimensions: Individual Differences Correlates and Meta-Analytic Incremental Validity," *International Journal of Selection and Assessment*, 2009, 17(3), pp. 254–270; H. J. Bernardin, R. Konopaske, and C. M. Hagan, "Impact Levels Based on Top-Down, Multisource, and Assessment Center Data: Promoting Diversity and Reducing Legal Challenges," *Human Resource Management*, 2012, 51, pp. 313–341.

28. D. J. Putka and B. J. Hoffman, "Clarifying the Contribution of Assessee-, Dimension-, Exercise-, and Assessor-Related Effects to Reliable and Unreliable Variance in Assessment Center Ratings," *Journal of Applied Psychology*, 2013, 98, pp. 114–133.

29. A. M. Gibbons and D. E. Rupp, "Dimension Consistency as an Individual Difference: A New (Old) Perspective on the Assessment Center Construct Validity Debate," *Journal of Management*, 2009, 35(5), pp. 1154–1180; C. E. Lance, "Why Assessment Centers Do Not Work the Way They Are Supposed To," *Industrial and Organizational Psychology*, 2008, 1, pp. 84–97; B. S. Connelly, D. S. Ones, A. Ramesh, and M. Goff, "A Pragmatic View of Assessment Center Exercises and Dimensions," *Industrial and Organizational Psychology*, 2008, 1, pp. 121–124.

30. M. S. Christian, B. D. Edwards, and J. C. Bradley, "Situational Judgment Tests: Constructs Assessed and a Meta-Analysis of Their Criterion-Related Validities," *Personnel Psychology*, 2010, 63(1), pp. 83–117.

31. F. Lievens, E. Van Keer, and E. Volckaert, "Gathering Behavioral Samples Through a Computerized and Standardized Assessment Center Exercise: Yes, It Is Possible," *Journal of Personnel Psychology*, 2010, 9(2), pp. 94–98.

32. D. E. Krause and G. C. Thornton III, "A Cross-Cultural Look at Assessment Center Practices: Survey Results From Western Europe and North America," *Applied Psychology: An International Review*, 2009, 58(4), pp. 557–585; I. J. van Emmerik, A. B. Bakker, and M. C. Euwema, "What Happens After the Developmental Assessment Center? Employees' Reactions to Unfavorable Performance Feedback," *Journal of Management Development*, 2008, 27(5), pp. 513–527; N. Anderson and V. Goltsi, "Negative Psychological Effects of Selection Methods: Construct Formulation and an Empirical Investigation Into an Assessment Center," *International Journal of Selection and Assessment*, 2006, 14(3), pp. 236–255.

33. J. E. Abueva, "Return of the Native Executive," *New York Times*, May 17, 2000, pp. B1, B8; P. Caligiuri and W. F. Cascio, "Sending Women on Global Assignments," *WorldatWork*, Second Quarter 2001, pp. 34–41; J. A. Hauser, "Filling the Candidate Pool: Developing Qualities in Potential International Assignees," *WorldatWork*, Second Quarter 2000, pp. 26–33; M. Mukuda, "Global Leaders Wanted . . . Apply Within," *Workspan*, Apr. 2001, pp. 36–41; C. Patton, "Match Game," *Human Resource Executive*, June 2000, pp. 36–41.

34. G. C. Thornton III, *Assessment Centers in Human Resource Management* (Reading, MA: Addison-Wesley, 1992).

35. Equal Employment Opportunity Commission, EEOC Compliance Manual—Section 15: Race and Color Discrimination, 2006 (*www.eeoc.gov/policy/docs/race-color.html*); J. A. Segal, "Land Executives, Not Lawsuits," *HR Magazine*, Oct. 2006, pp. 123–130.

# The Staffing Organizations Model

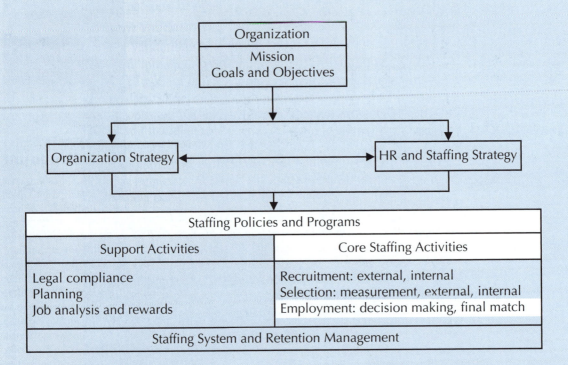

Organization

Mission
Goals and Objectives

Organization Strategy ⟷ HR and Staffing Strategy

Staffing Policies and Programs

| Support Activities | Core Staffing Activities |
|---|---|
| Legal compliance<br>Planning<br>Job analysis and rewards | Recruitment: external, internal<br>Selection: measurement, external, internal<br>Employment: decision making, final match |

Staffing System and Retention Management

# PART FIVE

## Staffing Activities: Employment

# CHAPTER ELEVEN

# Decision Making

**Learning Objectives and Introduction**
Learning Objectives
Introduction

**Choice of Assessment Method**
Validity Coefficient
Face Validity
Correlation With Other Predictors
Adverse Impact
Utility

**Determining Assessment Scores**
Single Predictor
Multiple Predictors

**Hiring Standards and Cut Scores**
Description of the Process
Consequences of Cut Scores
Methods to Determine Cut Scores
Professional Guidelines

**Methods of Final Choice**
Random Selection
Ranking
Grouping
Ongoing Hiring

**Decision Makers**
Human Resource Professionals
Managers
Employees

**Legal Issues**
Uniform Guidelines on Employee Selection Procedures
Diversity and Hiring Decisions

**Summary**

**Discussion Questions**

**Ethical Issues**

**Applications**

**Endnotes**

# LEARNING OBJECTIVES AND INTRODUCTION

## Learning Objectives

- Be able to interpret validity coefficients
- Estimate adverse impact and utility of selection systems
- Learn about methods for combining multiple predictors
- Establish hiring standards and cut scores
- Evaluate various methods of making a final selection choice
- Understand the roles of various decision makers in the staffing process
- Recognize the importance of diversity concerns in the staffing process

## Introduction

The preceding chapters described a variety of techniques that organizations can use to assess candidates. However, collecting data on applicants does not ultimately lead to a straightforward conclusion about who should be selected. Should interviews take precedence over standardized ability tests? Should job experience be the primary focus of selection decisions, or will organizations make better choices if experience ratings are supplemented with data on personality? What role should experience and education have in selection? In this chapter, we will discuss how this information can be used to make decisions about who will ultimately be hired. As we will see, subjective factors often enter into the decision process. Having methods to resolve any disputes that arise in the process of evaluating candidates in advance can greatly facilitate efficient decision making and reduce conflict among members of the hiring committee.

When it comes to making final decisions about candidates, it is necessary to understand the nature of the organization and the jobs being staffed. Organizations that have strong cultures and heavy needs for customer service might put a stronger emphasis on candidate personality and values. For jobs with a stronger technical emphasis, it makes more sense to evaluate candidates on the basis of demonstrated knowledge and skills. Throughout this chapter, you will want to consider how your own organization's strategic goals factor into staffing decision making.

The process of translating predictor scores into assessment scores is broken down into a series of subtopics. First, techniques for using single predictors and multiple predictors are discussed. The process used to determine minimum standards (a.k.a. "cut scores") will be described, as well as the consequences of cut scores and methods to determine cut scores. Methods of final choice must be considered to determine who from among the finalists will receive a job offer. For all the preceding decisions, consideration must be given to who should be involved in the decision process. Finally, legal issues should also guide decision making. Particular consideration will be given to the Uniform Guidelines on Employee Selection Procedures (UGESP) and to the role of diversity considerations in hiring decisions.

# CHOICE OF ASSESSMENT METHOD

In our discussions of external and internal selection methods, we listed multiple criteria to consider when deciding which method(s) to use (e.g., validity, utility). Some of these criteria require more amplification, specifically validity, correlation with other predictors (newly discussed here), adverse impact, and utility. In this section, we will consider a variety of techniques managers can use to assess how well various selection methods predict future performance, and which should therefore be retained in the measurement process.

Our discussion of how to choose an assessment method is based on the material we have already presented regarding the value of standardization, objectivity, and statistical decision tools. Despite a great deal of evidence supporting the use of these decision aids, managers often prefer to use their intuition when making important decisions. Although it is tempting to conclude that one's own subjective feeling and intuition will perform better than a mathematical formula for decision making, a very large body of research shows that experts seldom are as good as mathematical models when it comes to combining information and assessing across alternatives.[1] Intuitive decision making tends to rely on relatively little information, stories about past events that may not represent the current situation, and personal biases. One study that involved recording panels of managers making hiring decisions found that the managers often completely departed from the standardized information they were provided. They used very minor cues like intellectual ability from the speed of answering one question and attempted to read complex motives or personality traits from the subtle wording of answers to interview questions. Decision makers are strongly encouraged to focus their attention on objective, standardized assessment tools and decision-making aids as much as possible for important decisions like hiring.

## Validity Coefficient

Validity refers to the relationship between predictor and criterion scores. Often this relationship is assessed using a correlation (see Chapter 7). The correlation between predictor and criterion scores is known as a validity coefficient. The usefulness of a predictor is determined on the basis of the practical significance and statistical significance of its validity coefficient. As was noted in Chapter 7, reliability is a necessary condition for validity. Selection measures with questionable reliability will have questionable validity.

### Practical Significance
Practical significance refers to the extent to which the predictor adds value to the prediction of job success. It is assessed by examining the sign and the magnitude of the validity coefficient.

***Sign.***    The sign of the validity coefficient refers to the direction of the relationship between the predictor and the criterion. A useful predictor is one where the sign of the relationship is positive or negative and is consistent with the logic or theory behind the predictor.

***Magnitude.***    The magnitude of the validity coefficient refers to its size. It can range from 0 to 1.00, where a coefficient of 0 is least desirable and a coefficient of 1.00 is most desirable. The closer the validity coefficient is to 1.00, the more useful the predictor. Predictors with validity coefficients of 1.00 are not to be expected, given the inherent difficulties in predicting human behavior. Instead, as shown in Chapters 8 and 9, validity coefficients for current assessment methods range from 0 to about .60. Any validity coefficient above 0 is better than random selection and may be somewhat useful. Validities above .15 are moderately useful, and validities above .30 are highly useful.

### Statistical Significance

Statistical significance, as assessed by probability or p values (see Chapter 7), is another factor that should be used to interpret the validity coefficient. If a validity coefficient has a reasonable p value, chances are good that it would yield a similar validity coefficient if the same predictor were used with different sets of job applicants. That is, a reasonable p value indicates that the method of prediction, rather than chance, produced the observed validity coefficient. Convention has it that a reasonable level of significance is $p < .05$. This means there are fewer than 5 chances in 100 of concluding there is a relationship in the population of job applicants when, in fact, there is not.

Caution must be exercised in using statistical significance as a way to gauge the usefulness of a predictor. Research has clearly shown that nonsignificant validity coefficients may simply be due to the small samples of employees used to calculate the validity coefficient. Thus, a predictor should not be rejected solely on the basis of a small sample, since the predictor would likely be quite acceptable had a larger sample of employees been used to test for validity. These concerns over significance testing have led some researchers to recommend the use of "confidence intervals," for example, showing that one can be 90% confident that the true validity is no less than .30 and no greater than .40.[2]

## Face Validity

Face validity concerns whether the selection measure appears valid to the applicant. Face validity is potentially important to selection decision making in general, and choice of selection methods in particular, if it affects applicant behavior (willingness to continue in the selection process, performance, and turnover once hired). Judgments of face validity are closely associated with applicant reactions.[3]

## Correlation With Other Predictors

If a predictor is to be considered useful, it must add value to the prediction of job success. To add value, it must add to the prediction of success above and beyond the forecasting powers of current predictors. In general, a predictor is more useful if it has a *smaller* correlation with other predictors and a higher correlation with the criterion.

To assess whether the predictor adds anything new to forecasting, a matrix showing all the correlations between the predictors and the criteria should always be generated. If the correlations between the new predictor and the existing predictors are higher than the correlations between the new predictor and the criterion, the new predictor is not adding much that is new. There are also relatively straightforward techniques, such as multiple regression, that take the correlation among predictors into account.

Predictors are likely to be highly correlated with one another when their domain of content is similar. For example, both biodata and application blanks may focus on previous training received. Thus, using both biodata and application blanks as predictors may be redundant, and neither one may augment the other much in predicting job success. Instead, it might be more useful to supplement the application blank with a situational interview or a cognitive ability test.

## Adverse Impact

A predictor discriminates between people in terms of the likelihood of their success on the job. A predictor may also discriminate by screening out a disproportionate number of minorities and women. To the extent that this happens, the predictor has adverse impact, and it may result in legal problems. As a result, when the validity of alternative predictors is the same and one predictor has less adverse impact than the other predictor, the one with less adverse impact should be used.

A very difficult judgment call arises when one predictor has high validity and high adverse impact while another predictor has low validity and low adverse impact.[4] From the perspective of accurately predicting job performance, the former predictor should be used. From an equal employment opportunity and affirmative action (EEO/AA) standpoint, the latter predictor is preferable. Balancing the trade-offs is difficult and requires use of the organization's staffing philosophy regarding EEO/AA. Later in this chapter we consider some possible solutions to this important problem.

## Utility

Utility refers to the expected gains to be derived from using a predictor. Expected gains are of two types: hiring success and economic.

## Hiring Success Gain

Hiring success refers to the proportion of new hires who turn out to be successful on the job. Hiring success *gain* refers to the increase in the proportion of successful new hires that is expected to occur as a result of adding a new predictor to the selection system. If the current staffing system yields a success rate of 75% for new hires, how much of a gain in this success rate will occur by adding a new predictor to the system? The greater the expected gain, the greater the utility of the new predictor. This gain is influenced not only by the validity of the new predictor (as already discussed) but also by the selection ratio and base rate.

***Selection Ratio.***   The selection ratio is simply the number of people hired divided by the number of applicants (sr = number hired / number of applicants). The lower the selection ratio, the more useful the predictor. When the selection ratio is low, the organization is more likely to be selecting successful employees.

If the selection ratio is low, then the denominator is large or the numerator is small. Both conditions are desirable. A large denominator means that the organization is reviewing a large number of applicants for the job. The chances of identifying a successful candidate are much better in this situation than when an organization hires the first available person or reviews only a few applicants. A small numerator indicates that the organization is being very stringent with its hiring standards. The organization is hiring people likely to be successful rather than hiring anyone who meets the most basic requirements for the job; it is using high standards to ensure that the very best people are selected.

***Base Rate.***   The base rate is defined as the proportion of current employees who are successful on some criterion or human resource (HR) outcome (br = number of successful employees / number of employees). A high base rate is desired for obvious reasons. A high base rate may come about from the organization's staffing system alone or in combination with other HR programs, such as training and compensation.

When considering the possible use of a new predictor, one issue is whether the proportion of successful employees (i.e., the base rate) will increase as a result of using the new predictor in the staffing system. This is the matter of hiring success gain. Dealing with it requires simultaneous consideration of the organization's current base rate and selection ratio, as well as the validity of the new predictor.

The Taylor-Russell tables help address this issue. An excerpt is shown in Exhibit 11.1.

The cells in the tables show the percentages of new hires who will turn out to be successful. This is determined by a combination of the validity coefficient for the new predictor, the selection ratio, and the base rate. The top matrix (A) shows the percentage of successful new hires when the base rate is low (.30), the validity coefficient is low (.20) or high (.60), and the selection ratio is low (.10) or high (.70).

**EXHIBIT 11.1   Excerpt From the Taylor-Russell Tables**

A.

| | Base Rate = .30 Selection Ratio | |
|---|---|---|
| **Validity** | **.10** | **.70** |
| .20 | 43% | 33 |
| .60 | 77 | 40 |

B.

| | Base Rate = .80 Selection Ratio | |
|---|---|---|
| **Validity** | **.10** | **.70** |
| .20 | 89% | 83 |
| .60 | 99 | 90 |

Source: H. C. Taylor and J. T. Russell, "The Relationship of Validity Coefficients to the Practical Effectiveness of Tests in Selection," *Journal of Applied Psychology*, 1939, 23, pp. 565–578.

The bottom matrix (B) shows the percentage of successful new hires when the base rate is high (.80), the validity coefficient is low (.20) or high (.60), and the selection ratio is low (.10) or high (.70). Two illustrations show how these tables may be used.

The first illustration has to do with the decision whether to use a new test to select computer programmers. Assume that the current test has a validity coefficient of .20. Also assume that a consulting firm has approached the organization with a new test that has a validity coefficient of .60. Should the organization purchase and use the new test?

At first blush, the answer might seem to be yes, because the new test has a substantially higher level of validity. This initial reaction, however, must be gauged in the context of the selection ratio and the current base rate. If the current base rate is .80 and the current selection ratio is .70, then, as can be seen in matrix B of Exhibit 11.1, the new selection procedure will only result in a hiring success gain from 83% to 90%. The organization may already have a very high base rate due to other facets of HR management it does quite well (e.g., training, rewards). Hence, even though it has validity of .20, the base rate of its current predictor is already .80.

On the other hand, if the existing base rate of the organization is .30 and the existing selection ratio is .10, the organization should strongly consider the new test. As shown in matrix A of Exhibit 11.1, the hiring success gain will go from 43% to 77% with the addition of the new test.

A second illustration using the Taylor-Russell tables has to do with recruitment in conjunction with selection. Assume that the validity of the organization's current predictor, a cognitive ability test, is .60. Also assume that a new college recruitment program has been very aggressive. As a result, there is a large swell in the number of applicants, and the selection ratio has decreased from .70 to .10. Given this, the organization must decide whether to continue the college recruitment program.

An initial reaction may be that the program should be continued because of the large increase in applicants generated. As shown in matrix A of Exhibit 11.1, this answer would be correct if the current base rate is .30. By decreasing the selection ratio from .70 to .10, the hiring success gain increases from 40% to 77%. On the other hand, if the current base rate is .80, the organization may decide not to continue the program. The hiring success increases from 90% to 99%, which may not justify the very large expense associated with aggressive college recruitment campaigns.

The point of these illustrations is that when confronted with the decision of whether to use a new predictor, the decision depends on the validity coefficient, base rate, and selection ratio. They should not be considered independent of one another. HR professionals should carefully record and monitor base rates and selection ratios. Then, when management asks whether they should use a new predictor, the HR professionals can respond appropriately. The Taylor-Russell tables may be used for any combination of validity coefficient, base rate, and selection ratio values. The values shown in Exhibit 11.1 are excerpts for illustration only; when other values need to be considered, the original tables should be consulted to provide the appropriate answers.

## Economic Gain

Economic gain refers to the bottom-line or monetary impact of a predictor on the organization. The greater the economic gain the predictor produces, the more useful the predictor. Considerable work has been done over the years on assessing the economic gain associated with predictors. The basic utility formula used to estimate economic gain is shown in Exhibit 11.2.

At a general level, this formula works as follows. Economic gains derived from using a valid predictor versus random selection (the left-hand side of the equation) depend on two factors (the right-hand side of the equation). The first factor (the entry before the subtraction sign) is the revenue generated by hiring productive employees using the new predictor. The second factor (the entry after the subtraction sign) is the cost associated with using the new predictor. Positive economic gains are achieved when revenues are maximized and costs are minimized. Revenues are maximized by using the most valid selection procedures. Costs are minimized by using the predictors with the least costs. To estimate actual economic gain, values are entered into the equation for each of the variables shown. Values are usually generated by experts in HR research relying on the judgments of experienced line managers.

Several variations on this formula have been developed. For the most part, these variations require consideration of additional factors such as assumptions about tax rates and applicant flows. In all these models, the most difficult factor to estimate

**EXHIBIT 11.2 Economic Gain Formula**

$\Delta U \, (T \times N_n \times r_{xy} \times SD_y \times \bar{Z}_s) - (N_a \times C_y)$

Where:

$\Delta U$ = expected dollar value increase to the organization using the predictor versus random selection

$T$ = average tenure of employees in position

$N_n$ = number of people hired

$r_{xy}$ = correlation between predictor and job performance

$SD_y$ = dollar value of job performance

$\bar{Z}_s$ = average standard predictor score of selected group

$N_a$ = number of applicants

$C_y$ = cost per applicant

SOURCE: Adapted from C. Handler and S. Hunt, "Estimating the Financial Value of Staffing-Assessment Tools," *Workforce Management*, Mar. 2003 (*www.workforce.com*).

is the dollar value of job performance, which represents the difference between productive and nonproductive employees in dollar value terms. A variety of methods have been proposed, ranging from manager estimates of employee value to percentages of compensation (usually 40% of base pay).[5] Despite this difficulty, economic gain formulas represent a significant way of estimating the economic gains that may be anticipated with the use of a new (and valid) predictor.

## Limitations of Utility Analysis

Although utility analysis can be a powerful method to communicate the bottom-line implications of using valid selection measures, it is not without its limitations. Perhaps the most fundamental concern among researchers and practitioners is that utility estimates lack realism because of the following:

1. Determining the dollar value of an employee's performance is extremely subjective for many jobs and depends on untestable assumptions about how each employee contributes to a finished product.[6] This is especially difficult in team environments or for jobs that do not have tangible individual outcomes.

2. Many important variables are missing from the model, such as EEO/AA concerns and applicant reactions.[7]

3. The utility formula is based on many assumptions that are probably overly simplistic, including that validity does not vary over time;[8] that nonperformance criteria such as attendance, trainability, applicant reactions, and fit are irrelevant;[9] and that applicants are selected in a top-down manner and all job offers are accepted.[10]

Perhaps as a result of these limitations, several factors indicate that utility analysis may have a limited effect on managers' decisions about selection measures. For example, a survey of managers who stopped using utility analysis found that 40% did so because they felt that utility analysis was too complicated, whereas 32% discontinued use because they believed that the results were not credible.[11] Other studies have found that managers' acceptance of utility analysis is low; one study found that reporting simple validity coefficients was more likely to persuade HR decision makers to adopt a particular selection method than was reporting utility analysis results.[12]

These criticisms should not be taken as arguments that organizations should ignore utility analysis when evaluating selection decisions. However, decision makers are much less likely to become disillusioned with utility analysis if they are informed consumers and realize some of the limitations inherent in such analyses. Researchers have the responsibility of better embedding utility analysis in the strategic context in which staffing decisions are made, while HR decision makers have the responsibility to use the most rigorous methods possible to evaluate their decisions.[13] By being realistic about what utility analysis can and cannot accomplish, the potential to fruitfully inform staffing decisions will increase.

## DETERMINING ASSESSMENT SCORES

Once the predictors for final decision making have been selected, it is necessary to determine assessment scores for each candidate. This process is focused on developing a method to assign numerical scores to each candidate. These methods vary in complexity, from using a single predictor, to combining information from multiple predictors simultaneously, to sequentially eliminating candidates from consideration at each stage.

### Single Predictor

Using a single predictor in selection decisions simplifies the process of determining scores. In fact, scores on the single predictor *are* the final assessment scores. Thus, concerns over how to combine assessment scores are not relevant when a single predictor is used in selection decisions. Although using a single predictor has the advantage of simplicity, there are some obvious drawbacks. First, few employers would feel comfortable hiring applicants on the basis of a single attribute. In fact, almost all employers use multiple methods in selection decisions. A second and related reason for using multiple predictors is that utility increases as the number of valid predictors used in selection decisions increases. In most cases, using two valid selection methods results in more effective selection decisions than using a sole predictor. Unfortunately, in many cases, organizations rely entirely on an unstructured interview, which has already been described as less than desirable because it is inconsistent, low in validity, and potentially difficult to defend in a lawsuit. For these reasons, although basing selection decisions on a single predictor is a simple way to make decisions, it is rarely the best way.

## Multiple Predictors

Given the less-than-perfect validities of predictors, most organizations use multiple predictors in making selection decisions. With multiple predictors, decisions must be made about combining the resultant scores. These decisions can be addressed through compensatory, multiple hurdles, and combined approaches.

### Compensatory Model

With a compensatory model, scores on one predictor are simply added to scores on another predictor to yield a total score. This means that high scores on one predictor can compensate for low scores on another. For example, if an employer is using an interview and grade point average (GPA) to select a person, an applicant with a low GPA who does well in the interview may still get the job.

The advantage of a compensatory model is that it recognizes that people have multiple talents and that many different constellations of talents may produce success on the job. The disadvantage of a compensatory model is that, at least for some jobs, the level of proficiency for specific talents cannot be compensated for by other proficiencies. For example, a firefighter requires a certain level of strength that cannot be compensated for by intelligence.

In terms of using the compensatory model to make decisions, four procedures may be followed: clinical prediction, unit weighting, rational weighting, and multiple regression. The four methods differ from one another in terms of the manner in which predictor scores (raw or standardized) are weighted before being added together for a total or composite score.

Exhibit 11.3 illustrates these procedures. In all four methods, raw scores are used to determine a total score. Standard scores (see Chapter 7) may need to be used rather than raw scores if each predictor variable uses a different method of measurement or is measured under different conditions. Differences in weighting methods are shown in the bottom part of Exhibit 11.3, and a selection system consisting of interviews, application blanks, and recommendations is shown in the top part. For simplicity, assume that scores on each predictor range from 1 to 5. Scores on these three predictors are shown for three applicants.

*Clinical Prediction.* In the clinical prediction approach in Exhibit 11.3, note that managers use their expert judgment to arrive at a total score for each applicant. That final score may or may not be a simple addition of the three predictor scores shown in the exhibit. Hence, applicant A may be given a higher total score than applicant B even though simple addition shows that applicant B had one more point $(4 + 3 + 4 = 11)$ than applicant A $(3 + 5 + 2 = 10)$.

**EXHIBIT 11.3** **Raw Scores for Applicants on Three Predictors**

| | Predictor | | |
|---|---|---|---|
| Applicant | Interview | Application Blank | Recommendation |
| A | 3 | 5 | 2 |
| B | 4 | 3 | 4 |
| C | 5 | 4 | 3 |

**Clinical Prediction**

$P_1, P_2, P_3 \rightarrow$ Subjective assessment of qualifications

Example: Select applicant A based on "gut feeling" for overall qualification level.

**Unit Weighting**

$P_1 + P_2 + P_3$ = Total score

Example: All predictor scores are added together.

Applicant A = 3 + 5 + 2 = 10

Applicant B = 4 + 3 + 4 = 11

Applicant C = 5 + 4 + 3 = 12

**Rational Weighting**

$w_1P_1 + w_2P_2 + w_3P_3$ = Total score

Example: Weights are set by manager judgment at $w_1 = .5$, $w_2 = .3$, $w_3 = .2$

Applicant A = (.5 × 3) + (.3 × 5) + (.2 × 2) = 3.4

Applicant B = (.5 × 4) + (.3 × 3) + (.2 × 4) = 3.7

Applicant C = (.5 × 5) + (.3 × 4) + (.2 × 3) = 4.3

**Multiple Regression**

$a + b_1P_1 + b_2P_2 + b_3P_3$ = Total score

Example: Weights are set by statistical procedures at $a = .09$, $b_1 = .9$, $b_2 = .6$, $b_3 = .2$

Applicant A = .09 + (.9 × 3) + (.6 × 5) + (.2 × 2) = 6.19

Applicant B = .09 + (.9 × 4) + (.6 × 3) + (.2 × 4) = 6.29

Applicant C = .09 + (.9 × 5) + (.6 × 4) + (.2 × 3) = 7.59

Frequently, clinical prediction is done by initial screening interviewers or hiring managers. These decision makers may or may not have "scores" per se, but they have multiple pieces of information on each applicant, and they make a decision on the applicant by taking everything into account. In initial screening decisions, this summary decision determines whether the applicant gets over the initial hurdle and passes on to the next level of assessment. For example, when making an initial screening decision on an applicant, a manager at a fast-food restaurant might subjectively combine his or her impressions of various bits of information about the applicant on the application form and a quick interview. A hiring manager for a professional position might focus on a finalist's résumé and answers to the manager's interview questions to decide whether to extend an offer to the finalist.

The advantage of the clinical prediction approach is that it draws on the expertise of managers to weight and combine predictor scores. In turn, managers may be more likely to accept the selection decisions than if a mechanical scoring rule (e.g., add up the points) were used. Many managers believe that basing decisions on their experiences, rather than on mechanical scoring, makes them better at judging which applicants will be successful.[14] The problem with this approach is that the reasons for the weightings are known only to the manager. In addition, clinical predictions have been consistently shown to be less accurate than mechanical decisions. Research has shown, again and again, that experts who rely on intuition are less capable of accurately combining information compared to using a standardized system based on mathematical tools for combining information. This finding has been replicated in domains such as picking stocks, making medical diagnoses, granting university admission to students, and hiring employees.[15]

***Unit Weighting.*** With unit weighting, each predictor is weighted the same at a value of 1.00. As shown in Exhibit 11.3, the predictor scores are simply added together to get a total score. Therefore, the total scores for applicants A, B, and C are 10, 11, and 12, respectively. The advantage of unit weighting is that it is a simple and straightforward process and makes the importance of each predictor explicit to decision makers. The problem with this approach is that it assumes each predictor contributes equally to the prediction of job success, which often is not the case.

***Rational Weighting.*** With rational weighting, each predictor receives a differential rather than equal weighting. Managers and other subject matter experts (SMEs) establish the weights for each predictor according to the degree to which each is believed to predict job success. These weights (w) are then multiplied by each raw score (P) to yield a total score, as shown in Exhibit 11.3.

For example, the predictors are weighted .5, .3, and .2 for the interview, application blank, and recommendation, respectively. This means managers think interviews are the most important predictors, followed by application blanks and recommendations. Each applicant's raw score is multiplied by the appropriate weight to yield a total score. For example, the total score for applicant A is $(.5)3 + (.3)5 + (.2)2 = 3.4$.

The advantage of this approach is that it considers the relative importance of each predictor and makes this assessment explicit. The downside, however, is that it is an elaborate procedure that requires managers and SMEs to agree on the differential weights to be applied.

To simplify the process of rational weighting, some organizations are turning to computer-aided decision tools. Williams Insurance Service utilizes a program called ChoiceAnalyst to make it easier for hiring managers to integrate information on a variety of candidate characteristics into a single score.[16] Recruiters select the predictor constructs that will be used to judge applicants, and provide decision weights for how important they think each construct should be in making a final choice. Scores on a variety of predictor measures are entered into the software, which produces a rank ordering of candidates. One advantage of these software-based solutions is that they can be explicitly developed to consider a variety of managerial preferences and assess how differences in perceptions of predictor importance can lead to differences in final hiring decisions.

***Multiple Regression.***   Multiple regression is similar to rational weighting in that the predictors receive different weights. With multiple regression, however, the weights are established on the basis of statistical procedures rather than on judgments by managers or other SMEs. The statistical weights are developed from (1) the correlation of each predictor with the criterion, and (2) the correlations among the predictors. As a result, regression weights provide optimal weights in the sense that they will yield the highest total validity.

The calculations result in a multiple regression formula like the one shown in Exhibit 11.3. A total score for each applicant is obtained by multiplying the statistical weight (b) for each predictor by the predictor (P) score and summing these along with the intercept value (a). As an example, assume the statistical weights are .9, .6, and .2 for the interview, application blank, and recommendation, respectively, and that the intercept is .09. Using these values, the total score for applicant A is $.09 + (.9)3 + (.6)5 + (.2)2 = 6.19$.

Multiple regression offers the possibility of a higher degree of precision in the prediction of criterion scores than do the other methods of weighting. Unfortunately, this level of precision is realized only under a certain set of circumstances. In particular, for multiple regression to be more precise than unit weighting, there must be a small number of predictors, low correlations between predictor variables, and a large sample that is similar to the population that the test will be used on.[17] Many selection settings do not meet these criteria, so in these cases consideration should be given to unit or rational weighting, or to alternative regression-based weighting schemes that have been developed—general dominance weights or relative importance weights.[18] In situations where these conditions are met, however, multiple regression weights can produce higher validity and utility than the other weighting schemes.

***Choosing Among Weighting Schemes.***   Choosing among the different weighting schemes is important because how various predictor combinations are weighted is critical in determining the usefulness of the selection process. Despite the limitations of regression weighting schemes noted above, one analysis of actual selection measures revealed that when scores on cognitive ability and integrity tests were combined by weighting them equally, the total validity increased to .65, an increase of 27.6% over the validity of the cognitive ability test alone.[19] When scores were weighted according to multiple regression, however, the increase in validity became 28.2%. While these results do not prove that multiple regression weighting is a superior method in all circumstances, they do help illustrate that the choice of the best weighting scheme is consequential and likely depends on answers to the most important questions about clinical, unit, rational, and multiple regression schemes (in that order):

- Do selection decision makers have considerable experience and insight into selection decisions, and is managerial acceptance of the selection process important?
- Is there reason to believe that each predictor contributes relatively equally to job success?
- Are there adequate resources to use relatively involved weighting schemes such as rational weights or multiple regression?
- Are the conditions under which multiple regression is superior (relatively small number of predictors, low correlations among predictors, and large sample) satisfied?

Answers to these questions—and the importance of the questions themselves—will go a long way toward deciding which weighting scheme to use. We should also note that while statistical weighting is more valid than clinical weighting, the combination of both methods may yield the highest validity. One study indicated that regression-weighted predictors were more valid than clinical judgments, but clinical judgments contributed uniquely to performance controlling for regression-weighted predictors. This suggests that both statistical and clinical weighting might be used. Thus, the weighting schemes are not necessarily mutually exclusive.[20]

## Multiple Hurdles Model

With a multiple hurdles approach, an applicant must earn a passing score on each predictor before advancing in the selection process. Such an approach is taken when each requirement measured by a predictor is critical to job success. Passing scores are set using the methods to determine cut scores (discussed in the next section). Unlike the compensatory model, the multiple hurdles model does not allow a high score on one predictor to compensate for a low score on another predictor.

Many organizations use multiple hurdles selection systems to both reduce the cost of selecting applicants and make the decision-making process more tractable in the final selection stage. It would be very inefficient to process all the possible information the organization might collect on a large number of candidates, so some candidates are screened out relatively early in the process. Typically, the first stage of a selection process screens the applicant pool down to those who meet some minimal educational or years-of-experience requirement. Collecting information on such requirements is fairly inexpensive for organizations and can usually be readily quantified. After this stage, the pool of remaining applicants might be further reduced by administering relatively inexpensive standardized tests to those who passed the initial screen. This will further reduce the pool of potential candidates, allowing the organization to devote more resources to interviewing finalists and having them meet with managers at the organization's headquarters. This is the selection stage. There are many variations in how the multiple hurdles model can be implemented, and the exact nature of the "screen" versus "select" measures will vary based on the job requirements.

### Combined Model

For jobs where some but not all requirements are critical to job success, a combined method may be used involving both the compensatory and the multiple hurdles models. The process starts with the multiple hurdles model and ends with the compensatory method.

An example of the combined approach for the position of recruitment manager is shown in Exhibit 11.4. The selection process starts with two hurdles that applicants must pass in succession: the application blank and the job knowledge test. Failure to clear either hurdle results in rejection. Applicants who pass receive an

### EXHIBIT 11.4  Combined Model for Recruitment Manager

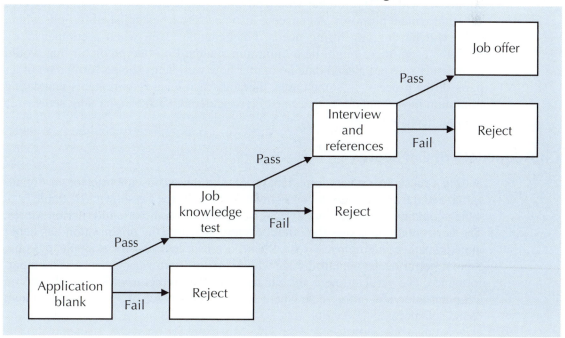

interview and have their references checked. Information from the interview and the references is combined in a compensatory manner. Those who pass are offered jobs, and those who do not pass are rejected.

## HIRING STANDARDS AND CUT SCORES

Hiring standards or cut scores address the issue of what constitutes a minimally qualified candidate. The score for a candidate may be from a single predictor or a total score from multiple predictors. To address this, a description of the process and the consequences of cut scores are presented. Then, methods that may be used to establish the actual cut score are described. These techniques include minimum standards, top-down hiring, and banding.

### Description of the Process

Once one or more predictors have been chosen for use in a multiple hurdles model, a decision must be made as to who advances in the selection process. This decision requires that one or more cut scores be established. A cut score is the score that separates those who advance in the process (e.g., applicants who become candidates) from those who are rejected. For example, assume a test is used on which scores range from 0 to 100 points. A cut score of 70 means that those applicants with a 70 or higher would advance, while all others would be rejected for employment purposes. A cut score also needs to be established for jobs where there will be ongoing hiring needs. For example, even when a compensatory model is used, there might be a minimum standard on one predictor that would completely rule out a candidate no matter how well he or she performed on other parts of the process. In some cases, there are also legal requirements mandating minimum hiring standards that must be considered, such as a passing score on a nursing licensure exam.

### Consequences of Cut Scores

Setting a cut score is a very important process, as it has consequences for the organization and the applicant. The consequences of cut scores are shown in Exhibit 11.5, which contains a summary of a scatter diagram of predictor and criterion scores. The horizontal line shows the criterion score at which the organization has determined whether an employee is successful or unsuccessful—for example, a 3 on a 5-point performance appraisal scale where 1 is low performance and 5 is high performance. The vertical line is the cut score for the predictor—for example, a 3 on a 5-point interview rating scale where 1 reveals no chance of success and 5 a high chance of success.

**EXHIBIT 11.5** **Consequences of Cut Scores**

| Criterion | Predictor Cut Score | |
|---|---|---|
| | D | A |
| **Successful** | False<br>negatives | True<br>positives |
| | C | B |
| **Unsuccessful** | True<br>negatives | False<br>positives |
| | | **Predictor** |
| | No hire | Hire |

The consequences of setting the cut score at a particular level are shown in each of the quadrants. Quadrants A and C represent correct decisions, which have positive consequences for the organization. Quadrant A applicants are called true positives because they were assessed as having a high chance of success using the predictor and would have succeeded if hired. Quadrant C applicants are called true negatives because they were assessed as having little chance for success and, indeed, would not be successful if hired.

Quadrants D and B represent incorrect decisions, which have negative consequences to the organization and affected applicants. Quadrant D applicants are called false negatives because they were assessed as not being likely to succeed, but had they been hired, they would have been successful. Not only was an incorrect decision reached, but also a person who would have done well was not hired. Quadrant B applicants are called false positives. They were assessed as being likely to succeed, but would have ended up being unsuccessful performers. Eventually, these people would need to receive remedial training, be transferred to a new job, or even be terminated.

How high or low a cut score is set has a large impact on the consequences shown in Exhibit 11.5, and trade-offs are always involved. Compared with the moderate cut score in the exhibit, a high cut score results in fewer false positives but a larger number of false negatives. Is this a good, bad, or inconsequential set of outcomes for the organization? The answer depends on the job open for selection and the costs involved. If the job is an astronaut position for NASA, it is essential that there be no false positives. The cost of a false positive may be the loss of human life.

Now consider the consequences of a low cut score, relative to the one shown in Exhibit 11.5. There are fewer false negatives and more true positives, but more false positives are hired. In organizations that gain competitive advantage in their industry by hiring the very best, this set of consequences may be unacceptable. Alternatively, for EEO/AA purposes it may be desirable to have a low cut score so that the number of false negatives for minorities and women is minimized.

In short, when setting a cut score, attention must be given to the consequences, as they can be very serious. As a result, different methods of setting cut scores have been developed to guide decision makers. These will now be reviewed.[21]

## Methods to Determine Cut Scores

Three methods may be used to determine cut scores: minimum competency, top-down, and banding. Each of these is described below, along with professional guidelines for setting cut scores.

### Minimum Competency

Using the minimum competency method, the cut score is set on the basis of the minimum qualifications deemed necessary to perform the job. SMEs usually establish the minimum competency score. This approach is often needed in situations where the first step in the hiring process is the demonstration of minimum skill requirements. Exhibit 11.6 illustrates the use of cut scores in selection. The scores of 25 applicants on a particular test are listed. The cut score is set at the level at which applicants who score below the line are deemed unqualified for the job. In this case, a score of 75 was determined to be the minimum competency level necessary. Thus, all applicants who scored below 75 are deemed unqualified and are rejected, and all applicants who scored 75 or above are deemed at least minimally qualified. Finalists and ultimately offer receivers can then be chosen from among these qualified applicants on the basis of other criteria.

A well-known example of a minimum competency approach is the Angoff method.[22] In this approach, SMEs set the minimum cut scores needed to proceed in the selection process. These experts go through the content of the predictor (e.g., test items) and determine the proportion of individuals with a minimum level of competence who would answer each item correctly. For example, experts might estimate that at least 75% of minimally qualified electricians would be able to define ampacity on a quiz. The experts might estimate that only 25% would be able to identify a bonding jumper. These ratings are then summed together to obtain a minimal cut score.

---

**EXHIBIT 11.6** **Use of Cut Scores in Selection Decisions**

| Rank | Test Score | Minimum Competency | | Top-Down | | | Banding* |
|------|------------|--------------------|--|----------|--|--|----------|
| 1 | 100 | 100⌐ | | 100 | 1st | choice | 100⌐ |
| 2 | 98 | 98 | | 98 | 2nd | choice | 98 |
| 3 | 97 | 97 | | 97 | 3rd | choice | 97 |
| 4 | 96 | 96 | | 96 | 4th | choice | 96 |
| T5 | 93 | 93 | | 95 | 5th | choice | 93 |
| T5 | 93 | 93 | | 95 | 5th | choice | 93 |
| 7 | 91 | 91 | | 91 | ′′ | | 91 ⌟ |
| T8 | 90 | 90 | | 90 | ′′ | | 90 ⌐ |
| T8 | 90 | 90 | | 90 | ′′ | | 90 |
| 10 | 88 | 88 | Qualified | 88 | ′′ | | 88 |
| 11 | 87 | 87 | | 87 | ′′ | | 87 |
| T12 | 85 | 85 | | 85 | ′′ | | 85 |
| T12 | 85 | 85 | | 85 | ′′ | | 85 |
| 14 | 83 | 83 | | 83 | ′′ | | 83 |
| 15 | 81 | 81 | | 81 | ′′ | | 81 ⌟ |
| 16 | 79 | 79 | | 79 | ′′ | | 79 ⌐ |
| T17 | 77 | 77 | | 77 | ′′ | | 77 |
| T17 | 77 | 77 | | 77 | ′′ | | 77 |
| 19 | 76 | 76 | | 76 | ′′ | | 76 |
| 20 | 75 | 75 ⌟ Min. competency | | 75 | ′′ | | 75 ⌟ |
| 21 | 74 | 74 ⌐ | | 74 | 21st | choice | 74 ⌐ |
| 22 | 71 | 71 | | 71 | 22nd | choice | 71 ⌟ |
| 23 | 70 | 70 | Unqualified | 70 | 23rd | choice | 70 ⌐ |
| 24 | 69 | 69 | | 69 | 24th | choice | 69 |
| 25 | 65 | 65 ⌟ | | 65 | 25th | choice | 65 ⌟ |

*All scores within brackets are treated as equal; choice of applicants within brackets (if necessary) can be made on the basis of other factors, such as EEO/AA considerations.

There are several problems with this particular approach and the subsequent modifications to it. First, it is a time-consuming procedure. Second, the results are dependent on the SMEs. It is very difficult to get members of the organization to agree on who "the" SMEs are. Which SMEs are selected may have a bearing on the actual cut scores developed. Finally, it is unclear how much agreement there must be among SMEs when they evaluate test items. There may also be judgmental errors and biases in how cut scores are set. If the Angoff method is used, it is important that SMEs are provided with a common definition of minimally competent test takers, and that SMEs are encouraged to discuss their estimates. Each of these steps has been found to increase the reliability of the SME.[23]

A variation of the minimum competency approach is hiring the first acceptable candidate. It is often used when candidates come to the attention of the hiring person sequentially, one at a time, rather than having a total pool of candidates from which to choose the finalists. It is also used when the organization is desperate for "warm bodies" and willing to hire anyone who meets some threshold. Although at times a rush to hire is understandable, the consequences can be most unfortunate. In one case, due to the difficulty of finding telemarketers, a home mortgage call center had a policy of hiring the first acceptable candidate. The hiring manager at this call center overheard a newly hired employee tell a customer, "If I had a rate as high as yours, I'd slit my wrists, then climb to the top of the highest building and jump off."[24] While hiring the first acceptable candidate may seem necessary, it is far from an ideal hiring strategy and the costs may not be revealed until it is too late.

Another variant on the minimum competency approach is to impose a sort of maximum competency on overqualified applicants. The assumption here is that the job will not be sufficiently rewarding and the overqualified employee will quickly quit. Evidence suggests that employees who perceive themselves to be overqualified for their jobs report lower levels of job satisfaction and higher intentions to leave.[25] This may be because individuals who feel that they are overqualified believe that they deserve a better job and that their present work does not sufficiently challenge them. Employers can use tactics like increasing employee empowerment to alleviate these feelings among overqualified employees and therefore allow the organization to retain individuals who have exceptional levels of skills.[26] Managers should exercise caution before automatically rejecting individuals who appear to be overqualified. Sometimes people are interested in a job for reasons unknown to the hiring manager. There are also legal dangers, as many apparently overqualified applicants are over age 40. As one manager said, "I think it's a huge mistake not to take a second look at overqualified candidates. Certainly there are valid reasons to reject some candidates, but it shouldn't be a blanket response."[27]

## Top-Down

Another method of determining the level at which the cut score should be set is to simply examine the distribution of predictor scores for applicants and then determine which proportion of applicants will be hired. These demands might include the number of vacancies to be filled and EEO/AA requirements. This top-down method of setting cut scores is illustrated in Exhibit 11.6. As the exhibit shows, under top-down hiring, cut scores are established by the number of applicants that need to be hired. Once that number has been determined, applicants are selected from the top based on the order of their scores until the number desired is reached. The advantage of this approach is that it is easy to administer. It also minimizes judgment required because the cut score is determined on the basis of the demand for labor. The big drawback is that validity is often not established prior to the use of the predictor. If the applicant pool is particularly low-quality and hiring needs are high, it is possible that in an effort to staff a position, the organization will hire individuals who are poorly qualified. In these situations, knowing a minimum competency score in advance might suggest that it would be better to continue recruiting than to hire some individuals. Also, there may be overreliance on the use of a single predictor and cut score, while other potentially useful predictors are ignored.

## Banding and Other Alternatives to Top-Down Selection

The traditionally selected cut score method is the top-down approach. For both external hiring and internal promotions, the top-down method will yield the highest validity and utility. This method has been criticized, however, for ignoring the possibility that small differences between scores are due to measurement error. Another criticism of the top-down method is its potential for adverse impact, particularly when cognitive ability tests are used. As we noted in Chapter 9, there is perhaps no greater paradox in selection than the fact that the single most valid selection measure (cognitive ability tests) is also the measure with the most adverse impact. The magnitude of the adverse impact is such that, on a standard cognitive ability test, if half the white applicants were hired, only 16% of the African American applicants would be expected to be hired.[28]

One suggestion for reducing the adverse impact of top-down hiring is to use different norms for minority and majority groups; thus, hiring decisions are based on normatively defined (rather than absolute) scores. For example, an African American employee who achieved a score of 75 on a test where the mean of all African American applicants was 50 could be considered to have the same normative score as a white applicant who scored a 90 on a test where the mean for white applicants was 60. However, this "race norming" of test scores, which was a common practice in the civil service and among some private employers, is expressly forbidden by the Civil Rights Act of 1991. As a result, another approach, termed "banding," has been promulgated.

Banding refers to the procedure whereby applicants who score within a certain score range or band are considered to have scored equivalently. A simple banding procedure is provided in Exhibit 11.6. In a 100-point test, all applicants who score within the band of 10-point increments are considered to have scored equally. For example, all applicants who score 91 and above could be assigned a score of 9, those who score 81–90 are given a score of 8, and so on. (In essence, this is what is done when letter grades are assigned based on exam scores.) Hiring within bands could then be done at random or, more typically, could be based on race or sex in conjunction with other factors (e.g., seniority or experience). Banding might reduce the adverse impact of selection tests because such a procedure tends to reduce differences between higher- and lower-scoring groups (as is the case with whites and minorities on cognitive ability tests). In practice, band widths are usually calculated on the basis of the standard error of measurement.

Research suggests that banding procedures result in substantial decreases in the adverse impact of cognitive ability tests, while, under certain conditions, the losses in terms of utility are relatively small. Various methods of banding have been proposed, but the differences between these methods are relatively unimportant.[29]

Perhaps the major limitation with banding is that it sacrifices validity, especially when the selection measure is reliable. Because the standard error of the difference between test scores is partly a function of the reliability of the test, when test reliability is low, band widths are wider than when the reliability of the test is high. For example, if the reliability of a test is .80, at a reasonable level of confidence, nearly half the scores on a test can be considered equivalent.[30] Obviously, taking scores on a 100-point test and lumping applicants into only two groups wastes a great deal of important information on applicants (it is unlikely that an applicant who scores a 51 on a valid test will perform the same on the job as an applicant who scores 99). Therefore, if the reliability of a test is even moderately high, the validity and utility decrements that result from banding become quite severe. There is also evidence that typical banding procedures overestimate the width of bands, which of course exacerbates the problem.[31]

The scientific merit of test banding is hotly debated.[32] It is unlikely that we could resolve here the myriad ethical and technical issues underlying its use. Organizations considering the use of banding in personnel selection decisions must weigh the pros and cons carefully, including the legal issues (a review of lawsuits concerning banding found that it was generally upheld by the courts[33]). In the end, however, there may be a values choice to be made: to optimize validity (to some detriment to diversity) or to optimize diversity (with some sacrifice in validity). As one review noted, though "there is extensive evidence supporting the validity [of cognitive tests], adverse impact is unlikely to be eliminated as long as one assesses" cognitive abilities in the selection process.[34]

In an effort to resolve this somewhat pessimistic trade-off, some researchers have developed nonlinear models that attempt to find optimal solutions that maximize validity and diversity. One effort produced a statistical algorithm that attempts to achieve an optimal trade-off between validity and adverse impact by differentially weighting the selection measures. Although such algorithms may reduce the price to be paid in the values (between optimizing validity and diversity), the silver bullet solution remains elusive.[35]

## Professional Guidelines

Much more research is needed on systematic procedures that are effective in setting optimal cut scores. In the meantime, a sound set of professional guidelines for setting cut scores is shown in Exhibit 11.7.

## EXHIBIT 11.7   Professional Guidelines for Setting Cutoff Scores

1. It is unrealistic to expect that there is a single "best" method of setting cutoff scores for all situations.
2. The process of setting a cutoff score (or a critical score) should begin with a job analysis that identifies relative levels of proficiency on critical knowledge, skills, abilities, or other characteristics.
3. The validity and job relatedness of the assessment procedure are crucial considerations.
4. How a test is used (criterion-referenced or norm-referenced) affects the selection and meaning of a cutoff score.
5. When possible, data on the actual relation of test scores to outcome measures of job performance should be considered carefully.
6. Cutoff scores or critical scores should be set high enough to ensure that minimum standards of job performance are met.
7. Cutoff scores should be consistent with normal expectations of acceptable proficiency within the workforce.

Source: W. F. Cascio, R. A. Alexander, and G. V. Barrett, "Setting Cutoff Scores: Legal, Psychometric, and Professional Issues and Guidelines," *Personnel Psychology*, 1988, 41, pp. 21–22. Used with permission.

## METHODS OF FINAL CHOICE

The discussion thus far has been on decision rules that can be used to narrow down the list of people to successively smaller groups that advance in the selection process from applicant to candidate to finalist. How does the organization determine which finalists will receive job offers? Discretionary assessments about the finalists must be converted into final choice decisions. The methods of final choice are the mechanisms by which discretionary assessments are translated into job offer decisions.

Methods of final choice include random selection, ranking, and grouping. Examples of each of these methods are shown in Exhibit 11.8 and are discussed here.

### Random Selection

With random selection, each finalist has an equal chance of being selected. The only rationale for selecting a person is the "luck of the draw." For example, the six names from Exhibit 11.8 could be put in a hat and the finalist drawn out and tendered a job offer. This approach has the advantage of being quick. In addition, with random selection, one cannot be accused of favoritism, because everyone has an equal chance of being selected. The disadvantage to this approach is that discretionary assessments are simply ignored.

**EXHIBIT 11.8    Methods of Final Choice**

| Random | Ranking | Grouping |
|---|---|---|
| Casey | 1. Keisha | Keisha |
| Keisha | 2. Meg | Meg ] Top choices |
| Buster | 3. Buster | |
| Lyn Aung  > Pick one | 4. Lyn Aung | Buster |
| Meg | 5. Casey | Lyn Aung ] Acceptable |
| Luis | 6. Luis | |
| | | Casey |
| | | Luis ] Last resorts |

## Ranking

With ranking, finalists are ordered from the most desirable to the least desirable based on results of discretionary assessments. As shown in Exhibit 11.8, the person ranked first (Keisha) is the most desirable, and the person ranked sixth (Luis) is the least desirable. It is important to note that desirability should be viewed in the context of the entire selection process. When this is done, persons with lower levels of desirability (e.g., ranks of 3, 4, and 5) should not be viewed necessarily as failures. Job offers are extended to people on the basis of their rank ordering, with the top-ranked person receiving the first offer. Should that person turn down the job offer or suddenly withdraw from the selection process, finalist number 2 receives the offer, and so on.

The advantage of ranking is that it indicates the relative worth of each finalist for the job. It also provides a set of backups should one or more of the finalists withdraw from the process.

Backup finalists may decide to withdraw from the process to take a position elsewhere. Although ranking gives the organization a cushion if the top choices withdraw from the process, it does not mean that the process of job offers can proceed at a leisurely pace. Immediate action needs to be taken with the top choices in case they decide to withdraw and there is a need to go to backups. This is especially true in tight labor markets, where there is a strong demand for the services of people on the ranking list.

## Grouping

With the grouping method, finalists are banded together into rank-ordered categories. In Exhibit 11.8, the finalists are grouped according to whether they are top choices, acceptable, or last resorts. The advantage of this method is that it permits ties among finalists, thus avoiding the need to assign a different rank to each person. The disadvantage is that decisions still have to be made from among the top choices. These decisions might be based on factors such as the probability of each person accepting the offer.

## Ongoing Hiring

In some organizations, the hiring process is continuous, meaning that there is never a final list of candidates to be selected. Instead, an organization that has continuous needs for employees in a variety of positions might continuously collect résumés from interested parties, and then when positions open up, call in for interviews everyone who passes the minimum qualifications for open jobs. In many ways, this is like the method of hiring the first acceptable candidate, described under the minimum competency approach. Jobs with very high turnover rates, like entry-level retail and food service positions, are typically staffed in this way. The advantage of an ongoing hiring method is that it generates a large quantity of applicants who can start in a relatively short period of time, which can be very important for organizations that frequently replace staff. The disadvantage of this system is that it seldom allows for careful consideration of the best possible candidates from a set of qualified applicants.

## DECISION MAKERS

A final consideration in decision making for selection is who should participate in the decisions. That is, who should determine the process to be followed (e.g., establishing cut scores), and who should determine the outcome (e.g., who gets the job offer)? The answer is that both HR professionals and line managers must play a role. Although the two roles are different, both are critical to the organization. Employees may play certain roles as well.

## Human Resource Professionals

As a general rule, HR professionals should have a high level of involvement in the processes used to design and manage the selection system. They should be consulted in matters such as which predictors to use and how to best use them. In particular, they need to orchestrate the development of policies and procedures in the staffing areas covered. These professionals have, or know where to find, the technical expertise needed to develop sound selection decisions, and they also have the knowledge to ensure that relevant laws and regulations are followed. Finally, they can represent the interests and concerns of employees to management.

Although the primary role HR professionals should play is in terms of the process, they should also have some involvement in determining who receives job offers. One obvious area where this is true is with staffing the HR function. A less obvious place where HR professionals can play an important secondary role is in terms of providing input into selection decisions made by managers.

HR professionals may be able to provide some perception on applicants that is not always perceived by line managers. For example, they may be able to offer some insight on the applicants' people skills (e.g., communications, teamwork). HR professionals are sensitive to these issues because of their training and experience. They may have data to share on these matters as a result of their screening interviews, knowledge of how to interpret paper-and-pencil instruments (e.g., personality test), and interactions with internal candidates (e.g., serving on task forces with the candidates).

The other area where HR professionals may contribute to outcomes is in terms of initial assessment methods. Many times, HR professionals are, and should be, empowered to make initial selection decisions, such as who gets invited into the organization for administration of the next round of selection. Doing so saves managers time in which to carry out their other responsibilities. In addition, HR professionals can ensure that minorities and women applicants are actively solicited and not excluded from the applicant pool for the wrong reasons.

## Managers

As a general rule, a manager's primary involvement in staffing is in determining who is selected for employment. Managers are the SMEs of the business, and they are thus held accountable for the success of the people hired. They are far less involved in determining the processes followed to staff the organization, because they often do not have the time or expertise to do so. The average manager can also be expected to have no knowledge of staffing research whatsoever, though that doesn't mean he or she is uninterested in learning.[36]

Although they may not play a direct role in establishing processes, managers can and should be periodically consulted by HR professionals on process issues. They should be consulted because they are the consumers of HR services. As such, they should be allowed to provide input into the staffing process to ensure that it meets their needs in making the best possible person/job matches.

An additional benefit of allowing management a role in process issues is that, as a result of their involvement, managers may develop a better understanding of why HR professionals prescribe certain practices. When they are not invited to be part of the process to establish staffing policy and procedures, line managers may view HR professionals as obstacles to hiring the right person for the job.

It should also be noted that the degree of managers' involvement usually depends on the type of assessment decisions made. Decisions made using initial assessment methods are usually delegated to the HR professional, as just discussed. Decisions made using substantive assessment methods usually involve some degree of input from the manager. Decisions made using discretionary methods are usually the direct responsibility of the manager. As a general rule, the extent of managerial involvement in determining outcomes should only be as great as management's knowledge of the job. If managers are involved in hiring decisions for jobs with which they are not familiar, legal, measurement, and morale problems are likely to be created.

## Employees

Traditionally, employees have not been considered part of the decision-making process in staffing, but this tradition is slowly changing. For example, in team assessment approaches (see Chapter 8), employees may have a voice in both the process and the outcomes. That is, they may have ideas about how selection procedures are established, and they may make decisions about, or provide input into, who gets hired. Involvement in the team approach is encouraged because it may give employees a sense of ownership of the work process and help them better identify with organizational goals. Also, it may result in selecting members who are more compatible with the goals of the work team. Google includes line managers and peers in its hiring process. Its consensus-based hiring process is seen as a valuable way to get a variety of perspectives on the fit between applicants and the organization.[37] In order for employee involvement to be effective, employees need to be provided with staffing training just as managers are (see Chapter 9).

## LEGAL ISSUES

One of the most important legal issues in decision making is that of cut scores or hiring standards. These scores or standards regulate the flow of individuals from applicant to candidate to finalist to new hire. Throughout this flow, adverse impact may occur. When it does, the UGESP come into play. In addition, the organization could form a multipronged strategy for increasing workforce diversity.

## Uniform Guidelines on Employee Selection Procedures

If the use of cut scores does not lead to adverse impact in decision making, the UGESP are essentially silent on the issue of cut scores. The discretion exercised by the organization as it makes its selection decisions is thus unconstrained legally. If adverse impact is occurring, the UGESP become directly applicable to decision making.

Under conditions of adverse impact, the UGESP require the organization to either eliminate its occurrence or justify it through the conduct of validity studies and the careful setting of cut scores:

> Where cutoff scores are used, they should normally be set as to be reasonable and consistent with normal expectations of acceptable proficiency within the workforce. Where applicants are ranked on the basis of properly validated selection procedures and those applicants scoring below a higher cutoff score than appropriate in light of such expectations have little or no chance of being selected for employment, the higher cutoff score may be appropriate, but the degree of adverse impact should be considered.

This provision suggests that the organization should be cautious in general about setting cut scores that are above those necessary to achieve acceptable proficiency among those hired. In other words, even with a valid predictor, the organization should be cautious that its hiring standards are not so high that they create needless adverse impact. This is particularly true with ranking systems. Use of random methods—or to a lesser extent, grouping methods—would help overcome this particular objection to ranking systems.

Whatever cut score procedure is used, the UGESP also require that the organization be able to document its establishment and operation. Specifically, the UGESP say that "if the selection procedure is used with a cutoff score, the user should describe the way in which normal expectations of proficiency within the workforce were determined and the way in which the cutoff score was determined."

The UGESP also suggest two options to eliminate adverse impact, rather than to justify it as in the validation and cut score approach. One option is use of "alternative procedures." Here, the organization uses an alternative selection procedure that causes less adverse impact (e.g., work sample instead of a written test) but has roughly the same validity as the procedure it replaces.

The other option is that of affirmative action. The UGESP do not relieve the organization of any affirmative action obligations it may have. Also, the UGESP strive to "encourage the adoption and implementation of voluntary affirmative action programs" for organizations that do not have any affirmative action obligations.

## Diversity and Hiring Decisions

There has been considerable controversy and litigation over the issue of whether it is permissible for a legally protected characteristic such as race or gender to enter into a staffing decision at all, and if so, under exactly what circumstances. At the crux of the matter is whether staffing decisions should be based solely on a person's qualifications or on qualifications and the protected characteristic. It is argued that allowing the protected characteristic to receive some weight in the decision would serve to create a more diverse workforce, which many public and private organizations claim is something they have a compelling interest in and responsibility to do (refer back to Chapter 3 and the discussion of affirmative action).

It can be concluded that unless the organization is under a formal affirmative action plan (AAP), protected characteristics (e.g., race, sex, and religion) should not be considered in selection decision making. This conclusion is consistent with Equal Employment Opportunity Commission (EEOC) policy that the organization should use job-related hiring standards and that the same selection techniques and weights must be used for all people.[38]

How should the organization proceed, especially if it wants to not only comply with the law but also increase the diversity of its workforce? Several things might be done. First, carefully establish KSAOs (knowledge, skill, ability, and other characteristics) for jobs so that they are truly job related; as part of that process, establish some job-related KSAOs that correlate with protected characteristics, such as diversity in experience and customer contacts. For example, a KSAO for the job of marketing manager might be "substantial contacts within diverse racial and ethnic communities." Both white and nonwhite applicants could potentially meet this requirement, increasing the chances of recruiting and selecting a person of color for the job. Second, use recruitment (both external and internal) as a tool for attracting a more qualified and diverse applicant pool. Third, use valid methods of KSAO assessment derived from a formal selection plan. Fourth, avoid clinical or excessively subjective prediction in making the assessment and deriving a total assessment or score for candidates. Instead, establish and use the same set of predictors and weights for them to arrive at the final assessment. Fifth, provide training in selection decision making for hiring managers and staffing managers. Content of the training should focus on overcoming usage of stereotypes, learning how to gather and weight predictor information consistently for all candidates, and looking for red flags about acceptance or rejection based on vague judgments about the candidate being a "good fit." Sixth, use a diverse group of hiring and staffing managers to gather and evaluate KSAO information, including a diverse team to conduct interviews. Finally, monitor selection decision making and challenge those decision makers who reject candidates who would enhance diversity to demonstrate that the reasons for rejection are job related.

When the organization is under an AAP, either voluntary or court imposed, the above recommendations are still appropriate. Attempts to go even further and provide a specific "plus" to protected characteristics should not be undertaken without a careful examination and opinion of whether this would be legally permissible.

## SUMMARY

The selection component of a staffing system requires that decisions be made in several areas. The critical concerns are deciding which predictors (assessment methods) to use, determining assessment scores and setting cut scores, making final decisions about applicants, considering who within the organization should help make selection decisions, and complying with legal guidance.

In deciding which assessment methods to use, consideration should be given to the validity coefficient, face validity correlation with other predictors, adverse impact, utility, and applicant reactions. Ideally, a predictor would have a validity coefficient with large magnitude and significance, high face validity, low correlations with other predictors, little adverse impact, and high utility. In practice, this ideal situation is hard to achieve, so decisions about trade-offs are necessary.

How assessment scores are determined depends on whether a single predictor or multiple predictors are used. In the case of a single predictor, assessment scores are simply the scores on the predictor. With multiple predictors, a compensatory, multiple hurdles, or combined model must be used. A compensatory model allows a person to compensate for a low score on one predictor with a high score on another predictor. A multiple hurdles model requires that a person achieve a passing score on each successive predictor. A combined model uses elements of both the compensatory and the multiple hurdles models.

In deciding who earns a passing score on a predictor or a combination of predictors, cut scores must be set. When doing so, the consequences of setting different levels of cut scores should be considered, especially those of assessing some applicants as false positives or false negatives. Approaches to determining cut scores include minimum competency, top-down, and banding methods. Professional guidelines were reviewed on how best to set cut scores.

Methods of final choice involve determining who will receive job offers from among those who have passed the initial hurdles. Several methods of making these decisions were reviewed, including random selection, ranking, and grouping. Each has advantages and disadvantages.

Multiple individuals may be involved in selection decision making. HR professionals play a role primarily in determining the selection process to be used and in making selection decisions based on initial assessment results. Managers play a role primarily in deciding whom to select during the final choice stage. Employees are becoming part of the decision-making process, especially in team assessment approaches.

A basic legal issue is conformance with the UGESP, which provide guidance on how to set cut scores in ways that help minimize adverse impact and allow the organization to fulfill its EEO/AA obligations. In the absence of an AAP, protected class characteristics must not enter into selection decision making. That prohibition notwithstanding, organizations can take numerous steps to increase workforce diversity.

## DISCUSSION QUESTIONS

1. Your boss is considering using a new predictor. The base rate is high, the selection ratio is low, and the validity coefficient is high for the current predictor. What would you advise your boss and why?

2. What are the positive consequences associated with a high predictor cut score? What are the negative consequences?

3. Under what circumstances should a compensatory model be used? When should a multiple hurdles model be used?

4. What are the advantages of ranking as a method of final choice over random selection?

5. What roles should HR professionals play in staffing decisions? Why?

6. What guidelines do the UGESP offer to organizations when it comes to setting cut scores?

## ETHICAL ISSUES

1. Do you think companies should use banding in selection decisions? Defend your position.
2. Is clinical prediction the fairest way to combine assessment information about job applicants, or are the other methods (unit weighting, rational weighting, and multiple regression) fairer? Why?

## APPLICATIONS

### Utility Concerns in Choosing an Assessment Method

Randy May is a 32-year-old airplane mechanic for a small airline based on Nantucket Island, Massachusetts. Recently, Randy won $2 million in the New England lottery. Because Randy is relatively young, he decided to invest his winnings in a business to create a future stream of earnings. After weighing many investment options, Randy chose to open up a chain of ice cream shops in the Cape Cod area. (As it turns out, Cape Cod and the nearby islands are short of ice cream shops.) Randy reviewed his budget and figured he had enough cash to open shops on each of the two islands (Nantucket and Martha's Vineyard) and two shops in small towns on the Cape (Falmouth and Buzzards Bay). Randy contracted with a local builder and the construction/renovation of the four shops is well under way.

The task that is occupying Randy's attention now is how to staff the shops. Two weeks ago, he placed advertisements in three area newspapers. So far, he has received 100 applications. Randy has done some informal HR planning and figures he needs to hire 50 employees to staff the four shops. Being a novice at this, Randy is unsure how to select the 50 people he needs to hire. Randy consulted his friend Mary, who owns the lunch counter at the airport. Mary told Randy that she used interviews to get "the most knowledgeable people possible" and recommended it to Randy because her people had "generally worked out well." While Randy greatly respected Mary's advice, on reflection several questions came to mind. Does Mary's use of the interview mean that it meets Randy's requirements? How can Randy determine whether his chosen method of selecting employees is effective or ineffective?

Confused, Randy also sought the advice of Professor Ray Higgins, from whom Randy took an HR management course while getting his business degree. After learning of the situation and offering his consulting services, Professor Higgins suggested that Randy choose one of two selection methods (after paying Professor Higgins's consulting fees, he cannot afford to use both methods). The two methods Professor Higgins recommended are the interview (as Mary recommended) and a work sample test that entails scooping ice cream and serving it to a customer. Randy estimates that it would cost $100 to interview an applicant and $150 per applicant to administer the work sample. Professor Higgins told Randy that the validity of the interview is $r = .30$ while the validity of the work sample is $r = .50$. Professor Higgins also informed Randy that if the selection ratio is .50, the average score on the selection measure of those applicants selected is $z = .80$ (.80 standard deviations above the mean). Randy plans to offer employees a wage of $8 per hour. (Over the course of a year, this would amount to $16,000 in income.)

Randy would really appreciate it if you could help him answer the following questions:

1. How much money would Randy make using each selection method?
2. If Randy can use only one method, which should he use?
3. If the number of applicants increases to 200 (more applications are coming in every day), how will your answers to questions 1 and 2 change?
4. What limitations are inherent in the estimates you have made?

## Choosing Entrants Into a Management Training Program

Come As You Are, a convenience store chain headquartered in Fayetteville, Arkansas, has developed an assessment program to promote nonexempt employees into its management training program. The minimum entrance requirements for the program are five years of company experience, a college degree from an accredited university, and a minimum acceptable job performance rating (3 or higher on a 1–5 scale). Anyone interested in applying for the management program can enroll in the half-day assessment program, where the following assessments are made:

1. Cognitive ability test
2. Integrity test
3. Signed permission for background test
4. Brief (30-minute) interview by various members of the management team
5. Drug test

At the Hot Springs store, 11 employees have applied for openings in the management training program. The selection information on the candidates is provided in the following exhibit. (The scoring key is provided at the bottom of the exhibit.) It is estimated that three slots in the program are available for qualified candidates from the Hot Springs location. Given this information and what you know about external and internal selection, as well as staffing decision making, answer the following questions:

1. How would you go about deciding whom to select for the openings? In other words, without providing your decisions for the individual candidates, describe how you would weigh the various selection information to reach a decision.
2. Using the decision-making process from the previous question, which three applicants would you select for the training program? Explain your decision.

**EXHIBIT**

Predictor Scores for 11 Applicants to Management Training Program

| Name | Company Experience | College Degree | Performance Rating | Cognitive Ability Test | Integrity Test | Background Test | Interview Rating | Drug Test |
|---|---|---|---|---|---|---|---|---|
| Radhu | 4 | Yes | 4 | 9 | 6 | OK | 6 | P |
| Merv | 12 | Yes | 3 | 3 | 6 | OK | 8 | P |
| Marianne | 9 | Yes | 4 | 8 | 5 | Arrest '95 | 4 | P |
| Helmut | 5 | Yes | 4 | 5 | 5 | OK | 4 | P |
| Siobhan | 14 | Yes | 5 | 7 | 8 | OK | 8 | P |
| Galina | 7 | No | 3 | 3 | 4 | OK | 6 | P |
| Raul | 6 | Yes | 4 | 7 | 8 | OK | 2 | P |
| Frank | 9 | Yes | 5 | 2 | 5 | OK | 7 | P |
| Osvaldo | 10 | Yes | 4 | 10 | 9 | OK | 3 | P |
| Byron | 18 | Yes | 3 | 3 | 7 | OK | 6 | P |
| Aletha | 11 | Yes | 4 | 7 | 6 | OK | 5 | P |
| Scale | Years | Yes–No | 1–5 | 1–10 | 1–10 | OK–Other | 1–10 | P–F |

3. Although the data provided in the exhibit reveal that all selection measures were given to all 11 candidates, would you advise Come As You Are to continue to administer all the predictors at one time during the half-day assessment program? Alternatively, should the predictors be given in a sequence so that a multiple hurdles or combined approach could be used? Explain your recommendation.

## ENDNOTES

1. R. Hastie and R. M. Dawes, *Rational Choice in an Uncertain World*, 2nd ed. (Thousand Oaks, CA: Sage, 2010); D. Kahneman, *Thinking, Fast and Slow* (New York: Farrar, Straus, and Giroux, 2011); P. Bolander and J. Sandberg, "How Employee Selection Decisions Are Made in Practice," *Organization Studies*, 2013, 34, pp. 285–311.

2. R. B. Kline, *Beyond Significance Testing: Statistics Reform in the Behavioral Sciences,* 2nd ed. (Washington, DC: American Psychological Association, 2013).

3. J. P. Hausknecht, D. V. Day, and S. C. Thomas, "Applicant Reactions to Selection Procedures: An Updated Model and Meta-Analysis," *Personnel Psychology*, 2004, 57, pp. 639–683.

4. W. De Corte, P. R. Sackett, and F. Lievens, "Selecting Predictor Subsets: Considering Validity and Adverse Impact," *International Journal of Selection and Assessment,* 2010, 18, pp. 260–270; W. De Corte, F. Lievens, and P. R. Sackett, "Combining Predictors to Achieve Optimal Trade-Offs Between Selection Quality and Adverse Impact," *Journal of Applied Psychology*, 2007, 92, pp. 1380–1393.

5. C. Handler and S. Hunt, "Estimating the Financial Value of Staffing-Assessment Tools," *Workforce Management*, Mar. 2003 (*www.workforce.com*); J. Sullivan, "The True Value of Hiring and Retaining Top Performers," *Workforce Management*, Aug. 2002 (*www.workforce.com*)

6. J. W. Boudreau, "'Retooling' Evidence Based Staffing: Extending the Validation Paradigm Using Management Mental Models," in N. Schmitt (ed.), *The Oxford Handbook of Personnel Assessment and Selection* (New York: Oxford University Press, 2012), pp. 793–813.

7. J. Hersch, "Equal Employment Opportunity Law and Firm Profitability," *Journal of Human Resources*, 1991, 26, pp. 139–153.

8. G. V. Barrett, R. A. Alexander, and D. Doverspike, "The Implications for Personnel Selection of Apparent Declines in Predictive Validities Over Time: A Critique of Hulin, Henry, and Noon," *Personnel Psychology*, 1992, 45, pp. 601–617; C. L. Hulin, R. A. Henry, and S. L. Noon, "Adding a Dimension: Time as a Factor in Predictive Relationships," *Psychological Bulletin*, 1990, 107, pp. 328–340; C. T. Keil and J. M. Cortina, "Degradation of Validity Over Time: A Test and Extension of Ackerman's Model," *Psychological Bulletin*, 2001, 127, pp. 673–697.

9. J. W. Boudreau, M. C. Sturman, and T. A. Judge, "Utility Analysis: What Are the Black Boxes, and Do They Affect Decisions?" in N. Anderson and P. Herriot (eds.), *Assessment and Selection in Organizations* (Chichester, England: Wiley, 1994), pp. 77–96.

10. K. M. Murphy, "When Your Top Choice Turns You Down," *Psychological Bulletin*, 1986, 99, pp. 133–138; F. L. Schmidt, M. J. Mack, and J. E. Hunter, "Selection Utility in the Occupation of US Park Ranger for Three Modes of Test Use," *Journal of Applied Psychology*, 1984, 69, pp. 490–497.

11. T. H. Macan and S. Highhouse, "Communicating the Utility of Human Resource Activities: A Survey of I/O and HR Professionals," *Journal of Business and Psychology*, 1994, 8, pp. 425–436.

12. K. C. Carson, J. S. Becker, and J. A. Henderson, "Is Utility Really Futile? A Failure to Replicate and an Extension," *Journal of Applied Psychology*, 1998, 83, pp. 84–96; J. T. Hazer and S. Highhouse, "Factors Influencing Managers' Reactions to Utility Analysis: Effects of SDy Method, Information Frame, and Focal Intervention," *Journal of Applied Psychology*, 1997, 82, pp. 104–112; G. P. Latham and G. Whyte, "The Futility of Utility Analysis," *Personnel Psychology*, 1994, 47, pp. 31–46; G. Whyte and G. Latham, "The Futility of Utility Analysis Revisited: When Even an Expert Fails," *Personnel Psychology*, 1997, 50, pp. 601–610.

13. C. J. Russell, A. Colella, and P. Bobko, "Expanding the Context of Utility: The Strategic Impact of Personnel Selection," *Personnel Psychology*, 1993, 46, pp. 781–801.

14. S. Highhouse, "Stubborn Reliance on Intuition and Subjectivity in Employee Selection," *Industrial and Organizational Psychology*, 2008, 1, pp. 333–342; D. L. Diab, S-Y Pui, M. Yankelevich, and S. Highhouse, "Lay Perceptions of Selection Decision Aids in US and Non-US Samples," *International Journal of Selection and Assessment*, 19, 2011, pp. 209–216.

15. Hastie and Dawes, *Rational Choice in an Uncertain World*; Kahneman, *Thinking, Fast and Slow*.

16. "ChoiceAnalyst Software Makes Hiring Decisions Easier on the Brain," *Recruiter*, Mar. 3, 2010, p. 12.

17. R. E. McGrath, "Predictor Combination in Binary Decision-Making Scenarios," *Psychological Assessment*, 2008, 20, pp. 195–205.

18. J. M. LeBreton, M. B. Hargis, B. Griepentrog, F. L. Oswald, and R. E. Ployhart, "A Multidimensional Approach for Evaluating Variables in Organizational Research and Practice," *Personnel Psychology*, 2007, 60, pp. 475–498.

19. D. S. Ones, F. L. Schmidt, and K. Yoon, "Validity of an Equally-Weighted Composite of General Mental Ability and a Second Predictor," and "Predictive Validity of General Mental Ability Combined With a Second Predictor Based on Standardized Multiple Regression," Working papers, University of Iowa, Iowa City, 1996.

20. Y. Ganzach, A. N. Kluger, and N. Klayman, "Making Decisions From an Interview: Expert Measurement and Mechanical Combination," *Personnel Psychology*, 2000, 53, pp. 1–20.

21. W. F. Cascio, R. A. Alexander, and G. V. Barrett, "Setting Cutoff Scores: Legal, Psychometric, and Professional Issues and Guidelines," *Personnel Psychology*, 1988, 41, pp. 1–24.

22. W. H. Angoff, "Scales, Norms, and Equivalent Scores," in R. L. Thorndike (ed.), *Educational Measurement* (Washington, DC: American Council on Education, 1971), pp. 508–600; R. E. Biddle, "How to Set Cutoff Scores for Knowledge Tests Used in Promotion, Training, Certification, and Licensing," *Public Personnel Management*, 1993, 22, pp. 63–79.

23. J. P. Hudson, Jr., and J. E. Campion, "Hindsight Bias in an Application of the Angoff Method for Setting Cutoff Scores," *Journal of Applied Psychology*, 1994, 79, pp. 860–865; G. M. Hurtz and M. A. Auerbach, "A Meta-Analysis of the Effects of Modifications to the Angoff Method on Cutoff and Judgment Consensus," *Educational and Psychological Measurement*, 2003, 63, pp. 584–601.

24. J. Bennett, "Scientific Hiring Strategies Are Raising Productivity While Reducing Turnover," *Wall Street Journal*, Feb. 10, 2004, p. B7.

25. W. R. Johnson, P. C. Morrow, and G. J. Johnson, "An Evaluation of Perceived Overqualification Scales Across Work Settings," *Journal of Psychology*, 2002, 136, pp. 425–441; D. C. Maynard, T. A. Joseph, and A. M. Maynard, "Underemployment, Job Attitudes, and Turnover Intentions," *Journal of Organizational Behavior*, 2006, 27, pp. 509–536.

26. B. Erdogan and T. N. Bauer, "Perceived Overqualification and Its Outcomes: The Moderating Role of Empowerment," *Journal of Applied Psychology*, 2009, 94, pp. 557–565.

27. S. J. Wells, "Too Good to Hire?" *HR Magazine*, Oct. 2004, pp. 48–54.

28. P. R. Sackett and S. L. Wilk, "Within-Group Norming and Other Forms of Score Adjustment in Preemployment Testing," *American Psychologist*, 1994, 49, pp. 929–954.

29. K. R. Murphy, K. Osten, and B. Myors, "Modeling the Effects of Banding in Personnel Selection," *Personnel Psychology*, 1995, 48, pp. 61–84.

30. K. R. Murphy, "Potential Effects of Banding as a Function of Test Reliability," *Personnel Psychology*, 1994, 47, pp. 477–495.

31. P. Bobko, P. L. Roth, and A. Nicewander, "Banding Selection Scores in Human Resource Management Decisions: Current Inaccuracies and the Effect of Conditional Standard Errors," *Organizational Research Methods*, 2005, 8, pp. 259–273.

32. W. F. Cascio, I. L. Goldstein, and J. Outtz, "Social and Technical Issues in Staffing Decisions," in H. Aguinis (ed.), *Test-Score Banding in Human Resource Selection: Technical, Legal, and Societal Issues* (Westport, CT: Praeger, 2004), pp. 7–28; K. R. Murphy, "Conflicting Values and Interests in Banding Research and Practice," in Aguinis (ed.), *Test-Score Banding in Human Resource Selection: Technical, Legal, and Societal Issues*, pp. 175–192; F. Schmidt and J. E. Hunter, "SED Banding as a Test of Scientific Values in I/O Psychology," in Aguinis (ed.), *Test-Score Banding in Human Resource Selection: Technical, Legal, and Societal Issues*, pp. 151–173.

33. C. A. Henle, "Case Review of the Legal Status of Banding," *Human Performance*, 2004, 17, pp. 415–432.

34. P. R. Sackett, N. Schmitt, J. E. Ellingson, and M. B. Kabin, "High-Stakes Testing in Employment, Credentialing, and Higher Education," *American Psychologist*, 2001, 56, pp. 302–318.

35. De Corte, Lievens, and Sackett, "Combining Predictors to Achieve Optimal Trade-Offs Between Selection Quality and Adverse Impact"; H. Aguinis and M. A. Smith, "Understanding the Impact of Test Validity and Bias on Selection Errors and Adverse Impact in Human Resource Selection," *Personnel Psychology*, 2007, 60, pp. 165–190.

36. M. D. Nowicki and J. G. Rosse, "Managers' Views of How to Hire: Building Bridges Between Science and Practice," *Journal of Business and Psychology*, 2002, 17, pp. 157–170.

37. "Google Goes for Consensus in Hiring," *Recruiter*, Apr. 28, 2010, p. 5.

38. D. D. Bennett-Alexander and L. P. Hartman, *Employment Law for Business*, 6th ed. (New York: McGraw-Hill-Irwin, 2009), pp. 207–243; R. K. Robinson, G. M. Franklin, and R. E. Wayland, *Employment Regulation in the Workplace* (Armonk, NY: M. E. Sharpe, 2010), pp. 182–212; US Equal Employment Opportunity Commission, "EEOC Compliance Manual," 2006 (*www.eeoc.gov/policy/docs/race-color.html*), accessed 7/27/10.

# CHAPTER TWELVE

## Final Match

**Learning Objectives and Introduction**
Learning Objectives
Introduction

**Employment Contracts**
Requirements for an Enforceable Contract
Parties to the Contract
Form of the Contract
Disclaimers
Contingencies
Other Employment Contract Sources
Unfulfilled Promises

**Job Offers**
Strategic Approach to Job Offers
Job Offer Content

**Job Offer Process**
Formulation of the Job Offer
Presentation of the Job Offer
Timing of the Offer
Job Offer Acceptance and Rejection
Reneging

**New Employee Orientation and Socialization**
Orientation
Socialization
Examples of Programs

**Legal Issues**
Employment Eligibility Verification
Negligent Hiring
Employment-at-Will

# LEARNING OBJECTIVES AND INTRODUCTION

## Learning Objectives

- Learn about the requirements for an enforceable contract
- Recognize issues that might arise in the employment contract process
- Understand how to make strategic job offers
- Plan for the steps of formulating and presenting a job offer
- Know how to establish a formal employment relationship
- Develop effective plans for new employee orientation and socialization
- Recognize potential legal issues involving final matches

## Introduction

In the previous chapter, we described how to reduce the initial applicant pool to a smaller set of candidates and identify one or more job finalists. In this chapter we move to the next stage—the process of actually hiring the individuals who have been selected. A final match occurs when the offer receiver and the organization have determined that there is sufficient overlap between the person's knowledge, skill, ability, and other characteristics (KSAOs) and the job's requirements and rewards. Once the decision to enter the employment relationship has been made, the organization and the candidate become bound through mutual agreement on the terms and conditions of employment.

The initial theme of this chapter is setting the stage for a legally sound employment relationship. Organizations often get into legal trouble when they fail to understand the contractual nature of many employment relationships. As we show, careless promises or guarantees made during the job offer can come back to haunt an organization when it needs to alter the employment relationship later. This chapter also discusses the process of convincing promising job finalists to take the job offer, and developing the grounds of the relationship that will persist throughout this individual's employment through "onboarding" or socialization activities.

This chapter begins with an overview of employment contract concepts and principles, emphasizing the essential requirements for establishing a legally binding employment contract. A strategic approach to job offers is then presented, followed by a discussion of the major components of a job offer and points to address in it. Through the job offer process, these terms and conditions are proposed, discussed, negotiated, modified, and, ultimately, agreed on. Once agreement on the terms and conditions of employment has been reached, the final match process is completed, and the formal employment relationship is established. To phase the new hire into his or her job, it is vital to develop appropriate techniques for orienting and socializing the newcomer. The chapter concludes with a discussion of specific legal issues that pertain not only to the establishment of the employment contract but also to potential long-term consequences of the contract that must be considered at the time it is established.

## EMPLOYMENT CONTRACTS

The establishment and enforcement of employment contracts is a very complex and constantly changing undertaking. Covered next are some very basic, yet subtle, issues associated with this undertaking. It is crucial to understand the elements that compose a legally enforceable contract and be able to identify the parties to the contract (employees or independent contractors, third-party representatives), the form of the contract (written, oral), disclaimers, fulfillment of other conditions, reneging on an offer or acceptance, and other sources (e.g., employee handbooks) that may also constitute a portion of the total employment contract.

### Requirements for an Enforceable Contract

Three basic elements are required for a contract to be legally binding and enforceable: offer, acceptance, and consideration.[1] If any one of these is missing, there is no binding contract.

#### Offer

The offer is usually made by the employer and is composed of the terms and conditions of employment desired and proposed by the employer. The terms must be clear and specific enough to be acted on by the offer receiver. Vague statements and offers are unacceptable (e.g., "Come to work for me right now; we'll work out the details later"). The content of advertisements for the job and general written employer material, such as a website describing the organization, are probably too vague to be considered offers. Both the employer and the offer receiver should have a definite understanding of the specific terms proposed.

#### Acceptance

To constitute a contract, the offer must be accepted on the terms as offered. Thus, if the employer offers a salary of $70,000 per year, the offer receiver must either accept or reject that term. Acceptance of an offer on a contingency basis does not constitute an acceptance. If the offer receiver responds to the salary offer of $70,000 by saying, "Pay me $75,000, and I'll come to work for you," this is not an acceptance. Rather, it is a counteroffer, and the employer must now either formally accept or reject it.

The offer receiver must also accept the offer in the manner specified in the offer. If the offer requires acceptance in writing, for example, the offer receiver must accept it in writing. Similarly, if the offer requires acceptance by a certain date, it must be accepted by that date.

### Consideration

Consideration entails the exchange of something of value between the parties to the contract. Usually, it involves an exchange of promises. The employer offers or promises to provide compensation to the offer receiver in exchange for labor, and the offer receiver promises to provide labor to the employer in exchange for compensation. The exchange of promises must be firm and of value, which is usually quite straightforward. Occasionally, consideration can become an issue. For example, if the employer makes an offer to a person that requires a response by a certain date, and then does not hear from the person, there is no contract, even though the employer thought that they "had a deal."

## Parties to the Contract

Two issues arise regarding the parties to the contract: whether the employer is entering into a contract with an employee or with an independent contractor, and whether an outsider or third party can execute or otherwise play a role in the employment contract.[2]

### Employee or Independent Contractor

Individuals are hired by the organization as either employees or independent contractors. Both of these terms have definite legal meanings that should be reviewed (see Chapter 2) before entering into a contractual relationship. The organization should be clear in its offer whether the relationship being sought is that of employer–employee or employer–independent contractor. Care should be taken to avoid misclassifying the offer receiver as an independent contractor when in fact the receiver will be treated practically as an employee (e.g., subject to specific direction and control by the employer). Such a misclassification can result in substantial tax and other legal liability problems for the organization. Experts report that companies have been increasingly claiming that individuals who should be classified as employees are being reported as independent contractors. As a result, the Department of Labor has been working to identify organizations that are misclassifying employees. This push has resulted in the collection of millions of dollars in unpaid taxes, as well as payouts of millions of additional dollars due to underpayments and insufficient benefits provision.[3] Therefore, understanding how to maintain the distinction between an employee and an independent contractor will be of great importance.

### Third Parties

Often, someone other than the employer or the offer receiver speaks on their behalf in the establishment or modification of employment contracts. These people serve as agents for the employer and the offer receiver. For the employer, this may mean the use of outsiders such as employment agencies, executive recruiters, or search consultants; it also usually means the use of one or more employees, such as the human resource (HR) department representative, the hiring manager, higher-level managers, and other managers within the organization. For the offer receiver, it may mean the use of a special representative, such as a professional agent for an athlete or an executive. These possibilities raise three important questions for the employer.

First, who, if anyone, speaks for the offer receiver? This is usually determined by checking with the offer receiver as to whether any given person is indeed authorized to be a spokesperson, and what, if any, limits have been placed on that person regarding terms that may be discussed and agreed on with the employer.

Second, who is the spokesperson for the employer? In the case of its own employees, the employer must recognize that from a legal standpoint, any of them could be construed as speaking for the employer. Virtually anyone could thus suggest and agree to contract terms, knowingly or unknowingly. This means that the employer should formulate and enforce explicit policies as to who is authorized to speak on its behalf.

Third, exactly what is that person authorized to say? Here, the legal concept of apparent authority is relevant. If the offer receiver believes that a person has the authority to speak for the employer, and there is nothing to indicate otherwise, that person has the apparent authority to speak for the employer. In turn, the employer may be bound by what that person says and agrees to, even if the employer did not grant express authority to do so to this person. It is thus important for the organization to clarify to both the offer receiver and the designated spokespersons what the spokesperson is authorized to discuss and agree to without approval from other organizational members.

## Form of the Contract

Employment contracts may be written (whether documented through paper or electronic media), oral, or a combination of the two.[4] All may be legally binding and enforceable. Within this broad parameter, however, are numerous caveats and considerations.

### Written Contracts

As a general rule, the law favors written contracts over oral ones. This alone should lead an organization to use only written contracts whenever possible.

A written contract may take many forms, and all may be legally enforceable. Examples of a written document that may be construed as a contract include a letter of offer and acceptance (the usual example), a statement on a job application blank (such as an applicant voucher to the truthfulness of information provided), internal job posting notices, e-mail messages, and statements in employee hand-books or on websites. The more specific the information and statements in such documentation, the more likely they are to be considered employment contracts.

Unintended problems may arise with this documentation. They may be inter-preted as enforceable contracts even though that was not their intent (perhaps the intent was merely informational), or statements on a given term or condition of employment may contradict one another in various documentation.

An excellent illustration of these kinds of problems involves the issue of employment-at-will. Assume an employer wishes to be, as a matter of explicit pol-icy, a strict at-will employer. That desire may be unintentionally undercut by docu-mentation that implies something other than an employment-at-will relationship. For example, electronic correspondence with an applicant may talk of "continued employment after you complete your probationary period." This statement might be legally interpreted as creating something other than a strict at-will employment relationship. To muddy the waters further, employment policies may contain an explicit at-will statement, thus contradicting the policy implied in the correspon-dence with the applicant.

Care must thus be taken to ensure that all communication accurately conveys only the intended meanings regarding terms and conditions of employment. To this end, the following suggestions should be heeded:[5]

- Before putting anything in writing, ask, "Does the company mean to be held to this?"
- Choose words carefully; where appropriate, avoid using words that imply bind-ing commitment.
- Make sure all related documentation is internally consistent.
- Always have a second person, preferably a lawyer, review what another has written.
- Form the habit of looking at the entire hiring procedure and consider any writ-ings within that context.

### Oral Contracts

While oral contracts may be every bit as binding as written contracts, there are two notable exceptions that support placing greater importance on written contracts.

The first exception is the one-year rule, which comes about in what is known as the statute of frauds.[6] Under this rule, a contract that cannot be performed or fulfilled within a one-year interval is not enforceable unless it is in writing. Thus, oral agreements for any length greater than one year are not enforceable. Because of this rule, the organization should not make oral contracts that are intended to last more than one year.

The second exception involves the concept of parole evidence, which pertains to oral promises made about the employment relationship.[7] Legally, parole evidence (e.g., the offer receiver's claim that "I was promised that I wouldn't have to work on weekends") may not be used to enforce a contract if it is inconsistent with the terms of a written agreement. Thus, if the offer receiver's letter of appointment explicitly stated that weekend work was required, the oral promise of not having to work weekends would not be enforceable.

Note, however, in the absence of written statements to the contrary, oral statements may indeed be enforceable. In the preceding example, if the letter of appointment was silent on the issue of weekend work, the oral promise of no weekend work might well be enforceable.

More generally, oral statements are more likely to be enforceable as employment contract terms in the following situations:[8]

- When there is no written statement regarding the term (e.g., weekend work) in question
- When the term is quite certain ("You will not have to work on weekends," as opposed to, "Occasionally, we work weekends around here")
- When the person making the oral statement is in a position of authority to do so (e.g., the hiring manager as opposed to a coworker)
- The more formal the circumstances in which the statement was made (the manager's office as opposed to around the bar or dinner table as part of a recruiting trip)
- The more specific the promise ("You will work every other Saturday from 8:00 to 5:00," as opposed to, "You may have to work from 8:00 to the middle of the afternoon on the weekends, but we'll try to hold that to a minimum")

As this discussion makes clear, from a legal perspective, oral statements are a potential minefield in establishing employment contracts. They obviously cannot be avoided (the employer and the applicant have to speak to each other), and they may serve other legitimate and desired outcomes, such as providing realistic recruitment information to job applicants. Nonetheless, the organization should use oral statements with extreme caution and alert all members to its policies regarding their use. As further protection, the organization should include in its written offer that, by accepting the offer, the employee agrees the organization has made no other promises than those contained in the written offer.

## Disclaimers

A disclaimer is a statement (oral or written) that explicitly limits an employee right and reserves that right for the employer.[9] Disclaimers are often used in letters of appointment, job application blanks, and employee handbooks.

A common, and increasingly important, employee "right" that is being limited by a disclaimer is that of job security. Here, through its policy of employment-at-will, the employer explicitly makes no promise of any job security and reserves the right to terminate the employment relationship at its own will. The following is an example of such a disclaimer suggested by the Society for Human Resource Management:

> Your employment with [company name] is a voluntary one and is subject to termination by you or [company name] at will, with or without cause, and with or without notice, at any time. Nothing in these policies shall be interpreted to be in conflict with or to eliminate or modify in any way the employment-at-will status of [company name] employees. This policy of employment-at-will may not be modified by any officer or employee and shall not be modified in any publication or document. The only exception to this policy is a written employment agreement approved at the discretion of the President or the Board of Directors, whichever is applicable. These personnel policies are not intended to be a contract of employment or a legal document.[10]

An employment-at-will disclaimer should appear in the job offer letter. It should also appear on the application blank, along with two other disclaimers. First, there should be a statement of consent by the applicant for the organization to check provided references, along with a waiver of the right to make claims against them for anything they say. Second, there should be a so-called false statement warning, indicating that any false statement, misleading statement, or material omission may be grounds for dismissal.

Disclaimers are generally enforceable. They can thus serve as an important component of employment contracts. Their use should be guided by the following set of recommendations:[11]

1. They should be clearly stated and conspicuously placed in appropriate documents.
2. The employee should acknowledge receipt and review of the document and the disclaimer.
3. The disclaimer should state that it may be modified only in writing and by whom.
4. The terms and conditions of employment, including the disclaimer, as well as limits on their enforceability, should be reviewed with offer receivers and employees.

It would be wise to obtain legal counsel for drafting language for all disclaimers.

## Contingencies

The employer may wish to make a job offer that is contingent on certain other conditions being fulfilled by the offer receiver.[12] Examples of such contingencies include (1) passage of a particular test, such as a licensure exam (e.g., CPA or bar exam), (2) passage of a medical exam, including alcohol/drug/screening tests, (3) satisfactory background and reference checks, and (4) proof of employability under the Immigration Reform and Control Act (IRCA).

Though contingencies to a contract are generally enforceable, contingencies to an employment contract (especially those involving any of the preceding examples) are exceedingly complex and may be made only within defined limits. For this reason, contingencies should not be used in employment contracts without prior legal counsel.

## Other Employment Contract Sources

As alluded to previously, employment contract terms may be established through multiple sources, not just the letters of job offer and acceptance. Such establishment may be the result of both intentional and unintentional acts by the employer. Moreover, these terms may come about not only when the employment relationship is first established but also during the course of the employment relationship.[13]

The employer thus must constantly be alert to the fact that terms and conditions of employment may come into being and be modified through a variety of employment contract sources. Sources worth reiterating here are employee handbooks (and other written documents) and oral statements made by employer representatives. Job advertisements and job descriptions are generally not considered employment contracts.

In the case of employee handbooks, the employer must consider whether statements in them are legally enforceable or merely informational. While there is legal opinion on both sides of this question, handbooks are increasingly being considered as a legally enforceable part of the employment contract. To avoid this occurrence, the employer may wish to place an explicit disclaimer in the handbook that states the intent to provide only information to employees and that the employer will not be bound by any of the statements contained in the handbook.

In the case of oral statements, their danger and the need for caution in their use have already been addressed. Oral statements may present legal problems and challenges when made, not only at the time of the initial employment contract but also throughout the course of the employment relationship. Of particular concern here are oral promises made to employees regarding future events, such as job security ("Don't worry, you will always have a place with us") or job assignments ("After training, you will be assigned as the assistant manager at our new store"). With oral statements, there is thus a constant need to be careful regarding the messages being delivered to employees, as well as who delivers those messages.

## Unfulfilled Promises

Since the staffing process in general, and the job offer process in particular, involve making promises to offer receivers about terms and conditions of employment, it is important for the organization to (1) not make promises it is unwilling to keep, and (2) be sure that promises made are actually kept. Unfulfilled promises may spur the disappointed person to pursue a legal action against the organization. Three types of claims might be pursued.[14]

The first claim is that of breach of contract, and it may be pursued for both written and oral promises. The employee has to show that both parties intended to be legally bound by the promise and that it was specific enough to establish an actual oral agreement. The second claim is that of promissory estoppel. Here, even if there is no enforceable oral contract, employees may claim that they relied on promises made by the organization, to their subsequent detriment, since the actual or presumed job offer was withdrawn (such withdrawal is known as reneging). Examples of detrimental effects include resigning from one's current employer, passing up other job opportunities, relocating geographically, and incurring expenses associated with the job offer. When the offer receiver experiences such detrimental reliance, the person may sue the employer for compensatory damages; actual hiring of the person is rarely sought. The final claim is that of fraud, where the employee claims the organization made promises it had no intention of keeping. Employees may legally pursue fraud claims and seek both compensatory and punitive damages.

## JOB OFFERS

A job offer is an attempt by the organization to induce the offer receiver into the establishment of an employment relationship. Assuming that the offer is accepted and that consideration is met, the organization and the offer receiver will have established their relationship in the form of a legally binding employment contract. That contract is the culmination of the staffing process. The contract also signifies that the person/job match process has concluded and that the person/job match is now about to become a reality. That reality, in turn, becomes the start of, and foundation for, subsequent employee effectiveness on the various HR outcomes. For these reasons, the content and extension of the job offer become critical final parts of the overall staffing process.

This section discusses a strategic approach to job offers, along with the numerous factors that should be considered in the determination of the content of job offers. Then the actual content of job offers is discussed, along with some of the complexities associated with it.

### Strategic Approach to Job Offers

The organization has considerable discretion in the content of the offers that it puts together to present to finalists. Rather than hastily crafting job offers, often in the heat of the hiring moment and with a desire to fill the vacancy now, it is better to think a bit more strategically as to job offer content. Such an approach has a better possibility of serving the interests of both the organization and the finalists and not locking them into a contract that either will come to regret. Another benefit of the strategic approach is that it will help the organization decide whether all finalists will receive a standard offer or whether some finalists will receive enhanced offers, and the circumstances that will give rise to such offers.

Shown in Exhibit 12.1 is the strategic approach to job offers, or the employee value proposition (EVP). The EVP is the total package of extrinsic and intrinsic rewards that the offered job will provide to the finalist if the job offer is accepted. Technically, the job offer is not the same as the EVP, because it is difficult to write in the job offer letter the nature of the intrinsic rewards that will be provided, and because a job offer contains information in addition to job rewards (e.g., starting date, date the offer lapses, and disclaimers). Nonetheless, the major thrust and purpose of the job offer is to convey to the finalist the nature of the rewards "deal" being promised if the offer is accepted. First and foremost, the job offer must be a compelling one—an EVP the finalist will find enticing and difficult to turn down. The offer thus must present a package of rewards with the right combination of magnitude, mix, and distinctiveness to be compelling to the offer receiver.

Exhibit 12.1 indicates that labor market conditions, organization needs, applicant needs, and legal issues are forces to consider in the creation of job offers. As to labor markets, the simple availability of potential offer receivers needs to be considered, for there may be shortages that will require the organization to sweeten the deal if it is to fill vacancies. Coupled with that is consideration of the overall tightness or looseness of the labor market. Tight labor markets will serve to exacerbate limited supply availability, for applicants in the limited supply pool will likely have many job offer alternatives. On the other hand, with plentiful supply and a

**EXHIBIT 12.1   Strategic Approach to Job Offers**

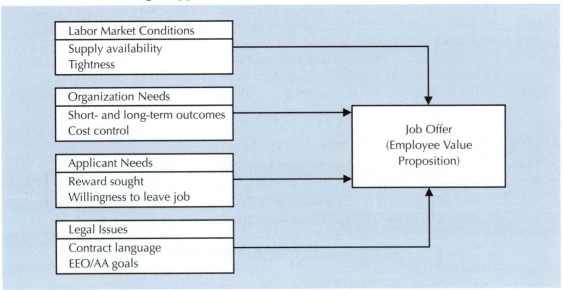

loose labor market, the organization will be in a position to provide standard offers, and ones that are lower in cost.

The organization has multiple needs it must seek to identify and fulfill in the formation of the employment relationship. Some of these are short-term outcomes—such as filling vacancies quickly or at any cost. To what extent does the organization want to respond to such pressures? The answer will clearly shape the content of job offers. Long-term outcomes such as the likely performance level of the new employee, the extent to which the employee fits in with the organization and work unit, the promotion success of the employee, and employee job satisfaction and retention all need to be considered. To what extent does the organization wish to craft job offers that are likely to enhance these longer-term outcomes? Finally, cost control must come into play. All job offers, if accepted, will cost the organization, so how much is it willing to spend? Moreover, is the organization willing to spend more for finalists that it thinks will more likely deliver the short-term and/or long-term outcomes it seeks?

In terms of applicant needs, the organization must seek to identify the rewards likely sought by applicants. Here, it is useful to consider the full range of rewards possible and to gather information about reward preferences of applicants. Strategically, it will be helpful to identify some rewards with a distinctiveness that may be particularly alluring. For example, Red Frog Events emphasizes factors that set it apart from alternative employers. The extrinsic features of the EVP include not just competitive pay and benefits but also unlimited vacation days and a four-week, all-expenses-paid sabbatical for travel after five years of service. Unique intrinsic features of the EVP include a casual environment, energized and motivated teams, and one-on-one job coaching. Having a compelling EVP is especially important for firms like Red Frog that are rapidly expanding and need a flow of qualified new employees.[15] The EVP should also be tailored to the types of employees being sought. One study of over 1,000 individuals in the United States demonstrated some of the different types of preferences employees have.[16] About 33% of respondents were identified as stabilizers and preferred team-based rewards, communication, and work-value balance. Another 26% of respondents were pioneers who were more intrinsically motivated and most valued work that allowed them to learn and contribute. Drivers, who made up 24% of respondents, valued achievement and success and so preferred work with a clear track to promotions. Finally, 17% of respondents were most interested in social work environments in which they could make a positive impact on others. Organizations should consider what types of employees they are recruiting for each job and make sure their EVP fits for these individuals.

Coupled with the assessment of applicant needs should be an assessment of the finalists' willingness to leave their current jobs. If the finalist is relatively willing, or even eager to leave, the job offer may not need to be very compelling in magnitude, mix, or distinctiveness. On the other hand, if the finalist is satisfied with the current job and current geographic location, the need to craft a compelling offer rises dramatically. Essentially, such offers must provide an EVP that stirs in the finalist a dissatisfaction with the current job and boosts the willingness to change locations, both by pointing out positive features of the new location and by minimizing the costs of making the move.

## Job Offer Content

The organization has considerable latitude in the terms and conditions of employment that it may offer to people. That latitude, of course, should be exercised within the organization's particular applicant attraction strategy.

With some degree of latitude in terms and conditions offered for almost any job, it is apparent that job offers should be carefully constructed. There are definite rewards that can, and for the most part should, be addressed in any job offer. Moreover, the precise terms or content of the offer to any given finalist requires careful forethought. What follows is a discussion of the types of rewards to address, as well as some of their subtleties and complexities.

### Starting Date

Normally, the organization controls when the employment relationship begins. To do so, it must provide a definite starting date in its offer. If it does not, acceptance and consideration of the offer occur at the time the new hire actually begins work. Oftentimes, the starting date is one that allows the offer receiver at least two weeks to provide notification of resignation to a current employer.

### Duration of Contract

Employment contracts may be of a fixed term (i.e., have a definite ending date) or an indeterminate term (i.e., have no definite ending date). The decision about duration is intimately related to the employment-at-will issue.

A fixed-term contract provides certainty to both the new hire and the organization regarding the length of the employment relationship. Both parties decide to and must abide by an agreed-on term of employment. The organization can then (according to common law) terminate the contract prior to its expiration date for "just cause" only. Determination and demonstration of just cause can be a complicated legal problem for the organization.

Most organizations are unwilling to provide such employment guarantees. They much prefer an employment-at-will relationship, in which either party may terminate the employment relationship at any time without having to demonstrate just cause.[17] Should the organization decide to have indeterminate-term employment contracts, it should carefully state in its written offer that the duration is indeterminate and that it may be terminated by either party at any time, for any reason. Because of the overriding importance of this issue, all wording should be approved at the highest organizational level.

Although employers can request that employees give advance notice (e.g., two weeks' notice) before quitting, employment-at-will generally does not allow employers to compel employees to give advance notice. Some employers specify in their policies that employees who do not give notice will be ineligible for rehire or will be denied accumulated vacation time, but some state laws prohibit these actions.[18]

## Compensation

Although recent research suggests that organizational characteristics and perceived working conditions are the strongest predictors of applicant attraction in the final stages of the job choice process, compensation remains a powerful predictor of employee interest at the point of a job offer.[19] Compensation is a multifaceted set of rewards that may be presented to the offer receiver in many forms. Sometimes it consists of a standard pay rate and benefits package, which must be simply accepted or rejected. Other times the offer may be more tailor-made, often negotiated in advance.

Job seekers carry with them a set of pay preferences and expectations that shape how they respond to the compensation components of the job offer. A survey of around 600 employees conducted in 2012 across diverse industries and jobs found that employees thought being paid competitively while the local market was the most important feature of a pay plan, while opportunities for variable pay (e.g., bonuses or commissions) and stock options ranked substantially lower.[20] The same survey also found that health care and paid time off were the most important benefits, while family-friendly benefits were the least important. So contrary to some speculation in the popular press, most employees are still seeking a strong conventional compensation package as their highest priority. The compensation portion of the job offer should thus be carefully thought out and planned in advance. This pertains to starting pay, variable pay, and benefits.

***Starting Pay: Flat Rate.***   In flat-rate job offers, all persons are offered an identical rate of pay, and variance from this is not permitted. Starting pay is thus offered on a "take it or leave it" basis.

Use of flat rates is appropriate in many circumstances, such as the following examples:

- Jobs for which there is a plentiful supply of job applicants
- Where applicants are of quite similar KSAO quality
- Where there is a desire to avoid creating potential inequities in starting pay among new employees

Note that under some circumstances, use of flat rates may be mandatory. Examples here include pay rates under many collective bargaining agreements and for many jobs covered by civil service laws and regulations.

*Starting Pay: Differential Rates.*   Organizations often opt out of flat rates, despite their simplicity, and choose differential starting pay rates. In general, this occurs under three sets of circumstances.

First, there are situations where the organization thinks there are clear qualitative (KSAO) differences among finalists. Some finalists are thus felt to be worth more than others, and starting pay differentials are used in recognizing this. A good example here involves new college graduates. Research clearly shows that highly educated individuals get higher compensation. After taking parents' level of income and education into account, college graduates earn 66% more than high school graduates and those holding masters' degrees earn 106% more than high school graduates.[21] It's also clear that workers with different fields of study have significant differences in income. Science and technology majors make more than humanities majors, and the returns on a science or technology degree are even greater for individuals with higher levels of cognitive ability.[22] Finally, some market conditions lead employers to devote more money to hiring "stars." As an example, software companies that develop products for fast-moving and evolving markets tend to pay especially high premiums to experienced and highly skilled workers.[23]

The second situation occurs when the organization is concerned about attraction outcomes, almost regardless of applicant KSAO differences. Here, the organization is under intense pressure to acquire new employees and fill vacancies promptly. To accomplish these outcomes, flexibility in starting pay rate offers is used to respond to finalists' demands, to sweeten offers, and to otherwise impress applicants with an entrepreneurial spirit of wheeling and dealing. Hence, the organization actively seeks to strike a bargain with the offer receiver, and differential starting pay rates are a natural part of the attraction package.

The third situation involves geographic pay differentials. For organizations with multiple facilities in different geographic areas, the starting pay rate for any particular job may need to vary because of average pay differentials across geographic areas. For example, for the job of HR manager, which had an average national rate of $99,270 in 2013, pay varied from $65,500 in Mississippi to $118,300 in Delaware.[24] Clearly, starting pay must take into account geographic pay variation.

Use of differential starting pay rates requires attention to several potential problems.[25] One problem is that offer receivers, though similarly qualified, may have different pay "mix" preferences. Some offer receivers may place higher (or lower) value on salary than on stock options or benefits, leading them to demand higher (or lower) salaries. The organization must decide how much it is willing to provide offer receivers salary trade-offs for other forms of compensation. A second problem, often heightened by the first one, is that issues of fairness and internal equity among employees may arise when there is too much discretion in the range of starting salaries. Naturally, similarly qualified employees receiving wide differences in starting pay is a guaranteed recipe for perceived pay inequities, and paying new hires starting salaries that exceed those of current "leapfrogged" employees also fuels the perceived inequity flames. Research shows that women are less likely than men to negotiate for higher wages at the time of hire, leading to lower starting wages. If these behaviors shape early compensation rates, the average starting pay for women will be lower than that for men, and "catch up" for women may be difficult since raises are usually a percentage of one's salary. These represent potential salary discrimination issues confronting the organization.

For such reasons, whenever differential rates of starting pay are used, the organization must carefully consider what is permissible and within bounds. At times, the organization may choose to provide minimal guidance to managers making the offers. Often, however, there is a need for some constraints on managers. These constraints may specify when differential starting pay offers may be made and where within a pay range starting pay rates must fall. Exhibit 12.2 contains examples of such starting pay policies.

***Variable Pay: Short Term.*** Short-term variable pay may be available on jobs, and if so, the organization should address this in the job offer.

Prior to the job offer, the organization should determine whether there should be variable pay. This is not a major issue that transcends staffing per se, but it does have important implications for the likely effectiveness of staffing activities.

Consider an organization with sales jobs, a classic example of a situation in which incentive or commission pay systems might be used. The mere presence/absence of such a pay plan will likely affect the motivation/job rewards part of the

**EXHIBIT 12.2**  **Example of Starting Pay Policies**

**The Wright Company**

The following policies regarding starting pay must be adhered to:

1. No person is to be offered a salary that is below the minimum, or above the midpoint, of the salary range for the job.
2. Generally, persons with reasonable qualifications should be offered a salary within the first quartile (bottom 25%) of the salary range for the job.
3. Salary offers above the first quartile, but not exceeding the midpoint, may be made for exceptionally well-qualified persons, or when market conditions dictate.
4. Salary offers should be fair in relation to other offers made and to the salaries paid to current employees.
5. Salary offers below the first quartile may be made without approval; offers at or above the first quartile must be approved in advance by the manager of compensation.
6. Counteroffers may not be accepted without approval of the manager of compensation.

matching process. Different "breeds of cats" may be attracted to jobs providing incentive plans as opposed to those that do not.

More generally, research shows that the use of short-term incentive pay is quite common, with almost 90% of private sector, 76% of partnerships, and 44% of public sector organizations offering incentive pay plans of various sorts. Of these organizations, 95% provide cash payments via individual incentive pay and bonuses, based on financial, customer service, production, goal attainment, efficiency, and cost reduction measures. Two of the major reasons these organizations provide for such short-term incentive offerings are to compete for qualified employees and to retain employees.[26] Use of short-term incentives is continually increasing, with one study finding that over half of surveyed companies provide hiring bonuses.[27]

If there are to be short-term variable pay plans, the organization should communicate this in the offer letter. Beyond that, the organization should carefully consider how much detail about such plans, including payout formulas and amounts, to include in the job offer. The more specific the information, the less flexibility the organization will have in the operation or modification of the plan.

**Variable Pay: Long Term.** Long-term variable pay plans provide employees ownership opportunity and the opportunity to increase their income as the value of the organization increases. Applicable only in the private sector, stock options—either an incentive stock option or a nonqualified stock option—are the most commonly used long-term variable pay plan.[28] A stock option is a right to purchase a share of stock for a predetermined price at a later date; there is both a time span during which the right may be exercised (e.g., 10 years) and a waiting period before the employee is eligible (vested) to make purchases (e.g., 1 year).

Though stock options provide potential incentive value to offer receivers, some may prefer cash in the form of base pay or short-term variable pay incentives. In addition, stock options only have actual value to the recipient if the value of the stock appreciates beyond the purchase price and if the employee remains eligible to participate in the plan—such as through remaining with the organization for a specified time period. Research suggests that stock options tend to impact employee performance only *after* the options have been exercised.[29] In other words, stock options are motivational only for workers who have already been paid. This undermines the whole premise of giving stock options, which are supposed to motivate workers to perform better in order to increase stock prices so they can exercise their options in the future. It also suggests that only companies that are doing well enough to have options that are worth more than the predetermined price will receive any motivational benefits. In sum, all of this evidence suggests that most employees put stock options fairly low on their list of priorities when evaluating jobs, and options are not likely to increase motivation or retention.[30]

Perhaps because managers have also noticed that stock options do not achieve their stated goals, their use has been waning. Taking the place of stock options are numerous other long-term variable pay plans—performance options, stock appreciation rights, stock grants, restricted stock, delayed issuance awards, employee stock ownership, and employee stock purchase. Each of these types of plans has both strong and weak points, and careful analysis of the objectives sought (e.g., employee retention) should occur prior to its use and presentation to job offer receivers.[31] As with short-term variable pay plans, the job offer letter should mention the right or requirement to participate in these plans, but not go into too much detail about them.

**Benefits.**   A job is usually accompanied by a fixed benefits package that is offered to all offer receivers. Examples include health insurance and retirement and work/life plans. When a fixed or standard benefits package is offered, the offer letter should not spell out all of the specific benefit provisions. Rather, it should state that the employee would be eligible to participate in the benefit plans maintained by the organization, as provided in written descriptions of these plans. In this way, the job offer letter does not inadvertently make statements or promises that contradict or go beyond the organization's actual benefits plan.

**Hours.**   Statements regarding hours of work should be carefully thought out and worded. For the organization, such statements will affect staffing flexibility and cost. In terms of flexibility, a statement such as "Hours of work will be as needed and scheduled" provides maximum flexibility. Designation of work as part time, as opposed to full time, may affect cost because the organization may provide restricted, if any, benefits to part-time employees.

Factors other than just number of hours may also need to be addressed in the job offer. Any special arrangements for work hours should be clearly spelled out. Examples include "Weekend work will not be required of you" and "Your hours of work will be from 7:30 to 11:30 a.m. and 1:30 to 5:30 p.m." Overtime hours requirements and overtime pay, if applicable, could also be addressed.

**Hiring Bonuses.**   Hiring, signing, or "up-front" bonuses are one-time payments offered and subsequently paid upon acceptance of the offer. Typically, the bonus is in the form of an outright cash grant; the bonus may also be in the form of a cash advance against future expected earnings. Top executives are likely to receive not only a cash bonus but also restricted stock and/or stock options. Roughly half (46.4%) of college recruiters say they use hiring bonuses to recruit new graduates.[32]

Offers of hiring bonuses should be used judiciously. For example, while it is desirable to be flexible as to the use and amount of hiring bonuses, it is necessary to carefully monitor them so that they do not get out of control. Also, it is important to avoid getting into overly spirited hiring bonus bidding wars with competitors—the other rewards of the job need to be emphasized in addition to the bonus. A danger is that hiring bonuses might give rise to feelings of jealousy and inequity, necessitating retention bonuses if existing employees learn of the bonuses being given to new hires. To avoid this possibility, hiring bonuses should be confidential. Another potential problem is that bonus recipients may be tempted to "take the money and run," and their performance motivation may be lessened because their bonus money is not contingent on their job performance.

To address these problems, the organization may place restrictions on the bonus payment, paying half up front and the other half after some designated time period, such as 6 or 12 months; another option is to make payment of a portion or all of the bonus contingent on meeting certain performance goals within a designated time period. Such payment arrangements should help other employees see the hiring bonus as not a total "freebie" and should encourage only serious and committed offer receivers to accept the offer. Although such "clawbacks" are awkward, and some employers have had difficulties enforcing such agreements, they are generally necessary in some form because the labor markets in which bonuses are most likely to be used (tight labor markets) are the same markets in which job-hopping is very easy to do.[33]

***Relocation Assistance.***   Acceptance of the offer may require a geographic move and entail relocation costs for the offer receiver. The organization may want to provide assistance to conduct the move, as well as totally or partially defray moving costs. Thus, a relocation package may include assistance with house hunting, guaranteed purchase of the applicant's home, a mortgage subsidy, actual moving cost reimbursement, and a cost-of-living adjustment if the move is to a higher-cost area. To simplify things, a lump-sum relocation allowance may be provided, thus reducing record keeping and other paperwork.[34] Managers should be especially attentive to the potential needs of dual-career couples and may find offering job search assistance as part of the package a valuable enticement.[35] An increasing number of companies are giving employees relocation counseling prior to a formal job offer, to ensure that applicants know all the costs and benefits of moving in advance. If applicants are well informed about the likely outcome of a move, those who might drop out of the process can be eliminated from consideration before an expensive investment in selection and hiring is made.[36]

***Hot Skill Premiums.***   A hot skill premium is a temporary pay premium added to the regular base pay to account for a temporary market escalation in pay for certain skills in extreme shortage. Hiring bonuses are also frequently used to attract in-demand talent. The job offer should clearly indicate the amount of base pay that constitutes the premium, the length of time the premium will be in effect, and the mechanism by which the premium will be halted or phased out. Before offering such premiums, it is wise to recognize that there will likely be pressure to maintain rather than discontinue the premium and that careful communication with the offer receiver about the temporary nature of the premium will be necessary.[37]

***Severance Packages.*** Terms and conditions that the organization states the employee is entitled to upon departure from the organization constitute a severance package. Content of the package typically includes one or two weeks of pay for every year of service, earned vacation and holiday pay, extended health insurance coverage and premium payment, and outplacement assistance in finding a new job.[38] What is the organization willing to provide?

In pondering this question, a few points should be borne in mind. Severance packages for top executives are usually expected and provided, and their provisions can be quite complex. Lower-level managers and non-managers also appear to be aware of and expect severance packages. In other words, job applicants consider these packages as part of the EVP. This expectation is probably due to a realization of how marketable their KSAOs are, as well as increased concerns about job security and layoff protection. Unmet severance expectations may translate into demands by candidates for a severance package to be included in their job offer, or a refusal to even consider a job offer that does not provide some form of severance benefit.[39]

Other thorny issues surround these packages. When does an employee become eligible for the package? Will severance be granted for voluntary or involuntary termination, or both? If involuntary, are there exceptions, such as for unacceptable job performance or misconduct? Questions such as these illustrate the need to very carefully craft the terms that will govern the package and define its contents.

## Idiosyncratic Deals

While most of our discussion up to this point has centered around negotiating common contract terms, with an emphasis on salary and benefits, many organizations find that employees wish to engage in a discussion of unique terms that go beyond the traditional menu. The results of these negotiations are "idiosyncratic deals," and they can have important consequences.[40]

What makes a deal idiosyncratic? The most important features are that it is individually negotiated, concerns issues unique to the specific employee, is mutually beneficial for the employee and the employer, and varies in its scope. The main goal here is to strike an integrative or "win-win" arrangement in which both the employer and the employee expand the terms of the negotiation process to capture positive outcomes that benefit both parties.[41] Unlike traditional negotiation, which asks "how much" employees get from a job (e.g., how much money), idiosyncratic negotiations are about "what" employees get (e.g., a variety of different work and benefit items).

There are four broad topics that cover the content of most idiosyncratic deals.[42] They are described in Exhibit 12.3, along with potential examples for each category. Because of the nature of idiosyncratic deals, it is impossible to list all the possible elements of these deals: each situation is unique.

Idiosyncratic deals have resulted in a number of unique positive outcomes. Research has shown that employees who have negotiated tasks, work responsi-

**EXHIBIT 12.3   Elements and Examples of Idiosyncratic Deals**

| Category | Examples |
| --- | --- |
| Tasks and work responsibilities that are specially tailored to the employee's unique KSAOs | • Allow an engineer with an interest and background in marketing to participate in marketing meetings<br>• Give a salesperson who is especially familiar with a certain product line paid time to share expertise with other workers<br>• Give a customer service provider who is interested in management paid time to attend skill development workshops |
| Flexible schedules to accommodate individual employee needs | • Allow an employee to come in later in the day and leave later to accommodate child care needs<br>• Allow an employee whose spouse works a nonstandard workweek to work a Tuesday to Saturday schedule<br>• Allow a nonexempt employee to work variable hours from week to week |
| The ability to work outside of the main office | • Use a virtual private network or cloud-based servers to allow employees to access work data remotely<br>• Provide a mobile device like a tablet computer or smartphone and pay for connectivity fees for an employee who travels frequently with family |
| Financial incentives that are particular to the employee and match his or her unique contribution to the organization | • Compensate an especially productive research developer based on patent applications<br>• Designate an employee with well-developed social networks a "rainmaker" and pay him a bonus for each new client he brings in<br>• Pay a bonus to a manager with strong developmental skills for each person successfully mentored |

bilities, and schedule flexibility to fit their needs are particularly satisfied, committed to their employers, and engaged in their work.[43] Because we know that satisfied and committed employees are less likely to quit, employers should definitely take these deals into account during the negotiation process. Other research has shown that employees who have idiosyncratic deals help their coworkers and pitch in with extra effort above and beyond what is generally required, further demonstrating the importance of taking a broader perspective on the job negotiation process.[44]

## Restrictions on Employees

In some situations, the organization may want to place certain restrictions on employees to protect its own interests. These restrictions should be known, and agreed to, by the new employee at the time of hire. Thus, they should be incorporated into the job offer and resultant employment contract. Because of the potential complexities in these restrictions and because they are subject to state contract laws, legal counsel should be sought to guide the organization in drafting appropriate contract language. Several types of restrictions are possible.[45]

One form of restriction involves so-called confidentiality clauses that prohibit current or departing employees from the unauthorized use or disclosure of confidential information during or after employment. Confidential information is any information not made public and that gives the organization an advantage over its competitors. Examples of such information include trade secrets, customer lists, secret formulas, manufacturing processes, marketing and pricing plans, and business forecasts. It will be necessary to spell out, to some degree, exactly what information the organization considers confidential, as well as the time period after employment for which confidentiality must be maintained.

Another restriction, known as a noncompete agreement, seeks to keep departed employees from competing against the organization. For example, former Microsoft VP Kai-Fu Lee signed a noncompete agreement when he first joined Microsoft. When Lee left Microsoft to run a Google research facility in China, Microsoft sued Google and Lee for violating his noncompete agreement. Google and Microsoft eventually settled out of court, but the case showed that not all noncompete agreements are enforceable. For example, some states (Alabama, California, Georgia, Montana, Nebraska, North Dakota, Oklahoma, and Texas) do not favor noncompetes. If an employee signs a noncompete agreement in a state that allows them, but relocates to a state that disfavors them, the employer may be out of luck—which is exactly what happened to Convergys Corp. when an employee signed a noncompete agreement with Convergys in Ohio and then moved to work for a competitor in Georgia, which bars such agreements.[46]

More generally, noncompete agreements cannot keep departed employees from practicing their trade or profession completely or indefinitely, for this would in essence restrict the person from earning a living in a chosen field. Accordingly, the noncompete agreement must be carefully crafted in order to be enforceable. The agreement should probably not be a blanket statement that applies to all employees; rather, the agreement should apply to those employees who truly could turn into competitors, such as high-level managers, scientists, and technical staff. Additionally, the agreement must be limited in time and geography. The time should be of short duration (less than two years), and the area should be limited to the geographic area of the organization's competitive market. For example, the VP of sales for an insurance agency with locations in two counties of a state might have a noncompete agreement that prohibits working with any other agencies within the two counties, and the solicitation of the agency's policyholders, for one year.

A final type of restriction is the "golden handcuff," or payback agreement. The intent of this restriction is to retain new hires for some period of time and to financially discourage them from leaving the organization, particularly soon after they have joined. A typical golden handcuff requires the employee to repay (in full or pro rata) the organization for any up-front payments made at the time of hire if the employee departs within the first year of employment. These payments might include hiring bonuses, relocation expenses, tuition reimbursements, or any other financial hiring lures. Executive pay packages might contain even more restrictions designed to tie the executive to the organization for an extended period of time. Annual bonuses might be deferred for two or three years and be contingent on the executive not leaving during that time, or an executive may forfeit accrued pension benefits if he or she departs before a particular date.

### Acceptance Terms

The job offer should specify terms of acceptance required of the offer receiver. For reasons previously noted regarding oral contracts, acceptances should normally be required in writing only. The receiver should be required to accept or reject the offer in total, without revision. Any other form of acceptance is not an acceptance, merely a counteroffer. Finally, the offer should specify the date, if any, by which it will lapse. A lapse date is recommended so that certainty and closure are brought to the offer process.

### Sample Job Offer Letter

A sample job offer letter is shown in Exhibit 12.4 that summarizes and illustrates the previous discussion and recommendations regarding job offers. This letter should be read and analyzed for purposes of becoming familiar with job offer letters, as well as gaining an appreciation for the many points that need to be addressed in such a letter. Remember that, normally, whatever is put in the job offer letter, once accepted by the receiver, becomes a binding employment contract. Examples of more complex job offer letters, more relevant to executives, might also be consulted.

**EXHIBIT 12.4** **Example of Job Offer Letter**

### The Wright Company

Mr. Vern Markowski
152 Legion Lane
Clearwater, Minnesota

Dear Mr. Markowski:

We are pleased to offer you the position of Human Resource Specialist, beginning March 1, 2014. Your office will be located here in our main facility at Silver Creek, Minnesota.

This offer is for full-time employment, meaning you will be expected to work a minimum of 40 hours per week. Weekend work is also expected, especially during peak production periods.

You will receive a signing bonus of $2,500, half payable on March 1, 2014, and the other half on August 1, 2014, if you are still an employee of the company. Your starting pay will be $3,100 per month. Should you complete one year of employment, you will then participate in our managerial performance review and merit pay process. You will be eligible to participate in our benefit plans as provided in our written descriptions of those plans.

Should you choose to relocate to the Silver Creek area, we will reimburse you for one house/apartment hunting trip for up to $1,000. We will also pay reasonable and normal moving expenses up to $7,500, with receipts required.

It should be emphasized that we are an employment-at-will employer. This means that we, or you, may terminate our employment relationship at any time, for any reason. Only the president of the Wright Company is authorized to provide any modification to this arrangement.

We must have your response to this offer by February 1, 2014, at which time the offer will lapse. If you wish to accept our offer as specified in this letter, please sign and date at the bottom of the letter and return it to me (a copy is enclosed for you). Should you wish to discuss these or any other terms prior to February 1, 2014, please feel free to contact me.

Sincerely yours,

Mary Kaiser
Senior Vice President, Human Resources

I accept the employment offer, and its terms, contained in this letter. I have received no promises other than those contained in this letter.

_____          _____

Signed                                                                              Date

## JOB OFFER PROCESS

Besides knowing the types of issues to address in a job offer, it is equally important to understand the total job offer process. The content of any specific job offer must be formulated within a broad context of considerations. Once these have been taken into account, the specific offer must be developed and presented to the finalist. Following this, there will be matters to address in terms of either acceptance or rejection of the offer. Finally, there will be an occasional need to deal with the unfortunate issue of reneging, either by the organization or by the offer receiver.

## Formulation of the Job Offer

When the organization puts together a specific job offer, several factors should be explicitly considered: knowledge of the terms and conditions offered by competitors, applicant truthfulness about KSAOs and reward information provided, the receiver's likely reaction to the offer, and policies on negotiation of job offer content with the offer receiver.

### Knowledge of Competitors

The organization competes for labor within labor markets. The job offer must be sensitive to the labor demand and supply forces operating, for these forces set the overall parameters for job offers to be extended.

On the demand side, this requires becoming knowledgeable about the terms and conditions of job contracts offered and provided by competitors. Here, the organization must confront two issues: exactly who are the competitors, and exactly what terms and conditions are they offering for the type of job for which the hiring organization is staffing?

Assume the hiring organization is a national discount retailer, and it is hiring recent (or soon-to-be) college graduates for the job of management trainee. It may identify as competitors other retailers at the national level (e.g., Sears), as well as national discount retailers (e.g., Target, Wal-Mart, and Kmart). There may be fairly direct competitors in other industries as well (e.g., banking, insurance) that typically place new college graduates in training programs.

Once such competitors are identified, the organization needs to determine, if possible, what terms and conditions they are offering. This may be done through formal mechanisms such as performing salary surveys, reading competitors' ads and websites, or consulting with trade associations. Information may be gathered informally as well, such as through telephone contacts with competitors, and conversations with actual job applicants, who have firsthand knowledge of competitors' terms.

The organization may quickly acquire salary information through the use of free online salary sites or ones that charge fees. Salary information is also available through O*Net. Listings of the sites and discussions of their advantages and disadvantages are available.[47] Generally, the user should be cautious in his or her use of these data, being careful to assess salary survey characteristics such as sample nature and size, currency of data, definitions of terms and job descriptions, and data presentation. The organization should remember that a job seeker can and will access these data, making this individual a very knowledgeable "shopper" and negotiator.

Through all the above mechanisms, the organization becomes "marketwise" regarding its competitors. Invariably, however, the organization will discover that for any given term or condition, a range of values will be offered. For example, starting pay might range from $50,000 to $70,000 per year, and the length of the training program may vary from three months to two years. The organization will thus need to determine where within these ranges it wishes to position itself in general, as well as for each particular offer receiver.

On the labor supply side, the organization will need to consider its needs concerning both labor quantity and quality (KSAOs and motivation). In general, offers need to be attractive enough that they yield the head count required. Moreover, offers need to take into account the KSAOs each specific receiver possesses and what these specific KSAOs are worth in terms and conditions offered the person. This is illustrated in Exhibit 12.2, which shows an example of an organization's policies regarding differential starting pay offers among offer receivers. Such differential treatment, and all the issues and questions it raises, applies to virtually any other term or condition as well.

## Applicant Truthfulness

Throughout the recruitment and selection process, the applicant provides information about KSAOs and other factors (e.g., current salary). Initially, this information is gathered as part of the assessment process, whose purpose is to determine which applicants are most likely to provide a good fit with job requirements and rewards. For applicants who pass the hurdles and are to receive job offers, the information that has been gathered may very well be used to decide the specific terms and conditions to include in a job offer. Just how truthful or believable is this information? The content and cost of job offers depend on how the organization answers this question.

Indications are that deceit may be common. Applicants may be tempted to embellish or enhance not only their reported salaries but also their KSAOs to provide an artificially high base or starting point for the organization as it prepares its job offer. Some companies specialize in providing job applicants with tips and assistance in fabricating educational qualifications, embellishing prior work tasks and responsibilities, and overstating previous salaries and even provide contacts who will "verify" that an applicant performed well at a job he or she may have never held.[48]

To combat such deceit by applicants, organizations are increasingly verifying all applicant information, including salary, and may go to extremes to do so. At the executive level, for example, some organizations require people to provide copies of their W-2 income forms. The organization should not act on finalist-provided information in the preparation of job offers unless it is willing to assume, or has verified, that the information is accurate.

## Likely Reactions of Offer Receivers

Naturally, the terms and conditions presented in an offer should be based on some assessment of the receiver's likely reaction to it. Will the receiver jump at it, laugh at it, or respond somewhere in between?

One way to gauge likely reactions to the offer is to gather information about various preferences from the offer receiver during the recruitment/selection process. Such preliminary discussions and communications will help the organization construct an offer that is likely to be acceptable. At the extreme, the process may lead to almost simultaneous presentation and acceptance of the offer. Another way to assess likely reactions to offers from offer receivers is to conduct research on reward importance to employees and applicants.

## Policies on Negotiations and Initial Offers

Before making job offers, the organization should decide whether it will negotiate on them. In essence, the organization must decide whether its first offer to a person will also be its final offer. If there will be room for negotiation, the style of negotiation should also be determined.

To help make this decision, it is useful to consider what components of the salary and benefits part of the offer are considered open to negotiation by organizations. An example of such data, based on a survey of 418 HR professionals in organizations of all sizes, is shown in Exhibit 12.5. It can be seen that salary is almost uniformly considered negotiable. A majority also considers the following components negotiable: payment for relocation costs, flexible work schedules, and early salary reviews with the possibilities for increases. The openness to negotiation of other components trails off from there.

Several considerations should be kept in mind when formulating strategies and policies for making job offers. First, remember that job offers occur for both external and internal staffing. For external staffing, the job offer is intended to convert the offer receiver into a new hire. For internal staffing, the job offer is being made to induce the employee to accept a new job assignment or to attempt to retain the employee by making a counteroffer to an offer the employee has received from another organization. These separate types of job offers (new hire, new assignment, and retention) will likely require separate job offer strategies and policies.

Second, consider the costs of the offer receiver not accepting the job offer. Are other equally qualified individuals available as backup offer receivers? How long can the organization afford to let a position remain vacant? How will current employees feel about job offers being rejected—will they, too, feel rejected, or will they feel that something they are unaware of is amiss in the organization? Will those next in line to receive an offer feel like second-class citizens or choices of desperation and last resort? Answers to such questions often suggest it may be desirable to negotiate (up to a point) with the offer receiver.

Third, recognize that many people to whom you will be making offers may in turn be seeking and receiving counteroffers from their current employer. Although

**EXHIBIT 12.5** **Negotiable Components of Salary and/or Benefits According to HR Professionals**

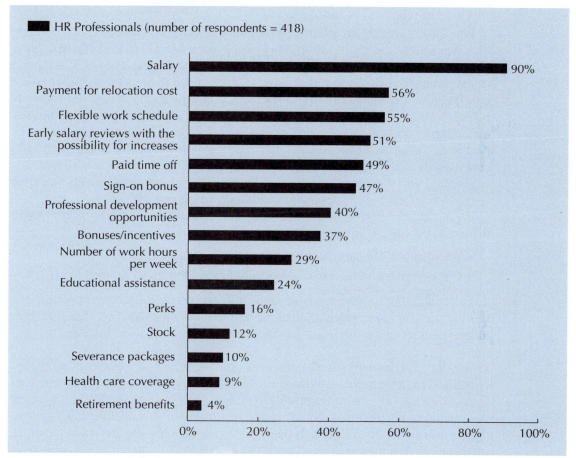

SOURCE: E. Esen, *Job Negotiation Survey Findings: A Study by SHRM and CareerJournal.com* (Alexandria, VA: Society for Human Resource Management, 2004), p. 9. Used with permission.

counteroffers are less likely in a poor economy, many organizations do seek to keep their employees by making counteroffers even during down times.[49] Hence, the organization should recognize that any offer it makes might lead to a bidding war of sorts with other organizations.

Fourth, a currently employed offer receiver normally incurs costs for leaving and will expect a "make whole" offer from the organization. Often these costs can amount to 20%–30% of the offer receiver's current base pay. In addition to relocation or higher commuting costs, the offer receiver may forfeit employer contributions to a retirement plan, vacation time and holidays, various perks, and so forth. In addition, there may be waiting periods before the offer receiver is eligible for various benefits, leading to opportunity costs of lost coverage and possibly paying the costs (e.g., health insurance premiums) out of pocket until coverage begins.

Finally, job seekers are often quite sophisticated in formulating and presenting their demands to the organization. They will know what it truly costs them to leave their current job and will frame their demands accordingly. They will be aware of the particular KSAOs that they have to offer, make these acutely known to the organization, and demand a high price for them. The terms demanded (or more politely, proposed) may focus not only on salary but on myriad other possibilities, including vacation time, a flexible work schedule to help balance work and family pressures, guaranteed expenditures on training and development, higher employer matching to a 401(k) retirement plan, and so on. In short, unless it is illegal, it is negotiable, and the organization must be prepared to handle demands from job seekers on virtually every term and condition of employment.

Presumably, each term or condition contained in an offer is a mini-offer in itself; therefore, the organization must decide the following:

- Whether it will negotiate on this term or condition
- If it negotiates, what are its lower and (especially) upper bounds

Once these questions have been answered, the organization may determine its posture regarding the presentation of the initial offer to the receiver. There are three basic strategies to choose from: lowball, market-matching, and best shot.

*Lowball.* The lowball strategy involves offering the lower bounds of terms and conditions to the receiver. Advantages of this strategy include getting acceptances from desperate or unknowledgeable receivers, minimizing initial employment costs, and leaving plenty of room to negotiate upward. Dangers of the lowball strategy include failing to get any acceptances, driving people away from and out of the finalist pool, developing an unsavory reputation among future potential applicants, and creating inequities and hard feelings that the reluctant accepter may carry into the organization, which may then influence postemployment attraction outcomes such as retention. This strategy is often adopted during periods of economic downturn, when applicants have relatively few alternatives.[50]

*Market Matching.* With a market-matching strategy, the organization prepares an offer that corresponds to the average salary for a given job based on salary survey information. The market-matching strategy should yield a sufficient number of job offer acceptances overall, though not all of the highest-quality (KSAO) applicants. This strategy leaves room for subsequent negotiation, should it be necessary. Market-matching offers are unlikely to offend or excite the receiver, and they probably will not have negative consequences for postemployment outcomes.

***Best Shot.***    With the best-shot strategy, the organization goes for broke and gives a high offer, one right at the upper bounds of feasible terms and conditions. Accompanying this offer is usually a statement to the receiver that this is indeed the organization's best shot, thus leaving little or no room for negotiation. These offers should enhance both preemployment attraction outcomes (e.g., filling vacancies quickly) and postemployment outcomes (e.g., job satisfaction). Best-shot offers obviously increase employment costs. They also leave little or no room for negotiation or for sweetening the offer. Finally, they may create feelings of inequity or jealousy among current employees.

None of these initial offer strategies is inherently superior, but the organization will need to choose one of them. It could also choose to tailor a strategy to fit the finalist pursued, as well as other circumstances. For example, the best-shot strategy may be chosen (1) for high-quality finalists, (2) when there are strong competitive hiring pressures from competitors, (3) when the organization is pressured to fill vacancies quickly, and (4) as part of an aggressive EEO/AA recruitment program.

Policies for how negotiations will be conducted should also be discussed in advance. After the initial offer is made—either lowball, market-matching, or best shot—the job offer maker will have to know which style of negotiation is appropriate. Research has generally suggested that individuals are more satisfied with a give-and-take negotiation than a hardline "take it or leave it" approach.[51] In other words, offer receivers may be more satisfied with their offer if they feel as though they have a chance to move the initial figure somewhat. This argues against setting in stone all components of the job offer in advance. A nonconfrontational tone may also generate more positive outcomes down the road. Research also suggests that individuals who are more satisfied with their job negotiation process and outcomes are more satisfied with their subsequent compensation and jobs in general and have lower intentions to leave a year later.[52]

## Presentation of the Job Offer

Presentation of the offer may proceed along many different paths. The precise path chosen depends on the content of the offer, as well as factors considered in formulating the offer. To illustrate, two extreme approaches to presenting the job offer—the mechanical approach and the sales approach—are detailed.

### Mechanical Approach

The mechanical approach relies on simple one-way communication from the organization to the offer receiver. Little more than a standard, or "form," written offer is sent to the person. The organization then awaits a response. Little or no input about the content of the offer is received from the person, and after the offer has been made, there is no further communication with the person. If the person rejects the offer, another form letter acknowledging receipt of the rejection is sent.

Meanwhile, the offer process is repeated anew, without modification, for a different receiver. Although there are obvious disadvantages to such an approach, it is highly efficient and inexpensive. It also ensures that all applicants are treated in exactly the same manner, which may improve the legal defensibility of the process.

### Sales Approach

The sales approach treats the job offer as a product that must be developed and sold to the customer (i.e., receiver). There is active interaction between the organization and the receiver as the terms and conditions are developed and incorporated into an offer package. Informal agreement unfolds between the receiver and the organization, and reduction of that agreement into an actual job offer is a mere formality. After the formal offer has been presented, the organization continues to have active communication with the receiver. In this way, the organization can be alert to possible glitches that occur in the offer process and can continue to sell the job to the receiver. The sales approach is much more expensive and time-consuming, but it may have a higher chance of the receiver accepting the offer. It is more likely to be employed for high-value employees who likely have more varied KSAO sets than entry-level employees.

## Timing of the Offer

Another issue that must be considered in the process of presenting an offer is the timing of the offer. In general, organizations will want to deliver the offer as quickly as possible after a final decision has been reached. Post-interview delays in communication with candidates have been linked to negative perceptions of the organization.[53] Research has also demonstrated that organizations that make offers more quickly are more likely to have their offers accepted than organizations that wait to make an offer.[54] This same research has shown that individuals who accept these quicker offers have similar levels of performance and turnover relative to those who received later offers. In sum, it appears that organizations can increase acceptance rates and reduce vacancy times if they make offers in a timely manner.

## Job Offer Acceptance and Rejection

Ultimately, of course, job offers are accepted and rejected. How this happens and how it is handled are often as important as the outcomes themselves.

Provided next are some general suggestions and recommendations about acceptances and rejections. They are intended to serve as advice about additional practices and issues involved in the job offer process.

### Acceptance

When the offer receiver accepts a job offer, the organization should do two important things. First, it should check the receiver's actual acceptance to ensure that it has been accepted as required in the offer. Thus, the acceptance should not come in the form of a counteroffer or with any other contingencies attached to it. Also, the acceptance should occur in the manner required (normally in writing), and it should arrive on or before the date specified.

Second, the organization must maintain contact with the new hire. Initially, this means acknowledging receipt of the acceptance. Additional communication may also be appropriate to further "cement the deal" and build commitment to the new job and organization. Examples of such continued communication include soon-to-be coworkers calling and offering congratulations to the new hire, sending work materials and reports to the new hire to help phase the person into the new job, and inviting the new hire to meetings and other activities prior to that person's starting date.

### Rejection

The organization may reject the finalist, and the finalist may reject the organization.

***By the Organization.*** Depending on the decision-making process used, the acceptance of an offer by one person means that the organization will have to reject others. This should be done promptly and courteously. Moreover, the organization should keep records of those it rejects. This is necessary for legal purposes (e.g., applicant flow statistics) and for purposes of building and maintaining a pool of potential applicants that the organization may wish to contact about future vacancies.

The content of the rejection message (usually a letter) is at the discretion of the organization. Most organizations opt for short and vague content that mentions a lack of fit between the applicant's KSAOs and the job's requirements. Providing more specific reasons for rejection should only be done with caution. The reasons provided should be candid and truthful, and they should match the reasons recorded and maintained on other documents by the organization.

***By the Offer Receiver.*** When the receiver rejects the job offer, the organization must decide whether to accept the rejection or extend a new offer to the person. If the organization's position on negotiations has already been determined, as ideally it should, the organization simply needs to carry out its plan to either extend a new offer or move on to the next candidate.

The organization should accept the rejection in a prompt and courteous manner. Moreover, records should be kept of these rejections, for the same reasons they are kept when rejection by the organization occurs.

## Reneging

Occasionally, and unfortunately, reneging occurs. Organizations rescind offers extended, and receivers rescind offers accepted. Solid evidence on reneging, and exactly why it occurs, is lacking. Sometimes reneging is unavoidable. The organization may experience a sudden downturn in business conditions, which causes planned-on jobs to evaporate, or the offer receiver may experience sudden changes in circumstances requiring reneging, such as a change in health status.

As an example of reneging, consider the case of Ford Motor Company, which extended offers of employment as assemblers to hundreds of individuals in its Oakville plant in Ontario, Canada.[55] A sudden drop in demand for vehicles led Ford to withdraw these job offers soon after they had been made. As a result, the individuals who had lost their offers brought a class-action lawsuit, claiming that they had faced considerable economic difficulties because of this repudiation of the employment agreement. Economic damages included lost wages for individuals who had terminated work at another employer in anticipation of these jobs with Ford. In addition to the legal concerns, there are also reputational concerns that come with reneging. As word of the Oakville plant problems spread, Ford could anticipate problems in staffing future positions because applicants might be worried about the company's tendency to not keep its word.

While some reneging by the organization may be necessary, we believe that the organization can and should take steps to lessen its occurrence. If these steps are insufficient, we believe the organization should take other actions to handle reneging. Examples of these actions are shown in Exhibit 12.6. They represent attempts to be fair to the offer receiver while still representing the interests of the organization.

For the offer receiver, high standards of fairness are also required. The receiver should not be frivolous and should not go through the application process just "for

**EXHIBIT 12.6**   **Organization Actions to Deal With Reneging**

### A. To Lessen the Occurrence of Reneging

- Extend offers only for positions known to exist and be vacant
- Require top management approval of all reneging
- Conduct thorough assessments of finalists prior to job offer
- Honor outstanding offers but make no new ones
- Discourage offer receiver from accepting offer
- Defer starting date and provide partial pay in interim
- Keep offer open but renegotiate or reduce salary and other economic items
- Stagger new hire starting dates to smooth out additions to payroll

### B. To Handle Reneging

- Communicate honestly and quickly with offer receiver
- Provide consolation or apology package (e.g., hiring bonus, three months' salary)
- Pay for any disruption costs (e.g., relocation)
- Hire as consultant (independent contractor), convert to employee later
- Guarantee priority over other applicants when future vacancies occur

the experience." Nor should the receiver accept an offer as a way of extracting a counteroffer out of his or her current employer. Indeed, organizations should be aware that some people to whom they make job offers will receive such counter-offers, and this should be taken into account during the time the offer is initially formulated and presented. Finally, the receiver should carefully assess the probable fit for the person/job match prior to accepting an offer.

## NEW EMPLOYEE ORIENTATION AND SOCIALIZATION

Establishment of the employment relationship through final match activities does not end a concern with the person/job match. Rather, that relationship must now be nurtured and maintained over time to ensure that the intended match becomes and remains effective. The new hires become newcomers, and their initial entry into the job and organization should be guided by orientation and socialization activities. Orientation and socialization may be concurrent, overlapping activities that occur for the newcomer. Orientation is typically more immediate, while socialization is more long term.

Despite the importance of a quality orientation program, many organizations do not invest substantial resources into helping new employees get on board.[56] A survey conducted by Harris Interactive found that only 29% of employers give managers training in techniques to facilitate orientation for newcomers, and 15% leave the process of getting new employees on board entirely in the hands of the hiring manager. Experts agree that this short-sighted approach can be very costly, as turnover rates for new hires tend to be much higher than for established employees. Programs that continue to challenge and develop employees are an especially important element in effective orientation and socialization processes.

As an example of a comprehensive "onboarding" program, Sun Microsystems has jettisoned the typical orientation program that involves filling out mountains of paperwork.[57] Instead, new employees learn about the company through an interactive video game. When they arrive at their desks, new hires receive welcome notes and other company-themed paraphernalia. There are also opportunities to join online social networks to form relationships with established employees. Filling out forms must be accomplished during orientation, of course, but the entire process has been integrated with the company's human resource information systems, and hiring managers can guide employees through a checklist of requirements relatively quickly and efficiently. This level of attention and guidance is certainly not typical—many companies still engage in minimal, low-cost efforts to facilitate newcomer engagement—but Sun believes that the returns for the system are well worth the expenditures.

It should be remembered that the newcomer is likely entering a situation of uncertainties and unknowns. Research indicates that how the organization responds to this situation will have an important impact on how well the newcomer adapts to the job and remains with the organization. Several factors have been identified as influencing the likely effectiveness of orientation and socialization:[58]

- Providing realistic recruitment information about job requirements and rewards (orientation begins before the job does)
- Clarifying for the newcomer the job requirements, knowledge, and skills to be acquired
- Encouraging the newcomer to actively seek out information and build relationships
- Ensuring that managers and coworkers provide assistance to the newcomer
- Conducting active mentoring for the newcomer

Elaboration on these points, as well as many examples, is provided below.

## Orientation

Orientation requires considerable advanced planning in terms of topics to cover, development of materials for the newcomer, and scheduling of the many activities that contribute to an effective program. Often, the HR department is responsible for the design and conduct of the orientation, and it will seek close coordination of actual orientation activities and schedules with the newcomer's supervisor. This is also the organization's first opportunity to welcome new hires and to emphasize the opportunities it can provide.

Exhibit 12.7 contains a far-ranging set of suggested topics of information for an orientation program, delivery of which is accomplished via written materials, online services, training programs, meetings with various people, and visual inspection. Note that these activities are spaced out rather than concentrated in just the first day of work for the newcomer. An effective orientation program will foster an understanding of the organization's culture and values, help the new employee understand his or her role and how he or she fits into the total organization, and help the new employee achieve objectives and shorten the learning curve.

Some organizations see the orientation program as a crucial part of their culture formation process.[59] For example, Accenture Consulting puts new employees through a two-week orientation at headquarters, followed by an additional two-week "New Joiner Orientation" program. During the orientation program, new employees learn about the company's methods for interacting with clients, go through mock client engagement sessions, make presentations to clients, and implement systems to solve client problems. As a follow-up, each new hire has a career counselor who reinforces orientation materials in the workplace and helps the new employee throughout his or her career. Although this extensive orientation program is costly, representatives from the organization argue that it has helped create a unified culture among employees who work in offices around the world. Some experts argue that in addition to making sure the first few weeks

**EXHIBIT 12.7**   **New Employee Orientation Guidelines**

**Before the Employee Arrives**

- Notify everyone in your unit that a new person is starting and what the person's job will be; ask the other staff members to welcome the new employee and encourage their support
- Prepare interesting tasks for the employee's first day
- Provide the new employee with a copy of the job description, job performance standards, organization chart, and your department's organization chart
- Enroll the employee in any necessary training programs
- Make sure the employee's work location is available, clean, and organized
- Make sure a copy of the appropriate personnel policy manual or contract is available for the employee
- Have a benefits information package available
- If possible, identify a staff member to act as a peer mentor for the first week
- Put together a list of key people the employee should meet and interview to get a broader understanding of their roles
- Arrange for a building pass, parking pass, and IDs if necessary
- Draft a training plan for the new employee's first few months

**First Day on the Job**

- Give a warm welcome and discuss the plan for the first day
- Tour the employee's assigned work space
- Explain where restrooms, vending machines, and break areas are located
- Provide required keys
- Arrange to have lunch with the new employee
- Tour the building and immediate area and introduce the new employee to other staff members
- Introduce the new employee to the person you've identified as a peer mentor (if appropriate)
- Review the job description
- Review the department's (or office's) organizational chart
- Review your office's policies and procedures involving working hours, telephone, e-mail and Internet use, office organization, office resources, and ethics

**During the First Week**

- Check the employee's work area to ensure needed equipment is in place
- Set up a brief meeting with the employee and the assigned peer mentor to review the first week's activities (if appropriate)
- Schedule a meeting with the human resources office to complete required paperwork, review personnel policies and procedures, learn about benefits, obtain credentials, and explain other policies and procedures

*(continued)*

**EXHIBIT 12.7   Continued**

### Within the First Month of Employment

- Meet with the employee to review:
    - ❏ Job description
    - ❏ Performance standards
    - ❏ Work rules
    - ❏ Organization structure
    - ❏ Health and safety
    - ❏ Benefits

### Within Six Months of Starting

- Revisit performance standards and work rules
- Schedule a performance appraisal meeting

SOURCE: Based on "Guide to Managing Human Resources: New Employee Orientation," Human Resources, University of California, Berkeley (*http://hrweb.berkeley.edu/guide/orient.htm*).

are successful, organizations should conduct routine follow-up sessions with new employees throughout the first year of employment as a means of enhancing newcomer engagement and retention. This extended check-in period bridges the gap between orientation and socialization.

## Socialization

Socialization of the newcomer is a natural extension of orientation activities. Like orientation, socialization aims to achieve effective person/job and person/ organization matches. Whereas orientation focuses on the initial and immediate aspects of newcomer adaptation, socialization emphasizes helping the newcomer fit into the job and organization over time. The emphasis is on the long haul, seeking to gain newcomers' adaptation in ways that will make them want to be successful, long-term contributors to the organization.[60] Research has shown that when socialization programs are effective, they facilitate new employee adjustment by increasing employees' role clarity (clarify job duties and performance expectations), by enhancing their self-efficacy (their belief that they can do the job), and by fostering their social acceptance (making employees believe that they are valued members of the team).[61]

To increase new employees' role clarity, self-efficacy, and social acceptance, two key issues should be addressed in developing and conducting an effective socialization process. First, what are the major elements or contents of socialization that should occur? Second, how can the organization best deliver those elements to the newcomer?

## Content

While the content of the socialization process should obviously be somewhat job- and organization-specific, several components are likely candidates for inclusion. From the newcomer's perspective, these components are the following:[62]

1. *People*—meeting and learning about coworkers, key contacts, informal groups and gatherings, and networks; becoming accepted and respected by these people as "one of the gang"
2. *Performance proficiency*—becoming very familiar with job requirements; mastering tasks; having impacts on performance results; and acquiring necessary KSAOs for proficiency in all aspects of the job
3. *Organization goals and values*—learning of the organization's goals; accepting these goals and incorporating them into the line of sight for performance proficiency; learning about values and norms of desirable behavior (e.g., working late and on weekends; making suggestions for improvements)
4. *Politics*—learning about how things really work; becoming familiar with key players and their quirks; taking acceptable shortcuts; schmoozing and networking
5. *Language*—learning special terms, buzzwords, and acronyms; knowing what not to say; learning the jargon of people in the trade or profession
6. *History*—learning about the origins and growth of the organization; becoming familiar with customs, rituals, and special events; understanding the origins of the work unit and the backgrounds of people in it

Many of these topics overlap with the possible content of an orientation program, suggesting that orientation and socialization programs be developed in tandem so that they are synchronized and seamless as the newcomer passes from orientation into socialization.

## Delivery

Helping to socialize the newcomer should be the responsibility of several people. First, the newcomer's supervisor should be personally responsible for socializing the newcomer, particularly in terms of performance proficiency and organization goals and values. The supervisor is intimately familiar with and the "enforcer" of these key elements of socialization. It is important that the newcomer and the supervisor communicate directly, honestly, and formally about these elements.

Peers in the newcomer's work unit or team are promising candidates for assisting in socialization. They can be most helpful in terms of politics, language, and history, drawing on their own accumulated experiences and sharing them with the newcomer. They can also make their approachability and availability known to the newcomer when he or she wants to ask questions or raise issues in an informal manner.

To provide a more formal information and support system to the newcomer, but one outside a chain of command, a mentor or sponsor may be assigned to (or chosen by) the newcomer. The mentor functions as an identifiable point of contact for the newcomer, as well as someone who actively interacts with the newcomer to provide the inside knowledge, savvy, and personal contacts that will help the newcomer settle into the current job and prepare for future job assignments. Mentors can also play a vital role in helping shatter the glass ceiling of the organization.

Given the advances in computer technology and the increasing geographic dispersion of an organization's employees, organizations might be tempted to conduct their orientation programs online. Web-based recruiting tools make it easy to track and monitor new hires, provide new hires with an online tour complete with streaming video, provide mandatory training, and automate processes like signing up for insurance, e-mail addresses, and security badges.[63] Though some of this may be necessary, depending on the job, research suggests that socialization programs are less effective when conducted entirely online—in the eyes of both the employees and their supervisors. As would be expected, when compared with in-person programs, online socialization programs do a particularly poor job of socializing employees to the personal aspects of the job and organization, such as organizational goals and values, politics, and how to work well with others.[64]

Finally, the HR department can be very useful to the socialization process. Its representatives can help establish formal, organization-wide socialization activities such as mentoring programs, special events, and informational presentations. Also, representatives may undertake development of training programs on socialization topics for supervisors and mentors. Representatives might also work closely, but informally, with supervisors and coach them in how to become successful socializers of their own newcomers.

## Examples of Programs

The Sonesta Hotels chain developed a formal program to help newcomers adapt to their jobs during their first 100 days. After 30 days, the hotel site HR director meets with the newcomer to see whether his or her expectations are being met and whether he or she has the resources needed to do the job. At 60 days, the newcomer participates in a program called the Booster, which focuses on developing customer service and communication skills. Then at the end of 90 days, the newcomer meets with the supervisor to do performance planning for the rest of the year. In addition, managers are encouraged to take the newcomer and the rest of the department out to lunch during the first month.[65]

The president and CEO of Southcoast Hospitals Group in Fall River, Massachusetts, decided to develop an "owner's manual" about himself that was to be given to the new VP of performance improvement that he was recruiting for. The one-page manual gave tips to the new VP on how to work for the president. It was developed on the basis of self-assessment and feedback from colleagues and direct reports.

These people began using the completed manual immediately in their interactions with the president. The manual was given to the finalist for the VP job two days before the job offer was actually extended. The finalist took the job and commented on how helpful the manual was in saving him time figuring out what the president thinks of things.[66]

The National City Corporation in Cleveland, a bank and financial services organization, experienced high turnover among newcomers within the first 90 days on the job. These early-exiting employees were referred to as "quick quits" in the HR department. To combat this problem, a program called Early Success was designed for entry-level, nonexempt newcomers. Newcomers attend a series of custom-made training programs that provide them the necessary knowledge and skills. Examples of the programs are Plus (overview of the organization's objectives, employee benefits, and brand); People, Policies, and Practices (augment the employee handbook and reinforce the organization as an employer of choice); and Top-Notch Customer Care (focus on customer service delivery and how to be a team player). Another component of the program matches a newcomer with a peer; peer mentors then attend workshops to learn coaching skills. Finally, the hiring managers of the newcomers also attend workshops on such topics as how to select a peer mentor for the newcomer, how to communicate and create a supportive work environment, and how to help the newcomer assume more job responsibilities and achieve career goals. The program has reduced turnover by 50% and has improved attendance by 25%, saving over $1.6 million per year.[67]

## LEGAL ISSUES

The employment contract establishes the actual employment relationship and the terms and conditions that will govern it. In the process of establishing the relationship, the organization must deal with certain obligations and responsibilities. These pertain to (1) employing only those people who meet the employment requirements under the IRCA, (2) avoiding the negligent hiring of individuals, and (3) maintaining the organization's posture toward employment-at-will. Each of these is discussed in turn.

### Employment Eligibility Verification

Under the IRCA (see Chapter 2), the organization must verify each new employee's identity and employment eligibility (authorization). The verification cannot begin until after the job offer has been accepted. Specific federal regulations detail the requirements and methods of compliance.

For each new employee, the employer must complete the newest I-9 form. Section One, seeking employee information, must be completed no later than the first day of employment. Section Two, requiring the employer to examine evidence of the employee's identity and employment authorization, must be completed within three business days of the date employment begins. Both identity and employment authorization must be verified. The I-9 form shows only those documents that may be used for verification. Some documents (e.g., US passport) verify both identity and authorization; other documents verify only identity (e.g., state-issued driver's license or ID card) or eligibility (e.g., original Social Security card or birth certificate). Section Three deals with reverification and rehires.

E-Verify is an Internet-based system that allows the employer to determine employment eligibility and the validity of Social Security numbers, based on the I-9 information. The information is checked against federal databases, usually yielding results in a few seconds. E-Verify verifies only employment eligibility, not immigration status. Federal contractors and subcontractors, along with employers in some states, are required to use E-Verify. Other employers may voluntarily participate in E-Verify. Users must first complete an E-Verify tutorial and pass a mastery test. Employers may not use E-Verify to prescreen applicants or selectively verify only some new employees.

I-9 records should be retained for three years after the date of hire or one year after the date of employment ends, whichever is later. Use of paper or electronic systems or a combination of these is permitted, as are electronic signatures. Employees must be given a copy of the record if they request it.

Finally, since the IRCA prohibits national origin or citizenship discrimination, it is best not to ask for proof of employment eligibility before making the offer. The reason for this is that many of the identity and eligibility documents contain personal information that pertains to national origin and citizenship status, and such personal information might be used in a discriminatory manner. As a further matter of caution, the organization should not refuse to make a job offer to a person based on that person's foreign accent or appearance.

## Negligent Hiring

Negligent hiring is a claim made by an injured party (coworker, customer, client, or the general public) against the employer. The claim is that an injury was the result of the employer hiring a person it knew, or should have known, was unfit and posed a threat of risk. In short, negligent hiring is a failure to exercise "due diligence" in the selection and hiring of employees.[68] Injuries may include violence, physical damage, bodily or emotional injury, death, and financial loss. For example, elderly patients in a long-term care facility may suffer injury from a health care attendant due to overmedication or failure to provide adequate food and water, or an accountant might divert funds from a client's account into his or her own personal account.

What should the organization do to minimize negligent hiring occurrences? Following are several straightforward recommendations.[69] First, staffing any job should be preceded by a thorough analysis that identifies all the KSAOs required by the job. Failure to identify or otherwise consider KSAOs prior to the final match is not likely to be much of a defense in a negligent hiring lawsuit.

Second, particular attention should be paid to the *O* part of KSAOs, such as licensure requirements, criminal records, references, unexplained gaps in employment history, and alcohol and illegal drug usage. Of course, these should be derived separately for each job rather than applied identically to all jobs.

Third, methods for assessing these KSAOs that are valid and legal must be used. This is difficult to do in practice because of lack of knowledge about the validity of some predictors, or their relatively low levels of validity. Difficulties can also arise because of legal constraints on the use of preemployment inquiries, credit checks, and background checks (see Chapter 8).

Fourth, require the applicant to sign a disclaimer statement allowing the employer to check references and otherwise conduct a background investigation. In addition, have the applicant sign a statement indicating that all provided information is true and that no requested information has been withheld.

Fifth, apply utility analysis to determine whether it is worthwhile to engage in the preceding recommendations to try to avoid the (usually slight) chance of a negligent hiring lawsuit. Such an analysis will undoubtedly indicate great variability among jobs in terms of how many resources the organization wishes to invest in negligent hiring prevention.

Finally, when in doubt about a finalist and whether to extend a job offer, do not proceed until those doubts have been resolved. Acquire more information from the finalist, verify existing information more thoroughly, and seek the opinions of others on whether to proceed with the job offer.

## Employment-at-Will

As discussed in this chapter and in Chapter 2, employment-at-will involves the right of either the employer or the employee to unilaterally terminate the employment relationship at any time, for any legal reason. In general, the employment relationship is at-will, and usually the employer wishes it to remain that way. Hence, during the final match (and even before), the employer must take certain steps to ensure that its job offers clearly establish the at-will relationship. These steps are merely a compilation of points already made regarding employment contracts and employment-at-will.

First, ensure that job offers are for an indeterminate time period, meaning that they have no fixed term or specific ending date. Second, include in the job offer a specific disclaimer stating that the employment relationship is strictly at-will. Third, review all written documents (e.g., employee handbook, application blank) to ensure that they do not contain any language that implies anything but a strictly at-will relationship. Finally, take steps to ensure that organizational members do not make any oral statements or promises that would serve to create something other than a strictly at-will relationship.[70]

## SUMMARY

During the final match, the offer receiver and the organization move toward each other through the job offer/acceptance process. They seek to enter into the employment relationship and become legally bound to each other through an employment contract.

Knowledge of employment contract principles is central to understanding the final match. The most important principle pertains to the requirements for a legally enforceable employment contract (offer, acceptance, and consideration). Other important principles focus on the identity of parties to the contract, the form of the contract (written or oral), disclaimers by the employer, contingencies, reneging by the organization or the offer receiver, other sources that may also specify terms and conditions of employment (e.g., employee handbooks), and unfulfilled promises.

Job offers are designed to induce the offer receiver to join the organization. Offers should be viewed and used strategically by the organization. In that strategy, labor market conditions, organization and applicant needs, and legal issues all converge to shape the job offer and EVP.

Job offers may contain virtually any legal terms and conditions of employment. Generally, the offer addresses terms pertaining to starting date, duration of contract, compensation, hours, special hiring inducements (if any), other terms (such as contingencies), and acceptance of the offer.

The process of making job offers can be complicated, involving a need to think through multiple issues before making formal offers. Offers should take into account the content of competitors' offers, potential problems with applicant truthfulness, likely reactions of the offer receiver, and the organization's policies on negotiating offers. Presentation of the offer can range from a mechanical process all the way to a major sales job. Ultimately, offers are accepted and rejected, and all offer receivers should receive prompt and courteous attention during these events. Steps should be taken to minimize reneging by either the organization or the offer receiver.

Acceptance of the offer marks the beginning of the employment relationship. To help ensure that the initial person/job match starts out and continues to be effective, the organization should undertake both orientation and socialization activities for newcomers.

From a legal perspective, the organization must be sure that the offer receiver is employable according to provisions of the IRCA. Both identity and authorization for employment must be verified. The potential negligent hiring of individuals who, once on the job, cause harm to others (employees or customers) is also of legal concern. Those so injured may bring suit against the organization. The organization can take steps to help minimize the occurrence of negligent hiring lawsuits. There are limits on these steps, however, such as the legal constraints on the gathering of background information about applicants. Finally, the organization should have its posture, policies, and practices regarding employment-at-will firmly developed and aligned. Numerous steps can be taken to help achieve this.

## DISCUSSION QUESTIONS

1. If you were the HR staffing manager for an organization, what guidelines might you recommend regarding oral and written communication with job applicants by members of the organization?
2. If the same job offer content is to be given to all offer receivers for a job, is there any need to use the strategic approach to job offers? Explain.
3. What are the advantages and disadvantages of the sales approach in the presentation of the job offer?
4. What are examples of orientation experiences you have had as a new hire that have been particularly effective (or ineffective) in helping to make the person/job match happen?
5. What steps should an employer take to develop and implement its policy regarding employment-at-will?

## ETHICAL ISSUES

1. A large financial services organization is thinking of adopting a new staffing strategy for entry into its management training program. The program will provide the trainees all the knowledge and skills they need for their initial job assignment after training. The organization has therefore decided to do college recruiting at the end of the recruiting season. It will hire those who have not been fortunate enough to receive any job offers, pay them a salary 10% below market, and provide no other inducements such as a hiring bonus or relocation assistance. The organization figures this strategy and EVP will yield a high percentage of offers accepted, low cost per hire, and considerable labor cost savings due to below-market salaries. Evaluate this strategy from an ethical perspective.
2. An organization has a staffing strategy in which it hires 10% more employees than it actually needs in any job category in order to ensure its hiring needs are met. It reasons that some of the new hires will renege on the accepted offer and that the organization can renege on some of its offers, if need be, in order to end up with the right number of new hires. Evaluate this strategy from an ethical perspective.

## APPLICATIONS

### Making a Job Offer

Clean Car Care (3Cs) is located within a western city of 175,000 people. The company owns and operates four full-service car washes in the city. The owner of 3Cs, Arlan Autospritz, has strategically cornered the car wash market, with his only competition being two coin-operated car washes on the outskirts of the city. The unemployment rate in the city and surrounding area is 3.8%, and it is expected to dip even lower.

Arlan has staffed 3Cs by hiring locally and paying wage premiums (above-market wages) to induce people to accept job offers and to remain with 3Cs. Hiring occurs at the entry level only, for the job of washer. If they remain with 3Cs, washers have the opportunity to progress upward through the ranks, going from washer to shift lead person to assistant manager to manager of one of the four car wash facilities. Until recently, this staffing system worked well for Arlan. He was able to hire high-quality people, and a combination of continued wage premiums and promotion opportunities meant he had relatively little turnover (under 30% annually). Every manager at 3Cs, past or present, had come up through the ranks. This is now changing with the sustained low unemployment and the new hires, who just naturally seem more turnover-prone. The internal promotion pipeline is thus drying up, since few new hires are staying with 3Cs long enough to begin climbing the ladder.

Arlan has a vacancy for the job of manager at the north-side facility. Unfortunately, he does not think any of his assistant managers are qualified for the job, and he reluctantly concluded that he has to fill the job externally.

A vigorous three-county recruitment campaign netted Arlan a total of five applicants. Initial assessments resulted in four of those being candidates, and two candidates became finalists. Jane Roberts is the number-one finalist, and the one to whom Arlan has decided to extend the offer. Jane is excited about the job and told Arlan she will accept an offer if the terms are right. Arlan is quite certain Jane will get a counteroffer from her company. Jane has excellent supervisory experience in fast-food stores and a light manufacturing plant. She is willing to relocate, a move of about 45 miles. She will not be able to start for 45 days, due to preparing for the move and the need to give adequate notice to her present employer. As a single parent, Jane wants to avoid working weekends. The number-two finalist is Betts Cook. Though she lacks the supervisory experience that Jane has, Arlan views her as superior to Jane in customer service skills. Jane told Arlan she needs to know quickly if she is going to get the offer, since she is in line for a promotion at her current company and she wants to begin at 3Cs before being offered and accepting the promotion.

Arlan is mulling over what kind of offer to make to Jane. His three managers make between $38,000 and $48,000, with annual raises based on a merit review conducted by Arlan. The managers receive one week of vacation the first year, two weeks of vacation for the next four years, and three weeks of vacation after that. They also receive health insurance (with a 20% employee co-pay on the premium). The managers work five days each week, with work on both Saturday and Sunday frequently occurring during peak times. Jane currently makes $40,500, receives health insurance with no employee co-pay, and has one week of vacation (she is due to receive two weeks shortly, after completing her second year with the company). She works Monday through Friday, with occasional work on the weekends.

Betts earns $47,500, receives health insurance fully paid by her employer, and has one week of vacation (she is eligible for two weeks in another year). Weekend work, if not constant, is acceptable to her.

Arlan is seeking input from you on how to proceed. Specifically, he wants you to:

1. Recommend whether Jane should receive a best-shot, market-matching, or lowball offer, and why.
2. Recommend other inducements beyond salary, health insurance, vacation, and schedule that might be addressed in the job offer, and why.
3. Draft a proposed job offer letter to Jane, incorporating your recommendations from items 1 and 2 above, as well as other desired features that should be part of a job offer letter.

## Evaluating a Hiring and Variable Pay Plan

Effective Management Solutions (EMS) is a small, rapidly growing management consulting company. EMS has divided its practice into four areas: management systems, business process improvement, human resources, and quality improvement. Strategically, EMS has embarked on an aggressive revenue growth plan, seeking a 25% revenue increase in each of the next five years for each of the four practice areas. A key component of its plan involves staffing growth, since most of EMS's current entry-level consultants (associates) are at peak client loads and cannot take on additional clients; the associates are also at peak hours load, working an average of 2,500 billable hours per year.

Staffing strategy and planning have resulted in the following information and projections. Each practice area currently has 25 associates, the entry-level position and title. Each year, on average, each practice area has five associates promoted to senior associate within the area (there are no promotions or transfers across areas, due to differing KSAO requirements), and five associates leave EMS, mostly to go to other consulting firms. Replacement staffing thus averages 10 new associates in each practice area, for a total of 40 per year. To meet the revenue growth goals, each practice area will need to hire 15 new associates each year, or a total of 60. A total of 100 associate new hires will thus be needed each year (40 for replacement and 60 for growth).

Currently, EMS provides each job offer receiver a generous benefits package plus what it deems to be a competitive salary that is nonnegotiable. About 50% of such offers are accepted. Most of those who reject the offer are the highest-quality applicants; they take jobs in larger, more established consulting firms that provide somewhat below-market salaries but high-upside monetary potential through various short-term variable-pay programs, plus rapid promotions.

Faced with these realities and projections, EMS recognizes that its current job offer practices need to be revamped. Accordingly, it has asked Manuel Rodriguez, who functions as a one-person HR "department" for EMS, to develop a job offer proposal for the EMS partners to consider at their next meeting. The partners tell Rodriguez they want a plan that will increase the job offer acceptance rate, slow down the outflow of associates to other firms, and not create dissatisfaction among the currently employed associates.

In response, Rodriguez developed the proposed hiring and variable pay (HVP) program. It has as its cornerstone varying monetary risk/reward packages through a combination of base and short-term variable (bonus) pay plans. The specifics of the HVP program are as follows:

- The offer receiver must choose one of three plans to be under, prior to receiving a formal job offer. The plans are high-risk, standard, and low-risk.
- The high-risk plan provides a starting salary that is 10% to 30% below the market average and participation in the annual bonus plan, with a bonus range from 0% to 60% of current salary.
- The standard plan provides a starting salary that is 10% below the market average and participation in the annual bonus plan, with a bonus range from 0% to 20% of current salary.
- The low-risk plan provides a starting salary that is 5% above the market average and no participation in the annual bonus plan.
- The average market rate will be determined by salary survey data obtained by HR.
- The individual bonus amount will be determined by individual performance on three indicators: number of billable hours, number of new clients generated, and client-satisfaction survey results.
- The hiring manager will negotiate the starting salary for those in the high-risk and standard plans, based on likely person/job and person/organization fit and on need to fill the position.
- The hiring manager may also offer a "hot skills" premium of up to 10% of initial starting salary under all three plans—the premium will lapse after two years.
- Switching plans is permitted only once every two years.
- Current associates may opt into one of the new plans at their current salary.

Evaluate the HVP program as proposed, answering the following questions:

1. If you were an applicant, would the HVP program be attractive to you? Why or why not? If you were an offer receiver, which of the three plans would you choose, and why?
2. Will the HVP program likely increase the job offer acceptance rate? Why or why not?
3. Will the HVP program likely reduce turnover? Why or why not?
4. How will current associates react to the HVP program, and why?

5. What issues and problems will the HVP plan create for HR? For the hiring manager?

6. What changes would you make in the HVP program, and why?

## ENDNOTES

1. M. W. Bennett, D. J. Polden, and H. J. Rubin, *Employment Relationships: Law and Practice* (New York: Aspen, 2004), pp. 3-3 to 3-4; A. G. Feliu, *Primer on Individual Employee Rights*, 2nd ed. (Washington, DC: Bureau of National Affairs, 1996), pp. 7–29; G. P. Panaro, *Employment Law Manual* (Boston: Warren, Gorham and Lamont, 1993), pp. 4-2 to 4-4; Society for Human Resource Management, "How to Create an Offer Letter Without Contractual Implications," Sept. 15, 2010 (*www.shrm.org*).

2. Panaro, *Employment Law Manual*, pp. 4-61 to 4-63; D. Cadrain, "Coming to Terms," *Staffing Management Magazine*, Oct. 2009 (*www.shrm.org*).

3. S. Greenhouse, "U.S. Cracks Down on 'Contractors' as a Tax Dodge," *New York Times*, Feb. 17, 2010 (*www.nytimes.com*).

4. Bennett, Polden, and Rubin, *Employment Relationships: Law and Practice*, pp. 3-22 to 3-23; Panaro, *Employment Law Manual*, pp. 4-5 to 4-60.

5. Panaro, *Employment Law Manual*, pp. 4-18 to 4-19; Society for Human Resource Management, "How to Create an Offer Letter Without Contractual Implications."

6. Feliu, *Primer on Individual Employee Rights*, pp. 23–25; Panaro, *Employment Law Manual*, pp. 4-30 to 4-31.

7. Feliu, *Primer on Individual Employee Rights*, pp. 26–28.

8. Feliu, *Primer on Individual Employee Rights*, pp. 48–51.

9. Bennett, Polden, and Rubin, *Employment Relationships: Law and Practice*, pp. 3-30 to 3-32; Feliu, *Primer on Individual Employee Rights*, pp. 22–25.

10. Society for Human Resource Management, "At Will: Policy Statement," Mar. 2010 (*www.shrm.org*).

11. Feliu, *Primer on Individual Employee Rights*, p. 26.

12. Panaro, *Employment Law Manual*, pp. 4-66 to 4-136.

13. Bennett, Polden, and Rubin, *Employment Relationships: Law and Practice*, pp. 3-24 to 3-34; Feliu, *Primer on Individual Employee Rights*, pp. 39–50; Society for Human Resource Management, "How to Create an Offer Letter Without Contractual Implications."

14. J. A. Segal, "An Offer They Couldn't Refuse," *HR Magazine*, Apr. 2001, pp. 131–144.

15. M. M. Breslin, "Why Companies Are Embracing the Employee Value Proposition," *Workforce*, Feb. 28, 2013 (*www.workforce.com*).

16. M. Pokorny, "Getting to Know Your Employees and What Motivates Them," *Employment Relations Today*, 2013, 39, pp. 45–52.

17. Bennett, Polden, and Rubin, *Employment Relationships: Law and Practice*, pp. 2-11 to 2-49.

18. R. Mayhew, "Can My Boss Keep My Last Paycheck if I Don't Put My Two Weeks Notice In?" *Houston Chronicle*, Aug. 15, 2013 (*http://work.chron.com/can-boss-keep-last-paycheck-dont-put-two-weeks-notice-in-8946.html*).

19. K. L. Uggerslev, N. E. Fassina, and D. Kraichy, "Recruiting Through the Stages: A Meta-Analytic Test of Predictors of Applicant Attraction at Different Stages of the Recruiting Process," *Personnel Psychology*, 2012, 65, pp. 597–660.

20. Society for Human Resource Management, *2012 Employee Job Satisfaction and Engagement* (Alexandria, VA: author, 2012).

21. L. Reisel, "Is More Always Better? Early Career Returns to Education in the United States and Norway," *Research in Social Stratification and Mobility*, 2013, 31, pp. 49–68.

22. M. Hout, "Social and Economic Returns to College Education in the United States," *Annual Review of Sociology*, 2012, 38, pp. 379–400.

23. F. Andersson, M. Freedman, J. Haltiwanger, J. Lane, and K. Shaw, "Reaching for the Stars: Who Pays for Talent in Innovative Industries?" *The Economic Journal*, 2009, 119, pp. F308–F332.

24. O*NET OnLine (*www.onetonline.org*).

25. Y. J. Dreazen, "When #$%+! Recruits Earn More," *Wall Street Journal*, July 25, 2000, p. B1; K. J. Dunham, "Back to Reality," *Wall Street Journal*, Apr. 12, 2001, p. R5; L. Babcock and S. Laschever, *Women Don't Ask: The High Cost of Avoiding Negotiation* (New York: Bantam Books, 2007); V. Slavina, "Why Women Must Ask," *Forbes*, June 17, 2013 (*www.forbes.com/sites/dailymuse/2013/06/17/why-women-must-ask-the-right-way-negotiation-advice-from-stanfords-margaret-a-neale/*).

26. Society for Human Resource Management, *Strategic Compensation Survey* (Alexandria, VA: author, 2000), pp. 35–47.

27. Society for Human Resource Management, "Use of Short Term Incentives Up," *SHRM Online*, Nov. 9, 2012 (*www.shrm.org*).

28. M. A. Jacobs, "The Legal Option," *Wall Street Journal*, Apr. 12, 2001, p. R9; Society for Human Resource Management, *Strategic Compensation Survey*, pp. 48–57.

29. P. Cappelli and M. J. Conyon, "Stock Option Exercise and Gift Exchange Relationships: Evidence for a Large US Company," NBER Working Paper No. 16814 (Cambridge, MA: National Bureau of Economic Research, 2012).

30. Society for Human Resource Management, *2012 Employee Job Satisfaction and Engagement* (Alexandria, VA: author, 2012).

31. B. Jones, M. Staubus, and D. N. Janich, "If Not Stock Options, Then What?" *Workspan*, Fall 2003, pp. 26–32; R. Simon, "With Options on the Outs, Alternatives Get a Look," *Wall Street Journal*, Apr. 28, 2004, p. D2.

32. "Employers Say Increased Competition Not Likely to Translate Into Signing Bonuses for New College Graduates," *IPMA-HR Bulletin*, Dec. 1, 2006, p. 1.

33. L. Morsch, "Return of the Signing Bonus?" CNN.com, Aug. 18, 2006 (*www.cnn.com/2006/US/Careers/08/18/cb.signing.bonus/*).

34. L. G. Klaff, "Tough Sell," *Workforce Management*, Nov. 2003, pp. 47–50; J. S. Lublin, "The Going Rate," *Wall Street Journal*, Jan. 11, 2000, p. B14.

35. J. M. Vick and J. S. Furlong, "The Logistics of a Dual-Career Search," *Chronicle of Higher Education*, Mar. 14, 2012 (*http://chronicle.com/article/the-logistics-of-a-dual-career/131140/*).

36. H. O'Neill, "Relocation Benefits Are on the Move," *Workforce*, Feb. 6, 2012 (*www.workforce.com*).

37. J. Barthiaume and L. Culpepper, "Hot Skills: Most Popular Compensation Strategies for Technical Expertise," Jan. 14, 2008 (*www.shrm.org*).

38. J. S. Lublin, "You Should Negotiate a Severance Package—Even Before the Job Starts," *Wall Street Journal*, May 1, 2001, p. B1.

39. C. Patton, "Parting Ways," *Human Resource Executive*, May 20, 2002, pp. 50–51.

40. D. M. Rousseau, V. T. Ho, and J. Greenberg. "I-Deals: Idiosyncratic Terms in Employment Relationships," *Academy of Management Review*, 2006, 31, pp. 977–994.

41. M. A. Wheeler, "The Art of Haggling," Harvard Business School *Working Knowledge*, May 7, 2012 (*http://hbswk.hbs.edu/item/6922.html*).

42. C. C. Rosen, D. J. Slater, C. Chang, and R. E. Johnson, "Let's Make a Deal: Development and Validation of the Ex Post I-Deals Scale," *Journal of Management*, 2013, 39, pp. 709–742.

43. Rosen, Slater, Chang, and Johnson, "Let's Make a Deal: Development and Validation of the Ex Post I-Deals Scale"; S. Hornung, D. M. Rousseau, J. Glaser, P. Angerer, and M. Weigel, "Beyond

Top-Down and Bottom-Up Work Redesign: Customizing Job Content Through Idiosyncratic Deals," *Journal of Organizational Behavior*, 2010, 31, pp. 187–215.

44. S. Anand, P. R. Vidyarthi, R. C. Liden, and D. M. Rousseau, "Good Citizens in Poor-Quality Relationships: Idiosyncratic Deals as a Substitute for Relationship Quality," *Academy of Management Journal*, 2010, 53, pp. 970–988.

45. J. J. Meyers, D. V. Radack, and P. M. Yenerall, "Making the Most of Employment Contracts," *HR Magazine*, Aug. 1998, pp. 106–109; D. R. Sandler, "Noncompete Agreements," *Employment Management Today*, Fall 1997, pp. 14–19; S. G. Willis, "Protect Your Firm Against Former Employees' Actions," *HR Magazine*, Aug. 1997, pp. 117–122.

46. A. Smith, "Noncompetes Can Be Tough to Enforce When Former Employees Move," *HR News*, Apr. 10, 2006 (*www.shrm.org*).

47. M. Orgel, "Web Sites That Provide Salary Help," *Wall Street Journal*, Oct. 16, 2008, p. D5.

48. F. Dawkins, "Foiling Résumé Fraud," *Workforce*, Aug. 6, 2009 (*www.workforce.com*).

49. M. Himmelberg, "Counteroffers Grow More Commonplace," *Knight-Ridder Tribune Business News*, Feb. 6, 2007, p. 1.

50. J. S. Lublin, "How to Handle the Job Offer You Can't Afford," *Wall Street Journal*, Dec. 2, 2008, p. B9; J. Sammer, "Money Matters in the Hiring Process," *HR Magazine*, Sept. 2009, pp. 93–95.

51. S. Kwon and L. R. Weingart, "Unilateral Concessions From the Other Party: Concession Behavior, Attributions, and Negotiation Judgments," *Journal of Applied Psychology*, 2004, 89, pp. 263–278.

52. J. R. Curhan, H. A. Elfenbein, and G. J. Kilduff, "Getting Off on the Right Foot: Subjective Value Versus Economic Value in Predicting Longitudinal Job Outcomes From Job Offer Negotiations," *Journal of Applied Psychology*, 2009, 94, pp. 524–534.

53. D. S. Chapman and J. Webster, "Toward an Integrated Model of Applicant Reactions and Job Choice," *International Journal of Human Resource Management*, 2006, 17, pp. 1032–1057.

54. W. J. Becker, T. Connolly, and J. E. Slaughter, "The Effect of Job Offer Timing on Offer Acceptance, Performance, and Turnover," *Personnel Psychology*, 2010, 63, pp. 223–241.

55. T. Stefanik, "Ford Hit With Class-Action Lawsuit After Backing out of 100s of Jobs," *Canadian HR Reporter*, Mar. 8, 2010, p. 5.

56. K. Gurchiek, "Many Employers Wing Support of New Hires," *HR News*, Sept. 18, 2007 (*www. shrm.org*).

57. L. G. Klaff, "New Emphasis on First Impressions," *Workforce Management Online*, Mar. 2008 (*www.workforce.com*).

58. T. N. Bauer, T. Bodner, B. Erdogan, D. M. Truxillo, and J. S. Tucker, "Newcomer Adjustment During Organizational Socialization: A Meta-Analytic Review of Antecedents, Outcomes, and Methods," *Journal of Applied Psychology*, 2007, 92, pp. 707–721; J. D. Kammeyer-Mueller, C. R. Wanberg, A. L. Rubenstein, and Z. Song, "Support, Undermining, and Newcomer Socialization: Fitting in During the First 90 Days," *Academy of Management Journal*, 2013, 56, pp. 1104–1124.

59. J. Marquez, "Connecting a Virtual Workforce," *Workforce Management*, Sept. 22, 2008, pp. 23–25; F. Hansen, "Onboarding for Greater Engagement," *Workforce Management Online*, Oct. 2008 (*www.workforce.com*).

60. C. L. Adkins, "Previous Work Experience and Organizational Socialization: A Longitudinal Examination," *Academy of Management Journal*, 1995, 38, pp. 839–862.

61. Bauer et al., "Newcomer Adjustment During Organizational Socialization: A Meta-Analytic Review of Antecedents, Outcomes, and Methods."

62. G. T. Chao, A. M. O'Leary-Kelly, S. Wolf, H. J. Klein, and P. D. Gardner, "Organizational Socialization: Its Content and Consequences," *Journal of Applied Psychology*, 1994, 79, pp. 730–743.

63. A. D. Wright, "Experts: Web-Based Onboarding Can Aid Employee Retention," July 14, 2008 (*www.shrm.org*).

64. M. J. Wesson and C. I. Gogus, "Shaking Hands With a Computer: An Examination of Two Methods of Organizational Newcomer Orientation," *Journal of Applied Psychology*, 2005, 90, pp. 1018–1026.

65. J. Mullich, "They're Hired: Now the Real Recruiting Begins," *Workforce Management Online*, Feb. 9, 2004 (*www.workforce.com*).

66. J. S. Lublin, "Job Candidates Get Manual From Boss: How to Handle Me," *Wall Street Journal*, Jan. 7, 2003, p. B1.

67. M. Hammers, "Optimas Award Financial Impact: National City Corporation," *Workforce Management Online*, Feb. 9, 2004 (*www.workforce.com*).

68. USLegal, "Negligent Hiring Law and Legal Definition" (*http://definitions.uslegal.com/n/negligent-hiring/*), accessed 9/13/10; S. Smith, "Negligent Hiring" (*http://sideroad.com/human_resources/negligent_hiring.html*), accessed 9/13/10; R. K. Robinson, G. M. Franklin, and R. F. Wayland, "Employment Regulation in the Workplace" (Armonk, NY: M. E. Sharpe, 2010), pp. 334–336.

69. Bureau of National Affairs, "Recruiting Exposure to Negligent Hiring Suits Requires Preventive Action, Practitioner Says," *Daily Labor Report*, June 18, 1998, p. C1; F. Hansen, "Taking 'Reasonable Action' to Avoid Negligent Hiring Claims," *Workforce Management*, Dec. 11, 2006, pp. 31–33.

70. Bennett, Polden, and Rubin, *Employment Relationships: Law and Practice*, pp. 2-1 to 2-65.

# The Staffing Organizations Model

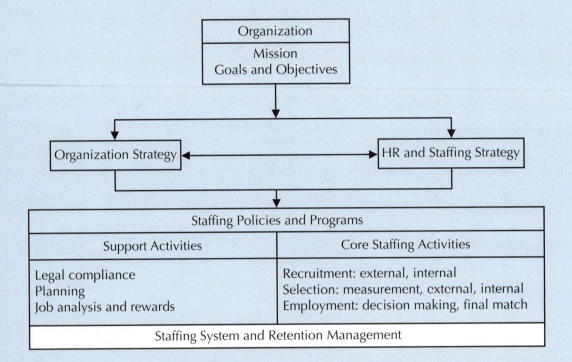

# PART SIX

## Staffing System and Retention Management

# CHAPTER THIRTEEN

## Staffing System Management

**Learning Objectives and Introduction**
    Learning Objectives
    Introduction

**Administration of Staffing Systems**
    Organizational Arrangements
    Policies and Procedures
    Human Resource Information Systems
    Outsourcing

**Evaluation of Staffing Systems**
    Staffing Process
    Staffing Process Results
    Calculating Staffing Metrics
    Customer Satisfaction

**Legal Issues**
    Record Keeping and Privacy
    EEO Report
    Legal Audits
    Training for Managers and Employees
    Dispute Resolution

**Summary**

**Discussion Questions**

**Ethical Issues**

**Applications**

**Endnotes**

## LEARNING OBJECTIVES AND INTRODUCTION

### Learning Objectives

- Recognize the importance of effective policies and procedures for staffing
- Understand the importance of concrete, fair policies and procedures in selection
- Evaluate the advantages and disadvantages of outsourcing staffing processes
- Understand how to evaluate the various results of staffing processes
- Develop metrics for the measurement of staffing systems
- Recognize the legal issues involving record keeping and applicant/employee privacy
- Plan for effective dispute resolution

### Introduction

Up to this point, we have covered how organizations plan for effective staffing system implementation, recruit candidates, evaluate candidates, select from candidates, and make a final match. We now take a step back from these operational issues and evaluate whether an overall staffing system is functioning effectively. Staffing systems involve complex processes and decisions that require organizational direction, coordination, and evaluation. Most organizations must create mechanisms for managing their staffing system and its components. Management of staffing systems requires consideration of both administration and evaluation, as well as legal issues.

The evaluation of the effectiveness of a staffing system as a whole has become a central issue for human resource (HR) managers. An increased push for accountability in all areas of HR that began over 20 years ago has become a permanent feature of the organizational landscape. Staffing managers who are successfully adapting to this environment focus on analytics, which demonstrate relationships between a variety of staffing functions and organizational performance.[1]

The chapter starts by describing how the staffing function operates within the HR department of many organizations. The role and nature of staffing policies and procedures in administering the staffing function are explained, as is the use of human resource information systems (HRISs) to enhance efficient operation of staffing systems. Next, a discussion of ways to evaluate the effectiveness of the staffing function is presented. Various results of the staffing process are examined to gauge the effectiveness of staffing systems. Compilation and analysis of staffing system costs are also suggested as an evaluation technique. Finally, assessment of customer (hiring manager, applicant) satisfaction is presented as an important approach to the evaluation of staffing systems. Legal issues surround the management of staffing systems. Partly, this involves matters of compiling various records and reports and of conducting legal audits of staffing activities. Also discussed are training for managers and employees, and mechanisms for dispute resolution.

# ADMINISTRATION OF STAFFING SYSTEMS

## Organizational Arrangements

An organizational arrangement refers to how the organization structures itself to conduct HR and staffing activities, often within the HR department. The arrangements vary considerably, and both organization size and type (integrated or multiple business) make a difference in the arrangement used.

Consider the following data from the US Census Bureau on organization size. The vast majority of organizations (5.9 million) have fewer than 100 employees, and those organizations employ about 36% of total employees. At the other extreme, only 18,000 organizations have 500+ employees, and they employ about 50% of total employees. In between are about 89,000 organizations, each one employing between 100 and 499 employees.[2]

In organizations with fewer than 100 employees, staffing is most likely to be conducted by the owner, the president, or the work unit manager. Only a small percentage (13%) of these organizations have an HR department that is responsible for staffing. Among these small organizations, staffing activities are quite varied in terms of establishing job requirements, recruitment sources, recruitment communication techniques, selection methods, decision making, and job offers. As organization size increases, so does the likelihood of there being an HR department and a unit within it responsible for staffing. But the exact configuration of the HR department and staffing activities will depend on whether the organization is composed of business units pursuing a common business product or service (an integrated business organization) or a diverse set of products or services (a multiple-business organization).[3] Because of its diversity, the multiple-business organization will likely not try to have a major, centralized corporate HR department. Rather, it will have a small corporate HR department, with a separate HR department within each business unit. In this arrangement, staffing activities will be quite decentralized, with some guidance and expertise from the corporate HR department.

An integrated business organization will likely have a highly centralized HR department at the corporate level, with a much smaller HR presence at the plant, store, or site level. As pertains to staffing, such centralization creates economies of scale and consistency in staffing policies and processes, as well as hiring standards and new hire quality.

A more detailed example of a centralized organizational arrangement for an integrated-business, multiplant manufacturing organization is shown in Exhibit 13.1. As can be seen, the vice president of HR oversees the work of several corporate HR functions, including the director of employment and EEO/AA. Under this specific function, which is most directly involved in staffing activities, there are also specialists in areas including recruiting, internal placement, testing, and interviewing. The site manager reports directly to the vice president of operations. Each site's HR activities are a combination of corporate policies and procedures as coordinated

**EXHIBIT 13.1    Example of HR Department and Employment (Staffing) Function**

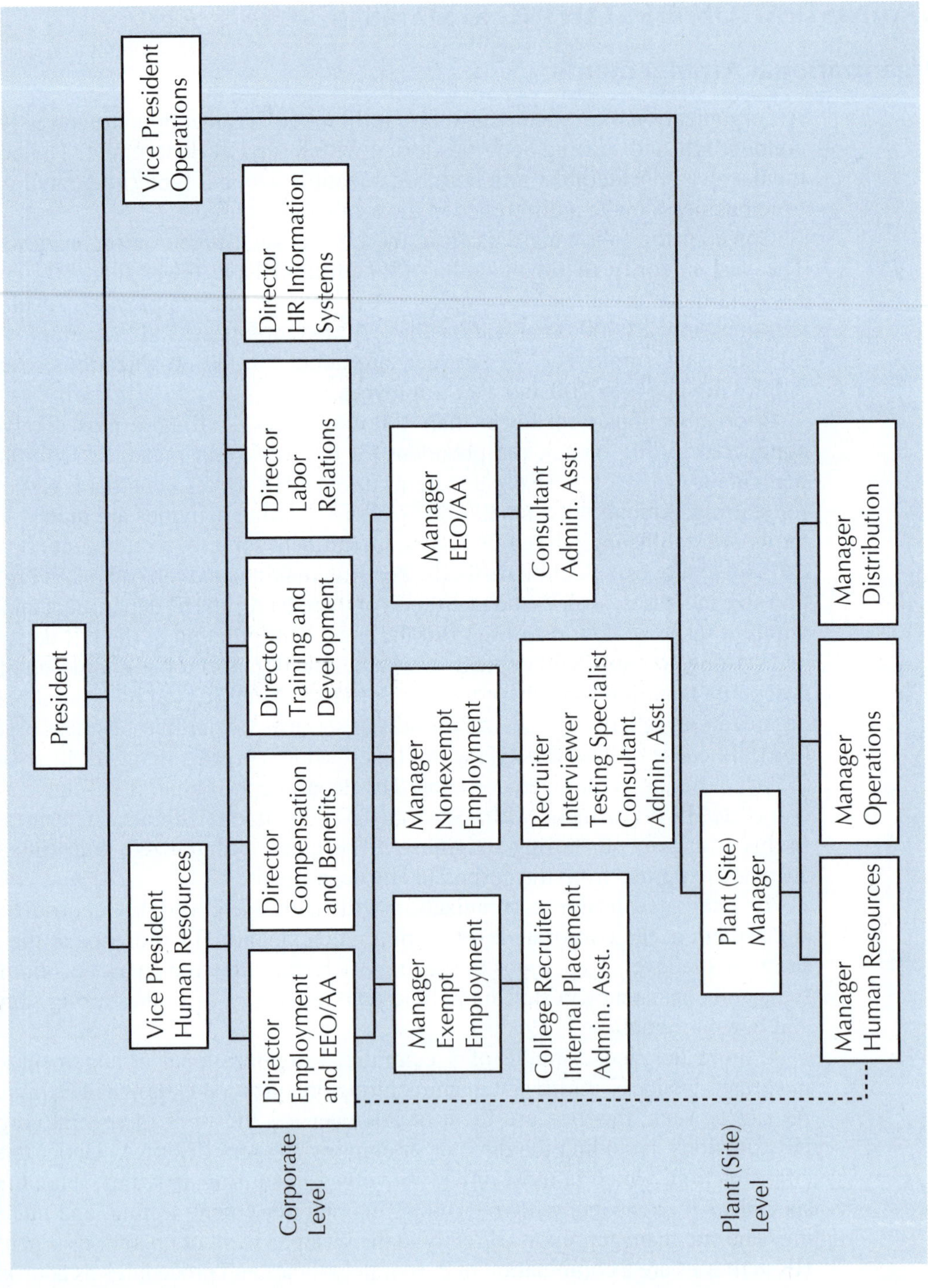

Corporate Level

- President
- Vice President Operations
- Vice President Human Resources
  - Director Employment and EEO/AA
    - Manager Exempt Employment
      - College Recruiter
      - Internal Placement
      - Admin. Asst.
    - Manager Nonexempt Employment
      - Recruiter
      - Interviewer
      - Testing Specialist
      - Consultant
      - Admin. Asst.
  - Director Compensation and Benefits
  - Director Training and Development
  - Director Labor Relations
    - Manager EEO/AA
      - Consultant
      - Admin. Asst.
  - Director HR Information Systems

Plant (Site) Level

- Plant (Site) Manager
  - Manager Human Resources
  - Manager Operations
  - Manager Distribution

by the site manager. The HR manager reports directly to the site manager but implements strategies for recruiting, placement, testing, and interviewing established at the corporate level to meet needs identified by the site manager.

This close relationship between the corporate HR function and operational management points to a critical issue. Experts emphasize that an effective HR function must be aware of organizational strategy, build capabilities to execute strategies, integrate talent and organizational practices, and advocate for effective implementation of policies and procedures.[4] For the operational and staffing functions to work well together in organizations, there must be frequent communication among all managers in the process. If the staffing function is successful, it will help site managers and line managers easily and quickly fill vacancies with qualified individuals. A failure in coordination and communication, on the other hand, can make the staffing function little more than an administrative hurdle that managers will try to circumvent whenever possible.

Those employed within the staffing function must also work closely with members of all the other HR function areas. Staffing can contribute to organizational success only if it complements practices in the compensation, training and development, and employee relations areas.[5] For example, staffing members must coordinate their activities with the compensation and benefits staff in developing policies on the economic components of job offers, such as starting pay, hiring bonuses, and special perks. Staffing activities must also be closely coordinated with the training and development function. This will be needed to identify training needs for external, entry-level new hires, as well as for planning transfer and promotion-enhancing training experiences for current employees. The director of employee relations will work with the staffing area to determine how policies and practices will be combined with corporate communications and other programs to improve employee morale and motivation. Record keeping, staffing software, and EEO/AA statistics requirements will be worked out with the director of HR information systems.

## Policies and Procedures

It is highly desirable to have written policies and procedures to guide the administration of staffing systems. Understanding the importance of policies and procedures first requires definition of these terms.

A policy is a selected course or guiding principle. It is an objective to be sought through appropriate actions. For example, the organization might have a promotion-from-within policy as follows: "It is the intent of XXX organization to fill from within all vacancies above the entry level, except in instances of critical, immediate need for a qualified person unavailable internally." This policy makes it clear that promotion from within is the desired objective; the only exception is in the absence of an immediately available, qualified current employee.

A procedure is a prescribed routine or way of acting in similar situations. It provides the rules that govern a particular course of action. To carry out the promotion-from-within policy, for example, the organization may follow specific procedures for listing and communicating the vacancy, identifying eligible applicants, and assessing the qualifications of the applicants.

Policies and procedures can improve the strategic focus of the staffing area.[6] When there are clearly articulated systems of policies and procedures, it is possible to consider the meaning and function of the entire system at a strategic level. On the other hand, poorly thought out or inconsistent policies and procedures result in HR managers spending an inordinate amount of time playing catch-up or "putting out fires," as inconsistent behavior across organizational units inevitably leads to employee complaints. Without clear staffing policies, managers scramble to develop solutions to recruiting or selection needs at the last minute. Dealing with these routine breakdowns in procedures leaves less time to consult organizational goals or consider alternatives. The final result is inefficiency and wasted time.

Policies and procedures can also greatly enhance the perceived justice of staffing activities. Research conducted in a wide variety of organizations has consistently shown that employees perceive organizational decision making as most fair when decisions are based on facts rather than social influence or personal biases, when decision-making criteria are clearly communicated, and when the process is consistently followed across all affected individuals.[7] The use of well-articulated policies and procedures can increase perceived justice considerably if they meet all of the requirements for perceived justice. There are bottom-line implications: employee perceptions of organizational justice have been linked to increased intention to pursue a job in the recruiting context, increased intention to accept a job in the selection context, increased satisfaction and commitment in job assignments, and decreased intention to sue a former employer in the layoff context.[8]

What are the keys to writing staffing policies and procedures that enhance organizational effectiveness? Exhibit 13.2 summarizes the most important principles.[9] The examples provided in the figure are not meant to be exhaustive; at every stage there are many alternative elements of the staffing policy and procedure development process. Each organization needs to consider its business context to know what the right elements of this process will be.

The single most important idea underlying every one of these principles is maintaining a clear linkage between organizational goals and staffing policies and procedures. The policy and procedure process really is a cycle, in which existing practices are continually revised to match environmental demands. The plan is therefore based on identifying strategic goals, employing specific methods to achieve these goals, measuring the success of these methods, and responding to ongoing information.

The first stage is determining the overarching HR strategy, as described in Chapter 3. The second stage involves defining specific objectives for staffing policies and procedures. The third stage is communicating policies and procedures to employees and ensuring that they are implemented correctly. As we noted previously, one of the major benefits of policies and procedures is the clarity they provide to employees and the perceived justice that comes from explicit rules

---

**EXHIBIT 13.2**   **Guidelines for Creating Effective Staffing Policies and Procedures**

| Planning Process Stage | Example Elements of the Process |
| --- | --- |
| Stage 1: Determine the overarching HR strategy and priorities that guide all policies and procedures | • Align employee capabilities and efforts with annual strategic plans<br>• Maintain diversity of employee expertise and perspectives<br>• Deliver services in a timely and cost-effective manner |
| Stage 2: Define specific objectives for staffing policies and procedures | • Evaluate KSAOs and competencies that will guide the recruiting and selection process<br>• Recruit highly qualified individuals from a variety of sources<br>• Use standardized and validated selection processes and tools<br>• Coordinate all facets of the staffing process with managers to ensure positions are filled quickly and effectively |
| Stage 3: Communicate policies and procedures to all employees and ensure their implementation | • Provide all employees with links to policy and procedure statements on the company intranet or through a policy and procedure manual<br>• Train managers in techniques for implementing policies and procedures<br>• Provide experts who can explain policies and procedures, answer questions, and take suggestions<br>• Monitor ongoing compliance with policies and procedures |
| Stage 4: Evaluate and revise existing policies and procedures | • Analyze staffing metrics<br>• Perform periodic reviews of manager opinions regarding policy and procedure outcomes<br>• Review changes to organizational and HR strategy to determine new staffing strategy and priorities<br>• Assess new technology and techniques for improving staffing outcomes |

for decision making. Organizations that communicate the content of policies and procedures make the most of this benefit. The fourth stage is evaluating whether policies and procedures are effective in achieving goals. Based on this evidence, new policies and procedures will be implemented when HR strategy and priorities change (such as a shift toward a focus on competencies linked to innovation), when existing policies and procedures are not effective (such as finding that not enough qualified individuals are being recruited through current methods), or when new methods for achieving goals are developed (such as the development of more accurate or informative measures of employee KSAO levels).

## Human Resource Information Systems

Staffing activities generate and use considerable information. Job descriptions, application materials, résumés, correspondence, applicant profiles, applicant flow and tracking, and reports are examples of the types of information that are necessary ingredients for the operation of a staffing system. Naturally, problems regarding what types of information to generate, along with how to file, access, and use it, will arise when managing a staffing system. Thus, management of a staffing system involves management of an HRIS.

Most organizations with a sufficient number of employees to warrant a dedicated HR department have integrated the staffing function with HRISs. Many vendors have developed specialized HRIS interfaces that can track the critical processes and outcomes involved in staffing, as shown in Exhibit 13.3. The features listed in the exhibit are meant to be illustrative rather than exhaustive; new functionality is continually being added to HRISs. Providing hard data on staffing system outcomes can increase the credibility of staffing services in organizations. The increased availability of data on staffing processes following from the use of HRISs means that organizations will also be able to track the efficacy of policies and procedures with accuracy. Staffing policies that do not show returns on investments can be eliminated, whereas those that show positive results can be expanded. Organizations that have outsourced staffing functions should also be aware of the information provided by HRISs and should ensure that they are receiving accurate and comprehensive reports from their vendor's HRIS database. Organizations considering outsourcing options should request historical data showing the efficacy of staffing systems in other organizations before committing resources toward any particular vendor. If an outsourcing service provider cannot provide these data, this may be a sign that it does not communicate well or may not be very rigorous about evaluating the quality of its services.

Web-based staffing management systems are also available from application service providers (ASPs) or software-as-a-service (SaaS) providers. With such systems, the vendor provides both the hardware (e.g., servers, scanners) and the software, as well as day-to-day management of the system. Recruiters and hiring managers access the system through a web browser. Kenexa's BrassRing system is an example of what an ASP can provide. Designed to facilitate the management of all aspects of the selection system, this customizable set of staffing tools can be designed to work for a wide variety of organizations. For example, the system can link an organization with a variety of online and social media applications to advertise a position. Applicants can then directly enter their qualifications into the system. Other tools facilitate the management of recruiting events, like campus visits or job fairs, including rapid screening of applicants and interview schedules. Alternatively, for organizations that outsource recruiting, tools are available to

**EXHIBIT 13.3** **Human Resources Information Systems for Staffing Tasks**

| Staffing Task | HRIS Functionality |
|---|---|
| Legal compliance | EEO data analysis and reports<br>Policy and procedure writing guides<br>Statistical analysis for demonstrating job relatedness |
| Planning | Tracking historical demand for employees<br>Forecasting workforce supply<br>Replacement and succession planning |
| Job analysis | Database of job titles and responsibilities<br>Database of competencies across jobs<br>Comparing job descriptions with O*Net |
| External recruitment and selection | Job posting reports<br>Time-to-fill hiring requisitions<br>Applicant logs and status and tracking reports<br>Recruitment source effectiveness<br>Electronic résumé routing<br>Keyword scanning of applications<br>New hire reports (numbers, qualifications, assignments)<br>Validation of selection systems |
| Internal recruitment and selection | Employee succession planning<br>Intranet for job postings<br>Skills databases<br>Tracking progress through assessment centers<br>Job performance reports<br>Individual development plans |
| Final match | Tracking job acceptance rates<br>Contract development<br>Tracking employee socialization progress |
| Staffing system management | System cost reports<br>Return on investments<br>Record-keeping functions |
| Retention | Collection and analysis of job satisfaction data<br>Tracking differences in turnover rates across locations and time<br>Documenting performance management and/or progressive discipline |

manage information flow across multiple hiring agencies or consulting companies. Managers can then access these applications directly and use a variety of search criteria to identify applicants who best match the job requirements. Once individuals are in the system, screening tests can be performed prior to face-to-face interviews. Some modules are even able to facilitate the onboarding process by creating hiring checklists, online forms, and so forth. Several trends continue to alter the landscape of HRISs.[10] Many systems now allow frontline managers and employees to access their HR records and engage with the system directly rather than working through a centralized HR employee. These processes are implemented to facilitate internal staffing functions. Employees can use self-service pages to stay up to date with skills needed in the organization through succession management plans, find training that will help them prepare for higher-level positions, and submit applications for openings. The increased availability of web-based solutions also makes it easier for even small employers with limited resources to provide a full suite of automated HRIS solutions for staffing.

Social networking applications for information sharing, mirroring Facebook or Twitter, have become much more common elements in HRISs. They have been particularly popular elements of employee orientation or "onboarding" programs because they allow newcomers to interact with established employees quickly.

### Effectiveness

When assessing HRISs for staffing tasks, HR managers must carefully consider their needs and goals for the entire HRIS today and in the future.[11] Some of the key factors that differentiate HRISs include whether the system is hosted on-site or as SaaS on a remote server run by an HRIS provider, the degree and nature of custom reporting provided by the HRIS, the ability to generate reports that integrate a variety of HR functions, and the degree to which systems for recruiting, selection, record keeping, orientation, benefits, and compensation are integrated with one another. Other factors to consider include how long the service provider has been in business, how often it upgrades its system, how many other customers the provider has, who those clients are, and, of course, costs. The sheer complexity of deciding which HRIS to use means that the decision is seldom made by a single individual; rather, the decision is made by joint committees made up of executives, members of the HR staff, and information technology professionals.

Staffing technologies have a multitude of potential positive and negative effects. Many of these effects extend beyond process improvement (e.g., speed of staffing) and cost reduction. While these two potential advantages are very important, they need to be considered within the context of other potential advantages, and especially the myriad potential disadvantages. The organization should proceed with caution and due diligence in deciding how to use new staffing technologies, evaluating products and vendors, establishing service agreements with vendors, and conducting planning prior to implementation. It is also clear that even once the staffing technologies are implemented, monitoring and system improvement will need to be periodically undertaken.

## Outsourcing

Outsourcing refers to contracting out work to a vendor or third-party administrator. In Chapter 3, we discussed outsourcing work for noncore organizational processes. Here, we consider the case when certain staffing functions are outsourced. Examples of specific staffing activities that are outsourced include a search for temporary employees, an executive search, drug testing, skill testing, background checks, job fairs, employee relocation, assessment centers, and affirmative action planning. A number of factors that influence the decision of whether to outsource are reviewed in Exhibit 13.4. Outsourcing decisions require consideration of organizational strategy, size of the organization, and the skills required. Thus, the

**EXHIBIT 13.4**   **Comparison of Outsourced and In-House Staffing**

|  | Outsourced | In-House |
|---|---|---|
| Strategy | Staffing functions not linked to core organizational competencies | Staffing functions linked to core organizational competencies |
| Size | Small organizations, organizations without a centralized HR function, or organizations with continual hiring needs | Large organizations where economies of scale will pay off or for executive selection tasks where knowledge of the organization is crucial |
| Skills required | General human capital, such as that easily obtained through education | Firm-specific human capital, such as required knowledge of organizational policies or specific personality traits |
| Examples | • Recruiting packaging employees in a small warehouse<br>• Screening registered nurses for a long-term care facility<br>• Developing a website for automatically screening entry-level candidates<br>• Providing temporary employees for a highly cyclical manufacturing organization | • Recruiting creative talent for an advertising firm<br>• Selecting members of the organization's executive team<br>• Providing employee orientation<br>• Recruiting and selecting employees for a large retail organization<br>• Recruiting and selecting individuals for an interdependent work team |

decision about whether to outsource is not an all-or-nothing proposition. Some staffing functions are more easily outsourced, so many organizations use outsourcing for some tasks but not for others.

One of the benefits of outsourcing is that it frees the internal HR department from performing day-to-day administrative activities that could be more efficiently managed by an external organization. Reviews of best practices show that the major advantages of outsourcing include access to superior information from specialists, access to technology and services that are difficult to implement internally, and general cost reduction.[12] By eliminating the day-to-day work of maintaining staffing systems, it is possible to dedicate more energy to analyzing and improving the effectiveness of the staffing system as a whole. Because specialized staffing firms work with the same processes all the time, they can develop specialized, highly efficient systems that deliver results more quickly and more cheaply than an organization's in-house staffing services. An external staffing firm will have more resources to keep up with developments in its area. For example, a firm that specializes in EEO compliance will always have the latest information regarding court decisions and changing precedents.

These advantages of outsourcing should always be weighed against the potential downfalls of outsourcing too many staffing functions or outsourcing functions too rapidly. Experts in this area warn that the expected benefits will not materialize if the decision to outsource is not accompanied by a complete transformation of the way HR is delivered.[13] Organizations that outsource should hold external providers accountable by keeping track of staffing metrics, especially since specialized staffing firms should have access to better systems for managing and reporting staffing data. Someone inside the organization should have final, bottom-line accountability for any outsourced services. In many organizations, there is resistance to outsourcing, and employees may feel that the company is treating them impersonally if questions or concerns about employment are directed to an external vendor. Thus, if employees have complaints or concerns about staffing services, they should be able to discuss their concerns with someone inside the organization who can respond to them.

One increasingly popular type of vendor is a professional employer organization (PEO). It is similar to a staffing firm, but unlike a staffing firm, a PEO provides a wider range of HR services and has a long-term commitment to the client. Under a typical arrangement, the client organization enters into a contractual relationship with a PEO to conduct some or all HR activities and functions. The client and the PEO are considered co-employers of record. A PEO is particularly appealing to small employers because it can provide special HR expertise and technical assistance, conduct the administrative activities and transactions of an HR department, provide more affordable employee benefits, meet legal obligations (payroll, withholding, workers' compensation, and unemployment insurance), and manage legal compliance. A survey of over 740 small businesses suggests that using a PEO was associated with higher levels of satisfaction with HR outcomes and more efficient implementation of HR processes relative to small businesses that did not use a PEO, and that the more functions the company outsourced to the PEO, the greater the results.[14]

The health care industry has often turned to outsourcing for staffing needs, with individual hospitals hoping to learn best practices that have worked in other facilities. For example, Fauquier Health, a small hospital in Virginia, was experiencing difficulty in finding and retaining qualified staff. It turned to three HR outsourcing firms that had expertise in the areas of situational assessments, standardized testing, and health care hiring practices. The firms worked in concert to develop a selection tool that incorporated simulations to assess interpersonal skills, cognitive ability and personality tests, and medical knowledge. These different selection tools, when used together, helped Fauquier achieve a 98% retention rate for the year. Representatives from Fauquier note that the previous experience these firms had in implementing staffing solutions across other organizations greatly facilitated the process.[15]

Another example of successful staffing outsourcing comes from Chequed, a firm that specializes in applicant assessment. By studying competencies required for hundreds of positions over time, it was able to create a standardized questionnaire that can assess qualifications quickly, with assessments tailor-made to specific job requirements. In addition to gathering information regarding which applicants are most qualified, it can also note competency gaps that might need to be addressed in the future. Because it has data across so many different jobs and companies—data that are much more comprehensive than the data of an in-house HR function—it can more easily identify which characteristics are associated with success. As with the previous example, the goal of using this deep knowledge of job fit is to allow the HR department to focus its attention on organization fit and its unique strategic needs.[16]

At the outset, it is important to remember that the agreement (often called a service-level agreement, or SLA) with the vendor is usually negotiable, and that flaws in the negotiating stage are often responsible for many problems that may subsequently occur in the relationship. Using some form of legal or consulting assistance might be desirable, especially for the organization that has little or no staffing outsourcing experience.

There are many issues to discuss and negotiate. Awareness of these factors and advance preparation with regard to the organization's preferences and requirements are critical to a successful negotiation with a potential vendor. The factors include the actual staffing services sought and provided, client control rights (e.g., monitoring of the vendor's personnel and the software to be used), fees and other costs, guaranteed improvements in service levels and cost savings, benchmarking metrics and performance reviews, and willingness to hire the organization's own employees to provide expertise and coordination. On top of these factors, the choice of vendor should take into account the vendor's past track record and familiarity with the organization's industry.[17]

## EVALUATION OF STAFFING SYSTEMS

Evaluation of staffing systems entails an examination of the effectiveness of the total system. The evaluation should focus on the operation of the staffing process, the results and costs of the process, and the satisfaction of customers of the staffing system.

### Staffing Process

The staffing process establishes and governs the flow of employees into, within, and out of the organization. Evaluation of the process itself requires mapping the intended process, identifying any deviations from the intended process, and planning corrective actions to reduce or eliminate the deviations. The intent of such an evaluation is to ensure standardization of the staffing process, remove bottlenecks in operation, and improve speed of operation.

Standardization refers to the consistency of operation of the organization's staffing system. Use of standardized staffing systems is desirable for several reasons. First, standardization ensures that the same KSAO information is gathered from all job applicants, which, in turn, is a key requirement for reliably and validly measuring these KSAOs. Second, standardization ensures that all applicants receive the same information about job requirements and rewards. Thus, all applicants can make equally informed evaluations of the organization. Third, standardization will enhance applicants' perceptions of the procedural fairness of the staffing system and of the decisions made about them by the organization. As noted previously, perceived fairness is closely associated with employees' attitudes toward the organization and their motivation to perform. Finally, standardized staffing systems are less likely to generate legal challenges and more likely to maintain diversity; both statutes and case law advocate for consistent treatment of all employees.

Mapping out the staffing process involves constructing a staffing flowchart. The staffing flowchart shown in Exhibit 13.5 depicts the staffing system of a medium-sized (580 employees) high-tech printing and lithography company. It shows the actual flow of staffing activities, and both organization and applicant decision points, from the time a vacancy occurs until the time it is filled with a new hire.

A detailed inspection of the chart reveals the following information about the organization's staffing system:

1. It is a generic system used for both entry-level and higher-level jobs.
2. For higher-level jobs, vacancies are first posted internally (thus showing a recruitment philosophy emphasizing a commitment to promotion from within). Entry-level jobs are filled externally.
3. External recruitment sources (colleges, advertising, and employment agencies) are used only if the current applicant file yields no qualified applicants.

**EXHIBIT 13.5   Staffing Flowchart for Medium-Sized Printing Company**

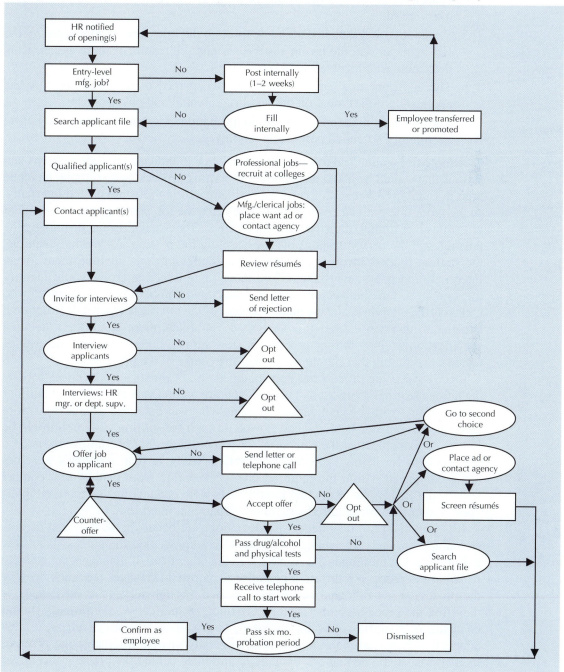

4. Initial assessments are made using biographical information (application blanks, résumés), and the results of these assessments determine who will be interviewed.

5. Substantive assessments are made through the interview(s) conducted by the HR manager and the hiring supervisor, and the results of these assessments determine who receives the job offer.

6. The applicant may counteroffer, and acceptance of the final offer by the applicant is conditional on passing drug/alcohol and physical tests.

7. The new hire undergoes a six-month probationary employment period before becoming a so-called permanent employee.

A more fine-grained analysis is then conducted to indicate the specific steps and actions that should be taken throughout the staffing process. For example, it can be seen in Exhibit 13.5 that non-entry-level manufacturing jobs are posted internally, so the more fine-grained analysis would describe the job posting process—content of the posting, timing of the posting, mechanisms for circulating and displaying the posting, and the person responsible for handling the posting. As another example, the staffing process involves contacting qualified applicants, inviting them for an interview, and interviewing them. The more fine-grained analysis would identify the amount of time between the initial contact and completion of interviews, who conducts the interview, and the nature/content of the interview (such as a structured, situational interview). After this analysis is complete, there would be a detailed specification of the staffing process in flow terms, along with specific events, actions, and timing that should occur over the course of the process.

Once the staffing process has been mapped out, the next step is to check for any deviations that have occurred. This will require an analysis of some past staffing "transactions" with job applicants, following what was done and what actions were taken as the applicants entered and flowed through the staffing system. It might be found, for example, that the content of the job postings did not conform to specific requirements for listing tasks and necessary KSAOs, or that interviews were not being conducted within the required one-week period from date of first contact with a qualified applicant, or that interviewers were conducting unstructured interviews rather than the required structured, situational interview.

It is important to understand why deviations are occurring so they can be corrected appropriately. If managers simply do not know what the process is or how to implement it, training is the solution. On the other hand, if managers are actively resisting the process, a different response is required. Manager feedback on why the process is not followed should be solicited through surveys or interviews. If they find the process cumbersome, inefficient, or ineffective, the process should be changed: if staffing does not contribute to organizational effectiveness, it must adapt. If it is not possible or if it is strategically unwise to change the process, then efforts should be made to explain the rationale behind the process; incentives might be considered to align manager motivation with organizational interests.

Getting managers to participate in the process is crucial, because managers are much more engaged when they are directly involved.[18]

## Staffing Process Results

In the past, it was commonly argued that most of the processes involved in staffing were too subjective or difficult to quantify. As a result, staffing managers could not provide representatives from finance and accounting with the hard cost-effectiveness data they were looking for. Fortunately, a dramatic increase in the availability and functionality of database software in recent years means that staffing system effectiveness can be assessed much more readily. HRISs can catalog and quickly display recruiting, hiring, retention, and job performance data. HR scholars have developed standardized metrics based on these sources of information that can help staffing managers communicate the business case for staffing services across the organization.[19]

Exhibit 13.6 provides a flowchart for using metrics to evaluate and update staffing processes. The first step is to collect and synthesize the objectives of the staffing process that were developed in Stage 2 of policy and procedure creation (reviewed in Exhibit 13.2). The second step is to develop metrics that are associated with those objectives. There should be a very close relationship between the objectives of the staffing process and the objectives that are selected. Simply because an HR-related outcome is readily available in the HRIS does not necessarily mean that assessing and analyzing it will be informative. The third step is to actually gather, analyze, and evaluate metrics. Both internal and external benchmarks can be useful here. An internal benchmark can evaluate whether some business units

**EXHIBIT 13.6   Using Metrics for Staffing Process Evaluation**

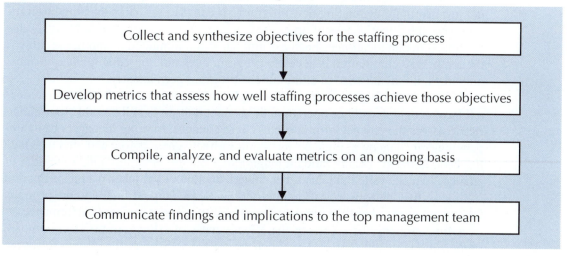

are in greater need of attention than others, and it can evaluate trends in HR outcomes over time. External benchmarks can evaluate whether your organization is achieving exceptional, average, or poor results relative to other organizations in your industry or area. Finally, it is essential that these findings be communicated effectively to top management teams. Steps for correcting any problems identified in the process should be highlighted, along with suggestions for how to improve.

This strategic planning and evaluation process is an essential component of staffing system management. If there are no attempts to monitor and check the outcomes of staffing systems, it is likely that systems that may have been effective in the past will remain in place long after they have failed to obtain desired results. Of course, there is no guarantee that HR programs will prove to be effective when put to the test; experienced managers who have used staffing system metrics often find that new staffing systems may not represent a significant improvement.

One method for evaluating the efficacy of staffing programs is to use the scientific technique of split samples.[20] As an example, a split sample analysis might begin with the premise that a new recruiting program will affect operational outcomes by attracting more qualified employees, improving the organization's ability to respond to staffing requisitions quickly, and reducing long-range turnover. The specific metrics for this proposed program include measures of employee qualifications, time-to-hire for position openings taken from the organization's HRIS, and unit turnover rates. In a split sample analysis, the target employee population is split in half, and the new HR program is initiated with only one of these halves. In this case, perhaps one region of a national chain would serve as the experimental group for the new recruiting program. This group's outcome would be compared with the rest of the organization, which did not use the new recruiting program. After the program has had an opportunity to work, representatives from HR can compare the metrics from the experimental sample with areas of the company where the new recruiting system was not employed. The split sample technique is not just useful for evaluating new programs; it can also assess an existing program. To assess the effectiveness of an existing program, the program is selectively discontinued in one location or business unit but still maintained in another section. If the temporary elimination of a costly program does not appreciably alter business outcomes, it may be wise to eliminate the program permanently.

If it is not possible to use the split sample technique because the workforce does not have geographically or operationally distinct units, it is still possible to use metrics to assess the efficacy of proposed system changes. Staffing managers can compare long-run data on a single business unit's effectiveness before and after a change has been initiated. This is called a longitudinal design, or simply put, a measure of change. To make valid inferences, benchmark data should be taken over a long period of time so that changes in staffing metrics can be reliably attributed to the program implementation rather than just routine variability in organizational performance.

A final strategy for assessing the effectiveness of HR programs is to compare organizational results with external benchmarks. The Society for Human Resource

Management (SHRM) provides a number of guidelines for developing and interpreting staffing metrics. Its website lists a number of benchmarking studies every year, including surveys that outline the use and perceived efficacies ranging across a number of practices, such as retention initiatives, e-recruiting, and diversity management. More detailed metrics can also be obtained from SHRM surveys of human capital benchmarks. Learning what other organizations are doing may not always be especially informative for determining the effectiveness of these policies and procedures for the organization. Many practices that work in one context may not be as useful in another context, and the research on HR bundling suggests that policies need to be implemented into a comprehensive system rather than just implementing individual practices in isolation. Therefore, although it is helpful to have some benchmark information, any new policies should be investigated for how well they are working in one's own organization.

The use of scientific methods with data from HRISs can help investigate whether common assumptions about staffing are supported in an organization.[21] For example, Thrivenet financial managers had assumed that new hires who had substantial prior experience in the industry were less likely to leave in their first year, but analysis of HR metrics showed that the exact opposite was true. Managers at Metropolitan Life assumed that there was no common profile of individuals who were most likely to succeed in their organization, but they found that they could identify future high performers by looking at the variety of job experiences employees had in the company. Although managers at the food service company Wawa Inc. suspected that hourly wage rates were influencing turnover among clerks, analysis of their staffing data found that part-time workers were more prone to turnover than full-time employees. This led the company to change its staffing mix to include a higher proportion of full-timers than it had previously. As these examples illustrate, HR metrics and associated analytics can be powerful tools for testing and refining beliefs about the effectiveness of a variety of practices related to staffing.

Over the course of the staffing process it is possible to develop quantitative indicators that show how effectively and efficiently the staffing system is operating. For example, how many applicants does a given vacancy attract on average? What percentage of job offers are accepted? What is the average number of days it takes to fill a vacancy? What percentage of new hires remain with the organization for one year posthire? Answers to such questions can be determined by tracking and analyzing applicant flows through the staffing pipeline.

In Exhibit 13.7 we offer some suggestions for the types of financial and process data that might be most useful for assessing the effectiveness of staffing systems overall. These suggestions are based on established research on best practices in the field. Following from several other writers, we divided the outcomes into four key categories: cost, timeliness, outcomes, and reactions. For each category, we present some representative metrics that might be useful, although there are many other measurable outcomes that might be relevant depending on an organization's goals.

**EXHIBIT 13.7**   **Common Staffing Metrics**

| | Cost | Timeliness | Outcomes | Reactions |
|---|---|---|---|---|
| Staffing system | Staffing budget<br>Staffing-to-employee ratios<br>Staffing expenses for full-time equivalents (FTEs) | Time to respond to requests | Evaluation of employee readiness for strategic goals | Communication<br>Satisfaction with services provided |
| Recruiting | Advertising expenses<br>Cost per applicant | Recruits per week | Number of recruits | Applicant quality |
| Selection | Test costs per candidate<br>Interview expenses<br>Cost per candidate | Time to hire<br>Days to fill | Competence<br>Workforce diversity | Candidate quality<br>Satisfaction with tests |
| Final match | Training costs per hire<br>Cost per hire | Days to start<br>Time to perform | Number of positions filled<br>Job performance | New employee satisfaction |
| Retention | Exit interview expenses<br>Replacement costs | Timely response to external offers | Voluntary separation rate<br>Involuntary separation rate | Employee job satisfaction |

Exhibit 13.8 shows the required layout for this tracking and analysis, as well as some staffing process results that may be easily calculated. In part A, the steps in the staffing process start with the announcement of a vacancy and run through a sequential flow of selection, job offer, offer acceptance, start as new hire, and retention. A timeline shows the average number of days to complete each step. For illustration purposes, it is assumed that 25 vacancies attracted 1,000 applicants who proceeded through the staffing process. Ultimately, all 25 vacancies were filled, and these new hires were tracked to see how many remained with the organization for six months and one year posthire.

In part B of Exhibit 13.8 are staffing process results indicators, also referred to as metrics, along with their calculations using data from the example. The first indicator is applicants per vacancy, which averaged 40. This is an indication of the effectiveness of recruitment activities to attract people to the organization. The second indicator is the yield ratio; it indicates the percentage of people who

**EXHIBIT 13.8**  **Evaluation of Staffing Process and Results: Example**

### A. Staffing Process Example
No. of vacancies filled = 25

| Process step | Vacancy announced (1) | Applicants (2) | Candidates (3) | Finalists (4) | Offer receiver (5) | Offer acceptance (6) | Start as new hire (7) | On the job | |
| | | | | | | | | Six months (8) | One year (9) |
|---|---|---|---|---|---|---|---|---|---|
| No. of people | 0 | 1,000 | 200 | 125 | 30 | 25 | 25 | 20 | 13 |
| Process time (avg. no. of days) | 0 | 14 | 21 | 28 | 35 | 42 | 44 | | |

### B. Staffing Process Results

Applicants/Vacancy = 1,000/25 = 40

Yield ratio:  candidates/applicant = 20%; new hires/applicant = 2.5%; offers accepted/received = 83.3%

Time lapse:  avg. days to offer = 35; avg. days to start = 44
(cycle time)

Retention rate:  $\dfrac{\text{on job six months}}{\text{new hires}}$ = 80% for six months;  $\dfrac{\text{on job one year}}{\text{new hires}}$ = 52% for first year moved on to one or more of the next steps in the staffing process. For example, the percentage of applicants who became candidates is 20%; the percentage of job offers accepted is 83.3%. The third indicator, time lapse (or cycle time), shows the average amount of time lapsed between each step in the staffing process. It can be seen that the average number of days to fill a vacancy is 44. The final indicator is retention rate; the six-month retention rate for new hires is 80% and the one-year rate is 52%.

These types of metrics are very useful barometers for gauging the pulse of the staffing flow. They have an objective, bottom-line nature that can be readily communicated to managers and others in the organization. These types of data are also very useful for comparative purposes. For example, the relative effectiveness and efficiency of staffing systems in two different units of the organization could be assessed by comparing their respective yield ratios. Additionally, the metrics of one staffing system could be compared over time. Such time-based comparisons are useful for tracking trends in effectiveness and efficiency. These comparisons are also used to help judge how well changes in staffing practices have worked to improve staffing process performance.

Increasingly, organizations are emphasizing time to fill vacancies as a key indicator of staffing effectiveness, because the shorter the vacancy time, the less the employee contribution forgone. Vacancies in sales jobs, for example, often mean lost sales and revenue generation, so shortening the time to fill means lessening the revenue forgone. Filling vacancies more quickly has led organizations to develop "speed hiring" and continuous hiring programs, in which they redesign their staffing systems to eliminate any excessive delays or bottlenecks in the process.[22]

Surveys of organizational practice in calculating staffing metrics should be consulted to learn about the many nuances involved.[23]

## Calculating Staffing Metrics

We have already outlined methods for assessing the costs and benefits of staffing policies and procedures. Below we present more specific methods for calculating these metrics.[24] Number of positions filled is a straightforward count of the number of individuals who accepted positions during the fiscal year. These data are collected for both internal and external candidates. Time to fill openings is estimated by assessing the number of days it takes for a job requisition to result in a job acceptance by a candidate. Hiring cost estimates are the sum of advertising, agency fees, employee referrals, travel costs for applicants and staff, relocation costs, and pay and benefits for recruiters. Hiring cost estimates are often indexed by dividing by the number of positions filled. As we noted in the chapters on recruiting, these cost estimates may be subdivided in a number of ways to get a better idea of which portions of the staffing process are comparatively more expensive. Turnover rates are also often used as staffing metrics. The annual turnover rate is estimated by dividing the number of separations per month by the average number of individuals employed each month and then taking the sum of these average month rates. Turnover rates are often differentiated based on whether they represent voluntary or involuntary turnover, which we cover in the next chapter. Other cost data, and how to calculate them, are also available.[25]

Another staffing metric is the staffing cost or efficiency ratio.[26] It takes into account that recruiting applicants for jobs with a higher compensation level might cost more due to such costs as executive search fees, recruitment advertising, relocation, and so forth. The formula is total staffing cost ratio = total staffing costs / total compensation recruited. Though the cost per hire may be greater for one job category than for another, their staffing cost ratios may be the same. This is illustrated in Exhibit 13.9. If just cost per hire is considered, it appears that recruitment for the repair job is more effective than for the sales manager job. But by also calculating the staffing cost ratio, it can be seen that recruitment is at the same level of efficiency for both job categories. That is, recruitment for each source incurs the same relative expense to "bring in" the same amount of compensation via new hires.

## Customer Satisfaction

Managers and employees can be thought of as customers of the system. Managers look to the staffing system to provide them the right numbers and types of new hires to meet their own staffing needs. Job applicants expect the staffing system to recruit, select, and make employment decisions about them in ways that are fair and legal. Line employees count on the staffing system to keep them informed regarding position openings. Thus, it is important to know how satisfied these customers are with the staffing systems that serve them. Customer satisfaction can reinforce the usage of current staffing practices. Customer dissatisfaction, alternately, may serve as a trigger for needed changes in the staffing system and help pinpoint the nature of those changes.

### Managers

In the state of Wisconsin, the Department of Employment Relations houses the Division of Merit Recruitment and Selection (DMRS), which is the central agency responsible for staffing the state government. Annually, it helps the 40 state agencies

---

**EXHIBIT 13.9   Comparison of Cost per Hire and Staffing Cost Ratio**

| Job Category | New Hires | Staffing Cost | Cost per Hire | Compensation per Hire | Staffing Cost Ratio |
|---|---|---|---|---|---|
| Repair | 500 | $500,000 | $1,000 | $20,000 | 5% |
| Sales manager | 100 | $300,000 | $3,000 | $60,000 | 5% |

fill about 4,000 vacancies through hiring and promotions. Managers within these agencies are customers of the DMRS and its staffing systems.

To help identify and guide needed staffing system improvements, the DMRS decided to develop a survey measure of managers' satisfaction with staffing services. Through the use of focus groups, managers' input on the content of the survey was solicited. The final survey contained 53 items that were grouped into five areas: communication, timeliness, candidate quality, test quality, and service focus. Examples of the survey items are shown in Exhibit 13.10.

The survey was administered via internal mail to 645 line and HR managers throughout the agencies. Statistical analyses provided favorable psychometric evidence supporting usage of the survey. Survey results served as a key input to implementation of several initiatives to improve staffing service delivery. These initiatives led to increases in the speed of filling vacancies, elimination of paperwork, higher reported quality of job applicants, and positive applicant reactions to the staffing process.[27]

### Job Applicants

As with managers, it is best to develop a tailor-made survey for job applicants, one that reflects the specific characteristics of the staffing system used and the types of contacts and experiences job applicants will have with it. Consulting a staffing flowchart (Exhibit 13.5) would be helpful in this regard. If possible, the survey should be given to three different applicant groups: candidates who were rejected, candidates who accepted a job offer, and candidates who declined a job offer. Examples of questions that might be included in the survey are in Exhibit 13.11. Separate analysis of responses from each group should be done. Many web-based recruiting systems provide applicants with surveys or open-ended text boxes where they can share their reactions to the recruiting process. Because these systems provide immediate feedback to the organization, it may be possible to make real-time improvements to a recruiting drive.

## LEGAL ISSUES

### Record Keeping and Privacy

In staffing systems, substantial information is generated, used, recorded, and disclosed. Numerous legal constraints and requirements surround staffing information. These pertain to record keeping and privacy concerns.

#### Record Keeping

The organization creates a wide range of information during staffing and other HR activities. Examples include personal data (name, address, date of birth, dependents, etc.), KSAO information (application blank, references, test scores, etc.), medical information, performance appraisal and promotability assessments, and

**EXHIBIT 13.10**   **Examples of Survey Items for Assessing Managers' Satisfaction With Staffing Services**

**Communication:** How well are you kept informed on the staffing process?

How satisfied are you with:

1. The clarity of instructions and explanation you receive on the staffing process
2. Your overall understanding of the steps involved in filling a vacancy
3. The amount of training you receive in order to effectively participate in the total staffing process

**Timeliness:** How do you feel about the speed of recruitment, examination, and selection services?

How satisfied are you with the time required to:

1. Obtain central administrative approval to begin the hiring process
2. Score oral and essay exams, achievement history questionnaires, or other procedures involving scoring by a panel of raters
3. Hire someone who has been interviewed and selected

**Candidate Quality:** How do you feel about the quality (required knowledges and skills) of the job candidates?

How satisfied are you with:

1. The number of people you can interview and select from
2. The quality of candidates on new register
3. Your involvement in the recruitment process

**Test Quality:** How do you feel about the quality of civil service exams (tests, work samples, oral board interviews, etc.)?

How satisfied are you with:

1. Your involvement in exam construction
2. The extent to which the exams assess required KSAOs
3. The extent to which the exams test for new technologies used on the job

**Service Focus:** To what extent do you believe your personnel/staffing representatives are committed to providing high-quality service?

How satisfied are you with:

1. The accessibility of a staffing person
2. The expertise and competence of the staffing representative
3. Responses to your particular work unit's needs

Source: H. G. Heneman III, D. L. Huett, R. J. Lavigna, and D. Ogsten, "Assessing Managers' Satisfaction With Staffing Services," *Personnel Psychology*, 1995, 48, pp. 170–173. © *Personnel Psychology*, 1995. Used with permission.

**EXHIBIT 13.11** **Sample Job Applicant's Satisfaction Survey Questionnaire**

1. What prompted you to apply to Organization X?

    ___ Company website ___ Advertisement ___ Employee referral
    ___ Job fair ___ Campus recruitment ___ Other (indicate)

2. Was the information you got from this source valuable?

    ___ Very ___ Somewhat ___ No

3. Please indicate your level of agreement with each of the following on the 1–5 scale, where 1 = strongly disagree and 5 = strongly agree.

|  | Strongly disagree |  |  |  | Strongly agree |
|---|---|---|---|---|---|
| The applicant process was easy to use. | 1 | 2 | 3 | 4 | 5 |
| I received a prompt response to my application. | 1 | 2 | 3 | 4 | 5 |
| My first interview was promptly scheduled. | 1 | 2 | 3 | 4 | 5 |
| My first interview covered all my qualifications. | 1 | 2 | 3 | 4 | 5 |
| The test I took was relevant to the job. | 1 | 2 | 3 | 4 | 5 |
| The test process was fair. | 1 | 2 | 3 | 4 | 5 |
| I received prompt feedback about my test scores. | 1 | 2 | 3 | 4 | 5 |
| I always knew where I stood in the selection process. | 1 | 2 | 3 | 4 | 5 |
| My interview with the hiring manager was thorough. | 1 | 2 | 3 | 4 | 5 |
| The hiring manager represented Organization X well. | 1 | 2 | 3 | 4 | 5 |
| I was treated honestly and openly. | 1 | 2 | 3 | 4 | 5 |
| Overall, I am satisfied with the selection process. | 1 | 2 | 3 | 4 | 5 |
| I would recommend Organization X to others as a place to work. | 1 | 2 | 3 | 4 | 5 |

4. Please describe what you liked most about your experience seeking a job with Organization X.

5. Please describe what you liked least about your experience seeking a job with Organization X.

changes in employment status (promotions, transfers, etc.). Why should records of such information be created?

Records should be created and maintained for two major legal purposes in staffing. First, they are necessary for legal compliance. Federal, state, and local laws specify what information should be kept and for how long. Second, having records allows the organization to provide documentation to justify staffing decisions or to defend these decisions against legal challenge. For example, performance appraisal and promotability assessments might be used to explain to employees why they were or were not promoted. Or, these same records might be used as evidence in a legal proceeding to show that promotion decisions were job related and unbiased.

It is strongly recommended that two sets of records be created. These records can be kept in paper or electronic form. The first set should be the individual employee's personnel file. It should comprise only those documents that relate directly to the job and the employee's performance of it. To determine which documents to place in the personnel file, ask if it is a document on which the organization could legally base an employment decision. If the answer is "no," "probably no," or "unsure," the document should not be placed in the employee's personnel file. The second set of records should contain documents that cannot be used in staffing decisions. Examples include documents pertaining to medical information (both physical and mental), equal employment opportunity (e.g., information about protected characteristics such as age, sex, religion, race, color, national origin, and disability), and information about authorization to work (e.g., I-9 forms).[28]

Any document that is to be placed in an employee's personnel file should be reviewed before it becomes part of that record. Examine the document for incomplete, inaccurate, or misleading information, as well as potentially damaging notations or comments about the employee. All such information should be completed, corrected, explained, or, if necessary, eliminated. Remember that any document in the personnel file is a potential court exhibit that may work either for or against the employer's defense of a legal challenge.[29]

Federal EEO/AA laws contain general record-keeping requirements. Though the requirements vary somewhat from law to law, major subject areas for which records are to be kept (if created) are shown in Exhibit 13.12. Requirements by the Office of Federal Contract Compliance Programs (OFCCP) are broader than those shown, and records must be maintained for at least two years.

The various laws also have requirements about length of retention of records. As a general rule, most records must be kept for a minimum of one year from the date a document is made or a staffing action is taken, whichever is later. Exceptions to the one-year requirements all provide for even longer retention periods. If a charge of discrimination is filed, the records must be retained until the matter is resolved.

## EXHIBIT 13.12 Federal Record-Keeping Requirements

Records that should be kept include the following:

- Applications for employment (hire, promote, or transfer)
- Reasons for refusal to hire, promote, or transfer
- Tests and test scores, plus other KSAO information
- Job orders submitted to labor unions and employment agencies
- Medical exam results
- Advertisements or other notices to the public or employees about job openings and promotion opportunities
- Requests for reasonable accommodation
- Impact of staffing decisions on protected groups (adverse impact statistics)
- Records related to filing of a discrimination charge

All records should be kept for a minimum of one year.

### Privacy Concerns

The organization must observe legal requirements governing employees' and others' access to information in personnel files, as well as guard against unwarranted disclosure of the information to third-party requesters (e.g., other employers). Information access and disclosure matters raise privacy concerns under both constitutional and statutory law.[30]

Several states have laws guaranteeing employees reasonable access to their personnel files. The laws generally allow the employee to review and copy pertinent documents; some documents such as letters of reference or promotion plans for the person may be excluded from access. The employee may also have a right to seek to correct erroneous information in the file. Where there is no state law permitting access, employees are usually allowed access to their personnel file only if the organization has a policy permitting it. Disclosure of information in personnel files to third parties is often regulated as well, requiring such procedures as employees' written consent for disclosure.

At the federal level, numerous laws and regulations restrict access to and disclosure of employee personnel information. An example is the Americans With Disabilities Act (ADA) and its provisions regarding the confidentiality of medical information. There is, however, no general federal privacy law covering private employees. Public employees' privacy rights are protected by the Privacy Act of 1974.

## EEO Report

Under the Civil Rights Act and Affirmative Action Programs Regulations, private employers with more than 100 employees (50 for federal contractors) are required to file an annual report with the Equal Employment Opportunity Commission (EEOC). The basis of the report is the revised EEO-1 form, especially the section requesting employment data, shown in Exhibit 13.13.[31] Data are to be reported for combinations of job categories and race/ethnicity classifications. The data may be gathered from organization records, visual inspection, or a self-report. Detailed instructions and questions and answers are available online. They cover issues such as definitions of job categories and race/ethnicity classification, and data collection. The EEOC has a web-based system for reporting and will accept paper forms only in extreme cases where the employer does not have Internet access.

## Legal Audits

It is highly desirable to periodically conduct audits or reviews of the organization's degree of compliance with laws and regulations pertaining to staffing. The audit forces the organization to study and specify its staffing practices and to compare these current practices against legally desirable and required practices. Results can be used to identify potential legal trouble spots and to map out changes in staffing practices that will serve to minimize potential liability and reduce the risk of lawsuits being filed against the organization. Note that development of AAPs and reports includes a large audit and review component. They do not, however, cover the entire legal spectrum of staffing practices, nor do they require sufficient depth of analysis of staffing practices in some areas. For these reasons, AAPs and reports are not sufficient as legal audits, though they are immensely important and useful inputs to a legal audit.

The audit could be conducted by the organization's own legal counsel. Alternately, the HR department might first conduct a self-audit and then review its findings with legal counsel. Conducting an audit after involvement in employment litigation is also recommended.[32]

## Training for Managers and Employees

Training for managers and employees in employment law and compliance requirements is not only a sound practice but also increasingly a defense point for the organization in employment litigation. The following statement illustrates this:

> Recent judicial and agency activity make clear that training is no longer a discretionary HR activity—it is essential. The question is not whether your company is going to provide it, but how long will it have to suffer the costly consequences of neglect. A carefully crafted, effectively executed, methodically measured, and frequently fine-tuned employment practices training program for managers and employees is a powerful component of a strategic HRD (human resource development) plan that aligns vital corporate values

**EXHIBIT 13.13**   Employer Information Report EEO-1 Form

| Job Categories | | Number of Employees (Report employees in only one category) | | | | | | | | | | | | | | |
|---|---|---|---|---|---|---|---|---|---|---|---|---|---|---|---|---|
| | | Race/Ethnicity | | | | | | | | | | | | | | |
| | | Hispanic or Latino | | Not-Hispanic or Latino | | | | | | | | | | | | Total Col A–N |
| | | | | Male | | | | | | Female | | | | | | |
| | | Male | Female | White | Black or African American | Native Hawaiian or other Pacific Islander | Asian | American Indian or Alaska Native | Two or more races | White | Black or African American | Native Hawaiian or other Pacific Islander | Asian | American Indian or Alaska Native | Two or more races | |
| | | A | B | C | D | E | F | G | H | I | J | K | L | M | N | O |
| Executive/Senior Level Officials and Managers | 1.1 | | | | | | | | | | | | | | | |
| First/Mid-Level Officials and Managers | 1.2 | | | | | | | | | | | | | | | |
| Professionals | 2 | | | | | | | | | | | | | | | |
| Technicians | 3 | | | | | | | | | | | | | | | |
| Sales Workers | 4 | | | | | | | | | | | | | | | |
| Administrative Support Workers | 5 | | | | | | | | | | | | | | | |
| Craft Workers | 6 | | | | | | | | | | | | | | | |
| Operatives | 7 | | | | | | | | | | | | | | | |
| Laborers and Helpers | 8 | | | | | | | | | | | | | | | |
| Service Workers | 9 | | | | | | | | | | | | | | | |
| TOTAL | 10 | | | | | | | | | | | | | | | |
| PREVIOUS YEAR TOTAL | 11 | | | | | | | | | | | | | | | |

Source: EEO-1 Joint Reporting Committee, *Employer Information Report EEO-1*, n.d. (*www.eeoc.gov/employers/eeo1survey/upload/instructions_form.pdf*).

with daily practices. The costs of neglect are serious. The benefits are compelling and fundamental to long-term success. . . . Adequate, effective, and regularly scheduled employment law and practices training is now the rule, not the exception.[33]

The constantly changing employment law landscape reinforces the need for training. New laws, regulations, and court rulings can all redefine permissible and impermissible staffing practices.[34]

Though the requirements for employment law training are still being developed, it appears there are several desirable components to be incorporated into it: (1) the training should be for all members of the organization; (2) basic harassment and discrimination training should be given immediately to new employees, managers should receive additional training, and refresher training should occur periodically and when special circumstances arise, such as a significant change in policy or practice; (3) the trainers should have special expertise in employment law and practice; (4) the training content should be substantive and cover EEO practices in several staffing areas—such as recruitment, hiring, succession planning, and promotion—as pertains to the numerous EEO laws and regulations; training in other areas of HR, such as compensation and benefits, should also be provided; and (5) the training materials should also be substantive, incorporate the organization's specific harassment and discrimination policies, and allow for both information presentation and active practice by the participants.[35] Trainees should learn which EEO actions they can implement on their own and which actions should be referred to the HR department. Finally, the training should be matched with diversity initiatives to avoid an overly legalistic perspective.[36]

## Dispute Resolution

Employment laws and regulations naturally lead to claims of their violation by job applicants and employees. If the claim is filed with an external agency, such as the EEOC, the dispute resolution procedures described in Chapter 2 ("Laws and Regulations" section) are applied. By providing mediation as an alternative dispute resolution (ADR) procedure, the EEOC seeks to settle disputes quickly and without formal investigation and litigation. The EEOC provides, without a fee, a trained mediator to help the employer and the job applicant (or employee) reconcile their differences and reach a satisfactory resolution. The process is confidential, any records or notes are destroyed at its conclusion, and nothing that is revealed may be used subsequently in investigation or litigation should the dispute not be resolved.

For claims of discrimination (or other grievances) made internally, the organization will likely offer some form of ADR to resolve the dispute. Exhibit 13.14 shows the numerous approaches to ADR that might be used.

---

**EXHIBIT 13.14** **Alternative Dispute Resolution Approaches**

| Approach | Description |
| --- | --- |
| Negotiation | Employer and employee discuss complaint with goal of resolving complaint. |
| Fact finding | A neutral person from within or outside the organization investigates a complaint and develops findings that may be the basis for resolving the complaint. |
| Peer review | A panel of employees and managers work together to resolve the complaint. |
| Mediation | A neutral person (mediator) from within or outside the organization helps the parties negotiate a mutually acceptable agreement. Mediator is trained in mediation methods. Settlement is not imposed. |
| Arbitration | A neutral person (arbitrator) from within or outside the organization conducts formal hearing and issues a decision that is binding on the parties. |

Sometimes new hires are required as part of an employment contract to sign a provision waiving their protected rights under civil rights laws to file or participate in a proceeding against the organization and to instead use only a specified ADR system to resolve complaints. The EEOC has issued guidance indicating that such waiver provisions are null and void, and that their existence cannot stop the EEOC from enforcing the law.[37] The EEOC may pursue a discrimination claim even when the employee has signed an ADR waiver.

## The Special Case of Arbitration

With arbitration as the ADR procedure, the employer and the job applicant (or employee) agree in advance to submit their dispute to a neutral third-party arbitrator, who will issue a final and binding decision. Such arbitration agreements usually include statutory discrimination claims, meaning that the employee agrees not to pursue charges of discrimination against the employer by any means (e.g., lawsuit) except arbitration. The courts have ruled that such arbitration agreements generally are legally permissible and enforceable. However, such agreements do not serve as a bar to pursuit by the EEOC of a discrimination claim seeking victim-specific relief.

The arbitration agreement and process must meet many specific, suggested standards in order to be enforceable.[38] For example, the agreement must be "knowing and voluntary," meaning that it is clearly written, obvious as to purpose, and presented to the employee as a separate document for a signature. Other suggested standards include the following:

- The arbitrator must be a neutral party.
- The process should provide for more than minimal discovery (presentation of evidence).
- The same remedies as permitted by the law should be allowed.
- The employee should have the right to hire an attorney, and the employer should reimburse the employee a portion of the attorney's fees.
- The employee should not have to bear excessive responsibility for the cost of the arbitrator.
- The types of claims (e.g., sex discrimination, retaliation) subject to arbitration should be indicated.
- The arbitrator should issue a written award.

These points are complex, indicating that legal counsel should be sought prior to use of arbitration agreements.

## SUMMARY

The multiple and complex set of activities collectively known as a staffing system must be integrated and coordinated throughout the organization. Such management of the staffing system requires both careful administration and evaluation, as well as compliance with legal mandates.

To manage the staffing system, the usual organizational arrangement in all but very small organizations is to create an identifiable staffing or employment function and place it within the HR department. That function then manages the staffing system at the corporate and/or plant and office levels.

The myriad staffing activities require staffing policies to establish general staffing principles and procedures to guide the conduct of those activities. Lack of clear policies and procedures can lead to misguided and inconsistent staffing practices, as well as potentially illegal ones. Staffing technology can help achieve these consistencies and aid in improving staffing system efficiency. Outsourcing of staffing activities is also being experimented with as a way of improving staffing system operation and results.

Evaluation of the effectiveness of the staffing system should proceed along several fronts. First is assessment of the staffing system from a process perspective. Here, it is desirable to examine the degree of standardization (consistency) of the process, as well as a staffing flowchart in order to identify deviations in staffing practice and bottlenecks. The results of the process according to indicators such as yield ratios and time lapse (cycle time), along with the costs of staffing system operation, should also be estimated. Finally, the organization should consider assessing the satisfaction of staffing system users, such as managers and job applicants.

Various laws require maintenance of numerous records and protection of privacy. It is desirable to conduct a legal audit of all the organization's staffing activities periodically. This will help identify potential legal trouble spots that require attention. Employment law training for managers and employees is increasingly becoming necessary. Methods for addressing employment disputes, known as ADRs, should be explored.

## DISCUSSION QUESTIONS

1. What are the advantages of having a centralized staffing function, as opposed to letting each manager be totally responsible for all staffing activities in his or her unit?
2. What are examples of staffing tasks and activities that cannot or should not be simply delegated to a staffing information system?
3. What are the advantages and disadvantages of outsourcing an entire staffing system to a vendor?
4. In developing a report on the effectiveness of a staffing process for entry-level jobs, what factors would you address and why?
5. How would you encourage individual managers to be more aware of the legal requirements of staffing systems and to take steps to ensure that they themselves engaged in legal staffing actions?

## ETHICAL ISSUES

1. It has been suggested that the use of staffing technology and software is wrong because it dehumanizes the staffing experience, making it nothing but a mechanical process that treats applicants like digital widgets. Evaluate this assertion.
2. Since there are no standard ways of creating staffing process results and cost metrics, is there a need for some sort of oversight of how these data are calculated, reported, and used within the organization? Explain.

## APPLICATIONS

### Learning About Jobs in Staffing

The purpose of this application is to have you learn in detail about a particular job in staffing currently being performed by an individual. The individual could be a staffing job holder in the HR department of a company or public agency (state or local government), a nonprofit agency, a staffing firm, an employment agency, a consulting firm, or the state employment (job) service. The individual may perform staffing tasks full time, such as a recruiter, interviewer, counselor, employment representative, or employment manager. Or, the individual may perform staffing duties as part of the job, such as the HR manager in a small company or an HR generalist in a specific plant or site.

Contact the job holder and arrange for an interview with that person. Explain that the purpose of the interview is for you to learn about the person's job in terms of job requirements (tasks and KSAOs) and job rewards (both extrinsic and intrinsic). To prepare for the interview, review job descriptions for HR managers and specialists on O*Net, obtain any information you can about the organization, and develop a set of questions to ask the job holder. Either before or at the interview, be sure to obtain a copy of the job holder's job description if one is available. Use the written and interview information to prepare a report of your investigation that covers the following:

1. The organization's products and services, size, and staffing (employment) function
2. The job holder's job title, and why you chose that person's job to study
3. A summary of the tasks performed by the job holder and the KSAOs necessary for the job
4. A summary of the extrinsic and intrinsic rewards received by the job holder
5. Unique characteristics of the job that you did not expect to be part of the job

## Evaluating Staffing Process Results

The Keepon Trucking Company (KTC) is a manufacturer of custom-built trucks. It does not manufacture any particular truck lines, styles, or models. Rather, it builds trucks to customers' specifications; these trucks are used for specialty purposes such as snow removal, log hauling, and military cargo hauling. One year ago, KTC received a new, large order that would take three years to complete and required the external hiring of 100 new assemblers. To staff this particular job, the HR department manager of nonexempt employment hurriedly developed and implemented a special staffing process for filling these new vacancies. Applicants were recruited from three sources: newspaper ads, employee referrals, and a local employment agency. All applicants generated by these methods were subjected to a common selection and decision-making process. All offer receivers were given the same terms and conditions in their job offer letters and were told there was no room for any negotiation. All vacancies were eventually filled.

After the first year of the contract, the manager of nonexempt employment, Dexter Williams, decided to pull together some data to determine how well the staffing process for the assembler jobs had worked. Since he had not originally planned on doing any evaluation, Dexter was able to retrieve only the following data to help him with his evaluation:

### Exhibit
### Staffing Data for Filling the Job of Assembler

| Recruitment Source | Applicants | Offer Receivers | Start as New Hires | Remaining at Six Months |
|---|---|---|---|---|
| Newspaper ads | | | | |
| No. apps. | 300 | 70 | 50 | 35 |
| Avg. no. days | 30 | 30 | 10 | |
| Employee referral | | | | |
| No. apps. | 60 | 30 | 30 | 27 |
| Avg. no. days | 20 | 10 | 10 | |
| Employment agency | | | | |
| No. apps. | 400 | 20 | 20 | 8 |
| Avg. no. days | 40 | 20 | 10 | |

1. Determine the yield ratios (offer receivers / applicants, new hires / applicants), time lapse or cycle times (days to offer, days to start), and retention rates associated with each recruitment source.
2. What is the relative effectiveness of the three sources in terms of yield ratios, cycle times, and retention rates?
3. What are some possible reasons for the fact that the three sources differ in their relative effectiveness?
4. What would you recommend Dexter do differently in the future to improve his evaluation of the staffing process?

## ENDNOTES

1. T. H. Davenport, J. Harris, and J. Shapiro, "Competing on Talent Analytics," *Harvard Business Review*, Oct. 2010, pp. 52–58.
2. US Census Bureau, "Statistics About Business Size (Including Small Business) From the US Census Bureau" (*www.census.gov/epcd/www/smallbus.html*), accessed 1/28/11.
3. E. E. Lawler III and A. A. Mohrman, *Creating a Strategic Human Resources Organization* (Stanford, CA: Stanford University Press, 2003), pp. 15–20.
4. D. Ulrich, J. Younger, W. Brockbank, and M. Ulrich, *HR From the Outside In* (New York: McGraw-Hill, 2012).
5. S. T. Hunt, *Driving Business Execution Through Integrated Talent Management* (Brisbane, QLD, Australia: SuccessFactors, 2012); D. Zielinski, "Total Integration," *HR Magazine*, 2011, 56(11), pp. 69–72.

6. M. Fiester, "Practicing Strategic Human Resources," *SHRM Templates and Toolkits*, Mar. 21, 2013 (*www.shrm.org*).

7. J. A. Colquitt, B. A. Scott, J. B. Rodell, D. M. Long, C. P. Zapata, D. E. Conlon, and M. J. Wesson, "Justice at the Millennium, A Decade Later: A Meta-Analytic Test of Social Exchange and Affect Based Perspective," *Journal of Applied Psychology*, 2013, 98, pp. 199–236.

8. D. M. Truxillo, T. N. Bauer, M. A. Campion, and M. E. Paronto, "Selection Fairness Information and Applicant Reactions: A Longitudinal Field Study," *Journal of Applied Psychology*, 2002, 87, pp. 1020–1031; K. L. Uggerslev, N. E. Fassina, and D. Kraichy, "Recruiting Through the Stages: A Meta-Analytic Test of Predictors of Applicant Reaction at Different Stages of the Recruiting Process," *Personnel Psychology*, 2012, 65, pp. 597–660; S. Schinkel, A. van Vianen, and D. van Dierendonck, "Selection Fairness and Outcomes: A Field Study of Interactive Effects on Applicant Reactions," *International Journal of Selection and Assessment*, 2013, 21, pp. 22–31; C. W. Wanberg, L. W. Bunce, and M. B. Gavin, "Perceived Fairness of Layoffs Among Individuals Who Have Been Laid Off: A Longitudinal Study," *Personnel Psychology*, 1999, 52, pp. 59–84.

9. D. Ulrich, J. Allen, W. Brockbank, J. Younger, and M. Nyman, *HR Transformation: Building Human Resources From the Outside In* (New York: McGraw Hill, 2009); S. A. Smith and R. Mazin, *The HR Answer Book* (New York: American Management Association, 2011).

10. H. Williams, "e-HR 2010: Key HR Software Developments Ahead," *Personnel Today*, Dec. 1, 2009, p. 10; Anonymous, "What Are the Latest Trends in HR Applications Adoption," *HR Focus*, Dec. 2009, pp. 10–11; E. Frauenheim, "Core HR Technology Takes Center Stage," *Workforce Management*, Oct. 2007 (*www.workforce.com*).

11. B. Roberts, "How to Get Satisfaction From SAAS," *HR Magazine*, Apr. 2010 (*www.shrm.org*); L. Grensing-Pophal, "Mission: Organized HR!" *Credit Union Management*, Oct. 2008, pp. 36–39; E. Frauenheim, "Talent Tools Still Essential," *Workforce Management*, Apr. 2009, pp. 20–26.

12. WorldatWork, *The State of Human Resources Outsourcing: 2004–2005* (Scottsdale, AZ: author, 2005); A. Collis, "Outsourcing the HR Function," *SHRM Toolkits*, Mar. 2013 (*www.shrm.org*).

13. E. Van Slyke, "Laying the Groundwork for HR Outsourcing," *Workforce Management*, Jan. 2010 (*www.workforce.com*); P. Meskanik, "Critical Success Factors for Recruiting Process Outsourcing," *Oil and Gas Journal*, Jan. 1, 2009, pp. 8–11.

14. B. S. Klaas, H. Yang, T. Gainey, and J. A. McClendon, "HR in the Small Business Enterprise: Assessing the Impact of PEO Utilization," *Human Resource Management*, 2005, 44, pp. 433–448.

15. B. E. Rosenthal, "Coopitition Is an Rx for Success for Three HR Suppliers in the Healthcare Arena," *Outsourcing Center*, Jan. 2013 (*www.outsourcing-center.com*).

16. B. E. Rosenthal, "Employers Make Better Hiring Decisions Using an Online Reference Checking App That Uses Logic," *Outsourcing Center*, Jan. 2013 (*www.outsourcing-center.com*).

17. P. Babcock, "Slicing Off Pieces of HR," *HR Magazine*, July 2004, pp. 71–76; J. C. Berkshire, "Seeking Full Partnership," *HR Magazine*, July 2004, pp. 89–96; D. Dell, *HR Outsourcing* (New York: The Conference Board, 2004); E. Esen, *Human Resource Outsourcing* (Alexandria, VA: Society for Human Resource Management, 2004).

18. D. Ulrich, J. Younger, W. Brockbank, and M. Ulrich, *HR Transformation* (New York: McGraw-Hill, 2009); P. M. Wright, J. W. Boudreau, D. A. Pace, E. Sartain, P. McKinnon, and R. L. Antoine, *The Chief HR Officer: Defining the New Role of Human Resource Leaders* (San Francisco: Wiley, 2011).

19. S. Overman, "Staffing Management: Measure What Matters," *Staffing Management Magazine*, Oct. 1, 2008 (*www.shrm.org*); B. Roberts, "Analyze This!" *HR Magazine*, Oct. 1, 2009 (*www.shrm.org*); J. Fitz-enz, *The ROI of Human Capital: Measuring the Economic Value of Employee Performance* (New York: AMACOM, 2000); M. A. Huselid, B. E. Becker, and R. W. Beatty, *The Workforce Scorecard: Managing Human Capital to Execute Strategy* (Boston: Harvard Business

School Press, 2005); Society for Human Resource Management, *SHRM Human Capital Benchmarking Study* (Alexandria, VA: author, 2007).

20. J. Sullivan, "HR's Burden of Proof," *Workforce Management*, Jan. 2007, p. 26; I. L. Goldstein and Associates, *Training and Development in Organizations* (San Francisco: Jossey-Bass, 1991).

21. Roberts, "Analyze This!"; B. Roberts, "How to Put Analytics on Your Side," *HR Magazine*, Oct. 1, 2010 (*www.shrm.org*).

22. L. Micco, "Lockheed Wins the Best Catches," *Employment Management Association Today*, Spring 1997, pp. 18–20; E. R. Silverman, "The Fast Track," *Human Resource Executive*, Oct. 1998, pp. 30–34.

23. L. Klutz, *Time to Fill/Time to Start: 2002 Staffing Metrics Survey* (Alexandria, VA: Society for Human Resource Management, 2003).

24. Fitz-enz, *The ROI of Human Capital: Measuring the Economic Value of Employee Performance*; Society for Human Resource Management, *SHRM Human Capital Benchmarking Study*.

25. Society for Human Resource Management, *2002 SHRM/EMA Staffing Metrics Study* (Alexandria, VA: author, 2003); Staffing.Org, *2003 Recruiting Metrics and Performance Benchmark Report* (Willow Grove, PA: author, 2003).

26. K. Burns, "Metrics Are Everything: Why, What and How to Choose," in N. C. Burkholder, P. J. Edwards, Sr., and L. Sartain (eds.), *On Staffing* (Hoboken, NJ: Wiley, 2004), pp. 364–371.

27. H. G. Heneman III, D. L. Huett, R. J. Lavigna, and D. Ogsten, "Assessing Managers' Satisfaction With Staffing Service," *Personnel Psychology*, 1995, 48, pp. 163–173.

28. H. P. Coxson, "The Double-Edged Sword of Personnel Files and Employee Records," *Legal Report*, Society for Human Resource Management, 1992; Warren Gorham Lamont, *How Long Do We Have to Keep These Records?* (Boston: author, 1993).

29. Coxson, "The Double-Edged Sword of Personnel Files and Employee Records."

30. M. W. Finkin, *Privacy in Employment Law*, 3rd ed. (Washington, DC: BNA Books, 2009), pp. 650–657; International Personnel Management Association, "Employee Privacy and Recordkeeping—I and II," *IPMA News*, Aug. and Sept. 1998, pp. 16–18.

31. V. J. Hoffman, "Equal Opportunity Reporting: New Requirements, New Best Practices," *Legal Report*, Society for Human Resource Management, July–Aug. 2006 (*www.shrm.org*); R. Zeidner, "EEO-1 Changes," *HR Magazine*, May 2006, pp. 61–64.

32. J. W. Janove, "It's Not Over, Even When It's Over," *HR Magazine*, Feb. 2004, pp. 123–131.

33. W. K. Turner and C. S. Thrutchley, "Employment Law and Practices Training: No Longer the Exception—It's the Rule," *Legal Report*, Society for Human Resource Management, July–Aug. 2002, p. 1.

34. A. Smith, "Managerial Training Needed as Hiring Resumes," (*www.shrm.org*), accessed 3/16/10; D. G. Bower, "Don't Cut Legal Compliance Training," *Workforce Management*, Feb. 2009 (*www.workforce.com*).

35. S. K. Williams, "The New Law of Training," *HR Magazine*, May 2004, pp. 115–118.

36. J. A. Segal, "Unlimited Check-Writing Authority for Supervisors?" *HR Magazine*, Feb. 2007, pp. 119–124; J. C. Ramirez, "A Different Bias," *Human Resource Executive*, May 16, 2006, pp. 37–40.

37. Equal Employment Opportunity Commission, *EEOC Enforcement Guidance on Non-Waivable Employee Rights Under EEOC Enforcement Statutes* (Washington, DC: author, 1997).

38. M. E. Bruno, "The Future of ADR in the Workplace," *Compensation and Benefits Review*, Nov.–Dec. 2001, pp. 46–59; C. Hirschman, "Order in the Hearing," *HR Magazine*, July 2001, pp. 58–64; L. P. Postol, "To Arbitrate Employment Disputes or Not, That Is the Question," *Legal Report*, Society for Human Resource Management, Sept.–Oct. 2001, pp. 5–8.

# CHAPTER FOURTEEN

## Retention Management

**Learning Objectives and Introduction**
Learning Objectives
Introduction

**Turnover and Its Causes**
Nature of the Problem
Types of Turnover
Causes of Turnover

**Analysis of Turnover**
Measurement
Reasons for Leaving
Costs and Benefits

**Retention Initiatives: Voluntary Turnover**
Current Practices and Deciding to Act
Desirability of Leaving
Ease of Leaving
Alternatives

**Retention Initiatives: Discharge**
Performance Management
Progressive Discipline

**Retention Initiatives: Downsizing**
Weighing Advantages and Disadvantages
Staffing Levels and Quality
Alternatives to Downsizing
Employees Who Remain

**Legal Issues**
Separation Laws and Regulations
Performance Appraisal

**Summary**

**Discussion Questions**

**Ethical Issues**

**Applications**

**Endnotes**

# LEARNING OBJECTIVES AND INTRODUCTION

## Learning Objectives

- Be able to differentiate among the types and causes of employee turnover
- Recognize the different reasons employees leave their jobs
- Evaluate the costs and benefits of turnover
- Learn about the variety of techniques companies use to limit turnover
- See how performance management and progressive discipline limit discharge turnover
- Understand how companies manage downsizing
- Recognize a variety of legal issues that affect separation policies and practices

## Introduction

Even the best recruiting and selection system in the world will be of little value to an organization if employees leave their jobs soon after being hired. Therefore, the establishment of effective systems for retaining employees is a crucial part of the staffing process. While some loss of employees is both inevitable and desirable, retention management seeks to ensure that the organization is able to keep enough employees with important knowledge, skill, ability, and other characteristics (KSAOs) to generate future success.

From a strategic perspective, some turnover of employees is actually good. For example, when an employee who lacks strategic competencies leaves, an opportunity arises to find a more suitable replacement. On the other hand, if a highly productive employee with unique skills leaves, the organization may have trouble finding a suitable replacement. In this case, turnover can severely limit the organization's ability to achieve strategic goals. Therefore, throughout the chapter we will highlight how turnover is a complex phenomenon with both positive and negative aspects.

The chapter begins with a look at three types of turnover—voluntary, discharge, and downsizing. Retention management must be based on a thorough analysis of these three types of turnover. Analyses include measuring turnover, determining employees' reasons for leaving, and assessing the costs and benefits of turnover. Attention then turns to retention initiatives. As we will see, organizations often encourage retention by focusing on the extrinsic nature of jobs; this involves enacting policies like generous compensation plans, matching job offers from competitors, developing unique benefits programs, and providing incentives for long-term service. Organizations can also improve the intrinsic quality of jobs by providing more satisfying working conditions, improving the social nature of interactions with coworkers, and ensuring that supervisors engage in effective and motivational leadership behaviors. Next, we discuss how to reduce employee discharges through both performance management and progressive discipline initiatives. Although layoffs are generally avoided in most organizations, at times downsizing is necessary; thus, we will discuss some strategies for effectively and ethically reducing head count. The final topic involves the myriad laws and regulations pertaining to employee separation from the organization.

# TURNOVER AND ITS CAUSES

## Nature of the Problem

The focus of this book so far has been on acquiring and deploying people in ways that contribute to organizational effectiveness. Attention now shifts to retaining employees as another part of staffing that can contribute to organizational effectiveness. Although turnover is often seen as a detriment to organizational performance, there are several positive functional outcomes. Thus, an extremely important part of employee retention strategy and tactics is careful assessment of both retention costs and benefits and the design of retention initiatives that provide positive benefits at a reasonable cost to the organization. Moreover, retention strategies and tactics must focus on not only how many employees are retained but exactly who is retained. Both within and between jobs and organization levels, some employees are "worth" more than others in terms of their contributions to job and organizational effectiveness. Thus, another important matter for the retention agenda is making special efforts to retain what we call "high-value" employees.

Retention must be tackled realistically, however, since some amount of employee turnover is inevitable.[1] People constantly move out of organizations voluntarily, and organizations shed employees as well. The Department of Labor estimates that employees between the ages of 18 and 44 have held an average of 11 jobs, and among employees aged 33–38, 58% of jobs lasted less than two years. In some industries, high voluntary turnover is a continual fact of life and cost of doing business. Turnover among sit-down restaurant managers, for example, hovers around 50% annually year after year. A final example is that in 2009, the Department of Labor estimated there were over 28,000 mass layoffs (those involving 50 or more employees), creating nearly 3 million unemployed workers. This was a relatively high number of mass layoffs due to generally poor economic conditions that year.

When people voluntarily leave an organization, they do so for a variety of reasons, only some of which are potentially avoidable (controllable) by the organization. Sound retention management thus must be based on a gathering and analysis of employees' reasons for leaving. Specific retention initiatives must be tailor-made to address these reasons in a cost-effective way. Against this backdrop we now turn to a more detailed discussion of the types of turnover and their causes.

## Types of Turnover

There are many different types of employee turnover. Exhibit 14.1 provides a basic classification of these types.[2] It can be seen that turnover is either voluntary (initiated by the employee) or involuntary (initiated by the organization).

### Voluntary

Voluntary turnover is broken down into avoidable and unavoidable turnover. Avoidable turnover is that which potentially could have been prevented by certain organization actions, such as a pay raise or a new job assignment. Unavoidable turnover represents employee quits that the organization probably could not have prevented, such as people who quit and withdraw from the labor force through retirement or by returning to school. Other examples of unavoidable turnover are people quitting due to dual career problems, pursuit of a new and different career, health problems that require taking a different type of job, child care and elder care responsibilities, or leaving the country. The line of demarcation between avoidable and unavoidable turnover is fuzzy and depends on decisions by the organization as to exactly what types of voluntary turnover it thinks it could prevent.

A further line of demarcation involves just avoidable turnover, in which the organization explicitly chooses to either try to prevent or not try to prevent employees from quitting. As shown in Exhibit 14.1, the organization will try to prevent high-value employees from quitting—those employees with high job performance, strong KSAOs, key intellectual capital, high promotion potential, high training and development invested in them, and high experience and who are difficult to replace. The organization is less likely to try to retain low-value employees.

### Involuntary

Involuntary turnover is split into discharge and downsizing types. Discharge turnover is aimed at the individual employee, due to discipline and/or job performance problems. Downsizing turnover typically targets groups of employees and is also known as a reduction in force (RIF). It occurs as part of an organizational restructuring or cost-reduction program to improve organizational effectiveness and increase shareholder value (stock price). RIFs may occur as permanent or temporary layoffs for the entire organization, or as part of a plant or site closing or relocation. RIFs may also occur as the result of a merger or acquisition, in which some employees in the combined workforces are viewed as redundant in the positions they hold. Even if the organization has to terminate employees through discharge or downsizing, it can take steps to minimize the negative reactions of the employees who were not terminated.

The different types of turnover have different underlying causes, so the organization must think very selectively in terms of the different types of retention strategies and tactics it wishes to deploy. It is first necessary to explore the underlying causes of turnover, since knowledge of those causes is necessary for developing and implementing retention strategies and tactics.

**EXHIBIT 14.1** **Types of Employee Turnover**

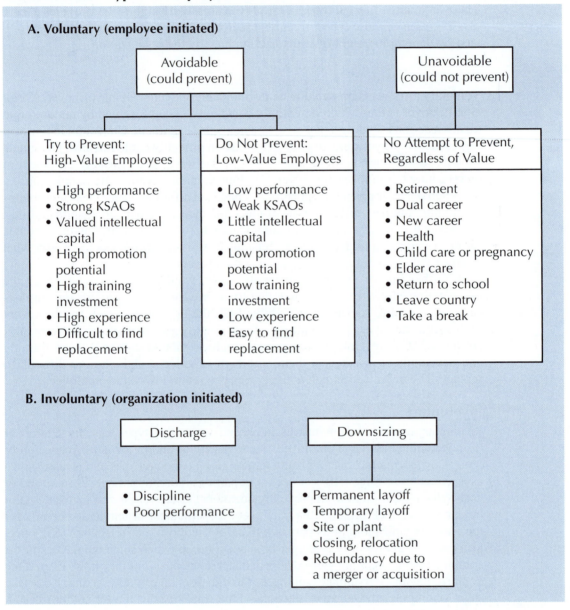

**A. Voluntary (employee initiated)**

| Avoidable (could prevent) | | Unavoidable (could not prevent) |
|---|---|---|

| Try to Prevent: High-Value Employees | Do Not Prevent: Low-Value Employees | No Attempt to Prevent, Regardless of Value |
|---|---|---|
| • High performance<br>• Strong KSAOs<br>• Valued intellectual capital<br>• High promotion potential<br>• High training investment<br>• High experience<br>• Difficult to find replacement | • Low performance<br>• Weak KSAOs<br>• Little intellectual capital<br>• Low promotion potential<br>• Low training investment<br>• Low experience<br>• Easy to find replacement | • Retirement<br>• Dual career<br>• New career<br>• Health<br>• Child care or pregnancy<br>• Elder care<br>• Return to school<br>• Leave country<br>• Take a break |

**B. Involuntary (organization initiated)**

| Discharge | Downsizing |
|---|---|
| • Discipline<br>• Poor performance | • Permanent layoff<br>• Temporary layoff<br>• Site or plant closing, relocation<br>• Redundancy due to a merger or acquisition |

## Causes of Turnover

Separate models of turnover causes are presented for each of the three turnover types that the organization may seek to influence with its retention strategies and tactics. These are voluntary, discharge, and downsizing turnover.

### Voluntary Turnover

Through considerable research, various models of voluntary turnover have been developed and tested.[3] The model shown in Exhibit 14.2 is a distillation of that research.

The employee's intention to quit depends on three general factors: the perceived desirability of leaving, the perceived ease of leaving, and alternatives available to the employee. The perceived desirability of leaving is often an outgrowth of a poor person/job or person/organization match. One form of this mismatch may be a difference between the rewards provided by the job and the rewards desired

---

**EXHIBIT 14.2   Causes (Drivers) of Voluntary Turnover**

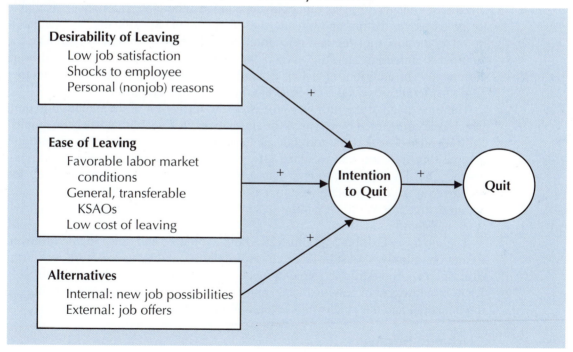

NOTE: The relative importance of the drivers and how they interact to determine the decision to quit varies across situations.

by the employee, leading to job dissatisfaction. In addition to mismatches, certain shocks may occur to the employee that trigger a more impulsive intention to quit, such as finding out that the organization is being acquired and one's job might be eliminated. Interpersonal conflicts with coworkers or supervisors are another type of shock that could lead to turnover. Finally, employees may find it desirable to leave for personal, nonjob reasons that are unavoidable.

The perceived ease of leaving represents a sense of a lack of barriers to leaving and a high likelihood of finding a new job. The ease of leaving will be higher when labor market conditions provide plentiful job opportunities with other organizations, when the employee possesses KSAOs that are transferable to other organizations, and when the departure is not a very costly proposition for the employee. Employees who are highly embedded in their jobs, organizations, and communities are less likely to leave. Some of the factors that increase embeddedness can be influenced by the organization, such as interpersonal relationships with supervisors and coworkers or levels of training in company-specific human capital. As will be discussed later, the turnover of friends and colleagues can significantly reduce embeddedness and lead to "turnover contagion." Other factors are beyond the organization's control, such as ties to the local community.[4]

Finally, the intention to quit will depend on other job alternatives available to the employee within and outside the organization. Specifically, the availability of promotion, transfer, and relocation alternatives may lessen or eliminate the employee's intentions to quit, even if the employee is very dissatisfied with the current job. In addition, actual or potential receipt of a job offer from another employer represents a clear external alternative for the employee.

The final stage of the turnover process is the formation of the intention to quit, which is accompanied by a search for alternatives. Job searching has been empirically identified as a close correlate of turnover. However, employers should not assume that it is too late to make efforts to keep an employee who is seeking another job. Directly addressing what changes would be necessary to keep the employee is a good strategy in this case. Many employees who are looking for an alternative job would be willing to stay with their current employer if their job were sufficiently modified.

The model in Exhibit 14.2 illustrates both avoidable and unavoidable turnover. Retention initiatives must be directed toward the avoidable types of turnover: turnover due to job dissatisfaction, employee possession of general and transferable KSAOs, a low cost of leaving, the availability of other job opportunities within the organization, and the employee's receipt of a job offer.

### Discharge Turnover

Discharge turnover is due to extremely poor person/job matches, particularly a mismatch between job requirements and KSAOs. One form of mismatch involves the employee failing to follow rules and procedures. These infractions can range from the relatively minor (e.g., dress code violations, horseplay) to the very serious (e.g., bringing a firearm to work). Often it is the cumulative effect of multiple incidents that results in the discharge.

The other form of discharge turnover involves unacceptable job performance. Here, the KSAO/job requirements mismatch is severe. In fact, the employee's performance is so deficient that the organization has decided that it is intolerable and the only solution is termination.

### Downsizing Turnover

Downsizing turnover reflects a staffing level mismatch in which the organization is, or is projected to be, overstaffed. In other words, the head count available exceeds the head count required. Overstaffing may be due to (1) a lack of forecasting and planning, (2) inaccuracies in forecasting and planning, or (3) unanticipated changes in labor demand and/or labor supply. For example, optimistic forecasts of demand for products and services that do not materialize may lead to overstaffing, as may sudden unanticipated downturns in demand that create sudden excess head count. Alternatively, a change in the labor market may reduce ease of movement, causing fewer employees to leave the organization—an unanticipated decrease in the voluntary turnover rate and thus a change in workforce head count available. Quite naturally, these types of demand/supply imbalances create strong downsizing pressure on the organization, to which it must respond.

## ANALYSIS OF TURNOVER

Analysis of turnover requires that the three types of turnover be measured and benchmarked, that specific reasons for employees leaving be identified, and that costs and benefits of each type of turnover be assessed.

## Measurement

### Formula

Since turnover involves the discrete action of leaving or staying with the organization, it is expressed as the proportion or percentage of employees who leave the organization in some time period. Thus:

$$\text{turnover rate} = \frac{\text{number of employees leaving}}{\text{average number of employees}} \times 100$$

Use of this formula to calculate turnover rates will require data on, and decisions about, the following: (1) what is the time period of interest (e.g., month, year), (2) what type of employee "counts" (e.g., full time only, part time, seasonal), and (3) how to calculate the average number of employees over the time period, such as straight or weighted average.

## Breakouts and Benchmarks

Analysis and interpretation of turnover data are aided by breaking out the data according to various factors, including (1) type of turnover: voluntary (avoidable and unavoidable) or involuntary (discharge and downsizing), (2) type of employee (e.g., exempt/nonexempt, demographics, KSAOs, and performance level), (3) job category, and (4) geographic location. Such breakouts help in identifying how much variation in turnover there is around the overall average and pockets of the most and least severe turnover. Human resources information systems (HRISs) are designed to process and track employee departures, so data are often readily available regarding when, where, and even why employee turnover is occurring.

It is also useful to benchmark turnover data in order to have comparative statistics that will aid in the interpretation of the organization's turnover data. One type of benchmark is internal, looking at trends in the organization's own turnover data over time. Such trend analysis is very useful for identifying where turnover problems are worsening or improving and for evaluating the effectiveness of retention initiatives.

The other form of benchmarking is external, in which the organization compares its own data with the current turnover rates and trends of other organizations. One major external benchmarking source is the data from the Job Openings and Labor Turnover Survey (JOLTS), collected and published by the US Department of Labor. The JOLTS is conducted monthly among 16,000 business establishments and provides data on total employment, job openings, hires, quits, layoffs and discharges, and other separations. Exhibit 14.3 provides representative data from the JOLTS for the period between 2005 and 2012. On the website, the data are broken down by region and industry but not by occupation.

**EXHIBIT 14.3**   Data From the JOLTS

| Annual | Hires | Quits | Layoffs and Discharges | Other Terminations |
|--------|-------|-------|------------------------|--------------------|
| 2005 | 48.2% | 26.2% | 17.0% | 3.3% |
| 2006 | 47.7% | 26.7% | 15.8% | 3.6% |
| 2007 | 46.1% | 25.5% | 16.4% | 3.2% |
| 2008 | 41.1% | 22.7% | 17.9% | 2.9% |
| 2009 | 37.2% | 16.8% | 21.2% | 3.0% |
| 2010 | 37.4% | 16.9% | 16.8% | 3.0% |
| 2011 | 37.8% | 17.7% | 15.5% | 3.0% |
| 2012 | 38.9% | 18.8% | 15.4% | 3.0% |

SOURCE: Bureau of Labor Statistics, "Job Openings and Labor Turnover Survey," Sept. 10, 2013 (*www.bls.gov/jlt/*).
NOTE: Percentages of total nonfarm employment.

# Reasons for Leaving

It is important to ascertain, record, and track the various reasons why employees leave an organization. These data are essential for measuring and analyzing turnover. At a minimum, the departure of each employee should be classified as a voluntary, discharge, or downsizing exit, thus permitting the calculation of turnover rates. To learn more about the specific reasons underlying exit decisions, however, more in-depth probing of employee motivations is necessary. Tools for conducting such probing are exit interviews, post-exit surveys, and employee satisfaction surveys.[5] All three tools can be used to help gauge whether the decision to leave was voluntary, and if so, what the specific reasons were—thus allowing a determination of avoidable or unavoidable turnover.

## Exit Interviews

Exit interviews are formally planned and conducted interviews with departing employees. In addition to providing an opportunity to learn the employee's reasons for leaving, exit interviews are used to explain such things as rehiring rights, benefits, and confidentiality agreements. Because of the major implications of a potentially inaccurate measurement, the organization should not dramatically alter its retention strategies based on any one interview. Rather, the overall pattern of results that emerges over many interviews should be used.

It is important to ensure that exit interviews are conducted carefully. Research suggests that there are differences between the reasons for turnover that employees provide in exit interviews and the reasons they provide in anonymous surveys.[6] Departing employees are reluctant to complain about their employer because they do not want to burn any bridges or jeopardize future references. Thus, employees may claim that they are leaving for higher pay when in fact they are leaving because of poor working conditions or interpersonal conflicts with supervisors or coworkers.

The following are suggestions for conducting an appropriate interview that will hopefully elicit accurate information from the interviewee: (1) the interviewer should be a neutral person (normally someone from the human resources [HR] department or an external consultant) who has been trained in how to conduct exit interviews; (2) the training should cover how to put the employee at ease and explain the purposes of the interview, how to follow the structured interview format and avoid excessive probing and follow-up questions, the need for taking notes, and how to end the interview on a positive note; (3) there should be a structured interview format that contains questions about unavoidable and avoidable reasons for leaving, and for the avoidable category, the questions should focus on desirability of leaving, ease of leaving, and job alternatives (Exhibit 14.4 contains an example of structured exit interview questions, with questions focused on these three aspects); (4) the interviewer should prepare for each exit interview by reviewing the interview format and the interviewee's personnel file; (5) the interview

**EXHIBIT 14.4 Examples of Exit Interview Questions**

1. Current job title _____ Department/work unit _____
2. Length of time in current job _____ Length of time with organization _____
3. Are you leaving for any of the following reasons?
   retirement _____ dual career _____ new career _____ health _____
   child care or pregnancy _____ elder care _____ return to school _____
   leave the country _____ take a break _____
4. Do you have another job lined up? _____ New employer _____
5. What aspects of your new job will be better than your current job? _____
6. Before deciding to leave did you check the possibility of:
   job transfer _____ promotion _____ relocation _____
7. Was it easy to find another job? _____ Why? _____
8. Do many of your current skills fit with your new job? _____
9. What aspects of your job have been most satisfying? _____
   least satisfying? _____
10. What could the company have done to improve your job satisfaction? _____
11. How satisfactory has your job performance been since your last review? _____
12. What are things the company or your manager could have done to help you improve your performance? _____
13. If you could have had a different manager, would you have been more likely to stay with the company? _____
14. Are you willing to recommend the company to others as a place to work? _____
15. Would you be willing to hire back with the company? _____
16. Is there anything else you would like to tell us about your decision to leave the company? _____

should be conducted in a private place, before the employee's last day; and (6) the interviewee should be told that the interview is confidential and that only aggregate results will be used to help the organization better understand why employees leave and to possibly develop new retention initiatives. Conducting the interview before an employee's last day can sometimes bring up issues that, if addressed, could prevent the employee from leaving. For example, if an exit interview reveals that an employee is only leaving for higher pay, the organization can make a counteroffer.

**Post-Exit Surveys**

To increase confidentiality, anonymous post-exit surveys might be used. It is recommended that the survey cover the same areas as the exit interview and that the survey be sent shortly after the employee's last day. Open-ended surveys can be used to gather more detailed information from the employee's individual point of view, while surveys with specific questions and standardized response options make it easier to quickly compile and compare responses. Because of these trade-offs, a combination of both approaches is usually best.

### Employee Satisfaction Surveys

Since employee job dissatisfaction (desirability of leaving) is known to be a potent predictor of voluntary turnover, conducting job satisfaction surveys is a good way to discover the types of job rewards that are most dissatisfying to employees and might therefore become reasons for leaving. Conducting job satisfaction surveys has the advantage of learning from all employees (at least those who respond to the survey), rather than just those who are leaving. Satisfaction survey results also give the organization information it can use to hopefully preempt turnover by making changes that will increase job satisfaction. Designing, conducting, analyzing, and interpreting results from these surveys requires substantial organizational resources and should only be undertaken with the guidance of a person explicitly trained in job satisfaction survey techniques. Oftentimes a consultant is retained for this purpose. Online surveys allow managers to quickly and conveniently collect information from geographically dispersed employees.

## Costs and Benefits

Costs, both financial and nonfinancial in nature, and benefits may be estimated for each of the three turnover types. Most involve actual costs or benefits, though some are potential, depending on how events transpire. Some of the costs and benefits may be estimated financially, a useful and necessary exercise. Such financial analysis must be supplemented with a careful consideration of the other costs and benefits to arrive at a reasonable estimate of the total costs and benefits of turnover. It may well turn out that the nonfinancial costs and benefits outweigh the financial ones in importance and impact for the development of retention strategies and tactics.

### Voluntary Turnover

Voluntary turnover can be extremely expensive for organizations. Research consistently shows that organizations with high turnover have a low stock price, a low return on investment, low revenues, and other low financial returns.[7] Exhibit 14.5 shows the major types of costs and benefits that can occur when an employee leaves the organization.[8] An assessment of these costs and benefits will help determine whether a retention attempt should be made, and if so, how far the organization is willing to go in that attempt. Alternatively, at the aggregate level, the costs and benefits assessment could be developed for the work or business unit, division, or total organization. The results could be used to communicate with top management about the nature and severity of employee turnover and to help develop retention strategies and tactics.

---

**EXHIBIT 14.5   Voluntary Turnover: Costs and Benefits**

**I. Separation Costs**
  **A. Financial Costs**
   • HR staff time (e.g., exit interview, payroll, benefits)
   • Manager's time (e.g., retention attempts, exit interview)
   • Accrued paid time off (e.g., vacation, sick pay)
   • Temporary coverage (e.g., temporary employee, overtime pay for current employees)

  **B. Other Costs**
   • Production and customer service delays or quality decreases
   • Lost or unacquired clients
   • Employee goes to competitor or forms competitive business
   • Contagion—other employees decide to leave
   • Teamwork disruptions
   • Loss of workforce diversity

**II. Replacement Costs**
   • Staffing costs for new hire (e.g., cost-per-hire calculations)
   • Hiring inducements (e.g., bonus, relocation, perks)
   • Hiring manager and work-unit employee time
   • Orientation program time and materials
   • HR staff induction costs (e.g., payroll, benefits enrollment)

**III. Training Costs**
   • Formal training (trainee and instruction time, materials, equipment)
   • On-the-job training (supervisor and employee time)
   • Mentoring (mentor's time)
   • Socialization (time of other employees, travel)
   • Productivity loss (loss of production until full proficient employee)

**IV. Benefits**
   • Replacement employee better performer and organization citizen than last employee
   • New KSAO and motivation infusion to organization
   • Opportunity to restructure work unit
   • Savings from not replacing employee
   • Vacancy creates transfer or promotion opportunity for others
   • Replacement less expensive in salary and seniority-based benefits

Exhibit 14.5 shows that on the cost side there are separation, replacement, and training costs, both financial and nonfinancial. The financial costs mainly involve the cost of people's time, the cost of materials and equipment, cash outlays, and productivity losses. The other costs are less discernible and harder to estimate but may entail large negative impacts on organizational effectiveness, such as loss of clients. On the benefits side, a number of positive things may occur, including finding a higher-quality, less expensive replacement for the departing employee.

Accurate cost and benefit calculations require diligence and care in development, particularly those involving people's time. To estimate time costs, it is necessary to know the average amount of time each person spends in the specific activity, plus each person's compensation (pay rate plus benefits). Consider the case of an exit interview, a separation cost. Assume that (1) the staffing manager spends one hour conducting the interview and writing up a brief summary for the voluntary turnover data file, (2) the staffing manager's salary is $46,000 ($23/hour) and the employee's salary is $50,000 ($25/hour), and (3) benefits are 30% of pay ($6.90/hour for the staffing manager and $7.50/hour for the employee). The time cost of the exit interview is $62.40. At the aggregate level, if the staffing manager conducts 100 exit interviews annually, and the average pay rate of those interviewed is $20/hour, the annual time cost of exit interviews is $5,590 (staffing manager pay = $2,300 and benefits = $690; employee's pay = $2,000 and benefits = $600).

Materials and equipment costs are likely to be most prevalent in replacement and training costs. Recruitment brochures and testing materials, orientation program materials, and induction materials such as benefits enrollment forms all add to staffing costs. Formal training may involve the use of both materials and equipment that must be accounted for. Cash outlays include paying for (1) the departing employee's accrued but unused paid time off, (2) possible temporary coverage for the departing employee, and (3) hiring inducements for the replacement employee.

On the benefits side, the primary immediate benefit is the labor cost savings from not having the departing employee on the payroll. This will save the organization labor costs until a permanent replacement is hired (if ever). The organization will also save on labor costs if a temporary replacement at a lower pay rate can fill the position until a permanent replacement is acquired. The hired permanent replacement may be hired at a lower wage or salary than the departing employee, resulting in additional pay and benefit savings. The other benefits shown in Exhibit 14.5 are less tangible but potentially very important in a longer-run sense of improved work-unit and organizational effectiveness.

Exhibit 14.6 shows the cost estimates for a single incident of voluntary turnover in a hypothetical industrial supplies organization that employs 40 salespeople who receive $20/hour on average and bring in approximately $8 million in total annual sales. The three categories of the turnover and replacement process (separation, replacement, and training) are described in terms of their time costs, materials and equipment costs, and other costs.

Separation costs include the time of the employees who process turnover ($25 + $15) and the former employee's manager ($120). There is also accrued time off paid to the departing individual ($2,400). Replacement costs include both a temporary fill-in and a permanent replacement. It takes an average of four weeks to find a permanent replacement. During these four weeks (160 hours), a temporary replacement is hired through a staffing firm for $15/hour plus a 33.3% markup.

**EXHIBIT 14.6** Example of Financial Cost Estimates for One Voluntary Turnover

| | Time | | Materials and Equipment ($) | Other Costs ($) |
|---|---|---|---|---|
| | Hours | Cost ($) | | |
| **A. Separation Costs** | | | | |
| Staffing manager | 1 | 25 | | |
| HR staff | 1 | 15 | | |
| Employee's manager | 3 | 120 | | |
| Accrued paid time off | 160 | 2,400 | | |
| Processing | | | 30 | |
| **B. Replacement Costs** | | | | |
| Temporary replacement | | | | |
| Compensation difference | 160 | (800) | | |
| Staffing manager | 1 | 25 | | |
| Employee's manager | 1 | 40 | | |
| Staffing firm fee (markup) | | | | 800 |
| Permanent replacement | | | | |
| Compensation difference | 960 | (4,800) | | |
| Cost-per-hire | | | | 4,500 |
| Hiring bonus | | | | 3,000 |
| Laptop computer | | | | 2,000 |
| Employee's manager | 3 | 120 | | |
| Orientation | 8 | 160 | | |
| **C. Training Costs** | | | | |
| Training program | | | 1,000 | |
| Trainee | 80 | 1,200 | | |
| Instructor | 100 | 1,600 | | |
| Mentor | 52 | 1,040 | | |
| Productivity/sales loss | | | | |
| Permanent replacement | | | | 50,000 |
| Temporary replacement | | | | 2,000 |
| **D. Total Costs** | | 1,145 | 1,030 | 62,300 |

While this temporary employee is paid less than the average salesperson, temporary salespeople typically make $2,000 less in sales over the four-week period. A permanent new hire receives an average of $15/hour for the first six months of employment until he or she gets up to speed ($5/hour less × 960 hours = $4,800 in savings). Each new hire costs $4,500, and newcomers receive a hiring bonus of $3,000 and a laptop computer worth $2,000. Each new salesperson's manager typically has an additional three hours devoted to orienting the newcomer, and the new employee also attends an eight-hour organizational orientation session. The additional orientation cost of $40 per new hire, beyond the $120 wage cost, reflects the per employee cost of orientation trainers and classroom materials.

Training costs include the materials and equipment required for the program ($1,000), two weeks (80 hours) of paid time in the class, and the instructor's pay (100 hours). Additionally, an experienced salesperson acts as a mentor during the transition period, averaging one hour per week over the course of a year. It takes the new permanent replacement 24 weeks (24 weeks × 40 hours = 960 hours) to reach the average sales proficiency of $200,000; this means that $50,000 in sales is lost during this period. Overall, the estimated total other costs for this organization for a single salesperson turnover incident come to $62,300. The data for this organization also suggest that time costs and material costs are a fairly trivial contribution to the total expense of turnover. Lost productivity makes up 81% of the cost of turnover (i.e., $52,000 / $64,475 = 81%). This figure will, of course, vary considerably depending on the job under consideration.

It should be recognized that turnover cost estimates require considerable judgment and guesstimates. Nonetheless, this example illustrates that many turnover costs are hidden in (1) the time demands placed on the many employees who must handle the separation, replacement, and training activities, and (2) the sales or productivity losses experienced. Such costs might be offset, at least in part, through the acquisition of less expensive temporary and permanent replacement employees, at least for a while. Also note that when turnover costs for a single employee loss are aggregated to an annual level for multiple losses, the costs can be substantial. In this example, if the sales unit experienced just a 20% annual voluntary turnover rate, it would lose eight employees at a total cost of $519,000, or 6.5% of annual sales.

## Discharge

In the case of an employee discharge, some of the costs and benefits are the same as for voluntary turnover. However, at the aggregate level, there is not a relationship between involuntary turnover rates and firm performance.[9]

Exhibit 14.7 shows that separation, replacement, and training costs are still incurred. There may be an additional separation cost for a contract buyout of guarantees (salary, benefits, and perks) made in a fixed-term contract. Such buyouts are common for high-level executives and public sector leaders such as school superintendents. These guarantees are negotiated and used to make the hiring package

---

**EXHIBIT 14.7    Discharge: Costs and Benefits**

**I. Separation Costs**

    **A. Financial Costs**

- Same as for voluntary turnover plus possible contract buyout (salary, benefits, perks)

    **B. Other Costs**

- Manager and HR staff time handling problem employee
- Grievance, alternative dispute resolution
- Possibility of lawsuit, loss of lawsuit, settlement or remedy
- Damage to labor–management relations

**II. Replacement Costs**

- Same as for voluntary turnover

**III. Training Costs**

- Same as for voluntary turnover

**IV. Benefits**

- Departure of low-value employee
- High-value employee replacement possibility
- Reduced disruption for manager and work unit
- Improved performance management and disciplinary skills

---

more attractive and to reduce the financial risk of failure for the new hire. Such guarantees can drive up the costs of discharge substantially, reinforcing the need for careful selection decisions followed by support to help the new hire become a successful performer who will remain with the organization for at least the full term of the contract.

A discharge is usually preceded by the manager and others spending considerable time, often unpleasant and acrimonious, with the employee, seeking to change the person's behavior through progressive discipline or performance management activities. The discharge may be followed by a lawsuit, such as a claim that the discharge was tainted by discrimination based on the race or sex of the dischargee. The time costs for handling the matter, and the potential cash outlays required in a settlement or court-imposed remedy, can be substantial.[10] In short, compared with voluntary turnover, discharge is a more costly, and unpleasant, type of turnover to experience. Moreover, in unionized settings, discharge problems may pose a serious threat to labor–management relations.

Accompanying these often substantial costs are many potential benefits that may offset them. First and foremost is that the organization will be rid of a truly low-value employee whose presence has caused considerable disruption, ineffective performance, and possibly declines in organizational effectiveness. Another benefit is the opportunity to replace this person with a high-quality new hire who will hopefully turn out to be a high-value employee. A side benefit of a discharge experience is that many members of the organization will gain improved disciplinary and performance management skills, and the HR department's awareness of the need for better discipline and performance management systems may be heightened and lead to these necessary changes.

## Downsizing

Downsizing costs are concentrated in separation costs for a permanent RIF since there will presumably be no replacement hiring and training. These costs are shown in Exhibit 14.8, along with potential benefits.[11] The major economic cost areas are time costs, cash outlays for various severance and buyout packages, and increased unemployment compensation insurance premiums. The time costs involve both HR staff and managers' time in planning, implementing, and handling the RIF. RIF turnover has an especially strong negative relationship with organizational performance relative to other forms of involuntary turnover.[12]

Severance costs may take numerous forms. First, employees can be paid for accrued time off. Second, early retirement packages may be offered to employees as an inducement to leave early. Third, employees ineligible for early retirement may be offered a voluntary severance package as an inducement to leave without being laid off. A typical severance package includes one week's pay for each year of service, continued health insurance coverage and premium payment, and outplacement assistance. A danger with both early retirement and voluntary severance packages is that their provisions may turn out to be so attractive that more employees take them and leave than had been planned for in the RIF.

If the early retirement and voluntary severance packages do not induce a sufficient number of employees to leave, the organization may also institute an involuntary RIF with a severance package. Some employees may receive special severance consideration. For those on a fixed-term contract, a contract buyout will be necessary. Others, usually key executives, may have change in control (CIC) clauses in their contracts that must be fulfilled if there is a merger or acquisition; CICs are also known as "golden parachutes." In addition to the terms in typical severance packages, a CIC may provide for immediate vesting of stock options, a retirement payout sweetener or buyout, bonus payments, continuation of all types of insurance for an extended time period, and maintenance of various benefits.

Other costs of downsizing shown in Exhibit 14.8 may also be considerable. Shareholder value (stock price) may not improve, suggesting the stock market views the probable effectiveness of the restructuring as low. There will be a critical talent loss and an inability to respond quickly to the need for workforce additions

---

**EXHIBIT 14.8** **Downsizing: Costs and Benefits**

### I. Separation Costs

#### A. Financial Costs

- HR staff time in planning and implementing layoff
- Managers' time in handling layoff
- Accrued paid time off (e.g., vacation, sick pay)
- Early retirement package
- Voluntary severance package (e.g., one week's pay/year of service, continued health insurance, outplacement assistance)
- Involuntary severance package
- Contract buyouts for fulfillment of guarantees
- Higher unemployment insurance premiums
- Change in control (CIC) guarantees for key executives during a merger or acquisition

#### B. Other Costs

- Shareholder value (stock price) may not improve
- Loss of critical employees and KSAOs
- Inability to respond quickly to surges in product and service demand; restaffing delays and costs
- Contagion—other employees leave
- Threat to harmonious labor–management relations
- Possibility of lawsuit, loss of lawsuit, costly settlement or remedy
- Decreased morale, increased feelings of job insecurity
- Difficulty in attracting new employees

### II. Benefits

- Lower payroll and benefits costs
- Increased production and staffing flexibility
- Ability to relocate facilities
- Improved promotion and transfer opportunities for stayers
- Focus on core businesses, eliminate peripheral ones
- Spread risk by outsourcing activities to other organizations
- Flatten organization hierarchy—especially among managers
- Increase productivity

to cover new demand surges. Moreover, a reputation for job instability will create added difficulties in attracting new employees. Terminated employees may pursue legal avenues, claiming, for example, that decisions about whom to lay off were tainted by age discrimination. Employees who survive the job cuts may have damaged morale and may fear even more cuts, which may harm performance and cause them to look for another job with a more secure organization. Against this backdrop of heavy costs are many potential benefits. There will in fact be lower payroll and benefits costs. The organization may gain production and staffing flexibility, an ability to outsource parts of the business that are not mission critical, and opportunities to redesign and relocate facilities. The restructuring may also entail a flattening of the organization hierarchy by eliminating management layers, leading to increased speed in decision making as well as productivity boosts.

### Summary

Despite their many potential benefits, voluntary turnover, discharges, and downsizing are typically costly propositions. Time costs, materials costs, performance and revenue losses, severance costs, legal costs, and so forth can create substantial cost challenges and risks for the organization. Potentially even more important are the human costs of frayed relationships, critical talent losses, performance declines, disruptive discipline, the contagion effect of other employees leaving along with the departing employee, and the risk of not being able to locate, attract, and hire high-quality replacements.

The organization must carefully weigh these costs and benefits generally for each type of turnover, as well as specifically for separate employee groups, job categories, and organizational units. Clear cost–benefit differences in turnover will likely emerge from these more fine-grained analyses. Such analyses will help the organization better understand its turnover, determine where and among whom turnover is most worrisome, and learn how to fashion tailor-made retention strategies and tactics.

## RETENTION INITIATIVES: VOLUNTARY TURNOVER

For most organizations, of the three types of turnover, voluntary turnover is the most prevalent and the one they choose to focus on in the continual "war for talent." Described below are examples of retention initiatives undertaken by organizations. These are vast in number, but little is known about how organizations actually decide to act on a turnover problem and go forward with one or more retention initiatives. To fill this void, a retention decision process is described that will help the organization more systematically and effectively pursue the right retention initiatives. Based on the causes of turnover model (Exhibit 14.2), ways to influence the three primary turnover drivers—desirability of leaving, ease of leaving, and alternatives—are suggested for retention initiatives.

## Current Practices and Deciding to Act

Turnover analysis does not end with the collection and analysis of data. These activities are merely a precursor to the critical decision of whether to act to solve a perceived turnover problem, and if so, how to intervene to attack the problem and ultimately assess how effective the intervention was. Presented first are some examples of organization retention initiatives that illustrate the breadth and depth of attempts to address retention concerns. Then a systematic decision process for retention initiatives is provided as a framework to help with deciding whether to act. Such decision guidance is necessary given the complexity of the retention issue and the lack of demonstrated best practices for improving retention.

## What Do Organizations Do?

Several descriptive surveys provide glimpses of the actions that organizations take to address retention. These examples come mostly from relatively large organizations, so what happens in small organizations is more of an unknown. Nonetheless, the data provide interesting illustrations of organization tenacity and ingenuity, along with a willingness to commit resources, in various approaches to retention.

***Review of Organizational Practices.*** Although there are many anecdotal stories about which retention practices are or are not effective, the most compelling evidence on this topic comes from a comprehensive examination that correlated various organizational practices with organizational turnover rates across thousands of different workplaces.[13] The results of this study showed that some practices were clearly more effective than others. The most and least effective retention initiatives are listed in Exhibit 14.9. We discuss the specific components of retention bundles in greater detail later in this chapter, but for now, it should be emphasized that these initiatives included not just single, isolated practices but a combined

---

**EXHIBIT 14.9** **Most and Least Effective Retention Initiatives**

**Most Effective Retention Initiatives**

- Retention bundles (high-commitment HR systems)
- Benefits
- Dispute resolution
- Participation-enhancing work design

**Least Effective Retention Initiatives**

- Relative pay
- Sophisticated selection system
- Variable pay
- Training

system of practices that worked together to encourage employees to remain. It is also interesting to note that increased investment in training as a stand-alone practice was actually associated with increases in turnover. This is consistent with our earlier discussion proposing that higher levels of general, transferable KSAOs can increase the ease of leaving.

***WorldatWork Survey.*** WorldatWork conducts regular surveys of HR managers regarding the implementation and success of retention initiatives. A survey conducted with a sample of 526 respondents in 2012 focused on the role of rewards in retaining key talent.[14] The great majority of respondents indicated that their organizations identified their key talent and focused their retention efforts on those individuals. Discussing future opportunities, creating succession plans, providing meaningful and enriching job designs, and paying key employees above the market rate were all identified as particularly effective retention methods. One of the least effective methods was providing tuition reimbursement and other educational opportunities. Such activities can actually increase the level of general human capital possessed by employees, thereby making it easier for them to find jobs elsewhere. Most managers also felt that simply tracking employee satisfaction was not particularly useful, perhaps because the tracking activities often were not accompanied by tangible efforts to improve problem situations.

***The 100 Best Companies.*** Each year *Fortune* magazine publishes the report "The 100 Best Companies to Work For."[15] Organizations apply to be on the list, and their score is based on randomly chosen employees' responses to the Great Place to Work Trust Index survey and an evaluation of a Culture Audit. Winners are ranked according to their final score, and brief descriptions are provided about the number of US employees (including the percentages of women and minorities), job growth, annual number of job applicants and voluntary turnover rate, average number of employee training hours, entry-level salary for production and professional employees, revenues, and what makes the organization stand out.

Unfortunately, the study does not provide specific information on patterns of usage and effectiveness of retention initiatives among the 100 organizations. However, comments about what makes the organization stand out provide intriguing tidbits as to special practices that might enhance retention. Google, the top-rated organization for 2013, was highlighted for having a particularly appealing array of perquisites, including a gourmet cafeteria, swimming pools, volleyball courts, laundry facilities, on-site physicians, and language classes. The company also emphasizes a culture of employee collaboration, learning, and development, which increases employees' intrinsic enjoyment of the work they do. Also, Google engineers are required to spend one day per week developing their own new ideas for projects that can be implemented. For individuals who are eager to pursue new and exciting ideas, this might be the most valuable perk of all. *Fortune* also profiled the candy maker Mars. As you might expect, there are vending machines that dispense free M&Ms to employees, and there are additional programs that further sweeten the deal. Rather than investing in luxurious offices, the company concentrates its efforts on providing employees with long-term project development and development plans that help them envision spending their career within the company. Mars boasts an annual turnover rate of 5%, which is exceptionally low. It is not uncommon for individuals from multiple generations of the same family to be employees. This suggests that investing in employees and their futures can lower turnover and attract new employees who are well acquainted with the company's culture and values.

***Retention Bundles.*** The retention initiatives up to this point have been described in terms of individual practices, such as providing rewards linked to tenure or matching offers from other organizations. This should not be taken to suggest that retention initiatives should be offered in isolation. To be effective, retention practices need to be integrated into a comprehensive system, or as a "bundle" of practices. As an example, research has shown that the best performers are least likely to quit when an organization both rewards performance with higher compensation *and* widely communicates its compensation practices. Focusing on only compensation or communication does not have these effects—the procedures are much more effective as a bundle.[16] Other research found that the level of both voluntary and involuntary turnover was lower in organizations that made long-term investments in employees through a combination of employment security, internal mobility opportunities, and pensions for long-term employees.[17] In sum, large-scale reviews of organizational practices and turnover rates clearly indicate that the most effective tool for improving retention is to provide integrated systems that involve careful selection, adequate training, satisfying work conditions, and rewards for retention.[18]

In practical terms, managers need to examine all the characteristics in the work environment that might lead to turnover and address them in a comprehensive manner. Organizations with strong investments in their staffing methods may find their investments are lost if they do not support this strategy with an equally strong commitment to providing newcomers with sufficient orientation material to adjust to their new jobs. Organizations that provide numerous benefits in a poorly integrated fashion may similarly find that the intended effects are lost if managers and employees believe that the programs fail to address their needs.

***Specific Retention Initiatives.*** To further illustrate policies that organizations might adopt to control turnover, Exhibit 14.10 summarizes practices from a number of organizations that have been able to significantly improve retention outcomes.[19] One noteworthy feature of these programs is the use of both extrinsic and intrinsic rewards.

**EXHIBIT 14.10** **Retention Initiative Examples**

| Organization | Initiative | Results |
|---|---|---|
| Cendant | Flexible working schedule and work/life balance program designed around employee survey feedback | Annual turnover decreased from approximately 30% to less than 10% |
| Deloitte | Develop "mass career customization," which allows employees to customize their workload to suit their needs | Dramatic reduction in turnover of top-performing employees |
| Fleet Bank | Career growth opportunities and ensuring that employees are able to establish long-term relationships with their managers | Turnover fell by 40% among salaried employees and by 25% among hourly employees |
| Outback Steakhouse | Provide adequate information on job characteristics prior to hiring, extensive opportunities for employee voice | Turnover rates at approximately half of industry norms |
| SAP Americas | Increase communication regarding the organization's strategic direction and goals, provide rewards for retention, improve supervisor–employee relationship | Voluntary annual turnover rates fell from 14.9% to 6.1% |
| UPS | Provide well-above-market wages, ample vacation time, free health insurance, and pension | Typical annual turnover rate of 1.8% |
| Wegmans | Provide a comprehensive menu of health care benefits far above industry norms | Turnover rates at approximately 60% of industry norms |

## Decision Process

Exhibit 14.11 provides a suggested decision process that can help organizations navigate the complex trade-offs inherent in developing retention initiatives.

The first question—do we think turnover is a problem?—requires consideration and analysis of several types of data. It is necessary to judge whether turnover rates are increasing and/or high relative to internal and external benchmarks such as industry or direct competitor data. Additional information is necessary, such as whether managers are complaining about retention problems, whether mostly high-value employees are leaving, and whether there are demographic disparities

**EXHIBIT 14.11** **Decision Process for Retention Initiatives**

| Do We Think Turnover Is a Problem? | How Might We Attack the Problem? | What Do We Need to Decide? | How Should We Evaluate the Initiatives? |
|---|---|---|---|
| • Turnover high or increasing relative to internal and external benchmarks<br>• Managers complain about retention problems<br>• High-value employees are leaving<br>• Demographic disparities among those who leave<br>• Overall costs exceed benefits of turnover | • Lower desirability of leaving? Increase job satisfaction—yes Decrease shocks—no Personal reasons—no Improve organizational justice—yes Improve social environment at work—yes<br>• Lower ease of leaving? Change market conditions—no Decrease provision of general KSAOs—yes Make leaving more costly—yes<br>• Change alternatives? Promotion and transfers—yes Respond to outside job offers—yes | • Turnover goals<br>• Targeted to units and groups<br>• High-value employees<br>• General and targeted retention initiatives<br>• Lead, match, or lag the market<br>• Supplement or supplant<br>• HR and managers' roles | • Lower proportion of turnover if avoidable<br>• Turnover low or decreasing compared with benchmarks<br>• Fewer complaints about retention problems<br>• Fewer high-value employees leaving<br>• Reduced demographic disparities<br>• Lower turnover costs relative to benefits |

among those who leave. The final analysis should involve the type of costs/benefits described earlier. Even though turnover may be high, in the final analysis it is only a problem if its costs are judged to exceed its benefits.

The second question—how might we attack the problem?—requires consideration of desirability of leaving, ease of leaving, and alternative turnover causes. In addition, within each of these areas, which specific factors is it possible to change? In Exhibit 14.11, for desirability of leaving it shows that increasing job satisfaction, improving organizational justice, and improving the social environment are possible, but it is likely not possible to change personal shocks or personal reasons for leaving. Likewise, for ease of leaving it is possible to avoid providing general KSAOs and to increase the cost of leaving for the employee.

Question three—what do we need to decide?—crosses the boundary from consideration to possible implementation. First to be decided are specific numerical turnover (retention) goals in the form of desired turnover rates. Retention programs without retention goals are bound to fail. Then it must be decided whether the goals and retention programs will be applied across the board, targeted to specific organization units and employee groups, or applied to both. Examples of targeted groups include certain job categories in which turnover is particularly troublesome, women and minorities, and first-year employees (newcomers)—a group that traditionally experiences high turnover. Next to be considered is if and how high-value employees will be treated. Many organizations develop special retention initiatives for high-value employees on top of other retention programs, and it will have to be decided whether to follow this path of special treatment for such employees.[20] Having identified organizational units, targeted groups, and high-value employees (and established turnover goals for them), the retention program specifics must be designed. These may be general (across-the-board) initiatives applicable to all employees, or they may be targeted ones. It must then be decided how to position the organization's initiatives relative to the marketplace. Will it seek to lead, match, or lag the market? For example, will base pay on average be higher than the market average (lead), be the same as the market average (match), or be lower than the market average (lag)? Likewise, will new variable pay plans try to outdo competitors (e.g., a more favorable stock option plan) or simply match them? Adding to the complexity of the decision process is the delicate issue of whether new retention initiatives will supplement (add on to) or supplant (replace) existing rewards and programs. If the latter, the organization should be prepared for the possibility of employee backlash against what employees may perceive as "take backs" of rewards they currently have and must give up. Finally, the respective roles of HR and individual managers will have to be worked out, and this may vary among the retention initiatives. If the initiative involves responding to outside job offers, for example, line managers may demand a heavy or even exclusive hand in this process. Alternatively, some initiatives may be HR driven; examples here include hours of work and variable pay plans.

The final question—how should we evaluate the initiatives?—should be considered *before* any plan is implemented. Answers will lend focus to the design of the intervention and agreed-upon criteria on which to later judge intervention effectiveness. Ideally, the same criteria that led to the conclusion that turnover was a problem (question one) will be used to determine whether the chosen solution actually works (question four).

## Desirability of Leaving

Employees' desire to leave depends on their job satisfaction, shocks they experience, and personal (nonjob) reasons. Of these, only job satisfaction can usually be meaningfully influenced by the organization. Therefore, the first strategy for improving retention is to improve job satisfaction. The myriad examples of retention initiatives described above mostly represent attempts to improve job satisfaction through delivery of various rewards to employees.

It is critical to understand that merely throwing more or new rewards at employees is not a sound retention initiative. Which rewards are chosen, and how they are delivered to employees, will determine how effective they are in improving job satisfaction. Accordingly, guidelines for reward choice and delivery are also described here. Exhibit 14.12 summarizes the guidelines for increasing job satisfaction and retention.

As discussed in Chapter 4, a variety of extrinsic and intrinsic rewards can be brought to bear on the question of job satisfaction. Rather than reiterating these specific rewards here, we instead discuss how organizations can provide both categories of rewards in a manner that is consistent with the best practices identified by research and experience.

One important point must be borne in mind for both intrinsic and extrinsic rewards. The person/job match model emphasizes that job satisfaction results from a match between the rewards desired by the employee and the rewards provided by the job. Employee reward preferences may be assessed at all stages of the staffing process by (1) asking applicants what attracted them to the organization, (2) asking current employees about the most important sources of job satisfaction, and (3) assessing reasons for turnover during exit interviews.

---

**EXHIBIT 14.12**   **Guidelines for Increasing Job Satisfaction and Retention**

**A. Extrinsic Rewards**

- Make rewards meaningful and unique
- Match rewards to individual preferences
- Link rewards to retention behaviors
- Link rewards to performance

**B. Intrinsic Rewards**

- Assign employees to jobs that meet their needs for work characteristics
- Provide clear communication with employees
- Design fair reward allocation systems
- Ensure supervisors provide a positive environment
- Provide programs to enhance work/life balance

### Extrinsic Rewards

To have attraction and retention power, extrinsic rewards must be unique and unlikely to be offered by competitors. Surveys of employees consistently show that inadequate compensation and benefits are extremely powerful drivers of employee turnover decisions.[21] The organization must benchmark against its competitors to determine what others are offering. A survey of 1,223 employed adults also revealed that employee benefits were a key driver of employee retention. In particular, 40% of respondents indicated that 401(k) matching decreased their desire to leave; health care coverage and competitive salary also topped the list.[22] Surveys also suggest that in a down economy, many employees see benefits like health insurance as a vital part of their personal safety net.[23]

Rewards can be even more powerfully attached to employee retention if they explicitly take seniority into account. For example, employees who have been with the organization longer may receive more vacation hours, career advancement opportunities, and increased job security. A more subtle way of rewarding employee retention is to make the reward contingent on the person's base pay level. Base pay levels typically increase over time through a combination of promotions and merit pay increases. Specific retention bonuses are also used to encourage longer-term relationships.

Rewards can also be linked to employee job performance. Organizations with a strong performance management culture thrive on high performance expectations, coupled with large rewards (e.g., base pay raises, bonuses, commissions, and stock options) for high performers. Because lesser performers receive lower wages in these organizations, they are more likely to leave, whereas superior performers are more likely to stay.[24] Organizations may even more specifically target key performers by providing special retention bonuses, new job assignments, and additional perks if it appears that they are likely to leave.[25]

### Intrinsic Rewards

The intrinsic rewards listed in Exhibit 4.18 should not be overlooked. There is consistent evidence that employee dissatisfaction with the intrinsic quality of their job is strongly related to turnover.[26]

Improving the work environment involves assigning employees to jobs that better meet their intrinsic-reward preferences. For example, employees with high needs for skill variety could be assigned to more complex jobs or projects within a work unit, or employees with high autonomy needs could be assigned to supervisors with a very "hands-off" style of leadership. Job redesign can also improve the work environment. To increase skill variety, managers might broaden the scope of tasks and responsibility for longer-term employees, allowing for personal growth on the job. Job rotation programs also help reduce perceived monotony on the job. Enhancing job autonomy might be facilitated by establishing formal performance goals for the job while giving employees minimal direction or oversight as to the methods required to achieve these goals. A survey of over 700 nursing managers found that higher levels of training and development opportunities were associated with lower levels of establishment-level turnover.[27] Similar methods for improving task identity, task significance, and feedback should also be considered.

One of the closest correlates of employee commitment is the perception that the organization treats its employees fairly and provides them with support. Two forms of justice are necessary.[28] Distributive justice refers to perceptions that the individual reward levels are consistent with employee contributions to the organization. Procedural justice refers to perceptions that the process for allocating rewards and punishments is administered consistently, follows well-defined guidelines, and is free from bias. A sense that these justice principles have been violated can create dissatisfaction and may result in turnover or a lawsuit.

A crucial component to increasing employees' perception of justice is clear communication. Communication must begin early in the staffing process by providing employees with honest information about their job conditions. Evidence suggests that employees who receive adequate information regarding job conditions perceive their employers as more honest and may be less likely to leave.[29] If reward systems are to increase satisfaction, employees must know why the system was developed, the mechanics of the system, and the payouts to be expected. Such knowledge and understanding require continuous communication. Research shows that a very common form of employee dissatisfaction with reward systems is a failure to understand them, or actual misinformation about them.[30] Any retention initiative designed to increase job satisfaction must have a solid communication component. On a broader level, communication regarding the organization's strategic direction can reduce turnover. Surveys at SAP America indicated that employees who felt the organization had a clear vision for the future and believed that top management supported them were more likely to report that they were engaged in their work.[31]

Justice perceptions are also strongly influenced by reward system design. Distributive justice requires that there be a rational and preferably measurable basis for reward decisions. Objective measures of job performance, such as sales figures, are also likely to be accepted as legitimate. Rewards based on managerial performance reviews may be more problematic if employees question the legitimacy of the performance measurement system, or if they believe these rewards create divisive comparisons among employees. The importance of system fairness has been demonstrated in many contexts. Although much of the research on justice has been conducted in the United States and Canada, studies from China, Korea, Japan, and Pakistan have also shown that perceived justice increases job satisfaction and decreases turnover intentions.[32]

It is said that employees don't quit their jobs, they quit their bosses. Thus, interpersonal compatibility or chemistry between the employee and the supervisor can be a critical part of the employee's decision to stay or leave. The same could be said for coworkers. Employees who believe they fit with the social environment in which they work are more likely to see their job as a source of significant social rewards. The resultant sense of camaraderie with the supervisor and coworkers may make them reluctant to leave the organization. Research confirms that individuals whose coworkers are searching for alternative jobs will increase their own job search efforts.[33]

The supervisor is also a source of justice perceptions because of his or her role as a direct source of reward or punishment.[34] This is because the supervisor decides the process for assessing employees, as well as the amount of rewards to be provided based on these assessments. The supervisor also serves as a key communication conduit regarding reward systems. If supervisors communicate the purpose and mechanics of the system, employees will be able to understand the process of reward distribution and what they need to do to receive rewards in the future. Supervisors who treat subordinates with respect and concern can also help reduce turnover.

Supervisors and coworkers in the social setting can engage in abusive or harassing behaviors that are threatening or discomforting to an employee. Research suggests that employees who believe that their supervisors are abusive are more likely to leave.[35] Examples of abusive supervisor behavior that are frequently cited in surveys include "tells me my thoughts and feelings are stupid," "puts me down in front of others," and "tells me I'm incompetent." More extreme behaviors, such as sexual harassment, have even stronger negative impacts on an employee's desire to remain on the job. Turnover due to interpersonal conflicts at work tends to come especially quickly; many employees who have such conflicts will bypass the process of searching for and considering alternative jobs and will instead quit immediately. Employees who are isolated from others in their racial, ethnic, or gender group are more likely to leave, whereas pro-diversity workplace climates tend to reduce turnover intentions.

For many employees, trying to balance work tasks with their personal lives contributes to stress, dissatisfaction, and a desire to leave.[36] Therefore, many organizations hoping to reduce turnover have developed programs to help employees integrate their work and nonwork lives. These work/life balance programs allow employees to take time off from work if needed, create flexible scheduling options, and facilitate opportunities to work from remote locations. Many organizations have made family-friendly benefits and flexible work arrangements centerpieces of their retention strategies, and surveys suggest that making efforts to help employees balance their work and family lives can pay off in terms of lower turnover. Data from 2,769 individuals who responded to the National Study of the Changing Workforce revealed that employees who had access to family-friendly work benefits experienced less stress and had lower turnover intentions relative to employees who did not have access to these benefits.[37] In a survey of over 200 HR professionals, 67% of respondents believed that flexible work arrangements had a positive impact on employee retention.[38] Despite evidence supporting their use, it should be remembered that work/life programs do not come without costs. Restructuring the workforce can disrupt productivity and may require investments in new technology to facilitate off-site work. Research has also shown that some employees who choose not to take advantage of telecommuting options resent their coworkers who are not in the office regularly, and this resentment can lead to increased intention to leave.[39]

### Individual Dispositions

Although organizations often try to influence turnover rates by providing intrinsically and extrinsically satisfying working conditions, a growing body of evidence suggests that some employees are more likely to quit because of their personality dispositions. In other words, some people are just more prone to quit than others are. We have already noted that a variety of tools like standardized tests and interviews can be used to identify the characteristics of job applicants. Organizations that are especially concerned about turnover might consider assessing applicants' propensity to quit voluntarily as part of their selection system.

One approach to identifying individuals who are likely to quit is to explicitly ask applicants how often they have changed jobs and what their intentions are regarding staying in their current job. Although the effects are not large, these types of biodata questions are related to turnover rates.[40] Another approach to identifying employees with high turnover propensity is to assess conscientiousness, agreeableness, and emotional stability, as some research has shown that individuals with these traits are less likely to quit.[41]

## Ease of Leaving

The decision process (Exhibit 14.11) indicates two points of attack on ease of leaving—providing organization-specific training and increasing the cost of leaving. The third factor, labor market conditions, cannot be influenced and represents a variable that will continuously influence the organization's voluntary turnover.

### Organization-Specific Training

Training and development activities provide KSAOs to employees that they did not possess when they entered the organization as new hires. Training and development seek to increase labor quality in ways that enhance employees' effectiveness. As shown previously, training represents a substantial investment (cost) that evaporates when an employee leaves the organization.

The organization may invest in training to provide KSAOs that vary along a continuum of general to organization-specific. The more general the KSAOs, the more transferable they are to other organizations, thus increasing their likelihood of improving the employee's marketability and raising the probability of leaving. Organization-specific KSAOs are not transferable, and possession of them does not improve employee marketability. Hence, it is possible to lower the employee's ease of leaving by providing, as much as possible, only organization-specific training content that has value only as long as the employee remains with the organization.

This strategy needs to be coupled with a selection strategy in which any general KSAOs required for the job are assessed and selected on so that they will not have to be invested in once the employee is on the job. For example, applicants for an entry-level sales job might be assessed and selected for general sales competencies such as written and verbal communication and interpersonal skills. Those hired may then receive more specialized training in such areas as product knowledge, specific software, and knowledge of territories. To the extent that such organization-specific KSAOs become an increasingly large proportion of the employee's total KSAO package over time, they help restrict the employee's mobility.

This strategy entails some risk. It assumes that the general KSAOs are available and affordable among applicants. It also assumes these applicants will not be dissuaded if they learn about the organization-specific training and development they will receive.

### Increased Cost of Leaving

Driving up the cost of leaving is another way to make it less easy to leave. Providing above-market pay and benefits is one way to do this, since employees will have a hard time finding better-paying jobs elsewhere. Any form of deferred compensation, such as deferred bonuses, will also raise the cost of leaving, since the compensation will be lost if the employee leaves before he or she is eligible to receive it.

Retention bonuses might also be used. Normally, these are keyed to high-value employees whose loss would wreak organizational havoc. Such may be the case during mergers and acquisitions, when retention of key managers is essential to a smooth transition.

Another long-term way to make leaving costly is to locate the organization's facilities in an area where it is the dominant employer and other amenities (housing, schools, and health care) are accessible and affordable. This may entail location in the outer rings of suburban areas or relatively small and rural communities. Once employees move to and settle into these locations, the cost of leaving is high because of the lack of alternative jobs within the area and the need to make a costly geographic move in order to obtain a new job.

## Alternatives

In confronting outside alternatives available to employees, the organization must fashion ways to make even better internal alternatives available and desirable. Two key ways to do this involve internal staffing and responding to outside job offers.

## Internal Staffing

The nature and operation of internal staffing systems have already been explored. It is important to reiterate that open systems serve as a safety valve, retentionwise, in that employees are encouraged to look internally for new job opportunities, and managers benefit by seeking internal candidates rather than going outside the organization. The organization should also think of ways outside the realm of its traditional internal staffing systems to provide attractive internal alternatives to its employees.

For example, Mercer Management Consulting has developed a rotational externship program for some of its consultants. These consultants are allowed to take on a full-time operational role for a client for 6–24 months, rather than handle multiple clients. The consultant gets the satisfaction of seeing a project through to completion and gains valuable operating experience. In the spirit of the "if you love something, set it free" saying, it is hoped that these consultants will return to Mercer at the end of the project. Another example is a temporary internal transfer system used by Interbrand Group, a unit of Omnicom Group. Certain high-performing employees are offered short-term transfers to any of its 26 offices worldwide. The lateral moves can last from three months to one year. The transfers allow employees to make a change in their lives without quitting their jobs.[42] Illustrating this point, a study of 205 individuals employed in diverse work settings found that those who were unhappy with their work environments did not translate this dissatisfaction into an intention to leave if they believed that there were opportunities for mobility within their organization. In a sense, one could say that these dissatisfied individuals saw internal transfers as a way to quit a disliked job, but without the costs to the employer that typically come with turnover.[43]

## Response to Job Offers

When employees receive an outside job offer or are on the verge of receiving one, they clearly have a solid job alternative in hand. How should the organization respond, if at all, in order to make itself the preferred alternative?

The organization should confront this dilemma with a policy that has been carefully thought through in advance. This will help prevent impulsive, potentially regrettable actions being taken on the spot when an employee brings forth a job offer and wants to use it for leverage.

First, the organization should decide whether it will respond to job offers. Some organizations choose not to, thereby avoiding bidding wars and counteroffer games. Even if the organization successfully retains the employee, the employee may then lack commitment to the organization, and other employees may resent the special retention deal that was cut. Other organizations choose to respond to job offers, not wanting to automatically close out an opportunity to at least respond to, and hopefully retain, the employee. The price for such openness to outside offers is that it may encourage employees to actively solicit them in order to try to squeeze a counteroffer out of the organization, thus improving the "deal."

# RETENTION INITIATIVES: DISCHARGE

## Performance Management

Many organizations use performance management to help ensure that the initial person/job match made during staffing yields an effectively performing employee, to facilitate employee performance improvement and competency growth, and to detect and hopefully remedy performance problems. Performance management systems focus most of their attention on planning, enabling, appraising, and rewarding employee performance.[44] Having a performance management system in place, however, also allows the organization to systematically detect and treat performance problems that employees exhibit before those problems become so harmful and intractable that discharge is the only recourse. The discharge prevention possibilities of a performance management system make it another important retention initiative to use within an overall retention program. In addition, a sound performance management system can be very useful in helping an organization successfully defend itself against legal challenges to discharges that do occur.

Exhibit 14.13 portrays the performance management process. Organization strategy drives work-unit plans, which in turn become operational for employees through a four-stage process. Stage one—performance planning—involves setting performance goals for each employee and identifying specific competencies the employee will be evaluated on. In stage two—performance execution—the focus is on the employee actually performing the job. Assistance to the employee could or should be made in the form of resources to aid in job performance coupled with coaching and feedback from the employee's manager, peers, and others. To be effective, performance feedback should be provided frequently and should always be accompanied by specific suggestions for improvement. At the end of the performance period, such as a quarter or a year, stage three begins and a formal performance review is conducted, usually by the manager. In this stage, the employee's success in reaching established goals is assessed, ratings of the employee's competencies are made, written comments are developed to explain ratings and provide suggestions for performance improvement, and feedback from the assessment is provided to the employee. In stage four, the information developed during the performance review is used to help make decisions that will affect the employee. These decisions will likely pertain to pay raises and to training and career plans. They may also pertain to formal identification of performance problems, where the employee has shown, or is headed toward, unacceptable performance.

Specifically, it may be decided that an employee has severe performance problems (stage four), and this can set in motion a focused performance-improvement

**EXHIBIT 14.13**   **Performance Management Process**

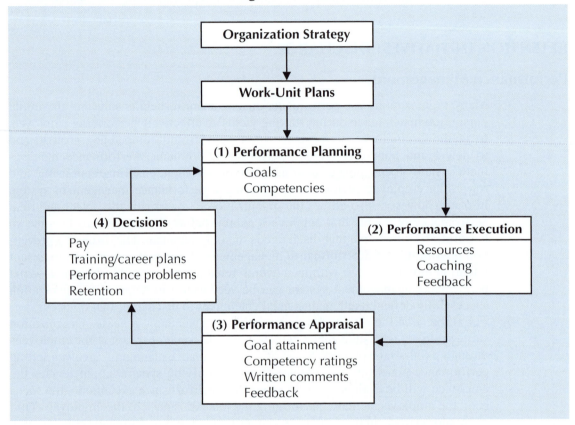

process throughout the next performance management cycle. The process of performance counseling and discipline can be conceptualized in six stages, as shown in Exhibit 14.14. It is important for managers to consider different types of performance problems when developing a counseling and disciplinary plan, because each dimension requires different responses. The model in Exhibit 14.14 breaks job performance into three categories.[45] Task performance includes the completion of job tasks that are specifically included in the job description. Citizenship reflects the psychological and social environment of work created by employees, which might be only indirectly reflected in written job descriptions but is important for maintaining a smoothly functioning work group. Counterproductivity represents actions that directly violate organizational rules or that undermine performance. The first imperative for managers is to continually monitor employee performance and identify problems. Next, managers should determine

**EXHIBIT 14.14** **Performance Counseling and Disciplinary Processes**

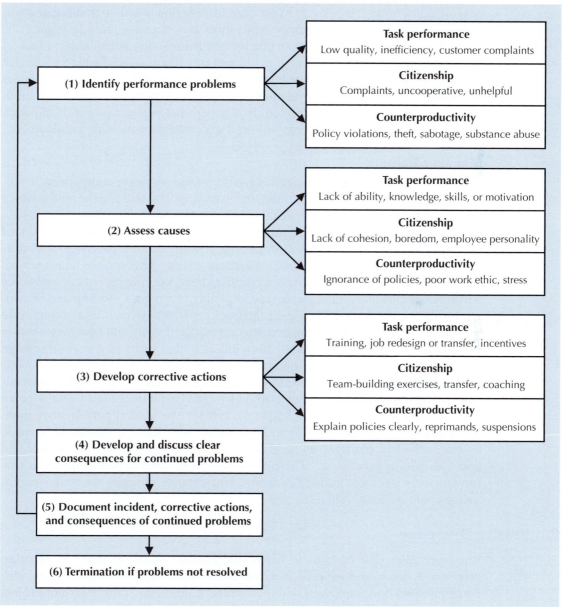

**(1) Identify performance problems**

> **Task performance**
> Low quality, inefficiency, customer complaints

> **Citizenship**
> Complaints, uncooperative, unhelpful

> **Counterproductivity**
> Policy violations, theft, sabotage, substance abuse

**(2) Assess causes**

> **Task performance**
> Lack of ability, knowledge, skills, or motivation

> **Citizenship**
> Lack of cohesion, boredom, employee personality

> **Counterproductivity**
> Ignorance of policies, poor work ethic, stress

**(3) Develop corrective actions**

> **Task performance**
> Training, job redesign or transfer, incentives

> **Citizenship**
> Team-building exercises, transfer, coaching

> **Counterproductivity**
> Explain policies clearly, reprimands, suspensions

**(4) Develop and discuss clear consequences for continued problems**

**(5) Document incident, corrective actions, and consequences of continued problems**

**(6) Termination if problems not resolved**

why employee performance has become unacceptable. This process should involve the employee's input as well. If problems are occurring because of a lack of knowledge or skills, it may be possible to use corrective action based on training or counseling. Problems involving lack of motivation or a negative attitude require the use of rewards and punishments, while problems involving personality or lack of ability may require reassignment to a different job. Regardless of which corrective actions are taken, employees need to be clearly informed about the consequences of continued failure to perform adequately, and the entire counseling and disciplinary process needs to be documented. It is hoped that performance will improve, but if it does not, the organization will need to consider terminating employment.

### Manager Training

A successful performance management system requires many components. Probably none is more critical than training the managers who will use the performance management system with employees in their work units.[46]

Performance management requires managers to possess a complex set of knowledge and skills. Examples of training content include purposes of performance management, policies and procedures of the performance management system, appraisal forms and how to complete them, keeping records of employee performance incidents, rating accuracy, coaching techniques, finding and providing resources, methods of providing feedback, goal setting, and legal compliance requirements. It is especially important to stress exactly why and how performance management is to be used as a retention initiative that seeks to prevent discharge through intensive performance improvement attempts.

Another important part of training should be concerned with employee termination. Here, managers must come to understand that a decision to discharge an employee for performance problems falls outside the normal performance management process (Exhibit 14.13) and is not a decision that can or should be made by the individual manager alone. Terminations require separate procedural and decision-making processes.[47] These could also be covered as part of a regular performance management training program, or a separate program devoted to termination could be conducted.

## Progressive Discipline

Employee discipline pertains to behavioral conduct problems that violate rules, procedures, laws, and professional and moral standards.[48] Discipline may also come into play for employees with performance problems. Progressive discipline involves a series of penalties for misconduct that increase in severity if the misconduct is repeated, starting with an informal warning and going all the way up to termination. In progressive discipline, employees are given notice of their misconduct and are provided the opportunity (and often the assistance) to change their behavior; termination is a last resort.

Progressive discipline systems are rooted in major principles of fairness and justice that can be summarized in the following five requirements for a progressive discipline system: (1) give employees notice of the rules of conduct and misconduct, (2) give employees notice of the consequences of violating the rules, (3) provide equal treatment for all employees, (4) allow for full investigation of the alleged misconduct and defense by the employee, and (5) provide employees the right to appeal a decision.[49]

### Actions to Take

Several things can be done to address the fairness requirements. First, establish what constitutes misconduct and the penalties for misconduct. The penalties start with an oral warning and progress through a written warning, suspension, and termination. Second, provide training to employees and managers so that they are aware of the types of misconduct, penalties, investigation and documentation requirements, and appeal rights. Third, work with managers to ensure that there is consistency in treatment of employees (i.e., no favoritism), meaning that similar misconduct results in similar penalties for all employees. Finally, establish an appeals procedure, if one is not already in place, in which employees may challenge disciplinary actions.

Documentation by the manager is critical in all but the least severe instances of misconduct (e.g., first-time minor offense with an oral warning).[50] Thus, the manager must investigate allegations of misconduct, gather evidence, write down what happened, and keep records of what was learned. Allegations of tardiness, for example, might involve inspection of time cards and interviews with other employees.

Performance problems could be incorporated into, or dovetailed with, the progressive discipline system.[51] Here, it would be wise (if possible) to first adhere to the normal performance management cycle so that correction of performance deficiencies is done in a consultative way between the employee and the manager, and the manager assumes major responsibility for providing resources to the employee, as well as for attentive coaching and feedback. If performance improvement is not forthcoming, then shifting to the progressive discipline system will be necessary.

Employee termination is the final step in progressive discipline. In an ideal world, it would never be necessary, but rarely, if ever, is this the case. The organization thus must be prepared for the necessity of conducting terminations. Termination processes, guidelines, training for managers, and so forth must be developed and implemented. Considerable guidance is available to help the organization in this regard.[52]

## RETENTION INITIATIVES: DOWNSIZING

Downsizing involves reducing the organization's staffing levels through layoffs. Many factors contribute to layoff occurrences: decline in profits, restructuring of the organization, substitution of the core workforce with a flexible workforce, an obsolete job or work unit, mergers and acquisitions, loss of contracts and clients, technological advances, productivity improvements, shortened product life cycles, and financial markets that favor downsizing as a positive organizational action.[53] While downsizing obviously involves the elimination of jobs and employees, it also encompasses several retention matters that involve balancing the advantages and disadvantages of downsizing, staffing levels and quality, alternatives to lay-offs, and dealing with employees who remain after downsizing.

## Weighing Advantages and Disadvantages

Downsizing has multiple advantages (benefits) and disadvantages (costs); refer back to Exhibit 14.8 for a review. A thoughtful consideration of these makes it clear that if downsizing is to be undertaken, it should be done with great caution. It is usually not an effective "quick fix" for financial performance problems confronting the organization.

Moreover, research suggests that the presumed and hoped-for benefits of downsizing might not be as great as they seem.[54] For example, one study looked at how employment level changes affected the profitability and stock returns of 537 organizations over a 14-year period. Downsizing did not significantly improve profitability, though it did produce somewhat better stock returns. In fact, organizations that combined downsizing with asset restructuring fared better.[55] Additional research has found that downsizing has negative impacts on employee morale and health, workgroup creativity and communication, and workforce quality.[56]

In short, downsizing is not a panacea for poor financial health. It has many negative impacts on employees and should be combined with a well-planned total restructuring if it is to be effective. Such conclusions suggest the organization should carefully ponder whether it should downsize, and if so, by how much, and which employees it should seek to retain.

## Staffing Levels and Quality

Reductions in staffing levels should be mindful of retention in at least two ways. First, enthusiasm for a financial quick fix needs to be tempered by a realization that, once let go, many downsized employees may be unlikely to return later if economic circumstances improve. The organization will then have to engage in costly restaffing as opposed to potentially less costly and quicker retention initiatives. At a minimum, therefore, the organization should consider alternatives to downsizing simultaneously with downsizing planning. Such an exercise may well lead to less downsizing and greater retention.

Second, staffing level reductions should be thought of in selective or targeted terms, rather than across the board. Such an approach is a logical outgrowth of HR planning, through which it is invariably discovered that the forecasted labor demand and supply figures lead to differing HR head-count requirements across organizational units and job categories. Indeed, it is possible that some units or job categories will be confronting layoffs while others are actually hiring.

If cuts are to be made, who should be retained? Staffing quality and employee acceptance concerns combine to produce some options to choose from. The first choice would be to retain the most senior employees in each work unit. Such an approach signals job security commitments to long-term employees. On the downside, the most senior employees may not be the best performers, and looking ahead, the most senior employees may not have the necessary qualifications for job requirement changes that will occur as part of the restructuring process.

A second alternative would be to make performance-based retention decisions.[57] Employees' current and possibly past performance appraisals would be consulted in each work unit. The lowest-performing employees would be designated for lay-off. This approach assumes that the current crop of best performers will continue to be so in the future, even though job requirements might change. It also assumes that the evaluation of who is or is not a high-quality employee is accurate. Legal challenges may also arise, as discussed later.

## Alternatives to Downsizing

A no-layoff or guaranteed employment policy as an organization strategy is the most dramatic alternative to downsizing. A no-layoff strategy requires considerable organization and HR planning, along with a commitment to a set of programs necessary for successfully implementing the strategy. This strategy also requires a gamble and a bet that, if lost, could severely damage employee loyalty and trust. During the deep recession of 2007–2009, many employers that had previously pursued a no-layoff strategy abandoned these policies and significantly reduced their workforces.[58]

Some organizations are unwilling to make a no-layoff guarantee but pursue layoff minimization through many different programs. Exhibit 14.15 provides an example based on a survey of 633 organizations. It can be seen that multiple steps were taken as alternatives to layoffs, headed by attrition (not replacing employees who leave), hiring freezes, and nonrenewal of contract workers. A series of direct and indirect pay changes (e.g., salary reduction, early retirement) also played a role in their layoff minimization. Other actions are also possible, such as a temporary layoff with some proportion of pay and benefits continued, substitution of stock options for bonuses, conversion of regular employees to independent contractors, temporary assignments at a reduced time (and pay) commitment, and off-site employees who temporarily work at home on a reduced time (and pay) basis.[59]

## Employees Who Remain

Employees who remain either in their pre-layoff job or in a redeployed job after a downsizing must not be ignored. Doing otherwise creates a new retention problem—survivors who are stressed and critical of the downsizing process. One survey of

**EXHIBIT 14.15**   **Alternative Methods for Cost Minimization**

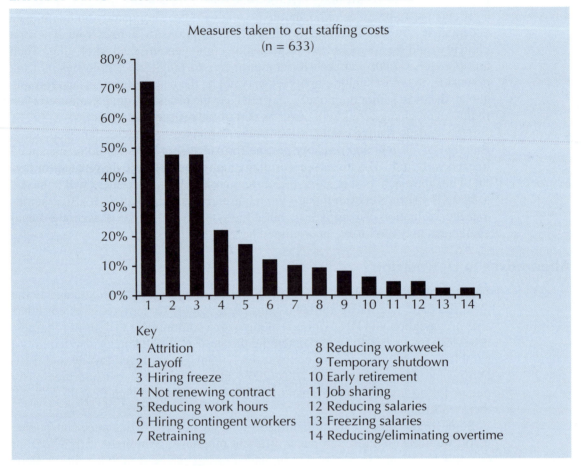

SOURCE: Society for Human Resource Management, *The Impact of 2008 U.S. Economy on Businesses* (Alexandria, VA: author, 2008). Used by permission.

workers employed at 318 companies found that 81% reported customer service had declined, 77% reported more errors and mistakes being made, and 64% reported that their coworkers' productivity had declined.[60] The survey authors attributed these negative results to layoff survivor stress, which was heightened by the loss of coworkers and friends, a heavier workload, new locations and work hours, new and/or more responsibilities, and fear of job loss just around the corner.

These examples of "survivor sickness" suggest a need to anticipate and attack it directly in downsizing planning. Experts recommend that organizations take active steps to reduce survivor stress. This can include active communication, involving the current workforce in redesigning jobs to accommodate lower staffing levels, and discussing career-related issues.[61] Unless steps are taken to help survivors plan for and adjust to the new realities they will confront, heightened job dissatisfaction seems inevitable. In turn, voluntary turnover may spike, further increasing the cost of downsizing.[62]

There are numerous examples of organizations that took steps to either help laid-off employees find new work or avoid layoffs altogether. When Circuit City announced plans to liquidate all of its stores in 2009, the organization took extraordinary steps to ensure that employees had assistance in their search for new jobs. Staff members established contacts with other organizations to help downsized employees find new jobs.[63] The organization also hosted résumé-writing and interviewing workshops for former associates. When HOK had to lay off a portion of its workforce, it offered transfers to other locations and held multiple training sessions with managers to teach them how to openly communicate about the layoffs with their employees.[64] As another example, following a steep drop in demand for its products during the recession, Piper Aircraft moved to a four-day workweek, which reduced employee compensation by 20%.[65]

## LEGAL ISSUES

Retention initiatives are closely entwined with the occurrence of employee separations, since the result of an unsuccessful retention initiative is the voluntary or involuntary separation of the employee from the organization. The organization's retention initiatives thus must be guided in part by the laws and regulations governing separations. A brief overview of these is provided. Then a detailed look at the role of performance appraisal in separation is presented, since performance-based retention is a thrust of this chapter.

## Separation Laws and Regulations

A desire to provide protection and safeguards to employees leaving an organization, especially as a result of discharge or downsizing, has led to myriad laws and regulations governing the separation process.[66] These include the following:

- Public policy restrictions on employment-at-will
- Employment discrimination laws and regulations
- Affirmative action requirements
- Employment contract principles
- Labor contract provisions
- Civil service laws and regulations
- Negligent supervision and retention
- Advanced warning about plant closings
- Severance agreements

A basic tenet underlying restrictions on employee separation is the need for fair and consistent treatment of employees. Included here are concerns for ensuring procedural fairness and having a legitimate basis for separations, such as merit, seniority, or performance. The organization should be thoroughly familiar with these numerous laws and regulations, and their underlying principles, as it designs and administers its separation initiatives.

## Performance Appraisal

Organizations often favor retention and separation systems and decisions that are driven by employee performance. Laws and regulations generally uphold or even encourage such a role for performance. However, the law as interpreted also insists that performance appraisals, and the performance appraisal system generally, be fairly and equitably applied to employees undergoing separation. Interpretations come about from a combination of court decisions and governmental regulations that have evolved around the issue of performance appraisal in practice.

Based on these decisions and regulations, numerous specific suggestions have been put forth to guide the organization in the design and use of its performance appraisal (or management) system:[67]

- Appraisal criteria should be job related, specific, and communicated in advance to the employee.
- The manager (rater) should receive training in the overall performance appraisal process and in how to avoid common rating errors.
- The manager should be familiar with the employee's job description and actual performance.
- There should be agreement among different raters in their evaluation of the employee's performance.
- Evaluations should be in writing.
- The employee should be able to review the evaluation and comment on it before it becomes final.
- The employee should receive timely feedback about the evaluation and an explanation for any outcome decision (e.g., retention or separation).
- There should be an upward review of the employee's appraisal.
- There should be an appeals system for employees who are dissatisfied with their evaluation.

Conforming to these recommendations will help provide (but not guarantee) a fair evaluation process and help defend decisions pertaining to retention and separation. If the organization wants to manage a performance-driven retention system, it would do well to ensure the adequacy of its performance appraisal system relative to the above recommendations.

## SUMMARY

Retention management seeks to control the numbers and types of employees who leave the organization and those who remain with the organization. Employee loss occurs through voluntary turnover or involuntary turnover in the form of discharge or downsizing. Voluntary turnover is caused by a combination of perceived desirability of leaving, ease of leaving, and alternatives to one's current job. Some of these reasons are avoidable, but others are not. Avoidable turnover can also be said to occur among high- and low-value employees. Discharge occurs for performance- and discipline-related problems. Downsizing or RIF occurs because the organization is, or is projected to be, overstaffed in head-count terms.

It is important for the organization to conduct thorough analyses of its turnover. Using a simple formula, turnover rates can be calculated, both overall and broken down by types of turnover, types of employees, job categories, and geographic location. It is also useful to benchmark the organization's turnover rates internally and externally. Another form of analysis is determining reasons that people leave. This can be done through exit interviews, post-exit surveys, and employee satisfaction surveys. Analysis of the costs and benefits of each of the three types of turnover should also be done. The three major cost categories are separation, replacement, and training. Within each category, numerous costs, both financial and nonfinancial, may be estimated. Likewise, each type of turnover has both financial and nonfinancial benefits associated with it that must be weighed against the many costs. A thorough understanding of costs and benefits will help the organization determine where and among whom turnover is the most worrisome, and how to fashion retention strategies and tactics.

To reduce voluntary turnover, organizations engage in numerous retention initiatives centered on direct and variable pay programs, benefits, work schedules, and training and development. Little is known about attempts to increase intrinsic rewards. A decision process may be followed to help decide which, if any, retention initiatives to undertake. The process is guided by four basic questions: Do we think turnover is a problem? How might we attack the problem? What do we need to decide? How should we evaluate the programs? To influence the desirability of leaving, the organization must raise job satisfaction by providing both extrinsic and intrinsic rewards. Ease of leaving can possibly be reduced by providing organization-specific training and increasing the cost of leaving. Finally, retention might be improved by providing more internal job alternatives to employees and by responding intentionally to other job offers they receive.

Discharges might be reduced through formal performance management and progressive discipline systems. The performance management system involves four stages—performance planning, performance execution, performance appraisal, and decisions about the employee. This helps prevent and correct performance problems. A progressive discipline system addresses behavioral conduct problems that violate rules, procedures, laws, and professional and moral standards. It has a series of penalties for misconduct that progress up to termination, which the system seeks to prevent if at all possible.

While downsizing seems to have some obvious benefits, research indicates that there are many costs as well, so the organization should carefully consider whether it really wants to downsize, and if so, by how much in terms of employee numbers and quality. Staffing levels should be achieved in a targeted way rather than across the board. From a staffing quality perspective, cuts could be based on seniority, job performance, or a more holistic assessment of who the high-value employees are that the organization wishes to retain. There are many alternatives to downsizing that could be pursued. Attention must be paid to employees who survive a downsizing, or they might create a new retention problem for the organization by starting to leave.

Legally, employee separation from the organization, especially on an involuntary basis, is subject to myriad laws and regulations that the organization must be aware of and incorporate into its retention strategy and tactics. If the organization wishes to base retention decisions on employees' job performance, it should recognize that laws and regulations require performance management systems to be fair and equitable to employees during separation. Based on regulations and court decisions, numerous recommendations must be followed in order for a performance management system to have a chance of withstanding legal challenges and scrutiny.

## DISCUSSION QUESTIONS

1. For the three primary causes of voluntary turnover (desirability of leaving, ease of leaving, alternatives), might their relative importance depend on the type of employee or type of job? Explain.
2. Which of the costs and benefits of voluntary turnover are most likely to vary according to type of job? Give examples.
3. If someone said to you, "It's easy to reduce turnover—just pay people more money," what would your response be?
4. Why should an organization seek to retain employees with performance or discipline problems? Why not just fire them?
5. Discuss some potential problems with downsizing as an organization's first response to a need to cut labor costs.

## ETHICAL ISSUES

1. Imagine your organization is doing exit interviews and has promised confidentiality to all who respond. You are responsible for conducting the exit interviews. Your supervisor has asked you to give her the name of each respondent so she can assess the information in conjunction with the per-

son's supervisor. What obligation do corporate HR employees have to keep information confidential in such circumstances?

2. Firing an employee has numerous potential negative organizational consequences, including the discomfort of the supervisor who delivers the termination information, conflict or sabotage from the departing employee, and the filing of a lawsuit. To avoid this, many supervisors give problem employees unpleasant work tasks, reduce their working hours, or otherwise negatively modify their jobs in hopes that they will simply quit. What are the ethical issues raised by this strategy?

## APPLICATIONS

### Managerial Turnover: A Problem?

HealthCareLaunderCare (HCLC) is a company that specializes in picking up, cleaning, and delivering laundry for health care providers, especially hospitals, nursing homes, and assisted care facilities. Basically, these health care providers have outsourced their total laundry operations to HCLC. In this very competitive business, a typical contract between HCLC and a health care provider is only two years, and HCLC experiences a contract nonrenewal rate of 10%. Most nonrenewals occur because of dissatisfaction with service costs and especially quality (e.g., surgical garb that is not completely sterilized).

HCLC has 20 laundry facilities throughout the country, mostly in large metropolitan areas. Each laundry facility is headed by a site manager, and there are unit supervisors for the intake, washing, drying, inspection and repair, and delivery areas. An average of 100 nonexempt employees are employed at each site.

The operation of the facilities is technologically sophisticated and very health- and safety-sensitive. In the intake area, for example, employees wear protective clothing, gloves, and eyewear because of all the blood, tissue, and germs on laundry that comes in. The washing area is composed of huge washers in 35-foot stainless steel tunnels with screws that move the laundry through various wash cycles. Workers in this area are exposed to high temperatures and must be proficient in the operation of the computer control systems. Laundry is lifted out of the tunnels by robots and moved to the drying room area, where it is dried, ironed, and folded by machines tended by employees. In the inspection and repair area, quality inspection and assurance occurs. Laundry is inspected for germs and pinholes (pinholes in surgical garb could allow blood and fluids to come into contact with the surgeon), and employees complete repairs on torn clothing and sheets. In the delivery area, the laundry is hermetically sealed in packages and placed in delivery vans for transport.

HCLC's vice president of operations, Tyrone Williams, manages the sites—and site and unit managers—with an iron fist. Williams monitors each site with weekly reports on a set of cost, quality, and safety indicators for each of the five areas. When he spots what he thinks are problems or undesirable trends, he has a conference call with both the site manager and the unit supervisor. In the decidedly one-way conversation, marching orders are delivered and are expected to be fulfilled. If a turnaround in the "numbers" does not show up in the next weekly report, Williams gives the manager and the supervisor one more week to improve. If sufficient improvement is not forthcoming, various punitive actions are taken, including base pay cuts, demotions, reassignments, and terminations. Williams feels such quick and harsh justice is necessary to keep HCLC competitive and to continually drive home to all employees the importance of working "by the numbers." Fed up with this management system, many managers have opted to say, "Bye-bye, numbers!" and leave HCLC.

Recently, the issue of site and unit manager retention came up on the radar screen of HCLC's president, Roman Dublinski. Dublinski glanced at a payroll report showing that 30 of 120 site and unit managers had left HCLC in the past year, though no reasons for leaving were given. In addition, Dublinski received copies of a few angry resignation letters written to Williams. Having never confronted or thought about possible employee retention problems or how to deal with them, Dublinski calls to ask you (the corporate manager of staffing) to prepare a brief written analysis that will then be used as the basis for a meeting between the two of you and the vice president of HR, Debra Angle (Angle recommended this). Address the following questions in your report:

1. Is the loss of 30 managers out of 120 in one year cause for concern?
2. What additional data should be gathered to learn more about managerial turnover?
3. What are the costs of this turnover? Might there be any benefits?
4. Are there any lurking legal problems?
5. If retention is a serious problem for HCLC, what are the main ways we might address it?

## Retention: Deciding to Act

Wally's Wonder Wash (WWW) is a full-service, high-tech, high-touch car wash company owned solely by Wally Wheelspoke. Located in a Midwestern city of 200,000 people (with another 100,000 in suburbs and more rural towns throughout the county), WWW currently has four facilities within the city. Wally plans to add four more facilities within the city in the next two years, and later on he plans to begin placing facilities in suburban locations and rural towns. Major competitors in the city include two other full-service car washes (different owners), plus three touchless automatic facilities (same owner).

Wally's critical strategy is to provide the very best to customers who want and relish extremely clean and "spiffy" vehicles and to have customers feel a positive experience each time they come to WWW. To do this, WWW seeks to provide high-quality car washes and car detailing and to generate considerable repeat business through competitive prices combined with attention to customers. To make itself accessible to customers, WWW is open seven days a week, 8:00 a.m. to 8:00 p.m. Peak periods, volumewise, are after 1:00 on weekdays and from 10:00 to 5:00 on weekends. In addition, Wally uses his workforce to drive his strategy. Though untrained in HR, Wally knows that he must recruit and retain a stable, high-quality workforce if his current businesses, let alone his ambitious expansion plans, are to succeed.

WWW has a strong preference for full-time employees, who work either 7:30 to 4:00 or 11:00 to 8:00. Part-timers are used occasionally to help fill in during peak demand times and during the summer when full-timers are on vacation. There are two major jobs at WWW: attendant (washer) and custom service specialist (detailer). Practicing promotion from within, WWW promotes all specialists from the attendant ranks. There are currently 70 attendants and 20 custom service specialists at WWW. In addition, each facility has a manager. Wally has filled the manager jobs by promotion from within (from either the attendant or custom service specialist ranks), but he is unsure if he will be able to continue doing this as he expands.

The job of attendant is a demanding one. Attendants vacuum vehicles from front to rear (and trunk if requested by the customer), wash and dry windows and mirrors, dry vehicles with hand towels, apply special cleaning compounds to tires, wipe down the vehicle's interior, and wash or vacuum floor mats. In addition, attendants wash and fold towels, lift heavy barrels of cleaning compounds and waxes, and perform light maintenance and repair work on the machinery. Finally, and very important, attendants consistently provide customer service by asking customers if they have special requests and by making small talk with them. A unique feature of customer service at WWW is that the attendant must ask the customer to personally inspect the vehicle before leaving to ensure that the vehicle is satisfactorily cleaned (attendants also correct any mistakes pointed out by the customer). The attendants work as a team, with each attendant expected to be able to perform all of the above tasks.

Attendants start at a base wage of $8.00/hour, with automatic $.50 raises at six months and one year. They receive brief training from the manager before starting work. Custom service specialists start at $9.00/hour, with $.50 raises after six months and one year. Neither attendants nor custom service specialists receive performance reviews. Managers receive a salary of $27,000, plus an annual "merit" raise based on a very casual performance review conducted by Wally (whenever he gets around to it). All attendants share equally in a customer tip pool; custom service specialists receive individual tips. The benefits package is composed of: (1) major medical health insurance with a 20% employee co-pay on the premium, (2) paid holidays for Christmas, Easter, July 4, and Martin Luther King Jr.'s birthday, and (3) a generous paid sick pay plan of two days per month (in recognition of high illness rates due to extreme working conditions).

In terms of turnover, Wally has spotty and general data only. In the past year WWW experienced an overall turnover rate of 65% for attendants and 20% for custom service specialists; no managers left. Though lacking data farther back, Wally thinks the turnover rate for attendants has been increasing. WWW's managers constantly complain to Wally about the high level of turnover among attendants and the problems it creates, especially in fulfilling the strong customer service orientation for WWW. Though the managers have not conducted exit interviews, the major complaints they hear from attendants are: (1) the pay is not competitive relative to the other full-service car washes and many other entry-level jobs in the area, (2) the training is hit-or-miss at best, (3) promotion opportunities are limited, (4) managers provide no feedback or coaching, and (5) customer complaints and mistreatment of attendants by customers are on the rise.

Wally is frustrated by attendant turnover and its threat to his customer service and expansion strategies. He calls on you for assistance in figuring out what to do about the problem. Use the decision process shown in Exhibit 14.11 to help develop a retention initiative for WWW. Address each of the questions in the process, specifically:

1. Do we think turnover is a problem?
2. How might we attack the problem?
3. What do we need to decide?
4. How should we evaluate the initiatives?

# ENDNOTES

1. US Department of Labor, "Employee Tenure in 2012," *News*, Sept. 18, 2012; US Department of Labor, "Number of Jobs Held, Labor Market Activity, and Earnings Growth Among the Youngest Baby Boomers," *News*, Sept. 10, 2010.

2. D. G. Allen and P. C. Bryant, *Managing Employee Turnover: Dispelling Myths and Fostering Evidence-Based Retention Strategies* (New York: Business Expert Press, 2012).

3. R. W. Griffeth, P. W. Hom, and S. Gaertner, "A Meta-Analysis of Antecedents and Correlates of Employee Turnover," *Journal of Management*, 2000, 26, pp. 463–488; Allen and Bryant, *Managing Employee Turnover*; J. D. Kammeyer-Mueller, C. R. Wanberg, T. M. Glomb, and D. A. Ahlburg, "Turnover Processes in a Temporal Context: It's About Time," *Journal of Applied Psychology*, 2005, 90, pp. 644–658; R. P. Steel and J. W. Lounsbury, "Turnover Process Models: Review and Synthesis of a Conceptual Literature," *Human Resource Management Review*, 2009, 19, pp. 271–282; P. W. Hom, L. Roberson, and A. D. Ellis, "Challenging Conventional Wisdom About Who Quits: Revelations From Corporate America," *Journal of Applied Psychology*, 2008, 93, pp. 1–34; J. G. March and H. A. Simon, *Organizations* (New York: Wiley, 1958); C. O. Trevor, "Interactions Among Actual Ease of Movement Determinants and Job Satisfaction in the Prediction of Voluntary Turnover," *Academy of Management Journal*, 2001, 44, pp. 621–638.

4. C. D. Crossley, R. J. Bennett, S. M. Jex, and L. Burnfield, "Development of a Global Measure of Job Embeddedness and Integration Into a Traditional Model of Voluntary Turnover," *Journal of Applied Psychology*, 2007, 92, pp. 1031–1042; W. S. Harman, T. W. Lee, T. R. Mitchell,

W. Felps, and B. P. Owens, "The Psychology of Voluntary Employee Turnover," *Current Directions in Psychological Science*, 2007, 16, pp. 51–54; F. Niederman, M. Sumner, and C. P. Maertz, Jr., "Testing and Extending the Unfolding Model of Voluntary Turnover to IT Professionals," *Human Resource Management*, 2007, 46, pp. 331–347; K. Jiang, D. Liu, P. F. McKay, T. W. Lee, and T. R. Mitchell, "When and How Is Job Embeddedness Predictive of Turnover? A Meta-Analytic Investigation," *Journal of Applied Psychology*, 2012, 97, pp. 1077–1096.

5. R. W. Griffeth and P. W. Hom, *Retaining Valued Employees* (Cincinnati, OH: South-Western, 2001), pp. 203–222; K. Fernandez, "Tie Up Loose Ends," *Staffing Management*, Jan. 2007 (*www.shrm.org*); E. Agnvall, "Exit Interviews with the Click of a Mouse: Exit Interviews Go High-Tech," SHRM Online HR Technology Focus Area, Oct. 2006 (*www.shrm.org*).

6. M. A. Campion, "Meaning and Measurement of Turnover: Comparison and Recommendations for Research," *Journal of Applied Psychology*, 1991, 76, pp. 199–212; H. R. Nalbantian and A. Szostak, "How Fleet Bank Fought Employee Flight," *Harvard Business Review*, Apr. 2004, pp. 116–125; S. Wescott, "Goodbye and Good Luck," *Inc.*, Apr. 2006, pp. 40–41.

7. J. P. Hausknecht, C. O. Trevor, and M. J. Howard, "Unit Level Voluntary Turnover Rates and Customer Service Quality Implications of Group Cohesiveness, Newcomer Concentration, and Size," *Journal of Applied Psychology*, 2009, 94, pp. 1068–1075; T-.Y. Park and J. D. Shaw, "Turnover Rates and Organizational Performance: A Meta-Analysis," *Journal of Applied Psychology*, 2013, 98, pp. 268–309.

8. W. F. Cascio, *Costing Human Resources*, 4th ed. (Cincinnati, OH: South-Western, 2000), pp. 23–57; Griffeth and Hom, *Retaining Valued Employees*, pp. 10–22; R. Williams and L. Arnett, "Retaining Employees by Sticking to the Basics," *Workforce Management*, Dec. 2008 (*www.workforce.com*).

9. Park and Shaw, "Turnover Rates and Organizational Performance: A Meta-Analysis."

10. Cascio, *Costing Human Resources*, pp. 83–105; L. B. Rassas, *Employment Law: A Guide to Hiring, Managing, and Firing for Employers and Employees* (Austin, TX: Aspen Publishers, 2011).

11. J. N. Barron and D. M. Kreps, *Strategic Human Resources* (New York: Wiley, 1999), pp. 421–445; Cascio, *Costing Human Resources*, pp. 23–57; L. Uchitelle, *The Disposable American: Layoffs and Their Consequences* (New York: Vintage Books, 2007).

12. Park and Shaw, "Turnover Rates and Organizational Performance."

13. A. L. Heavey, J. A. Holwerda, and J. P. Hausknecht, "Causes and Consequences of Collective Turnover: A Meta-Analytic Review," *Journal of Applied Psychology*, 2013, 98, pp. 412–453.

14. *Retention of Key Talent and the Role of Rewards* (Scottsdale, AZ: author, 2012).

15. *Fortune 100 Best Companies to Work For 2013* (*http://money.cnn.com/magazines/fortune/best-companies/*); D. A. Kaplan, "Mars Incorporated: A Pretty Sweet Place to Work," *Fortune*, Jan. 17, 2013 (*http://management.fortune.cnn.com/2013/01/17/best-companies-mars/?iid=bc_sp_lead*).

16. J. D. Shaw and N. Gupta, "Pay System Characteristics and Quit Patterns of Good, Average, and Poor Performers," *Personnel Psychology*, 2007, 60, pp. 903–928.

17. R. Batt and A.J.S. Colvin "An Employment Systems Approach to Turnover: Human Resources Practices, Quits, Dismissals, and Performance," *Academy of Management Journal*, 2011, pp. 695–717.

18. Heavey, Holwerda, and Hausknecht, "Causes and Consequences of Collective Turnover: A Meta-Analytic Review."

19. E. R. Demby, "The Insider: Benefits," *Workforce Management*, Feb. 2004, pp. 57–59; Nalbantian and Szostak, "How Fleet Bank Fought Employee Flight"; S. Overman, "Outback Steakhouse Grills Applicants, Caters to Employees to Keep Turnover Low," *SHRM News Online*, Oct. 2004 (*www.shrm.org*); T. Rutigliano, "Tuning Up Your Talent Engine," *Gallup Management Journal*, Fall 2001, pp. 12–14; G. Strauss, "UPS' Pay, Perks Make It a Destination Job for Many," *Wall Street Journal*, Oct. 14, 2003, pp. B1–B2; E. Zimmerman, "The Joy of Flex," *The Workforce*

*Management 2004 Optimas Awards*, pp. 4–5; J. T. Marquez, "Tailor-Made Careers," *Workforce Management*, Jan. 2010, pp. 16–21.

20. P. Cappelli, "A Market-Driven Approach to Retaining Talent," *Harvard Business Review*, Jan.–Feb. 2000, pp. 103–111; P. K. Zingheim and J. R. Schuster, "Retaining Scarce, Critical Talent," *HR Pulse*, Fall 2008, pp. 38–44.

21. S. Miller, "What Do Employees Want? Not Always What Employers Think," Mar. 2007 (*www.shrm.org*); Williams and Arnett, "Retaining Employees by Sticking to the Basics."

22. Harris Interactive, *Working in America: The Key to Employee Satisfaction* (Rochester, NY: author, 2007).

23. M. Schoeff, "Retention Edges Cost Reduction as Benefits Objective," *Workforce Management Online*, Mar. 24, 2009 (*www.workforce.com*).

24. J. D. Shaw, B. R. Dineen, R. Fang, and R. F. Vellella, "Employee-Organization Exchange Relationships, HRM Practices, and Quit Rates of Good and Poor Performers," *Academy of Management Journal,* 2009, 52, pp. 1016–1033; S. J. Peterson and F. Luthans, "The Impact of Financial and Nonfinancial Incentives on Business-Unit Outcomes Over Time," *Journal of Applied Psychology*, 2006, 91, pp. 156–165; Shaw and Gupta, "Pay System Characteristics and Quit Patterns of Good, Average, and Poor Performers"; J. D. Shaw, N. Gupta, and J. E. Delery, "Alternative Conceptualizations of the Relationship Between Voluntary Turnover and Organizational Performance," *Academy of Management Journal*, 2005, 48, pp. 50–68.

25. Cappelli, "A Market-Driven Approach to Retaining Talent"; B. S. Klaas and J. A. McClendon, "To Lead, Lag, or Match: Estimating the Financial Impact of Pay Level Policies," *Personnel Psychology*, 1996, 49, pp. 121–140.

26. S. L. Peterson, "Managerial Turnover in U.S. Retail Organizations," *Journal of Management Development*, 2007, 26, pp. 770–789; Griffeth and Hom, *Retaining Valued Employees*, pp. 31–45; Kammeyer-Mueller, Wanberg, Glomb, and Ahlburg, "Turnover Processes in a Temporal Context: It's About Time"; Harman, Lee, Mitchell, Felps, and Owens, "The Psychology of Voluntary Employee Turnover"; Niederman, Sumner, and Maertz, "Testing and Extending the Unfolding Model of Voluntary Turnover to IT Professionals."

27. K. V. Rondeau, E. S. Williams, and T. H. Wagar, "Developing Human Capital: What Is the Impact on Nurse Turnover?" *Journal of Nursing Management*, 2009, 17, pp. 739–748.

28. R. Folger and R. Cropanzano, *Organizational Justice and Human Resource Management* (Thousand Oaks, CA: Sage, 1998); R. A. Postuma, C. P. Maertz, Jr., and J. B. Dworkin, "Procedural Justice's Relationship With Turnover: Explaining Past Inconsistent Findings," *Journal of Organizational Behavior*, 2007, 28, pp. 381–398.

29. G. Paré and M. Tremblay, "The Influence of High-Involvement Human Resources Practices, Procedural Justice, Organizational Commitment, and Citizenship Behaviors on Information Technology Professionals' Turnover Intentions," *Group & Organization Management*, 2007, 32, pp. 326–357; N. P. Podsakoff, J. A. LePine, and M. A. LePine, "Differential Challenge Stressor-Hindrance Stressor Relationships With Job Attitudes, Turnover Intentions, Turnover, and Withdrawal Behavior: A Meta-Analysis," *Journal of Applied Psychology*, 2007, 92, pp. 438–454.

30. N. E. Day, "Perceived Pay Communication, Justice, and Pay Satisfaction," *Employee Relations*, 2011, 33, pp. 476–497.

31. Rutigliano, "Tuning Up Your Talent Engine."

32. J. Choi and C. C. Chen, "The Relationships of Distributive Justice and Compensation System Fairness to Employee Attitudes in International Joint Ventures," *Journal of Organizational Behavior*, 2007, 28, pp. 687–703; A. A. Chughtai and S. Zafar, "Antecedents and Consequences of Organizational Commitment Among Pakistani University Teachers," *Applied H.R.M.*

*Research*, 2006, 11, pp. 39–64; T. Kim and K. Leung, "Forming and Reacting to Overall Fairness: A Cross-Cultural Comparison," *Organizational Behavior and Human Decision Processes*, 2007, 104, pp. 83–95; D. G. Allen, R. W. Griffeth, J. M. Vardaman, K. Aquino, S. Gaertner, and M. Lee, "Structural Validity and Generalizability of a Referent Cognitions Model of Turnover Decisions," *Applied Psychology: An International Review*, 2009, 58, pp. 709–728.

33. W. Felps, T. R. Mitchell, D. R. Hekman, T. W. Lee, B. C. Holtom, and W. S. Harman, "Turnover Contagion: How Coworkers, Job Embeddedness and Job Search Behaviors Influence Quitting," *Academy of Management Journal*, 2009, 52, pp. 545–561.

34. J. Mayfield and M. Mayfield, "The Effects of Leader Communication on a Worker's Intent to Stay: An Investigation Using Structural Equation Modeling," *Human Performance*, 2007, 20, pp. 85–102; C. Donoghue and N. G. Castle, "Leadership Styles of Nursing Home Administrators and Their Association With Staff Turnover," *The Gerontologist*, 2009, 49, pp. 166–174; L. H. Nishii and D. M. Mayer, "Do Inclusive Leaders Help to Reduce Turnover in Diverse Groups?" *Journal of Applied Psychology*, 2009, 94, pp. 1412–1426.

35. B. J. Tepper, "Consequences of Abusive Supervision," *Academy of Management Journal*, 2000, 43, pp. 178–190; J. S. Leonard and D. I. Levine, "The Effect of Diversity on Turnover: A Large Case Study," *Industrial and Labor Relations Review*, 2006, 59, pp. 547–572; P. F. McKay, D. R. Avery, S. Toniandel, M. A. Morris, M. Hernandez, and M. R. Hebl, "Racial Differences in Employee Retention: Are Diversity Climate Perceptions the Key?" *Personnel Psychology*, 2007, 60, pp. 35–62.

36. C. A. Thompson and D. J. Prottas, "Relationships Among Organizational Family Support, Job Autonomy, Perceived Control, and Employee Well-Being," *Journal of Occupational Health Psychology*, 2006, 11, pp. 100–118; Podsakoff, LePine, and LePine, "Differential Challenge Stressor-Hindrance Stressor Relationships With Job Attitudes, Turnover Intentions, Turnover, and Withdrawal Behavior: A Meta-Analysis"; L. B. Hammer, E. E. Kossek, W. K. Anger, T. Bodner, and K. L. Zimmerman, "Clarifying Work-Family Intervention Processes: The Roles of Work-Family Conflict and Family-Supportive Supervisor Behaviors," *Journal of Applied Psychology,* 2011, 96, pp. 134–150; T. D. Golden, "Avoiding Depletion in Virtual Work: Telework and the Intervening Impact of Work Exhaustion on Commitment and Turnover Intentions," *Journal of Vocational Behavior*, 2006, 69, pp. 176–187; Society for Human Resource Management, *Workplace Flexibility in the 21st Century* (Alexandria, VA: author, 2008).

37. K. Aumann and E. Galinsky, *The State of Health in the American Workforce* (New York: Families and Work Institute, 2009).

38. Society for Human Resource Management, *Workplace Flexibility in the 21st Century* (Alexandria, VA: author, 2008).

39. B. A. Lautsch, E. E. Kossek, and S. C. Eaton, "Supervisory Approaches and Paradoxes in Managing Telecommuting Implementation," *Human Relations*, 2009, 62, pp. 795–827.

40. M. R. Barrick and R. D. Zimmerman, "Reducing Voluntary, Avoidable Turnover Through Selection," *Journal of Applied Psychology*, 2005, 90, pp. 159–166; J. B. Becton, M. C. Matthews, D. L. Hartley, and D. H. Whitaker, "Using Biodata to Predict Turnover, Organizational Commitment, and Job Performance in Healthcare," *International Journal of Selection and Assessment*, 2009, 17, pp. 189–202.

41. R. D. Zimmerman, "Understanding the Impact of Personality Traits on Individuals' Turnover Decisions: A Meta-Analytic Path Model," *Personnel Psychology*, 2008, 61, pp. 309–348; M. R. Barrick and R. D. Zimmerman, "Hiring for Retention and Performance," *Human Resource Management*, 2009, 48, pp. 183–206.

42. E. R. Silverman, "Mercer Tries to Keep Its Employees Through Its 'Externship' Program," *Wall Street Journal*, Nov. 7, 2000, p. B18.

43. A. R. Wheeler, V. C. Gallagher, R. L. Brover, and C. J. Sablynski, "When Person-Organization (Mis)Fit and (Dis)Satisfaction Lead to Turnover: The Moderating Role of Perceived Job Mobility," *Journal of Managerial Psychology*, 2007, 22, pp. 203–219.

44. M. Armstrong, *Performance Management*, 2nd ed. (London: Kogan-Page, 2000); D. Grote, *The Complete Guide to Performance Appraisal* (New York: AMACOM, 1996); G. P. Latham and K. N. Wexley, *Increasing Productivity Through Performance Appraisal*, 2nd ed. (Reading, MA: Addison-Wesley, 1994); E. E. Schuttauf, *Performance Management Manual for Managers and Supervisors* (Chicago: Commerce Clearing House, 1997).

45. M. Rotundo and P. R. Sackett, "The Relative Importance of Task, Citizenship, and Counterproductive Performance to Global Ratings of Job Performance: A Policy Capturing Approach," *Journal of Applied Psychology*, 2002, 87, pp. 66–80; P. R. Sackett, C. M. Berry, S. A. Wiemann, and R. M. Laczo, "Citizenship and Counterproductive Behavior: Clarifying Relations Between the Two Domains," *Human Performance*, 2006, 19, pp. 441–464; F. Lievens, J. M. Conway, and W. De Corte, "The Relative Importance of Task, Citizenship, and Counterproductive Performance to Job Performance Ratings: Do Rater Source and Team-Based Culture Matter?" *Journal of Occupational and Organizational Psychology*, 2008, 81, pp. 11–27.

46. K. Tyler, "Train Managers, Maximize Appraisals," *HR Magazine*, December 2012, pp. 68–69.

47. F. T. Coleman, *Ending the Employment Relationship Without Ending Up in Court* (Alexandria, VA: Society for Human Resource Management, 2001); P. C. Gibson and K. S. Piscitelli, *Basic Employment Law Manual for Managers and Supervisors* (Chicago: Commerce Clearing House, 1997).

48. Gibson and Piscitelli, *Basic Employment Law Manual for Managers and Supervisors*, pp. 51–53.

49. R. R. Hastings, "Designing a Progressive Discipline Policy," 2010 (*www.shrm.org*); R. R. Hastings, "Is Progressive Discipline a Thing of the Past?" 2010 (*www.shrm.org*).

50. Schuttauf, *Performance Management Manual for Managers and Supervisors*, pp. 43–45.

51. Gibson and Piscitelli, *Basic Employment Law Manual for Managers and Supervisors*, pp. 48–53; Hastings, "Is Progressive Discipline a Thing of the Past?"

52. Coleman, *Ending the Employment Relationship Without Ending Up in Court*, pp. 51–84.

53. D. K. Datta, J. P. Guthrie, D. Basuil, and A. Pandey, "Causes and Effects of Employee Downsizing: A Review and Synthesis," *Journal of Management*, 2010, 36, pp. 281–348.

54. J. P. Guthrie and D. K. Datta, "Dumb and Dumber: The Impact of Downsizing on Firm Performance as Moderated by Industry Conditions," *Organization Science*, 2008, 19, pp. 108–123.

55. W. F. Cascio, C. E. Young, and J. R. Morris, "Financial Consequences of Employment-Change Decisions in Major US Corporations," *Academy of Management Journal*, 1997, 40, pp. 1175–1189.

56. Datta, Guthrie, Basuil, and Pandey, "Causes and Effects of Employee Downsizing: A Review and Synthesis."

57. A. Fox, "Prune Employees Carefully," *HR Magazine*, Apr. 2008 (*www.shrm.org*).

58. C. Tuna, "No Layoff Policies Crumble," *Wall Street Journal*, Dec. 29, 2008, p. B1.

59. B. Mirza, "Look at Alternatives to Layoffs," *HR News*, Dec. 29, 2008 (*www.shrm.org*).

60. K. Gurchiek, "Layoffs Pack Punch to 'Surviving' Employees," *HR News*, Dec. 22, 2008 (*www.shrm.org*).

61. Gurchiek, "Layoffs Pack Punch to 'Surviving' Employees."

62. C. O. Trevor and A. J. Nyberg, "Keeping Your Headcount When All About You Are Losing Theirs: Downsizing, Voluntary Turnover Rates, and the Moderating Role of HR Practices," *Academy of Management Journal*, 2008, 51, pp. 259–276; A. K. Mishra, K. E. Mishra, and G. M. Spreitzer, "Downsizing the Company Without Downsizing Morale," *MIT Sloan Management Review*, 2009, 50(3), pp. 39–44.

63. A. Fox, "Pulling the Plug on Circuit City," *HR Magazine*, June 1, 2009 (*www.shrm.org*).

64. J. T. Marquez, "How HOK Builds Engagement Despite the Downturn," *Workforce Management Online*, Dec. 2009 (*www.workforce.com*).

65. R. Zeidner, "Cutting Hours Without Increasing Risk," *HR Magazine*, Apr. 1, 2009 (*www.shrm.org*).

66. Coleman, *Ending the Employment Relationship Without Ending Up in Court*; J. G. Frierson, *Preventing Employment Lawsuits* (Washington, DC: Bureau of National Affairs, 1997)*;* S. C. Kahn, B. B. Brown, and M. Lanzarone, *Legal Guide to Human Resources* (Boston: Warren, Gorham and Lamont, 2001), pp. 9-3 to 9-82; D. P. Twomey, *Labor and Employment Law*, 11th ed. (Cincinnati, OH: South-Western, 2001); E. Lipsig, M. E. Dollarhide, and B. K. Seifert, *Reductions in Force in Employment Law*, 2nd ed. (Washington, DC: BNA Books, 2010).

67. Kahn, Brown, and Lanzarone, *Legal Guide to Human Resources*, pp. 6-2 to 6-58; J. M. Werner and M. C. Bolino, "Explaining U.S. Courts of Appeals Decisions Involving Performance Appraisals: Accuracy, Fairness, and Validation," *Personnel Psychology*, 1997, 50, pp. 1–24; J. Marquez, "Is G.E.'s Ranking System Broken?" *Workforce Management*, June 25, 2007, pp. 1–3; M. Orey, "Fear of Firing," *BusinessWeek*, Apr. 23, 2007, pp. 52–62; D. J. Walsh, *Employment Law for Human Resource Practice*, 4th ed. (Mason, OH: South-Western), pp. 547–567.

# NAME INDEX

# SUBJECT INDEX